Exploring the Past

Exploring the Past

Readings in Archaeology

Edited by

James M. Bayman
and
Miriam T. Stark

University of Hawai'i

Carolina Academic Press
Durham, North Carolina

Library of Congress Cataloging-in-Publication Data

Exploring the past : readings in archaeology / [edited by] James M.
    Bayman and Miriam T. Stark.
        p.   cm.
    Includes bibliographical references and index.
    ISBN 0-89089-699-2
    1. Archaeology. 2. Archaeology—Methodology. 3. Excavations
(Archaeology) 4. Antiquities, Prehistoric.   I. Bayman, James M.
II. Stark, Miriam T.
    CC165.E88   1999
    930—dc21   98-52051
                                                            CIP

CAROLINA ACADEMIC PRESS
700 Kent Street
Durham, North Carolina 27701
Telephone (919) 489-7486
Fax (919) 493-5668
E-mail: cap@cap-press.com
www.cap-press.com

Printed in the United States of America

Contents

Preface   ix

Acknowledgments   xi

Photograph and Illustration Credits   xv

Part One — Defining Archaeology

Introduction   3

1   Yes, Wonderful Things
William Rathje and Colleen Murphy   7

2   The Wet Frontier: Underwater Archaeology
Lawrence H. Robbins   25

3   Proving Ground of the Nuclear Age
William Gray Johnson and Colleen M. Beck   45

4   The Archaeology of Contemporary Mass Graves
Melissa Connor   51

5   A Love for the Ages
Bruce Goldfarb   55

Commentary   63

Part Two — Archaeology's Past

Introduction   65

1   The Discovery of Prehistory
William H. Stiebing   67

2   The Enlightened Archaeologist
Jeffrey L. Hantmann and Gary Dunham   85

Commentary   91

Part Three — The Archaeology of Human Origins and the Human Diaspora

Introduction   93

1   Old Flame
Andrew Sillen and C.K. Brain   95

2   Ape at the Brink
Sue Savage-Rumbaugh and Roger Lewin   99

3   The First Europeans
Jean-Jacques Hublin   109

4   New Evidence Challenges Traditional Model of How the New World Was Settled
Kim A. McDonald   119

Commentary   125

Part Four — Conducting Fieldwork in Archaeology

Introduction   127

1   Surveying Ancient Cities
    Anthony M. Snodgrass and John L. Bintliff   131

2   Diving into the Wreck
    Andrew Todhunter   141

3   Thailand's Good Mound
    Charles Higham and Rachanie Thosarat   147

Commentary   159

Part Five — Measuring Time in Archaeology

Introduction   161

1   The Dating Game
    James Shreeve   165

2   A Modern Riddle of the Sphinx
    Robert M. Schoch   177

3   The Earliest Art Becomes Older—and More Common
    Virginia Morell   183

Commentary   187

Part Six — New Techniques in Archaeology

Introduction   189

1   Blood From Stones: Tests for Prehistoric Blood
    Cast Doubt on Earlier Results
    Jocelyn Kaiser   191

2   Tales from the Crypt
    Karen Wright   195

3   Tracking Ohio's Hopewell Road
    Bradley T. Lepper   203

4   Who Was the Iceman?
    Sandy Fritz   211

Commentary   219

**Part Seven — Archaeological
Approaches to Technology**

Introduction   221

1   Ice Age Lamps
    Sophie A. de Beaune and Randall White   223

2   Late Ice Age Hunting Technology
    Heidi Knecht   231

3   Bamboo and Human Evolution
    Geoffrey G. Pope   239

4   Moving the Moai: Transporting the Megaliths
    of Easter Island
    Jo Anne Van Tilburg   249

Commentary   259

Contents

Part Eight — Making a Living

Introduction   261

1   Polynesian Ancestors and Their Animal World
Tom Dye and David W. Steadman   265

2   Finding the First Farmers
Bruce Fellman   279

3   Raised Field Agriculture in the Titicaca Basin:
Putting Ancient Agriculture Back to Work
Clark L. Erickson   289

4   Household Craft Specialization and Shell Ornament
Manufacture in Ejutla, Mexico
Gary M. Feinman and Linda M. Nicholas   303

Commentary   315

**Part Nine — Social and Political Life
in the Ancient World**

Introduction   317

1   Cemetery Reveals Complex Aboriginal Society
Graeme O'Neill   321

2   Masters and Slaves in an Iron Age Cave?
Michael Balter   323

3   Platform Mounds of the Arizona Desert:
An Experiment in Organizational Complexity
Glen Rice and Charles Redman   325

4   Mighty Cahokia
William Iseminger   343

5   Settlement Patterns and Community Organization
in the Maya Lowlands
Jeremy A. Sabloff   351

6   Empires in the Dust
Karen Wright   361

Commentary   367

Part Ten — Art, Ritual, and Ideology

Introduction   369

1   Reading the Minds of Rock Artists
David S. Whitley   373

2   Neptune's Ice Age Gallery
Jean Clottes and Jean Courtin   381

3   The Dawn of Adornment
Randall White   391

4   Rise and Fall of the City of the Gods
John B. Carlson   397

Commentary   411

viii   Contents

✓ **Part Eleven — Experiment and Ethnography
in "Living Archaeology"**

Introduction   413

1   The Last Stone Ax Makers
    Nicholas Toth, Desmond Clark, and Giancarlo Ligabue   417

2   Ethnoarchaeology at the Top of the World:
    New Ceramic Studies Among the Kalinga of Luzon
    William Longacre, James M. Skibo, and Miriam T. Stark   425

3   Understanding the Past Through Hopi Oral History
    Kurt Dongoske, Leigh Jenkins, and T.J. Ferguson   441

4   Putting Voyaging Back into Polynesian Prehistory
    Ben Finney   447

Commentary   465

**Part Twelve — Archaeology and
the Contemporary World**

Introduction   467

1   The Past as Propaganda
    Bettina Arnold   471

2   Bones and Bureaucrats: New York's Great
    Cemetery Imbroglio
    Spencer P.M. Harrington   481

3   Collaboration at Inyan Ceyaka Atonwan
    (Village of the Rapids)
    Janet D. Spector   491

4   Archaeology Returns to the Public
    Charles R. Redman   499

5   Signatures Across the Landscape:
    The El Pilar Archaeological Reserve for Maya
    Flora and Fauna — Belize/Guatemala
    Anabel Ford   507

Commentary   515

✓ **Part Thirteen — Archaeology's Future**

Introduction   517

1   In Our Grandmother's House
    Sharman Russell   521

2   The Destruction of the Past
    Catherine M. Cameron   529

3   Fingerprints in the Sand: Federal Agents Use
    Dirty Evidence Against Archaeological Thieves
    Richard Monastersky   547

4   Lost City in the Jungle
    Fergus M. Bordewich   553

Commentary   557

Index   559

Preface

We created this reader as a teaching aide for introductory archaeology classes. We intend this reader to serve as a supplement to an introductory textbook on archaeological methods, with recent articles that illustrate archaeological applications. Growing teaching loads and research demands in today's universities and community colleges, and the heightened levels of specialization in the discipline, make it more difficult for instructors to keep abreast of current advances in anthropological archaeology. As we have taught classes in introductory archaeology, we have used articles to supplement textbook assignments, since even the best textbooks cannot sufficiently illustrate many fundamental archaeological methods and techniques. Although "course packets" were once a favorable solution, increased copyright restrictions are diminishing the value of this approach. Our goal, in this reader, is to provide a collection of readings in one package that interests students and that saves instructors the time involved in securing copyright permissions to develop a coursepack.

We designed *Exploring the Past: Readings in Archaeology* to help university and community college instructors, who, like ourselves, find it imperative to expose students to "real world" examples of how contemporary archaeologists do their work. In creating this reader, we have sought to learn from our own experience in teaching archaeology to students from a variety of backgrounds (majors and non-majors), different life experiences, and different motivations for enrolling in such a course. Students today are exposed to archaeology through a public lens: students tell us that they learn about archaeology first through television programs and articles in popular magazines, and these media have been successful in conveying the excitement and intrinsic interest of our field. While using popular media to teach archaeology might have provoked strong resistance thirty years ago, the wealth of well-written popular articles makes such attitudes counter-productive today.

As we have developed our archaeology courses in the last five years, we have collectively examined a few hundred popular and scholarly articles for consideration as supplemental readings. For *Exploring the Past* we chose those readings that best capture the excitement and breadth of contemporary archaeology. Readings in this collection are drawn from academic and popular venues to introduce today's introductory student to the rapidly changing character of the dynamic field of archaeology. Several of our selections illustrate actual case studies in which archaeologists deployed a particular method or technique as part of a problem-oriented research program, and some of them present controversial debates to display the dynamic, scientific nature of our field. The relatively high number of articles included in most sections of the reader enables instructors to assign their students those readings that best complement the content of course lectures.

We have divided *Exploring the Past: Readings in Archaeology* into thirteen topical sections that define archaeology, identify its goals and purpose, consider its origins and growth, and illustrate several key methods, techniques, and topics of study. Many selections highlight how archaeological concepts and methods are practically applied, from site discovery and excavation to artifact analysis and interpretation. We preface each major section of readings with an opening discussion that orients students to the issues at hand, and a brief synthetic commentary follows each section. The concluding sections contain articles that explore the relevance of archaeology to contemporary society as it seeks to interpret humanity's past, and as it looks to the future. In several instances these commentaries evaluate the merits of differing viewpoints, and seek to forecast upcoming developments in the field in light of current trends. Although most students who use this reader will probably study at North American universities, we have tried to make the reader global in its coverage on the archaeology of Asia, Africa, North and South America, Europe, Australia, and the Pacific.

Acknowledgments

4-1 Surveying Ancient Cities by Anthony M. Snodgrass and John L. Bintliff. *Scientific American* 264(3):88–93, 1991.

4-2 Copyright © 1996 Andrew Todhunter. This piece appears in *Preservation* 48(4):60–65 under the title "Diving into the Wreck." Reprinted by permission of the author.

4-3 With permission from *Natural History* (December 1994). Copyright © the American Museum of Natural History (1994).

5-1 The Dating Game by James Shreeve. *Discover* magazine, September 1992. Reprinted by permission.

5-2 A Modern Riddle of the Sphinx by Robert M. Schoch. *Omni* 14(11):46–48, 68–69, 1992.

5-3 Reprinted with permission from The Earliest Art Becomes Older—and More Common by Virginia Morell. *Science* 267(31):1908–1909. Copyright © 1995 American Association for the Advancement of Science.

6-1 Reprinted with permission from *Science News*, the weekly newsmagazine of science. Copyright © 1995 by Science Service.

6-2 Tales from the Crypt by Karen Wright. *Discover* magazine, July 1991. Reprinted by permission.

6-3 Reprinted with permission of *Archaeology* Magazine, vol. 48 no. 6. Copyright © 1995 by the Archaeological Institute of America.

6-4 Reprinted with permission from *Popular Science* magazine. Copyright © 1993, Times Mirror Magazines Inc.

7-1 Ice Age Lamps by Sophie A. de Beaune and Randall White. *Scientific American*, vol. 266, no. 3.

7-2 Late Ice Age Hunting Technology by Heidi Knecht. *Scientific American* 271(1):82–87, 1994.

7-3 With permission from *Natural History* (October 1989). Copyright © the American Museum of Natural History (1989).

7-4 Reprinted with permission of *Archaeology* Magazine, vol. 48 no. 1. Copyright © 1995 by the Archaeological Institute of America.

8-1 Reprinted by permission of *American Scientist*, magazine of Sigma Xi, The Scientific Research Society.

8-2 Finding the First Farmers by Bruce Fellman. *Yale* magazine, October 1994. Reprinted by permission.

8-3 Raised Field Agriculture in the Lake Titicaca Basin: Putting Ancient Agriculture Back to Work by C.L. Erickson. *Expedition* 30(3):8–16, 1988. Reprinted by permission.

8-4 Household Craft Specialization and Shell Ornament Manufacture by Gary P. Feinman and Linda M. Nicholas. *Expedition* 37(2):14–25, 1995. Reprinted by permission.

9-1 Reprinted with permission from Cemetery Reveals Complex Aboriginal Society by Graeme O'Neill. *Science* 264(5164):1403. Copyright © 1994 American Association for the Advancement of Science.

9-2 Reprinted with permission from Masters and Slaves in an Iron Age Cave? by Michael Balter. *Science* 268(5214):1132–1133. Copyright © 1995 American Association for the Advancement of Science.

9-3 Platform Mounds of the Arizona Desert: An Experiment in Organizational Complexity by Glen Rice and Charles Redman. *Expedition* 35(1):53–63, 1993. Reprinted by permission.

9-4 Reprinted with permission of *Archaeology* Magazine, vol. 49 no. 3. Copyright © 1996 by the Archaeological Institute of America.

9-5 Settlement Patterns and Community Organization in the Maya Lowlands by Jeremy A. Sabloff. *Expedition* 38(1):3–13, 1996. Reprinted by permission.

9-6 Empires in the Dust by Karen Wright. *Discover* magazine, March 1998. Reprinted by permission.

10-1 Reading the Minds of Rock Artists by David S. Whitley. *American Archaeology*, Fall 1997. Reprinted by permission.

10-2 With permission from *Natural History* (April 1993). Copyright © the American Museum of Natural History (1993).

10-3 With permission from *Natural History* (May 1993). Copyright © the American Museum of Natural History (1993).

10-4 Reprinted with permission of *Archaeology* Magazine, vol. 46 no. 6. Copyright © 1993 by the Archaeological Institute of America.

11-1 The Last Stone Ax Makers by Nicholas Toth, Desmond Clark, and Giancarlo Ligabue. *Scientific American* 267(1):88–93, 1992. Reprinted by permission

11-2 Ethnoarchaeology at the Top of the World: New Ceramic Studies Among the Kalinga of Luzon by William A. Longacre, James M. Skibo, and Miriam T. Stark. *Expedition* 33(1):4–15, 1991. Reprinted by permission.

11-3 Understanding the Past Through Hopi Oral History by Kurt Dongoske, Leigh Jenkins, and T.J. Ferguson. *Native Peoples* 6(2):24–31, 1993. Reprinted by permission of the authors.

11-4 Putting Voyaging Back into Polynesian Prehistory by Ben Finney. In *Oceanic Culture History: Essays in Honour of Roger Green*, edited by J.M. Davidson, G. Irwin, B.F. Leach, A. Pawley, and D. Brown, pp. 365–376. New Zealand Journal of Archaeology Special Publication, 1996.

12-1 Reprinted with permission of *Archaeology* Magazine, vol. 45 no. 4. Copyright © 1992 by the Archaeological Institute of America.

12-2 Reprinted with permission of *Archaeology* Magazine, vol. 46 no. 2. Copyright © 1993 by the Archaeological Institute of America.

12-3 Collaboration at *Inyan Ceyaka Atonwan* (Village at the Rapids) by Janet D. Spencer. *Society for American Archaeology Bulletin* 12(3):8–10, 1994.

12-4 Archaeology Returns to the Public by Charles L. Redman. *Native Peoples* 2(3):28–33, 1989. Reprinted by permission of the author.

12-5 Signatures Across the Landscape: The El Pilar Archaeological Reserve for Maya Flora and Fauna—Belize/Guatemala by Anabel Ford. *Anthropology Newsletter* 39(1). January 1998. Copyright © by the American Anthropological Association.

13-1 S. Apt Russell, *When the Land Was Young*, (pages 187–202). © 1996 Sharman Russell. Reprinted by permission of Addison Wesley Longman.

13-2 The Destruction of the Past: Nonrenewable Cultural Resources by Catherine M. Cameron. *Nonrenewable Resources* 3(1):6–24, 1994. Reprinted by permission.

13-3 Reprinted with permission from *Science News*, the weekly newsmagazine of science, copyright © 1990, 1995 by Science Service.

13-4 Reprinted with permission from the May 1998 *Reader's Digest*. Copyright © 1998 by The Reader's Digest Assn., Inc.

Photograph and Illustration Credits

Part 1

Article 1: p. 8 courtesy of Masakazu Tani, The Garbage Project; p. 14 courtesy of Douglas Wilson, The Garbage Project; p. 23 courtesy of The Garbage Project.

Article 3: p. 46 courtesy of Bette Duke; pp. 48 and 49 courtesy of William K. Geiger.

Article 4: p. 52 courtesy of Melissa Connor.

Article 5: p. 57 courtesy of Dennis Stanford and Pegi Jodry; p. 59 Alison Whitter; p. 60(t, b) courtesy of Dennis Stanford and Pegi Jodry; p. 61(t) Vic Krantz; p. 61(b) courtesy of Dennis Stanford and Pegi Jodry.

Part 2

Article 2: pp. 86 and 87 Martin Gallivan.

Part 3

Article 3 pp. 112 and 115 reprinted with the permission of *Archaeology* Magazine, vol. 49 no. 1. Copyright © 1996 by the Archaeological Institute of America.

Article 4 p. 120 courtesy of *The Chronical of Higher Education*.

Part 4

Article 1 pp. 132, 134, 135, and 137 courtesy of Hank Iken.

Article 3 pp. 148, 149, 150, 151(t, b), 152, 154, 156, and 157 courtesy of Charles Higham.

Part 5

Article 1 pp. 166, 169, and 172 courtesy of Alison Brooks.

Part 6

Article 1 p. 192 courtesy of Greg Byrne/Harper's Ferry Conservation Laboratory; p. 193 courtesy of Margaret Newman.

Article 2   p. 196 courtesy of Bill Wiegand/University of Illinois News Bureau; p. 198 courtesy of Richard Keen/College of Veterinary Medicine, University of Illinois.

Article 3   p. 204 courtesy of Ohio Historical Society, p. 205 courtesy of Bette Duke, adapted by Ronald Beckwith; pp. 207 and 208 courtesy of Ohio Historical Society.

Article 4   p. 215 Mark Zug.

Part 7

Article 1   pp. 224 and 226 courtesy of Randall White.

Article 2   pp. 233 and 234(l) courtesy of Heidi Knecht; p. 234(r) courtesy of Patricia Wynne; p. 235 (l, r) courtesy of Heidi Knecht.

Article 3   pp. 240, 241, 244, and 246 Miriam T. Stark.

Article 4   p. 250 Jo Anne Van Tilburg; p. 252 (t, b) Mike Ohara.

Part 8

Article 1   pp. 266, 268, and 272 courtesy of Tom Dye.

Article 2   pp. 280, 281, 282, 283, 284, 285, 286, and 287 courtesy of A.M.T. Moore, G.C. Hillman, and A.J. Legge.

Article 3   p. 290 courtesy of Clark L. Erickson; p. 291 courtesy of Clark L. Erickson, adapted by Ronald Beckwith; pp. 293, 294, 297, 299, and 301 courtesy of Clark L. Erickson.

Article 4   pp. 304 and 306 courtesy of Gary P. Feinman and Linda M. Nicholas; pp. 308, 309, and 310(t, b) Linda M. Nicholas.

Part 9

Article 3   p. 326 courtesy of the Bureau of Reclamation, U.S. Dept. of the Interior; p. 327 courtesy of Brenda Shears; p. 328 Glena Cain; p. 329 courtesy of Sharon Vaughn; p. 331 Sharon Vaughn; p. 332 Lynn Simon; p. 333 Greg Phillips; pp. 336 and 337(t) Lynn Simon; p. 337(b) Glena Cain; p. 338 Greg Phillips; p. 339 courtesy of Brenda Spears; p. 340 (t, b) Glena Cain.

Article 4   p. 344 L.K. Townsend, courtesy of Cahokia Mounds State Historic Site; p. 348 Peter Bostrom, courtesy of Cahokia Mounds State Historic Site.

Article 5   p. 353 courtesy of Jeremy Sabloff; pp. 355 and 356 courtesy of the Sayil Archaeological Project.

Part 10

Article 1   pp. 374, 377, and 378 David Whitley.

Article 2   p. 382(t) courtesy of Ministère de la Culture, Direction du Patrimoine, photo A. Chené, CNRS; p. 382(b) Ronald Beckwith; pp. 384, 385, and 386 courtesy of Ministère de la Culture, Direction du Patrimoine, photo A. Chené, CNRS; p. 388(t) Ronald Beckwith; pp. 388(b) and 390 courtesy of Ministère de la Culture, Direction du Patrimoine, photo A. Chené, CNRS.

Article 3   pp. 392 and 393 Randall White.

Article 4   pp. 399, 404, and 405 Joe Le Monnier.

Part 11

Article 2   p. 427 Brigid Sullivan; p. 428 Miriam T. Stark; p. 432 Ronald Beckwith; pp. 433 and 434 Miriam T. Stark.

Article 3   p. 442 T.J. Ferguson.

Article 4   p. 448 courtesy of the Bishop Museum; pp. 452, 454, and 455 courtesy of Ben Finney.

Part 12

Article 1   pp. 472, 473, 475, 476, and 479 courtesy of Bettina Arnold.

Article 2   pp. 483 and 488 courtesy of the U.S. General Services Administration.

Article 3   p. 494 Ronald Beckwith; p. 496 courtesy of Janet Spector.

Article 4   pp. 502, 503, 504, 506, and 508 Brenda Shears/Arizona State University.

Article 5   pp. 510, 511, 512(t, b), and 515 courtesy of Anabel Ford.

Part 13

Article 2   p. 539 Stephen H. Lekson.

Article 3   pp. 550 and 551 courtesy of Martin McAllister/Archaeological Resource Investigations.

Article 4   pp. 556 and 558 courtesy of Wilhelm Solheim.

Exploring the Past

Part One

Defining Archaeology

Introduction

What is archaeology? Why is archaeology important? Is archaeology relevant to the field of anthropology? How is archaeology relevant to our world today? Archaeology is one of the most misunderstood scholarly disciplines in the world. Popular images of archaeologists in movies and TV shows, detective novels, and even computer games often portray the glamorous and adventurous lives of men and women in single-minded pursuit of antiquities from remote and exotic reaches of the world. In many respects, nothing could be further from the truth. Far from being the "…the cowboys of science…" archaeologists are highly systematic (and sometimes obsessed!) social scientists within the broader field of anthropology. More often than not, our work is time-consuming and repetitive, and we relish those rare moments of true discovery.

Most archaeologists study physical remains of the past, whether they focus on sherds or stone tools, or on architecture and remnants of farm systems. We use these physical remains to attempt to understand how people lived and how societies organized themselves. Equally important in our research is the study of change: what we have found in our work is that human societies are remarkably fluid, and change in response to many different pressures. Archaeologists come in many varieties, and the public is familiar with Biblical and Classical archaeologists who rely on ancient histories to study the past. Some people are more familiar with Near Eastern archaeologists and Egyptologists, who link their translations of ancient documents to material remains to write ancient history. Articles in this reader focus instead on anthropological archaeology, and how thinking anthropologically reveals many aspects of past cultures.

Anthropological archaeologists share the view with many sociocultural anthropologists that culture is most developed among human societies, and that culture is a kind of behavior that is learned and shared by members of a society. Culture plays a vital role in helping human societies develop and flourish in an ever-changing world. Consequently, archaeologists who work in the New World and western Europe are often described as "anthropological archaeologists," since they study human culture and processes of culture change. However, unlike their colleagues in anthropology who study language (linguistic anthropologists), customs of living cultures (sociocultural anthropologists), or human biological evolution (physical anthropologists), archaeologists study and interpret the human past by using artifacts and other material remains. These artifacts can be as old as several million years, or as recent as yesterday's garbage. It is true that most archaeologists study ancient artifacts, found in sites from highland areas, in river valleys, around lake margins, and under water. The methods we use vary from one setting to the next, but our goals and our use of the scientific method are similar no matter the locale.

Archaeology has its roots in an antiquarian past and "archaeologists" of the 17th, 18th, and early 19th centuries were antiquarians whose interests led them to view digging and collecting as hobbies and avocations, rather than as true professions. Since the mid-19th century, archaeology has become a profession and a scientific field of inquiry, dominated by individuals with years of academic and technical training. Today, thousands of archaeologists are employed in the public and private sectors, in universities, and in museums as professionals the world over. Today's archaeologists engage in a variety of activities in the field, in the lab, and in the classroom. Some work is decidedly academic in focus, but other archaeologists work actively with local communities to build museums, to protect cultural resources, to rebuild monuments, and—sometimes—to apply archaeological techniques to answering contemporary problems.

This section, called "Defining Archaeology," displays some of the various guises that archaeology assumes in today's world. Not only do archaeologists seek to answer a wide range of questions, but they find information in a wide range of materials. Articles in this section also display the amazing variety of techniques that archaeologists use to collect their information: they use all manner of tools, from tweezers and trowels to picks and air pumps, from bulldozers and augers to subsurface radar and scuba tanks. We move from fieldwork in contemporary garbage dumps to work under water; we see that what is called "historic" today involves places and experiences of our parents' and grandparents' lifetimes; and we see how archaeology can be used to solve mysteries created by contemporary political problems in different parts of the world.

We begin our quest by confronting the most common material of archaeologists: garbage. Humans have always made and discarded trash. Collections of discards create sites that archaeologists find and study. Most archaeologists spend some portion of their professional career mapping, excavating, measuring, and reporting on ancient garbage. We love garbage, for the richness of its finds and for the clues it contains to how people lived in the past. However, we often disguise this fact by discussing instead the "middens" of our site. William Rathje, and his Garbage Project at the University of Arizona, have never been embarrassed by archaeologists' love of garbage. In fact, they wallow in it and learn great insights about disposal behavior as a result. They argue convincingly that archaeology can tell us not only about the past, but also about how we live today.

Lawrence Robbins' article, entitled, "The Wet Frontier," illustrates how archaeologists work with waterlogged and underwater sites. Although we commonly associate archaeologists with large monuments like the pyramids of Egypt, archaeological sites are often found in less convenient places. We learn the history of research at European sites that a lake has now inundated, and about the drastic measures required to study these sites. Robbins describes the "wells of sacrifice" that the ancient Maya used as part of their religion, and how archaeologists have found ways to probe their contents. We hear about the oldest brain found in North America (in Little Salt Spring), and about the difficulties of studying sunken Viking ships. We follow the saga of the ill-fated 16th century ship called the Mary Rose, and more recent efforts to bring this ship and its contents back to light. Robbins' final section takes us one step farther to show us how archaeologists have learned to use water and flotation devices to yield organic remains.

Some archaeologists study artifacts that are much more recent than Bronze Age lake dwellings and Viking ships. Materials on public (Federal) lands that are more than fifty years in age are legally "historical" property and thus worthy of archae-ological attention. The article "Proving Ground of the Nuclear Age," by William Johnson and Colleen Beck, describes a fascinating study of military "artifacts" from the Cold War era of the 1950s and onward. Atomic test sites of the Cold War era are now historical places that the public may visit, and archaeologists have played an instrumental role in identifying and interpreting these strange landscapes. The authors acknowledge that their fieldwork investigations seem foreign to most archaeologists. Yet, their careful documentation of the architec-tural remains of a nuclear proving ground in Nevada provides answers for gener-ations a century from now.

Melissa Connor provides one of the most sobering articles in this collection, entitled, "The Archaeology of Contemporary Mass Graves." She explains how archaeologists can provide a service through using field techniques that are regu-lar parts of our work. Here, National Park Service archaeologists helped a non-profit physicians' group that engages in human rights work around the world. Po-litical turbulence in Rwanda in 1994 involved the deaths of hundreds of thousands of people in widespread interethnic conflict. These archaeologists worked at mass grave sites to recover information on some of the many dead, through mapping and the recovery of skeletons from a Catholic Church complex where 4,000-6,000 people died in April 1994. Working with physical anthropolo-gists, the archaeologists could identify at least six mass graves and make signifi-cant contributions to human rights investigations in this tragic part of the world.

We end this section on a more optimistic note, by showcasing a pair of archae-ologists who make a career of studying the Ice Age of North America. In Bruce Goldfarb's article, "A Love for the Ages," we meet archaeologists Dennis Stan-ford and Margaret Jodry and learn about the life of archaeologists. Why do ar-chaeologists do what we do? And what does it involve? In describing this particu-lar archaeology couple, the article identifies several qualities that archaeologists share in common: a passion for knowledge, a burning curiosity about the past, a patience for tedious and meticulous work, and a sense of humor about them-selves. It also begins to address the process of research and the use of the scientific method, which tests hypotheses and discards them as necessary, and proceeds to formulate new ones.

1

Yes, Wonderful Things

William Rathje and Colleen Murphy

On a crisp October morning not long ago the sun ascended above the Atlantic Ocean and turned its gaze on a team of young researchers as they swarmed over what may be the largest archaeological site in the world. The mound they occupied covers three thousand acres and in places rises more than 155 feet above a low-lying island. Its mass, estimated at 100 million tons, and its volume, estimated at 2.9 billion cubic feet, make it one of the largest man-made structures in North America. And it is known to be a treasure trove—a Pompeii, a Tikal, a Valley of the Kings—of artifacts from the most advanced civilization the planet has ever seen. Overhead sea gulls cackled and cawed, alighting now and then to peck at an artifact or skeptically observe an archaeologist at work. The surrounding landscape still supported quail and duck, but far more noticeable were the dusty, rumbling wagons and tractors of the New York City Department of Sanitation.

The site was the Fresh Kills landfill, on Staten Island, in New York City, a repository of garbage that, when shut down, in the year 2005, will have reached a height of 505 feet above sea level, making it the highest geographic feature along a fifteen-hundred-mile stretch of the Atlantic seaboard running north from Florida all the way to Maine. One sometimes hears that Fresh Kills will have to be closed when it reaches 505 feet so as not to interfere with the approach of aircraft to Newark Airport, in New Jersey, which lies just across the waterway called Arthur Kill. In reality, though, the 505-foot elevation is the result of a series of calculations designed to maximize the landfill's size while avoiding the creation of grades so steep that roads built upon the landfill can't safely be used.

Fresh Kills was originally a vast marshland, a tidal swamp. Robert Moses's plan for the area, in 1948, was to dump enough garbage there to fill the marshland up—a process that would take, according to one estimate, until 1968—and then to develop the site, building houses, attracting light industry, and setting aside open space for recreational use. ("The Fresh Kills landfill project," a 1951 report to Mayor Vincent R. Impelliteri observed, "cannot fail to affect constructively a wide area around it. It is at once practical and idealistic.") Something along these lines may yet happen when Fresh Kills is closed. Until then, however, it is the largest active landfill in the world. It is twenty-five times the size of the Great Pyramid of Khufu at Giza, forty times the size of the Temple of the Sun at Teotihuacan (see Figure 1-A). The volume of Fresh Kills is approaching that of the Great Wall of China, and by one estimate will surpass it at some point in the next few years. It is the sheer physical stature of Fresh Kills in the hulking world of landfills that explains why archaeologists were drawn to the place.

FRESH KILLS LANDFILL

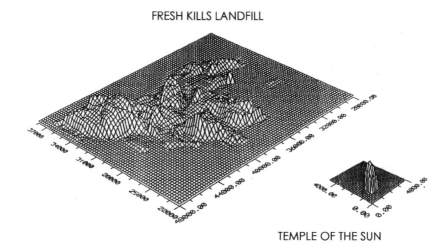

TEMPLE OF THE SUN

Figure 1-A. A comparison of the Pyramid of the Sun at Teotihuacan, in Mexico (right) and the Fresh Kills landfill, on Staten Island, in New York (left). The Pyramid of the Sun is roughly 800 feet to a side; the Fresh Kills grid as a whole represent an area roughly 2.8 miles by 3.8 miles. Elevations have been exaggerated for clarity but the relative volumes represented are accurate. (Grapic courtesy of Masakazu Tani, The Garbage Project)

To the archaeologists of the University of Arizona's Garbage Project, which is now entering its twentieth year, landfills represent valuable lodes of information that may, when mined and interpreted, produce valuable insights—insights not into the nature of some past society, of course, but into the nature of our own. Garbage is among humanity's most prodigious physical legacies to those who have yet to be born; if we can come to understand our discards, Garbage Project archaeologists argue, then we will better understand the world in which we live. It is this conviction that prompts Garbage Project researchers to look upon the steaming detritus of daily existence with the same quiet excitement displayed by Howard Carter and Lord George Edward Carnarvon at the unpillaged, unopened tomb of Tutankhamun.

"Can you see anything?" Carnarvon asked as Carter thrust a lighted candle through a hole into the gloom of the first antechamber. "Yes," Carter replied. "Wonderful things."

Garbage archaeology can be conducted in several ways. At Fresh Kills the method of excavation involved a mobile derrick and a thirteen-hundred-pound bucket auger, the latter of which would be sunk into various parts of the landfill to retrieve samples of garbage from selected strata. At 6:15 a.m. Buddy Kellett of the company Kellett's Well Boring, Inc., which had assisted with several previous Garbage Project landfill digs, drove one of the company's trucks, with derrick and auger collapsed for travel, straight up the steep slope of one of the landfill mounds. Two-thirds of the way up, the Garbage Project crew directed Kellett to a small patch of level ground. Four hydraulic posts were deployed from the stationary vehicle, extending outward to keep it safely moored. Now the derrick was raised. It supported a long metal rod that in turn housed two other metal rods; the apparatus, when pulled to its full length, like a telescope, was capable of penetrating the landfill to a depth of ninety-seven feet—enough at this particular spot to go clear through its bottom and into the original marsh that Fresh Kills had been (or into what was left of it). At the end of the rods was the auger, a large bucket made of high-tension steel: four feet high, three feet in diameter, and open at the bottom like a cookie cutter, with six graphite-and-steel teeth around the bottom's circumference. The bucket would spin at about thirty revolutions per minute and with such force that virtually nothing could impede its descent. At a Garbage Project excavation in Sunnyvale, California, in 1988, one of the first things the bucket hit in the cover dirt a few feet below the surface of the Sunnyvale Landfill was the skeleton of a car. The bucket's teeth snapped the axle, and drilled on.

The digging at Fresh Kills began. Down the whirring bucket plunged. Moments later it returned with a gasp, laden with garbage that, when released, spewed a thin vapor into the chill autumnal air. The smell was pungent, somewhere between sweet and disagreeable. Kellett's rig operator, David Spillers, did his job with the relaxation that comes of familiarity, seemingly oblivious to the harsh grindings and sharp clanks. The rest of the archaeological crew, wearing cloth aprons and heavy rubber gloves, went about their duties with practiced efficiency and considerable speed. They were veteran members of the Garbage Project's A-Team—its landfill-excavating arm—and had been through it all before.

Again a bucketful of garbage rose out of the ground. As soon as it was dumped Masakazu Tani, at the time a Japanese graduate student in anthropology at the University of Arizona (his Ph.D. thesis, recently completed, involves identifying activity areas in ancient sites on the basis of distributions of litter), plunged a thermometer into the warm mass. "Forty-three degrees centigrade," Tani called out. The temperature (equivalent to 109.4 degrees Fahrenheit) was duly logged. The garbage was then given a brusque preliminary examination to determine its generic source and, if possible, its date of origin. In this case the presence of telltale domestic items, and of legible newspapers, made both tasks easy. Gavin Archer, another anthropologist and a research associate of the Garbage Project, made a notation in the running log that he would keep all day long: "Household, circa 1977." Before the next sample was pulled up Douglas Wilson, an anthropologist who specializes in household hazardous waste, stepped up to the auger hole and played out a weighted tape measure, eventually calling out, "Thirty-five feet." As a safety precaution, Wilson, like any other crew member working close to the sunken shaft on depth-measure duty, wore a leather harness tethered to a nearby vehicle. The esophagus created by the bucket auger was just large enough to accept a human being, and anyone slipping untethered a story or two into this narrow, oxygen-starved cavity would die of asphyxiation before any rescue could be attempted.

Most of the bucketfuls of garbage received no more attention than did the load labeled "Household, circa 1977." Some basic data were recorded for tracking purposes, and the garbage was left on a quickly accumulating backdirt pile. But as each of what would finally be fourteen wells grew deeper and deeper, at regular intervals (either every five or every ten feet) samples were taken and preserved for full-dress analysis. On those occasions Wilson Hughes, the methodical and serenely ursine co-director and field supervisor of the Garbage Project, and the man responsible for day-to-day logistics at the Fresh Kills dig, would call out to the bucket operator over the noise of the engine: "We'll take the next bucket." Then Hughes and Wilson would race toward the rig in a running crouch, like medics toward a helicopter, a plywood sampling board between them. Running in behind came a team of microbiologists and civil engineers assembled from the University of Oklahoma, the University of Wisconsin, and Procter & Gamble's environmental laboratory. They brought with them a variety of containers and sealing devices to preserve samples in an oxygen-free environment—an environment that would allow colonies of the anaerobic bacteria that cause most of the biodegradation in landfills (to the extent that biodegradation occurs) to survive for later analysis. Behind the biologists and engineers came other Garbage Project personnel with an assortment of wire mesh screens and saw horses.

Within seconds of the bucket's removal from the ground, the operator maneuvered it directly over the sampling board, and released the contents. The pile was attacked first by Phillip Zack, a civil engineering student from the University of Wisconsin, who, as the temperature was being recorded, directed portions of the material into a variety of airtight conveyances. Then other members of the team moved in—the people who would shovel the steaming refuse atop the wire mesh; the people who would sort and bag whatever didn't go through the mesh; the people who would pour into bags or cannisters or jars whatever did go through the mesh; the people who would label everything for the trip either back to Tucson and the Garbage Project's holding bins or to the laboratories of the various microbiologists. (The shortest trip was to the trailer-laboratory that Procter & Gamble scientists had driven from Cincinnati and parked at the edge of the landfill.) The whole sample-collection process, from dumping to sorting to storing, took no more than twelve minutes. During the Fresh Kills dig it was repeated forty-four times at various places and various depths.

As morning edged toward afternoon the bucket auger began to near the limits of its reach in one of the wells. Down through the first thirty-five feet, a depth that in this well would date back to around 1984, the landfill had been relatively dry. Food waste and yard waste—hot dogs, bread, and grass clippings, for example— were fairly well preserved. Newspapers remained intact and easy to read, their lurid headlines ("Woman Butchered—Ex-Hubby Held") calling to mind a handful of yesterday's tragedies. Beyond thirty-five feet, however, the landfill became increasingly wet, the garbage increasingly unidentifiable. At sixty feet, a stratum in this well containing garbage from the 1940s and 1950s, the bucket grabbed a sample and pulled it toward the surface. The Garbage Project team ran forward with their equipment, positioning themselves underneath. The bucket rose majestically as the operator sat at the controls, shouting something over the noise. As near as anyone can reconstruct it now, he was saying, "You boys might want to back off some, 'cause if this wind hits that bucket...." The operator broke off because the wind did hit that bucket, and the material inside—a gray slime, redolent of putrefaction—thoroughly showered the crew. It would be an exaggeration to suggest that the victims were elated by this development, but their curiosity was certainly piqued, because on only one previous excavation had slime like this turned up in a landfill. What was the stuff made of? How had it come to be? What did its existence mean? The crew members doggedly collected all the usual samples, plus a few extras bottles of slime for special study. Then they cleaned themselves off.

It would be a blessing if it were possible to study garbage in the abstract, to study garbage without having to handle it physically.[1] But that is not possible. Garbage is not mathematics. To understand garbage you have to touch it, to feel it, to sort it, to smell it. You have to pick through hundreds of tons of it, counting and weighing all the daily newspapers, the telephone books, the soiled diapers, the foam clamshells that once briefly held hamburgers, the lipstick cylinders coated with grease, the medicine vials still encasing brightly colored pills, the empty bottles of scotch, the half-full cans of paint and muddy turpentine, the forsaken toys, the cigarette butts. You have to sort and weigh and measure the volume of all the organic matter, the discards from thousands of plates: the noodles and the Cheerios and the tortillas; the pieces of pet food that have made their own gravy; the hardened jelly doughnuts, bleeding from their side wounds; the half-eaten bananas, mostly still within their peels, black and incomparably sweet in the embrace of final decay. You have to confront sticky green mountains of yard waste, and slippery brown hills of potato peels, and brittle ossuaries of chicken bones and T-bones. And then, finally, there are the "fines," the vast connecting mixture of tiny bits of paper, metal, glass, plastic, dirt, grit, and former nutrients that suffuses every landfill like a kind of grainy lymph. To understand garbage you need thick gloves and a mask and some booster shots. But the yield in knowledge—about people and their behavior as well as about garbage itself—offsets the grim working conditions.

To an archaeologist, ancient garbage pits or garbage mounds, which can usually be located within a short distance from any ruin, are always among the happiest of finds, for they contain in concentrated form the artifacts and comestibles and remnants of behavior of the people who used them. While every archaeologist dreams of discovering spectacular objects, the bread-and-butter work of archaeology involves the most common and routine kinds of discards. It is not entirely fanciful to define archaeology as the discipline that tries to understand old garbage, and to learn from that garbage something about ancient societies and ancient behaviors. The eminent archaeologist Emil Haury once wrote of the aboriginal garbage heaps of the American Southwest: "Whichever way one views the mounds—as garbage piles to avoid, or as symbols of a way of life—they nevertheless are features more productive of information than any others." When the British archaeologist Sir Leonard Woolley, in 1916, first climbed to the top of the ancient city of Carchemish, on the Euphrates River near the modern-day Turkish-Syrian border, he moistened his index finger and held it in the air. Satisfied, he

---

1. A note on terminology. Several words for the things we throw away—"garbage," "trash," "refuse," "rubbish"—are used synonymously in casual speech but in fact have different meanings. *Trash* refers specifically to discards that are at least theoretically "dry"—newspapers, boxes, cans, and so on. *Garbage* refers technically to "wet" discards—food remains, yard waste, and offal. *Refuse* is an inclusive term for both the wet discards and the dry. *Rubbish* is even more inclusive: It refers to all refuse plus construction and demolition debris. The distinction between wet and dry garbage was important in the days when cities slopped garbage to pigs, and needed to have the wet material separated from the dry; it eventually became irrelevant, but may see a revival if the idea of composting food and yard waste catches on. We will frequently use "garbage" in this book to refer to the totality of human discards because it is the word used most naturally in ordinary speech. The word is etymologically obscure, though it probably derives from Anglo-French, and its earliest associations have to do with working in the kitchen.

scanned the region due south of the city—that is, downwind—pausing to draw on his map the location of any mounds he saw. A trench dug through the largest of these mounds revealed it to be the garbage dump Woolley was certain it was, and the exposed strata helped establish the chronological sequence for the Carchemish site as a whole. Archaeologists have been picking through ancient garbage ever since archaeology became a profession, more than a century ago, and they will no doubt go on doing so as long as garbage is produced.

Several basic points about garbage need to be emphasized at the outset. First, the creation of garbage is an unequivocal sign of a human presence. From Styrofoam cups along a roadway and urine bags on the moon there is an uninterrupted chain of garbage that reaches back more than two million years to the first "waste flake" knocked off in the knapping of the first stone tool. That the distant past often seems misty and dim is precisely because our earliest ancestors left so little garbage behind. An appreciation of the accomplishments of the first hominids became possible only after they began making stone tools, the debris from the production of which, along with the discarded tools themselves, are now probed for their secrets with electron microscopes and displayed in museums not as garbage but as "artifacts." These artifacts serve as markers—increasingly frequent and informative markers—of how our forebears coped with the evolving physical and social world. Human beings are mere place-holders in time, like zeros in a long number; their garbage seems to have more staying power, and a power to inform across the millennia that complements (and often substitutes for) that of the written word. The profligate habits of our own country and our own time—the sheer volume of the garbage that we create and must dispose of—will make our society an open book. The question is: Would we ourselves recognize our story when it is told, or will our garbage tell tales about us that we as yet do not suspect?

That brings up a second matter: If our garbage, in the eyes of the future, is destined to hold a key to the past, then surely it already holds a key to the present. This may be an obvious point, but it is one whose implications were not pursued by scholars until relatively recently. Each of us throws away dozens of items every day. All of these items are relics of specific human activities—relics no different in their inherent nature from many of those that traditional archaeologists work with (though they are, to be sure, a bit fresher). Taken as a whole the garbage of the United States, from its 93 million households and 1.5 million retail outlets and from all of its schools, hospitals, government offices, and other public facilities, is a mirror of American society. Of course, the problem with the mirror garbage offers is that, when encountered in a garbage can, dump, or landfill, it is a broken one: our civilization is reflected in billions of fragments that may reveal little in and of themselves. Fitting some of the pieces back together requires painstaking effort—effort that a small number of archaeologists and natural scientists have only just begun to apply.

A third point about garbage is that it is not an assertion but a physical fact—and thus may sometimes serve as a useful corrective. Human beings have over the centuries left many accounts describing their lives and civilizations. Many of these are little more than self-aggrandizing advertisements. The remains of the tombs, temples, and palaces of the elite are filled with personal histories as recorded by admiring relatives and fawning retainers. More such information is carved into obelisks and stelae, gouged into clay tablets, painted or printed on papyrus and paper. Historians are understandably drawn to written evidence of this kind, but garbage has often served as a kind of tattle-tale, setting the record straight.

It had long been known, for example, that French as well as Spanish forts had been erected along the coast of South Carolina during the sixteenth century, and various mounds and depressions have survived into our own time to testify to their whereabouts. Ever since the mid-nineteenth century a site on the tip of Parris Island, South Carolina, has been familiarly known as the site of a French outpost, built in 1562, that is spelled variously in old documents as Charlesfort, Charlesforte, and Charles Forte. In 1925, the Huguenot Society of South Carolina successfully lobbied Congress to erect a monument commemorating the building of Charlesfort. Subsequently, people in nearby Beaufort took up the Charlesfort theme, giving French names to streets, restaurants, and housing developments. Gift shops sold kitschy touristiana with a distinctly Gallic flavor. Those restaurants and gift shops found themselves in an awkward position when, in 1957, as a result of an analysis of discarded matter discovered at Charlesfort, a National Park Service historian, Albert Manucy, suggested that the site was of Spanish origin. Excavations begun in 1979 by the archaeologist Stanley South, which turned up such items as discarded Spanish olive jars and broken majolica pottery from Seville, confirmed Manucy's view: "Charlesfort," South established, was actually Fort San Marcos, a Spanish installation built in 1577 to protect a Spanish town named Santa Elena. (Both the fort and the town had been abandoned after only a few years.)

Garbage, then, represents physical fact, not mythology. It underscores a point that can not be too greatly emphasized: Our private worlds consist essentially of two realities—mental reality, which encompasses beliefs, attitudes, and ideas, and material reality, which is the picture embodied in the physical record. The study of garbage reminds us that it is a rare person in whom mental and material realities completely coincide. Indeed, for the most part, the pair exist in a state of tension, if not open conflict.

Americans have always wondered, sometimes with buoyant playfulness, what their countrymen in the far future will make of Americans "now." In 1952, in a monograph he first circulated privately among colleagues and eventually published in *The Journal of Irreproducible Results*, the eminent anthropologist and linguist Joseph H. Greenberg—the man who would one day sort the roughly one thousand known Native American languages into three broad language families—imagined the unearthing of the so-called "violence texts" during an excavation of the Brooklyn Dodgers' Ebbets Field in the year A.D. 2026; what interpretation, he wondered, would be given to such newspaper reports as "Yanks Slaughter Indians" and "Reese made a sacrifice in the infield"? In 1979 the artist and writer David Macaulay published *Motel of the Mysteries*, an archaeological site-report setting forth the conclusions reached by a team of excavators in the year A.D. 4022 who have unearthed a motel dating back to 1985 (the year, Macaulay wrote, in which "an accidental reduction in postal rates on a substance called third- and fourth-class mail literally buried the North Americans under tons of brochures, fliers, and small containers called FREE"). Included in the report are illustrations of an archaeologist modeling a toilet seat, toothbrushes, and a drain stopper (or, as Macaulay describes them, "the Sacred Collar...the magnificent 'plasticus' ear ornaments, and the exquisite silver chain and pendant"), all assumed to be items of ritual or personal regalia. In 1982 an exhibit was mounted

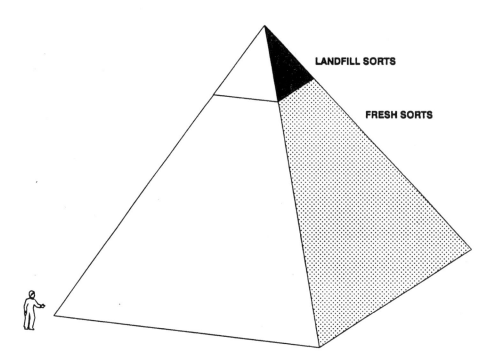

Figure 1-B. As of mid-1991, the volume of garbage that had been sorted by Garbage Project researchers was equivalent to 1,766 cubic yards—enough to create a pyramid 56 feet square and 45 feet high. The smaller pyramid at the pinnacle shows the percent of the total sorted garbage that had been obtained from landfills, as opposed to garbage fresh from the truck. (Graphic courtesy of Douglas Wilson, The Garbage Project)

in New York City called "Splendors of the Sohites"—a vast display of artifacts, including "funerary vessels" (faded, dusky soda bottles) and "hermaphrodite amulets" (discarded pop-top rings), found in the SoHo section of Manhattan and dating from the Archaic Period (A.D. 1950-1961), the Classical Period (1962-1975), and the Decadent Period (1976-c.1980).

Greenberg, Macaulay, and the organizers of the Sohites exhibition all meant to have some fun, but there is an uneasy undercurrent to their work, and it is embodied in the question: What are we to make of ourselves? The Garbage Project, conceived in 1971, and officially established at the University of Arizona in 1973, was an attempt to come up with a new way of providing serious answers. It aimed to apply *real* archaeology to this very question; to see if it would be possible to investigate human behavior "from the back end," as it were. This scholarly endeavor has come to be known as garbology, and practitioners of garbology are known as garbologists. The printed citation (dated 1975) in the *Oxford English Dictionary* for the meaning of "garbology" as used here associates the term with the Garbage Project.

In the years since its founding the Garbage Project's staff members have processed more than 250,000 pounds of garbage, some of it from landfills but most of it fresh out of garbage cans in selected neighborhoods (see Figure 1-B). All of this garbage has been sorted, coded, and catalogued—every piece, from bottles of furniture polish and egg-shaped pantyhose packaging to worn and shredded clothing, crumpled bubble-gum wrappers, and the full range of kitchen waste. A unique database has been built up from these cast-offs, covering virtually every aspect of American life: drinking habits, attitudes toward red meat, trends in the use of convenience foods, the strange ways in which consumers respond to shortages, the use of contraceptives, and hundreds of other matters.[2]

The antecedents of the Garbage Project in the world of scholarship and elsewhere are few but various. Some are undeniably dubious. The examination of fresh refuse is, of course, as old as the human species—just watch anyone who happens upon an old campsite, or a neighbor scavenging at a dump for spare parts or furniture. The first systematic study of the components of America's garbage dates to the early 1900s and the work of the civil engineers Rudolph Hering (in New York) and Samuel A. Greeley (in Chicago), who by 1921 had gathered enough information from enough cities to compile *Collection and Disposal of Municipal Refuse*, the first textbook on urban trash management. In academe, not much happened after that for quite some time. Out in the field, however, civil engineers and solid-waste managers did now and again sort and weigh fresh garbage as it stood in transit between its source and destination, but their categories were usually simple: paper, glass, metal. No one sorted garbage into detailed categories relating to particular consumer discard patterns. No one, for example, kept track of phenomena as specific as the number of beer cans thrown away versus the number of beer bottles, or the number of orange-juice cans thrown away versus the number of pounds of freshly squeezed oranges, or the amount of candy thrown away in the week after Halloween versus the amount thrown away in the week after Valentine's Day. And no one ever dug into the final resting places of most of America's garbage: dumps (where garbage is left in the open) and sanitary landfills (where fresh garbage is covered every night with six to eight inches of soil).

Even as America's city managers over the years oversaw—and sometimes desperately attempted to cope with—the disposal of ever-increasing amounts of garbage, the study of garbage itself took several odd detours—one into the world of the military, another into the world of celebrity-watching, and a third into the world of law enforcement.

The military's foray into garbology occurred in 1941, when two enlisted men, Horace Schwerin and Phalen Golden, were forced to discontinue a survey they were conducting among new recruits about which aspects of Army life the re-

---

2. A question that always comes up is: What about garbage disposers? Garbage disposers are obviously capable of skewing the data in certain garbage categories, and Garbage Project researchers can employ a variety of techniques to compensate for the bias that garbage disposers introduce. Studies were conducted at the very outset of the Garbage Project to determine the discard differential between households with and without disposers, and one eventual result was a set of correction factors for various kinds of garbage (primarily food), broken down by subtype. As a general rule of thumb, households with disposers end up discarding in their trash about half the amount of food waste and food debris as households without disposers. It should be noted, however, that the fact that disposers have ground up some portion of a household's garbage often has little relevance to the larger issues the Garbage Project is trying to address. It means, for example, not that the Garbage Project's findings about the extent of food waste (see chapter three) are invalid, but merely that its estimates are conservative.

cruits most disliked. (Conducting polls of military personnel was, they had learned, against regulations.) Schwerin and Golden had already discovered, however, that the low quality of the food was the most frequently heard complaint, and they resolved to look into this one matter with an investigation that could not be considered a poll. What Schwerin and Golden did was to station observers in mess halls to record the types of food that were most commonly wasted and the volume of waste by type of food. The result, after 2.4 million man-meals had been observed, was a textbook example of how garbage studies can produce not only behavioral insights but also practical benefits. Schwerin and Golden discovered that 20 percent of the food prepared for Army mess halls was eventually thrown away, and that one reason for this was simply excess preparation. Here are some more of their findings, as summarized in a wartime article that appeared in the *The Saturday Evening Post*:

> Soldiers ate more if they were allowed to smoke in the mess hall. They ate more if they went promptly to table instead of waiting on line outside—perhaps because the food became cold. They ate more if they fell to on their own initiative instead of by command. They cared little for soups, and 65 percent of the kale and nearly as much of the spinach went into the garbage can. Favorite desserts were cakes and cookies, canned fruit, fruit salad, and gelatin. They ate ice cream in almost any amount that was served to them.

"That, sergeant, is an excellent piece of work," General George C. Marshall, the Army chief of staff, told Horace Schwerin after hearing a report by Schwerin on the research findings. The Army adopted many of Schwerin and Golden's recommendations, and began saving some 2.5 million pounds of food a day. It is perhaps not surprising to learn that until joining the Army Horace Schwerin had been in market research, and, among other things, had helped CBS to perfect a device for measuring audience reaction to radio shows.

The origins of an ephemeral branch of garbage studies focused on celebrities— "peeping-Tom" garbology, one might call it—seem to lie in the work of A. J. Weberman. Weberman was a gonzo journalist and yippie whose interest in the songs of Bob Dylan, and obsession with their interpretation, in 1970 prompted him to begin stealing the garbage from the cans left out in front of Dylan's Greenwich Village brownstone on MacDougal Street. Weberman didn't find much—some soiled Pampers, some old newspapers, some fast-food packaging from a nearby Blimpie Base, a shopping list with the word vanilla spelled "vannilla." He did, however, stumble into a brief but highly publicized career. This self-proclaimed "garbage guerrilla" quickly moved on to Neil Simon's garbage (it included a half-eaten bagel, scraps of lox, the Sunday *Times*), Muhammad Ali's (an empty can of Luck's collard greens, an empty roach bomb), and Abbie Hoffman's (a summons for hitchhiking, an unused can of deodorant, an estimate of the cost for the printing of *Steal This Book*, and the telephone numbers of Jack Anderson and Kate Millet). Weberman revealed many of his findings in an article in *Esquire* in 1971. It was antics such as his that inspired a prior meaning of the term "garbology," one very different from the definition established today.

Weberman's work inspired other garbage guerrillas. In January of 1975, the *Detroit Free Press* Sunday magazine reported on the findings from its raids on the garbage of several city notables, including the mayor, the head of the city council, the leader of a right-wing group, a food columnist, a disk jockey, and a prominent psychiatrist. Nothing much was discovered that might be deemed out of the ordinary, save for some of the contents of the garbage taken from a local Hare Krishna temple: a price tag from an Oleg Cassini garment, for example, and four ticket stubs from the Bel-Aire Drive-In Theater, which at the time was showing *Horrible House on the Hill* and *The Night God Screamed*. Six months after the *Free Press* exposé, a reporter for the National Enquirer, Jay Gourley, drove up to 3018 Dumbarton Avenue, N.W., in Washington, D.C., and threw the five garbage bags in front of Secretary of State Henry A. Kissinger's house into the trunk of his car. Secret Service agents swiftly blocked Gourley's departure, but after a day of questioning allowed him to proceed, the garbage still in the trunk. Among Gourley's finds: a crumpled piece of paper with a dog's teeth marks on it, upon which was written the work schedules of the Secret Service agents assigned to guard the Secretary; empty bottles of Seconal and Maalox; and a shopping list, calling for a case of Jack Daniel's, a case of Ezra Brooks bourbon, and a case of Cabin Still bourbon. Gourley later returned most of the garbage to the Kissingers—minus, he told reporters, "several dozen interesting things."

After the Kissinger episode curiosity about the garbage of celebrities seems to have abated. In 1977 the *National Enquirer* sent a reporter to poke through the garbage of President Jimmy Carter's press secretary, Jody Powell. The reporter found so little of interest that the tabloid decided not to publish a story. In 1980 Secret Service agents apprehended A. J. Weberman as he attempted to abduct former President Richard Nixon's garbage from behind an apartment building in Manhattan. Weberman was released, without the garbage.

The third detour taken by garbage studies involves police work. Over the years, law enforcement agents looking for evidence in criminal cases have also been more-than-occasional students of garbage; the Federal Bureau of Investigation in particular has spent considerable time poring over the household trash of people in whom it maintains a professional interest. ("We take it on a case-by-case basis," an FBI spokesman says.) One of the biggest criminal cases involving garbage began in 1975 and involved Joseph "Joe Bananas" Bonanno, Sr., a resident of Tucson at the time and a man with alleged ties to organized crime that were believed to date back to the days of Al Capone. For a period of three years officers of the Arizona Drug Control District collected Bonanno's trash just before the regular pickup, replacing it with "fake" Bonanno garbage. (Local garbagemen were not employed in the operation because some of them had received anonymous threats after assisting law enforcement agencies in an earlier venture.) The haul in evidence was beyond anyone's expectations: Bonanno had apparently kept detailed records of his various transactions, mostly in Sicilian. Although Bonanno had torn up each sheet of paper into tiny pieces, forensic specialists with the Drug Control District, like archaeologists reconstructing ceramic bowls from potsherds, managed to reassemble many of the documents and with the help of the FBI got them translated. In 1980 Bonanno was found guilty of having interfered with a federal grand jury investigation into the business operations of his two sons and a nephew. He was eventually sent to jail.

Unlike law-enforcement officers or garbage guerrillas, the archaeologists of the Garbage Project are not interested in the contents of any particular individual's garbage can. Indeed, it is almost always the case that a given person's garbage is at once largely anonymous and unimaginably humdrum. Garbage most usefully comes alive when it can be viewed in the context of broad patterns, for it is mainly in patterns that the links between artifacts and behaviors can be discerned.

The seed from which the Garbage Project grew was an anthropology class conducted at the University of Arizona in 1971 that was designed to teach principles of archaeological methodology. The University of Arizona has long occupied a venerable place in the annals of American archaeology and, not surprisingly, the pursuit of archaeology there to this day is carried on in serious and innovative ways. The class in question was one in which students undertook independent projects aimed precisely at showing links between various kinds of artifacts and various kinds of behavior. For example, one student, Sharon Thomas, decided to look into the relationship between a familiar motor function ("the diffusion pattern of ketchup over hamburgers") and a person's appearance, as manifested in clothing. Thomas took up a position at "seven different hamburger dispensaries" and, as people came in to eat, labeled them "neat" or "sloppy" according to a set of criteria relating to the way they dressed. Then she recorded how each of the fifty-seven patrons she studied—the ones who ordered hamburgers—poured ketchup over their food. She discovered that sloppy people were far more likely than neat people to put ketchup on in blobs, sometimes even stirring it with their fingers. Neat people, in contrast, tended to apply the ketchup in patterns: circles, spirals, and crisscrosses. One person (a young male neatly dressed in a body shirt, flared pants, and patent-leather Oxfords) wrote with ketchup what appeared to be initials.

Two of the student investigations, conducted independently by Frank Ariza and Kelly Allen, led directly to the Garbage Project. Ariza and Allen, wanting to explore the divergence between (or correlation of) mental stereotypes and physical realities, collected garbage from two households in an affluent part of Tucson and compared it to garbage from two households in a poor and, as it happens, Mexican-American part of town. The rich and poor families, each student found, ate about the same amount of steak and hamburger, and drank about the same amount of milk. But the poor families, they learned, bought more expensive child-education items. They also bought more household cleansers. What did such findings mean? Obviously the sample—involving only four households in all—was too small for the results even to be acknowledged as representative, let alone to provide hints as to what lay behind them. However, the general nature of the research effort itself—comparing garbage samples in order to gauge behavior (and, what is more, gauging behavior unobtrusively, thereby avoiding one of the great biases inherent in much social science)—seemed to hold great promise.

A year later, in 1972, university students, under professorial direction, began borrowing samples of household garbage from different areas of Tucson, and sorting it in a lot behind a dormitory. The Garbage Project was under way. In 1973, the Garbage Project entered into an arrangement with the City of Tucson, whereby the Sanitation Division, four days a week, delivered five to eight randomly selected household pickups from designated census tracts to an analysis site that the Division set aside for the Project's sorters at a maintenance yard. (Wilson Hughes, who as mentioned earlier is the Garbage Project's co-director, was one of the first undergraduate garbage sorters.) In 1984 operations were moved to an enclosure where many of the university's dumpsters are parked, across the street from Arizona Stadium.

The excavation of landfills would come much later in the Garbage Project's history, when to its focus on issues of garbage and human behavior it added a focus on issues of garbage management. The advantage in the initial years of sorting fresh garbage over excavating landfills was a basic but important one: In landfills it is often quite difficult and in many cases impossible to get some idea, demographically speaking, of the kind of neighborhood from which any particular piece of garbage has come. The value of landfill studies is therefore limited to advancing our understanding of garbage in the aggregate. With fresh garbage, on the other hand, one can have demographic precision down to the level of a few city blocks, by directing pickups to specific census districts and cross-tabulating the findings with census data.

Needless to say, deciding just which characteristics of the collected garbage to pay attention to posed a conceptual challenge, one that was met by Wilson Hughes, who devised the "protocol" that is used by the Garbage Project to this day. Items found in garbage are sorted into one of 150 specific coded categories (see Figure 1-C) that can in turn be clustered into larger categories representing food (fresh food versus prepared, health food versus junk food), drugs, personal and household sanitation products, amusement-related or educational materials,

GARBAGE ITEM CODE LIST

The Garbage Project University of Arizona

Beef* 001	Non-Dairy Creamer
Other Meat (not bacon)* 002	& Whips 065
Chicken 003	Health Foods* 066
Other Poultry 004	Slops* 069
Fish (fresh, frozen,	Regular Coffee
canned, dried)* 005	(instant or ground)* 070
Crustaceans & Mollusks	Decaf Coffee 071
(shrimp, clams, etc.) 006	Exotic Coffee* 072
T.V.P. Type Foods* 007	Tea* 073
Unknown Meat....................008	Chocolate Drink Mix
Cheese (including	or Topping 074
cottage cheese) 010	Fruit or Veg Juice ....
Milk* 110	(canned or bottled)...............075
Ice Cream	Fruit Juice Concentrate 076
(also ice milk, sherbet)* 012	Fruit Drink, powdered or liquid
Other Dairy (not butter)......013	(Tang, Koolaid, Hi-C)* 077
Eggs (regular, pwdrd, lqd).....014	Diet Soda 078
Beans (not green beans)* 015	Regular Soda..........................079
Nuts 016	Cocktail Mix (carbonated).....080
Peanut Butter 017	Cocktail Mix
Fats: Saturated* 018	(non-carb. liquid) 081
Unsaturated* 019	Cocktail Mix (powdered).......082
Bacon, saltpork* 020	Premixed Cocktails
Meat trimming 021	(alcoholic) 083
Corn (also corn meal	Spirits (booze) 084
and masa)* 022	Wine (still & sparkling)..........085
Flour (also pancake mix)* ...023	Beer* 086
Rice* 024	Baby Food & Juice* 087
Other Grain (barley,	Baby Cereal (pablum) 088
wheat germ, etc.)...............025	Baby Formula (liquid)* 089
Noodles (pasta) 026	Baby Formula (powdered)* ...090
White Bread 027	Pet Food (dry) 091
Dark Bread 028	Pet Food
Tortillas* 029	(canned or moist) 092
Dry Cereals: Regular 030	TV Dinners (also pot pies) 094
High Sugar	Take Out Meals 095
(first ingredient only).......031	Soups* 096

Rolling Papers
(also smoking items) 128
Household & Laundry
Cleaners* 131
Household Cleaning Tools
(not detergents) 132
Household Maint. Items
(paint, wood, etc.)...............133
Cooking & Serving Aids 134
Tissue Container 135
Toilet Paper Container 136
Napkin Container 137
Paper Towel Container 138
Plastic Wrap Container 139
Bags (paper or plastic)*.........140
Bag Container 141
Aluminum Foil Sheets.............142
Aluminum Foil Package 143
Wax Paper Package 144
Mechanical Appliance
(tools)..................................147
Electrical Appliance
and Items 148
Auto Supplies 149
Furniture...............................150
Clothing: Child* 151
Adult*..................................152
Clothing Care Items
(shoe polish, thread)............153
Dry Cleaning (laundry also)...154
Pet Maintenance (litter)..........155
Pet Toys 156
Gate Receipts (tickets)...........157
Hobby Related Items 158
Photo Supplies 159
Holiday Value (non-food)* 160
Decorations (non-holiday) 161

Cooked Cereals	Gravy & Specialty Sauces 097	Plant and Yard Maint............162
(instant or regular) 032	Prepared Meals	Stationary Supplies................163
Crackers* 033	(canned or packaged)* 098	Jewelry...................................164
Chips (also pretzels) 034	Vitamin Pills and	Child School Related
Unknown Produce* 040	Supplements	Papers*...............................171
Fresh Vegetables* 041	(commercial)* 100	Child Educ. Books
Canned Vegetables	Prescribed Drugs 101	(non-fiction) 172
(dehydrated also)* 042	Aspirin* 102	Child Educ. Games (toys).......173
Frozen Vegetables*..............043	Commerical Stimulants	Child Amusement Reading.....174
Potato Peel* 044	and Depressants* 103	Child Amusement Toys
Fresh Fruit* 045	Commercial Remedies*..........104	(games) 175
Canned Fruit	Illicit Drugs* 105	Adult Books (non-fiction) 176
(dehydrated also)*.............046	Commerical Drug	Adult Books (fiction)..............177
Frozen Fruit* 047	Paraphenalia 106	Adult Amusement Games.......178
Fruit Peel* 048	Illicit Drug Paraphenalia 107	Local Newspapers* 181
Relish, Pickles, Olives..........049	Contraceptives:	Newspapers (other city,
Syrup, Honey, Jellies,	Male 108	national)* 182
Molasses 051	Female 109	Organizational Newspapers
Patries (cookies, cakes and	Baby Supplies	or Magazines
mix, pies, etc.) 052	(diapers, etc.).....................111	(also religion)*....................183
Sugar*..................................053	Injury Oriented	General Interest
Artificial Sweetners..............054	(iodine, bandaids, etc.) 111	Magazines* 184
Candy* 055	Personal Sanitation* 112	Special Interest Magazine
Salt*.....................................056	Cosmetics*............................114	or Newspaper* 185
Spices & Flavorings (catsup,	Cigarettes (butts)...................123	Entertainment Guide
mustard, pepper, etc.)........057	Cigarettes (pack)* 124	(TV Guide, etc.) 186
Baking Additives (yeast,	Cigarettes (carton)* 125	Miscellaneous Items
baking powder, etc.) 058	Cigars 126	(specify on back
Popsicles..............................060	Pipe, Chewing, Tobacco,	of sheet)* 190
Pudding...............................061	Loose Tobacco.....................127	
Gelatin 062		
Instant Breakfast 063		*See Special Notes
Dips (for chips) 064		

Figure 1-C. Garbage Project sorters use the codes displayed here to begin the process of transforming raw garbage into data. The code numbers are supplemented on the recording forms by much more detailed information, such as a discarded item's brand name (if applicable), its type, its weight, the census tract from which it originated, the date of collection, and so on. Not shown here are several pages of specialized instructions, such as this for the item with code number 044: "Do not count individual peels; weigh them as a group." (Table courtesy of The Garbage Project)

communications-related materials, pet-related materials, yard-related materials, and hazardous materials. For each item the following information is recorded on a standardized form: the date on which it was collected; the census tract from which it came; the item code (for example, 001, which would be the code for "Beef"); the item's type (for example, "chuck"); its original weight or volume (in this case, derived from the packaging); its cost (also from the packaging); material composition of container; brand (if applicable); and the weight of any discarded food (if applicable). The information garnered over the years from many thousands of such forms, filled out in pursuit of a wide variety of research objectives, constitutes the Garbage Project's database. It has all been computerized and amounts to some two million lines of data drawn from some fifteen thousand household-refuse samples. The aim here has been not only to approach garbage with specific questions to answer or hypotheses to prove but also to amass sufficient quantities of information, in a systematic and open-minded way, so that with the data on hand Garbage Project researchers would be able to answer any future questions or evaluate any future hypotheses that might arise. In 1972 garbage was, after all, still terra incognita, and the first job to be done was akin to that undertaken by the explorers Lewis and Clark.

From the outset the Garbage Project has had to confront the legal and ethical issues its research involves: Was collecting and sorting someone's household garbage an unjustifiable invasion of privacy? This very question has over the years been argued repeatedly in the courts. The Fourth Amendment unequivocally guarantees Americans protection from unreasonable search and seizure. Joseph Bonanno, Sr., tried to invoke the Fourth Amendment to prevent his garbage from being used as evidence. But garbage placed in a garbage can in a public thorough-fare, where it awaits removal by impersonal refuse collectors, and where it may be picked over by scavengers looking for aluminum cans, by curious children or neighbors, and by the refuse collectors themselves (some of whom do a thriving trade in old appliances, large and small), is usually considered by the courts to have been abandoned. Therefore, the examination of the garbage by outside par-ties cannot be a violation of a constitutional right. In the Bonanno case, U.S. Dis-trict Court Judge William Ingram ruled that investigating garbage for evidence of a crime may carry a "stench," but was not illegal. In 1988, in California v. Green-wood, the U.S. Supreme Court ruled by a margin of six to two that the police were entitled to conduct a warrantless search of a suspected drug dealer's garbage—a search that led to drug paraphenalia, which led in turn to warrants, arrests, and convictions. As Justice Byron White has written, "The police cannot reasonably be expected to avert their eyes from evidence of criminal activity that could have been observed by any member of the public."

Legal issues aside, the Garbage Project has taken pains to ensure that those whose garbage comes under scrutiny remain anonymous. Before obtaining garbage for study, the Project provides guarantees to communities and their garbage collectors that nothing of a personal nature will be examined and that no names or addresses or other personal information will be recorded. The Project also stipulates that all of the garbage collected (except aluminum cans, which are recycled) will be returned to the community for normal disposal.

As noted, the Garbage Project has now been sorting and evaluating garbage, with scientific rigor, for two decades. The Project has proved durable because its findings have supplied a fresh perspective on what we know—and what we think we know—about certain aspects of our lives. Medical researchers, for example, have long made it their business to question people about their eating habits in order to uncover relationships between patterns of diet and patterns of disease. These researchers have also long suspected that people—honest, well-meaning people—may often be providing information about quantities and types and even brands of food and drink consumed that is not entirely accurate. People can't readily say whether they trimmed 3.3 ounces or 5.4 ounces of fat off the last steak they ate, and they probably don't remember whether they had four, five, or seven beers in the previous week, or two eggs or three. The average person just isn't paying attention. Are there certain patterns in the way in which people wrongly "self-report" their dietary habits? Yes, there are, and Garbage Project studies have identified many of them.

Garbage archaeologists also know how much edible food is thrown away; what percentage of newspapers, cans, bottles, and other items aren't recycled; how loyal we are to brand-name products and which have earned the greatest loyalty; and how much household hazardous waste is carted off to landfills and incinerators. From several truckloads of garbage and a few pieces of ancillary data—most importantly, the length of time over which the garbage was collected—the Garbage Project staff can reconstruct the community from which it came with a degree of accuracy that the Census Bureau might in some neighborhoods be unable to match.

Garbage also exposes the routine perversity of human ways. Garbage archaeologists have learned, for example, that the volume of garbage that Americans produce expands to fill the number of receptacles that are available to put it in. They have learned that we waste more of what is in short supply than of what is plentiful; that attempts by individuals to restrict consumption of certain foodstuffs are often counterbalanced by extra and inadvertent consumption of those same foodstuffs in hidden form; and that while a person's memory of what he has eaten and drunk in a given week is inevitably wide of the mark, his guess as to what a family member or even neighbor has eaten and drunk usually turns out to be more perceptive.

Some of the Garbage Project's research has prompted unusual forays into arcane aspects of popular culture. Consider the matter of those "amulets" worn by the Sohites—that is, the once-familiar detachable pop-top pull tab. Pull tabs first became important to the Garbage Project during a study of household recycling practices, conducted on behalf of the federal Environmental Protection Agency during the mid-1970s. The question arose: If a bag of household garbage contained no aluminum cans, did that mean that the household didn't dispose of any cans or that it had recycled its cans? Finding a way to answer that question was essential if a neighborhood's recycling rate was to be accurately determined. Pull tabs turned out to hold the key. A quick study revealed that most people did not drop pull tabs into the cans from which they had been wrenched; rather, the vast majority of people threw the tabs into the trash. If empty cans were stored separately for recycling, the pull tabs still went out to the curb with the rest of the garbage. A garbage sample that contained several pull tabs but no aluminum cans was a good bet to have come from a household that recycled.

All this counting of pull tabs prompted a surprising discovery one day by a student: Pull tabs were not all alike. Their configuration and even color depended on what kind of beverage they were associated with and where the beverage had been canned. Armed with this knowledge, Garbage Project researchers constructed an elaborate typology of pull tabs, enabling investigators to tease out data about beverage consumption—say, beer versus soda, Michelob versus Schlitz—even from samples of garbage that contained not a single can (see Figure 1-D). Detachable pull tabs are no longer widely used in beverage cans, but the pull-tab typology remains useful even now. Amount other things, in the absence of such evidence of chronology as a newspaper's dateline, pull tabs can reliably help to fix the dates of strata in a landfill. In archaeological parlance objects like these that have been widely diffused over a short period of time, and then abruptly disappear, are known as horizon markers.

The unique "punch-top" on Coors beer cans, for example, was used only between March of 1974 and June of 1977. (It was abandoned because some customers complained that they cut their thumbs pushing the holes open.) In landfills around the country, wherever Coors beer cans were discarded, punch-top cans not only identify strata associated with a narrow band of dates but also separate two epochs one from another. One might think of punch-tops playfully as the garbage equivalent of the famous iridium layer found in sediment toward the end

THE GARBAGE PROJECTS PULL-TAB TYPOLOGY FOR TUCSON, AZ

Figure 1-D. Shown here is a portion of the Garbage Project's pull-tab typology for the city of Tucson, underscoring the widespread variation even in relatively standardized everyday items. The typology was originally developed to assist in a study of recycling behavior for the Environmental Protection Agency. (Grapic courtesy of The Garbage Project)

of the Cretaceous Era, marking the moment (proponents of the theory believe) when a giant meteor crashed into the planet Earth, exterminating the dinosaurs.

All told, the Garbage Project has conducted nine full-scale excavations of municipal landfills in the United States and two smaller excavations associated with special projects. In the fall of 1991 it also excavated four sites in Canada, the data from which remains largely unanalyzed (and is not reflected in this book). The logistics of the landfill excavations are complex, and they have been overseen in all cases by Wilson Hughes. What is involved? Permission must be obtained from a raft of local officials and union leaders; indemnification notices must be provided to assure local authorities that the Garbage Project carries sufficient insurance against injury; local universities must be scoured for a supply of students to supplement the Garbage Project team; in many cases construction permits, of all things, must be obtained in advance of digging. There is also the whole matter of transportation, not only of personnel but also of large amounts of equipment. And there is the matter of personal accommodation and equipment storage. The time available for excavation is always limited, sometimes extremely so; the research program must be compressed to fit it, and the staff must be "tasked" accordingly. When the excavation has been completed the samples need to be packed and shipped—frequently on ice—back to headquarters or to specialized laboratories. All archaeologists will tell you that field work is mostly laborious, not glamorous; a landfill excavation is archaeology of the laborious kind.

For all the difficulties they present, the Garbage Project's landfill digs have acquired an increasing timeliness and relevance as concerns about solid-waste disposal have grown. Even as the Garbage Project has trained considerable attention on garbage as an analytical tool it has also taken up the problem of garbage itself—garbage as a problem, garbage as symbolized by Mobro 4000, the so-called "garbage barge," which sailed from Islip, Long Island, on March 22, 1987, and spent the next fifty-five days plying the seas in search of a place to deposit its 3,168 tons of cargo. Strange though it may seem, although more than 70 percent of America's household and commercial garbage ends up in landfills, very little reliable data existed until recently as to a landfill's contents and biological dynamics. Much of the conventional wisdom about garbage disposal consists of assertions that turn out, upon investigation, to be simplistic or misleading: among them, the assertion that, as trash, plastic, foam, and fast-food packaging are causes for great concern, that biodegradable items are always more desirable than nonbiodegradable ones, that on a per capita basis the nation's households are generating a lot more garbage than they used to, and that we're physically running out of places to put landfills.

This is not to say that garbage isn't a problem in need of serious attention. It is. But if they are to succeed, plans of action must be based on garbage realities. The most critical part of the garbage problem in America is that our notions about the creation and disposal of garbage are often riddled with myth. There are few other subjects of public significance on which popular and official opinion is so consistently misinformed.

This book is a summary of the research conducted and discoveries made by the Garbage Project over the course of two decades. In the following chapters we will first step back for a moment into human history and look at the place of garbage in it. We will then move on to some of the insights into human behavior that an examination of garbage can yield. We will next venture inside a landfill and examine its actual contents, and try to understand what happens—and doesn't happen—to the garbage that winds up there. We will conclude by discussing a few issues that receive a great deal of vocal attention, such as incineration and recycling. Along the way there will be digressions large and small—about disposable diapers, about the demographics of garbage, about many other odd or essential things.

Gaps—large gaps—remain in our knowledge of garbage, and of how human behavior relates to it, and of how best to deal with it. But a lighted candle has at least been seized and thrust inside the antechamber.

2

The Wet Frontier Underwater Archaeology

Lawrence H. Robbins

I once did a study of an abandoned fisherman's camp along the shore of Lake Turkana in East Africa. The settlement had been abandoned for only eighteen months, yet none of the dome-shaped huts of thatched palm leaves that had originally dotted the sandy lake edge was left standing. In fact, the only evidence of the huts' existence were some clumps of palm leaves projecting a few inches above the sand, along with discarded fish bones scattered around the bases of several palm trees that had been used as dumps. I was not surprised to find that some of the bones were already covered by several inches of loose sand, which had been driven by the strong winds that blow off the lake and had accumulated around the bases of the trees.

Here was an archaeological site in the making. Virtually nothing in the way of wood or cloth was evident at the site because everything of value had been packed up and taken to the next camp. Probably nothing would be left after a century or two—unless the fish bones survived. By contrast, our inventory of an inhabited Turkana nomad's camp showed that about 90 percent of the items were made of wood, gourds, or animal skin. All of this material is perishable and normally does not appear in the archaeological record. In terms of use, the most important of the belongings inventoried were containers for food and beverages. Almost none of them would survive, with the exception of a plastic bottle obtained from my camp.

The above study, along with other archaeological studies of contemporary settlements (termed *ethnoarchaeology*), underscores clearly why wet sites are so important to archaeologists. Under the right conditions, wet or waterlogged deposits provide remarkably good preservation of wood, leather, and other materials that normally do not survive. The wet deposits seal the finds from air and decomposition brought about by bacteria, thus providing information that would otherwise be only speculation by archaeologists. In this chapter, we will explore the murky bottoms of Alpine lakes, several limestone wells, a fjord being drained, and an English shipwreck as well as a waterlogged site on land. We will see that the quest to explore the underwater frontier, like that in other areas, is punctuated with adventure and examples of unusual perserverance.

Perhaps more than any other area in archaeology, underwater research has been made possible because of technological advances. Pioneer explorers dived without any equipment at all or used primitive gear. The critical breakthrough came in 1943, when Jacques Cousteau and Emile Gagnon developed a workable Aqualung. Their invention, rooted in earlier efforts, increased dramatically the depths at, and operating time in, which divers could work safely. Archaeologists scoffed at the first efforts to do underwater archaeology with the newly developed equipment. They saw this work as little more than adventuresome treasure hunting, for the divers who were doing the work were not trained in archaeology and made little effort to record the context of the finds. In 1960 George Bass, an American archaeologist, turned the tables by learning to dive and demonstrating to skeptical colleagues that dry-land archaeological techniques could be adapted to underwater environments, especially shipwrecks. He blazed a new trail in archaeology by demonstrating on a Bronze Age shipwreck at Cape Gelidonya, Turkey, that one could effectively map, excavate, and recover artifacts from beneath the sea. Most recently he has directed excavations of a 3,000-year-old Bronze Age ship found by sponge divers off the coast of Turkey.

Shipwrecks have often been seen as miniature time capsules, in which events from particular periods were frozen, awaiting archaeological discovery. Unfortunately, a growing interest in diving also contributed to the romantic image of unspoiled shipwrecks lying on the ocean bottom, filled with treasure. In point of fact, relatively few ships have gone down with vast amounts of treasure compared to those that have been destroyed in the hopes of finding treasure. Archaeological finds in the sea are protected by rules established by the United Nations as well as by the laws of individual nations. In the United States, where conflict between treasure salvagers and archaeologists has been a long-standing problem, an act protecting abandoned shipwrecks was passed by Congress in 1988. This act gives individual states control over wrecks found within three miles of the coast. Under the new law, these sites can no longer be looted.

The Lake Dwellings

One of archaeology's first encounters with wet sites, excluding shipwreck finds, occurred in the middle of the last century when some unusually cold weather retarded the melting of snow in the Swiss Alps, thus greatly decreasing the volume of water in the rivers that fed the Alpine lakes. In the winters of 1853 and 1854, the lake levels receded to their lowest marks in recorded history, and farmers began to reclaim fertile land at the edge of the retreating water. Along the shore of Lake Zurich, near Ober Meilen, some workers were using mud from the lake edge to repair holes in a wall when their shovels began to strike cut logs, pieces of deer antler, and other artifacts. These logs had served as posts and building material for houses. Further search revealed that the log field extended out into the lake. As in the discoveries of both Lascaux and the first Neandertal, a local schoolteacher appeared on the scene, recognized the importance of the find, and notified the Antiquarian Society of Zurich, which was headed by Dr. Ferdinand Keller. Keller subsequently devoted much of his life to the study of lake dwellers. The lake dwellers lived in small villages and practiced a mixture of farming, livestock herding, and hunting.

Following the historically significant discovery at Ober Meilen, similar sites were found at other Alpine lakes. The preservation was remarkable and included large numbers of normally perishable finds such as seeds, leaves, pieces of cloth, wooden tools, and some stone implements that were still fastened to their handles. Collectors began to scan the lake bottoms from small fishing boats; they pulled up artifacts with long tongs and used specially rigged, rakelike tools to scrape through the mud, which was, in turn, brought up and sifted for relics. These nineteenth-century methods were crude and destructive, so very little could be learned about the context of the finds.

In addition, no one knew exactly how old the sites were. The pioneer Keller suggested that the oldest sites "had their origins in that dark time when, at least in these districts, the use of metal was yet unknown." Keller remarked that the earliest lake dwellers were pastoralists who kept "the dog, the cow, the sheep, the goat and the horse." A more specific estimate was suggested by Dr. Oswald Heer, a botanist who examined the plant remains in the 1860s. Interestingly, Heer used the Bible as a point of historical reference, noting that the cereals, beans, and lentils found at the Swiss sites thrived in Bible lands during Old Testament times, which he believed to be about 1100 B.C. He therefore concluded that the lake dwellings most likely dated to between 2000 and 1000 B.C. It is now generally accepted that the sites are either Neolithic or Bronze Age. Radiocarbon-dating suggests the year 3000 B.C. for the Neolithic settlements, while the Bronze Age sites are, in fact, very close to Heer's estimate.

One of the most interesting of the nineteenth-century discoveries was the site of Robenhausen, located near Zurich at the edge of a small lake known as Pffafikon. Robenhausen was discovered in 1858 by Jacob Messikomer, a self-educated farmer who had developed a passion for the new field of archaeology. When Messikomer learned that some local peat cutters had found artifacts at Robenhausen, he began many years of work at the site, slowly draining small areas of the waterlogged peat with a hand pump. In a synthesis of the newly discovered lake sites, Keller estimated that Robenhausen more than likely contained at least 100,000 logs of oak, beach, and pine, some of which were about ten feet long. Messikomer also recovered some complete wooden bows, a flint arrowhead still attached to the shaft of the arrow with cord and mastic, a twelve-foot dugout canoe, wooden knives, and a wide range of other finds. The wet peat deposits also preserved fish netting, balls of string, woven cloth, and seeds. The carbonized grains of wheat and barley were among the first found in an ancient settlement in Europe, and there were also pieces of bread, charred apples, pears, nuts and berries, fish scales, and dung from domesticated livestock.

Dr. Heer studied the plant remains of Robenhausen, asking some of the same kinds of questions that are currently being posed by researchers in archaeobotany. For instance, he compared the harvest seasons of the various fruits and nuts, considered the other data, and reasoned that the lake dwellings were more than likely inhabited on a year-round basis. He also compared the ancient plants with their modern counterparts to evaluate how much change had occurred in these plants through the centuries. Heer judged that the wild plants and fruits eaten by the lake dwellers were identical to their modern forms but that the cereals were quite different and must have been subjected to considerable selective breeding through the years. He concluded that the wheat and barley were of Mediterranean origin, reaching Switzerland as the result of "scattered rays" of diffusion. These observations were generally correct.

The discoveries in the Alps demonstrated that another frontier in archaeology was being penetrated that rivaled some of the other important breakthroughs of the nineteenth century. Each of the discoveries posed significant questions, especially about the interpretations of the sites. In the case of the lake dwellings, the views of the pioneer worker Keller came to dominate the field, much as the theories of the Abbé Breuil held sway over the early period of cave-art studies in the first part of the present century. Keller felt that because there were a large number of sites found at many of the Alpine lakes and because most of the logs were found either underwater, embedded in the lake bottom, or in places that were covered recently by water, the ancient villagers must have lived out on the lakes, ingeniously building their houses on platforms supported by stilts or piles driven into the bottom of the lakes. He believed that the settlements were connected to the shore by means of a pierlike walkway and that, as the finds at Robenhausen demonstrated, the people also used canoes. The various artifacts found on the lake bottom were either discarded as trash, fell through the cracks of the platforms, or resulted from the ultimate abandonment of the settlements. Since cow dung was found at the bottom of the lakes, it was assumed that the lake dwellers corralled their cattle out on the platforms. The motive for such a lifestyle appeared to be defense.

Keller supported his interpretation with what today's archaeologists call ethnographic analogies, the comparison of known human behavior with the archaeological record. He noted that both the famous early physician Hippocrates and the historian Herodotus describe ancient historical cases of pile dwellings. He also used contemporary travelers' accounts from areas as far afield as New Guinea and Africa. For example, a British officer's account of lake dwellers in Africa seemed to provide a fascinating analogy for Keller's interpretation, so much so that he used the officer's illustrations as a model in his own book. These reports gave Keller's interpretation increased credibility, and it survived unchallenged for decades. Nevertheless, unlike Lewis-Williams' careful comparison of South African rock paintings with known San customs, Keller found no direct, historical linkages between reported lake dwellers and the Swiss sites. Inconsistencies of this nature, however, were generally ignored by nineteenth-century pioneers in archaeology; only those examples supporting an interpretation were used as evidence.

Keller did consider another hypothesis—that the settlements were built on the shores and were abandoned when the lake levels rose and covered the villages, but he rejected this idea as an alternative that was "virtually set at rest." He simply did not think this was a reasonable explanation for the deeply submerged logs and other finds. Nevertheless, it was this rejected theory that eventually proved to be correct.

That the houses were built on the beaches rather than on platforms as envisioned by Keller is clearly revealed at Lake Paladru, near Grenoble, France. The first sites at Paladru were noticed in 1866, when Ernest Chantres dredged up cultural remains from Grand Roseaux, at the north edge of the lake. At that time, there was even a local Atlantis-type legend about an ancient city that had sunk beneath the lake after God punished the inhabitants for persecuting some monks. Chantres' reconstruction of the site followed the interpretations of Keller by concluding that the settlement was out in the lake and was connected to the shore via footbridges.

Chantres and, no doubt, Keller would have marveled at the ingenious underwater project that took place a little over a century later at the site of Baigneurs located at the opposite end of Lake Paladru. In 1972, Aimé Bocquet and his research team began to piece together an unusually detailed site reconstruction. The archaeological layers were buried beneath sterile (artifact-free) sediments that lay submerged beneath about nine feet of water. This sterile layer was removed by an air lift, which is essentially an underwater suction hose. (Such devices are now commonly employed in excavating shipwrecks.) The team also used a special kind of pressure hose that forces away the cloudy water from the excavation area. As in most underwater projects, much of the excavation was done by hand. The sense of touch enables underwater archaeologists to recover very delicate finds, which sometimes must be raised in containers of wet sand and kept wet until proper preservation techniques can be applied. At Baigneurs many perishable finds were recovered, including balls of thread, basketry, pieces of moss used for chinking the spaces in house walls, ax handles, and some stone knives still set in their handles. Probably most of these finds would have been missed or destroyed by the old dredging techniques used by early workers.

During Keller's time, the most serious problem hampering the understanding of the Alpine sites was that there was no way to map or otherwise document the context of the finds because of the crude techniques that were first used. In contrast, a modern underwater team is able to map the site precisely by using a grid placed over the submerged habitation area. All logs, bones, and artifacts are plotted accurately and the data recorded on plastic sheets. The various mapping sheets are then pieced together in the laboratory.

At Paladru, the mapping efforts were further enhanced by coloring the exposed logs so that they could be photographed from the air. The pattern that emerged from this work revealed a palisaded community consisting of a few log houses situated on the shore of the lake. The palisade formed an arc around the houses and ended at the lake edge. (Quite possibly, early investigators would have interpreted palisades like this one as supports for platforms and houses on the lake.) Interestingly, the underwater researchers were able to determine that the houses were rectangular by following discarded nut shells along the edges of the walls. Artifacts, along with animal bones and plant remains, indicate that the Neolithic peoples of Baigneurs herded livestock, farmed grains, hunted, and collected wild foods.

The Baigneurs settlement has been radiocarbon-dated to 2900 B.C. Paleoclimatic studies have confirmed that prolonged cold spells in the past inhibited thawing and lowered the lake levels even more dramatically than did the weather of the mid-nineteenth century. The ancient houses were evidently built on the lake shores when the water levels were low. A study of the tree rings in the logs indicates that the village survived for no longer than thirty years. Apparently a fire destroyed the first houses, and the people left. Climatic conditions changed, and the local forests began to thin out. Then the lake level rose and covered the abandoned village with several feet of water. About thirty years later the water receded, and people returned to the shore and built a new community on top of the silt layer that had buried the old settlement. Subsequent rises in the lakes again covered the structures with the sediments that preserved them.

Thus the modern excavations have allowed for a much more accurate reconstruction of these kinds of sites and contrast greatly with the archaeological assumptions of the nineteenth century. Such changing interpretations in archaeology are not that uncommon, and they are signs of a healthy science in which old ideas are discredited or modified substantially as more sophisticated techniques are developed. In hindsight, it is easy to discredit the ideas of early workers who lacked modern perspective, yet their discoveries and theories paved the way for future work.

Chichén Itzá: The Mayan Well of Sacrifice

Near the mid-nineteenth century, just before Ferdinand Keller began studying the Swiss lake sites, John Lloyd Stephens, U.S. ambassador to Central America, and Frederick Catherwood, an English architect, rediscovered the magnificent ruins of the lost Mayan civilization, choked in jungle vegetation. News of their incredible finds captured the imagination of one particularly adventurous student named Edward H. Thompson, who resolved to follow in their footsteps.

While researching Mayan lore, Thompson came across a then recently recovered document written by the bishop of Yucatan in 1566. In it was a vivid description of the Well of Sacrifice at the site of Chichén Itzá, in the northern Yucatan Peninsula of southern Mexico. The bishop wrote that the Mayas had thrown people into the well alive to appease the gods and that "they also threw into it many other things they prized, and so if this country had possessed gold it would be this Well that would have the greater part of it, so great is the devotion that the Indians show for it." Thompson was captivated by this description, and, in his own words, it became "an obsession." Chichén Itzá was a known site, which John Lloyd Stephens had already visited. He had described the well as "an immense circular hole, with cragged perpendicular sides." There was only one way to find out what lay at the bottom of the well, and that was to explore it. Thompson took the diplomatic route to Central America. In 1885 he was appointed U.S. consul to Yucatan, a post which made possible his intended archaeological explorations.

Thompson was a strong advocate of "going native" in his explorations. He wrote, "I was physically well endowed, fortunately possessed of a rugged physique, so I decided that the best and surest way to lay the foundation for future success was to live among the Mayans as much as possible, make them my friends, study their legends...and master their language." During his excursions he explored several ancient Mayan wells, called *chultuns*, some of which were decorated with artwork. On one occasion, his Indian assistants lowered him into one of these dimly lit pits with a hunting knife between his teeth and one hand on the rope. When he reached the bottom of the pit, he immediately heard the buzzing of a very large rattlesnake, coiled to strike. Thompson was trapped. Slowly, he backed against the wall of the well, as the snake's jaws "dripped saliva and a strong odor like musk" permeated the well. Thompson pushed against the wall and, with a great amount of strain, cracked off a rocklike piece of mortar. Somehow he managed to reach behind himself, grab the mortar and hurl it at the snake. Luckily, he hit it and stunned it. Quick follow-up throws killed the rattler, and he escaped from the well.

Unperturbed, Thompson arranged to visit Chichén Itzá in the northern Yucatan peninsula of Mexico. Originally a Mayan town founded in A.D. 530, not long after the fall of the Roman Empire, it was one of many important Mayan sites. Most experts believe that the site was conquered by the Toltecs or related northern peoples in A.D. 1201. Indeed, the architecture displays a fusion of native Mayan and Toltec influences. The site was finally abandoned in the fifteenth century. In addition to the Well of Sacrifice, the site is well known for its Temple of the Warriors, its remarkable *castillo* (castle) with its steep flight of steps, a large number of roofless colonnades, an observatory, and a spectacular ball court. The game played there was widespread in Mesoamerica. The goal was to knock the rubber ball, without the aid of feet or hands, through a stone ring. The game was very rough, and the losers were sometimes killed. The winners were allowed to chase the spectators after the game and claim the clothes of the ones they caught.

Chichén Itzá did not disappoint Thompson. In fact he arranged to buy the site and lived there so that he could carry out his research. While exploring one of the pyramids, he managed to open a blocked passage and followed it to a deep and dark pit. Once again, he descended into it on a rope with a knife between his teeth. This time there was no rattlesnake, but he and his workers lost track of time. When they emerged, it was nearly midnight, and the families of Thompson's workers were wailing, convinced that their men had been swallowed by "the Great Serpent!"

The Well of Sacrifice itself was a steep-sided limestone pit fed by underground waters. Such natural wells are called *cenotes*. They are similar to caves except that they are large sinkholes formed in limestone deposits rather than tunnel-like systems extending horizontally beneath the earth. To the ancient inhabitants of Chichén Itzá, the cenote must have been a formidable sight, one which was naturally and divinely appropriate for their rituals. It measured about 200 feet across and dropped steeply to the water, which was about thirty-five feet deep and covered a great thickness of sediments. The dark color of the water varied with the sunlight, giving the well an eerie appearance at times. Occasionally, snakes and large frogs would slip through the water.

Thompson pondered how to explore the well. Some of his friends argued strongly against his plans, saying, "If you want to commit suicide, why not seek a less shocking way of doing it?" Not to be deterred, Thompson took deep-sea-diving lessons in Boston and rigged up a dredge with cables and a "thirty foot swinging boom." However, since the well was so large, he did not know where to start. To find the "fertile zone" for the dredging operations, Thompson tied ropes to logs that each weighed about as much as a person, heaved them into the well, and judged the distances from the edge where the victims might have landed. The dredging went on for a long period without any success, and Thompson became "nervous by day and sleepless at night." Then one day he noticed some suspicious-looking lumps in the dredging bucket. He burned one of them, and the fumes demonstrated that the lumps were a form of incense used in Mayan religious rituals. Thereafter, the dredging produced many priceless artifacts, and the well became one of the most treasure-laden archaeological discoveries in the New World.

It became apparent that Bishop de Landa's sixteenth-century account of the Well of Sacrifice was, for the most part, correct. Besides a plethora of bones, the well contained copper bells, jewelry, exquisite works of gold and jade, pieces of basketry, textiles, rubber, wood, and a variety of other finds. There were wooden spear-throwers, carved sticks, benches, and a stone sacrificial knife with a carved handle, such as those most likely used to tear the hearts out of sacrificial victims.

Many of the artifacts had been broken intentionally before they were thrown into the well, possibly to "kill" the objects when sacrificing them to the gods. The Indians had coated the wooden artifacts with resin, which helped preserve them. Thompson kept them moist after removing them from the well and added preservatives.

The skeletons found were assumed to be those of the sacrificial virgins. A 1936 *National Geographic* article includes an artist's reconstruction of the terrifying sacrificial scene, showing the women being thrown into the well. Later analysis of the more complete skeletons revealed, however, that there were not only women in the well but also men, children, and even dogs, turkeys, deer, and other animals.

When the dredging failed to produce any significant new finds, the intrepid Thompson set up his diving operation. He employed two experienced Greek divers and trained the Mayas to run the pump. Thompson says that after he slipped into the water, it changed to a "purplish black," thick with "gruel"-like sediments. Unable to see, he and the Greek divers groped about in the darkness of the well and managed to find more artifacts and skeletons. He survived one close call when he forgot to adjust the air valves properly and rose too suddenly. Thompson's pioneering efforts in underwater chaeology made for a courageous, if somewhat foolhardy, adventure. From a modern archaeological perspective, we know that the dredging was certain to destroy much of the original context of the finds at the bottom of the well, as was the case with the Swiss lakes, but more sophisticated methods did not exist at that time.

In an effort to protect the remains, Thompson shipped them to the Peabody Museum at Harvard University. This was his undoing. The word got out that a substantial amount of treasure, including much gold, had been recovered from the well, and by the time the news reached the Mexican government, the value of the treasure had been blown out of proportion. The Mexicans were incensed and accused Thompson of stealing the artifacts. He was forced to flee the country on a jury-rigged schooner without the aid of proper navigation instruments. Luckily, he made it to Cuba after nearly two weeks at sea. Thompson was eventually vindicated, albeit posthumously, when the Mexican government found that he had not violated any laws. In 1960 the museum returned many of the artifacts to Mexico.

That was also the year of renewed efforts at the Well of Sacrifice. The National Geographic Society and the Water Sports Club of Mexico combined efforts, with the benefit of an airlift pump and scuba gear. This expedition recovered thousands of artifacts, but the work was discontinued because the powerful airlift, which sucked artifacts out of the murky bottom, was deemed too destructive.

Yet another project was carried out in 1967. The researchers' efforts to pump all the water out of the well failed after lowering the water level only fifteen feet. Chemically treating the murky water, described as being in a condition "worse than in a New York sewer," cleared it enough, however, to allow the workers to use scuba gear and exercise greater control over the excavations. They were also able to modify the airlift so that it was much less destructive. The divers recovered a great many artifacts, including wooden stools and buckets, textiles, worked jade, bells, and stone projectile points. The human bones found indicate that many more children than adults had been sacrificed.

In summary, the Well of Sacrifice was an important ritual center for generations of Mayans. Many artifacts, such as the jade and obsidian objects, came from distant sources via the widespread Mayan trade networks. The gold and copper originated far to the north. Although found in a disturbed context, the artifacts can be compared stylistically to specimens recovered from other sites that have been dated. This cross-dating suggests that the well was used, off and on, between A.D. 800 and 1539. The practice of human sacrifice was an ancient religious custom in Mesoamerica, and early evidence of it may go back to when peoples were beginning to farm. Sacrificial burials of children in the Tehuacan Valley, south of Mexico City, for example, date from 6500 to 4800 B.C. At the more recent end of this time span are the Aztec sacrifices, in which the victims were spread-eagled and their hearts torn out to appease their gods. In spite of this grisly aspect of their culture, the Mesoamericans made remarkable achievements in domesticating crops, developing writing and calendars, creating unique architectural styles, and perfecting a wide range of artistically pleasing crafts.

Little Salt Spring:
The Oldest Archaeological Site in Florida

One of the most debated issues in American archaeology concerns the question of when the ancestors of the Indians (the Paleoindians) first settled in the New World. It is clear that they entered North America by way of the Bering Strait land bridge, which connected Alaska to the eastern tip of Siberia during late Ice Age times, when world sea levels were lowered. Recent findings in the Meadowcroft rock shelter southwest of Pittsburgh suggests that the ancestral native Americans were settled as far south as western Pennsylvania by at least 19,000 years ago. Finally, new data from a waterlogged peat bog in Chile shows that they had reached southern South America 13,000 years ago. There are many other sites, especially in the western United States, which date between 11,000 and 12,000 years ago.

An interesting and potentially important Paleoindian site was discovered accidentally in 1959 when William Royal, a retired Air Force colonel, was scuba diving in a shallow pond known as Little Salt Spring, near Sarasota on the southwest coast of Florida. The surprised colonel found that the gently sloping pond bottom opened suddenly into a sinkhole, or cenote, more than 300 feet deep. Further investigation revealed old-looking bones on the sinkhole's sloping edge. While professional archaeologists were skeptical of these amateur finds, Royal continued to collect and exhibit bones from Little Salt Spring. According to the *Miami Herald*, he even built a fireplace with some of the fossils and dressed bones up in scuba gear for amusement. Eventually, Royal got a crippling case of the bends from diving in the cenote. For many years Royal was seen as perpetuating a hoax regarding his finds at Little Salt Spring.

Finally, in the 1970s, a team of underwater archaeologists, geologists, and paleontologists began to explore the spring and an adjacent slough, which contained peat deposits. The scientists determined that the water level in the cenote was substantially lower in late Ice Age times, roughly around 13,000 years ago, because much of the world's fresh water was contained in the ice sheets far to the north. At that time, the southern Florida climate was much drier. The springs in the area of the sinkhole must have made it an oasis in the arid landscape. The Paleoindian peoples who frequented the area camped and hunted along the edge of the fresh-water sinkhole, and some of their artifacts and animal bones were deposited on nearby dry slopes and ledges. When the glaciers began to melt and climates changed, heralding the close of the Ice Age, the water in the cenote rose, covering up all traces of those ancient Indians.

The research team made some unprecedented discoveries. While excavating a two-meter-wide trench on a ledge ninety feet underwater, archaeologists found the shell of an extinct giant tortoise that had a sharpened wooden stake driven into it. The stake was radiocarbon-dated as being about 12,030 years old and was proba-bly used either to kill the animal or to assist in cooking it over a fire on the ledge. The tortoise, and perhaps its hunter, may have fallen into the cenote; on the other hand, it is possible that the Indians lowered themselves down onto the ledge in order to catch and kill animals that had fallen into the natural trap. Whatever the case, the tortoise and the stake provided the earliest well-dated traces of human occupation of the southern United States. There were bones of other animals on the ledge, too, including those of various turtles, a diamondback rattlesnake, ground sloth, mastodon, and other species. An extraordinary wooden artifact found there is believed to be a boomerang. As the archaeologists worked higher up along the slope of Little Salt Spring, they found ancient wooden stakes, hearths, food refuse, and artifacts of wood and stone that had been driven into the pond's bottom. The wooden tools are the oldest known in North America. The stakes were dated as being about 9,572 years old; a mortar, about 9,080 years old.

The nearby slough, with its wet peat deposits, is in some ways even more inter-esting than the spring. Here the archaeologists found a very large cemetery, which dates to what is called the Archaic period in North American archaeology. This pe-riod follows the Paleoindian, and at Little Salt Spring the dates suggest an age of 6,000 to 7,000 years. The preservation conditions in the cemetery are exceptional. Wooden, shell, and bone artifacts were placed in the graves, and the bodies were placed on branches of myrtle and wrapped partially with grass. One of the skulls found contained "a substantial portion of a brain with still discernible convolutions and cellular processes." This is one of the oldest known examples of a human brain.

The Skudelev Finds:
Viking Ships Emerge From A Danish Fjord

Each year at low tide, the rock pile, with its projecting timbers, was visible at Skudelev, in the narrow, shallow channel of Roskilde Fjord. Local fishermen would find pieces of wood from Margrethe's ship among the rocks and would re-call the legend: Long ago, Queen Margrethe of Denmark had ordered the ship filled with rocks and sunk in the channel to prevent enemy ships from attacking the town of Roskilde, at the south end of the fjord. The ship had been there since the late Middle Ages. This local folk tradition accounted for the ancient timbers, but archaeology would show it was not correct.

Following the invention of the Aqualung there was considerable interest in in-vestigating this legendary site. Several divers visited the scene of Margrethe's wreck, and in 1956 a piece of the ship was brought to the Danish Museum. Much to everyone's surprise, the ship turned out to be much older than Queen Margrethe herself. In fact, it was judged to be a Viking ship. At that time, almost all archaeological evidence of Viking ships was from ship-burial sites on land, in particular the Oseberg and Gokstaad ships in Norway. These were rather like the Sutton Hoo find, which predated them by a few hundred years. These buried Viking ships were used to inter royalty and were not necessarily typical Viking vessels. People wondered how the Skudelev ship would compare.

Aware of the new potentials of underwater archaeology, the Danish Museum decided to excavate the site. The Skudelev project was headed by Olaf Olsen and Ole Crumlin-Pederson, who started by learning to dive. The work began in 1957 in water that was only a meter deep but cold, with low visibility and a strong current. Underwater archaeology was still a novelty; previous efforts by amateurs did not take into account the context of the finds and were seen as little more than treasure hunting. Olsen and Crumlin-Pederson had to devise many of their own methods. They stretched a long steel wire between concrete blocks for taking measurements and mapping the finds. Excavations were carried out largely by hand and by a firehose used to blow the sediments away. Gradually the rocks were removed, and the wood from the sunken ship was exposed and removed carefully.

As the work progressed, it became clear that the site was much more complex than was believed originally. There was not one but at least four ships buried in the channel. Work on the third ship was "the unsurpassed high point of the underwater excavation" to the Danish excavators, who wrote, "To lie in that ship in the underwater silence and uncover one magnificent piece of timber after another was a unique experience. The oak wood was hard and strong, so well preserved in many places that axe marks could be seen in the finely hewn timber." Nevertheless, it became increasingly apparent that the excavation methods were not suited to the task at hand. Only the larger pieces of wood could be removed safely; much of the rest was too fragile and would be destroyed if brought to the surface.

The unique and imaginative solution to this problem was to build a dam completely around the site and drain it—in other words, to create an island in the fjord. This was certainly an expensive and elaborate proposition, considering the fact that the dam might not be able to withstand winter ice and storms, meaning that the ship remains would have to be recorded and removed in a single season. Luckily, several wealthy Danish foundations came to the rescue of the Skudelev ships, and in 1962, an engineering firm carried out the task of building the dam at a relatively low cost. Most of the water was piped out slowly, creating an artificial island in the fjord that covered about 1,600 square meters (17,216 square feet). Enough water remained to keep the ancient wood wet during the excavation.

After lowering the water level came the slippery job of removing the seaweed and the eels that had made their home in the rocks. Next a series of small boardwalks were built out over the wrecks so that the excavators could lie down carefully on the walkways and work without putting any weight on the thin pieces of wood. A sprinkler system was installed at the site in order to keep the remains wet. The tangled mass of stones and wrecked ships was mapped, photographed, and removed carefully, piece by piece. The Viking ships, like most ships found underwater, were not complete. Yet the estimated 50,000 pieces recovered were labeled, sprayed with water, and put into large airtight plastic sacks to keep them wet and prevent deterioration.

An enormous puzzle was in the making for the boat-building specialist in the lab, and there were other problems as well. First, it was difficult to preserve the wood so that the ships could be reconstructed accurately. Secondly, the Danish Museum simply did not have the facilities to exhibit the ships. (A new museum with special atmospheric conditions was eventually built to house them at Roskilde, along the edge of the fjord.)

The Skudelev ships provide much detailed information about Viking shipbuilding. They were made from a variety of woods, especially oak, and their builders used axes mostly. The ships were "clinker built," which means that the planks overlap each other. The caulking, which was still preserved, consisted of animal hair and wood tar. Some of this material has been radiocarbon-dated, which indicates that the Skudelev ships were probably built between A.D. 950 and 1050.

Skudelev produced more information on Viking ships than any other site. Altogether, five ships were recovered, all different in detail. There were two trading ships, a fishing boat, and two warships. One of the warships, not well preserved, was a classic longship, estimated to have been about twenty-nine meters (ninety-five feet) long. At first, the excavators had believed this ship was actually two vessels because of the difficulty in correctly reading the evidence underwater. It is estimated that the Skudelev longship probably had between twenty and twenty-five oars. Like other Viking ships, it was also sail-powered. Agile on the open seas, the sleek Viking warships were also able to enter shallow rivers for surprise attacks.

The Vikings were engaged in widespread trading, which extended from the Middle East to Canada, yet no Viking trading ships had ever been found before Skudelev. According to Olsen and Crumlin-Pederson, the largest of the trading ships, measuring about seventeen meters (fifty-six feet) in length, was originally a sturdy vessel designed for major ocean voyages. They note that similar vessels were probably used by Leif Ericsson, the first European to visit North America. (Leif was the son of Eric the Red, who was noted for establishing settlements in Greenland.) Viking artifacts excavated at L'anse aux Meadows, in Newfoundland, date to around A.D. 1000. This was part of the larger area of North America known as Vinland in Viking literature. It is thought that opposition from the Indians, known as Skraelings to the Vikings, combined with the vast sailing distance caused the Vikings to abandon their plans to settle in the New World.

Unfortunately, the excavations did not reveal any clues about why or when the ships were sunk at Skudelev. They were evidently cleared of artifacts first, for, in contrast to the burial ships, next to nothing was found on these ships. It is known that there was considerable raiding in the area, especially by Vikings from Norway, and that Roskilde was an important and prosperous town. Perhaps the ships were sunk to protect the town after all, but not by Queen Margrethe.

The *Mary Rose*

In midsummer, 1545, a French fleet with more than 200 ships was poised for attack near the Isle of Wight, off England's south coast. The English fleet was outnumbered by more than three to one. As the wind picked up, Henry VIII watched from shore as his flagship, the *Mary Rose*, named after his sister Mary, set sail to meet the enemy with a crew of 700 led by Sir George Carew. It weighed about

600 tons, had four decks, and was heavily armed. The *Mary Rose* was the first English ship to be fitted with heavy cannon. Previously, most fighting at sea was done by a combination of archers and the use of light arms, but now it would be possible to sink ships at a distance. The ship was overloaded, however, carrying several hundred more people than usual, the heavy guns, and other gear.

Suddenly, the *Mary Rose* began to heel. Admiral Carew's uncle, commanding another English ship, passed within shouting distance and tried to find out what was wrong. Carew replied, "I have the sort of knaves I cannot rule." Then, in the sight of Henry VIII and others on the shore, the *Mary Rose* capsized. The open gunports, which may have been positioned too low, filled with water; the ship sank suddenly, drowning almost the entire crew. The screams of the trapped men could be heard briefly before the ship disappeared beneath the waves. The French forces were elated and, of course, claimed to have sunk the ship. Following this unexpected turn of events, a major battle did not really develop; instead, the French conducted a series of raids on the Isle of Wight. As it turned out, the British were in a sound defensive position despite the fact that their ships were greatly outnumbered. The invading fleet withdrew and returned to France.

Not long after these tragic events, there was an attempt to salvage the *Mary Rose* by securing two ships to it with cables and exploiting the rising tide to lift the sunken ship. The attempt failed, and the *Mary Rose* was eventually lost to the swirling currents and tides and covered by sediments.

The ship rested, undisturbed by humans, in her watery grave for nearly 300 years until some fishermen caught their lines on some protruding debris. In 1836, they notified the Deane brothers, who had developed a diving business by inventing and using a primitive diving helmet into which air was pumped from a boat. Working at depths approaching seventy feet, they recovered guns, bows, and some other artifacts. They knew they had found the site of the *Mary Rose*, but very little of the ship was actually exposed above the sediments. In the hope of salvaging more artifacts, they used powerful explosives and blew a large hole in the boat. Relatively little was recovered, and the quest for further artifacts was abandoned. A few years later, it was alleged that a demolition team blew up what was left of the wreck of the *Mary Rose*. The site was subsequently forgotten, and whatever might have been left of the ship was lost with the site itself.

Over a century later, Alexander McKee, a British journalist and historian, set his sights on finding the *Mary Rose*. McKee was not a treasure seeker. He was a member of the British Sub Aqua Club, an amateur diving society, and believed that the *Mary Rose* was, in some ways, a kind of missing link in a historical sense. As McKee pointed out, there was a fundamental gap in the record between the Viking ships and those built in the 1700s. The *Mary Rose* was especially significant because of the major changes that took place in the sixteenth century in the development of warships, both in construction and in the use of heavy cannon. McKee believed that finding the ship might shed new light on a critical period in naval history and on life during the Tudor period in England. Discovery of the ship would also be of major national interest because of its association with Henry VII, who had brought about many historical changes in England.

Few people believed that McKee or anyone else would ever find the *Mary Rose*. After all, it was assumed that the ship had been blown up. Furthermore experts, citing experience with Mediterranean shipwrecks, argued that very little could have survived anyway because of poor preservation conditions in English waters. A final problem was that the waters of The Solent, the channel between the Isle of Wight and the south coast of England where the ship went down, had low visibility, were rough, and constituted a major shipping lane. Nevertheless, Alexander McKee began planning his quest for the *Mary Rose*. He wrote, "Even in the local sub-aqua club I was regarded as something of an impractical visionary." Later on, one of his volunteer helpers admitted that he was once "convinced Mac was a crank and the idea of a Tudor warship was just a figment of his vivid imagination."

In 1965, McKee began a low-key exploration of The Solent with a small contingent of volunteer divers, trying to locate any shipwrecks. There was initially some competition with a rival group from the University of London, and the two groups decided to divide the underwater "turf" into two zones: McKee was convinced that the ship would be found at a depth of less than sixty feet, while his rivals believed it would be below this depth. McKee felt he had a reasonable idea of where to search, but his divers found no evidence of the ship. He soon reasoned that its remains were most likely buried due to the scouring effect of the currents. Moreover, he was aware that Harold Edgerton of the Massachusetts Institute of Technology had invented some new techniques for using sonar to penetrate the sea bottom and detect anomalies there. The technique had great potential for underwater archaeology, and so McKee decided to try it in his quest for the *Mary Rose*. In October 1967, as his ship passed over what he thought was the most likely search area, the side-scanning sonar device picked up an anomaly consistent with the size of the *Mary Rose*. The elated McKee wrote, "Optimistically I thought we had 85 percent proof already." Yet proving it was another matter. In addition, there was no law at the time to protect the promising site from looters. Following the results of the sonar, the *Mary Rose* Committee was formed and, under existing law, arranged to lease the site area for one pound a year.

The next task was to actually locate the elusive wreck. Working with long probes, the divers finally touched debris buried deeply in the sand. One of the divers describes the thrilling moment of this discovery: "In our excitement we had forgotten all the rules of diving, and I believe Mac nearly lost his mask and mouthpiece during our speed tour to our probe." But these probe contacts, while very exciting, were not proof that the ship was the *Mary Rose*. Stronger evidence was needed. It came in the form of a heavily encrusted cannon discovered by McKee himself in 1970. It appeared to be similar to those recovered by the Deanes more than a hundred years earlier, before the location of the ship was lost. It was later found to be loaded, as would have been the case in the *Mary Rose*. Once the gun was raised, McKee radioed the news to colleagues on the shore. In what must have been a triumphant moment, he writes, "After so many years of being denigrated behind my back as a mad chaser of wild geese, it was with great satisfaction that I saw that message go off."

The discovery of the gun stimulated a great deal of public interest and eventually helped to pave the way for large-scale funding, which was essential to excavate the site properly. The *Mary Rose* project included everyone from volunteer divers to some of the wealthiest British industries, all combined to give their support. Even royal interest was kindled in King Henry VIII's flagship. Lord Mountbatten was a bastion of support, and Prince Charles, who had studied archaeology at Cambridge, became the president of the *Mary Rose* Trust, formed in 1979. Prince Charles even made numerous dives to visit the excavations. He wrote the foreword to archaeologist Margaret Rule's 1982 book *The Mary Rose* and made cogent remarks about the ship's significance to British history.

With the necessary funding and equipment, the excavations proceeded under the astute direction of Rule. The base of operations for the divers was a large ship that had been used in the raising of the *Wasa*, a Swedish warship that sank in 1628. First, the interior of the surviving section of the *Mary Rose*, estimated by Rule to have included slightly less than half of the shell, was excavated carefully. The structure was incompletely preserved because of the action of currents, sediments, and destructive undersea organisms. The deeply buried portions of the ship were exposed by removing the sediments with airlifts. As is standard for land excavations, the site was mapped and the finds were plotted on the map, an essential procedure allowing archaeologists to place the artifacts in their original context and to reconstruct the original nature of the site.

The thousands of artifacts recovered have enhanced our knowledge of Tudor culture and lifestyles and is providing a wealth of new information on a critical period in shipbuilding and armament. Wood, leather, seeds, and other normally perishable objects were found, and the preservation was aided by the pitch that was used in the ship. Chemical analysis has shown that the pitch came from pine tar most likely imported from Russia.

One of the more interesting finds was a chest discovered in an area identified as the surgeon's cabin. The chest contained razors, syringes, and other medical equipment. The diver who opened the chest underwater reported that it contained "clay pigeons." This seemed bizarre to Margaret Rule, who subsequently went down to have a look for herself. She found a medicine chest filled with sealed wooden "pigeon-shaped" jars. The sixteenth-century medicine from the jars is being analyzed and compared with historical sources. They appear to have been resin-based ointments, probably used for treating wounds and various ship-board ailments.

Even though the *Mary Rose* dates to a well-known historical period, there were many artifacts found on the ship that modern people had never seen before. For instance, archery was of major importance during the Tudor period but, surprisingly, almost no archery gear has survived. The *Mary Rose* has changed this by providing a very large number of the famous longbows, as well as arrows and wrist guards. Margaret Rule notes that one chest contained 1,238 arrows. She feels that it will now be possible to re-create the famous English longbow and conduct tests of its strength and accuracy. Numerous guns have also been recovered, along with gun carriages and stores of shot. Leather shoes and other items of clothing, barrels, leather book covers, musical instruments, games such as backgammon and chess, food, and a wide variety of other Tudor artifacts were found. Many of these have had to be handled with utmost care when removed from the protective environment of the sea bottom. Even the bronze artifacts will eventually deteriorate with what is known as bronze disease if not treated properly. The preservation experts working on the *Mary Rose* have used a variety of chemicals and freeze-drying techniques to preserve the finds.

The ship itself yielded wooden sail-rigging parts, the ship's bell engraved with its year of manufacture, and the oldest actual specimen of a mariner's compass. Researchers are studying the nature of the planking, the gunports, the brick galley (which had collapsed, contributing to the sinking of the ship), the size of the officers' quarters, and other aspects of the ship's construction.

Inevitably, skeletons of the people, manning their battle stations or attempting to escape, were found. There were four decks in the ship and most of the men were not on the uppermost deck when the ship pitched over. Two archers were doomed after falling on the steps in a desperate attempt to escape. People were trapped in the sick bay, where they had absolutely no chance to get away; they were kept far removed from the scene of action so that their moans and screams would not have a negative impact on the crew. Study of the skeletons has provided new information about the health conditions of Tudor seamen. In recent years, physical anthropologists have made major breakthroughs in methods of studying human bones, with the objective of gleaning detailed information about past diseases, nutritional stress, and other aspects of diet. Other than poor dental conditions, the crew of the *Mary Rose* was generally healthy.

The great dream of McKee and others on the project was to raise the ship itself following the excavations and return her to the shore, where she could eventually be exhibited in a museum. The overall plan was to use a specially built lifting frame, coupled with a protective cradle for holding the ship. The lifting of the *Mary Rose* took place in October 1982 in front of hundreds of newspaper reporters and with full international television coverage. Things were upbeat until one of the legs on the lifting frames developed problems. The operation was suspended while a crew of engineers worked feverishly through the night repairing the leg. The next day, the *Mary Rose* was lifted. When she came to the surface after more than 400 years, Alexander McKee was elated to note that the ship's hull was still watertight and had to be pumped out. Prince Charles was to be the first one to step out on the emergent *Mary Rose*, but just then, the frame collapsed and miraculously stopped just short of demolishing the ship. In fact, the frame was held by a single bolt until a skillful crane operator managed to bring the *Mary Rose* successfully to shore amidst fireworks and a massive celebration.

Once ashore, the ship needed a proper home, as did the Viking ships at Skudelev. A specially designed museum was constructed at Portsmouth, where the ship was built. This museum features a spraying system to keep the ship wet and ensure its preservation. The *Mary Rose* is perhaps as much a marvel today as it was in the time of Henry VIII. A final comment is that the unfortunate victims of the *Mary Rose* disaster have been buried with an appropriate religious ceremony based on Tudor practices as re-created through historical research.

Gwisho Hot Springs

A southern-African waterlogged site is found at the Gwisho Hot Springs, situated near the Kafue River in Central Zambia. Gwisho is a Late Stone Age site, radiocarbon-dated to between 3000 and 15000 B.C. The Late Stone Age in Africa has much in common with the European Mesolithic. It marks the last period of "pure" hunting and foraging for wild foods. As we have seen, Late Stone Age peoples are renowned for their beautiful rock paintings, especially in southern Africa, where the sites are linked to the ancestors of the San (Bushmen). For the most part, these Late Stone Age hunters are known archaeologically by the stone tools they made, which frequently include numerous small geometrically shaped pieces called microliths. The Gwisho Hot Springs site, in which the unique wet conditions preserved much more than the usual stones and bones, is the only one of its kind in Africa.

The hot springs were formed originally by faulting. This produced a series of vents, which issue forth nearly boiling water at various places spread over a square mile. The spring vents have shifted about, and through time the hot water has forced its way up at different places. Late Stone Age peoples camped in the area beginning about 3000 B.C., which is roughly about the time the first Pharaoh established his rule in Egypt, far to the north. The Gwisho people lived in the area intermittently for about 1,500 years. The shifting hot-spring deposits eventually penetrated and covered the lower levels of the camp sites with water, preserving much of the organic material. When archaeologists appeared on the scene, the sites appeared as a series of low mounds.

The Gwisho site was located by J. Desmond Clark in the 1950s, and the water-logged spring deposits were eventually excavated by Brian Fagan and Francis Van Noten in the early 1960s. Their excavations revealed more than two meters of deposits, which they exposed by lowering the water table substantially with a pump. The excavators uncovered the remnants of a shelter consisting of grass, posts, and a semicircle of stones. There was also a V-shaped arrangement of posts, which may have been an animal trap. Wooden tools, which are rarely found on most sites, were numerous. They were highlighted by arrowheads, link shafts (a part which connects the arrowhead to the shaft), and digging sticks. Interestingly, the arrow parts, which also include bone points, are similar to those used recently by the San of neighboring Botswana.

More than 10,000 plant remains were recovered from the waterlogged deposits. Richard Lee, a noted expert on the San, visited Gwisho while the excavations were in progress. With him came one of his San informants who could recognize and identify the ancient plants and tell the archaeologists how these plants are used in San society today. This is one of the few prehistoric archaeological sites known where this kind of direct bridge between past and present has been used. They found, for instance, that the San drink the liquid from the ivory palm seed and eat the roots and fruit of the bauhinia shrub, both prevalent at the site. They use gourds for containers and eat the fruit of the baobab. One of the trees at Gwisho yields pods that are used to make poison. If it was used in this way by the ancient campers, it is among the oldest traces of poison use known.

Nearly 200,000 bone fragments were uncovered at the spring site. The small proportion of those that could be identified belonged to buffalo, antelope, zebra, rhino, hippo, and elephant as well as other animals. Fagan calculated the approximate number of fauna at the site, considered the body weight of each species, and, finally, estimated the amount of usable meat. By estimating as well the number of inhabitants at the site and the period of occupation, he figured that each person may have had more than a pound of meat a day, supplemented by an abundance of plant foods. This is better than many of us do at the supermarket today.

Flotation Techniques

This chapter has progressed from a variety of underwater sites to a water-logged site on land. It is fitting to carry this transition from water to land a step further with a brief account of how the usual dry sites can often be made to yield organic remains, some not even visible to the naked eye, through the application of water and certain chemicals. Such methodology in the field and in the laboratory, has had a fundamental impact on findings in archaeology.

The fundamental breakthrough in the development of flotation methods happened about the same time that the techniques of underwater archaeology were being refined. In 1960 Stuart Struever, an American archaeologist, excavated an ashy pit in a prehistoric Indian site in the midwestern United States. Following the advice of a colleague in botany, he immersed material from the pit in water to see if any small plant fragments might float to the surface. He says, "To our surprise, we screened from the surface a few charred seeds whose presence had been masked in the fill." Struever then went on to pioneer the new recovery technique that is known as flotation. Following the lead of a geologist, he added a zinc-chloride solution to the flotation process and found that this quickly separated extremely small bone fragments from plants. Then he proved to colleagues at prehistoric Indian sites in the Illinois valley that he could recover thousands of seeds and small fishbones through flotation from soils that already had been dry-screened by archaeologists. Amazingly, standard excavation techniques, which employ screens to sieve the soil, fail to retrieve about 90 percent of the plant materials. Small seeds and other plant fragments either pass through the screens or are seen only rarely in the soils, which are ordinarily discarded.

One early use of the flotation method in 1963 illustrates the importance of this technique in archaeological interpretation. At that time, a group of archaeologists was investigating the origins of farming and the development of early villages on the Deh Luran plain of southwestern Iran, just below the hill ranges where the wild ancestors of wheat and barley thrive. A test pit at one of the key sites, Tepe Ali Kosh, led the investigators to believe that "no concentrated deposits of plant material could be expected." Indeed, one of the paramount problems in researching the origins of farming was that few sites in the Near East appeared to contain plant remains. Hans Helbaek, a Danish expert on the domestication of plants, sought to remedy this situation by trying a basic water-flotation method. He notes "that when called in on the excavation I made up my mind to transfer to the field, for the first time, the laboratory technique for segregating plant remains from mineral samples by means of buoyancy." This was no easy task, since the scarce water had to be trucked into the site.

The results were a great success. Samples of carbonized plant materials were recovered both from ashy areas, where meals had been spilled on ancient house floors, and in other areas. From this refuse, Helbaek's flotation methods recovered about 45,000 plant fragments. The number of finds was unprecedented for the area and provided major new information on the development of early farming communities. There were numerous species of cultivated plants, mostly wheat and barley, and a wide variety of wild grasses, legumes, and other plants.

Helbaek was able to estimate the average grain weights and quantify the relative importance of various plants, wild and domestic, through time. For example, between 7500 and 6750 B.C., the first villagers collected an abundance of edible wild plants (about 94 percent legumes). Only 3.4 percent of the plants were domesticated, including emmer wheat and two-hulled barley. From other information, we know that they also kept goats and sheep and hunted wild game. All evidence suggests that these earliest Tepe Ali Kosh inhabitants brought their domesticates from the nearby mountains, where it is reasoned that the first steps in the domestication of wheat and barley, along with sheep and goats, occurred. By the next phase, dated to between 6750 and 6000 B.C., the ratio of wheat and barley rose to 40 percent of the plants, while the wild plants declined in significance. Later, other detailed changes in plant usage occurred, including the advent of a new hybrid strain of barley that was adapted to irrigation techniques. This detailed study of plant remains, coupled with studies of fauna, helped to confirm that the advent of food production and the village way of life was a gradual process, not a sudden revolution.

In the United States we have learned more about when Indians started to practice plant cultivation by floating bulk samples from key sites. Such samples indicate that Midwest Indians domesticated indigenous plants by about 3000 B.C. Squash, derived from Mexico, was cultivated even earlier. At the deeply stratified Koster site in Illinois, domesticated squash-rind fragments were recovered "in three of the 239 flotation samples" at a depth of nearly four meters. The squash has been dated to about 5000 B.C. by the technique of accelerator radiocarbon-dating, which allows for the dating of extremely small samples. Other sites, such as those along the Green River in Kentucky and in southwest Missouri, indicate a younger age for squash cultivation, about 23000 B.C.

The flotation process is now used at digs throughout the world and has even undergone various refinements, such as pumping air into the water to aid in the separation and recovery of organic materials. Before the process was used, large bone fragments were the most visible traces of evidence at most sites. But now flotation has corrected the flawed concept that the food of ancient peoples was obtained predominantly by hunting.

3

Proving Ground of the Nuclear Age

William Gray Johnson and Colleen M. Beck

The desert flats of central Nevada offer an eerie landscape of twisted I-beams, bent towers and deformed bridges, frame buildings ripped apart, and stretches of land scarred by craters—one so vast it rivals depressions on the moon. Welcome to the Nevada Test Site, 1,350 square miles of landscape indelibly marked by hundreds of atomic bomb experiments. Here, for some 40 years during the Cold War between the West and the former Soviet Union and its allies, scientists experimented with various forms of nuclear weaponry. Today, with moratoriums on both underground and aboveground testing, the Test Site is a silent wasteland, its devastation a legacy of that time.

We work for the Desert Research Institute (DRI), a branch of the University of Nevada system set up in 1959 to investigate arid land problems such as water availability and air quality. Since then our focus has broadened to include past environments and archaeology. Working for the United States Department of Energy (DOE), which owns the Test Site, and for state and private agencies in Nevada, we also regularly study Native American cultures as well as early settlements of miners and ranchers. The Native American ruins span some 10,000 years and include scatters of stone artifacts and pottery, occasionally associated with rock-shelters, caves, and rock outcrops decorated with petroglyphs and pictographs. Most of the mining and ranching occurred between 1905 and 1940, and claim markers and shafts can be seen in the hilly regions nearby, where springs, stone and wood cabins, outhouses, corrals, and fencing still remain.

We began recording these sites in 1978 in an effort to help the DOE comply with the National Historic Preservation Act of 1966, which directs federal agencies to inventory archaeological and historical property under their jurisdiction and to determine the effects of their activities—in the DOE's case the testing of nuclear weapons—on these properties. It soon became clear that what remained of the testing program itself was the most important component of the archaeological record. Like most artifacts left unused on the landscape, the Test Site structures and associated debris have begun to disappear. Weathering, recycling of items, and the need to reuse areas for other activities are slowly stripping the landscape of its Cold War artifacts. In 1982 Nevada's State Historic Preservation Office acknowledged the years of testing as an important period in the state's history and recommended that specific artifacts be preserved as testaments to the nuclear bomb experiments spawned by the Cold War.

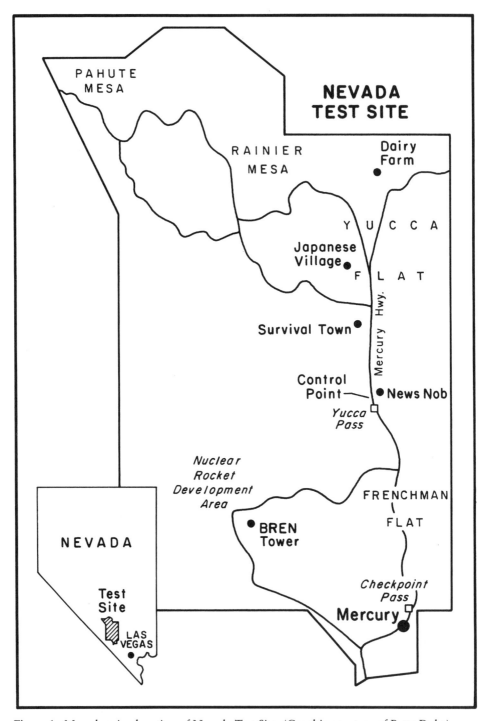

Figure 1. Map showing location of Nevada Test Site. (Graphic courtesy of Bette Duke)

In 1988 we proposed to the DOE that we survey the area. The proposal was well received, and in 1991 we were asked to evaluate two structures, a 1,527-foot tower used in a study of radiation released from an unshielded reactor, and an underground parking garage tested for possible lateral and vertical displacement in a nuclear blast. We felt both were eligible for the National Register of Historic Places, the official list of the nation's cultural resources deemed worthy of preservation. Soon after we were asked to inventory all Test Site structures to determine their eligibility for the National Register. This program continues today. Surprisingly, many of the artifacts and even some of the structures we have researched are not recorded in any official documents. Instrumentation stands and temporary storage bunkers, for example, were important for the instruments they held or stored, but were not considered worth documenting.

To enter the Test Site, one takes U.S. Highway 95 north from Las Vegas to Mercury, a complex of scientific laboratories and warehouses, a building that houses radiation monitoring equipment and staff, dormitory-style housing, a cafeteria, a post office, a fire station, a hospital, a bowling alley, and a chapel. This is where scientists and support staff lived and worked during the nuclear testing period, which began January 27, 1951, with an air-drop event code-named Able. Aboveground testing ended in 1963 with the Limited Test Ban Treaty, which prohibited atmospheric, underwater, and outer-space nuclear testing. The current moratorium, which includes underground testing, took effect October 2, 1992. It has been extended twice, most recently to October 1995. Scientists still work here, but their efforts are focused on tracking residual radiation in the environment and cleaning it up. Mercury is still closed to the casual tourist, and a gate is manned by guards 24 hours a day. The DOE began conducting public tours in the early 1980s in recognition of the need to communicate the nature and extent of the testing program and in acknowledgment of the taxpayers' contributions to the program. Monthly tours continue to be available to individuals and groups.

Those who visit the site follow the Mercury Highway north. A sign indicates that cameras are not allowed in the forward areas. Another warns workers to be cautious of posted radiation areas. Driving through Checkpoint Pass, a guard station no longer used, one enters Frenchman Flat, a dry lake bed surrounded by rolling hills leading to distant mountains. Blown-out buildings and twisted metal litter the landscape. Fourteen aboveground nuclear devices were detonated here; Grable, Priscilla, and Met were the code names of three. The largest, Priscilla, left most of the wreckage. Bunkers, motels, and homes, grouped at different distances from ground zero, were subjected to a blast equivalent to 37,000 tons of TNT. A steel-reinforced, concrete-sided bank vault at the center of the blast survived pressures of 600 pounds per square inch. We have recommended that the entire area be considered a historic district.

Continuing north, the highway cuts through Yucca Pass and a collection of gray windowless buildings that once served as the Test Site's electronic Control Point. Nearby, a faded sign on a boulder-covered hill identifies the site of News Nob, "where on April 22, 1952, the American press and radio first covered, and the nation first viewed by the medium of television, the firing of a nuclear device known as 'Operation Big Shot.'" At the foot of the hill are 11 rows of weather-beaten benches where reporters and dignitaries observed multiple explosions, some as close as 14 miles away.

Figure 2. This radar reflector served as a navigational aid for pilots flying through mushroom clouds to collect radioactive dust. (Photo courtesy of William K. Geiger)

Yucca Flat, whose cratered surface resembles the surface of the moon, witnessed more aboveground and underground tests than Frenchman Flat. One huge crater, known as Sedan, measures 320 feet deep and 1,280 feet across, and is a regular stop on the DOE tours. It was created in the Plowshare Program, a project designed to find peaceful uses for nuclear bombs, such as large-scale excavation. (A redigging of the Panama Canal was under consideration at the time.) Sedan Crater was listed on the National Register last year, the first Test Site area to be so designated.

Yucca Flat bears the remains of two-story houses located 6,600 and 8,000 feet southeast from ground zero of a test code-named Apple II. They were part of "Survival Town," a 1955 Civil Defense exercise designed to study the durability of typical civilian buildings subjected to nuclear weapons. Test targets also included industrial buildings and shelters, electrical power systems, communications equipment, a radio broadcasting station, trailer homes, fire equipment, cars,

Figure 3. Walls are all that remain of a motel subjected to a nuclear blast in 1953. (Photo courtesy of William K. Geiger)

and food supplies placed at varying distances from ground zero. The force of the blast was the equivalent of 29,000 tons of TNT. Only the two-story houses and the frames of a few ranch-style homes survived.

Yucca Flat was also the site of radiation experiments. Bare Reactor Experiment, Nevada, or BREN, was part of Operation Ichiban, a program intended to determine radiation exposures experienced by the survivors of the Hiroshima and Nagasaki bombings. In these tests an unshielded reactor was placed in an elevator that rode up and down a 1,527-foot tower. The reactor released radiation on a mock Japanese village whose frame houses contained dosimeters for measuring exposure. Raising or lowering the reactor enabled scientists to change the angle and range of the radiation. Ichiban data allowed scientists to determine relationships between radiation doses and health problems associated with radiation sickness. Though the tower was moved to another part of the Test Site in 1965, our research at the Japanese village and the relocated tower has determined that both are National Register candidates. Also eligible is an experimental dairy farm designed to study the effects of radioactive fallout on the fodder-cow-milk food chain. A number of small dairy farms were located downwind from the Test Site, and there was concern at the time that children drinking milk from these dairies might be affected by the fallout.

Farther north, Rainier Mesa rises 7,000 feet above sea level. Underground nuclear testing began here in 1957. Code-named Rainier, the first blast shook the mesa and surrounding areas with the force of 1,700 tons of TNT. Rainier Mesa and its neighbor, Pahute Mesa, were the sites of numerous underground tests. Some nuclear devices were placed in long shafts, others in tunnels. We know of underground bunkers, similar to bomb shelters, and we have heard about structures shaped like submarines with periscoping elevators. What condition are they in today? We hope to find out. Elsewhere there are remarkable structures associated with nuclear rocket development. We believe they too are significant.

Is this archaeology? We think it is. Our instincts lead us to believe that these artifacts of the Cold War are historically important and need to be studied. Can anyone honestly call them nonarchaeological? Scholars traditionally time-trek through millennia. Casually discussing similarities between the migrations of hunters and gatherers of 50,000 years ago and the peopling of the New World at the end of the last Ice Age some 10,000 years ago, they have grown accustomed to thinking in large blocks of time. It is the short blocks of time, especially our own, that we have difficulty understanding.

4

The Archaeology of Contemporary Mass Graves

Melissa Connor

Archaeologists and forensic investigators overlap in their need to reconstruct past events from the material culture and physical remains at a site, or "scene." The Physicians for Human Rights (PHR), a Boston-based nonprofit group, conducts forensic investigations for the United Nations and occasionally requests the assistance of professional archaeologists in its investigations. The National Park Service's Midwest Archeological Center has been privileged to assist PHR in its investigations for the United Nations in Croatia, El Salvador, and most recently Rwanda.

The violence in Rwanda began when President Juvenal Habyarimana of Rwanda was killed in an airplane crash on April 6, 1994. Within four months, an estimated half a million people were dead. By September 1994 the United Nations established the International Tribunal for Rwanda (ITR) to investigate the claims that these killings were genocide, rather than the result of civil war as maintained by the former government. The UN's ITR is actively investigating these accusations at the Kibuye Catholic Church and the Home St. Jean, located in central eastern Rwanda. The Home St. Jean is a complex adjacent to the church that includes a priest's house, a small hostel, workshops, and classrooms. It is estimated that 4,000-6,000 people were killed at the church and the Home St. Jean in April 1994.

The Midwest Archeological Center sent a team of three archaeologists, Douglas Scott, Ralph Hartley, and Melissa Connor, to assist in investigations at the massacre site, joining a larger team put together by PHR and ITR. The team was headed by William Hagland (ITR), a forensic anthropologist, and Robert Kirshner (PHR), a forensic pathologist. Hagland had divided the mission into three phases, all of which incorporated archaeological techniques to varying degrees: (1) mapping and initial documentation of the site, (2) recovery and analysis of the skeletal remains on the surface of the site, and (3) excavation and testing of the mass graves at the site.

Phase 1: Initial Mapping and Documentation

The archaeologists from the Midwest Archeological Center arrived in Rwanda in mid-December 1995 to begin mapping and initial site documentation. At this point, they were the only team members on site. The area of the Kibuye Catholic Church and the Home St. Jean was mapped using a coordinate system based on the 1,000-m Universal Transverse Mercator (UTM) grid, World Geodetic System

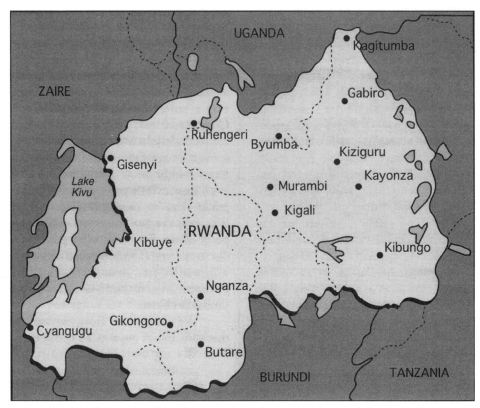

Figure 1. Map of Rwanda, illustrating population centers and major lakes and rivers.

1984 Ellipsoid (WGS84). The UTM points for the initial datum were derived from the Belgium GS3 GEO 1:50,000 topographic map of Kibuye. This was checked using a Magellan Trailblazer GPS. The site was mapped using a Sokkia Set 4B total station. Mapping data were collected in an SDR33 data collector that electronically captured the horizontal angle, vertical angle, slope distance, and elevation for each reading. It also converted the raw data into coordinate data, which would be the approximate UTM of the point. These data were downloaded into a computerized mapping program (Sokkia Map and Design V.6). Initial plotting, feature code processing, and contour computation were completed in this program, and the data were then transferred to AutoCAD Light for final editing and processing.

Ralph Hartley acted as team photographer and photographed the exteriors of all 23 buildings on the site area. In addition, he photographed any potential evidence remaining in the interiors of the buildings.

Phase 2: Recovery of Surface Skeletons

In early January 1996 six forensic physical anthropologists arrived. In an earlier trip to the site, William Haglund had identified the location of a number of surface skeletons and conducted an initial analysis of the material. The archaeologists had also walked transects around the site to determine site boundaries. In the course of this and the mapping of the site, they had flagged all skeletons encountered on the surface of the site. With the arrival of the forensic anthropologists, the skeletons were assigned a number, mapped, photographed in place, and carefully removed. The physical anthropologists set up a field laboratory and analyzed the skeletal remains for gender, age, race, and trauma.

Phase 3: Excavation of Mass Grave 1

The site area contained a minimum of six potential mass graves. The largest had been tested in October 1995 by Haglund and the ITR's senior scientific consultant, Andrew Thomsen. They had used local labor to hand-excavate two perpendicular trenches across the grave area and were able to estimate the size of the grave and the depth of the bodies. In mid-January 1996 the team began to open the grave. A mechanical excavator with a backhoe attachment was used to remove as much of the overburden as possible. When remains were encountered, shovels and entrenching tools were used to remove further overburden. Final delineation of the remains were accomplished using trowels and whisk brooms, and using hands to separate the interface between adjacent remains.

When a body was ready for removal, it was assigned a case number from a master list, which included a brief description of the remains, associated evidence, and possible commingling. Remains were frequently too commingled to be easily separated in the field. When this occurred, the remains were bagged together, case number(s) assigned, and a notation to this effect made in the master log. Photographs were taken according to the condition of the remains, and notes made on how much of the body was in its original position when it was possible to remove it. Crania were mapped as often as possible. Initially, all body outlines were mapped; as time became constrained, however, this was done for a lower percentage of the bodies to show generally how they lay in a specific area.

Four forensic pathologists and two autopsy technicians arrived in late January. All remains removed from the grave received a postmortem examination conducted by a team consisting of a forensic pathologist and a physical anthropologist. Remains were examined to determine sex, age, patterns of trauma, and cause of death.

The results of the examinations were entered into a database that is still under analysis. The conclusions of the excavations and examinations cannot be shared due to the ongoing medicolegal investigation. However, several hundred individuals were removed from the grave, making this one of the largest exhumations ever conducted for human rights investigations.

In December 1995 the International Tribunal for Rwanda issued indictments for eight people accused of genocide at four sites, including the Kibuye Catholic Church and Home St. Jean. Further indictments are pending. In late January relatives and friends of potential victims were allowed to view select personal items from the excavations, in the hope they might recognize something that could lead to the identification of a body. DNA testing is planned to match the victims with potential relatives. The Catholic Church is no longer used as a church and the prefecture of Kibuye is planning a memorial there to recognize those who died at the Kibuye Catholic Church and the Home St. Jean.

Meanwhile, teams of lawyers and investigators from the Tribunal continue working throughout Rwanda. Additional excavations are planned, and again, a professional archaeologist will be part of the team. The use of archaeological techniques and technology to meticulously document the collection of forensic data is an important addition to forensic investigations. The tendency of mainstream archaeology to interpret the findings in terms of cultural behavior is set aside in these cases in favor of the more circumspect medicolegal statement required for legal actions. Sound archaeological documentation adds materially in making a strong case both in the court of the ITR and the court of public opinion.

5

A Love for the Ages

Bruce Goldfarb

Dennis Stanford unrolls a three-by-five-foot photograph in the anthropology lab at the Smithsonian's National Museum of Natural History. Often dressed in a plaid shirt and jeans, Stanford might be mistaken for a woodsman rather than one of the nation's preeminent scientists. The large image before him is an overhead view of the Jones-Miller site in northeastern Colorado—a mosaic pieced together from individual photographs of excavation units. Investigations here have yielded the remains of some 300 butchered bison, plus tools left behind by the butchers. "This will be one of my life's major projects," Stanford says.

Nearly 26 years earlier, Colorado rancher Robert Jones Jr. leveled off a ridge above the Arikaree River flood-plain, exposing unusual bones and what appeared to be spear points. After local anthropologist Jack Miller examined the site, he quickly notified the Smithsonian Institution and a new associate curator named Dennis Stanford. The course of a career changed almost overnight. Stanford excavated Jones-Miller from 1973 to 1975, and he has spent the last quarter of a century processing the data he gathered there. His monograph on the subject runs over 1,400 pages, with hundreds of graphs and charts. "And I still have three chapters to go," he says.

This is the life of an archaeologist—the meticulous, diligent, and often compulsive search for clues to the past. Stanford has devoted his career to the investigation of North America's early inhabitants, a subject that has proven especially exciting during the past few years (see "On the Trail of the First Americans," *American Archaeology*, Summer 1997).

From his black-and-white photograph of thousands of jumbled bones, Stanford evokes a vivid story. Around 10,000 years ago a group of hunters at Jones-Miller may have constructed a corral out of brush, then herded bison inside for the kill. During at least two kills—one in early winter and one in the spring—the people worked cooperatively while butchering the meat and discarding the bones.

"You can see mandibles stacked like Lincoln Logs where children may have played," Stanford says, pointing. "Over here somebody put leg bones together as though it were an anatomy lesson."

Scientific Teamwork

Stanford's interest in prehistoric cultures dates to childhood, when he hunted for arrow points and other artifacts on the mesas near Albuquerque, New Mexico. As a professional archaeologist he has conducted fieldwork at dozens of sites throughout the Americas since 1966, including major projects in Colorado, Alaska, Wyoming, and New Mexico. Today, among other duties, he chairs the anthropology department at the Smithsonian's Museum of Natural History in Washington, D.C.

He is also partner in a unique husband-and-wife team. Margaret Jodry, field director of the museum's Paleo-Indian program, closely shares Stanford's goal of fleshing out the story of the first Americans: When did they arrive? How did they get here? What were their lives like?

"We just really want to know," Stanford says as he walks through a museum corridor, stacked to the ceiling with cabinets containing millions of artifacts. Down the hall in Jodry's office is a tray holding four stone projectile points. The largest is a four-inch Eden point, a slender tool painstakingly chiseled out of yellow-brown chert by a craftsman who lived some 9,000 years ago. The glass-like stone is chipped to a keen edge that gracefully tapers to a sharp tip. Also in the tray are colorful fragments of Folsom points: jasper tinted green and red, silicified palm wood with clear and yellow bands, cream and maroon swirling in Alibates chert. Clearly the people who made these points valued artistry in their work, not just the mere utility of a tool.

"They took the extra time to make it beautiful as well as useful," Jodry explains. Like Stanford, she has a gift for bringing prehistory to life. "You get a sense of the care and aesthetic quality that brought these tools into existence. It took ability and desire. I really admire their efforts to make hunting weapons beautiful, perhaps out of respect for the animals that gave them life."

Jodry spent five months on the road last year, directing projects in the field, attending conferences, and meeting with researchers, Native Americans, and collectors. She leads excavations at Stewart's Cattle Guard, a Folsom site in Colorado's San Luis Valley, and Black Mountain, the highest excavated Folsom site at 10,100 feet. She and Stanford married in 1988 but have worked together since 1979, when she joined an excavation team in Texas.

"We were salvaging a Clovis site then," she recalls. "We worked 13 hours a day in 38 straight days of rain. Dennis wanted to work every day, and I thought, 'This man is crazy.' But I was so happy to be working for the Smithsonian that I didn't want to say anything."

Working under adverse conditions is the rule rather than the exception in archaeology. Crews often operate in remote locations far from modern conveniences. The work is meticulous and physically demanding, and the risks range from foul weather to encounters with wild predators. It comes as no surprise, then, that fieldwork is a true test of any relationship.

"If you really want to know someone, take them to the bush in Alaska," Jodry says. But even in the museum halls of Washington, it takes an understanding spouse to accept the odd hours and the preoccupation with events that occurred thousands of years ago. Stanford and Jodry take turns assuming responsibility for field projects, which can involve months of preparation to arrange funding and assemble a team of archaeologists, geologists, soil scientists, pollen experts, and other specialists. "Archaeology is a team sport," Jodry says.

Figure 1. The husband-and-wife team of Dennis Stanford and Pegi Jodry at the field camp at Stewart's Cattle Guard site. (Photo courtesy of Dennis Stanford and Pegi Jodry)

The Lure of a Question

A passion for science and a mutual willingness to consider bold concepts has bound this duo together. "We like to throw out audacious ideas," Stanford says. "We may be wrong, but it spawns new directions in research and the ultimate resolution of questions." Stanford's interest in bone breakage, for example, spurred years of study by many archaeologists that added significantly to the body of knowledge about early Americans.

"There were a lot of ideas in the late '60s and early '70s about bone breaks—what was cultural and what was natural," Jodry explains. "Many of the ideas had not been tested experimentally, and they needed to be." Archaeologists knew that early hunters broke open the long bones of animals to eat the rich marrow, which typically resulted in a spiral fracture of the bone shaft. Many researchers concluded that all spiral fractures were man-made, a leap of logic that had no solid scientific basis, according to Jodry. Additional studies showed that carnivores such as wolves can create spiral fractures.

Stanford's work at three Colorado sites during the mid- to late-1970s examined bones broken before 11,500 years ago, the age of the state's oldest known Clovis hunting camps. Two of the possible pre-Clovis sites, Dutton and Selby, yielded mammoth bones with spiral fractures, flaking, and other signs of butchering. Was this the work of humans, some other carnivore, or a natural process? If human hunters had produced the marks, the evidence would suggest that Paleo-Indians had settled the Great Plains up to 3,000 years earlier than once believed.

An opportunity to test this theory presented itself in the winter of 1978, when Ginsberg, a 23-year-old elephant, died at a Boston zoo. The zoo donated the elephant to the Smithsonian, which transported the carcass to the National Zoological Park's Conservation and Research Center. Using stone knives made by modern flint knappers, Stanford and associates butchered the animal, slicing easily through the tough tissue. He used rocks to fracture long bones, producing marks similar to those found at Dutton and Selby.

A year later Stanford began excavations at a third site, Lamb Spring, located in a Denver suburb and now an Archaeological Conservancy preserve. In this mammoth bone bed dating before 11,500 years ago, some of the thickest, heaviest bones had been broken, while, strangely, the more fragile bones in the deposit were intact. Although the presence of humans at each of these early sites remains open to question, Stanford believes the greatest value in his work comes in stimulating intellectual thought and generating ideas that allow archaeologists to think about things in a new way.

Among Jodry's current research interests are thin knives found at Stewart's Cattle Guard and other Folsom sites, which she suspects may have been women's knives. Jodry thinks these tools may have been designed to jerk meat, work often done by women. The knives could be a stepping stone to greater understanding of Paleo-Indian social structure and behavior, or, Jodry admits, she may be wrong. But like Stanford, she perceives greater value in the open-ended pursuit of answers than in being right at every step along the way.

"Even if the evidence comes in and they're not women's tools, we'll have learned so much more about these tool types that it doesn't matter," she says. "We get to the same spot. We ask new questions about these tools and suggest new methods of inquiry. And in the end that's our goal—to learn more about pre-historic people by asking better questions."

Figure 2. A test excavation trench at the Jones-Miller archaeological site. Note the high number of bones from butchered bison. (Photo by Alison Whitter)

Figure 3. Dennis Stanford excavating bison bones at the Jones-Miller archaeological site. (Photo courtesy of Dennis Stanford and Pegi Jodry)

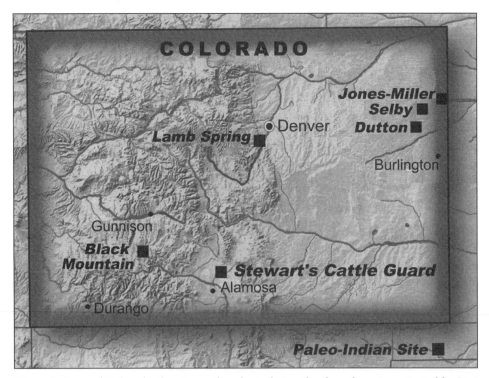

Figure 4. Map of Colorado showing archaeological sites that have been investigated by Pegi Jodry and Dennis Stanford. (Graphic courtesy of Dennis Stanford and Pegi Jodry)

Figure 5. Folsom bifaces from Stewart's Cattle Guard (1, 2, 3, 5) and Lindenmiere (4) in Colorado and the La Manga site in New Mexico. (Photo by Vic Krantz)

Figure 6. Excavation-in-progress at Stewart's Cattle Guard site (Pegi Jodry to left, Dennis Stanford in center, and Barbara Munford to right). (Photo courtesy of Dennis Stanford and Pegi Jodry)

Commentary

At the end of their article on the archaeology of atomic test sites, Johnson and Beck ask whether their work is archaeology, and argue forcefully that it is. What has traditionally defined archaeology is its focus on "material culture" to reconstruct and explain past life ways; few other anthropologists place such stock on the material, and devote their careers to studying objects and their associations. Archaeologists' emphasis on examining artifacts or material culture also makes their work quite different from other social sciences like political science, sociology, and psychology. In these other fields, scholars study living people and rely on written records and verbal accounts of human behavior. Scientific anthropological archaeology is also different from the humanities such as literature or art history that often emphasize individual creativity and imagination. While ingenuity and creative energies play an important role in formulating scientific hypotheses, scientific anthropological archaeologists ultimately evaluate their hypotheses with empirical evidence, i.e., artifacts and material culture.

In some respects, therefore, archaeology is extremely difficult, since some kinds of material remains are often poorly preserved in the archaeological record. Moreover, archaeologists (unlike a sociologist or sociocultural anthropologist) cannot interview members of an ancient society to find out how they lived. Archaeologists must use mute artifacts. In other respects, however, archaeology is uniquely valuable. Although people may lie, artifacts are silent. In spite of their silence, artifacts frequently offer unique insights on past events to archaeologists that understand how to "read" them. Archaeology does not always operate in an "ivory tower," since it is sometimes directly relevant to contemporary life. "The Archaeology of Contemporary Mass Graves" (Melissa Connor) describes an unusual application of archaeological methods for documenting human atrocities such as genocide.

No other scholarly discipline can study the ancient human past as effectively and reliably as anthropological archaeology. Furthermore, only archaeologists can provide the larger field of anthropology with a significant degree of time depth. No other specialty in anthropology—besides archaeology—can tell us about many of the ancient human societies and cultures that existed hundreds and thousands of years ago. Moreover, archaeology can provide a unique and valuable perspective on much more recent events. After reading these articles, the reader might well ask what, exactly, makes archaeology a single discipline. What unites archaeology into a single field? We hope, in the following sections, to answer this question by demonstrating how dozens of archaeologists, working in field settings all over the world, approach their work in a similar fashion.

Part Two

Archaeology's Past

Introduction

Perhaps humans have always been interested in their pasts: origin myths and religious belief systems are found among cultures throughout the world. Although we do not know exactly how long humans have had such origin myths and religious belief systems, contemporary scientific archaeology emerged relatively recently in the Western world where the Biblical account of human creation dominated most people's thinking for several centuries. In "The Discovery of Prehistory," William Stiebing examines European ideas concerning human antiquity and the earth's origin. He describes the origins of archaeology in western culture as part of a broader history of the development of western science, and talks about the changing nature of archaeology through the centuries.

Between the 16th and 19th centuries, European interpretations were deeply influenced by the Bible, and by accounts of the classical Greeks and Romans. Most scholars believed that antiquity extended back in time no more than 6000 years, based on Bishop Ussher's literal interpretation of the Bible. This account was not seriously questioned until the 19th century when the biologist, Charles Darwin, and the geologist, Charles Lyell, argued that life on earth probably developed over a much longer period of time than the 6000 years conjectured by Biblical interpretations. Even before Darwin and Lyell, however, other scholars in the Old and New World engaged in scientific studies that implicitly, if not explicitly, recognized the possibility of human antiquity.

The 18th and 19th centuries were characterized not only by scientific advances, but also by colonial expansion that brought Europeans into contact with indigenous peoples whose societies looked very different from those in Europe. Descriptions of traditional societies in the New World who used only stone tools changed European interpretations of the stone artifacts that farmers found on the surfaces of their fields. Objects previously viewed as "elf-stricking" and "fairy arrows" were now understood as ancient tools. Farming and construction activities throughout western Europe (in particular, gravel quarrying) unearthed fossilized bones of extinct animals, stone tools, and human remains. We can truly say that archaeology as we know it today was born in the 19th century with such discoveries. Stiebing's section describes the growing tensions between followers of Church doctrine and advocates of an emergent school of western science.

A key example of early scientific research involving archaeology was undertaken during the 19th century in early America. Thomas Jefferson, who we often call the "Father of American Archaeology," conducted one of the first stratigraphic archaeological excavations in the New World. His investigations focused on ancient Indian burial grounds on his estate. "The Enlightened Archaeologist," by Jeffrey Hantman and Gary Dunham, examines the historical context of Jefferson's work at a Native American burial mound in the state of Virginia. Although Jefferson's work lacked many of the specialized analytical techniques that are available to archaeologists today, his study foreshadowed a scientific archaeology in the use of hypotheses and empirical observations, rather than undisciplined speculation or reliance on a Biblical viewpoint. Apart from illustrating an early application of scientific procedures for studying the past, Jefferson's work also hinted at a continuity between present and past Indian cultures. Continuity of the sort he implied was one step toward convincing the scientific community of the significant antiquity of humans in the Americas.

1

The Discovery of Prehistory

William H. Stiebing, Jr.

Phase I — Exploration, Antiquarianism, and Early Excavation (1450-1860)

The Six-Thousand-Year History of the Earth

One of the most popular hobbies in America today is collecting Indian arrowheads. But this is a new interest, new at least when considered in terms of the centuries. For hundreds of years Europeans seem to have been oblivious even to the existence of such things. Millions of people must have seen stone axes, spear points, and arrowheads in plowed fields and dried-up stream beds or on eroded hillsides, but they did not notice them. To them such things were just so many more rocks. However, by the sixteenth and seventeenth centuries many people in Europe began recognizing the differences between ordinary rock formations and ancient stone artifacts. They then felt the need to explain the origin of the stone implements found throughout the continent.

These objects were commonly called "elf-stricking" or "fairy arrows," and many believed that fairies, on occasion, shot them from the heavens to injure humans. Others of a less superstitious mentality believed them to be freaks of nature, "thunderbolts" produced in storm clouds and rained upon the earth.

However, narratives by New World explorers often described the stone tools and weapons used by American Indians. These reports led a minority of scholars to argue that "elfshot" or "thunderbolts" were really implements produced by ancient people. Sir William Dugdale, an early British antiquary, declared in his *History of Warwickshire* (1650) that they were "weapons used by the Britons before the art of making arms of brass or iron was known."[1]

In 1699 another antiquary, Edward Lhwyd, wrote,

> I doubt not but you have often seen of these Arrow-heads they ascribe to elfs or fairies: they are just the same chip'd flints the natives of New England head their arrows with at this day; and there are also several stone hatchets found in this kingdom, not unlike those of the Americans....They were not invented for charms, but were once used in shooting here, as they are still in America. The most curious as well as the vulgar throughout this country, are satisfied they

---

1. Quoted in Glyn Daniel, *The Idea of Prehistory* (New York: World, 1963), p. 47.

often drop out of the air, being shot by fairies, and relate many instances of it; but for my part I must crave leave to suspend my faith, until I see one of them descend.[2]

A few years later, a German historian named Johann von Eckart also recognized the true nature of stone tools. But, in addition, he presented for the first time a clear description of the Three Age system of archaeological chronology. Eckart had been investigating the rise of the ancient Teutons, and as part of his research he had examined many burial mounds in Germany. To his great surprise, he found that none of them contained iron weapons or tools. Rather, many barrows (as such mounds are often called) produced bronze swords, shields, pins, and jewelry while others contained only bone and stone objects with no trace of metal. Eckart correctly interpreted his finds as evidence that there had been a Stone Age when metal was not used followed by a Bronze Age and an Iron Age, each heralding advances in technology and civilization. Dugdale had suggested a similar idea, but he did not go on to develop its implications as Eckart did. Unfortunately, the publication in which Eckart set forth his theory did not attract wide notice, and it was soon forgotten. A century would pass before the Three Age hypothesis would be proposed again as a system for understanding the development and relative chronology of European antiquities.

Not even those who accepted a human origin for the stone tools and weapons found in Western Europe realized just how ancient they were. These scholars thought that the peoples who had occupied the northern and western portions of Europe when Rome was ruling the Mediterranean world had made all the stone implements. Scholars also believed that people of the classical period had built the megalithic monuments such as Stonehenge that were also being studied at that time.

Europeans derived their knowledge of ancient history from only two sources, the Bible and the accounts of the classical Greeks and Romans. Chronologies based on these writings allowed the earth such a short span of existence that there simply was no time for prehistory. Most scholars agreed that the world was only about six thousand years old, though there was considerable disagreement over the exact date of the creation. Jewish rabbinical calculations from the Hebrew Massoretic Text showed that the world began 3,740 years before the Christian Era. Roman Catholic tradition, based on the Latin Vulgate translation of the Bible, placed the creation in 5199 B.C. And most English-speaking Protestants accepted the seventeenth-century Archbishop James Ussher's calculation of the time of creation, 4004 B.C. Ussher's dates were placed in the margins of early eighteenth-century editions of the King James version of the Bible, making them seem even more authoritative.

The conflict between supporters of science and those who believed in the complete accuracy of all parts of the Bible had not yet begun. Most seventeenth- and eighteenth-century scientists saw nothing in their work that contradicted the Bible. They agreed that science, in uncovering the truths of nature, would produce deeper reverence for nature's God. Thus, anyone who interpreted scientific or archaeological evidence in a way that challenged religious doctrine or the historical

---

2. From a letter to Dr. Richard Richardson on December 17, 1699. It was later published in the *Philosophical Transactions of the Royal Society* 28 (1713): p. 97.

reliability of the Bible had to fight an uphill battle for acceptance, not only among the general public, but also within the scientific community.

Throughout Europe scholars fit pre-Roman antiquities into the presumed six-thousand-year-long history of the world and assigned them to people known to have occupied various areas during the classical era. Many monuments (including Stonehenge and Avebury) were thought to be the work of Druids, the priestly class of the Celtic peoples of France, Spain, and Britain in Roman times. Other remains were credited to the Slavs or Teutons. A few people might have wondered about the many different kinds of artifacts that antiquarians assigned to the same people and time. However, most scholars continued to believe in a six-thousand-year history for mankind until the middle of the nineteenth century.

Hints of Human Antiquity

Developments in the field of geology eventually forced scholars to recognize the antiquity of the human race. Like stone tools, fossil remains of plants and animals were often found in Europe in early modern times, but their true nature and importance was seldom realized. As early as the fifteenth century Leonardo da Vinci recognized that fossils represented once-living creatures. He also saw that the occurrence of marine fossils on dry land showed that areas of the continent had once been beneath the sea. But during the next two centuries few investigators continued along the path blazed by Leonardo.

Many educated persons of the sixteenth and seventeenth centuries accepted the theory of the medieval Arab philosopher Avicenna. These people argued that a "plastic force" was at work in nature shaping stones in imitation of living things. A few supporters of the *vis plastica* theory combined it with the concept of spontaneous generation, an idea popular since the days of Aristotle. They claimed that fossils were nature's "false starts," so to speak. Supposedly the creative force within nature modeled creatures in stone and, when the formations were complete, generated life within them. If the process was interrupted or faulty in some way, fossils rather than living beings resulted.

Other people interpreted fossils of large prehistoric creatures as the remains of unicorns, giants, or dragons. The fossil ivory from the skeletons of such fabled beasts commanded very good prices from apothecaries. These early druggists ground up the material to produce potions believed to have miraculous healing properties or mounted fragments of it in gold or silver to make amulets thought to possess exceptional power.

But the most popular explanation of fossils was that they were the remains of living creatures killed and fossilized during the biblical Flood. Skeletons of fish or other marine creatures found far inland or on mountain slopes were thought to provide evidence of the absolute veracity of the Genesis account.

Among the earliest and most perceptive of the pioneers in geological theory was the seventeenth-century scholar Robert Hooke. Like Leonardo da Vinci, Hooke was interested in all aspects of knowledge. Besides dabbling in painting, music, and architecture, Hooke worked seriously in chemistry and biology. His *Micrographia* (1665) suggested several promising lines of investigation in microbiology. He proposed a wave theory of light, discovered the fifth star in the constellation Orion, worked with Sir Isaac Newton in optics, originated a kinetic theory of gases, invented several scientific instruments, devised a practical system of telegraphy, and was the first to use spiral springs to regulate watches. When he turned his attention to the study of fossils, Hooke perceived "that there have been Species of Creatures in former Ages, of which we can find none at present; and that 'tis not unlikely also but that there may be divers new kinds now, which have not been from the beginning."[3] He also noted that fossils consistently differed from one rock stratum to another. This fact led him to suggest that fossils could be used to formulate a chronology for the earth much longer than that suggested by Genesis.

Even more important than Hooke's geological observations were those published in Florence in 1669 by a young physician named Nicholas Steno. Like Hooke, Steno believed that fossils were the remains of once-living creatures. Also like Hooke, he noted that successive strata of sedimentary rock contained different types of fossils. More significant, however, was his demonstration that the flora and fauna represented in each layer of rock were types that could be expected to occur together in the same environment. Fossils of animal families inhabiting shallow coastal waters were found with those of plants growing in shallow water; remains of animals living in the depths of the sea occurred with fossils of deep-sea vegetation (if remains of vegetation were present at all).

Furthermore, the type of sedimentary rock in which each group of fossils was found tended to suggest the same environmental conditions as those suggested by the flora and fauna. Sandstone would have resulted from deposits near shore, shale from deposits in deeper water, and so on. Thus, the strata and their fossil contents suggested deposition by a natural process and could be used to show changes in the earth's climate and in the positions of the oceans in the distant past. Steno ascribed many of these changes in the earth's crust to natural causes, though he thought some were the result of the Flood described in Genesis. However, the time was not yet ripe for widespread public acceptance of Steno's geological principles.

Meanwhile, various discoveries suggested that humans had been contemporary with some of the extinct species of fossilized animals. But generally these finds were misinterpreted, explained away, or ignored. In 1690 John Conyers, a London apothecary, made the first such discovery of which we have a record. While digging for gravel near London, Conyers came upon several pieces of "fossil ivory" with a flint spearhead lying nearby. After an examination of the bones he concluded that they weren't those of a unicorn, but rather those of an elephant. How had an elephant gotten to England, he wondered? Were these the remains of beings that had lived before the Flood?

Scholars had not yet recognized the mammoth as an extinct species of elephant, so there seemed to be little reason to posit great antiquity for the bones or stone weapon. Conyers took the objects to his shop in London where one of his friends examined them. The man remembered that according to ancient Roman historians the Emperor Claudius had used elephants during his conquest of Britain in A.D. 43. He speculated that a heroic ancient Briton having no bronze or iron weapons had used a stone-tipped spear to kill one of the Romans' elephants. This explanation satisfied Conyers and the public. The bones and spearhead were stored away and forgotten.

---

3. Richard Waller, ed., *The Posthumous Works of Robert Hooke* (London, 1705), p. 291.

Over three quarters of a century passed before another discovery again raised the question of human contact with extinct species. A priest named Johann Friedrich Esper spent much of his free time searching the caves near Bamberg, Germany, for proofs of the Deluge account in Genesis. In one cave he found a layer of clay containing bones of a large animal that Esper recognized as an extinct type of bear. In the same clay stratum near the remains of the cave bear he dug up an unquestionably human lower jawbone and shoulder blade. The priest carefully removed his finds and continued to examine the nearby caves making notes and drawings of all that he uncovered. Finally, he dug up a well-preserved human skull. In 1774 he published his discoveries, claiming that he had found the remains of humans who had lived before the Great Flood.

However, Esper did not conclude that the human remains were as old as the bones of the extinct cave bear. Genesis made no mention of the disappearance of many species as a result of the Flood. In fact, the biblical account stated that Noah saved representatives of all species so that no such extinctions would take place. Thus, the extinct creatures represented in the fossil record probably had been destroyed long before the time of Noah.

In the first half of the eighteenth century scholars had also discovered that the earth was hot at its center. This fact suggested that the earth had once been in a molten state and that its surface gradually had cooled and hardened. However, experiments showed that the amount of time needed for a body the size of the earth to cool to its present state was much longer than the roughly six thousand years allowed by biblical chronology. So, by the time Esper made his discovery, scholars were coming to recognize that the Genesis account of the world's early history was not complete.

In 1778 such considerations led French naturalist Georges Louis Leclerc, Compte de Buffon, to postulate a series of "epochs" in the earth's history, each lasting a considerable period of time. He reconciled this view with the Bible by arguing that the "days" of creation mentioned in Genesis were six time periods of unknown duration, not ordinary twenty-four-hour days. According to Buffon, fossils, coal, and other geological deposits had been formed in earlier "epochs," thousands of years before the creation of human beings. He insisted that the six thousand years of biblical chronology were valid for the history of mankind, the end of the creative process, but not for the world itself.

Other naturalists proposed similar ideas. One group, the Neptunists, agreed that there had been stages in the creation of the earth, but held that all geological formations had been precipitated out of a primeval briny sea. Another school of thought, known as catastrophism, argued that there had been cataclysms separating the various epochs in the earth's history. The lack of overlap of fossil species from one rock layer to another seemed to prove that total destructions separated the geological periods these strata represented. After each great catastrophe, these theorists argued, God recreated living beings similar to (but not identical with) those from the previous era. Present-day species, including human beings, belonged to the last of these creations, the one described in the Bible; fossils belonged to earlier ones. While these naturalists and geologists disagreed over the details of how the earth's features had been formed, they agreed that the Genesis account of the last stage of creation was essentially accurate. They also agreed that present-day species, especially humans, could not have been associated with any of the vanished forms of life exhibited in the rock strata.

Thus, when Esper's account of his discovery of human bones in the same layer as remains of extinct species began to circulate in scholarly circles it was surmised that humans must have buried their dead in the caves long after the bones of the extinct creatures had gotten stratified in the clay layer. Even Esper concluded that there was not sufficient reason to presume that the human and animal remains were of the same age; they must have come to lie together by chance. So, the significance of Esper's finds generally went unrecognized.

Opposing the ideas of Buffon, the Neptunists, and the catastrophists were a few scholars who accepted the principle of uniformitarianism. This doctrine stated, in the words of its founder, Scottish geologist James Hutton, "No processes are to be employed that are not natural to the globe; no action to be admitted except those of which we know the principle."[4] In his major work, *Theory of the Earth* (1788 and 1795), Hutton described the earth as a delicately balanced system in which some forces constantly destroyed the land surfaces while others were slowly building future continents. Rivers carried the sediments worn from land masses to large bodies of water and deposited them there. Eventually the deposits would be consolidated into strata of sandstone, limestone, shale, or other types of rock by the pressure of the water and the weight of other material above them and by heat from the core of the earth. The heat would gradually cause the rock strata to expand and the pressure from that expansion would uplift them until they rose above the surface of the waters to form new land masses.

It was known that there had been little change in the geography of Europe since classical times, so these operations must take exceedingly long periods of time to complete. "The result, therefore, of our present enquiry," concluded Hutton, "is that we find no vestige of a beginning—no prospect of an end."[5]

Attacks were hurled against Hutton both by Neptunist and catastrophist geologists and by theologians who classed Hutton's theory with the atheistic materialism of various Enlightenment philosophers. As the geologists tried to explain away the evidence Hutton had presented to support his views, it became clear that their objections were not based primarily on scientific considerations but rather on religious ones. Richard Kirwan, president of the Royal Irish Academy and leader of the scientific opposition to Hutton, explained his long attack on *Theory of the Earth* by stating, "I have been led into this detail by observing how fatal the suspicion of the high antiquity of the globe has been to the credit of the Mosaic history, and consequently to religion and morality."[6]

In vain did Hutton and his few supporters argue that his system did not deny the existence of God nor did it state that the world had no beginning. Hutton claimed only that the earth must have originated an extremely long time ago and had gone through so many changes that one could discover no mark of that beginning. He had simply applied to study of the earth the same scientific assumptions and mechanical principles that Copernicus, Kepler, Galileo, Newton, and

4. Quoted in Glyn Daniel, *The Idea of Prehistory* (New York: World, 1963), p. 44.
5. "Theory of the Earth; or an Investigation of the Laws Observable in the Composition, Dissolution, and Restoration of Land Upon the Globe," *Transactions of the Royal Society of Edinburgh* 1 (1788): p. 304. Hutton revised this work, added rejoinders to his critics, and republished it in two volumes in 1795.
6. "Examination of the Supposed Igneous Origin of Stony Substances," *Transactions of the Royal Irish Academy* 5 (1793): p. 307.

others had already incorporated into astronomy and physics. But while scientists had accepted mechanistic views to explain the operation of the rest of the universe, the areas of geology, biology, and human cultural development were still studied on the basis of miracles and biblical history.

Hutton's views were opposed, but at least they were read and discussed. A different fate awaited a discovery made in England nine years later, in 1797. John Frere, a Fellow of the Royal Society, found many flint tools and weapons at Hoxne in Suffolk county. He wrote a letter to the Society of Antiquaries of London to announce the results of his excavations, stating that the flints were "evidently weapons of war, fabricated and used by a people who had not the use of metals."[7]

However, Frere realized that these artifacts were important because of the position in which he had discovered them. He had found them in a gravel deposit twelve feet from the surface and under three other clearly differentiated layers of soil. The sand layer immediately overlying this gravel deposit contained marine shells and bones of large extinct animals. Frere stated the conclusions to be drawn from these facts:

> The situation in which these weapons were found may tempt us to refer them to a very remote period indeed; even beyond that of the present world; but, whatever our conjectures on that head may be, it will be difficult to account for the stratum in which they lie being covered with another stratum, which, on that supposition, may be conjectured to have been once the bottom, or at least the shore, of the sea. The manner in which they lie would lead to the persuasion that it was a place of their manufacture and not of their accidental deposit; and the numbers of them were so great that the man who carried on the brick-work told me that, before he was aware of their being objects of curiosity, he had emptied baskets full of them into the ruts of the adjoining road.[8]

Frere realized that his conclusions contradicted the prevailing theories. So he met in advance the charge of "accidental association" that he knew would be used to explain away his finds. He carefully pointed out that the flints could not have been washed into their present position and then covered by earlier material eroded from higher ground. The strata he had found were *higher* than the surrounding terrain and were themselves being washed away by erosion. Furthermore, the earth strata were horizontal, ending abruptly at the place where the high ground sloped down to the surrounding bog. If the weapons and fossils had been eroded from another area and carried to the spot where Frere found them, they would have been deposited on the slopes of the hill in an uneven pattern and not in the successive horizontal layers he had observed. There seemed to be no way to avoid the conclusion that people had existed before or during the time that some types of extinct creatures had flourished.

Current geological theory and a six-thousand-year history for mankind could not explain the materials he had uncovered. As he had stated, they must have belonged "to a very remote period indeed, *even beyond that of the present world*"

---

7. "Account of Flint Weapons Discovered at Hoxne in Suffolk," *Archaeologia 13* (1800): p. 204.

8. "Account of Flint Weapons," pp. 204-5.

(that is, the world known from Genesis). Frere's letter appeared in 1800 in *Archaeologia*, the journal of the Society of Antiquaries, but the response he expected never came. His conclusions were not attacked or explained away. They were simply ignored.

Resolution of the Conflict

The validity of uniformitarianism, evolution of species, and the extremely long prehistory of the human race was not generally recognized by scholars until the third quarter of the nineteenth century. That victory for these ideas did not come sooner was largely because of the vast influence of one man, the great French natural scientist Georges Cuvier. Cuvier's lectures and writings brought catastrophist geological theory to its zenith both in popularity and in the scope and persuasiveness of the evidence presented to support it. His ideas dominated thought in biology and geology during his lifetime and for more than a decade after his death in 1832.

Based on his study of comparative anatomy, early in his career Cuvier formulated his "Law of Correlation," which stated that when one organ of an animal develops along certain lines, a corresponding development will be noted in its other organs. For example, hoofed animals will always have teeth suitable for eating vegetation while beasts with the interlocking teeth and fangs of carnivores will possess claws as well. Cuvier insisted that so detailed was this correlation that he could usually reconstruct the form of an entire animal from only one or two bones.

The well-known story of his encounter with the "devil" illustrates his commitment to the absolute validity of this law. Some of Cuvier's students decided to play a prank on their normally imperturbable professor. One night one of them dressed in a devil outfit complete with horns and shoes resembling cloven hooves. The others waited outside Cuvier's window to enjoy his discomfiture when this apparition burst upon him. Into the room rushed the devil roaring, "Wake up, thou man of catastrophes! I am the Devil. I have come to devour you!" Cuvier opened his eyes, glanced at the intruder, then calmly replied, "I doubt whether you can. You've got horns and hoofs. According to the Law of Correlation you only eat plants."[9] Upon hearing this, the students outside who had come to laugh at their professor instead burst into admiring applause.

To previous statements of catastrophism, Cuvier brought his thorough knowledge of fossil remains, which has earned him the title, "founder of vertebrate paleontology." Cuvier noted that there was only a small amount of variation between individuals within given species (either living or fossil). Because of this fact he could see no means by which one species might gradually change into another. He, therefore, affirmed that species were immutable, and steadfastly opposed hypotheses (such as that of his contemporary Lamarck) that suggested an evolution of present forms of life from extinct species found in the fossil record.

Cuvier found additional support for his views in the work of an Englishman, William Smith, who in 1816 published a table of thirty-two strata, each contain-

---

9. Herbert Wendt, In Search of Adam (Boston: Houghton Mifflin, 1956), p. 149.

ing different fossils. The lack of overlap of species from one stratum to another, Cuvier argued, proved that the geological periods represented by these layers of rock had been separated by total destructions and that life had been created anew after each great catastrophe. The fact that fossil life, like living species, had been subject to the Law of Correlation seemed to suggest that an intelligent Creator, following laws which he himself had laid down, had recreated life along similar lines several times in the past. Like Buffon, Cuvier claimed that Mosaic chronology and history were correct, but that they applied only to the present geological period in which presently existing species, including humans, had appeared. Cuvier confidently asserted that human fossils did not—could not—exist!

So firmly established was Cuvier's reputation as a paleontologist and so obviously valid was his Law of Correlation that many scholars came to regard all of Cuvier's conclusions as unquestionably correct. But the evidence stubbornly refused to conform to catastrophist doctrines. In 1828-29 M. Tournal, the curator of the Narbonne Museum, announced that in a cave in France he had found human bones and pottery with the remains of vanished species. Furthermore, some of the bones of the extinct animals even bore the marks of cutting tools. At about the same time other scholars made similar discoveries in Austria and in other southern French caves.

The most significant such finds, however, were made in Belgium by a physician named P. C. Schmerling and in England by a Roman Catholic priest named J. MacEnery. Dr. Schmerling investigated several caves near Liége. In one of them under a stalagmite crust he uncovered seven human skulls, other assorted human bones, and flint implements. Furthermore, he found these human remains lying with the skeletal remains of cave bears, mammoths, and rhinoceroses.

Father MacEnery's excavations in Kent's Cavern, Torquay, from 1824 to 1829, produced almost identical evidence. Under an unbroken floor of stalagmite was a layer of soil containing flint implements along with remains of extinct animals. In both instances, the stalagmite covering above the remains seemed to provide irrefutable evidence for the great antiquity of the finds. It also precluded the possibility that recent human material had been accidentally mixed with ancient animal remains.

However, most scholars ignored Schmerling's publication for a quarter of a century, while MacEnery decided against publishing his results at all. MacEnery had written about his discovery to William Buckland, the leading geologist in England and a strong supporter of Cuvier's catastrophism. Buckland informed the priest that ancient Britons must have dug ovens in the stalagmite floor of the cave, allowing some of their tools to fall through those holes and become mixed with the antediluvian skeletons of extinct species. MacEnery had found no such holes in the cave floor. But what was the word of an amateur explorer against that of a professor of geology at Oxford? He continued to dig in Kent's cavern until his death in 1841, but his manuscript remained unknown and unpublished until after other discoveries proved the antiquity of human beings.

The turning point in the battle against catastrophist and Neptunist geology came with the publication of Charles Lyell's three-volume work, *Principles of Geology, Being an Attempt to Explain the Former Changes of the Earth's Surface by Reference to Causes Now in Action* (1830-33). This work supported uniformitarianism and provided such a wealth of geological data to illustrate that principle that even its most unyielding opponents were impressed.

Lyell pointed out that geologists had failed to note gaps in the succession of strata and to appreciate the duration of past time. This failure had led them to misinterpret the breaks between strata as evidence for global cataclysms and violent convulsions. If the events of thousands of years of human history were compressed into the span of a few centuries, the appearance would also be one of constant and unnatural change and revolution rather than of slow and gradual development. Once one accepts the immensity of geological time, Lyell argued, there is no need to postulate supernatural catastrophes to explain the shaping of the earth's features. Given millions of years in which to operate, the agencies of wind, water, ice, and volcanism were sufficient to produce even the most dramatic alterations of the earth's surface. Of course, Lyell's arguments did not convince everyone. But they did force most geologists to reevaluate their positions, and they had a strong influence on the generation of young scientists (including Charles Darwin) who in the early 1830s were completing their education or just beginning their careers.

One aspect of the geology of Europe that seemed to support the views of the catastrophists was the occurrence of huge boulders or piles of smaller stones on the plains, miles away from the nearest mountains. How had such stones gotten there if not by the agency of some tremendous upheaval, such as a cataclysmic volcanic eruption or a universal Deluge? Soon after the appearance of *Principles of Geology* the question was answered by Swiss professor Louis Agassiz, who led a team of men into the Alps to study glaciers. Through his investigations, Agassiz was able to show that ice sheets had carried the erratic boulders found on European plains. He also proved that the advance and retreat of one or more great glaciers had produced many other features of the European landscape. Geological features formerly attributed to the Flood were now seen to be products of an Ice Age that must have lasted for a very long time.

The opposition to evidence of the existence of human fossils now began to wane. In 1837 Jacques Boucher de Crévecoeur de Perthes, a French customs official, started excavating in the gravel deposits of the Somme Valley near Abbeville. Like several explorers before him, he found flint tools and weapons side by side with the remains of extinct Ice Age creatures like mammoths, cave bears, woolly rhinoceroses, and bison. But this time scholars did not ignore the finds, and attempts to explain them away failed. Some opponents of Boucher de Perthes's claims went to France to examine the evidence for themselves or undertook their own excavations to prove him wrong. One by one they accepted the view that humans had been coeval with extinct animals of the Ice Age.

In 1859, two eminent British scholars, Joseph Prestwich and John Evans, were sent to examine and evaluate Boucher de Perthes's discoveries. After seeing the excavations for themselves, they returned to England and presented papers at meetings of the Royal Society and the Society of Antiquaries. In these reports, Prestwich and Evans stated their conviction of humanity's antiquity.

The year 1859 turned out to be decisive in the long conflict over the validity of Mosaic chronology and the biblical view of mankind's early history. It was the year in which Prestwich and Evans publicly accepted the finds of Boucher de Perthes. It was also the year in which William Pengelly substantiated the previous discoveries of Frere, Tournal, Schmerling, and MacEnery. Pengelly had excavated at Kent's Cavern in 1846, confirming the evidence found by MacEnery. But Buckland's suggestion that weapons of Britons had gotten mixed with earlier animal remains caused doubts to linger in many minds.

Virtually all doubt about human contemporaneity with vanished species was dispelled, however, by the evidence Pengelly obtained in 1858-59 from his excavations in Windmill Hill Cave overlooking Brixham Harbour, a coastal site about 165 miles southwest of London. Quarrying operations had accidentally uncovered this cave, and human occupants could not have used it since the Ice Age. From the beginning of the investigation a committee of prestigious members of the Royal and Geological Societies oversaw the work and could vouch for the accuracy of Pengelly's observations. Pengelly found the cave floor covered with a sheet of stalagmite from three to eight inches thick. Sealed within and just below this stalagmite floor he uncovered remains of lions, hyenas, bears, mammoths, rhinoceroses, and reindeer. In the layer of earth beneath the stalagmite, he found flint tools lying with the bones of Ice Age fauna. The antiquity of humans had finally been established beyond reasonable doubt.

Charles Darwin's *Origin of Species by Means of Natural Selection, or the Preservation of Favored Races in the Struggle for Life* also appeared in 1859. Lyell's arguments had strongly influenced Darwin and had removed one stumbling block encountered by earlier proponents of evolution, the short history of life on earth. If one accepted uniformitarian geological principles, then fossil remains in rock strata would suggest that life had existed on earth for a very long time—long enough to allow the slow development and modification of species to take place as assumed in evolutionary theories. Darwin cited a wealth of evidence from comparative anatomy studies and the fossil record to support the evolutionary hypothesis. But his major contribution to the theory was his presentation of a likely method by which evolution might occur. His description of the way "natural selection" and the "struggle for existence" determined which species or which individuals within a species would survive was extremely persuasive. Of course, many people, particularly some theologians and clergymen, objected to the theory of evolution because it eliminated the biblical concept of the special creation of living things. Nevertheless, in a short time the Darwinian hypothesis became the accepted view of most scientists and educated laymen.

Meanwhile, the first remains of Stone Age man had been found. In 1857 workmen digging in a cave in the Neanderthal Valley near Düsseldorf, Germany, found a human skullcap with prominently projecting browridges and a low, sloping forehead. A few supporters of evolution and the antiquity of man immediately recognized the find as genuine. Other scholars, however, argued that it was the congenitally deformed skull of an idiot, or that it belonged to an Irishman or a Cossack. But as acceptance of Darwin's ideas about evolution and natural selection grew, so did willingness to believe in the existence of humans with features more primitive than ours. Finally, when two more Neanderthal-like skeletons were found in 1887 in an Ice Age deposit in Belgium, almost all scholars were forced to accept the authenticity of Neanderthal man.

Within thirty years after 1859 the great antiquity of human beings, uniformitarian geology, and the evolution of species were all so widely accepted that their validity could be assumed in popular books on early man. Also, Neanderthal man and Cro-Magnon man (first found in 1868) had become recognized as our ancestors. The study of the past had at last been freed from the confinement of Mosaic chronology and a literal acceptance of the accounts in Genesis. Thus, the year 1859 marks a major turning point in the development of anthropology and archaeology. A new scholarly discipline, prehistoric archaeology, was born.

The Three Ages

While the battle over the antiquity of man was still raging, northern European scholars were showing that technological differences exhibited by human artifacts also had chronological significance. Much earlier Eckart had proposed that humans had passed successively through a series of technological stages, each more advanced than the preceding one. However, this idea wasn't taken seriously until a young man named Christian Jurgensen Thomsen applied it to Denmark's antiquities. Thomsen became the first curator of Denmark's newly created National Museum of Antiquities in 1816. Facing him was the task of organizing, labeling, and cataloging the royal collection, which at that time contained over one thousand pieces. When the museum opened three years later, visitors discovered that Thomsen had not followed the conventional practice of grouping artifacts primarily by their function or shape. Instead, he had grouped objects by the material of which they were made, producing three major classifications, stone, bronze, and iron. Within these groups, objects were subclassified in the familiar way by function and form.

Thomsen published a guidebook to the Danish museum in 1836. This work explained that his arrangement was not simply a convenient system for classifying museum collections, but represented three historical periods or technological stages through which early man had progressed. Thomsen's Three Age system began to attract the attention of antiquaries and museum curators in other areas of Europe, and soon museums in Sweden and Germany were using it. While it is possible that scholars in those countries independently developed the Three Age concept, it was not until Thomsen applied it to his museum collection and persuasively related Danish artifacts to stages of cultural development that the idea of a Stone, a Bronze, and an Iron Age received significant support.

Jens Worsaae, a student of Thomsen, soon showed the usefulness of the Three Age concept for understanding the relationship between primeval monuments and the history of a given area. In an 1840 article on Danish burial mounds, Worsaae distinguished the types of mounds and burial practices characteristic of each period, producing for the first time a relative chronology for these prehistoric barrows. After two more years of excavation and study, the young scholar published one of the most important books in the history of archaeology, *Danmarks Oldtid* (1842). This work was translated into English as *The Primeval Antiquities of Denmark* (1849). It gave a convincing account of the evidence for the Three Age system and related all the then-known Danish antiquities to either the Stone, Bronze, or Iron Age.

The Primeval Antiquities of Denmark also showed how careful study of archaeological discoveries could produce information on prehistoric population movements.

> In the stone-period and in that of bronze the funeral ceremonies and barrows were completely different; and we are therefore justified in concluding that the race who inhabited Denmark in the bronze-period was different from that, which during that of stone, laid the foundation for peopling the country. This is clearly shown by the antiquities, since there exists no gradual transition from

the simple implements and weapons of stone, the beautifully wrought tools and arms of bronze.[10]

Worsaae also stressed the importance of careful excavation and record-keeping, becoming one of the first to state the importance of noting stratigraphy and the position of finds. "Antiquities have a value with reference to the spot in which they are found," he stated.[11] In another place he remarked that it is "indispensably necessary to examine and compare with care the places in which antiquities are usually found; otherwise many most important collateral points can either not be explained at all, or at least in a very unsatisfactory manner."[12]

Perhaps Worsaae's greatest contribution to the development of archaeology was his recognition that the primary purpose of excavation should be to produce information on man's history and cultural development, rather than to gather specimens for museums or private collections. At a time when classical and Near Eastern monuments and antiquities were being plundered for the benefit of European and American collections, and more than fifty years before careful methodology would become common in excavations of European prehistoric sites, Worsaae declared,

> A very important rule is, that all antiquities, even those which appear the most trivial and the most common, ought to be preserved. Trifles often afford important information, when seen in connection with a large collection. That they are of common occurrence forms no objection; for historic results can be deduced only from the comparison of numerous contemporary specimens.[13]

Worsaae traveled throughout western Europe studying prehistoric remains and museum collections, and at every opportunity he explained and defended Thomsen's Three Age concept. Soon, in excavations in the Danish bogs and in the newly discovered prehistoric stilt-villages in the lakes of Switzerland, stone tools were found beneath strata containing artifacts of bronze or iron, providing stratigraphical proof of the Three Ages. By the middle of the 1860s the Three Age system had become widely accepted throughout Europe. Scholars then combined it with the concepts of evolution and the great antiquity of human beings to produce a clearer understanding of mankind's long journey from savagery to civilization.

As prehistorians began to compare the materials found in various parts of Europe it became clear that the ground and polished stone implements in the Scandinavian collections were quite different from the chipped stones found in France by Boucher de Perthes and in England by Frere, MacEnery, and Pengelly. This required the division of the Stone Age into two parts. John Lubbock in his *Prehistoric Times* (1865) named these eras the Paleolithic ("Old Stone") and Neolithic ("New Stone") periods. Specialists would gradually recognize subdivisions within each of these periods as well as within the Bronze and Iron Ages as they developed a more detailed picture of the movements and cultural history of pre-Roman groups in Europe. After a very long childhood, prehistoric archaeology now rapidly began to mature.

---

10. J. A. Worsaae, *The Primeval Antiquities of Denmark*, trans. William J. Thoms (London: John Henry Parker, 1849), p. 126.

11. Ibid., p. 156.

12. Ibid., p. 76.

13. Ibid., p. 156.

Phase II — European Prehistoric Archaeology Comes of Age (1860-1920)

Recognition of Ice Age Art

If there were any lingering doubts about early man's association with now-vanished Ice Age beasts, they should have been finally dispelled in the early 1860s. In France Eduard Lartet discovered bones engraved with animal likenesses, the most dramatic being a piece of mammoth tusk containing a portrait of the hairy mammoth itself. These finds revealed that early humans had possessed considerable artistic talent.

However, as acceptance of the doctrine of evolution spread, many had come to conceive of Stone Age people, especially the Neanderthal variety, as ape-like, primitive brutes only slightly more intelligent than their simian relatives. It seemed difficult to fit the idea of Ice Age artists into the picture of human development then current. So some authorities flatly denied the possibility that Stone Age people had produced the carvings. Others accepted the authenticity of the engraved pieces of bone only with strong reservations.

Scholars were still debating the issue when, on a spring day in 1879, Don Marcelino de Sautuola and his twelve-year-old daughter Maria set out to further explore a cave. For weeks the Spanish nobleman had been conducting excavations in the cave located on the de Sautuola estate at Altamira. He had found bones of bison, wild horses, a giant stag, and a cave bear along with flint and bone tools and mollusk shells with what seemed to be black and red pigment encrusted on their inside surfaces. While the amateur archaeologist renewed his digging in a side chamber of the cave, Maria wandered about, exploring the entire area illuminated by her father's lamp. Suddenly Don Marcelino's work was interrupted by a shout. "Papa, Papa, look! Colored bulls!"[14] Gazing upward in the direction his excited daughter was pointing, Don Marcelino was startled to see that beautiful paintings of great horned bison covered the roof of the chamber in which he had been working. In all the time he had spent exploring the cave, he had never before looked at its ceiling. Now, as he and his daughter examined the chamber's walls and roof more carefully, they discovered other paintings as wonderful as those Maria had first noticed. There was a charging wild boar, a large doe, a wild horse, and more bison—standing, running, crouching, dying.

Don Marcelino immediately reported his find to Vilanova y Piera, professor of paleontology at Madrid. After inspecting the cave and carefully questioning its excavator, Vilanova declared the paintings genuine. Vilanova's opinion was not enough, however, to stop the outcry of disbelief and ridicule that greeted the public announcement of the discovery. When they learned that Don Marcelino had befriended a penniless French painter a short time before discovering the cave paintings, many scholars accused the the nobleman of perpetrating a clumsy hoax. Others of a more generous nature were willing to believe that Don Marcelino and Vilanova had been innocent dupes who had been taken in by the real engineer of the fraud. Even those prehistorians who had given unqualified ac-

---

14. Geoffrey Bibby, *The Testimony of the Spade* (New York: Alfred A. Knopf, 1956).

ceptance to the previously discovered small engravings balked at crediting Upper Paleolithic inhabitants with the amount of artistic proficiency suggested by the Altamira paintings.

Don Marcelino's honor and Vilanova's judgment were not vindicated until 1895, when engravings were discovered on the walls of a cave at La Mouthe, France. Paleolithic and Neolithic deposits completely blocked the entrance to this cave, so no one could have entered it since the latter part of the Old Stone Age. Two years later excavators found paintings and engravings in another French cave at Pair-non-Pair. The discoverers noted that at several places in this cave Stone Age deposits that had accumulated on the cavern's floor covered the lower portions of the animal representations. This circumstance proved the Upper Paleolithic date of the art. Unfortunately, these discoveries came too late to be enjoyed by the men who had been maligned. Don Marcelino had died at the age of fifty-seven in 1888, followed by Vilanova in 1892.

Emile Cartailhac, professor of prehistory at the University of Toulouse and president of the Prehistoric Society of France, had been the most adamant opponent of the authenticity of Paleolithic cave art. But even he was convinced when cave paintings continued to be found at various French and Spanish sites. In 1902 he published a public confession of his longstanding error. Furthermore, he paid a visit to Don Marcelino's now married daughter, Maria, to apologize personally for the wrong he had done her father.

Stratigraphic Excavation and Improved Dating Techniques

The last decades of the nineteenth and first decades of the twentieth centuries also saw major advances in techniques of excavation and in methods of dating prehistoric finds. Between 1880 and 1900, a retired British general named Augustus Henry Lane-Fox Pitt Rivers developed the principles of modern archaeological excavation, recording, and publication. Pitt Rivers had become interested in the development of firearms while still in the army. This interest led him to amass a huge collection of weapons, which he arranged in typological sequences. Upon his retirement from the military in 1880 he shifted his antiquarian interests to the excavation of some prehistoric barrows and earthworks on his estate. In these digs he put into practice the principles he later stressed in his publications.

> Excavators, as a rule, record only those things which appear to them important at the time, but fresh problems in Archaeology and Anthropology are constantly arising, and it can hardly fail to have escaped the notice of anthropologists, especially those who, like myself, have been concerned with the morphology of art, that, on turning back to old accounts in search of evidence, the points which would have been most valuable have been passed over from being thought uninteresting at the time. *Every detail should, therefore, be recorded in the manner most conducive to facility of reference, and it ought at all times to be the chief object of the excavator to reduce his own personal equation to a minimum.*[15]

---

15. *Excavations in Cranborne Chase*, vol. 1 (privately published, 1887), p. xvii (emphasis added).

Pitt Rivers recognized the chronological value that seemingly worthless objects such as pottery sherds could have if their stratigraphical positions were accurately recorded. He insisted on careful, methodical excavation of entire sites instead of the grave robbing and tunneling which at that time often passed for archaeological excavation. He meticulously recorded all finds, and the publications of his results were models of archaeological reporting. Along with descriptions of his excavations he published drawings and lists of every object found, plans, and sections. He carefully cataloged the objects and exhibited them in a museum at Farnham with wooden models illustrating various stages in the excavation of each site. The achievement of Pitt Rivers is perhaps best summed up in the words of Glyn Daniel: "In fifteen years he transformed excavation from the pleasant hobby of barrow digging to an arduous scientific pursuit."[16]

While Pitt Rivers was improving excavation methods, others were developing the better ways to date prehistoric remains. Using the Three Age hypothesis, Thomsen, Worsaae, and others had worked out a relative chronology that could be applied to most antiquities within a given area. However, scholars recognized that the use of bronze and iron had come to different parts of Europe at different times. While one could say that Bronze Age barrows in Denmark were later than Stone Age mounds in the same area, no one could determine whether Danish Bronze Age remains were earlier than, later than, or contemporaneous with Bronze Age materials in Britain, France, or other parts of Europe.

This situation was transformed by the research of the Swedish archaeologist Gustav Oscar Montelius. By 1890 Montelius had linked together the local relative chronological schemes of various parts of Europe into a single complete system. Furthermore, by 1910 he managed to establish absolute dates for European Bronze and Iron Age cultures.

Montelius achieved these impressive results through the introduction of typological sequence dating into European prehistoric archaeology. This method required first a careful study of all finds from a given area. Then Montelius made lists noting objects that always occurred together and others never found together. From this study he would gradually discern several groups of contemporaneous objects, each group characteristic of a particular period. Next, Montelius studied a class of objects such as swords or axes, comparing the form of these objects from one group to another. Usually he could spot similarities between objects in different groups and arrange these objects into a sequence in which the change from one group to another was gradual, even though the objects at either end of the sequence might have little resemblance to one another. In order to determine which end of the sequence was the beginning and which the end, Montelius looked for evidence of technological advances or signs of vestigial features that had once served a useful function before degenerating into merely decorative elements. Once he had worked out several such typological sequences of individual objects and determined that the sequences were consistent with one another, then he could place the larger groups into sequential order. In this way he provided a relative chronology for the various cultures in a given area.

Trade items and mixtures of artifacts in border areas between cultures showed which artifact groups were contemporaneous with one another. This information

---

16. *A Hundred Years of Archaeology* (London: Duckworth, 1950), p. 173.

allowed Montelius to connect the relative chronologies of two or more different areas. Such evidence also gave him the key he needed to determine absolute dates for the European Bronze and Iron Age sequences. In the two decades between 1885 and 1905 archaeologists working in Greece and Egypt found many objects that evidenced Bronze Age trade between the two areas. Thus scholars were able to tie the Greek Bronze Age to the Egyptian absolute chronology, which was based on hieroglyphic inscriptions and ancient astronomical observations. Montelius was then able to use connections between the Greek material and assemblages in other parts of Europe to date European Bronze and Iron Age remains in absolute as well as relative terms.

During the early decades of the twentieth century another Swedish scholar, Baron Louis Gerhard de Geer, developed a method for dating past glacial movements. De Geer noticed that many clayey deposits were composed of many thin layers of soil. He discovered that these silt layers (called varves) were annual deposits caused by seasonal glacial melt waters flowing into quiet lakes or ponds. De Geer was able to relate various sequences of varves to one another and finally to a datable historical event. The chronology he created suggested that the last Ice Age ended about nine thousand years ago. Thus, artifacts found with remains of Ice Age animals had to be older. Varve chronology also provided the means for dating some of the Neolithic deposits in northern Europe.

Of course, over the years scholars have continued to improve these early chronological systems. The use of pollen analysis has allowed scholars to relate varve chronology to more archaeological deposits than had first been possible. Moreover, the development of dating systems based on the decay of radioactive material has provided absolute dates for much of the Stone Age as well as Bronze and Iron Age cultures. Nevertheless, the changes made in European archaeological chronology in recent years are minor compared to the great revolution in the scholarly understanding of prehistoric chronology wrought by Montelius, de Geer, and their colleagues in the late nineteenth and early twentieth centuries.

By the outbreak of World War I scholars had at last come to grips with the depth of mankind's past. Furthermore, with the development of methods for correctly recovering and interpreting that past, European prehistoric archaeology had become a mature discipline. The age of the amateur digger had ended, and the day of the professional prehistorian had begun.

2

The Enlightened Archaeologist

Jeffrey L. Hartman and Gary Dunham

Thomas Jefferson's Excavation of an Indian burial mound near Charlottesville, Virginia, has earned him the title "Father of American Archaeology." Jefferson described his dig on the South Fork of the Rivanna River in his book, *Notes on the State of Virginia*. He also reported that "many [mounds] are to be found all over this country [though] cleared of their trees and put under cultivation [they] are much reduced in their height, and spread in width, by the plough, and will probably disappear in time." In fact, the mound excavated by Jefferson has disappeared from view, despite several attempts to locate it earlier in this century. Jefferson's description of it remains the sole documentation that it existed at all.

In 1988, an opportunity arose to study a burial mound quite similar to the one dug by Jefferson. Known as the Rapidan Mound, it is located just 14 miles from the one Jefferson excavated. It had been placed on the endangered sites list of the Virginia Department of Historic Resources, and money was available to help excavate and preserve the remaining portions of it. Once prominent in the middle of a floodplain, it had been steadily eroded by the shifting course and destructive flooding of the Rapidan River. Early nineteenth-century accounts of the Rapidan Mound suggest it was then a 12 to 15-foot-high conical mound with a diameter of some 50 feet. In 1892, the Smithsonian's Gerard Fowke, who had been an assistant to Cyrus Thomas on the great mound surveys of the late nineteenth century, recorded the mound as being reduced to six feet in height, though the width had remained stable. Fowke dug a large trench through the mound, even then severely eroded by the river and partially leveled by farmers. In 1979, Archaeological Society of Virginia members Charlton G. Holland, Sandra Spieden, and David van Roijen opened two small excavation units on the river's edge and described apparently random deposits of human bone and a submound pit. By 1988 those units had been washed away, and only a small fragment of the mound's south edge remained. The rate of destruction had quickened even in the past few years, and there was no way possible to secure the site without flooding farm fields downstream.

On a cold spring day, we met with archaeologists Keith Egloff, David Hazzard, Randy Turner, and Catherine Slusser from the Virginia Department of Historic Resources and discussed by the possibility of salvaging the site. Because preservation was simply not possible, we decided to record what was left left of the mound, in accordance with Virginia's new burial laws that include a commitment to rebury human remains.

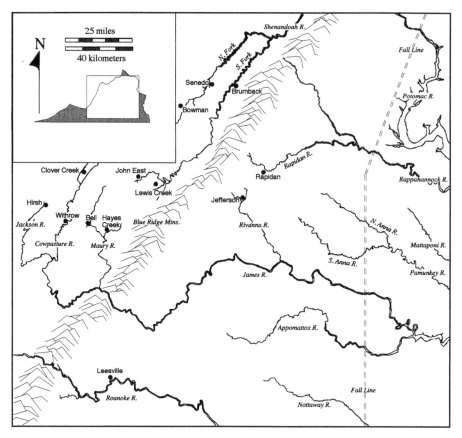

Figure 1. Location of the thirteen Monacan burial mounds in central and west-central Virginia. The two easternmost mounds—the Jefferson Mound on the Rivanna River and the Rapidan Mound on the Rapidan River—are discussed in the text. (Graphic by Martin Gallivan)

Initially we were skeptical that there would be anything left within the mound to record. Although respectfully protected in recent years by the family that owned the land on which it was located, the mound's condition was rapidly deteriorating. Recent floods had eroded the north face exposed to the river; a few abandoned cars buried off the south edge of the mound acted as a makeshift flood wall. Despite the erosion, we felt a season of testing was worth the effort. Funds from the Virginia Department of Historic Resources provided for a professional staff to oversee the excavation; students from the University of Virginia's summer field school joined in the dig after receiving extensive training at nearby sites. It would be three years before we finished our work.

Most of our first season was spent clinging to the riverbank, our feet in small rests cut into the submound soils, cleaning off flood debris and roots to reveal the mound's inner levels. We could see the clear outline of the trench that Fowke had made. Having located the old trench, we could focus our attention on undisturbed areas. What we discovered was an astonishing similarity between the profiles of our mound and the one excavated by Jefferson—layers of dark stained

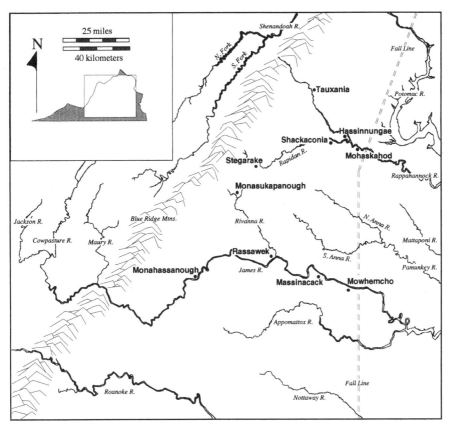

Figure 2. The territory of the Monacan of central Virginia, ca. 1607. This map identifies those villages which were identified by Jamestown colonist John Smith on his 1612 map of Virginia. (Graphic by Martin Gallivan)

soil with bone in it, interrupted by lighter colored soils brought to the site. Where Jefferson had seen seven such levels near the center of his mound, we could see three.

Jefferson had actually employed two excavation strategies. One was trenching, which allowed him to look at the internal structure of the mound and its stratigraphy. In this he was about 100 years ahead of his time. But he also wrote: "I first dug superficially in several parts of it, and came to collections of human bones, at different depths, from six inches to three feet below the surface. These were lying in the utmost confusion, some vertical, some oblique, some horizontal, and directed to every point of the compass, entangled, and held together in clusters by the earth. Bones of the most distant part were found together...." What Jefferson could not see or fully appreciate with his narrow trenching and random digging was the internal structure of each of the separate burial features he had carefully identified.

In 1989 and 1990 we excavated the Rapidan River mound by exposing broad horizontal areas in an effort to study the spatial relationships among the mound's burial features, as well as the internal configuration of each burial. We were able to identify six burial features, three of which we excavated completely. We found that the bones were not "lying in utmost confusion," as Jefferson described them, nor were they random placements as posited by later excavators. Instead, the bones, after an initial burial or exposure of the body to remove the flesh, had been recovered and reburied as part of a mortuary ritual. The skulls had been placed in concentric circles with long bones distributed around them in linear arrangements. Our excavations also revealed a pattern of change in burial practice over time from earlier individual or small multiple burials in pits, to later secondary burials containing up to 20 individuals. Jefferson did not record any submound pits, although they are common in most Virginia mounds, and we, as well as Fowke, found them at Rapidan Mound. Like the careful arrangement of bones, Jefferson probably missed them because he dug only narrow trenches and excavation pits.

We estimate that between 1,000 and 1,500 people were buried in the Rapidan Mound. Remarkably, with considerably less information in hand, Jefferson wrote of the Rivanna River mound, "I conjectured that in this barrow might have been a thousand skeletons." Based on our study of the Rapidan Mound, we now have good reason to believe his conjecture was accurate. The central Virginia mounds may not be extraordinary in terms of size, but the number of burials they contained and the generations it took for them to accumulate, is quite extraordinary.

Analysis of bones from Rapidan Mound has provided interesting new insights. Sandra Olsen, an archaeologist at the Carnegie Museum of Natural History, who was then on the staff of the Virginia Museum of Natural History, performed a scanning electron microscope analysis of five detached skull caps and two skulls missing caps that were found in a single burial feature. Separating skulls from skull caps, presumably with a sharp instrument, was a practice described in local histories relating to the treatment of an enemy prisoner after death. Of further interest was an intact cranium that had an unusual depressed fracture and V-shaped linear groove indicating a blow to the head with a sharp weapon. We inferred from this that some of those buried in the mound may have been killed in warfare. Such evidence, though tentative, contrasts with Jefferson's finding that "no holes were discovered in any of them, as if made by bullets, arrows or other weapons." In the absence of scanning electron microscopy, Jefferson may well have missed some tell-tale signs of violent death.

On so many other points, however, it is quite remarkable how well Jefferson's interpretations hold up in the late twentieth century. His reading of the stratigraphy of the mound has been well supported by excavations at other mounds in Virginia. Our own work also sheds light on the question of why Jefferson didn't mention any artifacts, and didn't appear to keep any from his excavation. At Rapidan Mound we found very little in the way of artifacts. Using screens and flotation, we did find small potsherds that appear to have been intentionally broken into small pieces as part of the burial ritual, and some stone tools including triangular projectile points. It is not likely that a trenching operation like Jefferson's, without screening, would have turned up such inconspicuous items.

Jefferson accurately described the variety of mounds in central Virginia, noting how they were of different sizes, some built of loose earth and others of stone. More than many twentieth-century archaeologists, he was aware of how the mound he was excavating fit into a regional archaeological perspective. He was also fairly accurate in describing the function of the mounds as community burial places, and the development of the mounds over an unstated period of time. He wrote: "Appearances certainly indicate that [the mound] has derived both origin and growth from the accustomary collection of bones, and deposition of them together; that the first collection had been deposited on the common surface of the earth, a few stones put over it, and then a covering of earth, that the second had been laid on this, had covered more or less of it in proportion to the numbers of bones, and was then also covered with earth, and so on."

To what extent did Jefferson's excavation contribute to an understanding of Native American history? The area in which his mound was located was the territory of the Monacan Indians. He noted that the mound was located across the river from an Indian town, most likely the Monacan town of Monasukapanough, or any one of a number of Late Woodland and possibly early contact period villages identified in archaeological surveys along the Rivanna. But of the Monacans, Jefferson only wrote that he thought they had merged with the Tuscarora and were now part of the Iroquois Confederacy to the north. He did not connect the mound to local Indian history. In fact, in his description of the excavation in *Notes*, Jefferson did not use archaeology to comment on Indian history at all. His focus was not on time, or cultural history, but on the inner construction of an odd feature on the landscape.

Why did he describe the mound at all? Because he was asked to do so. In 1780, a French diplomat in Philadelphia, Francois Marbois, circulated a letter to representatives of all the newly formed states requesting information on 22 separate topics such as their natural history, resources, population, climate, Indian population, etc. Jefferson was the Virginian who elected to answer this questionnaire, and his response became *Notes on the State of Virginia*. When Jefferson wrote *Notes*, he abbreviated the Indian question put to him by the Frenchman as: "A description of the Indians established in that state." In fact, Marbois' letter had requested: "A description of the Indians established in the state before the European settlements and of those who are still remaining. An indication of the Indian Monuments in that state."

Jefferson's chapter on Indians in *Notes*, titled "Aborigines," is in answer to these three questions posed by Marbois. First, he described the Indians established in the state before the Europeans, but he based this discussion entirely on his reading of colonist John Smith's account of Indians in the Jamestown area at the beginning of the seventeenth century—not on archaeological evidence. He then described the current distribution of the Indian tribes in Virginia, but argued that most had moved away, been greatly reduced in number or now "have more negro than Indian blood in them." Then he added, "I know of no such thing existing as an Indian monument for I would not honour with that name arrow points, stone hatchets, stone pipes, and half-shapen images." Jefferson then described his mound excavation. His archaeology was done in response to the request for information on Indian monuments, and was not undertaken as a matter of historical interest. In fact, in the section on Indian history in *Notes* he did not even mention the mounds. Jefferson concluded, however, with a moving personal memory that must have dated to his childhood: "But on whatever occasion they may have been made, they are of considerable notoriety among the Indians: for a party passing, about thirty years ago, through the part of the country where this barrow is, went through the woods directly to it, without any instructions or inquiry, and having staid about it some time, with expressions of sorrow, they returned to the high road, which they had left about half a dozen miles to pay this visit, and pursued their journey."

There is little reason to doubt the veracity of this account. We know that Indians were still living in central Virginia into the eighteenth century, even if they had relocated away from the Charlottesville area. The moundbuilder myth that would soon sweep the country and which denied any tie between ancient mounds and contemporary Indians was apparently not a temptation to Jefferson. Such myths are often attributed to the period of American expansion and the pushing west of American Indians, and Jefferson was, as governor of Virginia and later president, a prominent agent in such forced relocation. In 1781, the very year he wrote *Notes*, he was also authorizing and closely monitoring the removal of the Cherokees from the western of part of Virginia. Difficult as it is to comprehend such contradictory sides of Jefferson, we simply note here that he apparently did not rationalize his actions by manipulating his archaeological writing as some nineteenth-century scholars did.

At the time he wrote *Notes*, Jefferson did not see archaeological research as the key to understanding Native American origins. In *Notes* he followed the description of his archaeological excavation with a consideration of Indian origins based on linguistics, and suggested a close tie between Asians and Indians. However, seven years after publishing *Notes*, he wrote in a letter to a colleague that he would be interested in hearing more of his colleague's linguistic theory of the descent of the Creek Indians from the Carthaginians, noting that he "saw nothing impossible in this conjecture." Clearly, his archaeological excavations had not dissuaded him from considering rather spectacular theories of Indian origins. But his opinions were subject to change. By 1813, in a lengthy letter to John Adams, he dismissed as "really amusing" notions of Indian origins in a distant Trojan or Hebrew past, concluding that "the question of origins was so unresolved that it could not be deciphered; Thus it was not a very practical question to ask."

Jefferson's excavation stands as one of many original scientific achievements in a lifetime of remarkable achievements. That it was intended to answer a particular question, not merely to collect relics, is notable, although Jefferson *was* a notable relic collector. And the publication of his excavation strategy, hypotheses, observations, and conclusions was extraordinary for his time. In moving from speculation to empirical observation, his concern was with the inner construction of a man-made phenomenon. In this regard, as in his interest in architecture, landscape, and so much else, Jefferson was particularly concerned with form and function rather than history. Yet, in his sympathetic depiction of the mound visit by Indians, he hinted at a continuity between present and past Indian cultures. And his description of the mound excavation preserved information that would otherwise have been lost, and provides a comparative a comparative base for our own excavations and interpretations of the prehistoric and early historic period in Virginia.

Commentary

Compared with other scientific disciplines like biology or physics, archaeology is still a relatively young field. Despite human society's abiding interest in its own past, we see that systematic study of the ancient past began in earnest only three centuries ago. Since then, our knowledge of the past—and of the tools we use to investigate that past—has expanded tremendously. Not only do we embrace new techniques of data recovery with each passing year, but we reorganize our interpretations as new findings emerge in the world of science.

Studying the history of a particular discipline is common in the natural sciences, and some social sciences have a long tradition of historical study. In the field of archaeology, however, understanding the history of our field was until recently given relatively little attention. Learning the history of archaeology is necessary to understand the cultural basis of our scientific knowledge. What we learn, in reading about archaeology's origins in the 17th and 18th centuries, is that how archaeologists interpreted what they found was intimately tied to general ideas about the earth's antiquity and the relationship of humans to the divine. Progress in geology during the 18th and 19th centuries provided evidence that the world was far older than the 6,000 years described in the Bible. The growing recognition of this deep antiquity encouraged the development of archaeology to study what was clearly an ancient past.

We showcase one example of 18th century archaeology to illustrate how some of the approaches we now use were pioneered more than two hundred years ago. Yet we must also add that, despite the similarity in techniques and methods, much of what passed as archaeological interpretation was quite different during Jefferson's time. The public, both scientific and otherwise, was content to accept theories that monumental constructions throughout the New World and the European colonies were the work of foreigners rather than of the indigenous descendants whose lands the Europeans controlled. Today we know that those earlier interpretations were flawed, and deeply influenced by racist notions of their times. It has taken centuries of intellectual development, and of interchange between archaeologists and anthropologists, to develop more balanced and accurate interpretations of the past.

Part Three

The Archaeology of Human Origins and the Human Diaspora

Introduction

The concept of human antiquity was finally accepted by scholars in the late 19th century, due as much to advances in geological thinking as to archaeological finds. From that point onward, it was possible for archaeology to contribute to the study of human origins and human expansion out of Africa during the first human diaspora. The scientific study of human origins and diaspora is a multi-disciplinary undertaking that requires the expertise of archaeologists and physical anthropologists, along with specialists in other academic fields. Archaeology has played an important role in studying these topics: early human fossils must be recovered by using archaeological methods, and archaeologists are required to identify and interpret the artifacts, hearths, and other materials that early humans left behind in the archaeological record.

When we think about great accomplishments in human history, we often list the origins of agriculture, or metal, or the earliest cities. Yet one of humanity's greatest accomplishments occurred far earlier when human discovered and learned to control fire. When, exactly, did humans first learn to use fire for food preparation, for warmth, and for protection? Recent findings from the South African site of Swartkrans suggest that our hominid ancestors may have used fire as much as one million years ago. The signatures of human activity are often quite subtle and all but invisible to the careful archaeologist. As Andrew Sillen and C.K. Brain argue in "Old Flame," something as simple as burned bone may (but not always) be evidence of early human use of fire. Documenting something as seemingly mundane as fire use is highly significant to the study of human evolution since, with fire, humans could inhabit (and flourish in) a variety of natural environments. Since natural phenomena like lightning can also ignite fire, discriminating between natural and culturally ignited fire is essential.

Likewise, discriminating between naturally-flaked stone and human-modified stone (or tools) is an important problem that archaeologists must face in the study of early human origins. In "Ape at the Brink," Sue Savage-Rumbaugh and Roger Lewin illustrate the challenges that scientists face in identifying early human artifacts in the archaeological record by working with an exceptionally talented bonobo chimpanzee named Kanzi. They describe a series of experiments with Kanzi that explored the relationship between learning, toolmaking, anatomy and tested Kanzi's abilities to make and use stone tools. As it turned out, apes like

Kanzi can manufacture stone flakes, and use them for cutting purposes. Although Kanzi's remarkable ability allows him to make and use stone tools in a sophisticated fashion, the scientists found that his skills still fall short of those possessed by our australopithecine ancestors. Patterns in Kanzi's toolmaking left different artifacts than those we associate with Olduwan tools, and Kanzi's tools are not always discernibly different from naturally broken stones. Thus, how can archaeologists identify early human tools? Further study and experimentation by archaeologists can answer this difficult question. Already, research with Kanzi suggests that even two million years ago, our human ancestors behaved in fundamentally different ways than did their hominoid relatives.

In some respects, studying the diaspora of early humans is even more complicated than simply identifying the artifacts left behind. We know, from Jean-Jacques Hublin's article on "The First Europeans," that hominids had reached Europe by 800,000 years ago. What still remains unclear is the relationship between the earliest hominids found in Europe and the Neanderthals that appeared more than half a million years later. Is this a case of regional development over 300,000 years? Why did European Neanderthals develop, and why did they go extinct? Jean-Jacques Hublin wrestles with competing perspectives on this problem, and illustrates how human biological evidence and archaeological evidence coincide to produce a picture of localized evolution for Neanderthals. The spread of Neanderthals and, subsequently, modern humans, into Europe during the Pleistocene is one of the first well-defined examples of human expansion across the globe.

At least equally dramatic was the human settling of the New World, which may have occurred as much as 40,000 years ago; Kim McDonald describes this issue in "New Evidence Challenges Traditional Model of How the New World Was Settled." The discovery of 12,500 year old sites in South America prove that human populations reached this region far earlier than archaeologists traditionally assumed. Controversial interpretations of the early New World are being advanced with the discovery of unusually early sites such as Chile's Monte Verde, the application of DNA analyses, and sophisticated linguistic studies. Archaeologists previously believed that migrations took place across the Bering land bridge during periods of peak glaciation during the Pleistocene. With many early sites now documented across the New World, the process of migration now appears to have been more complex. Whatever the outcome of these new studies, it is certain that our views of how the New World was colonized will never be the same.

1

Old Flame

Andrew Sillen and C. K. Brain

The "discovery of fire," Darwin wrote in *The Descent of Man*, "probably the greatest ever made by man, excepting language, dates from before the dawn of history." Darwin was vague on the timing because he could cite no hard evidence. Today we have considerable archeological evidence, but still little agreement concerning the timing. Some traces of fire that turn up where there are early human remains or artifacts may be coincidental, the result of a natural conflagration.

Such coincidences do tell us something significant about the environment, and can be especially important if early humans exploited natural fires opportunistically, for example, by eating the cooked flesh of animals trapped in grass fires. Interested in just this possibility, a student at the University of Cape Town once arranged with park rangers to attend a controlled burn, where he placed a supermarket chicken in the path of the advancing fire. The meat was cooked perfectly, and the fire brigade ate every scrap of it for lunch!

The tricky thing is showing that early humans deliberately used fire in some way, especially by exercising some measure of control, for example, by feeding a fire with fuel, attempting to spread or carry it, or confining and maintaining it in a hearth. The ignition of fire, requiring special tools and skills, was an invention that almost certainly came about after humans had learned to use fire from natural sources.

Stephen James, a doctoral student at Arizona State University, has recently itemized the kinds of evidence for fire that are available to archeologists, such as burned layers of soil, ash, fire-cracked rock, and the charred remains of bones, tools, and shells. The best proof, he insists, is a hearth, some arrangement of stones that helped confine or enhance the fire and that may have been used repeatedly. Hearths are fairly common at archeological sites younger than 200,000 years, not only those of modern humans but also those of the Neanderthals, archaic humans that inhabited Europe until about 35,000 years ago.

For other species of hominids (the category of upright-walking creatures that includes humans, their ancestors, and other ancient relatives), the evidence is more sparse. Hearths from the more distant past are less likely to be preserved for the same reason that all archeological evidence becomes more fragmentary with the passage of time. One error made by archeologists earlier this century was to conclude that early hominids were primarily hunters because there was little evidence for consumption of plant foods. But the bones of animals survive better than plant remains; therefore, the further back in prehistory one goes, the better the evidence becomes for meat eating. This doesn't mean that early hominids didn't eat plants.

The first convincing evidence linking early hominids with fire came from Zhoukoudian in China, excavated under the direction of Davidson Black and

Franz Weidenreich in the interval between the two world wars. Along with the bones of *Homo erectus* (Peking man), the excavators uncovered patches of burned bones of deer and other animals, charcoal, burned chipped-stone artifacts, and thick layers of ash, which they interpreted as the remains of ancient hearths. Since Zhoukoudian is approximately 300,000 to 400,000 years old, this became the conventionally accepted date of the earliest use of fire by hominids. Even so, Zhoukoudian remains a source of controversy among archeologists, with some questioning the presence of hearths and thus of actual control of fire.

In the 1970s, Chinese archeologists reported finding ash associated with two *H. erectus* incisor teeth at the site of Yuanmou. While the stratigraphy is complex, the teeth are probably at least 500,000 years old, possibly older. Vértesszölös, a cave site in Hungary, has perhaps the best early evidence for Europe, with both hominid remains and burned animal bones at approximately 400,000 years ago, comparable to Zhoukoudian. At l'Escale Cave (Bouches-du-Rhône, France), traces of what seem to be hearths may well be more than 500,000 years old, but their association with human remains is uncertain. One unusual case for an early hearth comes from Southeast Asia, where a circular arrangement of fire-cracked basalt cobbles may be as much as one million years old (*see* "Bamboo and Human Evolution," by Geoffrey G. Pope, *Natural History*, October 1989).

Evidence that fire was used this early or even earlier in Africa has emerged only recently. Less than a decade ago, when French archeologist Catherine Perlés summarized the picture for *Natural History* (*see* "Hearth and Home in the Old Stone Age," October 1981), no early evidence had been published, and what has since accumulated remains contested. In some ways the reluctance to accept this evidence is reminiscent of the original resistance to the idea that Africa, rather than Asia, was the cradle of humanity. The late Raymond Dart, as a young anatomist in 1931, presented a paper to the Zoological Society of London in which he argued that a recently discovered specimen from Taung, South Africa, was a human ancestor. Most paleoanthropologists now agree that Dart was correct and recognize Taung as *Australopithecus africanus*, a small-brained hominid that was an ancestor of the genus *Homo*. But as Dart wrote in his autobiography, his paper was poorly received at the time, partly because the previous speaker had just stunned the audience with a compelling description of Peking man.

A case in point involves discoveries in East Africa dated to about 1.42 million years ago. At Chesowanja, near Kenya's Lake Baringo, archeologists John Gowlett and Jack Harris found flecks and lumps of reddish brown clay that proved to have been burned. Because most of the burned clay was concentrated within a square-yard area, intermixed with stone tools and animal bones, Gowlett and Harris reasoned that they had uncovered the remains of a hearth. Nearby they found fragments of a hominid cranium attributed to *A. boisei* (a very robustly built relative of *A. africanus*). Chesowanja is one of many East African sites in the period 1 to 1.5 million years ago where such traces of fire exist, but critics have argued that some natural event, such as a grass fire or lava flow, could have caused the burning.

We believe our recent discoveries from Swartkrans, a cave about 250 miles from Taung, now strengthen the case for fire being used in Africa at an early date. Swartkrans ("black cliff" in Afrikaans) first made headlines some forty years ago, when scientists learned that two different hominid species had lived there: *A. robustus* (a somewhat less robust species than *A. boisei*), and *H. erectus*. New excavations at the site began in 1965, under the direction of coauthor C. K. Brain. Among other discoveries, from 1984 to 1986, 270 pieces of bone were found that appeared to have been burned, either because they were partly turned to ash or because they were blackened. Most of the identifiable specimens were from antelopes; the rest were from other animals, including one bone from *A. robustus*.

The first thing we had to do was demonstrate that the blackened bones were actually the result of fire. Buried bone can also become blackened from soil manganese, commonly present in southern Africa. In fact, Raymond Dart once erroneously identified as burned some animal bones from the site of Makapansgat; he even named hominid remains found there *A. prometheus*, after Prometheus, the giver of fire in Greek myth. But *A. prometheus* was eventually shown to be the same as *A. africanus* from Taung, and the "burned" bones proved to be manganese stained.

Blackening in burned bones is caused by the incomplete combustion of organic molecules, which leaves free carbon atoms. The same process deposits soot in a chimney and causes char to form on overdone toast. When something being burned reaches high enough temperatures maintained over sufficient time, however, combustion goes to completion: the carbon burns off as carbon dioxide gas, and only ash remains. To prove that the blackened Swartkrans bones were burned, we simply had to identify free carbon as the source of the blackening. And in fact, all the blackened fossils we tested at the Archaeometry Laboratory at the University of Cape Town were found to contain free carbon, while others that didn't look burned contained none.

Unfortunately, no hearths exist at Swartkrans. How then can we prove that hominids were responsible for burning the bones? We have two reasons for believing that natural circumstances are a less likely explanation: the temperatures to which the bones were heated, and the distribution of the bones in the cave.

To find out the temperatures to which the Swartkrans bones had been heated, we heated bone samples from a modern hartebeest (a local species of antelope) to various temperatures, which were sustained for thirty minutes. We then examined the samples for discoloration and for microscopic changes. We found that char doesn't appear until bone reaches 450°F, and that bones heated to between 570° and 800° have the greatest amount of char. When viewed under a microscope, the concentric layers of hard tissue that in life form around the canals in the bone stand out especially clearly in charred samples. Bones heated to more than 800°, however, revert to a pale color as the char burns off and the bone converts to ash. In addition, such samples become severely cracked, and microscopic detail is lost.

These findings suggest that the burned bones at Swartkrans were heated to temperatures higher than could be expected in the natural surroundings, which consist of veld, or grassy plains with few trees. Scattered grass fires ignited by lightning sweep through this environment every summer. But they move rapidly, quickly consuming the fuel at any particular spot. While the flames may rage at 400°, normally an animal that perishes in such a fire will only briefly be engulfed by them. As a result, the flesh will retain some moisture, and the bones will not reach temperatures above the boiling point (212°). As in a roast taken out of the oven too soon, the bones may not even cook, let alone burn.

In contrast, campfires burn at hotter temperatures because wood rather than grass is selected for fuel, and the fire is maintained in one place longer, allowing a bed of coals to form. Coals may be anywhere between 900° and 1700°. As a result, bones that are tossed into campfires reach higher temperatures. Because some of the Swartkrans bones contain so much char and ash, campfires seem a much more likely explanation for them.

The distribution of burned bones in the cave provides a second line of evidence. The ancient Swartkrans hominids are found in three sequential deposits. Except for differences in age, the deposits are all fairly similar, each containing remains of *A. robustus* and worked stone and bone tools (*H. erectus* remains have also been found in the first two deposits and are assumed to be present in the third). But the burned bones are present only in the most recent of the three deposits. We suggest this is because hominids living there earlier did not know how to control fire. If burning had been a fully natural occurrence, one would expect to find burned bones in all three deposits.

The dating of the three ancient deposits is not precise, but falls within certain limits. Based on the types of animals found in it, the oldest deposit was created sometime between 1.6 and 1.8 million years ago. The other two deposits were each laid down following cycles of erosion, probably the result of Ice Age climatic fluctuations. Such fluctuations generally came at least 100,000 years apart. Finally, none of the deposits is likely to be younger than 1 million years old, because *A. robustus* is not known to have survived more recently than that anywhere else. This finding suggests that fire-using hominids appeared at Swartkrans no less than 1 million years ago, and possibly as much as 1.3 million years ago.

If fire at Swartkrans was not natural in origin, what was its purpose? The most practical uses in or near a cave include cooking, warmth, and protection from predators. Cooking is a possibility but is not indicated by the temperatures reached by the Swartkrans bones. By the time the bones became charred, any meat on them would have been inedible. Conceivably, however, the bones were tossed into the fire after the meat was first cooked and removed. Whether or not cooking was involved, using the bones as fuel would have provided warmth during the Transvaal's chilly winter nights.

We believe, however, that protection from predators is the most plausible explanation. We know from animal bones in the cave that leopards were a constant threat to Swartkrans hominids, and leopards are wary of fire. This is something hominids could have learned fairly easily by observing the effects of natural fires. In addition, by burning bones, hominids would have removed waste that otherwise would have attracted scavengers.

We don't know which—if not both—of the two hominid species at Swartkrans used fire. Since *H. erectus* had a larger brain and was more successful in leaving descendants (that's us), it seems the more likely candidate. Possibly, fire helped give our ancestors their competitive edge over *A. robustus*. Since one of the burned bones found at Swartkrans belonged to *A. robustus*, the competition may have been heated.

2

Ape at the Brink

Sue Savage-Rumbaugh and Roger Lewin

Threading my way along the sandy path toward the ocean shore, I sought out the rhythmic sound of shifting surf. The faint light of predawn arrived, and I could see the rocky coastline ahead, then the silhouette of distant mountains. I was near the small coastal village of Cascais, Portugal, attending a meeting organized by the Wenner-Gren Foundation, a group legendary in anthropological circles. Scientists invited to these meetings are kept away from the rest of the world and encouraged to examine each other's views in small, intense discussions.

Walking along the beach, I mused over the talk of the past few days. Bill Calvin, a neurobiologist at the University of Washington, had been telling us about the extraordinary accuracy and power with which humans can throw. We humans aren't the only primates with the raw ability—chimpanzees and gorillas can throw, too, as visitors to zoos sometimes discover to their chagrin. Apes do not enjoy being stared at and frequently throw things at visitors in an attempt to make them leave. But humans are far better at throwing than apes are, and the development of this skill, Bill had pointed out, was clearly important during man's evolution from an apelike ancestor. In particular, the accurate hurling of stones became a valuable means of hunting and self-defense against predators.

Another scientist in our group, archeologist Nick Toth of Indiana University, was also interested in throwing, but for a different reason. Nick, unlike the rest of us, knew how to make the stone tools that our prehuman ancestors had utilized.

Nick was not a typical scientist. I'd recognized this right away when, in the course of discussion, he began pulling fist-size rocks out of his briefcase. He riveted the group's attention with his display and with his demonstrations of how rocks can become tools. He explained the physics of conchoidal fracture by which rocks can be made to yield good, sharp tools. Then he challenged us to accompany him to the beach to try to make the "crude" stone tools that our hominid ancestors made 2 million years ago. That afternoon I gained a newfound respect for the feats of my forebears.

It was my first attempt to emulate a Paleolithic stone knapper, and I did not find it an easy task. Neither I nor most of the other "educated" scientists could coax even a single flake from the stones on the beach during our first half hour of trying. We even resorted to placing one stone on the ground and slamming another against it, but to no avail. Finally, instead of just watching Nick, I began to look closely at what he was doing. Why did the stones break so easily when he struck them together with such little force, while they just made a loud thud when I slammed them together as hard as I could?

I gradually recognized that Nick was not really hitting rocks together; instead he was throwing the rock in his right hand against the edge of the rock in his left hand, letting the force of the controlled throw knock off the flake. The "hammer rock" never really left his right hand, but it was nonetheless thrown, as a missile, against the "core," the rock held in place in his left hand. What had I been doing? Just slamming two rocks together as though I were clapping my hands with rocks in between.

Once I realized how Nick was actually flaking stone, I grasped the profound similarity between throwing and stone knapping. In each activity you must be able to snap the wrist rapidly forward at just the right moment during the downward motion of the forearm. This wrist-cocking action produces great force, either for achieving distance in throwing or for knocking a flake off a core. I also learned that it is important to deliver your blow to the core accurately. Several of us had bruised fingers after the afternoon's stone-knapping excursion, suggesting that, accurate though we might be as a species, as individuals we needed practice.

Bill Calvin was likely correct in his suggestion that throwing ability had been selected for in the course of human evolution. But now I saw that accurate throwers also had the potential skills for making stone tools. Could throwing as a defensive device have paved the way for the deliberate construction of stone tools?

Our conference was searching for evolutionary links between language, tools, and anatomy that could lead to the emergence of the bipedal, large-brained, technological creature that is *Homo sapiens*. The neurobiology of stone throwing and the skills of stone knapping were new to me, and as a psychobiologist, I was intrigued. Now as I walked on the beach, I attempted to integrate these ideas with my own knowledge of how apes understand language.

For the two decades I have known and studied chimpanzees, I have been attempting to discern the degree to which they can think and communicate as we do. The initial efforts of ape-language researchers, in the 1960s and early 1970s, were hurriedly greeted with acclaim. Newspapers and scientific journals declared the same message: apes can use symbols in a way that echoes the structure of human language, albeit in a modest manner. The symbols were not in the form of spoken words of course, but were produced variously as hand gestures from American Sign Language, as colored plastic shapes, and as arbitrary lexigrams on a computer keyboard.

But in the late 1970s and early 1980s this fascination turned to cynicism. Linguists asserted that apes were merely mimicking their caretakers and that they displayed no languagelike capacity at all. Most linguists and psychologists wanted to forget apes and move ahead with what they viewed as the "proper study of man"—generally typified by the analysis of the problem-solving strategies of freshman students.

From my earliest exposure to apes, I recognized that there would be considerable difficulty in determining whether or not they employed words with intent and meaning in the same way that we do. And so, in my research at the Language Research Center at Georgia State University, I searched for scientifically credible ways to approach the fundamental questions about apes and their intellectual and emotional capacities. By 1990, the year of the Wenner-Gren conference, I knew that at least some of this work was reaching an audience, or I would not have been invited to the conference. Perhaps there, I thought, I would have a chance to begin to tell my story—or, more accurately, Kanzi's story.

One ape out of the 11 that I have studied, a 150-pound bonobo (or pygmy chimpanzee) named Kanzi, began to learn language on his own, without drills or lessons. Kanzi, a male, was born on October 28, 1980, at the Yerkes Regional Primate Research Center's field station in Lawrenceville, Georgia. Before this time, no bonobo had been language trained. Matata, Kanzi's adoptive mother, was to be the first.

Matata proved to be a willing, though incompetent, study. She quickly understood that other chimpanzees used the keyboard to communicate and that pressing the lexigrams was what achieved this feat. However, after two years of training and 30,000 trials, she mastered only six symbols, in a limited way.

After Matata's departure, we set up the keyboard in the expectation that Kanzi would begin his language instruction—if he could learn to sit in one place long enough. Kanzi, however, had his own opinion of the keyboard, and he began at once to make it evident. Not only was he using the keyboard as a means of communicating, but he also knew what the symbols meant. For example, one of the first things he did that morning was to activate the symbol for "apple," then "chase." He then picked up an apple, looked at me, and ran away with a grin on his face. I was hesitant to believe what I knew I was seeing. Kanzi appeared to know all the things we had attempted to teach Matata, yet we had not even been attending to him. Could he simply have picked up his understanding through social exposure, as children do?

For 17 months we kept a complete record of Kanzi's utterances, either directly on the computer when he was indoors, or manually while outdoors. By the end of the period, Kanzi had a vocabulary of about 50 symbols. He was already producing combinations of words—spontaneous utterances such as "Matata group-room tickle" to ask that his mother be permitted to join in a game of tickle in the group room.

We first detected what seemed like spoken word comprehension when Kanzi was one and a half years old. We began to notice that often, when we talked about lights, Kanzi would run to the switch on the wall and flip it on and off. Kanzi seemed to be "listening in" on conversations that had nothing to do with him, in a manner that I had not experienced in other apes—even in those who had been reared in human homes. As time passed, Kanzi appeared able to understand more and more spoken words. In response, we had to do what many parents do when they don't want their children to overhear: we began to spell out some words around Kanzi. We were able to determine that Kanzi understood 150 spoken words at the end of the 17-month period.

"If an ape can begin to comprehend spoken English without being so trained," I later wrote in a scientific paper, "it would appear that the ape possessed speech and language abilities similar to our own." The dual lesson we learned from the project was that chimpanzees can acquire language skills spontaneously, through social exposure to a language-rich environment, as human children do. And, again as for humans, early exposure is critical. As Elizabeth Bates comments, "The Berlin Wall is down, and so is the wall that separates man from chimpanzee."

It was the end of a long day at the Wenner-Gren conference, and we had all eaten dinner at a restaurant in the nearby town. On our return to the hotel, I was sitting near the rear of the bus, and Nick Toth was in the very back, legs stretched out, arms folded across his chest, eyes closed, apparently asleep. Suddenly he opened an eye and beckoned me to join him. "I have something I want to ask you," he said. "Do you think Kanzi could learn to make stone tools, like early humans did?"

His question seemed to come right out of the blue. It was something I had never thought of trying. From my long experience with chimpanzees, I had gained a great respect for their abilities. But making stone tools seemed light-years beyond them. Indeed, even I could not make a worthwhile stone tool, and I'd had Nick there to teach me.

Nevertheless, I was intrigued. "What do you have in mind?" I asked. Nick sat up and quickly explained.

In 1949 the British anthropologist Kenneth P. Oakley published a classic book, *Man the Tool-Maker*. This short volume encapsulated what was widely held to set humans apart as unique: "Possession of a great capacity for conceptual thought...is now generally regarded by comparative psychologists as distinctive of man," he wrote. "The systematic making of tools...required not only for immediate use but for future use, implies a marked capacity for conceptual thought." The notion of man the tool-maker struck a receptive chord: alone among the world's species, toolmaking *Homo sapiens* fashions an elaborate culture and manufactures a powerful technology, through which the world is forever changed.

The shift to becoming a toolmaker has been seen as central to what differentiated humans from apes in an evolutionary sense. By definition, therefore, the very first members of the human family must have been toolmakers. This assumption has been challenged in the past several decades. The first members of the human family are now known to have evolved at least 5 million years ago, perhaps as many as 8 million. And yet the first recognizable stone artifacts date only to around 2.5 million years ago. The appearance of these stone tools coincides with the first appearance of the genus *Homo*, which eventually gave rise to modern humans.

This raises an important question: Were the earliest toolmakers doing something that was beyond the cognitive ability of apes? Or were they merely bipedal apes who were applying their apelike cognitive skills to non-apelike activities?

Nick told me that he had been musing over this question for a long time, and that he had an idea in search of a collaborator. His proposal was to motivate Kanzi to make stone flakes, not to teach him with structured lessons. "We want to avoid the criticism of classical conditioning," he said. He suggested we would need a box with a transparent lid. Something enticing would be put in the box, and the lid would be secured with a length of string. Kanzi could be shown by example how to make flakes, by knocking two rocks together, but there would be no active teaching, no shaping of his hands, no breaking the task down into component parts.

I made some suggestions about how the design of the food box, or "tool site" as we came to call it, could be improved; Nick had underestimated Kanzi's ability to tear flimsy objects apart, especially if there is food inside. Nick promised to get in touch with me after we returned to the United States. This he did within a couple of weeks, and I told him that we had made a tool site to his specifications. A week later he arrived at the Language Research Center in Atlanta with fellow archeologist Kathy Schick, their truck laden with a thousand pounds of rock.

At first we set up the tool site outside Kanzi's cage, so that Nick could show Kanzi how it was possible to gain access to the baited box. Nick struck a cobble with a hammerstone, selected a sharp flake, and then cut the string securing the lid to the box. Kanzi got the treat that was inside. Nick did this several times, after which we put the tool site inside Kanzi's enclosure. Nick knelt outside, making flakes. He handed sharp ones to me while I was inside with Kanzi, and I encouraged Kanzi to use them to cut the string. He very soon realized the utility of a sharp flake and eagerly took one from whoever was in with him. He then quickly went to the tool site to open the box. He even knocked two rocks together on several occasions, but in a rather desultory way, and without producing flakes. Nevertheless, he was clearly emulating Nick.

During that first afternoon, and throughout the project, Kanzi was never required to perform a task but was merely provided with the opportunity to participate if he wanted to. We wanted to motivate him to make and use flakes, and we hoped he would learn by example. As the days and weeks passed, he displayed a degree of persistence at the task that exceeded anything I'd seen him do.

Kanzi very quickly learned to discriminate between sharp flakes and dull ones, using visual inspection and his lips. On one occasion about three weeks into the project, one of our collaborators at Georgia State, psychologist Rose Sevcik, was striking a rock when—for the first time for her—it split, and several flakes flew off in different directions. Kanzi was watching closely and seemed to know which was the best of the flakes even before they had hit the ground. He let out a bonobo squeal of delight, rushed to pick up the sharpest flake, and was off to the tool site with it, all in one fluid motion.

Making flakes for himself, however, proved difficult. At first he was extremely tentative in the way he hit the rocks together. Almost always he used his right hand to deliver the hammer blow. He held the core in his left hand, often cradled against his chest, or sometimes braced against the floor, with his foot adding further support. Sometimes he put the core on the ground and simply struck it with the hammerstone. No one had demonstrated this "anvil" technique to him. But no matter how he held the core, he seemed unable or unwilling to deliver a powerful blow. Bonobos are three times stronger than a human of the same size, so there was no doubt that Kanzi had the muscle power to do the job. We wondered whether he was nervous about hitting his fingers; perhaps he lacked the correct wrist anatomy to produce a "snapping" action—the structure of a bonobo's arms, wrists, and hands is different from a human's (chimpanzees' wrists stiffened as they became adept knuckle walkers), and it constrains the animal's ability to deliver a sharp blow by snapping the wrist; or perhaps he was reluctant to deliver a hard blow because throughout his life we had discouraged him from slamming and breaking objects.

Then, one afternoon eight weeks into the project, I was sitting in my office when I was suddenly assailed with the sound of a BANG...BANG...BANG. I rushed to the tool-site room, and there was Kanzi, stone knapping with tremendous force. He had finally learned how to fracture rocks to make sharp flakes, albeit small ones.

During the first three months of the project Kanzi became steadily more proficient at producing flakes, in part because he seemed to have learned to aim the hammer blows at the edge of the core. But despite his willingness to deliver harder blows than he had initially, he still wasn't hitting hard enough to produce flakes bigger than about an inch long. Nevertheless, he persisted with his newfound concentration, and we in turn made the string that secured the tool site thicker and thicker, so that small flakes would wear out before they cut the string.

One day during the fourth month, Kanzi was having only modest success at producing flakes. He turned to me and held out the rocks, as if to say, "Here, you do it for me." He did this from time to time, and mostly I would encourage him to try some more, which is what I did that day. He just sat there looking at me, then at the rock, then at me again, apparently reflecting. Suddenly he stood up and, with clear deliberation, threw the rock on the hard tile floor. The rock shattered, producing a whole shower of flakes. Kanzi vocalized ecstatically, grabbed one of the sharpest flakes, and headed for the tool site.

There was no question that Kanzi had reasoned through the problem and had found a better solution to making flakes. No one had demonstrated the efficacy of throwing. Kanzi had just worked it out for himself. I was delighted, because it demonstrated his ingenuity in the face of a difficult problem. I quickly telephoned Nick and told him what had happened. I was so excited that I didn't give a thought to the fact that Nick might not be delighted, too. He wasn't. He was disappointed. "The Oldowan toolmakers used hard-hammer percussion, not throwing," he said.

"Oldowan" is the name applied to the earliest known stone-tool assemblages, which were found in Africa and date to 2.5 million years ago. The artifacts that make up Oldowan assemblages were produced from small cobbles, and they include about half a dozen forms of so-called core tools—such as hammerstones, choppers, and scrapers—and small, sharp flakes. The toolmakers were assumed to have had mental templates of these various tool types. The tools are often found in association with broken animal bones, which sometimes show signs of butchery. The clear inference is that, beginning about 2.5 million years ago, our human ancestors began exploiting their environment in a non-apelike way, by using stone tools as a means of including significant amounts of meat in their diet.

Until quite recently archeologists argued that the earliest toolmakers lived lives analogous to those of contemporary hunter-gatherers: they organized themselves into small, mobile bands, established temporary home bases, and divided the labor of hunting and gathering between male and female members of the band. This was a very humanlike way of life, albeit in primitive form, and most definitely unlike that of an ape.

In recent years, however, a reexamination of the archeological evidence has changed this picture dramatically, making it much less humanlike and more apelike. There is considerable debate over the extent to which these early members of the human family were active hunters as opposed to opportunistic scavengers. And the notion of home bases and a division of labor between the sexes has been abandoned as untenable. The earliest toolmakers are now viewed as bipedal apes who lived and foraged in social groups in a woodland-savanna environment, as baboons and chimpanzees do.

An equally important shift of perspective has taken place regarding the tool assemblages themselves. Nick Toth ran a program of experimental archeology in the 1970s, in which he became a proficient maker of Oldowan artifacts himself. "My experimental findings suggest that far too much emphasis has been put on cores at the expense of flakes," he wrote. "It seems possible that the traditional relationship might be reversed: the flakes may have been the primary tools and the cores often (although not always) simply the by-product of manufacture.... Thus the shape of many early cores may have been incidental to the process of manufacture and therefore indicative of neither the maker's purpose nor the artifact's function."

Nick's reassessment of the Oldowan artifacts revolutionized African archeology and further changed the perception of the humanness of the earliest toolmakers. According to this new theory, the half-dozen different tool types in Oldowan assemblages were not the product of mental templates in the minds of sophisticated toolmakers. The only skill required, therefore, was that of striking flakes off a core using a hammerstone.

"If Kanzi throws the rocks, the percussion marks will be random, and we won't learn anything," Nick protested. Our different reactions reflected, I suppose, the different interests of the psychologist and the archeologist. Nick said I had to discourage Kanzi from throwing, and I pointed out that that would be difficult. "Try," said Nick. I agreed to try.

Rose Sevcik came up with the obvious suggestion, which was to cover the floor with soft carpeting. The first time Kanzi went into the carpeted room, he threw the rock a few times and looked puzzled when it didn't shatter as usual. He paused a few seconds, looked around until he found a place where two pieces of carpet met, pulled back a piece, and hurled the rock. We have assembled a videotape of the toolmaking project, which I show to scientific and more general audiences. Whenever the tape reaches this incident there is always a tremendous roar of approval as Kanzi—the hero—outwits the humans yet again.

By this time, spring was approaching, and we decided to take the tool site outdoors, where there was no hard floor to throw against. Forced to abandon his throwing technique, Kanzi steadily became more efficient at hard-hammer percussion, delivering more forceful and more precisely aimed blows. Very consistently now, Kanzi was hitting the edge of the core and was more successful at producing flakes. The resulting cores were sometimes very simple, with just a couple of flakes removed, or, if Kanzi had persistently hammered at them, they had many small flake scars and steep, battered edges, some of which resembled eoliths, or "dawn stones," found in Europe in the decades around the turn of the century. There had been great controversy about these objects, with some arguing that they were true artifacts. They turned out to have been the product of natural forces, such as wave action or glaciation.

Just as Kanzi was becoming quite proficient at hard-hammer percussion, he foiled us yet again—which again delighted the psychologist and dismayed the archeologist. Kanzi discovered that even outside on soft ground he could exploit his throwing technique. This discovery seemed to be the result of a thoughtful analysis of the problem as well: he placed a rock carefully on the ground, stepped back, and took careful aim with the second rock, poised in his right hand. His aim was true, and the rock shattered. He continued to use this technique, and there was no way of stopping him. As far as I was concerned, we had presented Kanzi with a problem and he had figured out the best way to solve it—three times.

Kanzi had become a toolmaker. But our question was, how good a toolmaker? Could he have stood shoulder to shoulder with the makers of Oldowan tools, striking flakes off cores as effectively as they did? Nick's experience as an Oldowan toolmaker offered us a way of addressing these questions. On that beach in Portugal, I had been impressed by how very difficult it is to produce flakes. The initial inclination of the naive stone knapper is to hit the core hard enough so that a flake will pop out of the core, as if it were being chiseled out. But as Nick demonstrated, the flakes come from the bottom of the core, not the top.

The best everyday example of the principle of conchoidal fracture at work in stone toolmaking is the effect of a tiny pebble hitting a window: a cone of glass is punched out of the pane, and the exact shape of the cone is determined by the direction at which the stone hits the glass.

For effective flaking by hard-hammer percussion, three conditions have to be met. First, the core must have an acute edge (one with an angle of less than 90 degrees). Second, the core must be struck with a sharp, glancing blow, hitting about half an inch from the edge. And third, the blow must be directed through an area of high mass, such as a ridge or a bulge. With these conditions met, and starting with suitable raw material, you can form long, sharp flakes. Whatever forms are produced, they have the appearance of great simplicity. But as Nick correctly points out, "it is the process, not the product, that reveals the complexity of Oldowan toolmaking."

Nick and Kathy Schick recently drew up a list of criteria by which to assess the technological sophistication of simple tools. "It was necessary to get beyond relying on gut reaction for distinguishing between true artifacts and naturally fractured stone," explains Nick. The criteria include: flake angle, formed by its top and bottom surfaces; flake size, an indication of how efficiently flakes are being detached from the core; and the amount of step fractures and battering seen. Step fractures are unclean breaks. When a stone is hit at exactly the proper angle, a clean flake falls off, leaving the stone surface as smooth as if someone had run a knife through butter. If a stone is merely slammed into another hard surface, with little regard for the angle of the blow, it may break, but it will have a battered appearance. Well-flaked stone looks as though it has been sculpted or chiseled.

Measured against these criteria, the products of the earliest toolmakers score high. Their makers knew about angles required on the core, about sharp, glancing blows, and about seeking regions of high mass on the core. Therefore the Oldowan toolmakers displayed significant technological sophistication and perceptual skills.

What of Kanzi? His progress in hard-hammer percussion has been considerable, moving from the undirected, timid tapping together of rocks to forceful hammering. Nick describes the process of learning to make tools as being punctuational, with periods of slow change in between. "You suddenly get an insight into what is required and then slowly improve on that," he explains. Kanzi clearly had an insight into the importance of hitting the rock close to its edge; and he had important insights when he developed his throwing techniques. Despite this, however, he has not yet developed the stone-knapping skills of the Oldowan toolmakers.

Kanzi's relatively low degree of technological finesse seems to imply that these early humans had indeed ceased to be apes. It isn't yet certain, however, if Kanzi's poorer performance is the result of a cognitive or an anatomical limitation. I suspect that if Kanzi is limited in the quality of flaking through hard-hammer percussion, it is the result of biomechanical, not cognitive, constraints. Or simply lack of practice—certainly most of us working with Kanzi are unable to make stone tools ourselves. Without a good teacher and constant practice it is a very difficult skill to master. Making stone tools does not seem to be a skill that normal human beings acquire readily with little instruction, as we are asking Kanzi to do.

Nick hopes to learn whether or not Kanzi, with minimal demonstration, can acquire a skill that took, at best, many generations for our ancestors to perfect. If

Kanzi does not succeed in matching the skills of the Oldowan toolmakers in the span of one research career, it would still be foolish to rule out the potential of the ape mind to do so, given a few generations of exposure to a need to use such tools.

The greatest surprise of the toolmaking project was Kanzi's development of throwing as a way of obtaining sharp edges. Not only did it reflect a problem-solving process in Kanzi's mind, but it also produced material that addresses an important archeological problem: What did early humans do *before* they made Oldowan tools? The criteria mentioned earlier to identify genuine artifacts as compared with naturally fractured stone would reject Kanzi's flakes and cores as tools. And yet they are artifacts, and they can be used as cutting tools.

Some of Kanzi's cores look rather similar to Oldowan core tools, acknowledges Nick, but most do not. "If I were surveying a Stone Age site and found some of these things, I'd definitely check them out, but I would almost certainly conclude they were naturally flaked," he says. "But after seeing these incipient flaking skills with Kanzi, we certainly have to consider it as a possible model for the earliest stone-tool making. He has taught us what we should be looking for."

Nick joked that Kanzi should be awarded an honorary doctorate, pointing out that he would need a small cap and a gown with long arms. He wasn't joking, though, when in the spring of 1991 he conferred on Kanzi the inaugural CRAFT annual award for outstanding research. Nick and Kathy are codirectors of CRAFT, the Center for Research into the Anthropological Foundations of Technology, at Indiana University. "The award is justified," says Nick, "because the work with Kanzi has given us one of our most important insights into Paleolithic technology. It has given us a view of what is possible with apes, and an insight into the cognitive background of what is necessary to go further."

3

The First Europeans

Jean-Jacques Hublin

In the late 1850s the academic world and readers of daily newspapers were fascinated by Darwin's *On The Origin of Species*, stone tools discovered along the Somme by Jacques Boucher de Perthe, and a skullcap and long bones of a Neandertal unearthed near Düsseldorf. The following decades witnessed a virtual "flint-rush" during which adventurers, university professors, and country priests excavated (and often destroyed) many major European Ice Age sites. Nineteenth-century Europe was economically, politically, and scientifically the leader of Western civilization. For an intellect of the time, an "antediluvian" man, if he ever existed, had to have been European. In reality, during hundreds of thousands of years of human evolution, while the first hominids were emerging in Africa, Europe remained uninhabited.

The peopling of Europe took place in at least two waves. The best known involved modern humans, who moved into central and, later, western Europe from the Middle East more that 40,000 years ago. These people, popularly known as the Cro-Magnons, created the paintings found at Lascaux (France), Altamira (Spain), and the recently explored Chauvet Cave in southeastern France. When the caves were first painted, ca. 30,000 years ago, the last survivors of an older wave of colonization, the Neandertals, still existed in the western extreme of Europe. The Neandertals eventually became extinct, but recent discoveries demonstrate that their ancestors had occupied Europe for hundreds of thousands of years, evolving from archaic *Homo sapiens* as they became isolated from the mother population in Africa and the Near East.

Neandertals are generally assigned to the same biological species as modern humans, *Homo sapiens*, although some scientists consider them a separate species, *Homo neanderthalensis*. While they represent an essentially European group, they have close relatives in the Near and Middle East, from Israel to Uzbekistan. Neandertal skulls and mandibles display a singular morphology. Although some of their features can occasionally be found in other hominids, the combination of characteristic traits is unique. European Neandertals are rather short and sturdy, with a long trunk and short legs. The skeleton is robust, and the muscle attachments imply a powerful body. The head is remarkable. It is big, enclosing a brain comparable in volume to that of modern humans, but the braincase and face are very long, the forehead is low, and the browridges protrude. The mandible is strong and lacks a projecting chin. Seen from the rear, the braincase has a rounded, almost circular shape in contrast to the pentagonal shape observed in both the earlier *Homo erectus* and modern humans. The face is structured around a large nasal cavity, and its middle part projects forward. The bone below the eye sockets is flat or even convex, receding laterally. The cheekbones are weak and oriented obliquely. This projecting face contrasts strongly with the short, flat face of the first modern humans. Other anatomical details of the ear area and rear and base of the skull are unique to Neandertals. The occipital bone, at the back of the skull, is marked by a conspicuous depression called the supra-iniac fossa.

We know that the Neandertal lineage lasted from at least 127,000 to 30,000 years before present (B.P.), but during the last two decades a number of fossil discoveries and the reexamination of previously known specimens have fed discussion about the peopling of Europe before the Neandertals. One of the main issues has been the relationship of these first Europeans to their successors, Neandertals and modern humans. Another involves *Homo erectus*. Was this older species, known in Africa and Asia before 400,000 B.P., present in Europe before these two groups of *Homo sapiens*? The date of the first peopling of Europe has been hotly disputed. Hominids dating more than four million years old have been found in Africa, but the bulk of Palaeolithic remains in Europe are much later, from the Middle Pleistocene (780,000 to 127,000 B.P.) to the end of the Ice Age (10,000 B.P.). The debate has divided scholars into "short chronology" and "long chronology" camps.

Supporters of the short chronology dispute the human origin of stone tools from the earliest sites in Europe as well as the dating of the sites. Wil Roebroeks from the University of Leiden, The Netherlands, has, for example, even claimed that none of the European archaeological sites dated before 500,000 B.P. is valid. Until recently they could also point to a lack of human remains before 500,000 B.P. Rich fossil sites have been known for more than a century, especially in France's Massif Central, but amidst the thousands of large mammal remains not one single human bone or tooth was ever found. Why would humans have stayed out of Europe for such a long time? Climate seemed the most obvious reason, but other environmental factors were proposed to explain this limited expansion. Clive Gamble of the University of Southampton has suggested that hominids could not have successfully adapted to the temperate forest environment before 500,000 B.P. and were restricted to open areas to the south. According to Alan Turner of the University of Liverpool, the archaic humans who subsisted by hunting and scavenging could not compete with the numerous large carnivores then found in Europe.

Hominids, however, were at the gates of Europe long before 500,000 B.P. In North Africa, just beyond the Strait of Gibraltar, their artifacts are at least one million years old, and in the Near East, at Ubeidiya in Israel, stone artifacts and fragmentary human remains have been found with animal bones dated to ca. 1.4 million years ago. But the most striking evidence was found in 1991 on the southern side of the Caucasus mountains. A team from the Georgian Academy of Sciences and the Römisch-Germanisches Zentralmuseum of Mainz, Germany, excavating at Dmanisi, a medieval site near Tbilisi, unexpectedly found underlying strata with a well-preserved human mandible, stone artifacts, and animal remains. A basalt layer beneath these strata has been dated to about 1.8 million years ago. The paleomagnetism—the orientation of the earth's magnetic poles as reflected by the orientation of some particles in the deposits—of both the basalt and the bone-bearing layer confirms a date for the hominid just after 1.8 million years ago. Anatomically, the specimen is reminiscent of the contemporary early *Homo erectus* of Africa. The Dmanisi find suggests that early waves of people in the lowest latitudes of Europe are not unlikely, but before extended colonization was successful various attempts must have been made that left few archaeological traces.

Supporters of a long chronology believe that people reached Europe long before 500,000 B.P., and that traces of them are scarce because they were few in number and their sites were later destroyed by advancing glaciers. Still, some sites have been assigned to the Lower Pleistocene or even to the end of the Pliocene, between 5.5 and 1.7 million years ago. For example, in the French Massif Central, Saint-Eble has been dated between 2.2 and 2.5 million years ago and Blassac could be as old as 2.0 million years. But the flaked stones found at these sites are never flint but rather quartz or microgranites, and they are frequently interpreted as tephrofacts, stones naturally fragmented in the course of volcanic eruptions. In the same area, on the shores of an ancient lake, a more reliable archaeological site with flint tools and fossil remains of large mammals has been excavated by Eugene Bonifay of the Centre National de Récherche Scientifique. It is, however, more recent, no earlier than about one million years. Other sites roughly of the same age have been reported— Le Vallonet in the French Riviera and Stránská Skála in Moravia are the best known—but their dates and the human origin of their tools have been criticized.

The recent discovery of fossil hominids at the site of Gran Dolina at Atapuerca in northern Spain has now conclusively demonstrated that humans were present in Europe as early as 800,000 B.P. Atapuerca was already famous for the Sima de los Huesos, or Pit of Bones, which has yielded the largest number of Middle Pleistocene hominids ever found. A few hundred yards away, the Gran Dolina site, under investigation by Eudald Carbonell of Rovira y Virgili University, displays an extraordinary geological profile 60 feet deep that includes several archaeological layers. In 1994 a small area of a stratum known as TD6 was excavated and yielded 36 human fossils, including teeth, skull and jaw fragments, and foot and hand bones, belonging to at least four individuals; excavations in 1995 yielded more remains. The TD6 deposits immediately predate a paleomagnetic inversion (a reversal of the earth's magnetic poles) dating to 780,000 B.P. In addition, the site has two older archaeological layers below TD6. The TD6 remains are too fragmentary to be securely assigned to a species. However, the new evidence can hardly be rejected by even the most vigorous supporters of the short chronology.

It is likely that the early peopling of Europe occurred in the Mediterranean zone and only later extended northward. None of the oldest sites in northern Europe dates to a period of glacial expansion. These include Mauer, Miesenheim I, Kärlich, and Bilzingsleben in Germany; Cagny-l'Epinette in France; and Boxgrove, Hoxne, and Clacton-on-Sea in England. Three have yielded human remains. For almost a century, a human mandible discovered in a sand quarry at Mauer, near Heidelberg, in 1907 was said to be the oldest European human fossil. Study of the associated fauna indicates an age slightly before 500,000 B.P. A tibia found at Boxgrove in 1994 was declared, after a resounding announcement in the press and publication in the prestigious journal *Nature*, to be between 485,000 and 515,000 years old. It was only a matter of weeks, however, before the excavation of stratum TD6 at Atapuerca took the title away from Boxgrove and Mauer. The fragmentary remains found at Bilzingsleben are Middle Pleistocene in date, but more recent than Mauer and Boxgrove.

In the south the Middle Pleistocene fossil record is richer. An impressive series of hominid fossils from the cave of Tautavel, near the eastern end of the Pyrénées, is dated about 400,000 B.P. The Tautavel remains, unearthed by Henri de Lumley

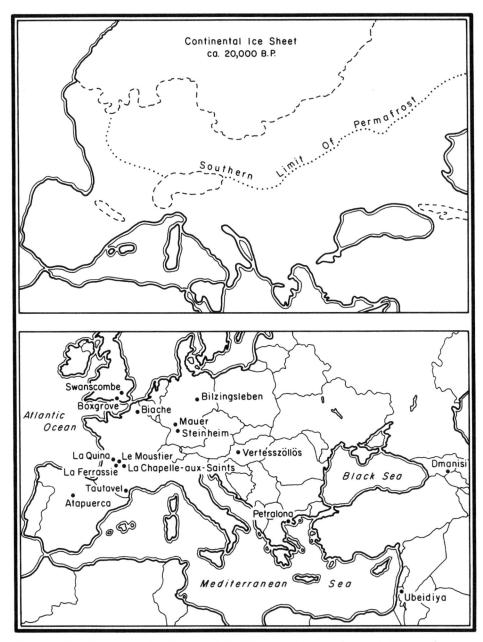

Figure 1. Neanderthals evolved from archaic *Homo sapiens* populations in Europe that were isolated from Africa and Asia, especially during periods of glacial advance. Map, top, shows Europe at the height of the last glacial peak, ca. 20,000 B.P. Though by this time Neanderthals had been replaced by modern humans, map does indicate how glacial advances could have isolated earlier European populations. Humans were able to move northward only during temperate interglacial or moderately cold periods. Key Neanderthal and pre-Neanderthal sites are on the map above (lower).

of the Institut de Paleontologie Humaine in Paris and his colleagues, includes a spectacular human face, an isolated parietal, two mandibles, a pelvic bone, many teeth, and fragments of post-cranial bones. Fragmentary human remains were also found at Vertésszöllös in Hungary.

What do these finds tell us about the peopling of Europe before the Neandertals? Was the older hominid, *Homo erectus*, present in Europe? Milford Wolpoff of the University of Michigan has claimed that the Mauer mandible, robust and chinless, is a European *Homo erectus*, comparable to the African and Asian representatives of this species. In terms of chronology this is not impossible, as 500,000 B.P. belongs to the transitional period between *Homo erectus* and archaic *Homo sapiens*. But there are no clear anatomical differences between the mandibles of the two species, so the identification of Mauer is very difficult. The development of clear Neandertal features begins only with later specimens.

The Tautavel-Vertésszöllös-Bilzingsleben remains provide us with a clear portrait of a 400,000-year-old European. (A complete skull found at Petralona Cave in northern Greece shows many similarities to this group, but it is difficult to date accurately.) According to Christopher Stringer of the British Museum they have a rather advanced expansion of the cranial vault, indicating that we are already dealing with archaic *Homo sapiens* rather than *Homo erectus*. The affinity of this group to the later Neandertals is obvious in that the specimens already display some Neandertal facial characteristics. The surface below the eye sockets is flat or even convex and the cheekbones are obliquely oriented, giving the face a laterally receding pattern. The large nasal aperture of the Petralona skull also evokes the Neandertal morphology, as do some mandibular features in Tautavel. All this suggests that the period between 500,000 and 400,000 B.P. could well be the beginning of Neandertal history.

The interpretation of later specimens was based, in part, on the hypothesis of a European origin of modern humans. The decade following 1910 was the golden age of Neandertal discoveries in southwestern France. The sites of La Chapelle-aux-Saints, La Quina, La Ferrassie, and Le Moustier yielded nearly complete skeletons on which our knowledge of European Neandertal anatomy is largely based. The description of the La Chapelle-aux-Saints remains by French paleontologist Marcellin Boule deeply influenced Neandertal studies, leading scholars to portray Neandertals as primitive, even apelike, compared to the succeeding Cro-Magnons. As a result, they were excluded from the ancestry of modern humans, while anthropologists hypothesized connections between the Cro-Magnon inhabitants of France and remote living populations. Late prehistoric dwellers of the Perigord were seriously considered as ancestors of the Eskimos, and inhabitants of the Riviera as forefathers of African people. Obviously, scholars at the time could not imagine that the ancestors of modern Europeans were to be found in southwestern Asia and Africa.

The rejection of Neandertals and the psychological need to find European roots of modern humankind led to the search for a new character in the Palaeolithic landscape, a European forerunner of the handsome Cro-Magnon hunters and a much more honorable and acceptable ancestor than the brutish Neandertal. So-called "Pre-sapiens" finds were for the most part dubious, fragmentary, and poorly dated. The acceptance of the Piltdown forgery—a recent skull and the mandible of an immature orangutan discovered in Sussex between 1912 and 1915—resulted mainly from this quest for a European Pre-sapiens.

The Pre-sapiens lineage did include two well-preserved, authentic and reasonably dated hominid fossils. One, found at Swanscombe in England, was an occipital and two parietal bones; the other was a more complete skull from Steinheim, Germany. These specimens are usually dated to ca. 250,000 B.P., but may be older. Both display some Neandertal features. In the late 1970s I argued that one could observe an incipient supra-iniac fossa, the depression on the back of the skull that is characteristic of the Neandertal lineage, on both specimens. This observation was rather well accepted for Swanscombe, but less so for Steinheim. The problem was that the general shape of the skulls was more similar to those of modern humans than those of Neandertals. Both display a pentagonal shape in rear view, somewhat reminiscent of a modern head and quite different from the rounded shape of the Neandertal skull. More detailed analysis of the evolution of the European hominids has finally resolved this contradiction. The pentagonal shape of the skull is a primitive trait shared by many archaic hominids, including *Homo erectus*, but still observed in modern humans. The ancestors of the Neandertals passed through a similar stage, but lost this pentagonal shape in the course of their evolution (in a sense modern humans are more primitive than Neandertals in this regard). The supra-iniac fossa suggests that Swanscombe and Steinheim are in the Neandertal ancestry, and the pentagonal occipital does not exclude them from the early stages of this lineage.

New discoveries have fully confirmed this interpretation. A skull found at Biache, in northern France, dating to ca. 175,000 B.P. provides a good intermediate between Swanscombe-Steinheim and later Neandertals in the shape of its braincase. On the other hand, the extraordinary specimens—hundreds of bones and three complete skulls—found in the Pit of Bones at Atapuerca by Juan Luis Arsuaga of Madrid's Complutense University and his colleagues fill the gap between the Tautavel-Vértésszöllös-Bilzingsleben group (400,000 B.P.) and Swanscombe-Steinheim (250,000 B.P.) The Pit of bones skulls have some midfacial projection but show an earlier stage of development of the supra-iniac fossa than the Swanscombe skull. In the rear view the Pit of Bones skulls also retain a pentagonal outline.

The evidence indicates that Neandertal traits developed continuously over the course of at least 300,000 years. In the beginning these characteristics were rare, but they became more common, more consistent, and more pronounced over the millennia. Different anatomical areas evolved at different rates. First the face changed, developing an incipient midfacial projection and receding cheeks. Then the occipital area developed a more Neandertal look. Finally the vault and the temporal bone took on Neandertal proportions. By 127,000 B.P. the Neandertal morphology was established.

This long biological continuity is echoed in the archaeological record. For nearly a century, archaeologists separated the Middle Palaeolithic (then thought to be limited to between 80,000 and 40,000 B.P.) from an earlier, more primitive Lower Palaeolithic. With the excavation and study of new sites, this boundary has become more and more difficult to draw. In contrast, the arrival of modern humans in Europe is reflected in the sharp division between the Middle Palaeolithic and the beginning of the Upper Palaeolithic (ca. 40,000 B.P.). The former, mainly represented by the Mousterian assemblages, are basically composed of side-scrapers, points, notches, and denticulates shaped from flint flakes. Bone objects are rare and very simple. The dwelling sites do not seem very structured. In the Upper

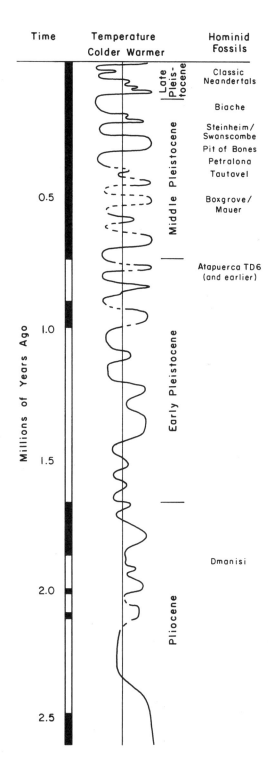

Figure 2. Periodic reversals of the earth's magnetic poles (indicated by black-and-white bar), recorded in cooling volcanic rocks, provide chronological markers. Fossil pollen from sites reflects temperature changes over the millennia. Oxygen isotopes in marine shells reflect the advance and retreat of ice caps and confirm the pollen data. Evidence from Dmanisi, Georgia, shows that humans were at the gates of Europe by ca. 1.8 million years ago. Artifacts and human bones from Atapuerca, Spain, indicate hominids reached Europe nearly one million years ago or earlier, but their remains are too fragmentary to be securely assigned to a species, as are those from Boxgrove and Mauer, dated ca. 500,000 B.P. By 400,000 years ago Europe was inhabited by archaic *Homo sapiens* whose remains have been found at Tautavel and elsewhere. As intense glacial periods isolated them from populations in Africa and Asia, these European populations evolved into classic Neanderthals through pre-Neanderthal forms such as Steinheim and Swanscombe, ca. 250.000 years ago.

Palaeolithic there is a large variety of flint tools, many shaped from elongated blades and bladelets. There are numerous bone and antler objects, especially spear points. It is the time of prehistoric art, of symbolism, of well-structured dwellings. It is quite likely the time of a new social organization.

Why and how did the Neandertals evolve? The evolution of living beings is mainly the result of two phenomena. One is natural selection, which, by favoring the transmission of characteristics, leads to an adaptation of the species to its environment. Others act at random. In the phenomenon called the founder effect, individual gene combinations of the few individuals that colonize a new territory strongly influence the genetic fate of their descendants. If a descendant population remains or becomes sparse, a haphazard phenomenon known as genetic drift can act on small groups. Relatively rare genes carried by some individuals can become rather frequent in their descendants.

To maintain its particular features, and eventually to become a new species, a diverging group needs to be isolated from its mother population. This segregation can happen in different ways, but it usually results from physical isolation created by a geographical barrier. European hominids evolving into Neandertals had to be somewhat isolated from nearby archaic *Homo sapiens* populations. Europe is a peninsula in the far west of Eurasia, and for hundreds of thousands of years the Mediterranean Sea seems to have been a nearly impassable barrier. The Strait of Gibraltar, in spite of its narrowness, was not a place of intense exchanges of people. The fossil hominids of northwestern Africa contemporary with the Neandertals followed a quite different evolutionary line. This does not mean that no human ever crossed the Strait during the second half of the Middle Pleistocene, just that such movements were not numerous and did not have a strong biological influence on the evolution of the resident population.

The gate of Europe was to the east, and the main path of colonization likely remained, for a long time, across the Bosphorus and along the northern Mediterranean coast. The first arrival of small groups of hominids may have created some founding effect. During temperate stages in the middle of the Middle Pleistocene, ca. 500,000 B.P., the descendants of these populations expanded to the north. However, pre-Neandertal bands may never have been able to survive in higher latitudes during the glacial maxima, when immense tundras developed hundred of miles south of the European ice sheet.

Archaic *Homo sapiens* began evolving into Neandertals at a time of major climatic change. After 400,000 B.P. there was an increase in the severity of climatic swings. Intense glaciations occurred after this date. Between 300,000 and 127,000 B.P., two glacial advances were separated only by a cool interglacial stage during which an extensive ice sheet persisted in northwestern Europe. That classic Neandertals were adapted to a cold environment is demonstrated by their body proportions, which Erik Trinkaus of the University of New Mexico has shown were similar to those of modern Eskimos or Lapps. Such physical adaptations may have been influenced by climate, abetted by a limited ability to make warm clothing, build protective dwellings, and use fire. The principal impact of cold or cool periods, however, was the isolation of the European population. During these times the bulk of the pre-Neandertals lived in the south. The frozen grounds to the north, the Mediterranean Sea, the ice sheets covering the mountains (especially the Caucasus), and the dramatic extension of the Caspian Sea to the northwest severely reduced the already limited genetic exchanges between Europe and nearby areas.

A climatic and geographic explanation of the Neandertal evolution was proposed in the 1950s by paleoanthropologist F. Clark Howell, then of the University of Chicago, who emphasized the role of the glaciation in isolating them. But the fact that Neandertals existed during the last interglacial provoked criticism of Howell's idea by other scholars. Recent discoveries and a better interpretation of the Neandertal features have shown the lineage to be much older than was thought. While Howell's proposed timing was wrong, his linking of human evolution with environmental changes during the Pleistocene in Europe appears to have merit. The astounding findings of the last few years, at Atapuerca and other sites, will allow us to test this theory. Undoubtedly the earliest Europeans and the origins of the Neandertals will remain matters of heated scientific discussion for years to come.

4

New Evidence Challenges Traditional Model of How the New World Was Settled

Kim A. McDonald

The long-standing belief that the first inhabitants of the New World arrived some 12,000 years ago is facing serious challenge from archaeologists, linguists, and geneticists whose findings suggest that humans may have traveled extensively in North and South America as long as 40,000 years ago.

According to the scholars, the new evidence also suggests that the first Americans did not come from a single area in Siberia, as had been assumed by many scientists, but in four distinct migrations, some of which had their origins in geographically distant regions of Asia.

"The peopling of the New World is a much more complicated issue than has been thought before," said Dennis Stanford, curator of Paleo-Indian anthropology at the Smithsonian Institution, in Washington. "The old model that we read about in our textbooks is no longer valid. The situation is extremely complex."

The researchers presented their evidence challenging the traditional model of the settlement of the Americas at last month's annual meeting here of the American Association for the Advancement of Science.

Their revisionist view is the culmination of a series of spectacular recent discoveries that have contradicted the accepted model and thrown the field of Paleo-Indian anthropology into turmoil.

"The last two years have been extremely exciting in the study of the first Americans," said Dr. Stanford.

According to the model that has held sway for more than 60 years, the first people to the New World were thought to have walked across the Bering Strait land bridge 12,000 years ago, and to have spread rapidly southward, reaching Central and South America in just a few centuries.

The 55-mile-long land bridge, which connected Siberia with Alaska, was exposed during the last Ice Age, when much of the earth's sea water was frozen in glaciers. While this glaciation was at its maximum for about 10,000 years—until about 12,000 years ago—many anthropologists believed that the settlement of the New World could not have occurred much before 12,000 years ago. They pointed out the presence, until that time, of an icecap over much of North America that would have hindered southerly migration. They also noted the paucity of well-documented archaeological sites from before 12,000 years ago in the Americas and before 18,000 years ago in Siberia.

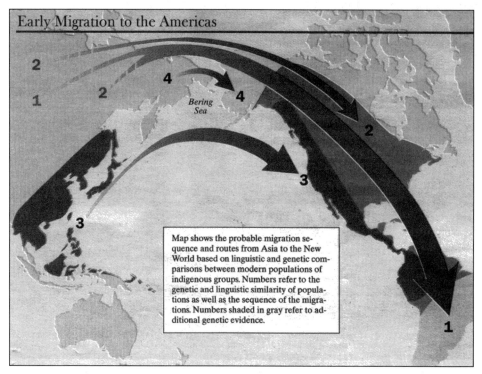

Figure 1. Map shows the probable migration sequence and routes from Asia to the New World based on linguistic and genetic comparisons between modern populations of indigenous groups. Numbers refer to the genetic and linguistic similarity of populations as well as the sequence of the migrations. Numbers shaded in gray refer to additional genetic evidence. (Graphic courtesy of The Chronicle of Higher Education)

Spear Points in New Mexico

Archaeologists had long agreed that the earliest human occupation in North America for certain was at a site near Clovis, N.M., containing spear points found to be 11,500 years old.

But last year, a team of eminent anthropologists ended a controversy over an excavation near Monte Verde, Chile, by concluding that the site showed that humans had lived there 12,500 years ago (*The Chronicle*, February 21, 1997).

The widespread acceptance of that date for the Monte Verde settlement—500 miles south of Santiago and 10,000 miles south of the Bering Strait—threw open the question of when and how the first Americans really did come to the New World.

It also lent credence to the authenticity of sites older than Monte Verde that have been bitterly contested by adherents of the traditional view of migration. The evidence at those sites includes the 15,000-to-20,000-year-old artifacts from Meadowcroft, in southwestern Pennsylvania; 16,000-year-old spear points from Cactus Hills, south of Richmond; 13,000-year-old fingerprints preserved in clay from the Pendejo Cave, in New Mexico; and 12,000-to-13,000-year-old mammoth bones found in proximity to stone tools at the Chesrow Complex, in Wisconsin.

Robson Bonnichsen, director of the Center for the Study of the First Americans, at Oregon State University, said the geographic diversity of those ancient settlements suggested that the first Americans may in fact have arrived thousands of years before those settlements existed, or that they made multiple migrations with separate points of entry into the New World.

In South America, a number of similarly diverse ancient settlements have been found. Besides the Monte Verde site—which contained more than 700 stone tools, remnants of hide-covered huts, and a child's footprint beside a hearth—archaeologists have recently found 11,000 year-old Paleo-Indian artifacts in a cave Brazil's Amazon rain forest, and 11,650 year-old stone tools in Peru.

Tom D. Dillehay, chairman of the anthropology department at the University Kentucky, who led the Monte Verde and Peru excavations, said another excavation at Monte Verde had revealed a deeper layer or artifacts, indicating that the site may have been occupied as long as 33,000 years ago.

"We Will Have Even More"

As more scholars become comfortable with the idea that humans wandered throughout the Americas more than 12,000 years ago, scientists say they expect many more ancient settlements to be unearthed.

"What I find extremely interesting that there have been a number of sites that were pretty good at first blush that the investigators have not wanted to publish having seen the kinds of academic attack that Dr. Dillehay and others have under gone in suggesting that the sites were that old," said Dr. Bonnichsen. "Now that there seems to be a consensus that there could be a pre-Clovis occupation in North America, a number of these sites are coming to light. I would predict that in the next year, we will have even more."

Some of the excavations are destroying the assumption that the first Americans resembled modern Native Americans. Paleo-Indian remains unearthed in Nevada and Washington State over the past two years have skeletal features so different from those of Native Americans that they bolster the view of scientists who believe that the settlement of the New World involved multiple migrations of genetically distinct populations.

According to Dr. Stanford, of the Smithsonian, the ancient skeletons possess what some have called Caucasoid features—such as a narrow face, prominent nose, and incisors that were not shovel-shaped—suggesting that the first Americans "were probably from a population that predated modern North American Indians."

The findings, however, do not mean that white people were among the first inhabitants of the Americas. "These are pretty general traits," Dr. Stanford explained, "that we think may have come from an original population in Asia out of which many different groups may well have developed, including the people of Europe."

4 Primary Lineages

Nevertheless, the idea that Paleo-Indians came not from a single population, but from diverse lineages, is supported by genetic studies of modern populations of indigenous groups in Asia and the Americas.

Studies conducted by Emory University scientists on the genes of American Indians from North, South, and Central America indicate that they descended from four primary lineages, originating in geographically distinct portions of Asia.

According to Douglas C. Wallace and Theodore G. Schurr, molecular geneticists at Emory, the first of the four groups came from the Baikal region of Siberia 25,000 to 35,000 years ago and eventually migrated to the interior of North and South America. The scientists based their conclusions on similarities in mitochondrial DNA—maternally inherited genetic material that remains largely unchanged from generation to generation—among native groups in Siberia and the Americas, and on estimated rates of change in the genes over time.

Mr. Schurr speculated that the second migration came from Eurasia and possibly coastal eastern Asia and made its way to the interior of North America and the northern portions of South America. The third migration originated in coastal eastern Asia and followed the western coast of the Americas to Peru. The final migration, which occurred after the last major glaciation period, and took place 8,000 to 10,000 years ago, involved the movement from Siberia into northern North America of Eskimo-Aleut and Athapaskan speakers, who now live in northern Canada and Alaska.

The pattern and timing of those migrations, inferred by genetic evidence, agree closely with the pattern inferred by linguistic studies.

Johanna Nichols, a professor of Slavic studies at the University of California at Berkeley, said about 150 families of native North American languages existed, each of which lasted for about 6,000 years.

Most of those languages share certain traits, with no evidence of outside influence for many thousands of years, she said. Only along the western coasts of the Americas do languages appear to have come from immigrants who arrived after 14,000 years ago. In addition, she said, the pattern of language spread suggests that migrations from Siberia did not go directly to the interior of North America, but first traveled south, then moved north and diversified as the icecap receded.

Shared Traits

Despite their long isolation, she said, many of the languages in the Americas share traits with languages in eastern Asia and the Pacific Islands. In contrast with languages in the interior of the Americas, those on the North and South American coasts share many grammatical traits with languages throughout the Pacific rim. The similarities include the use of verbs as the first word in a sentence, and the use of "n" in the words for "I" and "we" and "m" in the words for "you."

"As far as I can compute," Dr. Nichols said, the age of languages on the Pacific coast of the Americas is "at least 12,000 to 18,000 years," the result of a recent period of colonization, beginning after the end of glaciation. By calculating the rates of proliferation for the 150 families of languages, she also estimated that humans lived in the New World for at least 40,000 years.

While that figure compares favorably with the estimates made by the Emory scientists based on genetic data, both rely on assumptions of uniform rates of change—educated guesses that, if incorrect, could throw off the estimates by tens of thousands of years. Furthermore, Dr. Nichols assumed that the early settlers traveled by foot. But some scholars suspect that the early appearance of humans in South America may have been the result of travel by boat down the coast from Alaska, because the massive continental icecap covering the upper half of North America would have made overland travel impossible.

"That's a very active area of debate right now," said Mr. Schurr, of Emory. "There's a growing consensus that people who were coastally adapted probably used watercraft."

"Different Strands of Evidence"

To put together a complete picture of the settlement of the Americas, Dr. Bonnichsen said, scientists need hard data from the archaeological excavations. "We're at a stage where we really don't know the answers about where people came from and when. We have a lot of different strands of evidence that don't always seem to fit together."

At Oregon State, he said, researchers have developed techniques that allow them both to date and to sequence the genes of human hair found in ancient settlements. Often overlooked by archaeologists, hair is an ideal biological artifact, he said, because it is resistant to bacterial and fungal attack, contains the genetic history of those who lived at the settlement, and is often found in large quantity in Paleo-Indian excavations.

A person sheds more than 200 strands or fragments of hair a day, he noted, a rate that over a 60-year lifetime would leave 4.38 million strands of hair from just that one person at an archaeological site. Such remains can be easily extracted, according to scientists at Dr. Bonnichsen's center, who have found them in random samples of sediments collected at 25 excavations.

"Now what we need to do is to identify more archaeological sites, carefully excavate them, and use this new technology to examine human and animal hair that we find," he said. "Hopefully, we will be able to take archaeology and the search for the first Americans to the next level."

Commentary

Humans have an insatiable curiosity about our own past, and archaeologists have made significant contributions to understanding the multi-disciplinary problem of human origins and the human diaspora. Articles in this section report the latest models of human origins and diaspora, and each points out controversies that rage over particular interpretations. Archaeological findings, like scientific findings in general, are commonly superseded with new research and new discoveries. We may change our views and dates for the earliest use of fire, and for the sequence and genetic relationship of early European hominids to modern Homo sapiens. Each article raises still more unanswered questions, and what makes this section important is that its articles demonstrate the dynamic nature of archaeological research on our origins and spread.

It is often said that research on human origins and diaspora is some of the most contentious work in our field. Perhaps one reason this is true is that scientists offer hypotheses from different areas of the world and debate them, using multiple bodies of evidence. Key hominid fossil finds over a few field seasons, once dated, can overturn previous models of human evolution in ways that finds in the rest of the archaeological world cannot. The sheer distance in time between modern humans and our hominid ancestors also precludes the possibility of direct analogies with living human populations. Not only did pre-sapiens hominids look different from us, but they must have behaved quite differently too; efforts to model ancient behavior are criticized as much as are new models of Plio-Pleistocene hominid lineages.

One might reasonably conclude that it is in the area of human origins and diaspora that archaeology has some of its closest affinities to physical anthropology. Here, the linkage between the two subfields is intimate and necessary; results produced draw from both skeletal remains and contexts in which fossils were found. Debates in human origins research frequently escalate into full-pitched battles, which are won and lost over a few fossil finds. Science makes progress through such debates, and such lively disagreement has stimulated a burgeoning field of research on human origins and our spread throughout the world.

Part Four

Conducting Archaeological Fieldwork

Introduction

When most people think of archaeology, they envision large-scale excavations of ancient sites in remote areas of the world. Although such activity does take place in many instances, field archaeology is often highly variable from one research project to the next. In fact, contemporary field archaeology rarely entails the immense expeditions that took place fifty or eighty years ago. Why is this? There are variety of reasons. Unlike archaeology of a century ago, anthropological archaeologists now conduct their scientific research by developing and following "multistage" research designs. Multistage research designs require archaeological fieldwork to be undertaken through a series of different steps. Fieldwork and archaeological excavation are no longer the haphazard "digging" of antiquities from ancient ruins, nor is fieldwork commonly the grand field expedition that we associate with archaeology in the Near East. Field survey is less expensive and less destructive than is field excavation, provides information on a regional scale, and may even be used as an alternative to excavations for a particular area. Today, archaeological fieldwork includes a variety of systematic procedures that begin by studying the region through maps and previous reports; site excavation is only one—of several possible steps—that an archaeologist might follow.

Although each research design is unique to a particular place and problem, most field projects follow a series of basic steps. Many archaeological field projects begin with some sort of field reconnaissance before the archaeologist undertakes excavations. In land-based archaeology, this commonly involves a "pedestrian" survey, which finds surface evidence of archaeological sites. This first procedure requires archaeologists to examine systematically (by walking, hence the term"pedestrian survey") a specified area to locate and document as many archaeological sites as possible. For example, although an archaeologist may be particularly interested in studying a particular ancient site that was once a city, he or she often wants to know about other sites in neighboring areas that surround the ancient site. Pedestrian survey is an efficient and cost-effective way to find other archaeological sites that are scattered across a vast territory. Oftentimes, archaeologists discover that ancient sites and settlements are located near sources of potable water or areas with fertile soil for agriculture. Ancient foragers often placed their settlements near areas suitable for gathering undomesticated plant foods, or in areas where they could hunt small or large game animals.

Archaeological survey is occasionally undertaken within individual sites, especially large ones. Pedestrian survey can help archaeologists learn about the internal spatial organization of buildings, roadways, cemeteries, artifacts, and other ancient remains within ancient towns and cities. In their article, "Surveying Ancient Cities," Anthony Snodgrass and John Bintliff illustrate the value of systematic survey of Classical sites in central Greece. Their survey revealed changes in land use and trends in rural and urban development that were not reported in ancient histories of the two major cities of Thespiai and Haliartos. Their use of diagnostic artifacts recovered from survey transects enabled them to reconstruct major occupations at these two important settlements, without ever putting a spade to the earth. Their work shows how, in many areas of the world, pedestrian survey and surface recording of archaeological sites is sufficient to answer important questions about past life ways.

Although most people think of archaeology as a terrestrial (or land-based) undertaking, underwater archaeology is increasingly common in coastal areas of the world. "Diving into the Wreck," by Andrew Todhunter, describes ongoing archaeological research to recover a 17th century French shipwreck in Matagorda Bay, Texas, left by the explorer La Salle. We see, in this article, that underwater archaeologists also rely on survey and reconnaissance as one of the first steps of their fieldwork, and they use a variety of geomagnetic equipment. "Diving into the Wreck" vividly describes the sights and senses of an underwater archaeology project. Underwater archaeologists must combine a love of history with a desire to dive; like all archaeological fieldwork, underwater archaeology contains a mixture of tedium and discovery. Much (but not all) of the underwater archaeology done today explores shipwrecks, whether Viking Age (as in Robbins' discussion in section 1 of this reader; see "The Wet Frontier") or more recent in age. Fieldwork in underwater archaeology is expensive, time-consuming, and complicated. As J. Barto Arnold, a respected professional in this field comments, "Underwater archaeology is eighty percent logistics." It, like terrestrial archaeology, is a labor of love, and this article clearly conveys the passion that underwater archaeologists have for their fieldwork.

Field survey and reconnaissance, then, are increasingly important aspects of archaeological fieldwork. The excavations that we commonly associate with archaeological fieldwork are, however, alive and well: information recovered during excavations complements the information and data that are acquired during survey. By identifying areas with high densities of artifacts or buildings, archaeologists can streamline their excavations by focusing on the most promising areas of an ancient site, such as burials, which frequently have rich assemblages of artifacts that we can examine to interpret the past. Excavation projects today take many forms; some focus on randomly sampled small units across corn fields in the midwestern United States, others use bulldozers to strip topsoil off broad areas of a site, and still others involve broad-scale excavations that take many months and recover metric tons of archaeological materials.

Archaeological excavations are undertaken today all over the world, and for one example we turn our attention to northeast Thailand. In "Thailand's Good Mound," Charles Higham and Rachanie Thosarat describe their excavations at the site of Khok Phanom Di, an ancient village site along Thailand's Bang Pakong River. Field research at this site took place in several stages, and culminated in a seven-month field season that removed 28,000 cubic feet of prehistoric material and spanned a period of several thousand years. This large-scale excavation required the construction of a roof and the participation of dozens of archaeologists and Thai workers to reach the bottom of the site. Excavations recovered not only artifactual material, but animal remains, pollen, and macrobotanical evidence that enabled the researchers to study the development of Khok Phanom Di and its changing social organization.

1

Surveying Ancient Cities

Anthony M. Snodgrass and John L. Bintliff

In August 1981, near the end of our season in Greece, we discovered Askra, the home village of the early Greek poet Hesiod. Archaeologists had sought its location intermittently for a century. The 15-hectare site in the Boeotian highlands of central Greece was important for its literary associations and for the window it offered on rural Greek life. It was also far beyond our resources for full excavation.

The approach we took to investigating Askra—a surface survey—is not merely a low-budget alternative to traditional archaeological methods based on excavation. Surveys embody a fundamentally different approach to the study of how communities are born, grow and eventually die. They offer a broad sample of life throughout a given site rather than a statistically dubious (albeit exhaustive) slice of a few small plots. In some cases, surveys can give evidence that contradicts historical accounts. We found, for example, that rural Greece, commonly thought to have been deserted during the later stages of the Roman Empire, was in fact a thriving mix of diminished towns and intensively cultivated farmsteads.

Survey archaeology was first conceived as a technique for rural areas, and so we had to modify it for application to an urban site containing potentially unmanageable numbers of artifacts. Since investigating Askra, we have applied the methods we derived there to two larger Boeotian cities, Haliartos and Thespiai. In the meantime the technique has also been adapted to a small coastal township on the Cycladic island of Keos, a major Minoan city in Crete, a town in Etruria and an inland city in the Peloponnese.

The modern ground surface, as long as it is accessible and has not been altered, yields material representative of every period during which the site has been occupied. Potsherds and roof tiles are most common, followed by stone implements and building fragments, bronze coins and terra-cotta objects. By systematically covering the entire accessible area of a former city, picking up all distinctive material, recording its location and determining its identity, it is possible to construct a plot of the city's periods of occupation, growth, shrinkage and shifts in location.

To be sure, urban surveys are effective only under certain prescribed conditions. The site must be largely free of modern construction, and it must have been subjected to cultivation (the more intensive the better) at least intermittently since the abandonment of the city. The processes that bring pottery and other artifacts to the surface from the buried layers underneath are as yet understood only in a general way, but it is clear that they work. Cultivation plays a vital role in bringing material to the surface, as does the gradual erosion of topsoil. Material from the most recent periods is generally overrepresented in the surface layer, whereas ancient items are underrepresented.

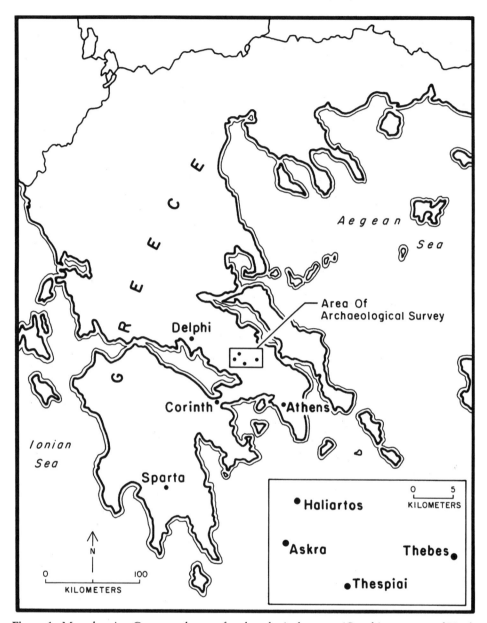

Figure 1. Map showing Greece and area of archaeological survey. (Graphic courtesy of Hank Iken)

Although they may be highly effective, surveys will never supplant excavation entirely. After all, the dating of artifacts found on the surface is possible in large part only thanks to decades of painstaking research by excavators, who have noted the sequences and associations of each class of material in their stratified deposits.

Moreover, there are many questions about the history of a city that surface surveys cannot answer. Unless the surface archaeologist is lucky enough to find the foundations of recognizable buildings—fortification walls, monumental public structures and the like—there is little the method can contribute to tracing changes in political power and independence, for example. (The relative abundance of imported pottery and similar items can furnish only indeterminate clues.)

Even when it was clear we had to survey Askra rather than trying to excavate it, the site still posed problems. Surface survey is a well-established archaeological practice, but surveys of areas that include urban centers had seldom been attempted because of the huge range in the concentration of artifacts. In Mediterranean lands the barren mountain slopes yield a handful of pieces per hectare, whereas the densest urban areas display 20 or even 200 artifacts per square meter.

Anyone but a Mediterranean archaeologist may find such figures hard to believe, but they are real enough. Furthermore, artifacts are not distributed in neat, discrete packets corresponding to ancient sites. Instead the nearly millionfold variation in artifact density takes the form of a gradual distribution extending hundreds or even thousands of meters from "primary" sites. The surveyor faces an extraordinarily rich body of data.

This embarrassment of riches poses problems, however, in devising collection strategies and determining what constitutes surface evidence for a site. Only after the highs and lows of the local distribution are known is it possible to place all the evidence in context. A concentration of artifacts that might pass for a rural farmstead at one site could represent only part of the general surface scatter at another. At the same time, there are limits to the amount of material from a single site that archaeologists can fruitfully catalogue and study. Early traverses of Askra yielded 10 or more artifacts per square meter, implying that a complete survey might yield 1.5 million artifacts.

We devised a sampling method that has since served well for larger sites in subsequent seasons. The work is done in two stages. The first stage covers the entire accessible surface area so that the site can reveal all its distinctive artifacts and so that its phases of occupation can be dated. (Askra, for example, proved to have been occupied intermittently for more than 4,000 years.) The second stage is a more precise examination that provides an accurate measure of the total density of artifacts and helps substantiate dates derived from the initial pass.

We divided Askra into a series of transects less than half a hectare in area and surveyed each in its entirety. Walkers 15 meters apart counted visible artifacts in a strip five meters wide and picked up any material they judged likely to provide a date. Then the team scoured a 300-square-meter subsection of each transect. Workers picked over every square centimeter of ground by hand and counted all the artifacts, again picking up items that appeared useful for dating.

On average, we retained about 20 distinctive pieces from the first walking of each transect, and we added a further 15 from each intensive sample. More than half of the approximately 2,000 artifacts collected form Askra turned out to have chronological value, vindicating the on-the-spot judgments of the walking teams. As a result, we could substantiate the mapping of times of occupation of even such a relatively small site by hundreds of accurately dated pieces for each period.

From the very start of our survey, we had noted that virtually every site, however small, was surrounded by a halo of finds whose density decreased as we moved away from the site itself. The most widely accepted explanation for such halos is the time-honored ancient practice of fertilizing the ground with the manure of animals kept in the vicinity of domestic premises. Pieces of discarded pottery became mixed with the dung; the density of items in a given location is in-

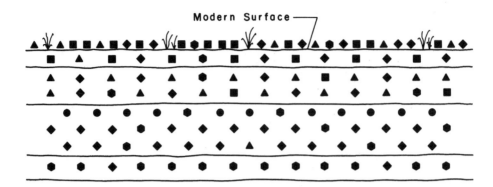

Figure 2. Ancient artifacts are brought to the surface by a continuous process of cultivation, erosion of topsoil and other geologic effects that are not yet fully understood. Older objects, from lower strata, are typically underrepresented at the surface. (Graphic courtesy of Hank Iken)

dicative of the density of cultivation. This hypothesis received striking confirmation in 1986, when Brian E. Davies and Andrew Waters of the University of Bradford found that concentration patterns of heavy metals in the soil across our sites matched the density patterns of ancient pottery.

It has long been known that heavy metals are deposited where people live and work. Davies and Waters's findings suggest that the refuse-deposition activities of 2,500 years ago have left clearly graded and quantifiable traces in both the form of visible potsherds and invisible pollutants. This reinforces our hypothesis that the rural sites were nuclei of intensive agricultural activity. On a vastly larger scale, the cities that we investigated have their own much broader and denser pottery halos. As economic historians have long maintained, Boeotian towns were occupied by cultivators.

Our technique had taken time to evolve, but it was ready by the time our survey carried us up to the walls of Thespiai and Haliartos, the two main cities in whose territory we were working. In particular, we were prepared to test the results of our surveys against written history. Whereas an obscure village like Askra, for all its literary associations, had no connected documentary history, these two towns had both been members of the Boeotian League and virtually independent political entities.

Thespiai earned a certain fame for its long opposition to Thebes, the most powerful city of the league. In 480 B.C., when Thebes prudently sided with the Persians invading Greece, Thespiai enjoyed its greatest moment of glory as it sent 700 soldiers (from a total population of perhaps 10,000) to die with Leonidas of Sparta in the attempt to hold the pass of Thermopylae.

In 424 B.C. Thespiai for once fought side by side with Thebes, winning a victory over the Athenians at Delion. The city again suffered heavy losses, however, and the following year the Thebans were able to exploit this weakness and compel Thespiai to dismantle its fortification walls. Not surprisingly, when Thebes achieved its military and political zenith by an unprecedented victory over Sparta in 371 B.C.—a battle actually fought on Thespiai territory—Thespiai supported Sparta. The loss put an end to the city's heyday.

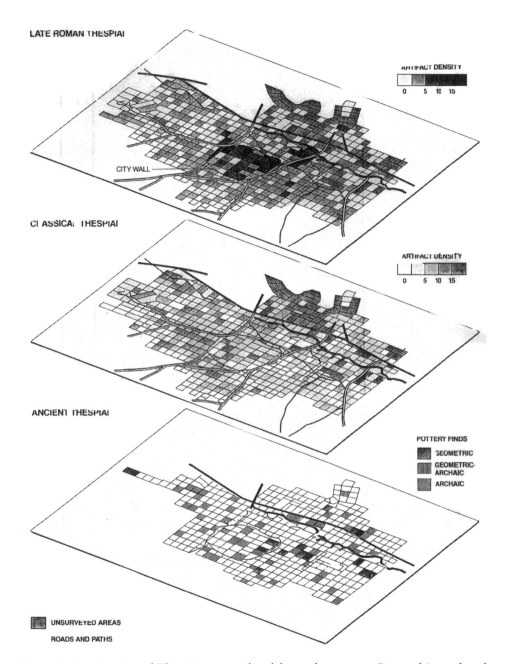

Figure 3. Ancient city of Thespiai was explored by surface survey. Dates of items found show that the settlement was occupied for more than 7,000 years. Archaeologists marked the site off into transects (*areas show by black lines*), which were then examined. A specified part of each transect was painstakingly searched to verify the conclusions of the broad survey. (Graphic courtesy of Hank Iken)

In the meantime Thespiai had produced its most famous daughter, the beautiful courtesan phryne, who became the mistress of the sculptor Praxiteles and posed for his most famous statue, a nude Aphrodite. She dedicated in her native city another of his works, a statue of Love that made Thespiai a tourist attraction for the rest of antiquity.

Haliartos was by comparison a smaller and less famous town. Its population numbered no more than 5,000 at its peak. It came to notice in 395 B.C. as the scene of a minor skirmish in which a force of Thebans and Athenians ambushed a group of Spartans. The Spartan General Lysander, then the most powerful individual in Greece, was among the few killed. The most memorable event in the city's official history was also the last: in 171 B.C. Haliartos backed the Macedonians and other enemies of Rome in a war fought on Greek soil. The town was razed, its inhabitants killed or sold into slavery and its land apportioned among the citizens of Athens, which had taken care to join the Roman side. The territory of both Thespiai and Haliartos is now entirely free of permanent human habitation. The land is cultivated from villages some distances away.

This official history furnished some crude guidelines for our work, even though some episodes were of the kind that a surface survey cannot expect to trace or illuminate. The story also left open many questions we hoped to illuminate. We hoped to establish, for example, how changes in total urban population affected the distribution of occupied farmsteads in the surrounding countryside—and how the extreme case of city destruction influenced the exploitation of the surrounding land. One important issue, of course, was whether the rural and urban sectors grew simultaneously or at each other's expense. We also wondered how the boundary between two states might be reflected in the surface evidence.

The picture that we were eventually able to construct was, in this and other ways, much more detailed than any available from documentary sources. For Askra, of course, there was hardly any documentary information, so any new knowledge was pure gain.

Askra gave clear indications of a long but interrupted occupation and a progressive shift of several hundred meters in the nucleus of the settlement over time. A small area of the site was first inhabited for a period around 2500 B.C. After a very long break, the same locale was first reoccupied and then enlarged into a substantial village of 1,000 people or more between about 900 B.C. and A.D. 100. A second, much shorter break seems to have intervened before the final period of settlement between about A.D. 300 and 1600; since then the site has reverted to open farmland.

The two breaks are inferred only from negative evidence: we found no material whose date fell within those time spans. The first interruption, however, is so long that there can be no doubt of it; furthermore, for part of the time, a neighboring hilltop site was inhabited, suggesting an alternative focus of local settlement. And the second break is corroborated by the Greek travel writer Pausanias, who visited the area around A.D. 170 and described it as deserted.

There is little to say about the first period of occupation. The second, 1,000 years long, embraces the life of the poet Hesiod (circa 700 B.C.) in the village's earlier stages, when Askra was no more than a few scattered dwellings. Ensuing centuries saw first a steady growth and filling in of the settlement, then a marked shrinkage of population and inhabited area.

Throughout the period, the nucleus of the settlement shifted to the south. When the site was reoccupied in the fourth century A.D., the shift resumed until, by the final phases of Askra's occupation in Late Byzantine and Turkish times, the

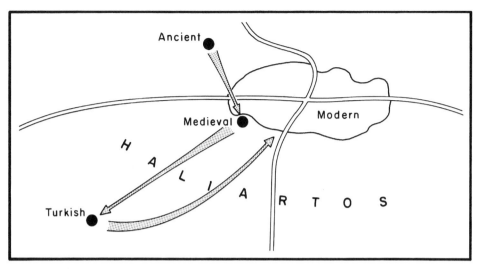

Figure 4. Odyssey of Haliartos show how towns migrate as well as growing or shrinking. The city encompassed nearly 30 hectares before it was razed by Roman troops. Subsequent settlements skirted the edges of the old city for two millennia; a new Haliartos was built to the east of the ancient site just under a century ago. (Graphic courtesy of Hank Iken)

settlement had no overlap at all with the original nucleus of prehistoric and early historical times.

Like Askra, Haliartos had a prehistoric forerunner, sited on the highest ground in the area. And a phase of apparent abandonment, although much shorter than that of Askra, preceded the establishment of the core of the historical city. Classical Haliartos spread progressively down the slopes to the south and north until it attained a population of 5,000 or more and an area approaching 30 hectares. The easternmost extremely is lost under the houses of the modern town that shares the same name.

One interesting discovery was that although by about 400 B.C. the territory of the more populous Thespiai was more densely covered with permanent structures than that of Haliartos, the reverse had been true three centuries earlier at the beginning of the historical period. Apparently the smaller town was faster to colonize its rural territory with independent farmsteads.

During the classical period, the ancient city was surrounded by walls whose foundations are still partially visible. The original nucleus on high ground became the city's acropolis and had an inner fortification of its own. (All these walls were most probably torn down in 171 B.C.)

As predicted from the official history, there is an abrupt break in the sequence of dated pottery in the second century B.C., and for the rest of antiquity the greater part of the site was entirely deserted. A short distance to the east, however, on the outer fringes of the classical city, a new settlement grew up in Byzantine and early Turkish times. From that point onward, in an unbroken cycle, the decline and desertion of one location has been accompanied by the simultaneous growth of an alternative center of population not far away. Two such shifts are traceable between the 17th and 19th centuries A.D., before the foundation of the modern town and the revival of the name "Haliartos" around 1900.

The unique feature of the story of Haliartos is the ruthlessness and thoroughness of the Roman sack of 171 B.C. More gradual shifts, in contrast, are typical of all the major settlements in the area we study. These shifts explain why the modern villages with the official names of Askraia, Thespiai and Haliartos all lie at a certain remove from their ancient forerunners.

Thespiai proved the most daunting of the urban surveys we undertook. We had expected it would be larger than Haliartos, but we were hardly prepared for a city that had exceeded 120 hectares—more than a square kilometer—in area during the period of its greatest extent in the fifth and fourth centuries B.C.

The two-stage procedure of observation and counting had to be repeated 598 times in all. It turned up well over 10,000 datable artifacts. We were able to draw up seven successive plans of the town's occupation and desertion over a span of some 7,000 years.

Unlike Haliartos, Thespiai did not grow from a single compact nucleus sited on top of a prehistoric settlement. The material of the eighth, seventh and sixth centuries B.C. is grouped in half a dozen separate clusters, suggesting a scatter of hamlets only welded into a single urban complex by the growth of the high classical era in the fifth and fourth centuries.

The inevitable sequel was a decline in size and, once again, a shift in the nucleus of occupation. One later phase stands out with special clarity: in the middle of the Roman Imperial period (between A.D. 30 and 300), Thespiai's inhabitants found it expedient to build a new fortification, enclosing a drastically reduced area of 12 hectares.

This polygonal circuit incorporated many blocks of classical stone; it stood until the late 19th century, when, ironically, it was destroyed by a classical epigraphist eager to get at its inscribed stones. Its outline is still faintly visible today. Not surprisingly, we found that material of the later Roman period (from about A.D. 300 to 600) was very heavily concentrated within and around this enclosure. Of the 32 transects that produced more than six later Roman pieces, 25 lay inside the fortified polygon and the rest immediately to the east and northeast.

Although late Roman Thespiai was much reduced in size, the large number of farmsteads we found in the surrounding countryside indicate that it lay at the center of a thriving rural economy. After the classical period, the late Roman is the most intensive period of rural settlement in the entire history of the central Grecian landscape—it was also the time of the reoccupation of Askra. This late Roman recovery is now being revealed by surveys elsewhere in Greece. It is a good example of a development for which the documentary sources, with their gloomy picture of the age, had done nothing to prepare us.

Thespiai also provides a corrective to widely held views of postclassical decline for later periods. A settlement survived there in Byzantine times, entirely to the east of the polygonal enclosure; the ruins of several churches bear witness to continued vitality.

In the end, although the city outlasted all its contemporaries, large and small, it died. When the British traveler Colonel Leake visited Thespiai in 1802, he found a few inhabited houses still standing on the eastern part of the site. A few years later the last inhabitants moved to the hilltop village just to the north, where their descendants still flourish. The ancient city on the plain was given over entirely to cultivation for the first time in nearly 3,000 years—a near-perfect condition for archaeological survey.

The results of our surveys in Boeotia cast light not only on the conditions there but also on the nature of the questions that archaeologists and historians attempt to answer. Official history presents events in a form that is memorable and, as far as the facts allow, gratifying to those who read it. Individuals and organizations appear to formulate consistent policies and carry them through either more or less successfully—as was once said of the *Times of London*, official history describes what ought to have happened rather than what did happen.

Additional constraints affect the case of ancient cities: the written sources that survived were chosen mostly for their literary quality rather than their faithfulness to events. Some ancient historians did share the modern desire for objective truth, and other kinds of documentary sources such as coins and inscriptions also survive. But all such records are vulnerable to distortions, and all too often the sum total of historical evidence yields a portrait of a city that begins with a foundation legend and ends with a visitation of the punishment of the gods. It is significant that some modern authorities have turned as often to poets and philosophers such as Homer, Plato or Aristotle as they have relied on the prose historians.

Conventional archaeology offers only limited help in augmenting the historical picture. Financial and political exigencies usually combine to prevent the excavation of more than a limited part of an ancient urban complex (in contrast with the potentially complete unearthing of small prehistoric settlements). Digs must be sited on land free of existing buildings and available for purchase or expropriation. Only by the rarest good fortune does excavation result in a valid cross section of urban life. Indeed, many investigators would openly disavow such a mundane objective. Better by far to locate the civic center or the main sanctuaries, where they may be able to make some spectacular finds and have a virtual certainty of forging some kind of link with the official history.

Furthermore, even with the best of intentions, the small samples of material and the peculiar nature of preserved deposits makes "commonsense" inferences from excavation notoriously unreliable. The contents of graves, for example, may present a poor picture of the structure of a society and its attitudes toward the living. The goods interred with a corpse may or may not correlate with social or economic standing. Implements found in a grave or scenes depicted in it may or may not match those in everyday life.

Conventional archaeology, then, runs the risk of tautology if excavations proceed only in areas designated by historical accounts. And it can yield a thoroughly skewed sample of ancient life if researchers rely on the contents of rare caches of well-preserved material. Surface survey, in contrast, extracts a limited but valid picture from the detritus and other evidence that human habitation cannot help leaving on the ground.

Those inside and outside archaeology have often asked us whether the results of surface investigation should not be put to the test by excavation. Ideally, perhaps they should. But even excavation yields findings that are often inconclusive, and they are only valid for the area actually dug. Furthermore, resources seldom extend to both survey and excavation, so the choice of one means excluding the other.

Our surface survey of Thespiai covered 99 percent of the city's maximum area in the initial transects and about 13 percent in the regularly spaced intensive samples. For the same cost, we could have excavated perhaps two or three trenches five meters square down to virgin soil: a total of about 0.005 percent of the city's area. Even if the excavation uncovered an equivalent body of dated material, there is no question which method produces a better statistical sample of the physical traces of a city's past.

Further Reading

ARCHAEOLOGICAL SURVEY IN THE MEDITERRANEAN AREA. Edited by Donald R. Keller and David W. Rupp. Oxford, British Archaeological Reports, International Series S155, 1983.

THE CAMBRIDGE/BRADFORD BOEOTIAN EXPEDITION: THE FIRST FOUR YEARS. John L. Bintliff and Anthony M. Snodgrass in *Journal of Field Archaeology*, Vol. 12, No. 2, pages 123-161; Summer 1985.

BEYOND THE ACROPOLIS: A RURAL GREEK PAST. Tjeerd H. van Andel and Curtis Runnels. Stanfor University Press, 1987.

OFF-SITE POTTERY DISTRIBUTIONS: A REGIONAL AND INTERREGIONAL PERSPECTIVE. John L. Bintliff and Anthony M. Snodgrass in *Current Anthropology* Vol. 29, No. 3, pages 506-513; June 1988.

2

Diving into the Wreck

Andrew Todhunter

Twelve feet beneath the wind-ruffled surface of Matagorda Bay in Texas, 75 miles northeast of Corpus Christi on the Gulf of Mexico, the silted bottom dissolves between my groping fingers like fine dust struck by a broom. The three-inch visibility drops to zero. The ambient light diminishes; pale mustard-green darkens into muddy rust. I raise my instrument console to within a finger's width of my face plate, strain to read the depth and pressure gauges, and see only a vague lump.

The water is warm; there is no appreciable current. The hydraulic hiss of the regulator and the gentle drumming of exhaled bubbles are the only sounds.

I hold a slender travel line between my fingertips; it connects 10 screw eyes buried in the sand in the approximate shape of a ship's hull. The line is my connection to the world, and I move along it, kicking gently with my fins.

My left hand sweeps across the rippled plain of silt as I continue. I find no stones, no vegetation. The barrenness of the terrain, the blindness, and the soundless solitude are alien but in some way profoundly comforting. I close my eyes, abandoning everything to touch, and move more quickly, the line slithering easily between thumb and forefinger. Suddenly my hand encounters something sharp and solid. I stare wide-eyed into the formless murk, reach out again, following the bottom, until my knuckles come to rest against the toothy mass. I release the line and with both hands carefully cross its surface. Protruding from the silt is a piece of the 17th-century French wreck *La Belle*.

In January of 1686, the 80-foot, three-masted *Belle*, gift of French King Louis XIV to explorer René-Robert Cavelier, Sieur de La Salle, was blown south by a storm across Matagorda Bay and wrecked some 12 miles northeast of present-day Port O'Connor. In what was hailed as "the most exciting nautical archaeology project ever in the U.S." by George Bass, the founder of underwater archaeology, Texas State Marine Archaeologist J. Barto Arnold III and his crew of archaeologists, students, and volunteers discovered the wreck in the summer of 1995. In early May 1996, I joined Arnold and his crew—a core of five plus a fluctuating number of volunteers—when they returned to the wreck to explore and excavate a number of smaller sites detected in the vicinity of the *Belle*'s hull.

Arnold's search for the *Belle* spanned 17 years. In 1978, he combed more than 15 square miles of Matagorda Bay with a magnetometer over a period of two-and-a-half months. The magnetometer, invented during World War II, measures variations—so-called anomalies—in the earth's magnetic field. Bodies of iron beneath the surface—submarines and mines, or, for the archaeologist, cannons and anchors—betray themselves as spikes or mounds on a scrolling map. Arnold's initial search produced two wrecks, but not the *Belle*, and he soon ran out of funding. Although his research continued, he didn't return to the field until 1991. "We just had to find the wreck in the bay," he says. "All the documentation, all the archival information indicated it was there. We just had to keep looking." With the help of donations, he expanded his search area in 1995 and discovered the site of the *Belle* within days.

Finding the wreck, says Arnold, was the most exciting moment of his 26-year career. In addition to the enormous significance of La Salle's expedition to Texan and American history, he says, very little is known about the design of the *Belle*'s class of ship—called a *barque longue*. As much as 20 percent of the hull may be preserved beneath the mud and sediment on the bay's bottom, promising to cast light on the techniques of 17th-century shipbuilding. Personal artifacts could reveal much about the lives of La Salle, his crew, and the colonists he brought to settle nearby. The rewards may be high, but finding such a site is hard work. "Underwater archaeology is eighty percent logistics," Arnold explains. "Many people don't think of that. There's a lot of drudgery leading up to the fun. The things that keep you going are the 'aha!' experiences. It's an incredible rush to shake the hand of someone from three hundred years ago."

Arnold, 46, born and raised in San Antonio, considered a law career but decided on archaeology while an undergraduate at the University of Texas at Austin. "I made a conscious decision to do something more personally rewarding," he explains. He landed his first job while still in graduate school, conserving and later excavating the remains of a 1554 Spanish shipwreck off the Texas coast.

He sees his role as an archaeologist in great part as public service. "I get a real kick out of presenting all this to people," he says. "The *Belle* is a tremendously important site—not just personally but for everyone." If Arnold shows a certain detachment from the objects of his search, it seems to lie in temperament and training. As he puts it, "The excitement is more intellectual than personal. From your first class in archaeology, you are taught not to want to possess artifacts. If you skim off the surface, you're like a politician on the take."

The smile is apropos: When not in the field, Arnold devotes much of his time to politics, including fundraising and professional service. He worked hard for the passage of the Abandoned Shipwreck Act of 1987, a federal law that gives states the right to protect shipwrecks older than 50 years from treasure hunters. Historic wrecks that lie outside national waters, however, enjoy no such protection and may be salvaged by entrepreneurs with no training or respect for archaeology. Salvage law that encourages individuals to return the property of ships in peril to "the stream of commerce" is intended to apply to modern shipping. But treasure hunters manipulate it to shield their operations on historic sites. "It is an insane legal fiction," says Arnold, "to treat a two-hundred-year-old archaeological site like a ship that went down yesterday." Ordinarily relaxed and easy-going, he becomes heated on the subject. "Every underwater archaeologist spends a lot of time thinking about, debating, and fighting the treasure hunters. They're destroying our cultural heritage."

La Salle was not, when all is said and done, a lucky man. Having discovered the mouth of the Mississippi and claimed half of the North American continent for France in 1682, he returned to the Gulf of Mexico two years later with 300 soldiers and colonists aboard four ships with the intention of founding a permanent colony at the river's mouth. After losing one of the ships to Spanish pirates in the Caribbean, La Salle's fleet subsequently missed the great river by more than 400 miles—a blunder that still baffles historians—and arrived at Matagorda Bay in early 1685. Brilliant and driven, La Salle apparently possessed an insufferable arrogance that made mortal enemies of his subordinates. Rather than obey La Salle's commands, one of his captains chose to run his ship, the *Aimable*, irretrievably aground while entering Matagorda Bay, sinking her in the Pass Cavallo and dealing the first of several deathblows to the expedition. (Archaeologists have failed to locate remnants of the *Aimable*.) Matters did not improve from there. La Salle's third ship, *Le Joly*, sailed back to France for supplies and never returned.

After founding Fort St. Louis, overlooking the bay on the banks of Garcitas Creek, La Salle continued northeast by canoe with 50 followers in search of the Mississippi. Guarded by a crew of 11 in La Salle's absence, the *Belle* awaited his return near the northeastern shore of Matagorda Bay. After La Salle did not show up on the agreed date, five crewmen went ashore for water and vanished. Out of water, the remaining crew resorted to the stores of wine and brandy. As the days wore on with no sign of La Salle, the drunken, panicked crew of six decided to return to Fort St. Louis. But a storm blew the vessel south and drove her aground across the bay. Three of the crew struck out for shore aboard a raft. It sank, drowning the men. The remaining three crewmen, including a priest, fashioned a second, superior raft and made it safely ashore. Back at Fort St. Louis, colonists fell by the score to syphilis, smallpox, dysentery, and other diseases until Indians overran the fort and massacred the last survivors in 1686.

In 1687, La Salle finally returned to discover the destruction. He again set out on an expedition but was assassinated by his men at the age of 43 between the Trinity and Bravos rivers. A mere handful of survivors, including the expedition's chronicler, Henri Joutel, found their way to Canada on foot.

More than 300 years later, two boats lie at anchor above the wreck of the *Belle*, some 550 yards north of the Matagorda peninsula—a narrow strip of sand, mesquite, and spartina marsh dotted with cattle and hunting cabins. The shallow bay is gray-green, opaque with the sediment stirred up by weeks of unrelenting wind.

One of the boats, the *Michael Jean*, is an abandoned shrimper donated to the project as a diving platform. The *Michael Jean* is weary and neglected but remains a pretty boat, well suited for the tasks at hand. A red and white diver-down flag flies from the antenna. Diving-gear bags rest like fitted bricks in the center of the broad aft deck. A dozen electric-blue scuba tanks form a neat row at the stern. Three five-gallon buckets, a cracked laundry basket, and a yellow ice chest await artifacts. A scattering of lead diving weights, a perfectly coiled length of fire hose, a submersible metal detector, a gas-powered water pump, hand tools, hand tools, gadgets, and assorted junk litter the deck.

From the deck of the *Michael Jean*, the expedition first addresses the so-called Anomaly B, detected by the magnetometer 25 yards southeast of the main wreck. Hopes run high that Anomaly B is the cargo of ordnance and stores from the sunken raft of the crewmen who tried to escape the *Belle*. Anomaly C, further to the east, may be one of the *Belle*'s anchors.

Beginning in late May, Arnold and his team will install a double-walled, rectangular, steel cofferdam around the hull remains, fill the space between the walls with sand, and drain the water from the dam's center. The resulting structure, rising eight feet above the surface of the bay, will allow the crew to excavate the wreck in plain air. This is only the third time a cofferdam has been employed in a nautical archaeological context.

In exploring the anomalies, nothing is guaranteed. The divers may find armaments from the *Belle*'s raft, or they may find modern "artifacts" from contemporary fishing boats. At the very least, they must determine that the construction of the cofferdam will not endanger historic remains outside the perimeter of the main hull.

During the next eight days, the crew attempts to pinpoint the anomalies. Outfitted in a wetsuit and fins, assistant archaeologist Layne Hedrick, 28, drags the magnetometer sensor, strapped to a Styrofoam surfboard, across the surface in the neighborhood of Anomaly B. Directing Hedrick's movements from the *Miss Kristi*, a transport vessel anchored near the *Michael Jean*, Arnold watches the needles rise and quiver on the scrolling graph. Readings taken on Anomaly B in 1995 peaked at 150 gammas. Hedrick kicks slowly over the site. "One-forty," Arnold announces, his voice rising with excitement. "One-fifty." The crew is quiet. "One-sixty." Once the readings begin to decline, Arnold signals Hedrick to reverse directions. When the needle soars back to 160, Arnold shouts, and Hedrick drops a weighted buoy on the position. Arnold leans back in his chair. "Far out," he says with a smile.

In the days that follow, divers work the site in pairs, sweeping the bottom with a metal detector, then dredging with a water-powered jet probe, its five-horsepower motor wailing on deck like a lawn mower. Crew members on board watch the divers' air bubbles, log their dive times and air consumption, and take careful notes on all tasks performed. Others organize artifact tags, spray-paint clipboards to be used as underwater slates, and fashion buoys from Gatorade bottles.

To an archaeologist, I discover, there is nothing that duct tape cannot fix. Drawing from every trade and discipline from plumbing to computer science, the archaeologist at sea, perpetually improvising, is the ultimate jerry-rigger. Underwater archaeology is still a new science, and its practitioners write the rule books as they proceed. This, of course, is one of the numerous appeals of the trade. "Nothing is ever standard in archaeology," says Arnold.

"Nothing," appends archaeologist and volunteer Laura Landry, "except the need to take meticulous notes." Throughout the week I hear of the affection, admiration, and wonder that the crew and volunteers feel for their work. They appear to live for history, for working with their hands, and for being on the water. Bill Pierson, 53, who left his job as a computer programmer to sign on as the crew's equipment and logistics manager, confesses "a serious weakness for gadgets." J. "Coz" Cozzi, 39, assistant project director and doctoral candidate at Texas A&M, specializes in shipwrecks and hull reconstruction. Aimée Green, 26, artist, project diver and archaeologist, abandoned a modeling career to pursue an anthropology degree at the University of Texas.

Intensely individual, the members of the crew nevertheless work easily together, while Arnold, a quart of Diet Coke in his hand, directs operations with the impenetrable detachment of a 19th-century military commander. His expression is usually inscrutable, but he is quick to laugh. Larry Sanders, a volunteer diver, surfaces and hands Arnold a thin strip of seaweed for identification. "That," says Arnold with a poker face, "is La Salle's shoelace." As the week wears on with no additional discoveries from the *Belle*, it pays to have a sense of humor.

The day before I joined Arnold's crew, I visited a Corpus Christi museum laboratory, where Toni Carrell, archaeologist and assistant project director, introduced me to artifacts collected from the *Belle*'s shipwreck site in 1995. Clear plastic trays contained 236 bronze bells ranging in size from peas to marbles, many of them still paired by twisted strands of fine wire. La Salle brought the bells, handmade in the Low Countries, as goods for barter with Indians. In other trays were hundreds of brass-wire pins, a pair of Jesuit rings, a boatswain's whistle, faience, majolica and stoneware ceramics, a bronze clasp, lead scatter shot, grindstones, scorched fire bricks from the *Belle*'s galley, a pewter button, a chunk of red ochre, a miraculously preserved wooden rigging block attached to a four-inch length of rope, a mysterious lead disk (part of the ship's pump?), and an object—still encased in shell and concreted mud—that resembles the head of a battle-ax.

The crowning discovery was a cannon. Five feet II inches long, 794 pounds of gleaming bronze, the gun is one of six four-pounders reported to have been aboard the *Belle*. After months of meticulous conservation, the barrel shows not a hint of age. The cannon is marked with the crests of Louis XIV and the Grand Adm. Le Comte de Vermandois, an illegitimate son of the king who assumed command of the French navy at age two.

Spread out across a table rested 23 pewter plates, stamped with their maker's circular "touch mark" and identified as the property of one "L.G.," believed to have been Sieur Le Gros in La Salle's party. Bitten by a rattlesnake, Le Gros contracted gangrene and died three months later. The plates before me were found in a neat stack within the hull's perimeter and lacked the scoring from cutlery usually found in the surface of used pewter. This, Carrell explains, is strong evidence that the plates had been manufactured for the anticipated French colony but were never used.

Marks on two other pewter plates resemble a coat of arms. One of the plates is bent and heavily corroded. On the other plate can be seen the crosshatched markings of sustained use. Does such a crest mean the plates belonged to La Salle? I lift one. The tin and lead alloy is heavy, cool to the touch. I run a finger firmly down the longest cut, imitating the pressure of the blade that produced it.

During eight days of diving from the *Michael Jean*, the expedition determines that no artifacts will be endangered by the cofferdam. But despite the high reading at Anomaly B, probes fail to locate artifacts. A search for the anchor produces nothing but a wad of fishing net. These artifacts may wait deeper in the silt than was expected, and the crew will continue the search with more powerful equipment later in the season. I, however, will see no piece of history retrieved from the shallow depths of Matagorda Bay. A diver emerges, at one point, with an object—the sole artifact found—rather like a chalice, choked with shells, concreted mud, and white coral. On closer inspection, the relic proves to be a 20th-century flange, dashing the excitement of the crew. Such is the game.

3

Thailand's Good Mound

Charles Higham and Rachanie Thosarat

About 650 feet wide and 40 feet high, Khok Phanom Di, "the good mound," stands out on the flat flood plain of Thailand's Bang Pakong River. Unoccupied in living memory except for a Buddhist temple, the site passed as a natural hill until a bulldozer, cutting a new path to the top, revealed a deep sequence of archeological deposits. These contained abundant remains of shellfish adapted to coastal mud flats, although nowadays the sea lies fourteen miles to the west. Damrongkiadt Noksakul, a staff member of the local teachers' college, excavated a small test square, which we visited in 1981. Peering into the inky gloom, we saw layer upon layer of hearths, ash, and discarded shellfish remains stretching down twenty-eight feet. This preliminary excavation had yielded eleven human burials, numerous pottery shards, abundant remains of rice, and shells from species of mollusks and crustaceans adapted to life in an estuary and along the seashore.

The site intrigued us because little was known of prehistoric settlements in Thailand so close to the sea. Most archeological work on early groups had been done along small tributary streams in the interior. Yet the wealth of resources on the coast or along major rivers probably played an important role in the spread of rice cultivation and in making mainland Southeast Asia the home of some of the world's great early civilizations. The best known of these civilizations had as its court center Angkor (in present-day Cambodia), a site that represented heaven in stone and incorporated vast temple mausoleums for its deified lords.

Toward the end of 1984, we returned to Khok Phanom Di with an archeological team to excavate a square measuring one hundred square meters, or about 1,075 square feet. We had no illusions about the ease of our undertaking, which eventually involved the removal of 28,000 cubic feet of prehistoric material. We chose this single large square, however, in hopes of discovering the spatial arrangement of ancient life—perhaps house plans, the layout of a cemetery, or distinct areas for different activities. Our research was designed to find out about the way of life of the occupants and how their environment may have changed over the generations.

We erected a steel roof to shelter the square from rain and sun and arranged for electrical wiring. Water was piped in to allow us to clean the finds before sorting and packing them. Jill Thompson, a member of the team, set up a large metal tank to float plant remains out of the archeological deposits. Brian Vincent processed much of the pottery as it was recovered, and Bernard Maloney was on hand to analyze the remains of pollen, a key to understanding the changing environment in the vicinity of the site. After seven months of digging, we reached a compacted, sandy layer at a depth of about twenty-one feet. At last, we were able to stand on the river flood plain that was first occupied in antiquity. The Thai

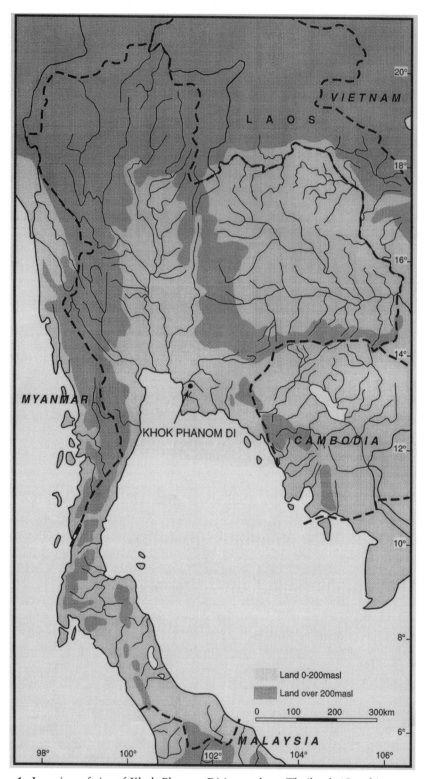

Figure 1. Location of site of Khok Phanom Di in southern Thailand. (Graphic courtesy of Charles Higham)

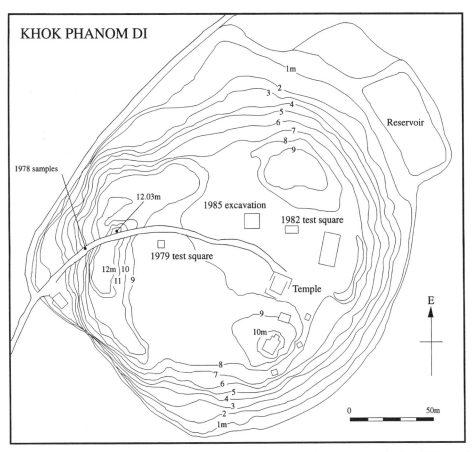

Figure 2. Planview of Khok Phanom Di showing location of excavations in the 1970s and 1980s. (Graphic courtesy of Charles Higham)

workers who were helping us—and who had shown as much interest in our discoveries as we did—were equally relieved to reach bottom.

In our square—still only a fraction of the total mound—we encountered part of a cemetery. We also observed that nearer the edge of the mound, the road-cut exposed layers of debris where prehistoric pots had been fired. The remains of houses probably lay elsewhere. In the earliest layers of the excavated material, we found extensive spreads of ash and much charcoal, along with pottery shards and blunted, well-used stone adz heads. Some of the pottery shards were encrusted with marine barnacles; judging from the species of ostracods and foraminifers, the earliest inhabitants established their settlement on a sheltered estuary of a major river near its entrance to the open sea. Dating of the charcoal showed that these early deposits were about 4,000 years old.

To determine the environment prior to the site's occupation, Bernard Maloney removed a series of cores from the natural sediments that surround the site (the base of the site itself was too hard for our equipment to penetrate). Beneath the present-day rice fields he found about eighteen feet of stiff, blue clay that had been laid down under a shallow sea. The clay contained microscopic fragments of charcoal and the remains of pollen. By dating samples of the charcoal taken at

Figure 3a. View of the excavation of Khok Phanom Di in 1985. (Photo courtesy of Charles Higham)

different levels in the cores, he was able to estimate that the clay was deposited between 8,000 and 4,000 years ago. And by identifying and counting the pollen grains in samples taken at intervals throughout the deposit, Maloney was also able to get a picture of the vegetation.

Mangrove pollen dominated, reinforcing other evidence that the area was near the seashore. At times, however, the quantity of charcoal rose spectacularly and the pollen of grasses and some plants that flourish in rice fields today became more prominent. Such episodes occurred sporadically beginning 7,800 years ago. Several explanations are possible: natural forest fires, burn-offs by local hunters and gatherers, and the clearing of land by rice cultivators. Possibly, people frequented the area long before they settled at Khok Phanom Di itself, about 4,000 years ago. A modern fish pond dug into the marine clay near the site revealed a deep layer of ash and pottery that may belong to this earlier time (we didn't venture to date this material, since it was not covered by our research permit).

Toward the top of the sediment cores, Maloney found evidence for a major episode of burning and the proliferation of grass pollen. This stratum was dated to the early period when Khok Phanom Di was occupied and surely reflects the activities of its inhabitants. They probably were cutting the coastal forests for fuel, including that needed to fire clay vessels, which they shaped from the rich local source of clay. They may also have been burning off dry-season plant growth in order to make way for their rice.

Because their estuary provided a wide range of renewable food resources, the inhabitants of Khok Phanom Di were probably rarely, if ever, short of food. At low tide they collected the abundant shellfish that lived on the mud flats. The clay net weights we have found tell us that they set nets in the estuary for the many species of passing fish. They also took their boats out to coastal waters to fish by

Figure 3b. View of the excavation of Khok Phanom Di in 1985. (Photo courtesy of Charles Higham)

Figure 3c. View of the excavation of Khok Phanom Di in 1985. (Photo courtesy of Charles Higham)

Figure 3d. View of the excavation of Khok Phanom Di in 1985. (Photo courtesy of Charles Higham)

line, using barbed fishhooks made of bone, and cultivated rice in the freshwater swamps behind the coastal mangrove belt. These ideal conditions favored permanent settlement, and during the ensuing years, from 4,000 until 3,500 years ago, twenty-one feet of cultural debris built up.

The inhabitants of Khok Phanom Di were in a good position to trade upriver with people inhabiting the interior and along the coast with other maritime settlements. A sedentary way of life means that trading partners know where to find one another. It permits the accumulation of weighty personal possessions and makes the construction of buildings worthwhile. And not least, it opens up the possibility of an expanding population. Where mobility is the rule, births need to be widely spaced, or there will be too many young children to carry. Permanence removes this constraint, and women can reduce the interval between pregnancies. The need to feed more mouths within such sedentary communities may help explain the rapid spread of agriculture that took place in many different parts of the world beginning 12,000 years ago.

Long-term occupation also allows for the maintenance of a cemetery as a resting place for dead ancestors. Such was the custom at Khok Phanom Di, where we found about twenty generations of burials (assuming an average interval of twenty-five years between generations). In preliterate times, the continuing presence of the ancestors may have helped signify the ownership of local land and resources.

Covered in red ocher and wrapped in shrouds fashioned from beaten bark cloth or sheets of asbestos fiber, the dead were interred face-up with their heads to the east. The oldest level of burials in the excavated part of the cemetery included only six interments, and they were very simple. Only one contained a durable grave offering—a necklace of twelve shell beads. Thereafter, burials accumulated steadily, and the accompanying grave goods became more elaborate, until the cemetery was abandoned.

The cemetery was arranged in a grid of at least six separate clusters. With time, new burials were placed over preceding ones, continuing the same pattern of clusters. We noted many post holes, the residue of building foundations. Their distribution is irregular, but some alignments hint that each of the grave clusters was housed within a wooden structure, forming, in effect, a collective tomb. Doubtless the wood decayed with time, and the structures had to be refurbished or replaced.

The space between the burials contained the remains of much activity. We found middens (refuse heaps), circular pits containing the remains of unopened—and therefore uneaten—shellfish, and thin layers of ash. Very likely burial was an occasion for funerary ritual, including graveside feasting and, perhaps, the placing of food in pits to provision the ancestors. At inland sites of comparable age, archeologists find bones from the legs of cattle or pigs, with no sign of cut marks from butchering. The animals were probably slaughtered for a mortuary feast and a limb placed with the dead. These practices seem to have disappeared with the introduction of Buddhism and cremation.

When one of our Thai colleagues, Praphid Choosiri, examined the human remains, she sometimes found rare or unusual bone structures thought to be genetically determined. Two examples of these, with the technical names *metopic suture* and *os inca*, concern the presence of extra sutures between bones in the skull. She noted that successive interments in the grave clusters sometimes exhibit the same rare characteristic, suggesting that each of the burial areas was devoted to a particular lineage. Based on this assumption, we set out to reconstruct prehistoric family trees and consider their ups and downs.

We found that two lineages were especially stable, in that they continued for the full complement of generations for the life of the cemetery. For one reason or another, however, some lineages failed to maintain themselves. In general, we observed that infant mortality was high for the first eight or so generations, so perhaps these families died out. An alternative explanation is that, as the number of inhabitants grew, the leaders of some lineages left with their relatives to found new settlements elsewhere.

In studying the two stable lineages, we found that the quantity of grave goods varied considerably between burials: some had nothing, while others were very rich. They included lustrously burnished and decorated pots, iridescent shell beads, translucent shell disks, and stone adz heads. Small clay anvils used in making pots were found only with the remains of women, children, and infants. (Such an anvil would have been held inside the vessel as it was shaped with a wooden paddle.) On the other hand, twelve-inch-wide plaques fashioned from sea turtle carapaces, apparently worn as chest ornaments, were found only with the skeletons of men. Both men and women were interred with the stones used to burnish pottery vessels until they shone.

Neither of the two stable lineages appeared consistently wealthier than the other. Fortunes rose or fell after a generation or two, or at most three. This suggests that esteem and status—assuming these translated into mortuary wealth—had to be attained into mortuary wealth—had to be attained through personal achievement. They were not inherited by right, except to the extent that when infants died, wealthy parents were able to endow them with rare and beautiful

Figure 4. Shell disks from mortuary phase five. (Photo courtesy of Charles Higham)

grave goods. (Interestingly, infants less than a month or two old were not accorded such attention; perhaps they were still too young to be regarded as official members of society.)

Evidence of important changes at Khok Phanom Di emerged after the actual excavation, as our team of specialists completed their analyses of various kinds of data. Up to the ninth or tenth generation, the inhabitants of the village continued to exploit both the river and seacoast. Men had strong muscular development in their upper bodies, and men and women apparently had somewhat different diets—women had more caries and tooth loss, while men kept their teeth longer and therefore showed more tooth wear. People were interred with beautifully decorated pots, and many wore shell jewelry. Infant mortality was high.

Then, about the tenth generation, something happened to the maritime connection. Marine and coastal shellfish gave way to species from freshwater or backwater mangrove stands. Mangrove wood became less common in the charcoal. From this time on, men appeared less muscular. Shell jewelry practically disappeared, and even pottery vessels became less common and lacked ornate decoration. Men and women shared a new diet pattern, probably including fewer shellfish. And infant mortality rates dropped.

We think these changes were a reaction to a swift alteration in the environment, probably a major flood followed by a shift in the river channel away from Khok Phanom Di. A gradual deposition of sediment also left the site farther from the sea. Men, whose previous strength probably reflected habitual paddling of boats, now embarked on fewer coastal voyages. The local source of high-quality shell for ornaments also suffered as the sediments killed off preferred species. And the change in habitat or diet may have reduced the danger of certain diseases, improving infant survival.

After three or four generations of relative poverty, yet another pattern emerged. We encountered a very large grave belonging to one of the two main clusters. It contained the remains of a woman in her midthirties. Her body was covered with a pile of clay cylinders, which may represent clay destined for conversion into pots, and the broken pieces of five ornately decorated vessels. Her personal jewelry included 120,000 shell beads, two shell disks, a headdress, and on her left wrist, a bangle made of an exotic shell. In life, this woman must have been dazzling in her finery. Beside her right ankle lay a shell containing two burnishing pebbles next to a clay anvil. We think that she must have been an outstanding potter. She had well-developed wrist muscles, consistent with preparing and molding clay.

Beside her was a matching grave containing the remains of a fifteen-month-old infant. Again, we encountered a pile of clay cylinders, the body festooned with 12,000 shell beads, a bangle placed over the left wrist, beautiful pots, and a miniature clay anvil beside the right ankle.

Despite the opulence of these two burials, the succeeding generation in what we believe was the same lineage displayed very little wealth. In contrast, the other main lineage now attained greater status within the community. We found the remains of two women and a nine-year-old child buried beneath the two-foot-high raised floor of a rectangular mortuary building. Both women were buried with clay anvils, and one was buried with 11,000 shell beads. The child was accompanied by a thick shell disk and at least 18,000 beads.

Our interpretation is that the community adapted to its now more inland habitat by expanding its ceramic industry, already established owing to the settlement's rich resources and favorable location. This craft, apparently the province of women, might have provided a valuable commodity for trade. Perhaps more than ever, a potter's skill became a source of individual prestige and a route to wealth. Jewelry came to include new styles of heavy bracelets and disks made of tridacna and trochus shell. These species of mollusks are adapted to a clean, coralline habitat and so must have been obtained by exchange from some distance away.

As before, while individuals might attain the prestige evident in a rich burial, they do not seem to have been able to convert this into inherited status and rank. Rather, one family might be successful in one generation, only to be followed by less able or less fortunate descendants in the next. This might have reflected success or failure in craftsmanship and in exchange dealings with other communities, depending on individual skill or charisma. Only when a mortuary tradition in a single community can be followed over so many generations can we gain such an intimate glimpse into its operating principles. No similar site exists elsewhere in Southeast Asia, and very few in the rest of the prehistoric world.

Any community that relies on female potters for making vessels for mortuary ritual and exchange would be reluctant to lose them to other communities through marriage. We believe that the custom at Khok Phanom Di, at least for this later period, was for women to remain at their place of birth. In such a "matrilocal" community, failure to produce a female heir would have spelled the end of the lineage. This may explain the attention given to the details of child or infant burials, some of whom, presumably the young girls, were interred with clay anvils.

We also noted that proportionately fewer men were buried in the cemetery during the later phase, although at least one was well provided with grave goods. A possibility is that men were now using sailing craft to engage in long-distance trade, taking pots and returning with shells. The present-day seafaring people of southern Thailand have a tradition of such voyaging, which is usually the work of men. When they die at sea, their bodies are interred in caves remote from their home base.

Despite its renewed prosperity, Khok Phanom Di was eventually abandoned, about 3,500 years ago. Perhaps the inhabitants chose to move closer to the coast. While we cannot say what happened to them, we have subsequently excavated another cemetery about eight miles to the south, at Nong Nor. This cemetery was in use from about 500 to 800 years after Khok Phanom Di was abandoned. In some ways it shows a similar mortuary ritual, with the bodies oriented with the head to the east and clusters containing men, women, and children (but there is no buildup of successive graves that would enable us to trace individual family groups through time). At Nong Nor, the men were buried with the potter's anvils and usually had the richest grave goods. The artifacts include ornaments cast in bronze and tin as well as jewelry of serpentine, talc, carnelian, and jade, indicating wider trade contacts.

Khok Phanom Di is one in a series of sites that mark the origins and expansion of rice-growing agriculturists in the hot, densely forested lands of Southeast Asia. The spread of agriculturists can be reconstructed by identifying similarities between many languages spoken in southern China and Southeast Asia today and by tracing them back to a common origin. According to this linguistic and associated radiocarbon evidence, there was a transition to rice farming in the Yangtze Valley of China about 8,500 years ago. The ancestors of the Vietnamese and Khmer, as well as the Munda speakers of eastern India, apparently moved down the major rivers, bringing their farming economy along with them.

Figure 5. The 1985 excavation under the roof. (Photo courtesy of Charles Higham)

Figure 6. View of the excavation of Khok Phanom Di in 1985. (Photo courtesy of Charles Higham)

Recent evidence suggests that the first farmers reached Thailand about 4,500 years ago. Occupied between 4,000 and 3,500 years ago, Khok Phanom Di has provided us with the clearest available evidence for their way of life. At the time the site was abandoned, Southeast Asia was entering the Bronze Age, as copper and tin began to be cast separately or alloyed to create ornaments, weapons, and tools. The later site of Nong Nor already includes some of these artifacts.

In terms of social organization, however, little changed in Southeast Asia until about 2,500 years ago, when the smelting of iron ores was discovered or introduced. Regional leaders began to control metal-working specialists, who cast a new range of luxury bronzes, including drinking vessels and drums. Over the next 500 years, Southeast Asia joined ever widening trade networks, and powerful regional chiefdoms arose as the rivalry and competition over luxury goods grew. The later chiefs forged the first states in Southeast Asia, a heritage that culminated 1,000 years ago in the founding of the great holy city of Angkor.

Commentary

Although most archaeologists do not engage in the dramatic exploits that the public associates with Indiana Jones, fieldwork continues to be an integral part of the research process. We have tried, in this section, to illustrate the wide range of field techniques that archaeologists use routinely on their field projects. What unites these diverse approaches is the careful and systematic way in which archaeologists do their fieldwork: above ground, below ground, and even under water. Archaeological materials that are recovered through fieldwork comprise the foundation of our interpretations of the past. If we have not carefully provenienced these materials, the information that they contain will have little or no interpretive value. One of the distinctive characteristics of professional archaeology that distinguishes our field is the scientific nature of our field investigations. Context, provenance, and association are as important to field archaeologists as are the objects themselves, and an object lacking context has little scientific value.

We know that people have used fieldwork to recover pieces of the past for a very long time. For example, Thutmose IV, pharaoh of Egypt in the 15th century B.C., ordered the excavation of the Great Sphinx at Giza, then already centuries old. In the 12th century A.D., monks at England's Glastonbury Abbey conducted excavations in search of King Arthur's grave, and were convinced that they had found his remains. Today, however, an important difference exists between archaeological fieldwork by trained professionals and fieldwork by untrained amateurs. Scientific archaeology relies on observable pieces of information (which we call data) to build plausible models of behaviors and events from the past. We are concerned with gaining knowledge about the past, and proceed in our search for knowledge in a systematic fashion that involves detailed observations and continuous self-correction.

Professional archaeologists are increasingly welcoming volunteers and nonprofessional archaeologists to work with them on projects. National archaeological societies (e.g, Archaeological Institute of America) welcome nonprofessionals to their ranks and local archaeological societies are found in nearly every major city in the United States today. Archaeological field opportunities (many of which involve formal training) are available throughout the world today, and joining professional archaeological projects has never been easier for amateur archaeologists. Times have changed since the 18th century, when gentlemen farmers like Thomas Jefferson could dabble in archaeology on their estates. We lack the funding today (and often the authorization) to undertake archaeological projects on the scale of those directed by archaeologists earlier in this century. Today we acknowledge that the archaeological record is a finite and delicate resource, and that undertaking fieldwork requires forethought, planning, and professional experience. It can also be a lot of fun!

Part Five

Measuring Time in Archaeology

Introduction

How old is it? Archaeologists all over the world are obsessed with this question! Time is one of the most important parameters that the archaeologist must control to explain events that happened in the past. Since a primary goal of anthropological archaeologists is the study of long-term change, we must determine reliable ages for our archaeological sites and artifacts. We have a variety of methods for assigning an age to a particular artifact or building, and our battery of techniques is growing with each passing decade. Archaeologists often draw a distinction between so-called "relative" versus "absolute" dates. Relative dating assigns an object's age compared with others within a series, that is, whether an object is older or younger than the others in a collection. The development of the "Three Age system" by Thomsen and Worsaae in 19th century Scandinavia marked the beginning of the formal use of a relative chronology for European materials.

Relative dating has always played an important role in archaeological research. During much of its history, for example, archaeologists could rely only on stratigraphic analyses or seriation to infer the age of an archaeological deposit and its associated artifacts. The stratigraphic method of dating was derived from the 19th century, when the geologist Charles Lyell proposed his law of superposition. Simply put, this "law" states that the earth's geological deposits are stacked on top of one another like a chocolate layer-cake. Moreover, it claims that the deeper layers are older than the upper layers. In applying this method to dating ancient sites, archaeologists presume that artifacts found in the deeper parts of a stratified site are older than artifacts found in shallow deposits. This method of relative dating has been extremely important for developing relative chronological frameworks for constructing culture histories. It can really only work, however, in archaeological sites like caves or tells that have deep deposits with well-developed stratigraphy. In many areas of the world (such as the Pacific region and parts of North America) archaeological sites are relatively shallow compared with areas where some sites are extremely deep, like the Near East. Consequently, this method is not always effective in areas of the world where sites are relatively shallow.

Although relative dating remains important to archaeology, the range of absolute dating techniques available to archaeologists has grown tremendously since A.E. Douglass pioneered dendrochronology (or tree-ring dating) in the 1920s. The development of radiocarbon dating method by Arnold and Libby in 1949 provided archaeology one of the best ways to figure out "absolute" (calendrical) dates for archaeological remains. Since Arnold and Libby's time, scientists have continued to develop increasingly sophisticated techniques for determining the "absolute" ages of archaeological sites and artifacts. Articles in this section illustrate how the application of these new methods—and also earlier methods—often yields unexpected (sometimes controversial) insights on the past.

We begin with James Shreeve's article entitled, "The Dating Game." Here we learn that thermoluminescence (TL, for short), a geochronological method for dating rocks, proved to be extremely important to archaeologists Allison Brooks and John Yellen in dating a fossilized harpoon point that was found in an early human site in Kenya. Thermoluminescence dating (an "absolute" dating method) is useful for archaeologists who work deposits that are older than 40,000 or 50,000 years. TL dating, if proven reliable, may revolutionize our understanding of the world at 60,000 years before the present. Brooks and Yellen wonder whether finds from their African site predate the celebrated human achievements of the European Paleolithic by some 40,000 years. Such a finding would suggest that modern humans evolved in Africa and then radiated north into the Middle East, Europe, and Asia. The use of TL dating has also muddied debates regarding the evolutionary relationship between Neanderthals and modern humans, since TL dates suggest that modern humans may coexisted with Neanderthals for at least 90,000 years. Can we trust this new dating technique, or might TL go the way of amino acid racemization? That technique proved so problematic in the 1970s that it has required substantial refinement to be useful today. In Brooks' and Yellen's African case study, they plan to employ an additional dating method called electron spin resonance (ESR) to test their provocative hypothesis regarding modern human origins.

Dates matter to archaeologists, and they are always experimenting with new approaches to assign ages to ancient sites, and we rely on our geology colleagues for help in this endeavor. "A Modern Riddle of the Sphinx," by Robert M. Schoch (a geology professor at Boston University) illustrates a somewhat different approach to relative dating. This geological approach to dating involved analyses of the stratigraphy, weathering, and erosion of rocks that ancient Egyptians used to build the Great Sphinx near the Pyramid of Giza. A lively debate followed from Schoch's controversial conclusion that ancient Egyptians might have constructed the Sphinx 2500 years earlier than most scholars previously believed. Schoch's careful description of his field methods illustrate how a geologist interprets this important archaeological treasure, and he makes it clear that his hypothesis requires additional testing. Whatever the outcome of debates concerning the age of the Great Sphinx, Shoch's study is a clear demonstration of how scientific hypotheses are formulated and evaluated by geologists and archaeologists.

Egypt is not the only hot spot for surprisingly early relative and absolute dates. In "The Earliest Art Becomes Older—and More Common," Virginia Morell describes how the application of thermoluminescence (TL) and optical dating to two rock shelters in northern Australia produced dates of 55,000 - 60,000 years. These dates suggest the possibility that humans entered Australia as early as 60,000 years ago, and the possibility that these early Australians created the rock art that was also found at these sites. In the world of Australian archaeology, such findings are highly controversial: these TL dates are approximately 30,000 years older than the radiocarbon dates previously produced for Australian sites. Such

dates, if proven, would be equally significant in the world of human origins research, since they are older than the earliest dates for modern humans in Europe.
These dates challenge the claim that modern humans evolved in Africa, moved
northward through the Middle East and Europe, and then onward to Asia and
the Pacific.

1

The Dating Game

James Shreeve

Four years ago archeologists Alison Brooks and John Yellen discovered what might be the earliest traces of modern human culture in the world. The only trouble is, nobody believes them. Sometimes they can't quite believe it themselves.

Their discovery came on a sun-soaked hillside called Katanda, in a remote corner of Zaire near the Ugandan border. Thirty yards below, the Semliki River runs so clear and cool the submerged hippos look like giant lumps of jade. But in the excavation itself, the heat is enough to make anyone doubt his eyes.

Katanda is a long way from the plains of Ice Age Europe, which archeologists have long believed to be the setting for the first appearance of truly modern culture: the flourish of new tool technologies, art, and body ornamentation known as the Upper Paleolithic, which began about 40,000 years ago. For several years Brooks, an archeologist at George Washington University, had been pursuing the heretical hypothesis that humans in Africa had invented sophisticated technologies even earlier, while their European counterparts were still getting by with the same sorts of tools they'd been using for hundreds of thousands of years. If conclusive evidence hadn't turned up, it was only because nobody had really bothered to look for it.

"In France alone there must be three hundred well-excavated sites dating from the period we call the Middle Paleolithic," Brooks says. "In Africa there are barely two dozen on the whole continent."

One of those two dozen is Katanda. On an afternoon in 1988 John Yellen—archeology program director at the National Science Foundation and Brooks's husband—was digging in a densely packed litter of giant catfish bones, river stones, and Middle Paleolithic stone tools. From the rubble he extricated a beautifully crafted, fossilized bone harpoon point. Eventually two more whole points and fragments of five others turned up, all of them elaborately barbed and polished. A few feet away, the scientists uncovered pieces of an equally well crafted daggerlike tool. In design and workmanship the harpoons were not unlike those at the very end of the Upper Paleolithic, some 14,000 years ago. But there was one important difference. Brooks and Yellen believe the deposits John was standing in were at least five times that old. To put this in perspective, imagine discovering a prototypical Pontiac in Leonardo da Vinci's attic.

"If the site is as old as we think it is," says Brooks, "it could clinch the argument that modern humans evolved in Africa."

Ever since the discovery the couple have devoted themselves to chopping away at that stubborn little word *if*. In the face of the entrenched skepticism of their colleagues, it is an uphill task. But they do have some leverage. In those same four years since the first harpoon was found at Katanda, a breakthrough has revived

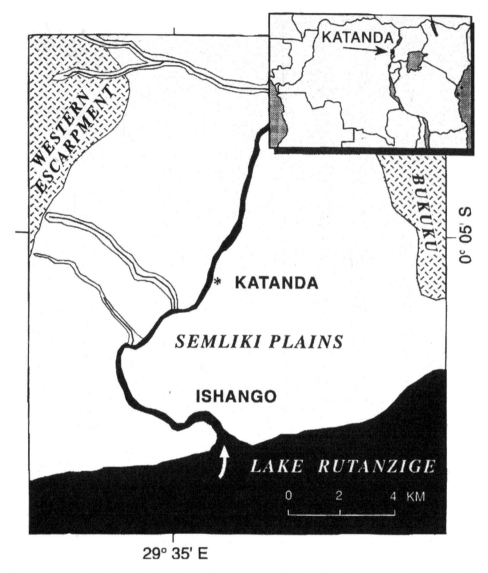

Figure 1. Map showing the location of Middle Paleolithic archaeological site of Katanda in Zaire, Africa. (Graphic courtesy of Alison Brooks)

the question of modern human origins. The breakthrough is not some new skeleton pulled out of the ground. Nor is it the highly publicized Eve hypothesis, put forth by geneticists, suggesting that all humans on Earth today share a common female ancestor who lived in Africa 200,000 years ago. The real advance, abiding quietly in the shadows while Eve draws the limelight, is simply a new way of telling time.

To be precise, it is a whole smorgasbord of new ways of telling time. Lately they have all converged on the same exhilarating, mortifying revelation: what little we thought we knew about the origins of our own species was hopelessly wrong. From Africa to the Middle East to Australia, the new dating methods are overturning conventional wisdom with insolent abandon, leaving the anthropological community dazed amid a rubble of collapsed certitudes. It is in this shell-shocked climate that Alison Brooks's Pontiac in Leonardo's attic might actually find a hearing.

"Ten years ago I would have said it was impossible for harpoons like these to be so old," says archeologist Michael Mehlman of the Smithsonian's National Museum of Natural History. "Now I'm reserving judgment. Anything can happen."

An archeologist with a freshly uncovered skull, stone tool, or bone Pontiac in hand can take two general approaches to determine its age. The first is called relative dating. Essentially the archeologist places the find in the context of the surrounding geological deposits. If the new discovery is found in a brown sediment lying beneath a yellowish layer of sand, then, all things being equal, it is older than the yellow sand layer or any other deposit higher up. The fossilized remains of extinct animals found near the object also provide a "biostratigraphic" record that can offer clues to a new find's relative age. (If a stone tool is found alongside an extinct species of horse, then it's a fair bet the tool was made while that kind of horse was still running around.) Sometimes the tools themselves can be used as a guide, if they match up in character and style with tools from other, better-known sites. Relative dating methods like these can tell you whether a find is older or younger than something else, but they cannot pin an age on the object in calendar years.

The most celebrated *absolute* method of telling archeological time, radiocarbon dating, came along in the 1940s. Plants take in carbon from the atmosphere to build tissues, and other organisms take in plants, so carbon ends up in everything from wood to woodchucks. Most carbon exists in the stable form of carbon 12. But some is made up of the unstable, radioactive form carbon 14. When an organism dies, it contains about the same ratio of carbon 12 to carbon 14 that exists in the atmosphere. After death the radioactive carbon 14 atoms begin to decay, changing into stable atoms of nitrogen. The amount of carbon 12, however, stays the same. Scientists can look at the amount of carbon 12 and—based on the ratio—deduce how much carbon 14 was originally present. Since the decay rate of carbon 14 is constant and steady (half of it disappears every 5,730 years), the difference between the amount of carbon 14 originally in a charred bit of wood or bone and the amount present now can be used as a clock to determine the age of the object.

Conventional radiocarbon dates are extremely accurate up to about 40,000 years. This is far and away the best method to date a find—as long as it is younger than this cutoff point. (In older materials, the amount of carbon 14 still left undecayed is so small that even the slightest amount of contamination in the experimental process leads to highly inaccurate results.) Another dating technique, relying on the decay of radioactive potassium rather than carbon, is available to date volcanic deposits *older* than half a million years. When it was discovered in the late 1950s, radiopotassium dating threw open a window on the emergence of the first members of the human family—the australopithecines, like the famous Lucy, and her more advanced descendants, *Homo habilis* and *Homo erectus*. Until now, however, the period between half a million and 40,000 years—a stretch of time that just happens to embrace the origin of *Homo sapiens*—was practically unknowable by absolute dating techniques. It was as if a geochronological curtain were drawn across the mystery of our species' birth. Behind that curtain the hominid lineage underwent an astonishing metamorphosis, entering the dateless, dark centuries a somewhat precocious bipedal ape and emerging into the range of radiocarbon dating as the culturally resplendent, silver-tongued piece of work we call a modern human being.

Fifteen years ago there was some general agreement about how this change took place. First, what is thought of as an *anatomically* modern human being—with the rounded cranium, vertical forehead, and lightly built skeleton of people today—made its presence known in Europe about 35,000 years ago. Second, along with those first modern-looking people, popularly known as the Cro-Magnons, came the first signs of complex human *behavior*, including tools made of bone and antler as well as of stone, and art, symbolism, social status, ethnic identity, and probably true human language too. Finally, in any one region there was no overlap in time between the appearance of modern humans and the disappearance of "archaic" humans such as the classic Neanderthals, supporting the idea that one group had evolved from the other.

"Thanks to the efforts of the new dating methods," says Fred Smith, an anthropologist at Northern Illinois University, "we now know that each of these ideas was wrong."

The technique doing the most damage to conventional wisdom is called thermoluminescence, TL for short. (Reader take heed: the terrain of geochronology is full of terms long enough to tie between two trees and trip over, so acronyms are a must.) Unlike radiocarbon dating, which works on organic matter, TL pulls time out of stone.

If you were to pick an ordinary rock up off the ground and try to describe its essential rockness, phrases like "frenetically animated" would probably not leap to mind. But in fact minerals are in a state of constant inner turmoil. Minute amounts of radioactive elements, both within the rock itself and in the surrounding soil and atmosphere, are constantly bombarding its atoms, knocking electrons out of their normal orbits. All this is perfectly normal rock behavior, and after gallivanting around for a hundredth of a second or two, most electrons dutifully return to their normal positions. A few, however, became trapped en route—physically captured within crystal impurities or electronic aberrations in the mineral structure itself. These tiny prisons hold on to their electrons until the mineral is heated, whereupon the traps spring open and the electrons return to their more stable position. As they escape, they release energy in the form of light—a photon for every homeward-bound electron.

Thermoluminescence was observed way back in 1663 by the great English physicist Robert Boyle. One night Boyle took a borrowed diamond to bed with him, for reasons that remain obscure. Resting the diamond "upon a warm part of my Naked Body," Boyle noticed that it soon emitted a warm glow. So taken was he with the responsive gem that the next day he delivered a paper on the subject at the Royal Society, noting his surprise at the glow since his "constitution," he felt, was "not of the hottest."

Three hundred years later another Englishman, Martin Aitken of Oxford University, developed the methods to turn thermoluminescence into a geophysical timepiece. The clock works because the radioactivity bombarding a mineral is fairly constant, so electrons become trapped in those crystalline prisons at a steady rate through time. If you crush the mineral you want to date and heat a few grains to a high enough temperature—about 900 degrees, which is more body heat than Robert Boyle's constitution could ever have produced—all the electron traps will release their captive electrons at once, creating a brilliant puff

Figure 2. Archaeologists recording finds during fieldwork at Katanda. (Photo courtesy of Alison Brooks)

of light. In a laboratory the intensity of that burst of luminescence can easily be measured with a device called a photomultiplier. The higher the spike of light, the more trapped electrons have accumulated in the sample, and thus the more time has elapsed since it was last exposed to heat. Once a mineral is heated and all the electrons have returned "home," the clock is set back to zero.

Now, our lineage has been making flint tools for hundreds of thousands of years, and somewhere in that long stretch of prehistory we began to use fire as well. Inevitably, some of our less careful ancestors kicked discarded tools into burning hearths, setting their electron clocks back to zero and opening up a ripe opportunity for TL timekeepers in the present. After the fire went out, those flints lay in the ground, pummeled by radioactivity, and each trapped electron was another tick of the clock. Released by laboratory heat, the electrons flash out photons that reveal time gone by.

In the late 1980s Hélène Valladas, an archeologist at the Center for Low-Level Radioactivity of the French Atomic Energy Commission near Paris, along with her father, physicist Georges Valladas, stunned the anthropological community with some TL dates on burned flints taken from two archeological sites in Israel. The first was a cave called Kebara, which had already yielded an astonishingly complete Neanderthal skeleton. Valladas dated flints from the Neanderthal's level at 60,000 years before the present.

In itself this was no surprise, since the date falls well within the known range of the Neanderthals' time on Earth. The shock came a year later, when she used the same technique to pin a date on flints from a nearby cave called Qafzeh, which contained the buried remains of early modern human beings. This time, the spikes of luminescence translated into an age of around 92,000 years. In other words, the more "advanced" human types were a full 30,000 years *older* than the Neanderthals they were supposed to have descended from.

If Valadas's TL dates are accurate, they completely confound the nation that modern humans evolved from Neanderthals in any neat and tidy way. Instead, these two kinds of human, equally endowed culturally but distinctly different in appearance, might have shared the same little nook of the Middle East for tens of thousands of years. To some, this simply does not make sense.

"If these dates are correct, what does this do to what else we know, to the stratigraphy, to fossil man, to the archeology?" worries Anthony Marks, an archeologist at Southern Methodist University. "It's all a mess. Not that the dates are necessarily wrong. But you want to know more about them."

Marks's skepticism is not entirely unfounded. While simple in theory, in practice TL has to overcome some devilish complications. ("If these new techniques were easy, we would have thought of them a long time ago," says geochronologist Gifford Miller of the University of Colorado.) To convert into calendar years the burst of luminescence when a flint is heated, one has to know both the sensitivity of that particular flint to radiation and the dose of radioactive rays it has received each year since it was "zeroed" by fire. The sensitivity of the sample can be determined by assaulting it with artificial radiation in the lab. And the annual dose of radiation received from *within* the sample itself can be calculated fairly easily by measuring how much uranium or other radioactive elements the sample contains. But determining the annual dose from the environment *around* the sample—the radioactivity in the surrounding soil, and cosmic rays from the atmosphere itself—is an iffier proposition. At some sites fluctuations in this environmental dose through the millennia can turn the "absolute" date derived from TL into an absolute nightmare.

Fortunately for Valladas and her colleagues, most of the radiation dose for the Qafzeh flints came from within the flints themselves. The date there of 92,000 years for the modern human skeletons is thus not only the most sensational number so far produced by TL, it is also one of the surest.

"The strong date at Qafzeh was just good luck," says Valladas. "It was just by chance that the internal dose was high and the environmental dose was low."

More recently Valladas and her colleague Norbert Mercier turned their TL techniques to the French site of Saint-Césaire. Last summer they confirmed that a Neanderthal found at Saint-Césaire was only 36,000 years old. This new date, combined with a fresh radiocarbon date of about 40,000 years tagged on some Cro-Magnon sites in northern Spain, strongly suggests that the two types of humans shared the same corner of Europe for several thousand years as the glaciers advanced from the north.

While Valladas has been busy in Europe and the Middle East, other TL timekeepers have produced some astonishing new dates for the first human occupation of Australia. As recently as the 1950s, it was widely believed that Australia had been colonized only some five thousand years ago. The reasoning was typically Eurocentric: since the Australian aborigines were still using stone tools when the first white settlers arrived, they must have just recently developed the capacity to make the difficult sea crossing from Indonesia in the first place. A decade later archeologists grudgingly conceded that the date of first entry might have been closer to the beginning of the Holocene period, 10,000 years ago. In the 1970s radiocarbon dates on human occupation sites pushed the date back again, as far as 32,000 years ago. And now TL studies at two sites in northern Australia drop that first human footstep on the continent—and the sea voyage that preceded it—all the way back to 60,000 years before the present. If these dates stand up, then the once-maligned ancestors of modern aborigines were building ocean-worthy craft some 20,000 years *before* the first signs of sophisticated culture appeared in Europe.

"Luminescence has revolutionized the whole period I work in," says Australian National University archeologist Rhys Jones, a member of the team responsible for the new TL dates. "In effect, we have at our disposal a new machine—a new time machine."

With so much at stake, however, nobody looks to TL—or to any of the other new "time machines"—as a geochronological panacea. Reputations have been too badly singed in the past by dating methods that claimed more than they could deliver. In the 1970s a flush of excitement over a technique called amino acid racemization led many workers to believe that another continent—North America—had been occupied by humans fully 70,000 years ago. Further testing at the same American sites proved that the magical new method was off by one complete goose egg. The real age of the sites was closer to 7,000 years.

"To work with wrong dates is a luxury we cannot afford," British archeologist Paul Mellars intoned ominously earlier this year, at the beginning of a London meeting of the Royal Society to showcase the new dating technologies. "A wrong date does not simply inhibit research. It could conceivably throw it into reverse."

Fear of just such a catastrophe—not to mention the risk that her own reputation could go up in a puff of light—is what keeps Alison Brooks from declaring

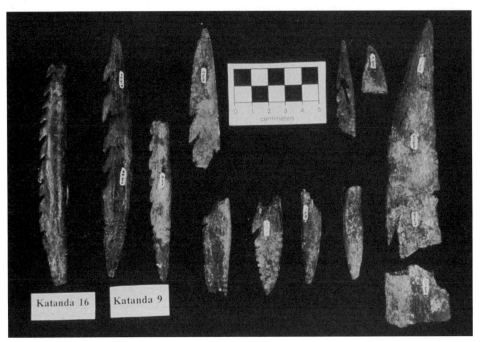

Figure 3. Middle Paleolithic bone tools (including harpoon points) from Katanda. (Photo courtesy of Alison Brooks)

outright that she has found exquisitely crafted bone harpoons in Zaire that are more than 40,000 years older than such creations are supposed to be. So far the main support for her argument has been her redating of another site, called Ishango, four miles down the Semliki River from the Katanda site. In the 1950s the Belgian geologist Jean de Heinzelin excavated a harpoon-rich "aquatic civilization" at Ishango that he thought was 8,000 years old. Brooks's radiocarbon dating of the site in the mid-1980s pushed the age back to 25,000. By tracing the layers of sediment shared between Ishango and Katanda, Brooks and her colleagues are convinced that Katanda is much farther down in the stratigraphy—twice as old as Ishango, or perhaps even more. But even though Brooks and Yellen talk freely about their harpoons at meetings, they have yet to utter such unbelievable numbers in the unforgiving forum of an academic journal.

"It is precisely because no one believes us that we want to make our case airtight before we publish," says Brooks. "We want dates confirming dates confirming dates."

Soon after the harpoons were discovered, the teams went to work with thermoluminescence. Unfortunately, no burned flints have been found at the site. Nevertheless, while TL works best on materials that have been completely zeroed by such extreme heat as a campfire, even a strong dose of sunlight can spring some of the electron traps. Thus even ordinary sediments surrounding an archeological find might harbor a readable clock: bleached out by sunlight when they were on the surface, their TL timers started ticking as soon as they were buried by natural processes. Brooks and Yellen have taken soil samples from Katanda for TL, and so far the results are tantalizing—but that's all.

"At this point we think the site is quite old," says geophysicist Allen Franklin of the University of Maryland, who with his Maryland colleague Bill Hornyak is conducting the work. "But we don't want to put a number on it."

As Franklin explains, the problem with dating sediments with TL is that while some of the electron traps might be quickly bleached out by sunlight, others hold on to their electrons more stubbornly. When the sample is then heated in a conventional TL apparatus, these stubborn traps release electrons that were captured perhaps millions of years before the sediments were last exposed to sunlight-teasing date-hungry archeologists with a deceptively old age for the sample.

Brooks does have other irons in the dating fire. The most promising is called electron spin resonance—or ESR, among friends. Like TL, electron spin resonance fashions a clock out of the steadily accumulating electrons caught in traps. But whereas TL measures that accumulation by the strength of the light given off when the traps open, ESR literally counts the captive electrons themselves while they still rest undisturbed in their prisons.

All electrons "spin" in one of two opposite directions—physicists call them up and down. (Metaphors are a must here because the nature of this "spinning" is quantum mechanical and can be accurately described only in huge mathematical equations.) The spin of each electron creates a tiny magnetic force pointing in one direction, something like a compass needle. Under normal circumstances, the electrons are paired so that their opposing spins and magnetic forces cancel each other out. But trapped electrons are unpaired. By manipulating an external magnetic field placed around the sample to be dated, the captive electrons can be induced to "resonate"—that is, to flip around and spin the other way. When they flip, each electron absorbs a finite amount of energy from a microwave field that is also applied to the sample. This loss of microwave energy can be measured with a detector, and it is a direct count of the number of electrons caught in the traps.

ESR works particularly well on tooth enamel, with an effective range from a thousand to 2 million years. Luckily for Brooks and Yellen, some nice fat hippo teeth have been recovered from Katanda in the layer that also held the harpoons. To date the teeth, they have called in Henry Schwarcz of McMaster University in Ontario, a ubiquitous, veteran geochronologist. In the last ten years Schwarcz has journeyed to some 50 sites throughout Europe, Africa, and western Asia, wherever his precious and arcane services are demanded.

Schwarcz also turned up at the Royal Society meeting, where he explained both the power and the problems of the ESR method. On the plus side is that teeth are hardy remains, found at nearly every archeological site in the world, and that ESR can test a tiny sample again and again—with the luminescence techniques, it's one-shot deal. ESR can also home in on certain kinds of electron traps, offering some refinement over TL, which lumps them all together.

On the minus side, ESR is subject to the same uncertainties as TL concerning the annual soaking of radiation a sample has received from the environment. What's more, even the radiation from *within* a tooth cannot be relied on to be constant through time. Tooth enamel has the annoying habit of sucking up uranium from its surroundings while it sits in the ground. The more uranium the tooth contains, the more electrons are being bombarded out of their normal positions, and the faster the electron traps will fill up. Remember: you cannot know how old something is by counting filled traps unless you know the rate at which the traps were filled, year by year. If the tooth had a small amount of internal uranium for 50,000 years but took in a big gulp of the hot stuff 10,000 years ago, calculations based on the tooth's current high uranium level would indicate the electron traps were filled at a much faster rate than they really were. "The big question is, When did the uranium get there?" Schwarcz says. "Did the tooth slurp it all up in three days, or did the uranium accumulate gradually through time?"

One factor muddying the "big question" is the amount of moisture present around the sample during its centuries of burial: a wetter tooth will absorb uranium faster. For this reason, the best ESR sites are those where conditions are driest. Middle Eastern and African deserts are good bets. As far as modern human origins go, the technique has already tagged a date of about 100,000 years on some human fossils from an Israeli cave called Skhul, neatly supporting the TL date of 92,000 from Qafzeh, a few miles away. If a new ESR date from a Neanderthal cave just around the corner from Skhul is right, then Neanderthals were also in the Middle East at about the same time. Meanwhile, in South Africa, a human jawbone from the site of Border Cave—"so modern it boggles the mind," as one researcher puts it—has now been dated with ESR at 60,000 years, nearly twice as old as any fossil like it in Europe.

But what of the cultural change to modern human behavior—such as the sophisticated technological development expressed by the Katanda harpoons? Schwarcz's dating job at Katanda is not yet finished, and given how much is at stake, he too is understandably reluctant to discuss it. "The site has good potential for ESR," he says guardedly. "Let's put it this way: if the initial results had indicated that the harpoons were not very old after all, we would have said 'So what?' to them and backed off. Well, we haven't backed off."

There are other dating techniques being developed that may, in the future, add more certainty to claims of African modernity. One of them, called uranium-series dating, measures the steady decay of uranium into various daughter elements inside anything formed from carbonates (limestone and cave stalactites, for instance). The principle is very similar to radiocarbon dating—the amount of daughter elements in a stalactite, for example, indicates how long that stalactite has been around—with the advantage that uranium-series dates can stretch back half a million years. Even amino acid racemization, scorned for the last 15 years, is making a comeback, thanks to the discovery that the technique, unreliable when applied to porous bone, is quite accurate when used on hard ostrich eggshells.

In the best of all possible worlds, an archeological site will offer an opportunity for two or more of these dating techniques to be called in so they can be tested against each other. When asked to describe the ideal site, Schwarcz gets a dreamy look on his face. "I see a beautiful human skull sandwiched between two layers of very pure flowstone," he says, imagining uranium-series dating turning those cave limestones into time brackets. "A couple of big, chunky hippo teeth are lying next to it, and a little ways off, a bunch of burned flints."

Even without Schwarcz's dream site, the dating methods used separately are pointing to a common theme: the alarming antiquity of modern human events where they are not supposed to be happening in the first place. Brooks sees suggestive traces of complexity not just at Katanda but scattered all over the African continent, as early as 100,000 years before the present. A classic stone tool type called the blade, long considered a trademark of the European Upper Paleolithic, appears in abundance in some South African sites 40,000 to 50,000 years before the Upper Paleolithic begins. The continent may even harbor the earliest hints of art and a symbolic side to human society: tools designed with stylistic meaning; colorful, incandescent minerals, valueless but for their beauty, found hundreds of miles away from their source. More and more, the Cro-Magnons of Europe are beginning to look like the last modern humans to show themselves and start acting "human" rather than the first.

That's not an easy notion for anthropologists and archeologists to swallow. "It just doesn't fit the pattern that those harpoons of Alison's should be so old," says Richard Klein, a paleoanthropologist at the University of Chicago. Then he shrugs. "Of course, if she's right, she has made a remarkable discovery indeed."

Only time will tell.

2

A Modern Riddle of the Sphinx

Robert M. Schoch

The Great Sphinx looms over the Egyptian desert, keeping silent watch over the tombs of the ancient Pharaohs. A human-headed lion carved from solid limestone, the Sphinx stretches for 240 feet and rises 66 feet above its base on the far-eastern edge of the Giza Plateau, facing the Nile River and the rising sun. For decades, Egyptologists have confidently dated the Sphinx to about 2500 B.C., when the Pharaoh Khafre, also known as Chephren, allegedly commissioned its construction. But new evidence challenges that long-held theory: Examining the great statue from a geological point of view rather than an Egyptological one suggests that much of it was built around 5000 B.C.—thousands of years earlier than previously thought.

Over the years, Egyptologists have held widely diverse opinions about the age of the Sphinx. At various points in their careers, such eminent scholars of the last century as Sir Flinders Petrie, Sir E. A. Wallis Budge, and Sir G. C. Maspero considered the Sphinx older than the pyramids it guards, as did the Egyptians themselves from about 1500 B.C. (the beginning of the period known as the New Kingdom) through Roman times. To this day, the villagers who live near Giza have an oral tradition that the Sphinx, which they call Abul Al-Hol, or "the Father of Terrors," is some 5,000 years older than the nearby Great Pyramid of Khufu, also called Cheops, and the smaller pyramids of Khafre and Menkaure (Mycerinus).

In recent years, the prime proponent of an older Sphinx has been John Anthony West, a writer, tour guide, and "independent Egyptologist" who has no formal degrees, credentials, or academic affiliations in Egyptology. He first came across the idea in the works of the late Orientalist, philosopher, and controversial Egyptologist R. A. Schwaller de Lubicz. Buried deep in one of his texts, Schwaller mentioned that the Sphinx showed geological weathering features that indicated it could be much older than most modern Egyptologists believed. But West has no training in geology and so could not convincingly pursue the subject on his own.

I first met West through a rhetoric professor at Boston University, where I am a science professor specializing in geology; I hold bachelor's, master's, and doctoral degrees in geology. The professor, Robert Eddy, had known West for many years and was well aware of West's ideas about the Sphinx's age. West asked Eddy to find an "open-minded" geologist to help explore his theory, and Eddy designated me as a potential candidate.

When I encountered West in the fall of 1989, I found his ideas concerning the Sphinx's age a bit outlandish, but interesting. At that time, West thought the Sphinx might have been built before the Sahara became a desert—the Giza

Figure 1. The Great Sphinx. Note the weathered and eroded areas below the head.

Plateau sits on the eastern edge of the Sahara, just west of Cairo—dating back to at least 10,000 B.C. He based this hypothesis on the severe weathering and erosion evident on the Sphinx's body but not on other nearby manmade structures.

West mumbled something about getting me over to Egypt to evaluate the evidence firsthand, but I figured he wouldn't fly me over there just to point out what was surely a simple error on his part. By June of 1990, though, West and I were indeed in Egypt, walking around the Giza Plateau. While I couldn't render a judgment after a week of simple observation, I became convinced that either the rocks were behaving in very strange ways or West was actually onto something.

The most persuasive piece of evidence for an older Sphinx that I found on that first trip involves the two-stage construction of the temples in front of the Sphinx. Rather than resting majestically on the top of the rocky plateau, as most people envision it, the Sphinx actually sits in a hollow—known as the Sphinx enclosure—formed when the ancient Egyptians carved away the limestone rock to shape its body. Large blocks of this limestone were used to construct two temples, and the Egyptians later covered the limestone with granite facing stones called ashlars. My field observations led me to conclude that the limestone was exposed to the elements and underwent considerable weathering and erosion before the granite was laid over it. In places, the workers cut the backs of the ashlars in an undulating pattern to complement the irregular surface—characteristic of weathering—of the limestone blocks from the Sphinx enclosure. Also, where the granite has fallen away, it's evident that the limestone beneath was not cut smoothly. Rather it shows a higgledy-piggledy surface pattern where apparently the ancient Egyptians, before resurfacing it with granite, attempted to cut back and even out the weathered surface, but didn't take off enough to make the wall perfectly smooth.

Egyptologists generally attribute the granite ashlars on the temples to Khafre: Carved into them are Old Kingdom inscriptions dating back to about 2500 B.C. It seems reasonable to assume that the limestone blocks would have been freshly cut—that is, their surfaces would have been unweathered—when initially used to construct the temples. But if the granite facing covers deeply weathered limestone, then the temples' core structures—which came from the Sphinx ditch—must predate the granite facing by a considerable degree. Since the granite ashlars date to Khafre's reign, the temples must have been erected earlier, meaning the Great Sphinx must also have been built prior to the reign of Khafre.

On my first trip to Egypt, I could only play tourist. I didn't have official permission to carry out scientific research on the Giza Plateau, and I couldn't enter the Sphinx enclosure. Upon my return to the United States, I spent several months drafting a lengthy proposal to the Egyptian Antiquities Organization (EAO), which oversees all research on the Sphinx and other monuments. I requested permission to carry out detailed, noninvasive geological studies of the rocks comprising the Sphinx and its adjacent structures, specifically looking at the stratigraphy (rock layers), weathering, erosion, and geomorphology (land forms). My studies didn't require collecting any samples, or breaking or disturbing any rocks.

In addition, I needed to examine the structure and weathering features beneath the rocks' surface and to find out what lay under piles of sand. But how could I see through 50 or more feet of sand? How could I probe nondestructively through rock to see how deeply it has weathered or whether it contains cavities, voids, or chambers? West and I ultimately decided to ask permission to pursue limited seismic investigations near the Sphinx, which the EAO granted along with the rest of our proposal.

West and I carried out the seismic work as well as other research when we returned to Egypt in April 1991. We were accompanied by Thomas L. Dobecki, a geophysicist with the Houston firm of McBride-Ratcliff, who had signed on to supervise the technical aspects of gathering and analyzing the geophysical data. The seismic research required hitting a steel plate with a sledgehammer to generate energy waves (essentially sound waves) that traveled below the surface of the rock and sand, reflecting off of whatever was underneath. Electronic geophones—microphones, more or less—picked up the resulting vibrations at the surface. The geophones fed their data into a sophisticated portable seismograph, which stored it on computer disks. From the seismic data, we reconstructed cross sections of the area beneath the rock and sand, creating pictures of what lay hidden underneath our feet without disturbing more than a few pebbles.

After collecting our data, we discussed our work with colleagues at Cairo University and returned to the United States to analyze the data. I returned to Egypt in June 1991 to collect more data and further check the information I'd already gathered.

Based on the data, I've concluded that the Sphinx was built in stages. The Egyptians carved the core of the Sphinx—the front and sides—first, in at least 5000 B.C. and perhaps earlier. Later, possibly in Khafre's time, workers chiseled out the rear of the Sphinx and recarved the head. No one knows what the original head looked like; many observers consider the current head too small for the body, and it shows signs of more recent cut marks than does the body. Furthermore, it has long been suggested that the face of the Sphinx portrays Khafre, but this assumption has recently been questioned: After detailed analysis, Frank Domingo, a senior forensic officer of the New York City Police Department, concluded that the face of the Great Sphinx does not match the face seen on statues of Khafre. Most Egyptologists agree that since Khafre's time, the Sphinx has been restored and refurbished many times, as evidenced by the layers of stone veneer covering much of the Sphinx's body and paws.

Geologists can date land forms by analyzing their weathering and erosion patterns. In examining the rocks of the Giza Plateau, including those incorporated into the Sphinx and nearby structures, I observed several distinct modes of weathering in identical rocks from the same formation of limestone. The Sphinx's body and the walls of the Sphinx enclosure exhibit mostly precipitation-induced weathering, giving a rolling, undulating, very deeply weathered profile to the vertical rock surface (Figure 1). By contrast, structures unambiguously attributed to early and middle Old Kingdom times (2600 B.C.-2300 B.C.), the same time the Sphinx was supposedly built, display primarily wind-induced weathering and fairly little precipitation-induced erosion. Weathering produced by the effects of the wind looks much different from that caused by precipitation: On these structures, much of the original surface remains intact, often with hieroglyphic inscriptions still legible, but in places, the rock is softer and has consequently been worn away by wind and sand abrasion, creating gaps in the vertical rock surface.

The precipitation-induced weathering evident on the Sphinx—clearly preserved under the oldest repairs to the statue's core, which date back to at least 1400 B.C.—harks back to an earlier, moister period of time preceding the current arid regime that has held sway on the Giza Plateau since middle and late Old Kingdom times. Both historical and geological data indicate that the area underwent a moist period, with sporadic heavy rains, between 5000 B.C. and 3000 B.C. Since then, the Giza area has simply not experienced the precipitation necessary to produce the erosional features found on the Sphinx's core body. For corroborative evidence, one need look no farther than the Saqqara Plateau, about ten miles from the Giza Plateau, where fragile mastabas, or tombs, built around 2800 B.C. of sun-dried mudbricks show no evidence of the precipitation-induced weathering seen on the Sphinx. Therefore, the Sphinx must predate these structures—by a considerable degree, given the depth of weathering seen in the Sphinx enclosure.

A few geologists have previously noticed the anomalous and very ancient weathering on the Sphinx's core body, but none seem to have drawn the conclusion that the Sphinx must be older than its traditional attribution of 2500 B.C. In fact, the well-known geologist Farouk El-Baz has suggested that the Great Sphinx is nothing more than a yardang—a natural erosional land form, essentially a wind-shaped hill—that the Old Kingdom Egyptians merely "dressed up" to look like a Sphinx. But El-Baz's yardang hypothesis is untenable, because in order to carve the Sphinx's body, the ancient Egyptians had to dig a ditch around it—the Sphinx enclosure, which is clearly artificial and manmade. Moreover, substantial evidence indicates that the Egyptians used the blocks removed from the Sphinx ditch to build the temples in front of the monument.

Seismic investigations conducted on the floor of the Sphinx enclosure suggest that on the north, south, and east sides (the Sphinx faces due east), the rock has undergone considerable weathering; from the surface to a depth of between six and eight feet, atmospheric moisture has made the rock more porous and caused some mineralogical changes. Along the back or west end, the identical limestone has weathered to a depth of only about four feet—compatible with a date of about 2500 B.C. If the Egyptians had carved the entire body of the Sphinx out of natural bedrock at one time, the limestone surrounding it should show the same depth of subsurface weathering everywhere. The data we collected indicates that initially only the sides and front of the Sphinx were carved free of the rock, while what would later become the back or rump originally merged with the natural rock. If the back end dates back to about 2500 B.C. and the other three sides exhibit about 50-percent to 100-percent more weathering, then they are probably at least that much older than 2500 B.C., dating the Sphinx's core body to about 5000 B.C. The seismic data is corroborated by the precipitation-induced weathering patterns evident on the Sphinx's body and the Sphinx enclosure.

In October, I presented my Sphinx work at the Annual Meeting of the Geological Society of America in San Diego. Geologists tend to be an honest lot, and I knew that someone would surely point out any major misinterpretation of the data. Much to my relief, no one found any errors in my work. In fact, many colleagues, intrigued by the research, suggested that I call on them if they could be of assistance.

My research on the Sphinx continues. Dobecki and I hope to gather more subsurface geological and geophysical data, and I plan to continue my stratigraphic, weathering, and geomorphologic studies in the Giza Plateau area. If the EAO permits, I'd like to collect a few very small samples of rocks from the plateau for certain mineralogical studies that could shed more light on weathering rates and regimes. More importantly, I'd like to pursue isotopic studies of such rocks that might accurately date the initial carving of the Sphinx. This procedure measures the concentration of isotopes produced *in situ* on the rock surface by the bombardment of cosmic rays—high-energy particles from outer space, like protons and neutrons, that constantly bombard the atmosphere. As these particles collide and interact with atoms on a rock surface, they produce numerous new isotopes, and in some cases, the accumulation of these isotopes reveals when a rock surface was initially exposed or, in this case, carved.

Finally, I hope to search Egypt for the remains of other major structures built back in 5000 B.C. by the same enterprising Egyptians who constructed the marvelous, enduring Sphinx. I predict that we will find them buried under the notorious Egyptian sands and Nile silts. The concept of an older Sphinx could herald the beginning of an exciting new era in the study of ancient Egypt.

3

The Earliest Art Becomes Older—and More Common

Virginia Morell

Rare and recent. When archaeologists discuss the earliest cave paintings and other symbols made by modern humans, those two terms are usually applied. In the consensus view, the spectacular red or black mammoths, horses, and geometric figures occasionally found on cave walls, which are among the first signs of fully modern human behavior—the ability to manipulate symbols—are at most 40,000 years old.

But these twin notions were severely undermined 2 weeks ago at a conference called "Upper Paleolithic Image and Symbol" at the California Academy of Sciences in San Francisco. Much of the undermining data came from the land down under: Australia. Researchers presented new results that may push the first signs of human artistic behavior—and Australia's first colonization—back an extra 20,000 years. Other scientists demonstrated that art may have been all around, both in Australia and Europe, and apparently was a part of everyday life for our ancestors rather than just a mysterious underground event.

Toss Another Paint Brush on the Barbie

Australians have long been viewed by archaeologists as Johnny-come-latelies to the human settlement scene. Based on genetics and the fossil record, many scientists believe modern humans evolved in Africa 100,000 to 140,000 years ago, arrived in Europe around 50,000 years ago, and found their way to Australia 10,000 years later. And it wasn't until 30,000 years ago, according to this consensus view, that early Australians began decorating rock shelters and cliff faces with elaborate paintings of animals and geometric shapes.

But Rhys Jones, an archaeologist from the Australian National University in Canberra, told the San Francisco gathering that he has concluded that human beings arrived in Australia at least 60,000 years ago. And, he suggested, they were already painting when they landed.

Jones drew on recently published data from two northern Australian sites, rock shelters known as Nauwalabila I and Malakunanja II. Both sites were excavated in the 1970s and early 1980s, but because their lowest occupation levels—3 meters down—lacked charcoal for radiocarbon dating, their age remained unknown. But in the last 15 years, geochronologists have developed and refined two dating techniques that don't require carbon samples and are not subject to the 40,000-year limit that applies to radiocarbon dating.

The methods, thermoluminescence (TL) and optical dating, rely on a type of quartz timing unused by even the finest Swiss watchmakers. In essence, the methods date sediments containing grains of quartz by counting electrons trapped by quantum mechanical or physical defects in the mineral. The electrons are bumped into these traps at a regular rate, providing the basis for a clock. They can be released by energy absorbed from sunlight, which sets the quartz timing to zero; if the grains are then buried safely in sediments, the clock starts ticking. Millennia later, by heating the quartz in a lab or flashing it with light, geochronologists can release the electrons. Before returning to their natural places within the material, the freed particles release energy in the form of photons, producing a brief glow whose intensity is in direct proportion to the number of released electrons. Measuring this light thus reveals the ticks of the clock, and the techniques can date deposits exposed to sunlight from 1000 to several hundred thousand years ago.

TL frees the electrons by heating them, and Jones's team first used the method in 1990, on deposits at Malakunanja II. He obtained an age of 55,000 to 60,000 years for the lowest level. That level contained flaked stone tools that resemble artifacts that have been dated to about the same period in Africa. But the fact that the Australian site was "20,000 years earlier than any modern human site in Europe...really caused people to raise their eyebrows," says Jones. Because the date was also more than 20,000 years older than any human site in Australia, many researchers just didn't believe Jones's dates.

In an effort to support his 60,000-year-old date, Jones's team decided to try optical dating. Unlike TL, optical dating uses light to eject the electrons from their traps. When Jones and his colleagues used optical dating on the lowest stratum at Nauwalabila I, the resulting dates of 53,000 to 60,000 years old seemed to confirm his earlier findings. Moreover, Jones found worn and faceted chunks of hematite—a mineral containing iron that many early human people ground into fine, red powder and used for painting—in the lowest artifact levels at both sites. He contends that the early Australians were probably painting rock walls even at that early date.

It's a striking idea, although claims of early artistry may be a bit premature, says Richard Klein, a Stanford University anthropologist. "Similar hematite fragments have been found in many Neanderthal sites and sites of comparable age in Africa without evidence for art," he says. But the issue of art aside, Klein notes that "if people were in Australia 60,000 years ago, then they must have been capable of fully modern behaviors," as they would have had to sail 80 to 100 kilometers across the open ocean to reach the continent—a complex task in any age.

But that notion creates a lot of theoretical headaches for anthropologists. Beyond changing the Australians' arrival time, Klein says, it upsets the "Out of Africa" paradigm for the emergence of fully modern humans. Sailors and painters on the Pacific Rim tens of thousands of years before they appeared in Europe give credence to the idea that modern people developed independently in different regions. And this unsettling development comes just when genetic tracking of population movements appears to firmly support the African origins of moderns (*Science*, 3 March, p. 1272).

For that reason, Klein, along with several geochronologists, wants additional sites dated. "I can't find any good reason to dispute these dates," says James

Bischoff, a geochronologist with the U.S. Geological Survey in Menlo Park, California. "But because of the importance of the issue I would like to see additional samples dated." If the dates hold up, says Klein, "it will force an enormous amount of rethinking."

Seeing the Invisible

The time when humans became artists isn't the only thing that will have to be rethought if other presentations at the meeting hold up. Alan Watchman, a geologist who heads Data-Roche Watchman, an independent consulting company on rock art in Quebec, Canada, thinks that rock art was also far more abundant than most other scholars have believed. Carefully prying small flakes off the surface of apparently bare walls of rock shelters in Australia, Watchman thinks he has found signs of paintings that may be 20,000 to 30,000 years old—but the paintings are invisible to the naked eye. "Most of the paintings on the surface are only a few thousand years old," says Watchman, but older signs of symbolic behavior lie hidden beneath hard crusty layers of gypsum and salts.

Watchman discovered the first clues to these older paintings when he pried flakes off a large, apparently blank boulder at one painted rock shelter site, Walkunder Arch. "Everyone has to pass by this boulder to reach the rock shelter," he says, "and I always thought it was curious that it was not painted, since it has a perfect surface and is in the right spot." And, in fact, Watchman discovered telltale yellow and reddish-brown layers in flakes from the rock, layers that have the hue and consistency of powdered ocher: "I can't prove it yet, but I suspect that there is a painting on that boulder that we just can't see." Layers of gypsum and salts have grown over it in the intervening years, he says.

Since that initial discovery, Watchman has sampled apparently blank walls at other rockshelters. He pries off 4-mm-thick flakes of crust and seals them with epoxy. After slicing the crust into thin vertical sections with a diamond saw, he polishes the surface, revealing stratified layers of rocks and minerals. Often sandwiched between two of these layers is a band of hematite or charcoal—the same materials Australian aborigines used for their painting. Watchman reports that preliminary radiocarbon dating on some of these samples has resulted in dates of "20,000 to 30,000, and older."

While Watchman's research intrigued the gathering, several scientists cautioned that traces of paint do not by themselves mean there are paintings beneath the crusty surfaces. "It may only mean that someone wiped his or her hand on a wall after rubbing their body with ocher," said David Lewis-Williams, an anthropologist from the University of Witwatersrand. "And there's a great difference between that and making a symbol." Watchman hopes to resolve this issue by examining a wider area of a wall, searching for patterns—figures, perhaps—via a geophysical, x-ray-like scan that might reveal the hidden shapes beneath the masking crust.

Such prospecting for invisible art may help archaeologists find symbolic works on other continents, where scientists have long suspected that there was more art than met archaeologists' eyes. "I've always thought that people were producing more art than what we saw in the caves," says Paul Bahn, a free-lance archaeologist in England and an expert on Ice Age art. Bahn and others suspect paintings or engravings on rocks in open air sites, rather than in caves, were common in Europe during the Upper Paleolithic (which lasted from 40,000 to 11,000 years ago), but have been obscured by erosion and sediment deposition. Randall White, an archaeologist at New York University, is co-excavating a rock shelter in France, Abri Castenet, that has "tantalizing fragments of black lines or smudges." Watchman's technique might bring them to light again.

At the meeting, Bahn provided more support for the notion of abundant open-air art when he described an extensive outdoor site of more than 150 rock engravings in Portugal. The site, discovered last October along the Coa River in northern Portugal, bears images of aurochs, horses, ibexes, and deer chiseled into rock walls beside the river up to 20,000 years ago. It is only the sixth such site known, and the largest, with animal images extending some 13 kilometers along the river.

Inside caves, paintings have a "mysterious air," says Bahn, so that they've been interpreted as being highly symbolic or religious and tied in to secret initiation rites. "But these outdoor sites are inherently less mysterious," he says, and imply that art was far more common and far better integrated into daily life than the cave painting alone would suggest. "It suggests that the 'sacred' was far less separate from their lives than the caves would have led us to believe," says Bahn.

Commentary

Human societies throughout the world use systems for measuring time, and some calendrical systems, like those of the Maya and the ancient Chinese, are at least as complex as the calendar in current use today. Measuring time and using dating techniques are indispensable to archaeologists. Without chronological information, we cannot do our research. We commonly distinguish between relative and absolute (or chronometric) dating techniques. Relative dating techniques, derived largely from stratigraphic interpretations by geologists, are a regular component of archaeological research. Patterns of stratigraphy, associations with particular faunal assemblages, and stratigraphically-based seriations provide three reliable means of assigning ages to some types of archaeological deposits. Absolute dates may involve the use of coins or inscriptions, histories or geochronology. Although archaeologists have relied on dating techniques since the early 19th century, we have seen a flurry of new techniques develop since the end of World War II that are often exciting and occasionally controversial.

Relative dating often lacks the precision and accuracy of absolute dating, but relative chronologies rarely undergo substantial revision once they have been established. Relative dating techniques, then, are basically reliable but coarse-grained. On the other hand, the world of absolute dates is unpredictable, changing, and full of discord. Two articles in this section have illustrated this situation in human origins research with respect to thermoluminescence (TL) dating. If the TL dates from Zaire are accepted, then scientists will be forced to consider whether fully modern humans originated first in Africa and then departed for the corners of the world. Should the TL dates be accepted from Australia, then archaeologists must figure out how modern humans reached this corner of the Pacific so long ago while bypassing Europe. And the riddle of the Sphinx clearly has not been solved.

The acrimony involved in debates over dating might surprise the non-archaeologist. Individual dates are subjected to scrutiny and occasionally rerun, and site excavation reports are studied in meticulous detail to understand the depositional context of samples. Why all this fuss over a handful of dates? Because that handful of dates provides the building blocks with which we construct models for key transitions in prehistory: the earliest modern humans, the origins of fire, the origins of agriculture, the beginning of metallurgy, and the birth of civilizations. It is true that archaeologists today concern themselves more with the processes by which humans adapted to these innovations than with the precise timing of each development. Yet often, new techniques produce still older dates than we imagined for some of these transitions. Archaeologists—just like the public—retain a powerful fascination for the "earliest" finds in our past.

Part Six

New Techniques in Archaeology

Introduction

Archaeologists have an intimate relationship with technology. On the one hand, ancient technology fascinates us and we devote enormous effort to studying it, replicating it, and describing the organizational systems in which such technologies were used. On the other, we are dependent upon modern technologies to conduct our research. We live in a rapidly changing world and new technological advances are continually modifying how we do archaeology. Highly specialized techniques are being applied to archaeology with such dizzying speed that archaeologists rely increasingly on the skills and expertise of scientists from ancillary disciplines, like chemistry, geophysics, and even medicine. Elaborate computer visualization programs and DNA analyses and blood hemoglobin tests provide exciting views of the past that most archaeologists never dreamed would be possible. While we are achieving stunning results with some new techniques, others are quite controversial and require further development and experimentation to assess their reliability.

New technologies have allowed archaeologists to study phenomena that our predecessors fifty years ago could only dream about. Today, we use medical techniques to study 6,000 year old brain tissues and to peer inside sarcophagi (crypts). We use geochemistry to study the composition of pottery and develop models of ancient economic systems. We use geophysical techniques to find sites under dense vegetation, under sand dunes, and even under water. These techniques produce impressive results, and allow us a rare glimpse into particular aspects of the past. Yet they are not without problems: at any given point in time, some specialized analytical methods are in an experimental stage of development, and are sometimes controversial. The article by Jocelyn Kaiser, "Blood from Stones: Tests for Prehistoric Blood Cast Doubt on Earlier Results," illustrates a promising method for identifying ancient blood on pieces of stone. Blood residue analysis may one day enable scientists to interpret what kinds of animals were hunted or butchered using ancient stone tools. Initial results using this method were exciting, and yielded results on materials that were dated as old as 180,000 years. Recently, this technique has come under scientific scrutiny that has raised important questions concerning the utility of blood residue studies in archaeology. This article shows how such techniques must undergo rigorous testing to test their validity and to refine their applications in archaeological studies of ancient subsistence systems.

Who would have imagined that archaeological materials would have found their way into modern hospital rooms for X-rays? And that this and similar technologies would enable us to study mummies from the inside out? Karen Wright's article, "Tales from the Crypt," describes how the use of medical technology provided a non-invasive and informative look at a 2000 year old mummy. The use of X-ray technology furnished information concerning the mummy's age, and archaeologists combined other X-ray information with historical information on embalming techniques to infer the socioeconomic status of this individual. Subsequent CAT scans suggested insights on the possible causes of death and the embalming practices. The deft work of a sculptor accustomed to making three-dimensional models of CAT scan images produced an image of an Egyptian child, who died young and was committed, through Egyptian mortuary practices, to a kind of eternity.

Some of these new techniques, such as aerial photography and satellite imagery, make it possible to study archaeological sites without damaging them by excavation. Remote sensing can be an efficient and cost-effective way to locate archaeological sites in areas that are difficult to examine using conventional methods of pedestrian survey. Similarly, subsurface radar enables archaeologists to learn important information about deeply buried archaeological sites without excavation. "Tracking Ohio's Great Hopewell Road," by Bradley T. Lepper, is an exciting account of how aerial reconnaissance and infrared photography were used to map an ancient road in south-central Ohio that dates between the first century B.C. and the fifth century A.D. Although 18th and 19th century residents of the region were already familiar with the mounded earthworks that dotted the landscape, we needed remote sensing to "see" the road that connected earthworks to each other. While these methods were useful for documenting the former existence of this 60 mile-long road, these methods cannot really tell us why the road was built—and what was its function. Lepper offers the intriguing idea that this road formed a ritual connection between the two communities, and with the dead.

One of the most sensational archaeological finds in recent decades is not an archaeological site at all. It is, instead, a mummified body from the southern Alps of Europe dubbed "the Iceman." Sandy Fritz' article, "Who Owns the Iceman," describes the application of a battery of modern techniques to this famous figure by a research team that included an anatomist, physiologist, ethnobotanist, conservators, and several archaeologists. Researchers used CAT scans to study the Iceman's skeletal structure and possible causes of death. The Iceman research is remarkable for the level of detail possible in the scientists' reconstruction of the Iceman's life. Not only could they reconstruct his entire wardrobe (from boots to a possible hat) and his hunting paraphernalia (including bow, arrow, and quiver), but they also concluded from his worn teeth and grains found in his clothes that he lived in a lowland farming community at the foot of the alps. With the Iceman, recent technological advances have been used to preserve and study this unusual example of a 5,300 year old human.

1

Blood from Stones

Jocelyn Kaiser

Forensic experts aren't the only scientists who mine bloodstains for clues. For more than a decade, archaeologists have been borrowing crime-lab techniques to hunt for ancient blood on scraps of stone.

Using antibodies to detect blood and the species it came from, some researchers have seemingly obtained astonishing results. Margaret E. Newman of the University of Calgary in Alberta and her colleagues reported finding buffalo blood on stone knives at a 5,600-year-old butchering spot in Canada. Thomas H. Loy's team picked up human blood in paint dating to 20,000 years ago on a cave wall in Australia. And at an Iraqi site, Loy says, he detected 180,000-year-old blood spilled by a man whittling wood.

It seems that dirt stuck in the grooves of a stone scraper or a dark spot on a rock slab can reveal such secrets as what creatures early peoples sacrificed and when they turned from hunting to farming.

But just as discoveries of ancient DNA have met with skepticism, researchers' zeal for archaeological blood tests, known as residue analysis, has begun to fizzle. In a recent spate of papers, scientists question not only one another's findings, but whether it's even possible for traces of buried blood to survive thousands of years.

"People are getting very capricious and puzzling and different results," says Christopher Chippindale, editor of ANTIQUITY, a journal on whose pages the debate is unfolding. "There's something in the biochemistry that is giving false positives. That really puts quite a question mark on the various studies."

Loy, now at the University of Queensland in Australia, leads the field in archaeological blood claims, having reported ancient blood on more than 1,000 tools since 1983. Initially, he identified prehistoric hemoglobin, a protein in blood, by crystallizing it. That test has come under heavy criticism, but Loy stands by his results.

When he and others began using immunological tests, they seemed to move to firmer ground. These tests, which detect blood proteins, date back more than 40 years. (Archaeological DNA tests, used since the 1980s, decode genetic material.) To devise a test for, say, deer blood, scientists inject fresh deer blood into a rabbit, which makes millions of antibodies to the blood. The antibodies in rabbit serum, called antiserum, can then be used to search for deer blood.

To test a stone tool for traces of such blood, a researcher would generally wash the tool, then pour the washing extract onto a solid to which the blood proteins stick—a plastic membrane, for example. At that point, he or she rinses the solid with deer antiserum, then with a second antibody that sticks to the antiserum. Because this second antibody is tagged with a fluorescent molecule or some other marker, it flags any deer blood in the sample.

191

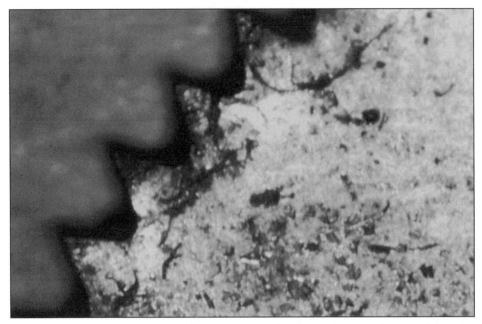

Figure 1. Close-up of a carpal saw from a surgeon's kit during the United States of America Civil War. (Photo courtesy of Greg Byrne/Harper's Ferry Conservation Laboratory)

In practice, the assays are more complicated. Because closely related species have similar blood proteins, the antiserum for, say, elk can react with blood from a deer or cow. So it's necessary to test each antiserum against many other species' blood for cross-reactions and to be aware of these reactions when testing a piece of stone.

The test itself varies from one laboratory to the next. Some people buy commercial antisera, while others make their own. Some testing methods are a thousand times more sensitive than others. An antiserum can be made to react with a single protein, such as albumin or hemoglobin, or even with one region of a protein instead of the many proteins in whole blood.

A chemist for 27 years, Judith A. Eisele had these things in mind 4 years ago when she began looking at blood residues on tools for an anthropology master's project at the University of Nevada at Reno. Working with biochemist Roger A. Lewis, she used a dozen antisera, from turkey to bear, to test for blood on more than 150 flaked stone tools from the Southwest.

When only seven tools tested positive for blood and these results proved ambiguous, she tried another experiment. She coated clean stone tools with deer blood and buried them for several months. The results, published in the March ANTIQUITY: Tools buried in dry dirt tested positive for blood for only 10 months. As for tools stored in damp dirt, the blood couldn't be detected after just a single month.

Eisele's adviser, archaeologist Donald D. Fowler, sent her master's thesis to researchers across the country a year ago. "The dovecotes were definitely fluttering," says Jerold M. Lowenstein, an immunologist at the University of California, San Francisco. Other reports added to these doubts. Researchers from the United Kingdom buried stone tools daubed with blood; only one tested positive for blood a year later. When scientists in Texas and New Mexico recently sent 54 tools dipped in *fresh* animal bloods to a commercial laboratory, it incorrectly identified half the samples.

Lowenstein and retired Boston physician Elinor F. Downs also reported confusing results in the January/February JOURNAL OF ARCHAEOLOGICAL SCIENCE. They split up washings from a set of stone tools, sending one-third to another university laboratory and keeping one-third each for themselves. Downs used crossover immunoelectrophoresis, Lowenstein radioimmunoassay, and the third group a dipstick clinicians use to detect hemoglobin in urine.

While the three groups agreed about tools that held fresh blood or nothing, their results for ancient blood didn't match. On a particular tool, for instance, one team found human blood, another bear blood, and the third nothing at all.

So is it possible to get ancient blood from a stone? The answer depends on whom you ask. Howard Ceri of Newman's group at the University of Calgary argues that the immunological techniques are valid, even on aged blood. "Look at the wealth of forensic evidence that's out there," he says.

Loy says others have gotten negative results because their tests aren't sensitive enough to detect minuscule amounts of blood and because they don't begin by screening for blood visually.

"They're either archaeologists using techniques that they really don't understand in terms of chemistry or immunology," he says, or they are immunologists who have never "actually looked at a tool." Loy tests for a single region of immunoglobin, and he is among the few who claim to have seen red blood cells on artifacts through a microscope.

At the other extreme is Eisele, who wonders whether blood can endure in prehistoric bone, much less on stone tools, except under freezing conditions. Those

Figure 2. Blood residue samples being prepared for analysis. (Photo courtesy of Margaret Newman)

who think they've found blood on artifacts, she says, more likely have picked up proteins from microbes or plants.

Lowenstein remains confident that he has detected blood on some tools. So does biochemist Noreen Tuross of the Smithsonian Institution in Washington, D.C. In the spring JOURNAL OF FIELD ARCHAEOLOGY, she and Tom D. Dillehay of the University of Kentucky, Lexington, reported a strong indication of hemoglobin, possibly from a mastodon, on a tool from a site in Chile dated to 11,000 B.C.

But Tuross speaks for many when she says, "Immunoreactivity to ancient, degraded molecules is an area we don't fully understand. To take modern techniques and to apply them to ancient results is inappropriate." Antibodies designed to find fresh, folded proteins could yield misleading results when used on old proteins that have lost their shape and broken into fragments or formed denser shapes, Tuross warns.

Adding to the confusion, there's no consistency across groups on how they test, how they deal with cross-reactions, or even how they wash possible blood from tools. And unlike chemists, researchers who publish in archaeological journals aren't accustomed to describing their procedures, Eisele says.

Blind tests may help iron out these problems. One has just been set up by University of Colorado Health Sciences Center in Denver researchers and a Golden, Colo., company, Paleo Research Laboratories. The group sent stone tools covered with modern blood to a half dozen research teams, which will analyze them using their usual methods and send back the results.

Lowenstein, a participant, says the study is a good first step. "I think we're just getting into the scientific phase of this work, and I think it's badly needed." But the real check will be blind tests for ancient blood, he says.

As complicated as ancient blood analysis is proving, it's a goal worth pursuing, Tuross adds. "The excavation record of early man is so overwhelmingly dominated by stone tools," she says. "Archaeologists really want this work done. What captivates them is that this is material they would normally [wash] away."

Such debris may yet yield intriguing surprises—the world just may have to wait a few years to be sure.

2

Tales from the Crypt

Karen Wright

You could call it the mummy in the plain brown wrapper. Reclining in a quiet corner of the World Heritage Museum at the University of Illinois in Urbana, basking in the amber aura of indirect lighting and artfully strewn sand, the four-and-a-half-foot treasure has all the aesthetic appeal of a hero sandwich packed to go.

It's a long, flat, mud-colored slab shaped only remotely like a human being, and it's broken off at the ankle, revealing the gray stubs of ancient leg bones. Two errant splotches of tar on the mummy's painted face give it an eerie, wide-eyed look. Around the tar you can still discern a faded gilt laurel wreath; across the torso you can still see the march of stiff-legged Egyptian gods. But there is no indication of pedigree, no inscription on the coverings supplying name, age, or sex of the person under wraps. No one even knows what Egyptian tomb this mummy came from. All that remains of it are its remains.

But across campus, in a swank new glass-and-brick building that houses the university's National Center for Supercomputing Applications, physician—computer scientist David Lawrance is peering inside those remains. Fiddling with a program that can reconstruct three-dimensional images from CT scans, Lawrance taps out a few commands to the Connection Machine humming in the building's heart. On the screen before him, in rosy hues, appear the contours of the mummy's skull. The teeth are solid white, and the bone a transparent sunset sinking into the milky clouds of the wrappings.

Even on the flat screen the skull appears fully rounded, but it's transparent; the surfaces aren't colored in to occlude what's behind them. "I sometimes compare it to looking through a bowl of Jell-O salad," Lawrance says. "You can see through the whole thing to the chunks of fruit and so on, but you kind of lose the surface detail."

He types a few more instructions to the computer, and the skull begins rolling chin over pate. In motion the rendering loses some of its visual ambiguity: it's more apparent which structures belong in the front and which in the back, as features are revealed and then concealed. Where the naked eye sees a plain brown wrapper, the computer supplies a peek inside—and a few more clues about who or what the mummy might have been.

"As far as we know, a supercomputer has never been used in this kind of three-dimensional reconstruction," says Sarah Wisseman, the archeologist who recruited Lawrance to be part of an interdisciplinary team investigating the mummy's identity. "It's unusual to use as much computing power as we've got here. We're getting views on the data that would not be possible just looking at two-dimensional stuff."

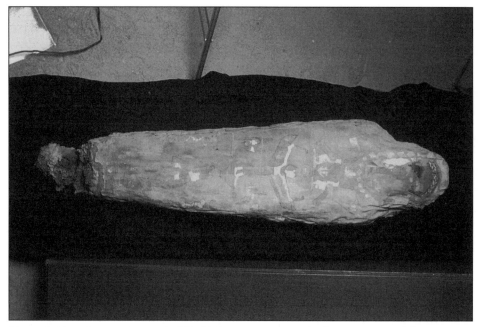

Figure 1. Egyptian mummy at the World Heritage Museum at the University of Illinois at Urbana-Champaign. (Photo courtesy of Bill Wiegand/University of Illinois News Bureau)

Wisseman, who works in the university's Ancient Technologies and Archaeological Materials program, was charged with the task of revealing the mummy's story in September 1989, shortly after the museum acquired the mummy from a Chicago antiquities dealer. The dealer knew nothing about his merchandise other than that it had been in the possession of a wealthy Illinois family for more than 60 years. Museum director Barbara Bohen wanted to know more. She went to Wisseman with her problem, along with a few opinions about how to solve it.

For one thing, Bohen stipulated, Wisseman would have to work fairly fast by archeological standards. "The mummy is probably one of the most spectacular artifacts the museum houses," Wisseman explains, and Bohen wanted to put it on display as soon as she could. Wisseman had about a year before her subject would be committed to the glass sarcophagus of a museum showcase.

And Bohen was especially concerned that the mummy remain intact, or relatively so—it had already suffered the unhappy loss of its feet. She wanted the mummy back in the same condition in which she'd found it. The details were not negotiable.

This edict dashed any hopes Wisseman had of performing an autopsy. "Because the resins and embalming fluids are practically petrified, there's no way you can unwrap the mummy, autopsy it, and then put it back together again for display," she says. Contrary to the Hollywood school of mummy extrication, you can't simply stand the deceased upright, grab one end of the gauze, and run. Instead, mummy "unwrappings" usually involve a sharp saw and a strong arm. Wisseman was going to have to find a different approach.

"I realized the emphasis was going to have to be on noninvasive testing," she says. "And I was really interested in seeing just how much we could find out without disturbing the wrappings."

So one afternoon Wisseman loaded the mummy in the back of her station wagon and drove to the university's Large Animal Clinic, where X-ray technician Richard Keen was waiting. Keen had worked with Wisseman in the past on various "items of fascination," as he puts it: an Italian painting, a Byzantine necklace, a Japanese statue. But the mummy was unusual, and he was exceptionally eager to help out. Within an hour the two were poring over the cloudy gray shapes on 15 new X-ray prints.

"The X-ray showed very clearly that the ends of the long bones—the epiphyses—weren't fused yet," Wisseman says. The epiphyses fuse with the shafts of the long bones (such as those in the arms and legs) when the bones stop growing, usually when a person is between 14 and 16 years old. Before that the region between the epiphyses and the shafts where growth occurs shows up darker on an X-ray than do the fully calcified bones.

"The epiphyses on the knee were just wide open," says Linda Klepinger, an anthropologist whom Wisseman consulted with the X-rays. The mummy had to be a preteen. Near the jawbone Klepinger could also see adult teeth coming in behind baby teeth, and she pegged the mummy's age at between seven and nine.

Wisseman had hoped that the X-rays would also reveal something about the mummy's sex, the cause of death, and the embalming practices that had committed it to eternity. But she couldn't tell much from the 15 prints. Although sex can sometimes be inferred from the shape of the pelvis, which is rounder in women than it is in men, the difference is not pronounced before puberty. And the mummy's hands were placed in its lap, obscuring the genitals.

The cause of death wasn't clear, either. "Radiographically he or she seems very healthy but unfortunately dead," says Klepinger. "Which gives you an idea of how much you can tell just by looking at the bone."

Wisseman did notice that something was conspicuously absent from any of the X-rays: amulets. "That's an interesting piece of information because wealthy burials in ancient Egypt generally included a lot of amulets and jewelry and other paraphernalia in the wrappings to ensure that things go well for the spirit. The fact that there are no amulets in the packing suggested that we were not dealing with an upper-class individual."

That wasn't a complete surprise. Wisseman had already deduced from the manner of wrapping and painting that the mummy was about 2,000 years old, from the time known as the Roman period, when mummification was no longer reserved for royalty alone. Embalming was mass-marketed by studios that offered their customers a selection of packages varying in extravagance and price.

"You would walk into an embalming studio," explains Wisseman, "and they'd say, 'Okay, what can you afford? There's the quick treatment, the slightly more detailed treatment, or the whole treatment.'" The whole treatment involved removing the lungs, liver, and bowels, and occasionally the brain; the body cavity would be packed with sundry materials such as myrrh, palm wine, honey, onions, sand, cedar chips, sawdust, and even mud, then dried with natron, a mixture of sodium salts. The organs were placed in canopic (for the Egyptian city Canopus) jars or wrapped in linen and returned to the body cavity or placed between the mummy's legs. The body was treated with molten resin, wrapped and soaked with resin again, and then decorated.

The Greek historian Herodotus, describing the procedure in the fifth century B.C., wrote that embalming took about 70 days from beginning to end. But

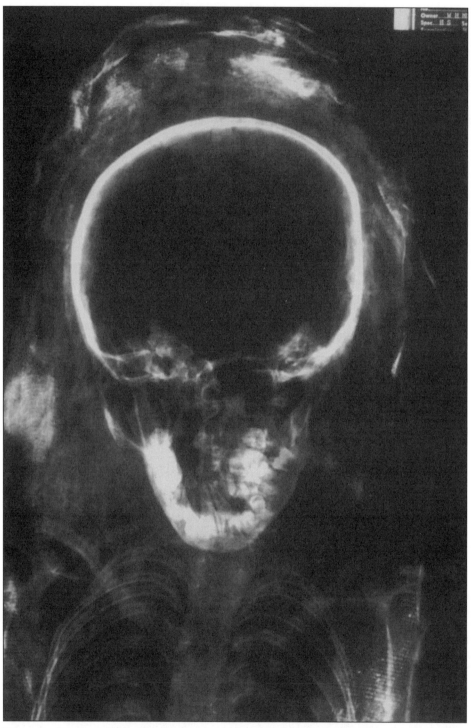

Figure 2. X-ray of Egyptian mummy studied by archaeologist Sarah Wisseman. (Image Courtesy of Richard Keen/College of Veterinary Medicine, University of Illinois)

through the years the practice became less formalized. By the Roman period, Wisseman says, the Egyptians were really cutting corners—or worse. One text suggests that families often retained the bodies of young females until decomposition had set in so as to discourage the advances of amorous embalmers. "The details of this stuff get increasingly gory," Wisseman admits.

Having exhausted the information in the X-rays, Wisseman decided to try more powerful imaging techniques. In October nearby Covenant Medical Center agreed to donate a CT scan for the mummy, along with a round-trip ambulance ride. The scan revealed not only the mummy's bones but the wrappings, resin, and tissue as well, all showing up as distinct and separate entities. And the board stuck out like a sore thumb.

The board was a big surprise," says Wisseman. The earlier X-rays hadn't even hinted at its existence. But the CT scan revealed a piece of wood running from head to what used to be toe along the back side of the mummy. The wood was tapered to follow the mummy's contours. Roman-period embalmers sometimes used such "stiffening boards," Wisseman says, to support bodies that had deteriorated before mummification.

Wondering whether any other surprises lurked within the CT images, Wisseman took them to Joe Barkmeier, a radiologist at the Carle Clinic in Urbana. Barkmeier pointed out that the scans of the head highlighted an anomaly, one that Wisseman and Klepinger had noticed on the X-rays but hadn't paid much attention to: the black of the mummy's skull was badly cracked, fractured in several places near where it joins the spine.

Could this be the cause of death? Barkmeier says that although the injury clearly occurred near the time of death—there was no evidence of healing—it could have easily been a postmortem accident. Wisseman thinks clumsy embalmers may have dropped the body or stacked one too many embalmees on top of it in the studio. But there's no way to be certain. In some ways, Barkmeier says, these CT scans are as cryptic to him as hieroglyphics.

"I know what I'm looking at when I see a scan of an ordinary human body," he says. The mummy, however, is far from ordinary. "There are things missing, and everything's dried up and moved around. It's like doing those hidden-picture puzzles: you know what things should look like, but trying to find them is something else." The remains of the brain, for example, had collapsed in the back of the skull like a heap of dead goldfish at the bottom of a dry bowl. And in one corner of the chest cavity the shriveled vestiges of a heart and a lung formed a silhouette you won't find in any anatomy textbook.

The presence of the heart is unremarkable; the Egyptians never disturbed the heart during mummification. They believed it was the seat of the emotions and the headquarters of the soul. That the lung and brain tissue remained in this mummy, on the other hand, strengthened Wisseman's suspicion that this was a low-budget embalming.

As Wisseman and Barkmeier puzzled over the scans for the next several months, winter turned into spring and the time for investigation grew short. Barbara Bohen had scheduled a museum exhibit for the mummy in October, and although Wisseman wanted to include some sort of concrete testimony to the mummy's identity, she had none. Wisseman had been talking with Clint Potter, a researcher at the supercomputing center who had written a program that displayed CT-scan data in three dimensions. Perhaps, she thought, a new way of displaying the data would give her the insight she needed. Potter told Wisseman that his program required images with better resolution than the ones that had been done on the mummy at Covenant. So Barkmeier persuaded Carle Clinic to contribute the services of its CT machine, one capable of providing scans with an exceptionally high resolution. The machine is in high demand for use on living patients, so the mummy team had to wait awhile for an opening in the schedule. But in August 1990 the mummy went via another ambulance ride to its second CT scan.

This time interpretation of the scan wasn't a matter of slapping black-and-white sections up on a light box. The day after the mummy's visit to the clinic Dave Lawrance ran the CT data through Potter's program and drew a portrait of the mummy's head and shrouds more ghostlike than the genuine article.

"It's what's called a volumetric rendering," says Lawrance, admiring the skull as it slowly spins on the screen before him. The CT scanner takes 66 images of the mummy's head at different depths, like slices of a tomato. The computer then stacks those slices one on top of the other and divides each slice into one-millimeter squares. The result is a cube of data, with each square in the cube corresponding to a point somewhere in the mummy's head. Lawrance can tell the computer to illuminate only those squares that correspond to the skull; he can also do cut-away sections of any part of slices in any orientation. He can even faintly illuminate the squares that represent the wrappings at the front of the head and brightly light the squares behind them to get a "ghosting" effect.

The image can be disorienting on the computer screen because there are no visual cues about each point's depth position relative to the other points. Lawrance brings up Jell-O salad again. "If there's a red cube of Jell-O somewhere in the middle, you can see it through the yellow and green cubes, but you don't really know how far in it is. You have to walk around the bowl to get a sense of perspective." Since he can't walk around the computer image, Lawrance instead turns every square in the data cube 5 degrees to the right again and again, so the whole image turns in front of his eyes.

Lawrance repeated the process for CT scans of the rest of the mummy's body. But some of the most interesting revelations had more to do with the preparation of the body than with the body of the mummy itself. When Wisseman saw the ancient child unveiled in three dimensions, she noticed for the first time that its hands had been wrapped individually and that the board had been carefully beveled.

"And underneath the broken skull in back was a whole wad of extra packing that had been put there to help support the head." she says. More packing had been placed around the chest, which appears to have collapsed a bit during shipping and handling. Wisseman says the packing was probably meant to make the outside contours of the mummy's wrapping look more robust or lifelike. The effort doesn't seem to have worked, but at least the embalmer's heart was in the right place—even if the mummy's isn't.

The evidence that came out of the computer visualization made Wisseman think twice about the socioeconomic status of her subject. "I've revised some of my own conclusions since I began," she says. "We originally thought this was a sloppy embalming job, because of the skull fracture and so forth." Instead, the wrapped hands, the beveled board, and the extra packing indicated that "this is probably an upper-middle-class kid whose family could afford to give it one of the better embalming jobs for its period."

By September Wisseman could tell Bohen a few things about her mummy: its posthumous age was 2,000 years; its age at the time of death was between seven and nine; and its demographics were probably *haut monde*. She still, however, didn't know anything about the sex; what one CT technician took for a penis turned out, after more careful examination, to be a thumb.

She was the on the verge of bidding her charge good-bye when Lawrance mentioned that the CT scans might be put to further use. He had been in contact with a biomedical visualization group at the nearby University of Illinois in Chicago. The group included sculptor Ray Evenhouse, who had made a three-dimensional model of a face from CT scans of a mummy housed at the Kalamazoo Public Museum in Michigan. Wisseman was intrigued and contacted Evenhouse. Evenhouse too was intrigued and asked to see the scans. Wisseman sent them off. "I called back a day or two later and said, 'I think I can do something with it,' " says Evenhouse. The museum was reserving space for the sculpture in its display, so Evenhouse dropped everything to build a face for the child mummy in record time. He constructed a plastic skull that conformed to the dimensions revealed in the CT scans and then began to flesh out the skull with modeling clay. Forensic anthropologists have determined characteristic depths of tissue at various points around the skull by measuring thousands of people, and Evenhouse drew on this information in his reconstruction. "You can almost connect the dots along those tissue depths to create the profile," he says.

From the size of the skull's nasal aperture he could determine how wide the nose was; two bony depressions, one at the top and one at the bottom of the aperture, indicated the nose's length. The spacing and size of the orbits—the bones that encircle the eye sockets—gave clues to the placement of the eyes, and the length of the teeth revealed how thick the lips were. Of course, Evenhouse couldn't tell the color of the eyes or hair from the mummy's skeleton, but he figured he wouldn't be too far off if he made both features a very dark brown.

"You're not creating an exact portrait of somebody here," Evenhouse cautions. "But you can be relatively certain that we're putting the kind of face back on the skull that *could've* existed on it. It may not look exactly like the person, but it should look like a close relative."

The most prominent feature of the fleshed-out World Heritage mummy, it turns out, is a pronounced overbite. Sadly, at its tender age, the hormones of puberty still hadn't molded the visage, and so Evenhouse's reconstruction gave no clues to the mummy's sex.

In one last attempt to resolve the issue, Evenhouse fed the specs on the mummy's appearance into a computer program, pioneered in his department, that ages children's faces based on the information in photographs. The program had been developed to aid in the identification of missing children who had been gone for years. Before his eyes the computer turned an androgynous eight-year-old into an 18-year-old who could've gone either way, too. Evenhouse thinks it looks more like a male, and Wisseman agrees. But, she says wistfully, "we can't prove it." And she was out of time.

In October 1990 the mummy exhibit opened, and for now at least, the book on its past is closed. There's been no shortage of suggestions about experiments Wisseman could perform should the museum ever relax its restrictions on invasive procedures: Klepinger mentions the possibility of doing DNA analysis of the mummy's tissue. Lawrance thinks it would be neat to stick a needle in the mummy's skull and sample the "ancient air" inside. "What I'd like them to do is turn the mummy over, drill a hole in the back side and put a little endoscope in there and look around at the pieces of tissue," Barkmeier offers.

But those ambitions seem strangely inappropriate now that the mummy lies secure and unmolested behind plate glass. On a gray December day the exhibit is deserted and still as a tomb. Amid the silence the hushed voices carrying in from adjoining halls seem to whisper the burial blessing that served as the Egyptians' farewell: *You live again, you revive always... You are young again, and forever.*

3

Tracking Ohio's Great Hopewell Road

Bradley T. Lepper

The Maya have long been known for their great network of roads, or *sacbeob*, that crisscrossed the Yucatan Peninsula, connecting one ceremonial center to another. In the southwestern United States the Anasazi built their own system of sacred pathways replicating a spiritual landscape described in their origin myths (see ARCHAEOLOGY, January/February 1994). Until recently such roads were unknown in eastern North America, though nineteenth-century observers had recorded short stretches of parallel earthen walls leading to and from the large geometric enclosures of the Hopewell, a people who thrived in the valleys of what is now southern Ohio from ca. 100 B.C. to ca. A.D. 400. Settlers assumed that these walls had been built to afford safe passage from one enclosure to another. It was a popular notion that their builders were a "lost race" vanquished by "savage" Indians and that their monumental earthworks—circles, squares, octagons, and a variety of less regular shapes—had been used for defense. I believe that the earthworks were used by priests and pilgrims for ritual purposes.

The founders of Marietta, Ohio, one of the earliest Euro-American settlements in the Ohio Valley, were veterans of the Revolutionary War. They knew that the ancient earthworks around which they laid out their city could never have served as fortifications—there were too many entrances to defend. They named the parallel walls leading 680 feet from the largest square enclosure in town to the Ohio River the *Sacra Via*, following a penchant for giving classical names to ancient remains. The walls of this sacred way were eight to ten feet high and 150 feet apart. Other Hopewell roads, such as those at Newark in east-central Ohio and Portsmouth, at the confluence of the Scioto and Ohio rivers in southern Ohio, were more extensive. At Portsmouth 16 miles of parallel walls, four feet high and 160 feet apart, led from a central cluster of circular embankments to two separate enclosures on the Kentucky side of the Ohio River. Only a few remnants of these earthworks survive.

For the past six years I have studied Newark's prehistoric roadway, which, I believe, stretched for nearly 60 miles across south-central Ohio—almost as long as the 60-mile Maya road from Cobá to Yaxuná and 30 miles longer than the Anasazi Great North Road. An industrial city of 45,000, Newark lies at the confluence of Raccoon Creek and the South Fork of the Licking River. Two Hopewell enclosures are preserved here in parks administered by the Ohio Historical Society: the Great Circle, an earthen enclosure 1,200 feet across with walls as high as 14 feet, at Moundbuilders State Memorial; and a circular earthwork 1,050 feet

203

Figure 1. Aerial photograph, circa 1930, of Octagon State Memorial, Newark, Ohio. The earthwork may have been the northern terminus of the Great Hope Hopewell Road. (Photo courtesy of Ohio Historical Society)

across with walls averaging five feet high connected to an eight-sided enclosure, at Octagon State Memorial.

In his 1820 *Descriptions of the Antiquities Discovered in the State of Ohio*, Caleb Atwater, an early student of the mounds and earthworks of the Ohio Valley, claimed that a set of parallel earthen walls projecting southwest from Newark's great octagonal enclosure might extend as far as 30 miles, linking up with a second complex of earthworks along the Hocking River. Ephraim Squier and Edwin Davis, in their *Ancient Monuments of the Mississippi Valley*, published in 1848, did not mention Atwater's claim, but noted on their map of the Newark works that parallel walls extended two and one-half miles south. Squier and Davis were well aware of Atwater's work, acknowledging him as a pioneer in the study of the ancient monuments of the Ohio Valley, so it is puzzling that they did not mention his claim concerning these walls, if only to refute it. Perhaps they were so intent on mapping the state's numerous mounds and earthworks that they were not inclined to follow the course of any parallel walls that would extend beyond the margins of their map.

In 1989 I discovered a manuscript in the American Antiquarian Society in Worcester, Massachusetts, written in 1862 by James and Charles Salisbury. They had followed the parallel walls two and one-half miles to Ramp Creek, a tributary of the South Fork of the Licking River, where Squier and Davis had decided the road ended. The Salisbury brothers crossed the creek and found that the walls continued south. They wrote: "We have traced them some six miles over fertile fields, through tangled swamps and across streams, still keeping their undeviating course." The Salisburys did not follow the road to its end, but they suggested that if it did continue it might well lead to the town of Chillicothe. Eight years later local historian Samuel Park observed in a pamphlet on the history of Union

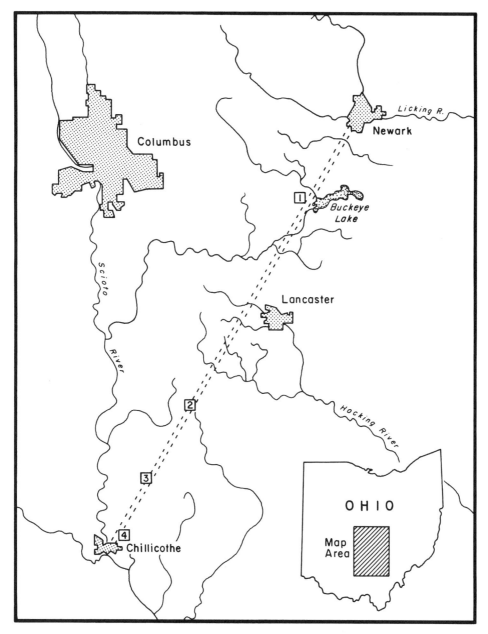

Figure 2. Map of south-central Ohio shows a projected Great Hopewell Road and four numbered areas where possible traces of the road have been observed. Visible in aerial photographs as parallel lines stretching across fields, the longest segment (3) is 1,025 feet long. (Graphic courtesy of Bette Duke, adapted by Ronald Beckwith)

Township in Licking County, Ohio, that if such a road ever existed cultivation of the land had erased all traces of it. Park did report the claim of one Jesse Thompson that "when he first settled on Walnut Creek [one-third of the way from Newark to Chillicothe], in Fairfield County, about the beginning of the present century, there was a graded road, easily traced in the timber...and he always thought it to be a road leading from the works near Newark to those at Circleville, as it was on a line between those points." Circleville, named for the circular earthworks around which the town was laid out, is about 35 miles southwest of Newark and about 18 miles north of Chillicothe. Park did not find the road and doubted that "in the present improved state of the country it could be found."

In 1930 a cold trail grew hot, thanks to Warren Weiant, Jr., a Newark businessman with an interest in local history who brought aerial reconnaissance to bear on the Hopewell past. In a 1931 letter to the Ohio Historical Society, Weiant wrote that from the air he had followed the remnants of the walls beyond Ramp Creek, "southwestward in a straight line for Millersport," a town about 12 miles southwest of Newark. Weiant corroborated James and Charles Salisbury's claim that the road was straight and that it extended far beyond its intersection with the creek. His letter, however, sparked little interest among archaeologists at the historical society, who felt there was little to be learned from flattened earthworks.

After I found the Salisbury manuscript, it occurred to me that this Hopewell road might share many of the characteristics of the sacred pathways of the Maya and the Anasazi. If it were a sacred road, it could be expected to follow a straight course toward its ultimate destination many miles away. The wall lines mapped by the Salisburys and photographed by Weiant might be used to project a hypothetical route, which could then be examined for road remnants. I placed a ruler on a map of Ohio, then angled it to parallel the orientation of the walls the Salisburys had mapped and that I could see on Weiant's aerial photos. The straight line I then drew extended from the Newark octagonal enclosure across central Ohio to the center of modern Chillicothe nearly 60 miles away.

Could the road have ended at Chillicothe? Dozens of Hopewell mounds and earthworks can be found in the Scioto River Valley. One earthen enclosure near Chillicothe in particular would have been quite familiar to the residents of ancient Newark. Known today as High Bank Works, it is a circular embankment 1,050 feet in diameter connected to an octagonal enclosure. The Hopewell built only two such earthworks, one near Chillicothe, the other in Newark. The circular embankments are virtually identical in size, though Newark's octagon is larger, enclosing 44 acres compared to High Bank Works' 20 acres. Archaeoastronomers Ray Hively and Robert Horn of Earlham College in Richmond, Indiana, have studied both of these sites and concluded that they could have functioned as astronomical observatories. A line drawn along the center axis of the Newark earthworks points to the northernmost spot on the eastern horizon where the moon would have risen, which happens only once every 18.6 years. A similar line drawn through the center of High Bank Works aligns at 90 degrees to the axis of Newark's earthworks, suggesting that the sites are not two versions of the same thing, but complimentary in their geometry and astronomical orientation.

In my search for traces of what I call the Great Hopewell Road, I have driven or walked across much of the route. I have studied Weiant's photographs and pored over aerial infrared images of the projected corridor. In recording reflected

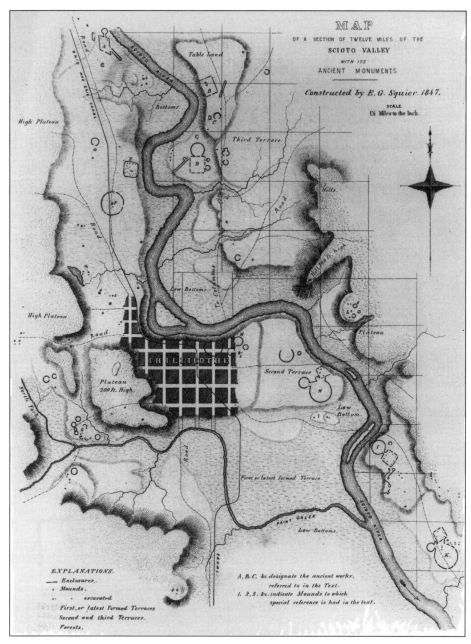

Figure 3. Map showing the locations of numberous earthworks in the Scioto River Valley. (Graphic from Whittlesey, Squier, and Davis 1837–47, courtesy of Ohio Historical Society)

heat, infrared photographs can reveal archaeological traces not apparent to the naked eye. I have also flown over the route twice—once in a small airplane with Roger Kennedy, now director of the National Park Service, and once in an Ohio Department of Transportation helicopter. From the air one can detect, in a few places and ever so faintly, parallel markings in the soil that might be the remains of parallel walls; most of the stretch between Newark and Chillicothe is a feature-

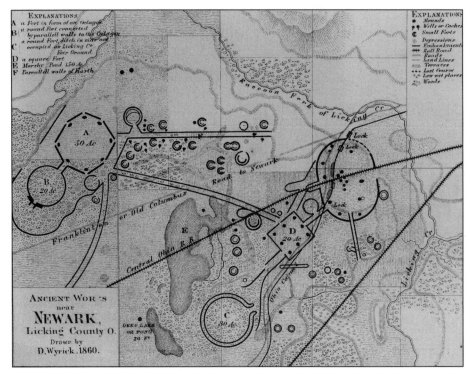

Figure 4. Newark earthworks point to the northernmost spot on the eastern horizon where the moon would have risen. Vintage plan shows a segment of the sacred road extending south. (Graphic from Whittlesey, Squier, and Davis 1837–47, courtesy of Ohio Historical Society)

less expanse of farmland. There is only one spot where one can actually stand between walls of the ancient road. Two miles southwest of Newark's great octagonal enclosure, in a wooded lot just north of the Licking County airport, lie two barely noticeable walls of earth, 200 feet apart and only about 12 inches high. The eastern segment is 290 feet long, the western portion 400 feet long. They end abruptly in farmland to the north and south.

So far I have identified four sites between Newark and Chillicothe where I think traces of the Great Hopewell Road can be detected. Infrared photographs obtained through the Ohio Department of Natural Resources reveal parallel lines along the predicted alignment about 12 miles southwest of Newark, some 800 feet long and 200 feet apart, cutting across agricultural fields. The Salisburys reported that the walls near Newark were 192 feet apart. In a series of photographs taken for me in 1993 by the Environmental Research Institute of Michigan (ERIM), two short straight lines are visible in the soil 36 miles southwest of Newark. The lines are each about 400 feet long. They are staggered, but if extended they would be about 200 feet apart. In another photograph taken by ERIM a single line about 1,025 feet long is visible 47 miles southwest of Newark. A shadowy parallel line is discernible about 200 feet to the east. In a ca. 1930 black-and-white photograph from the National Anthropological Archives of the Smithsonian Institution, two almost parallel lines are visible on the outskirts of Chillicothe, 56 miles southwest of Newark. One line is interrupted by a semicircular feature. Squier and Davis do not depict a parallel-walled roadway in this area on their 1845 map, but they do show a small semicircular earthwork. It is here, not far from High Bank Works, that the Great Hopewell Road seems to end. These indistinct and intermittent lines inscribed across the fields of south-central Ohio may or may not be remnants of a sacred road, but they are in the right place, at the right compass bearing, and are of the right dimensions to be traces of such a road.

We may never know why Ohio's Hopewell would have built such a pathway from Newark to Chillicothe. No surviving records or traditions can be reliably attributed to the Hopewell. In the sixteenth century, when the Spanish encountered the Maya of the Yucatán and asked of them the purpose of their long straight highways, the natives said they were sacred roads, routes of pilgrimage. The Maya name for them—and for the Milky Way—was *sacbe*, meaning "white road." Daniel Brinton, a nineteenth-century anthropologist, recorded an obscure tradition of the Lenni Lenape, or Delaware Indians, that, "in the good old times...a string of white wampum beads...stretched from the Atlantic to the Pacific, and on this white road their envoys travelled from one great ocean to the other, safe from attack." Among the eastern Algonquian peoples, wampum was not merely a form of money. It was also an instrument—or a sacrament—for negotiating peace, proposing marriage, or offering condolences at the death of a chief. Among the Iroquois, the "great white wampum belt" signified purity and peace. The Delaware referred to life's journey as the "Beautiful White Path," one ritually enacted in Big House ceremonies. American anthropologist Frank Speck believes the White Path also represented the Milky Way, the Spirit or Ghost Path, over which the souls of the dead would continue their journey into the spirit world. Perhaps the Great Hopewell Road was a spirit path ritually uniting two communities with each other and with the community of the dead.

The Hopewell participated in a trading network that spanned much of North America. They acquired copper from the upper Great Lakes, mica from the Carolinas, shells from the Gulf of Mexico, and obsidian from the Rocky Mountains. Diverse peoples from Missouri to New York, and from Michigan to Florida, adopted artistic and architectural motifs of the Hopewell. Although some items from Ohio, such as Licking County's Flint Ridge flint, trickled out to the ends of the Hopewell world, there is more evidence of exotic material coming into Ohio than of Ohio goods going out. Perhaps the mica and obsidian were not trade goods, but tribute or offerings from visiting dignitaries.

It is conceivable that Newark and Chillicothe were great religious centers, and that pilgrims came here from across eastern North America to leave rare and precious offerings of copper and mica. In return, they took away a blessing rather than a commodity. Such pilgrimages would have been facilitated by formal sacred roadways that may have been called, in the forgotten language of the Hopewell, "white roads." The timing of their rituals may have been based on a lunar calendar, which would explain the earthworks marking the lunar cycle that lie at each end of the Great Hopewell Road.

For now, the argument for the road's existence rests upon archival data, aerial photography, and ground survey. Much work remains to be done. More sophisticated remote-sensing techniques must be applied to the search. Telltale parallel lines must be excavated to see if they are the remnants of ancient earthworks or something else entirely—natural soil formations or, perhaps, historic drainage lines. Finally, ground surveys and excavations should focus on areas alongside and between the walls to gain a clearer understanding of how these roads were used.

There are precedents in prehistoric America for long, straight roadways connecting one sacred place with another. While analogies with cultures widely separated in space and time may be questionable, the knowledge that such roads were widespread in the Americas makes their presence in the Ohio Valley less of an anomaly. There are sound reasons for entertaining the possibility that the Great Hopewell Road did exist, a remarkable accomplishment by a remarkable people, and that this research has restored a page from a lost epic.

4

Who Was the Iceman?

Sandy Fritz

After forensic expert Rainer Henn found a flint-tipped knife in the slush, he told his assistants to stop working on the body. "When I saw this knife, I had the idea that this man was very old," Henn later reported. "From that moment I ordered all the people to be most careful while getting the body out of the ice."

Henn and his team had no idea that the man they were freeing from the ice could be the most important discovery in modern archaeology. The man had been sealed in the Similaun Glacier in the Tyrolean Oetztaler Alps for 5,300 years. He died wearing his buckskins and grass cape. His bow and arrows, a copper ax, and other tools were recovered nearby. His skin, internal organs, and even his eyes are still in place. Dubbed the Iceman by the public, but referred to in scientific literature as *Homo tyrolensis*, the Similaun man, and the Hauslabjoch mummy, he is the oldest and best-preserved human body ever found.

When the corpse and its bundle of artifacts arrived via helicopter at the University of Innsbruck's Institute of Forensic Medicine in October 1991, the university's dean of prehistory, Konrad Spindler, was on hand. "I felt like Howard Carter staring onto the likeness of King Tut," he recalls.

In fact, the find will probably prove to be far more important than the discovery of King Tutankhamen, because Tut's 3,344-year-old tomb only served to further illustrate the opulent lives of Egypt's well-known pharaohs. The Iceman is nearly 2,000 years older and his discovery illuminates a far more mysterious time period. Scant traces remain of the people who farmed and hunted in the forests of Europe during the late Neolithic Age. Now, a single individual from that shadowy time has emerged from a retreating alpine glacier completely outfitted with clothes, tools, and weapons.

The preservation of the body ranks among the true freaks of nature. In late summer or autumn around 3,300 B.C., a 25-to-35-year-old man wandering above the tree line at about 10,500 feet took shelter in a natural trench nearly six feet deep and 20 feet wide. He died there. Exposure to several weeks of cold winds mummified the body. Snowfall froze the mummy, and centuries of snowfall became a glacier. Sheltered in the trench, the frozen body was spared most of the shearing forces of the glacier. Then, during the unusually hot European summer of 1991, a pair of German hikers spotted a leathery skull and a shoulder poking out of the glacier and contacted the police.

Nobody rushed to the scene. The melting alpine glaciers had already released six corpses that summer. The others were 20th-century climbers whose bodies, full of moisture, had turned waxy and had been partially pulverized by the glacier's slow, ponderous movement. The Iceman's body, however, was virtually undamaged. That is, until his rescue. Unfortunately, the man who died fully clothed arrived at Innsbruck totally naked, except for a shoe.

"Thirty men with picks and compressors worked on him," groans Werner Platzer, dean of physiology at the University of Innsbruck and leader of the team studying the body. "The body froze at night and thawed during the hot sun for days while the rescue effort was under way. They had no idea how old he was."

The rescue caused the most prominent disfiguration of the body, tearing a sizable chunk from the left hip. The penis is missing, probably ripped off with his pants. What was most likely a backpack was largely destroyed, and what later turned out to be a long bow was broken. In their haste to ferry the find back to Innsbruck, the recovery team left some material behind. And by the time everyone had collected their wits after the first wave of excitement passed, ten feet of snow covered the site, sealing it for the winter.

The Iceman has spent most of the last 17 months swaddled in an icy cocoon at the University of Innsbruck's forensic laboratory. In life he stood five feet three inches tall, weighed about 110 pounds, and sported dark hair and a beard. Today he weighs 44 pounds and lies frozen in his death position, naked, shriveled, and bald. To slice off a section of skin for testing, researchers would need a saw, not a scalpel. "He's like a slab of meat that has been in the freezer for too long," is how Platzer describes the body.

A blanket of surgical gauze protects the Iceman's skin; on top of that is a layer of crushed ice rendered from sterilized water. A layer of plastic covers the ice, more sterilized ice is heaped on top, and a final plastic wrap encloses the body, guaranteeing humidity of 96 to 98 percent next to the skin. The cocoon sits inside a high-tech freezer maintained at a glacial temperature of –6°C (21.2°F) and monitored by an elaborate system of sensors. Six temperature sensors are rigged to set off alarms and portable pagers should the temperature rise by a few degrees.

Removing the body from its cocoon for inspection is somewhat traumatic. The uncovered mummy reclines inside a chilled glass box filled with filtered, sterilized

---

Bogman: Peat Moss of Britain

In 1984, a peat cutter spotted a foot protruding from a clod of peat near Manchester, England. But it wasn't until 1990 that the full story behind the body—preserved in an acidic bog rather than in ice—finally came to light.

Only the upper body and one foot were found; the other parts were probably chopped up with the surrounding peat and sold as fuel many years ago. The victim, estimated to be a 33-year-old man, was murdered in a particularly gruesome manner around 50 A.D.

Peat Moss, as the British public calls him, was brained so hard with an ax that the force of the blow sheared off the top of his molars. A thin leather noose was then twisted tightly around his neck with the aid of a stick, crushing his windpipe. At the same moment, an expertly placed jab lanced his jugular vein, apparently to drain his blood. Finally, Peat Moss was dumped into a pool of black water.

The overkill has been linked to a human sacrifice ritual that was held during the Celtic celebration of Beltain. Three blood-thirsty deities needed attention at this time of year, so it appears that Peat Moss was triple-killed in order to satisfy all of them. Folklore says that whoever selected the burned bread at the feast would be sacrificed. And indeed, Peat Moss had the remains of a burned grain pancake in his stomach—S. F.

air. Researchers have but 30 minutes for their work before the mummy is hurried back into its icy chamber. It takes 48 hours for the body to return to its storage temperature.

Because physical examination of the body endangers it, researchers are developing a comprehensive database that allows them to study the body in detail without touching it. Using computerized axial tomography (CAT) scans—three-dimensional images constructed by a computer from a series of cross-sectional X-ray pictures—researchers can view the Iceman's bones and organs on a computer screen. The same CAT scan data, combined with a computer-assisted drafting program, have allowed researchers to create a three-dimensional plastic skull that is an exact replica of the original.

Platzer has made a few tentative conclusions based on preliminary investigations: The man died lying on his left side, with his left arm extended across his rump. His current posture—face down with his left arm cushioning his forehead—is the result of the sliding glacier dragging his arm upward.

A CAT scan revealed that the Iceman's left arm is broken above the elbow. Initially, Platzer suspected the break occurred when the brittle body was rescued. "But his dry skin was not torn, so it might have taken place in ancient times," Platzer explains. "It may have been an old break that healed, or it may have happened just prior to his death. I just don't know at the moment."

Platzer also says the man has a deep groove in his right ear lobe, suggesting that he wore an earring. But a two-inch disc of white stone with a spray of leather fringe was the only jewelry found, and it was probably worn on a leather thong around his neck.

Other adornment includes a series of enigmatic tattoos: four three-inch-long stripes mark the top of his left foot, a cross dots the left kneecap, and 14 bars run down the small of the back. "His clothing would have covered the tattoos," observes Konrad Spindler, who is overseeing the entire investigation of the body and the equipment. "They were not meant to be seen publicly. In this sense, they are not like modern tattoos at all. They must have had significance to him alone."

A team of Dutch researchers will be studying the tattoos to ascertain how they were made. Some primitive peoples tattoo their bodies by pricking the skin with a needle and then rubbing ash or pigment into the wound. The Iceman could have used a similar technique to make the tattoos on his own foot and knee, but the bars on his back are clearly the work of another person.

Another visible clue about the man are his worn teeth, suggesting that his diet included gritty bread. Two grains of primitive wheat were recovered from the fur of his coat; the grains are evidence that he may have lived in or near a lowland farming community at the foot of the Alps.

Farming communities spread through the virgin lands of Neolithic Europe some 7,000 years ago. The first farmers slashed and burned hardwood trees, sowed wheat in the clearings, and pastured their sheep and oxen in the woods. The area was already peopled by a semi-nomadic folk skilled in hunting, tracking, and fishing. The two cultures eventually merged, as the idea and practice of farming spread throughout Europe. The Iceman reflects this hybridization: He probably subsisted on bread, yet could easily sustain himself with materials from the surrounding woods.

While the Iceman's body lies preserved in Innsbruck, his belongings are being housed and studied at the Roman-Germanic Central Museum in Mainz, Germany. Under the watchful eye of archaeologist Markus Egg, leather objects have been meticulously cleaned, greased, and dehydrated, and can now be handled. Artifacts of grass have been freeze-dried to dispel moisture. Wooden finds were cleaned and bathed in vats of thin, warm wax, which replaces moisture in the wood to prevent rotting.

One of the most remarkable wooden objects found was a long bow, hewn from the strong but flexible heartwood of a Tyrolian yew tree. Yews still grow in the valley below the Similaun Glacier where the Iceman was found, and in the past this valley was famed for the high-quality bow staves it produced. This, and the fact that the Iceman's bow was unfinished at the time of his death, suggests he had just cut his stave in the valley.

The sheer size of the bow tells us something about the man. Broken in half during the rescue, the bow originally spanned five feet ten inches—seven inches taller than its owner. "You can't make them much bigger than that," says Christopher Bergman, principal archaeologist with 3D/Environmental Services in Cincinnati.

Bergman is an experiential archaeologist who studies prehistoric bows from around the world. He crafts replicas in the same manner as the ancients, and then uses them in real-world settings to see how they perform. Bergman once made a five-foot-eight-inch yew bow and says it drew about 90 pounds: To pull the bow string back for firing required the same strength needed to lift 90 pounds with one hand. Bergman tested this weapon on a hunt. His shot blew a hole though a deer's chest cavity from 30 yards away, "and right out the other side, and still going," he recalls of the arrow's flight. "I wouldn't want to stand in front of it."

The bow's underbelly bears marks from the discovery's most striking find, a copper ax. The four-inch blade appears to have been cast from molten metal poured into a mold; when cooled, it was worked with a hammer. The blade was hafted in an L-shape crook of yew wood and lashed in place with leather thongs soaked in glue, probably derived from birch tree sap. The ax marks the end of one

---

Who Owns the Iceman?

When the Iceman was first found in the Oetztaler Alps, his 5,300-year-old body and equipment were presumed to be the property of Austria. But a closer inspection by surveyors revealed that the corpse was found about 100 yards inside the border of Italy's South Tyrol. He is therefore the property of Italy.

The body will remain in Innsbruck, Austria, and the equipment in Mainz, Germany, until Sept. 19, 1994—three years from the date the Iceman was discovered. If the researchers need more time to investigate the remains, they may petition for an extension. Meanwhile, it costs about $10,000 a month to maintain the body in its chilly preservation chamber.

Very few people have seen or examined the finds recovered from the site last summer. These artifacts are being held in South Tyrol, tangled in red tape. Provincial officials there plan to build an Iceman museum; they would like to display the body in a refrigerated case.

Werner Platzer, head of the University of Innsbruck's Anatomical Institute and leader of the team researching the body, says ownership of the body is meaningless. "Where he ends up is not important," Platzer says, "so long as he is well taken care of and receives the respect that is his due."—S. F.

The Iceman's unique grass cape is a masterpiece of utility and economy. In addition to serving as a water-repellent, insulating top coat, it may have doubled as a bedroll. It was almost certainly made by the man himself and shows considerable skill in the weaving, knotting, and splicing of the grass.

It is quite probable that the Iceman wore a hat. A ball of fur, still frozen in the ice that surrounded it, is among the objects being stored in Italy, and may prove to be his hat. Since there is not yet an official verdict on the object, this painting shows the Iceman bareheaded.

Deer skin made up most of the Iceman's clothing. Specialists have discovered that his garments were tanned in a vegetable-based solution. This painting depicts the coat as if it were worn with the fur side next to the skin, but it may have been worn with the fur side out.

An assortment of tools allowed the Iceman to exploit the natural resources around him. An ax, a knife, a drill, some scrapers, and bits of antler — along with an intimate knowledge of flora and fauna — were all that this man needed to survive. The man's powerful long bow was incomplete at the time of his death.

Leather work, absent from Neolithic record, can now be studied by examining the Iceman's clothing. Although most of his garments are in tatters, additional pieces of the puzzle may be revealed when artifacts being stored in Italy are officially released for study.

Clever expandable shoes had a multitude of eyelets. The design allowed the Iceman to wear the shoes snugly around his bare feet or to accommodate wads of insulating hay simply by relacing the strings.

Figure 1. Artistic interpretation of the Ice Man based on artifacts found with his body. (Graphic by Mark Zug)

age and the beginning of another. By 3,300 B.C., stone was giving way to metal as the material of choice for tools. The technological revolutions arising from the practice of metallurgy would change the world forever.

The Iceman was an expert at exploiting the natural resources around him; the gear he carried tells us that. Along with his ax he carried an ash-handled knife with a tiny flint blade, just 1 ½ cm inches long. "Had we found the blade without the handle attached," says Konrad Spindler, "we would have assumed it was an arrowhead."

The man also carried a small tool bag that held a bone awl, two flint blades, and what appears to be a flint drill. One of the blades bears pollen traces from some of the 46 species of grass he used to make strings, lashes, and other gear. Unique grass artifacts, including a woven sheath for his knife and a voluminous cape, were manufactured as needed. The cape seems to be made from strands of plaited grass that hung vertically from the collar, as if a poncho were cut into thin ribbons. "Running down to his knees, it looked like a grass skirt you would bind around your shoulders," says Egg.

World's Oldest Quiver

The Iceman's equipment includes a U-shape backpack frame made from hazel wood and the oldest quiver ever found. The quiver contained 12 dogwood arrow shafts and two finished arrows, tipped in expertly chipped flint held in place with gum derived from boiled birch tree roots. X-rays of the quiver's interior show a ball of string, a piece of deer antler, and a couple of raw flints. A puzzling tool—a willow dowel with horn or antler running through the center—may have been used to shape flints. Broad calfskin straps recovered from the glacier may be a belt for the quiver. Somewhere along his trek the Iceman harvested *Piptoporus betulinus*, a birch tree fungus that is used in folk medicine as an antibiotic.

All the equipment was found carefully stashed about 15 feet from the body, just beneath the lip of the trench. Near the body were charcoal remnants from six different types of wood. They could mean the spot was a hideaway that had been frequented in the past, or that the Iceman carried embers for starting a fire. No other fire-starter has been found, although a black, felt-like material laced with pyrite has been interpreted as tinder.

The Iceman was prepared for cold weather. His shoes, oval shapes cut from what is possibly cowhide, cunningly fold up around the foot and leave plenty of space for insulating hay. The hay, from grass that only grows at 10,000 feet in the Alps, was anchored with grass laces threaded though numerous eyelets. A leather flap on each shoe shielded the laces from moisture.

People at the scene of the find described leather pants that "wound around the legs," but only uncertain fragments survived. The Iceman's jacket, worn under the grass cape, is also in tatters. Small patches of finely stitched deer hide with the fur facing out seem to form the torso section, while broader strips probably served as long sleeves. The remaining fragments show many careful repairs over the jacket's lifetime—and one coarse repair. Egg thinks that the man may have been away from home for quite a while, damaged his coat during his trek, and quickly repaired it before he died.

A Shepherd or a Hunter?

When a team of researchers returned last summer to continue the investigation, the site was blanketed in 20 feet of snow. The sun melted 12 feet of it away, and volunteers shoveled through the remaining 600 tons of snow to reach rock. They found what may be a fur hat, or a cap for the quiver, along with the other half of the long bow and numerous scraps of leather and wood. Konrad Spindler collected many pellet-like animal droppings, tentatively identified as belonging to sheep. The Iceman may have been grazing a flock when he died.

An alternate scenario is that of a hunter, who hiked to the valley to cut a replacement for a broken bow and was forced to seek shelter when a storm struck. Experts studying the body speculate that the Iceman, perhaps exhausted as a consequence of adverse weather conditions, fell asleep in the trench and froze to death.

Researchers are reluctant to draw further conclusions about how the Iceman lived and died without more study. It will be many years before the frozen body reveals all of its secrets. Microscopic pieces of the Iceman's organs and equipment are spread among 120 researchers in Europe and the United States, and their work slowly progresses. A man who lost his life 53 centuries ago has become a messenger from the past, emerging from the ice to bring tidings of a world that has long since vanished.

Commentary

Archaeology, as a field, has a unique goal, which is to recover and interpret remains of the past. Although our goal is unique, the methods and techniques we use to pursue this goal commonly derive from other fields of science. Principles of archaeological stratigraphy and seriation derive directly from geology, and many systems of artifact classification follow the model of a binomial system not unlike that used in biology today. Our study of regional settlement systems uses geographic methods to interpret patterning, and we plumb the physical sciences for our techniques to measure time. Even the organization of field expeditions that General Pitt-Rivers and Sir Mortimer Wheeler pioneered in the 19th and early 20th centuries came from a military model. Archaeology's tools and methods often derive from other fields and develop in collaboration with specialists in those disciplines. Articles in this section have illustrated some recent techniques that archaeologists have borrowed to study the archaeological record, writ large (as roads) or small (as individuals). We archaeologists borrow techniques and methods constantly from other fields, and could not do our work effectively without such borrowing. One of the most important points in Kaiser's article on blood residue analysis is that this borrowing must be done just as rigorously and systematically as we conduct fieldwork. Occasionally, archaeologists caught up in the excitement of introducing a new technique will fail to test it adequately before publishing their results. In some cases like the blood residue study, such testing involves multiple scientists using the same technique. In others, testing involves the use of different approaches whose results support or challenge each other. Research described on the Egyptian mummy and on the Iceman illustrate how multiple lines of evidence reinforced a set of hypotheses that researchers advanced concerning their respective study objects. Occasionally, we find that new techniques prove less powerful than initially imagined and must be abandoned.

One of the most promising developments in the use of new techniques has been the array of methods now available to undertake research that involves nondestructive analysis. Not only are archaeological sites nonrenewable resources, but so are the materials recovered from them. Articles in this section illustrate some examples of this kind of work, while also proving that we can now collect a great deal of information from some archaeological remains (like mummies) that lack their original provenance. In the case of the Egyptian mummy, museum needs for an intact object precluded the kind of dissection work that would have yielded more insights on ancient embalming practices, among other topics. Use of radiography did not damage the mummy, just as several techniques used to study the Iceman used non-invasive forms of analysis. Remote sensing is a nondestructive form of analysis that grows increasingly accessible and useful to archaeologists, as we learn how to interpret and manipulate such data to produce meaningful results in our research.

The pace of technological change is rapid, and many specialists from nearly all fields are willing to work with archaeologists on problems out of pure curiosity about our past. As one example, radiocarbon dating was invented hardly more than fifty years ago, and revolutionized our knowledge of world archaeology. Who knows what kinds of new methods scientists will develop in the future? One thing is certain: our understanding of the human past will be greatly enriched with the application of new analytical methods. Ongoing development of scientific methods bodes well for the future of archaeology, when we will answer questions about the past that today we cannot even imagine!

Part Seven

Archaeological Approaches to Technology

Introduction

Some of the earliest archaeological work in the western world focused on the study of ancient technology, or how things were made and used. Archaeologists continue to have an active interest in the subject for several reasons. One is that technology—and the tools it produces—has been one of our most important cultural adaptations from the "Stone Age" of early human antiquity to the "Information Age" of the modern world system. Another is that some technological behavior produces material remains that archaeologists can study. In studying ancient technologies through replication, experiment, and analysis, we gain insights into the motivations and cognition of ancient peoples (see also articles in Part Eleven).

Humans (and our human ancestors) have made and used tools for at least two million years. The fabrication and use of tools for generating light, hunting wild game, transporting megalithic statues and for many other purposes, often accompanied remarkable changes in ancient societies. "Ice Age Lamps," by Sophie de Beaune and Randall White, describes how the technology of fat-burning lamps provided a source of light in the dark caverns of what is now southwestern France. Their study of Paleolithic lamps now housed in museum collections revealed three types of lamps, one of which (the closed-circuit variant) closely resembles those used by Arctic peoples as recently as the 20th century. Use of modern scientific techniques and replication yielded information on lamp fuel and gives some idea of just how much light individual lamps provided. Interestingly, these lamps were made during the Upper Paleolithic era (40,000 to 11,000 years ago), and are found in areas where cave painting was practiced in Ice Age Europe. Although Paleolithic lamps generate weak light compared with modern electrical lighting, the authors believe that such lamps were used to illuminate caves during the painting process. They also suggest that flickering light produced from fat-burning lamps may have generated powerful illusions as one viewed the images of animals. What we see today in our visits to magnificent caves containing Paleolithic art is thus much different from the perspective that their creators shared as they worked the walls of these important places.

Late Ice Age peoples developed several different technologies that enabled them to survive in Europe's harsh environment. While painters may have painted animal figures on cave walls to increase their hunting success, these people also made improvements in more mundane technologies like hunting equipment. Heidi Knecht's article, "Late Ice Age Hunting Technology," describes how experimental archaeological research changed our understanding of the design templates for spear points that humans developed during the Upper Paleolithic. Her replication and testing of different kinds of spear points (both bone and antler) suggests that many design changes during this period reflect distinct solutions to particular hunting problems. The Cro-Magnon case described here is an intriguing example of how ancient peoples experimented with different materials to improve their hunting technology.

Sometimes the absence of evidence (so-called "negative evidence") is as persuasive to archaeologists as its presence. We commonly study nonperishable artifacts from the Paleolithic, such as stone, bone, and antler. If studies of 20th century foragers is any guide, then Paleolithic populations also used perishable materials in their food procurement and preparation technologies. In his article entitled, "Bamboo and Human Evolution," Geoffrey Pope suggests a solution to a puzzle that the archaeologist Hallam Movius posed more than fifty years ago. Movius found that Lower Paleolithic sites across much of Asia (India, China, Japan, Korea and Southeast Asia) lacked sizable quantities of the bifacial tool (or Acheulean hand-axe) that characterizes the Lower Paleolithic in Europe, the Near East and Africa. Did this boundary, thereafter called "the Movius line," reflect lower levels of technological development in the East than in the West? Earlier anthropologists maintained this belief and dismissed Asia as a cultural backwater. Pope challenges this claim by using biogeography: it turns out that the Movius line corresponds closely to the westernmost boundary of bamboo species. Today in Asia, bamboo is used for many purposes, from making cooking and storage containers, knives, spears, traps, and ropes, to building structures. The only tools that cannot be made from bamboo are axes or choppers for working hard woods and harvesting bamboo itself. Pope argues that the stone axes and choppers that archaeologists find in Asia were used by ancient peoples to harvest the mainstay of their Paleolithic technology: bamboo.

Fewer archaeologists study transportation than they do tools, but it is no less important as a kind of ancient technology. "Moving the Moai," by Jo Anne Van Tilburg, is an exciting example of how an archaeologist used computer simulation, anthropological research, and experimentation to study and interpret the movement of megalithic monuments in ancient Polynesia. Easter Island is famous for its giant stone sculptures, or *moai;* nearly 900 of these enormous sculptures have been documented on the island through intensive archaeological research. One enduring question for archaeologists who study monument-building societies like Easter Island concerns how they moved these enormous rock statues from their quarries to their final resting places. This is not an easy task! Based on her studies, Van Tilburg argues that *moai,* which averaged 14 tons in weight, were most likely moved by using rollers made from wooden beams. Many archaeologists believe that ancient technologies were shaped by a variety of cultural values and ecological constraints. That ancient technologies often had unintended consequences is convincingly illustrated by the Easter Island case. The religious ideology that fueled the construction and movement of *moai* at Easter Island may have accelerated—rather than ameliorated—the depletion of environmental resources such as wood.

1

Ice Age Lamps

Sophie A. de Beaune and Randall White

The controlled use of fire, first achieved at least half a million years ago, is one of the great innovations in human culture. Although archaeologists and anthropologists generally emphasize the importance of fire for cooking, warmth and protection from predators, the light accompanying fire was also a precious resource, one that made it possible to extend human activity to times and places that are naturally dark. The invention of stone, fat-burning lamps, which happened in Ice Age Europe nearly 40,000 years ago, offered the first effective, portable means of exploiting this aspect of fire. The appearance of lamps broadly coincides with a number of other extraordinary cultural changes, including the emergence of art, personal adornment and complex weapons systems.

Many scholars have hypothesized about how Ice Age lamps functioned and were used, but nobody had ever undertaken a systematic study of them. One of us (de Beaune) therefore set out to examine these lamps in detail and to classify them by type. In conjunction with that project, we built working replicas of stone lamps in order to analyze their effectiveness as light sources and to learn about their design, fabrication and use. The results of this investigation provide a provocative insight into the technology and behavior of some of the earliest modern humans in Europe.

The first object explicitly identified as an Ice Age lamp was discovered in 1902, the year researchers authenticated the wall art in the cave at La Mouthe, France. Archaeologists had presumed that the creation of paintings and engravings hundreds of meters underground must have required an artificial light source. In the course of exploring La Mouthe, they uncovered compelling support of that notion: a carefully fabricated and heavily burned sandstone lamp bearing the engraved image of an ibex on its underside.

Since then, hundreds of more or less hollowed-out objects have been excavated and rather indiscriminately lumped into the category of lamps. The initial research goals were to sift through the potpourri, establish criteria for identifying lamps and examine variation within this category of objects. A search of the literature and of museum collections turned up 547 artifacts that had been listed as possible lamps. The first hurdle was to distinguish lamps from other similarly shaped implements, such as grinding stones. It quickly became obvious that the size and shape of an object are insufficient as defining criteria. For example, lamps need not have a bowl-shaped depression; many perfectly flat slabs show clear traces of localized burning, which in these and other instances provide the only incontrovertible evidence that an object served as a lamp.

We judged that 245 of the 547 putative lamps clearly served other purposes (mortars, ocher receptacles and so on). The remaining 302 objects were of uncer-

Figure 1. Ice Age lamp made from unaltered stone with natural crevices. (Photo courtesy of Randall White)

tain status as lamps. We then divided that sample (285 of which have a well-known site of origin) into two categories. We considered 169 of the items to be certain, probable or possible lamps. The other 133 we classified as doubtful or unavailable for study. Markings left by the burning of fuel and wick tend to disappear over time, so the oldest lamps were the most likely to fall into the dubious category. The lamps that we consider here all date from the Upper Paleolithic era, between 40,000 and 11,000 years ago.

The 285 lamps of known origin come from 105 different archaeological sites, mainly in southwest France. The Aquitaine basin has yielded 60 percent of the lamps, the Pyrenean region 15 percent. Considerably fewer lamps have been recovered from other parts of France, and lamps found outside France—in Spain, Germany and Czechoslovakia—are exceedingly rare. Although this pattern may be explained in part by the historically greater intensity of research and the greater number of sites in southwest France, it seems that lamp-producing cultures were in fact restricted to a particular European region.

The vast majority of the known stone lamps consist of limestone or sandstone, both of which are fairly abundant. Limestone has the advantage of often occurring naturally in slab-like shapes that require little alteration. Moreover, limestone conducts heat poorly, so lamps of this material do not get hot enough to burn the user's fingers. Sandstone is a much better heat conductor, so simple sandstone lamps quickly become too hot to hold after they are lit. Paleolithic people solved this problem by carving handles into most sandstone lamps. Perhaps part of the appeal of sandstone lay in its attractive red color and smooth texture.

Our experiments suggest that the size and shape of the bowl are the primary factors that control how well a stone lamp functions. Setting bowl shape as our primary criterion, we divided the 302 Upper Paleolithic lamps into three main types: open-circuit lamps, closed-circuit bowl lamps and closed-circuit lamps with carved handles.

Open-circuit lamps are the simplest kind. They consist of either small, flat or slightly concave slabs or of larger slabs having natural cavities open to one side to allow excess fuel to drain away as the fat melts; the largest ones are roughly 20 centimeters across. Because open-circuit lamps show no noticeable signs of carving or shaping, large numbers of them may have gone unrecognized in premodern excavations. As a result, open-circuit lamps probably are underrepresented in the current sample.

Any slab of rock will work as an open-circuit lamp, so fashioning one requires extremely little effort. The trade-off is that these kinds of lamps inevitably waste a lot of fuel. Open-circuit lamps may be best interpreted as makeshift or expedient devices, easily made and freely discarded. Studies of the modern Inuit show that human groups, even those capable of building large, elaborate lamps, occasionally burn a piece of fat on a stone slab when no alternative lies readily at hand.

Closed-circuit bowl lamps are the most common variety. They are found in all regions, in all periods and in all types of sites where lamps have been recovered. Closed-circuit bowl lamps have shallow, circular or oval depressions designed to retain the melted fuel. The recovered lamps of this kind range from crude to elaborate. Some bowl lamps are entirely natural, some have a slightly retouched bowl and others are completely fabricated. The exterior part of the lamp also may be natural, partly retouched or entirely sculpted. These lamps consist of oval or circular pieces of limestone that are usually the size of a fist or slightly larger. The bowl has sloping sides capable of retaining liquid when the lamp is placed on a horizontal surface. A typical bowl measures a few centimeters across but only 15 to 20 millimeters deep. The largest bowls can hold about 10 cubic centimeters of liquid.

Ice Age closed-circuit lamps resemble those employed by certain Inuit peoples—such as the Caribou, Netsilik and Aleut—who had access to wood for fuel and were therefore not dependent on lamps for heat. Inuit living north of the treeline, where wood was scarce, designed large lamps from slabs of soapstone that were up to a meter across. Those giant lamps (perhaps more correctly thought of as stoves) served many of the same functions as hearths elsewhere, including drying clothes, cooking and heating. There may be direct relations between the quality and abundance of locally available wood for fuel, the presence of fireplaces and the form of lamps at a site.

The most intricate lamps are those we classified as closed-circuit lamps with carved handles. The 30 such lamps in our sample are shaped, smoothed and finely finished entirely by abrasion. Each has a carved handle; 11 of them are decorated with engravings. These lamps appear in the archaeological record somewhat later than the others. The first carved-handle lamps show up in either the Solutrean (22,000 to 18,000 years ago) or Lower Magdalenian (18,000 to 15,000 years ago) cultures. They are particularly abundant in the Middle and Upper Magdalenian (15,000 to 11,000 years ago). Most carved-handle lamps are found in the Dordogne region of France. They are most abundant in rock-shelter sites but are also found in caves and open-air camps.

The elegant design, rarity and limited distribution in time and space of carved-handle lamps may imply that they served primarily ceremonial purposes. A well-

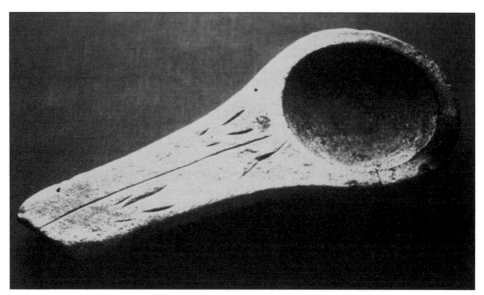

Figure 2. Ice Age lamp carved from stone. (Photo courtesy of Randall White)

known example from Lascaux, which has been dated to 17,500 years ago, was found on the cave floor at the bottom of a vertical shaft, below a drawing of a hunter confronting a wounded bison. This lamp was discovered by the Abbé Glory, a Catholic lay priest who suggested that such lamps were used to burn aromatic twigs and hence were analogous to incense burners. Too few chemical analyses have been performed, however, to test this hypothesis adequately. The other kinds of stone lamps probably served exclusively as sources of light.

To be effective, a fat-burning lamp must be reliable, easy to handle and bright enough to throw usable light a distance of a few meters in, for example, a darkened cave. The form of lamp that predominates in our sample of Paleolithic lamps is precisely that which our experiments revealed to be optimally efficient. It is a closed-circuit lamp having an oval or circular depression and gently sloping rather than vertical sides. Sloping the side of the bowl facilitates emptying the lamp (so that the wick does not become swamped in melted fat) without dislodging the wick. Carving a gap or notch in the rim of the lamp offers an alternative way to empty the bowl while keeping the wick in place. Eighty percent of the Paleolithic lamps we studied use the sloped-side approach.

Anthropologists have long assumed that animal fat was the fuel burned in Ice Age lamps. From our experiments, we learned that the best fats are those that melt quickly and at a low temperature. Also, they must not contain too much adipose tissue, the connective tissue in fat. Fat from seals, horses and bovids proved most effective in experimental lamps. But were these in fact the fuels favored by Paleolithic humans?

Guy L. Bourgeois of the University of Bordeaux and de Beaune analyzed residues from several Paleolithic lamps to identify the substances they contained. Using two sensitive chemical analysis techniques (vapor-phase chromatography and mass spectrometry), they measured the carbon isotope ratios in fatty acids in the residues. The abundance ratios resemble those in animal fats from modern herbivores, such as cattle, pigs and horses. Unfortunately, scientists have no samples of fat from the actual animals that lived during the late Pleistocene. Nevertheless, the observed ratios of carbon isotopes are quite unlike those in vegetable fats, proving that animals were indeed the source of fuel for Ice Age lamps.

Our investigations also provided new information about the materials from which wicks were made. A good wick must be able to attract melted fat by capillary action and convey it to the free, burning end without being too quickly consumed. Of the wicks we tested, lichen (known to be used by modern Inuit), moss and then juniper worked best. Fritz H. Schweingrüber of the Swiss Federal Research Institute for Forest, Snow and Landscape analyzed several lamp residues. He detected remnants of conifers, juniper and grass, as well as nonwoody residues, possibly lichen or moss. In our experience, juniper wicks are never completely consumed by the flame and so may be better preserved than wicks composed of other plants.

The traces of use on our experimental lamps make it possible to interpret with confidence the markings observed on Paleolithic lamps. Those signs of usage come in three broad forms: light accumulations of soot, deposits of charcoal and reddening of the rock itself, a process known as rubefaction. In 80 percent of all the lamps observed, soot and charcoal deposits are situated within or on the rim of the fuel chamber, where one would expect the wick to lie. Occasional blackening of the side or underside of the lamp can be produced by trickles of melted fat that carried with them small particles of soot. Charcoal deposits result from carbonization of the wick or from the heat alteration, or calcination, of adipose tissue in the burning fat.

Thermal reddening often appears on the sides and undersides of lamps, but it, too, most frequently appears in or on the rim of the fuel chamber (in 67.5 percent of the cases). Experience with modern replicas indicates that such reddening took place when hot, melted fat ran onto the side or bottom of the lamp, either as the lamp was being emptied or when it overflowed on its own. Thermal reddening evidently can occur after only a few uses and so provides a helpful indicator of which artifacts served as lamps.

Repeated reuse of a lamp leaves distinct patterns. If a standard open-or-closed-circuit lamp is lit on several occasions, the placement of the fat and wick tends to change from one time to the next. Because there is no preferred orientation for those simple lamps, they eventually become blackened and reddened over the entire bowl or surface. The carefully worked closed-circuit lamps that have handles display strikingly different signs of usage. They are oriented the same way each time they are lit, so soot deposits build up on one part of the bowl only, generally the area opposite the handle.

Open-circuit and simple closed-circuit lamps probably were lit only a few times before being discarded. They were so easy to manufacture that there would have existed little incentive to carry them from site to site; we found that we could make a decent lamp in about half an hour. Decorated, carved-handle lamps, which represent a greater investment of labor, were more likely to have been used repeatedly.

To evaluate the effectiveness of Paleolithic fat-burning lamps, one needs to know how much light those lamps could provide. De Beaune investigated this matter by measuring the light output of modern replicas in the metrology laboratories of Kodak-Pathé, France. In quantity, intensity and luminescence, the experimental lamps provided distinctly less light than a standard candle but nonetheless would have been sufficient to guide a person through a cave or to illuminate fine work when placed nearby—assuming, of course, that the visual acuity of Paleolithic people was the same as ours.

The limitations of Ice Age lamps suggest that the creators of cave drawings never saw them as they appear in modern photographs. Human color perception is constrained and distorted at levels less than 150 lux (for comparison, 1,000 lux is typical in a well-lit office). It seems doubtful that the creators of the cave art worked under such bright conditions. Achieving full and accurate color perception of the cave images along a five-meter-long panel would require 150 lamps, each of them placed 50 centimeters from the cave wall. Torches could have provided supplementary light, but few traces of torches have been found in deep caves. On the other hand, the absence or scarcity of lamps in vast cave galleries such as those at Rouffignac, Niaux and Les Trois Frères implies that the creator of the paintings had access to some alternative light sources.

Today when one views the famous cave art in France and Spain, the artificial illumination creates an effect fundamentally unlike that experienced by Paleolithic visitors. Electric lights in the cave of Font de Gaume yield a steady light level of about 20 to 40 lux across a full panel of drawings. Ten to 15 thoughtfully placed stone lamps would be needed to attain 20 lux. A person carrying a single lamp would get a very different impression of the cave art and could view only small portions of the wall at a time. The dim illumination produced by flickering lamps may well have been part of the desired effect of viewing art deep within a cave. The illusion of animals suddenly materializing out of the darkness is a powerful one, and some cave images are all the more convincing if one cannot see them too well.

Of course, fat-burning lamps were employed for many tasks other than creating and viewing cave art. Lamps are found in such abundance at sites throughout southwest France that they must have been a fairly ordinary item of day-to-day existence. Only about 30 percent of the known lamps were recovered in deep caves. Open-air sites, rock shelters exposed to plentiful daylight and cave entries have provided the rest. The number of lamps at each site (two to three, on average) does not differ significantly from caves to rock shelters to open-air sites.

The location of lamps within sites provides clues to how people exploited them. In deep caves, lamps are often recovered from places where people had to pass, such as cave entrances, the intersections of different galleries and along walls. It would seem that lamps were placed at strategic or predictable points where they could easily be found and reused. The discovery of many lamps lying together—most notably at Lascaux, where 70 lamps have been recovered—implies that lamps were stored in particular locations between uses. Unfortunately, one cannot deduce how many of the lamps were lit at any one time.

Lamps are frequently discovered near fireplaces. Perhaps they were preheated in the fire in order to warm the fat and make it easier to ignite or were abandoned and reused as hearthstones. More likely, fireplaces served as central points of heat and light from which people departed into and returned from the darkness. Many lamps are found inverted in the soil, implying that on returning, people extinguished them simply by turning them over.

In at least one location, a lamp seems to have provided a permanent, fixed source of light within a campsite. Archaeologists found two lamps in a small, natural cavity in the wall of the rock shelter of La Garenne. One lamp had been turned over as if to extinguish the flame. The other was placed upright in a nat-

Figure 3. Ice Age lamps have been found primarily in southwest France. Lamps in all eras of the Upper Paleolithic (40,000 to 11,000 years ago); more of them have been recovered from the later periods. Surprisingly, most lamps have been retrieved not from deep caves but from open-air sites and from under rock shelters.

ural hollow in the rock that held it level. The cavity itself would have served as a natural reflector that maximized the lamp's light output.

Sorting through the sample of fat-burning lamps, we sought to learn how their abundance and design changed over time. That analysis is somewhat restricted by the paucity of data. Accurate radioactive dates are available for only the most recently discovered lamps. In most cases, ages are inferred from the archaeological levels in which the lamps were found, and in many early excavations even that information was not recorded. Nevertheless, enough information exists for us to make some general observations.

Many more lamps appear in the last cultural period of the Upper Paleolithic, the Magdalenian, than in preceding periods. This may reflect the fact that there are simply more Magdalenian sites known than is the case for earlier periods, as well as the fact that most deep-cave painting took place in the Magdalenian. Older lamps are also harder to identify with certainty.

The form of lamps seems to have evolved surprisingly little through the ages. Some variation in form, material and design occurred, but there is no clear progression from crude to elaborate. Although carved-handle lamps are more common in the later eras, all three primary types of lamp are found throughout the Magdalenian, and even the most elaborate lamp designs date back to the earliest Upper Paleolithic periods, which roughly corresponds to the time when Cro-Magnon, anatomically modern humans, appeared in Europe. The various forms of lamp most likely represent functional responses to particular contexts of use; the need for both simple, easy-to-make lamps and carved, aesthetically pleasing ones apparently was common to all Paleolithic cultures in France.

It is difficult to overstate the importance of artificial light in freeing humans from their evolutionary adaptation to the daylight world. Cave art specialist Denis Vialou of the Museum of Natural History in Paris lauds the Magdalenian cave artists as the people who conquered the world of the underground. But perhaps it is more accurate to see them as the most daring of a long line of our Cro-Magnon ancestors, who, through intelligence and technological innovation, changed the human experience forever by domesticating the realm of darkness.

Further Reading

DARK CAVES, BRIGHT VISIONS: LIFE IN ICE AGE EUROPE. Randall White. American Museum of Natural History and W. W. Norton & Company, 1986.
PALEOLITHIC LAMPS AND THEIR SPECIALIZATION: A HYPOTHESIS. S. de Beaune in *Current Anthropology*, Vol. 28, No. 4, pages 569-577; August/October 1987.
TECHNOLOGICAL CHANGES ACROSS THE MIDDLE-UPPER PALEOLITHIC TRANSITION: ECONOMIC, SOCIAL AND COGNITIVE PERSPECTIVES. P. Mellars in *The Human Revolution: Behavioural and Biological Perspectives on the Origins of Modern Humans*. Edited by P. Mellars and C. Stringer. Princeton University Press, 1989.
NONFLINT STONE TOOLS OF THE EARLY UPPER PALEOLITHIC. Sophie de Beaune in *Before Lascaux: The Complex Record of the Early Upper Paleolithic*. Edited by H. Knecht, A. Pike-Tay and R. White. CRC Press, 1993.

2

Late Ice Age Hunting Technology

Heidi Knecht

Archaeologists try to piece together a complete picture of past events by examining objects left at the scene. Although artifacts buried under layers of sediment for long periods are often decayed, scattered and damaged, they offer a tremendous amount of information about the people who made them and about how and why they were produced. In recent years, archaeologists have increasingly adopted an experimental approach to gain fresh perspective on the clues they unearth. By trying to replicate certain objects and use them as our ancestors may have, researchers can test their theories and gain insight into the course of daily life millennia ago.

Using this method, I investigated the hunting tools and practices of the Cro-Magnons, who lived during the Late Ice Age (40,000 to 12,000 years ago). From studies of Cro-Magnon food debris and artifacts, workers have long known that those ancient people were highly successful at killing large game. All the same, until recently no one had considered how Late Ice Age humans had designed and used their sophisticated hunting weapons. Cro-Magnon arsenals may well have included traps and snares made from wood and plant or animal fibers. These hunters also used spears, consisting of a sharp point (made from stone, antler, bone or ivory) that was hafted, or fastened, to a wooden shaft. For the most part, only the spearpoints themselves have survived. Luckily, archaeologists have recovered such points from many different sites throughout Europe.

I analyzed in detail four distinct types of Late Ice Age spearpoints dating from between 40,000 and 22,000 years ago, hoping to rediscover some of the procedures our ancestors used to make them. Applying those same techniques, I then fashioned spearpoints in the laboratory identical to those found at archaeological sites and tested them in the field. Through these experiments, I have come to realize the specialized knowledge Cro-Magnon hunters must have had not only of their prey but also of the mechanical properties of their weaponry. They dramatically changed the design of their spearpoints during different periods of the Late Ice Age. By gaining a hands-on appreciation of each of these four designs, we can see more clearly the goals that inspired them so very long ago.

Archaeologists assume that Cro-Magnon hunters must have studied the habits of their prey extensively. They needed to know where herds of red deer, horses, ibexes and other large mammals roamed from season to season. They also had to be aware that the value of animals varied at different times of the year. In the early summer, for instance, reindeer may have been infested with insects that would have rendered their hides unsuitable for making clothing and tents. In addition, to take down animals as powerful as bison and mammoths, these hunters needed the skill to craft and use an array of lethal weapons.

During the beginning of the Late Ice Age, artisans most frequently created their deadly spearpoints from bone and antler. Several factors probably governed the selection of these two raw materials and the decision to use one instead of the other. The first factor was their relative availability. Bones, of course, came part and parcel with the rest of an animal after any successful kill. In contrast, only certain species, such as reindeer and red deer, carry antlers and only during certain seasons. Moreover, antlers are hardest and largest and therefore could supply more durable points in greater numbers during the fall rutting season or after they had been shed. And, except for reindeer, only the males of a species sport antlers.

The decision to use bone or antler for fashioning spearpoints also depended on whether either material was needed for some other purpose. For example, bone was often used to fuel fires kindled for warmth and cooking. Marrow, an excellent source of fat, which is needed to metabolize meat protein, resides in the center of a long bone and could be extracted only by breaking the bones apart. By shattering long bones and then boiling them, the Cro-Magnons could make bone grease—a kind of soup. All these activities destroyed long bones to such an extent that they could not be used for making tools or weapons.

Nevertheless, the choice between antler and bone does not seem to have been based solely on which materials were most available during any one season. Cro-Magnon hunters manipulated these two materials using different methods, in ways that imply that they understood the comparative advantages of each. Antler is a type of bone, but its pattern of growth and development differs dramatically from that of skeletal bone. As a result, antler and bone have distinct structural and mechanical properties. John D. Currey, a biologist at the University of York, has measured the bending strength, elasticity and fracture properties of the two materials and found significant differences between them. When force is applied along the longitudinal axis of bone and antler samples, they show nearly the same bending and compressive strengths. Bone, however, is stiffer and more mineralized, and so it is more likely to fracture on impact. The fact that Late Ice Age artisans developed specific ways for handling antler and bone does not suggest that they knew why the two products performed as they did. But, through experience, they no doubt would have accumulated quite a bit of knowledge about which of the two was more suitable for a given task.

During the Aurignacian period, 40,000 to 28,000 years ago (the earliest period during which anatomically modern humans were living in western Europe), Cro-Magnon artisans preferred antler for making weapons. They made antler spearpoints in three successive designs. The earliest ones were lozenge-shaped points with split bases; then, beginning around 30,000 years ago, thicker lozenge-shaped points having rounded bases were introduced; and 2,000 years after that, spindle-shaped points with gently tapered bases came into use. During the Gravettian period, which followed the Aurignacian, Cro-Magnon artisans introduced a fourth type of spearpoint, one that was made from bone and had a beveled base [see Figure 3].

What criteria guided those who fashioned these highly regular points? To try to answer that question, I first considered what characteristics these four basic variations share. Of necessity, the points are all shaped so that they can pierce the hide of an animal, penetrate muscles and internal organs, and inflict a life-threatening wound. The shapes of the bases, despite their dissimilarities, were also functional.

Figure 1. Lozenge-shaped projectile points recovered from Cro-Magnon archaeological sites were made from a variety of materials including bone and antler. (Photo courtesy of Heidi Knecht)

Cro-Magnon artisans developed the different forms so that the points could be firmly fastened to the wooden shaft and thus stay attached on impact.

Of course, the way a point was hafted onto its shaft affected the aerodynamics of the spear as a whole. To avoid making the finished product too heavy or unwieldy, Cro-Magnon hunters needed to take into account how forcefully the average hunter could throw a spear. During the Late Ice Age, spears were hurled either by hand or by atlatl, a handheld stick with a hook at one end that was inserted into a socket at the end of a spear. Prehistoric hunters began using atlatls at least as early as 22,000 years ago. Although archaeologists debate the precise reasons ancient people had for using atlatls, these devices clearly increased the force and accuracy with which a hunter could throw a spear.

All four points, whether thrown by hand or by atlatl, would have served equally well as the lethal end of a spear. Why did their design change over the course of the Late Ice Age? In search of an explanation, I conducted two series of experiments. First, I used Late Ice Age procedures to manufacture bone and antler spearpoints in the laboratory. I was able to reconstruct step by step the production process used by Cro-Magnons because archaeologists have been fortunate enough to recover spearpoints in different stages of completion, as well as waste and by-products from the process. To check that my method was accurate, at every opportunity I compared the scratches and other marks left on the surface of my objects with those found on archaeological specimens. If the marks did not match, I tried alternative techniques or tools until they did agree. I limited myself to using tools made only from stone, bone and antler. In the end, I was able to fabricate points nearly identical to the genuine artifacts from each period.

In the next stage of my experiments, working with several colleagues on a small farm near Les Eyzies in the southwest region of France, I measured the aerodynamics and durability of the replicated points, as well as how readily they penetrated an animal's hide and bones. We hafted our spearpoints to wooden shafts using strips of animal hide and natural resin and then shot them into goat carcasses suspended in lifelike positions. For the purpose of our exercises, we launched the spears using a calibrated crossbow, which allowed us to control the speed and force with which the spear hit the target. We could therefore be certain that the kinetic energy of the spear would be close to that of a spear thrown either by hand or by atlatl.

We tested each of our spearpoints several times in the hopes of breaking them. One goal of these trials was to determine whether bone and antler points break in telltale ways. Many Ice Age spearpoints excavated from archaeological sites are damaged, and it is often impossible to tell how, or even when, they broke. We

Figure 2. Replicated projectile points prior to hafting. (Photo courtesy of Heidi Knecht)

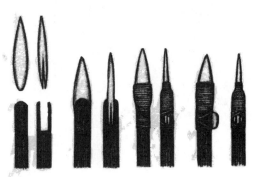

ANTLER SPLIT-BASED POINT
Early Aurignacian (35,000 to 32,000 years ago)

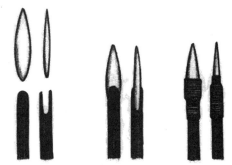

ANTLER LOZENGE-SHAPED POINT WITH SIMPLE BASE
Aurignacian (32,000 to 29,000 years ago)

TOP
VIEW

ANTLER SPINDLE-SHAPED POINT WITH SIMPLE BASE
Late Aurignacian (30,000 to 28,000 years ago)

Figure 3. Spearpoints changed dramatically during the Late Ice Age in form and in the way they were hafted onto a shaft (drawings). The later designs were more easily repaired. Spindle-shaped points could be reversed if the tip wore out. Because the bevels of the bone points were uniform, they could be interchanged. (Graphic courtesy of Patricia Wynne)

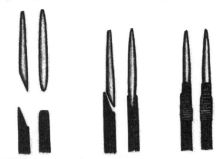

BONE POINT WITH BEVELED BASE
Gravettian (25,000 to 22,000 years ago)

Figure 5. Calibrated crossbow enabled experimenters to control the speed and force of a spear in target trials. They set the crossbow so that the kinetic energy of their spears equaled that of a spear thrown by hand or by atlatl. They could then be certain that the replicated weapons would not outperform those used by prehistoric hunters. (Photo courtesy of Heidi Knecht)

Figure 4. Replicated spears were formed by hafting points onto shafts using animal hide and natural resin. Cro-Magnon hunters most likely applied resin to the spearpoint and shaft to increase the adhesion between them. (Photo courtesy of Heidi Knecht)

learned that if the points were damaged when they hit bones inside the target, bone points usually broke along their midsection. Antler spearpoints, however, showed damage in the form of transverse snaps only near the tip. From such observations, we will be better able to judge whether certain points broke during manufacture or during use or whether instead they were crushed in the ground long after they had been deposited.

We also recorded how much damage the spearpoints did to the bones of the animal. Points made from bone and antler were far more rugged than we had expected. When they entered the animal at a force equivalent to that of a spear released from an atlatl, the points often passed unscathed through vertebrae, ribs and even femurs.

Producing bone and antler spearpoints similar to the Late Ice Age artifacts proved to be no simple task. In our efforts, it became ever more apparent that even during the earliest phase of the Aurignacian, Late Ice Age workers had mastered a highly coherent parcel of techniques. Over time, their methods changed to meet the needs of Late Ice Age hunting in innovative ways. Indeed, it seems from our exercises that the way in which the spearpoints changed shape over time offered more advantages to hunters, who were often on the move when in search of game. The later points were not only lethal, they were also more easily repaired, and during the Gravettian they were readily interchangeable as well.

At the beginning of the Aurignacian, Cro-Magnon hunters manufactured split-based points by splitting and wedging sections of antler. To extract a morsel of antler, the artisans halved a segment of antler along its length. To make the split in the base of the point, they gently struck a wedge held against a platform constructed at the base of the spearpoint. They controlled the direction and length of the split by shaping the point so that it was wider and thicker in that region where the split should end.

Given that splitting and wedging were common techniques for forming spearpoints, it is not surprising that the hunters apparently used another wedging tactic to haft the split-based points. They inserted the base of a spearpoint into a U-shaped slot cut into the end of a wooden shaft and then wrapped the assembly using a ligature made from plant or animal fiber. Next they forced a small wedge made from antler or wood into the split in the base of the point. Archaeologists have recovered antler wedges of this kind from one archaeological site, the Abri Castanet in the Vallon de Castelmerle, Sergeac, France. The wedge then splayed the wings of the split base open inside the shaft. A combination of the forces acting between the shaft, the point, the wedge and the ligature secured the attachment. Curiously, despite the care it took to execute this design, the makers of split-based points do not seem to have been primarily concerned with repairing their products. Although most split-based points have standardized, symmetrical shapes, reworked points found at archaeological sites appear unbalanced, lopsided or misshapen.

Thirty-two thousand years ago, split-based points suddenly disappeared, and lozenge-shaped points with simple bases took their place. In contrast to their forerunners, the lozenge-shaped points seem to have been designed so that they might be resharpened. To make lozenge-shaped points, the hunters cut a fragment of antler in half along its length. The artisans shaped the surfaces and sides of the lozenge-shaped point separately, as they did when making split-based points. They trimmed the sides of lozenge-shaped points by scraping them lengthwise. Then they scraped the top and bottom surfaces of the points until they were smooth. Because the lozenge-shaped points are much wider in the middle than at either end, the spear shaft probably needed to be slotted so that the girth of the point could extend past the diameter of the shaft. A spear shaft having a diameter as wide as a lozenge-shaped point would have been cumbersome to grasp or throw.

I found that lozenge-shaped points were less difficult to make because there was no need to split the base of the point first. Moreover, these points could easily be resharpened, without even removing them from the shaft. Every time we sharpened one of our points that had been damaged in the field, its form fell within the range of variation found in the archaeological sample. Therefore, the design of lozenge-shaped points may have been a response to a growing desire for easily maintained and reusable spearpoints.

Lozenge-shaped points gradually faded out, and spindle-shaped points emerged. Both the Aurignacian lozenge-and spindle-shaped points were usually made from antler, although occasionally some were fashioned from bone or ivory instead. Unlike the split-based points, they both have simple bases that taper gently to a blunt, rounded end. The artisans, however, could manufacture more spindle-shaped points from the same amount of antler than they could lozenge-shaped points. To form spindle-shaped points, Cro-Magnons scraped a segment of antler along its length. Rather than smoothing the sides of the point separately from shaping the upper and lower surfaces, they removed material from the entire circumference of the spindle-shaped point simultaneously. In other words, spindle-shaped points were formed "in the round." The spear maker probably inserted the tapered ends of the spindle-shaped points into a socket hollowed in the end of the shaft. In this way, the spindle-shaped points could be hafted very simply, again making no distinction between their surfaces and sides. The symmetrical design looked exactly the same all the way around the perimeter of the point and the shaft.

We resharpened spindle-shaped points attached to the shaft with the same ease that we experienced reworking damaged lozenge-shaped points. Moreover, because the two ends of spindle-shaped points are identical, a reworked spindle-shaped point could also be recycled by turning it around. The original base would then serve as a fresh point. Whereas only one side of a lozenge-shaped point could have been reused, both sides of a spindle-shaped point could have been resharpened repeatedly.

Spindle-shaped points prevailed for the remainder of the Aurignacian. Then, during the Gravettian, there appear single-beveled points made from long bones of large mammals rather than from antlers. The artisans broke the bones into large splinters and shaped them to a gently tapered point by scraping them along their length. Next they whittled or scraped the end of the piece to form the sloped base. The Gravettian designers probably beveled one end of a wooden shaft at the same angle as the bevel on the base of the point. The two faces, pointing toward each other, would then fit together perfectly. To increase adhesion, the spear maker applied resin to each of the beveled surfaces.

In addition, on virtually all single-beveled points, the surface of the bevel is textured and marked either by the pores of the remaining spongy bone or by purposefully scored grooves. This irregular surface further increased the hold between the base and the end of the shaft—smooth surfaces would have slid against each other, and the point could have come loose in the haft. The artisans sometimes flattened and scored the sides of single-beveled points as well, a feature that probably helped to secure the lashing or adhesive even more.

The shift from antler points to bone points is particularly curious. Given that antler is a tougher and more flexible material than bone, spearpoints made from antler are less likely to break. Moreover, according to the different manner in which antler and bone points fracture when they strike an animal or the ground, a bone point loses more of its length with each successive break. After several breaks, a bone point becomes too short to be resharpened. Therefore, it cannot be resharpened as many times as can an antler point of the same original length.

In designing single-beveled points, however, the artisans did in fact use bone in the best way possible to avoid breakage. They used segments of bone near the epiphyses, the ends of a long bone. Epiphyseal bone exhibits more uniform mechanical properties than does the material found along the middle of a long bone, regardless of the direction in which it experiences stress. As a result, this bone would have been less likely to fracture during impact, penetration and any subsequent movement of the wounded animal. Moreover, single-beveled points attached to a wooden shaft are more streamlined than are their antler predecessors, offering yet another advantage. Indeed, the cross-sectional shape of such a spear remains the same along its entire length, a characteristic that maximizes its elastic resilience.

In our experiments, we had no difficulty retooling broken single-beveled points while they were still attached to the shaft, as was the case for lozenge- and spindle-shaped points. As evidence that Gravettian hunters valued this characteristic, archaeologists have found broken single-beveled points from several Ice Age sites that look as though someone had been in the process of re-sharpening them. Also, if the single-beveled base of a spearpoint was damaged, we found that another bevel could readily be made on the remaining part of the shaft to accommodate the new haft. Significantly, the angle of the bevel was highly standardized. This uniformity meant that the same spear shaft could host a number of resharpened or new points. A hunter could carry spare points and replace a broken point while away from home on a hunting expedition. Of course, the few stone tools needed to repair a broken point could also be taken along.

These four types of spearpoints are but a small fraction of the myriad kinds that hunters manufactured during the Late Ice Age. In addition to bone and antler points, several types of points were made from stone as well. At sites dating to the Gravettian in southern Germany, archaeologists have found collections of points made from mammoth ribs. In addition, it appears that hunters eventually developed more sophisticated hafting mechanisms that were designed so that the point would detach from the shaft when it hit a target. Left inside the animal, the point could have caused even more internal damage.

Indeed, during different periods of the Late Ice Age, artisans explored a number of strategies to form lethal spearpoints. In their various designs, we can see distinct solutions to the same problem—that of manufacturing highly effective weapons. By continuing to reproduce these weapons and to test their performance capabilities, we can reach a fuller understanding of the manner in which our ancestors tackled the challenges that hunting presented.

Further Reading

OSSEOUS PROJECTILE POINTS: BIOLOGICAL CONSIDERATIONS AFFECTING RAW MATERIAL SELECTION AND DESIGN AMONG PALEOLITHIC AND PALEOINDIAN PEOPLES. R. Dale Guthrie in *Animals and Archaeology*, Vol. 1: *Hunters and Their Prey*. Edited by Juliet Clutton-Brock and Caroline Grigson. BAR International Series 163, pages 273-294; 1983.

THE OPTIMAL DESIGN OF HUNTING WEAPONS: MAINTAINABILITY OR RELIABILITY. Peter Bleed in *American Antiquity*, Vol. 51, No. 4, pages 737-747; October 1986.

VISUAL THINKING IN THE ICE AGE. Randall White in *Scientific American*, Vol. 261, No. 1, pages 92-99; July 1989.

HUNTERS OF THE RECENT PAST. Edited by Leslie B. Davis and Brian O. K. Reeves. Unwin Hyman, 1990.

BEFORE LASCAUX: THE COMPLEX RECORD OF THE EARLY UPPER PALEOLITHIC. Edited by Heidi Knecht, Anne Pike-Tay and Randall White. CRC Press, 1993.

HUNTING AND ANIMAL EXPLOITATION IN THE LATER PALEOLITHIC AND MESOLITHIC OF EURASIA. Edited by G. L. Peterkin, H. M. Bricker and P. Mellars. *Archaeological Papers of the American Anthropological Association*, No. 4; 1993.

SPEARS, DARTS, AND ARROWS: LATE WOODLAND HUNTING TECHNIQUES IN THE UPPER OHIO VALLEY. Michael Shott in *American Antiquity*, Vol. 58, No. 3, pages 425-443; July 1993.

3

Bamboo and Human Evolution

Geoffrey G. Pope

Today the seven-mile journey from the highway to our field camp in the Wang Valley seems almost too easy. In the ten years since I began paleoanthropological work in northern Thailand, roads have replaced bullock paths, and sugar cane fields lie where dense teak stands once towered. Taking only minutes to pass through the local village, our *song-tao*, or "two-bench" pickup truck, is well on the way to Kao Pah Nam (Wild Thorn Hill), a craggy spine of limestone clothed in treacherous thorn scrub. Everybody in the *song-tao* knows enough to lean into the center of the vehicle to avoid the razor-sharp thorns that rake the open sides.

Reaching our destination, we file out, impatient to flex cramped limbs, shake off the layers of cold dust, and rub new bruises. We are standing at the base of a karst ridge. Karst (first named for the Karst region of Yugoslavia) is an irregular terrain that develops when ground water saturated with carbonic acid erodes limestone. In tropical forests the effects are particularly striking because the dense root systems and thick layers of decaying organic matter give off a great deal of carbon dioxide, which in combination with water forms carbonic acid. All around us are imposing pinnacles with intriguing fissures and caves. For the paleoanthropologist, karst is especially inviting since caves attract animals seeking shelter, and early hominids—human ancestors and their relatives—would have been no exception. The caves trap bones and cement them in a limestone breccia, preserving fossils that would otherwise disintegrate on the tropical forest floor, with its acid soil and its active insect and microorganic life.

In prehistoric times the karst environment would have provided attractive resources for early humans. Today people still seek out caves during the hot dry season for their shaded, cool, subterranean waters. Bats, birds, snakes, and small mammals that live there are routinely collected for food. Karst towers also provide convenient points from which to survey the surrounding countryside and are important in the rainy season, when most rivers flood and the lowland country becomes inundated for months at a time. The limestone is also mined for phosphates, quicklime, and building stone.

From the forest around us comes the complacent, comforting cooing of "forest chickens." Suddenly, a series of explosions silences the birds. Some of the reports are as loud as dynamite blasts, but local inhabitants take no notice. For them the explosions are as natural as the sounds of the forest animals. They emanate from an unseen grove of bamboo that some villagers have set alight; the crackling sound of a brush fire accompanies them. The air in the sealed bases of the hollow

Figure 1. The Southeast Asian upland environment (Kalinga province, Philippines). (Photo by Miriam T. Stark)

bamboo trunks expands until they blow apart, felling the giant stalks (the word *bamboo* is Malay in origin and thought to be onomatopoeic for these explosions). This is the first step in the harvesting of a versatile raw material. For me, the explosions are fascinating, because I suspect that these same sounds have echoed in this valley for a million years, and that bamboo has shaped the course of human evolution in this part of the world.

Bamboo provides, I believe, the solution to a puzzle first raised in 1943, when the late archeologist Hallam Movius of Harvard began to publish his observations on paleolithic (Old Stone Age) cultures of the Far East. In 1937 and 1938 Movius had investigated a number of archeological localities in India, Southeast Asia, and China. Although most of the archeological "cultures" that he recognized are no longer accepted by modern workers, he made another, more lasting contribution. This was the identification of the "Movius line" (which his colleague Carleton Coon named in his honor): a geographical boundary, extending through northern India, that separates two long-lasting paleolithic cultures. West of the line are found collections of tools with a high percentage of symmetrical and consistently proportioned hand axes (these are called Acheulean tools, after the French site of Saint Acheul). More or less similar tool kits also occur in Mongolia and Siberia, but with few exceptions (which are generally relatively late in time), not in eastern China or Southeast Asia, where more crudely made tools known as choppers and chopping tools prevail.

Although both types of tools are attributed to our hominid ancestor *Homo erectus* and are of similar age (Acheulean tools are from 1.5 million to 200,000 years old; chopper-chopping tools from 1 million to 200,000 years old), Acheulean tools have long been regarded as more advanced than the more crudely made and less standardized tools of the Far East, which some have called a smash-and-grab technology. Movius was among the first to ponder the significance of this geographical division. In 1948 he published his conclusion that the Far East was a region of "cultural retardation," which he believed could never have played a vital and dynamic role in early human evolution, although very primitive forms of Early Man apparently persisted there long after types at a comparable stage of physical evolution had become extinct elsewhere.

For years this explanation was accepted and even, in the interpretations of Carleton Coon and others, taken as evidence of racial isolation and backwardness.

With the flowering of the civil rights movement in the 1960s, most anthropologists rejected the notion of cultural retardation, especially if it had racial overtones. Now some suggest that *all* early human ancestors (not just the Asian hominids) had minimal capacities for culture, that is, for toolmaking and other types of socially learned behavior. Lewis Binford, of the University of New Mexico, has been influential in this view. He has spent the last few years reexamining evidence from a number of archeological localities and has concluded that many characterizations of past cultural behavior are based on very little solid data. At any rate, Binford and others would attribute the crudeness of the artifacts from China to the general inability of early hominids to manufacture standardized stone tools.

The problem with this is that it doesn't really solve the mystery of the Movius line. Over the years, however, a few archeologists have put forward a very different line of reasoning, which I have found to be more fruitful. Their idea is that the early Asians may have relied heavily on tools that they made from raw materials other than stone, and since these are seldom preserved at archeological sites, we simply lack a balanced appreciation of their accomplishments. This suggestion

Figure 2. Bamboo is used for many purposes throughout Southeast Asia; here we see Kalinga men in the northern Philippines preparing bamboo for house construction. (Photo by Miriam T. Stark)

has not generally been pursued, primarily because it is hard to confirm—after all, there is not much use in going out to dig for what probably has not been preserved.

One promising method of detecting nonlithic technology is to study the cut marks on fossil bones. Jolee West, a graduate student at the University of Illinois, has been experimenting with using the electron microscope to differentiate between the kinds of damage left by stone and other cutting implements. Continued development of this approach should eventually offer a direct means to test for the prehistoric use of nonlithic tools.

My own research on the Movius line and related questions evolved almost by accident. During the course of my work in Southeast Asia, I excavated many sites, studied a variety of fossil faunal collections, and reviewed the scientific literature dealing with Asia. As part of this research I compared fossil mammals from Asia with those recovered from other parts of the world. In the beginning, my purpose was biostratigraphic—to use the animals to estimate the most likely dates of various sites used by early hominids. On the basis of the associated fauna, for example, I estimate that Kao Pah Nam may be as old as 700,000 years.

After years of looking at fossil collections and faunal lists, I realized that something was very strange about the collections from Southeast Asia: there were no fossil horses of Pleistocene age (1.6 million to 12,000 years ago) or for a considerable time before that. The only exceptions were a few horse fossils from one place in southern China, the Yuanmou Basin, which was and is a special small grassland habitat in a low, dry valley within the Shan-Yunnan Massif.

To mammalian biostratigraphers this is unusual, since members of the horse family are so common in both the Old and New World that they are a primary means of dating various fossil localities. Fossil horses have been reported from western Burma, but the last one probably lived there some twenty million years ago. Not a single fossil horse turns up later than that in Southeast Asia, although they are known from India to the west and China to the north and every other part of Europe and Asia.

I then began to wonder what other normally common animals might be missing. The answer soon became apparent: camels—even though they too were once widespread throughout the world—and members and relatives of the giraffe family. Pleistocene Southeast Asia was shaping up as a kind of "black hole" for certain fossil mammals! These animals—horses, camels, and giraffids—all dwell in open country. Their absence on the Southeast Asian mainland and islands (all once connected, along with the now inundated Sunda Shelf) is indicative of a forested environment. The mammals that are present—orangutans, tapirs, and gibbons—confirm this conclusion.

The significance of this is that most reconstructions of our evolutionary past have emphasized the influence of savanna grassland habitats, so important in Africa, the cradle of hominid evolution. Many anthropologists theorize that shrinking forests and spreading grasslands encouraged our primarily tree-dwelling ancestors to adapt to ground-dwelling conditions, giving rise to the unique bipedal gait that is the hallmark of hominids. Bipedalism, in turn, freed the hands for tool use and ultimately led to the evolution of a large-brained, cultural animal. Tropical Asia, instead, apparently was where early hominids had to readapt to tropical forest.

In studying the record, I noticed that the forested zone—the zone that lacked open-dwelling mammals—coincided generally with the distribution of the chopper-chopping tools. The latter appeared to be the products of a forest adaptation that, for one reason or another, deemphasized the utilization of standardized stone tools. At least this held for Southeast Asia; what at first I could not explain was the existence of similar tools in northern China, where fossil horses, camels, and giraffids were present. Finally, I came upon the arresting fact that the distribution of naturally occurring bamboo coincided almost perfectly with the distribution of chopper-chopping tools. The only exceptions that may possibly be of real antiquity—certain hand ax collections from Kehe and Dingcun, in China, and Chonggok-Ni, in Korea—fall on the northernmost periphery of the distribution of bamboo and probably can be attributed to fluctuation of the boundary.

Today there are, by various estimates, some 1,000 to 1,200 species of bamboo. This giant grass is distributed worldwide, but more than 60 percent of the species are from Asia. Only 16 percent occur in Africa, and those on the Indian subcontinent—to an unknown extent the product of human importation and cultivation—are discontinuous in distribution and low in diversity. By far, the greatest diversity occurs in East and Southeast Asia.

Based on these observations, I hypothesized that the early Asians relied on bamboo for much of their technology. At first I envisioned bamboo simply as a kind of icon representing all nonlithic technology. I now think bamboo specifically must have been an extremely important resource. This was not, in my opinion, because appropriate rock was scarce but because bamboo tools would have been efficient, durable, and highly portable.

There are few useful tools that cannot be constructed from bamboo. Cooking and storage containers, knives, spears, heavy and light projectile points, elaborate traps, rope, fasteners, clothing, and even entire villages can be manufactured from bamboo. In addition to the stalks, which are a source of raw material for the manufacture of a variety of artifacts, the seeds and shoots of many species can be eaten. In historical times, bamboo has been to Asian civilization what the olive tree was to the Greeks. In the great cities of the Far East, bamboo is still the preferred choice for the scaffolding used in the construction of skyscrapers. This incomparable resource is also highly renewable. One can actually hear some varieties growing, at more than one foot per day.

Some may question how bamboo tools would have been sufficient for killing and processing large and medium-size animals. Lethal projectile and stabbing implements can in fact be fashioned from bamboo, but their importance may be exaggerated. Large game accounts for a relatively small proportion of the diet of many modern hunters and gatherers. Furthermore, animals are frequently trapped, collected, killed, and then thrown on a fire and cooked whole prior to using bare hands to dismember the roasted carcass. There are many ethnographic examples among forest peoples of this practice.

The only implements that cannot be manufactured from bamboo are axes or choppers suitable for the working of hard woods. More than a few archeologists have suggested that the stone choppers and resultant "waste" flakes of Asia were created with the objective of using them to manufacture and maintain nonlithic tools. Bamboo can be easily worked with stone flakes resulting from the manufacture of choppers (many choppers may have been a throwaway component in the manufacture of flakes).

In addition to bamboo, other highly versatile resources such as liana, rattan, and various needs are also found in Asian forests. To really appreciate the wealth

Figure 3. Split bamboo is used for making floors and walls in many areas of Southeast Asia, including central Thailand. (Photo by Miriam T. Stark)

of resources one has to visit Southeast Asia today. Even though many forested areas have been disturbed or even destroyed by humans, those that remain offer an accurate picture of the variety of habitats that early hominids encountered when they first reached the Far East. Southeast Asia is dominated by tropical forest, but this is not necessarily rain forest. While evergreen rain forest exists in Indonesia, the monsoon forest in northern Thailand is deciduous. In northern China there is boreal woodland forest.

Most of my work has been in northern Thailand where the forests are burned every year, frequently not for agricultural reasons but to permit the passage of human foot traffic. Despite burning during the dry season (January-April), the forests are once again impenetrable at the end of the wet season (September-December). Many of the hardwood trees, such as the various kinds of teak, are fire resistant and seem little affected by these seasonal conflagrations, indicating that fire played an important role in their evolution. This may be evidence that fire, first used by our ancestors in tropical Africa, aided the colonization of the Asian forests by *Homo erectus*. Fire would also have been instrumental in the working and utilization of nonlithic resources such as bamboo. This relationship between humans, fire, and the forest is probably more than one million years old in Asia.

Our thorn-bedecked site of Kao Pah Nam, where we have been excavating a rock-shelter (shallow cave), itself preserves evidence of fire. Here we have discovered a roughly circular arrangement of fire-cracked basalt cobbles, in association with other artifacts and animal bones. These hearth stones had to have been brought in by early hominids, as very few nonlimestone rocks lie in the rock-shelter. At first I wondered why our early ancestors would have bothered to lug these heavy rocks into their shelter when limestone was abundant at the site.

The answer emerged as the result of a sort of accident in our field camp. For a number of days we had been cooking our meals on a hearth made of local limestone. A few days into the field season we began to notice that people were complaining of itchy and burning skin rashes. The symptoms were very unpleasant. At first we assumed the cause to be some sort of malevolent plant or fungus. By this time camp life had become uncomfortable and there were further complaints of shortness of breath and burning lungs. Finally, one of our Thai workers pointed out that the rocks of our cooking hearth, after numerous heatings and coolings from our fires, had begun to turn to quicklime. The heat, in conjunction with water from numerous spilled pots of soup and boiling kettles of coffee, had caused this caustic substance to become distributed throughout the dusty camp. We quickly replaced the limestone rocks with ones made of basalt. Only months later did it dawn on me that the early hominids that lived at Kao Pah Nam also must have known about the dangers of cooking on limestone. This explained why they bothered to bring in non-native rocks.

On the basis of our ongoing excavations we have concluded that Kao Pah Nam was occupied intermittently by both carnivores and hominids. Bones of extinct hyenas, tigers, and other carnivores are confined primarily to the deeper recesses of the rock-shelter, likely to have been preferred by denning animals. The hearth and other artifacts, on the other hand, are located near what was the entrance. Many of the prey animals that have been recovered are large by modern standards and include hippo and giant forms of ox, deer, bamboo rat, and porcupine. Nothing about the animals suggests anything but a forested environment.

Figure 4. Bamboo is used as drain pipe at an outdoor spring (note broken earthenware pottery in background). (Photo by Miriam T. Stark)

Artificial cut marks (as well as gnaw marks of large porcupines) are present on the bones associated with the hearth and artifacts. Bones that apparently had been burned have also been recovered. Other evidence that bears on the diet of early hominids consists of extinct freshwater oyster shells piled on top of one another against the rock-shelter wall. This area remains to be fully excavated.

As the result of our work at Kao Pah Nam and other early Pleistocene sites in Thailand, we are beginning to put together a picture of regional artifact types, frequency, and age. There appears to be a simple but systematic pattern of manufacturing choppers and other artifacts by removing a few flakes from one side of a lump of stone. A similar pattern is turning up in karst caves in southern China. In all these sites, small flakes are absent or rare. One interpretation is that the flakes were carried off into the forest for use in processing raw materials.

Of particular concern to paleoanthropologists is establishing the age of early Asian artifacts. In China, a number of sites are now reliably dated (by paleomagnetic evidence) to approximately one million years ago, and a variety of dating techniques suggest the earliest fossils and artifacts of *Homo erectus* on Java (so-called Java man) are somewhere between 800,000 and 1.3 million years old. In mainland Southeast Asia, however, artifacts demonstrably older than 100,000 years have long been elusive. Paleomagnetic studies have not yet been carried out to check our estimated biostratigraphic age of 700,000 years for Kao Pah Nam, but both radiometric and paleomagnetic studies were conducted at another site, Ban Don Mun. Artifacts beneath a basalt flow at that site can be assigned an early Pleistocene age of at least 700,000 years. For stratigraphic reasons, artifacts from a nearby site, Mae Tha, can also be accorded that antiquity.

One thing that still eludes us in mainland Southeast Asia are the fossils of the hominids that made the artifacts we have found. As we learn more about their environment, technology, and diet, however, we can see how capably they adapted to a land of bamboo and karst.

A Decade of Retrospect
Geoffrey G. Pope

When I first proposed that the archaeological evidence of the paleolithic record from East Asia was most parsimoniously explained in the context of non-lithic technology, people both derided it and passionately defended it. It was a time when what I call "Binfordism" (the lack of intelligence and cultural capacity in early species of Homo sp.) was on its ascendancy in archaeological thought and interpretation. Living and excavating with the people of Thailand, China and Indonesia finally led me to the hypothesis that tropically adapted modern people do not ordinarily leave traces of most of the daily technology on which they rely. Bamboo is the most conspicuous icon of making a living without stone or metal. In fact, while the rural peoples of all these countries now depend on metal, is also clear that they can substitute almost any metallic object for organic alternatives.

That conclusion from the present led me inevitably to considering how human ancestors could have spread so successfully into areas like Southeast Asia. After nearly a century of archaeological research in the Far East we continue to debate whether or not the unstandardized, stone "chopper-chopping tools" from Asia were manufacturing by hominids of less than human intelligence. My anthropological research, both archaeological and cultural, convinced me many years ago that survival in Southeast Asia would have been untenable for hominids lacking the ability to utilize nonlithic resources for the production of tools. Furthermore, over the course of the last decade, since the publication of "Bamboo and Human Evolution," no scholar that actually researches in East Asia has disagreed with this interpretation.

Hypotheses must stand the test of time in science. They are also subject to the political and social currents of the generations which follow them. To date, no better interpretation of the East Asian evidence has come along. I continue to believe that early Asian hominids were sentient primates whose simple material remains continue to evince their mental complexity.

The archaeological record from the Asian tropics is also one of the primary avenues for assessing the cultural and behavioral "capacities" of the earliest Asians. At the same time it is extremely important to realize that the geological and ecological contexts of these hominids differed substantially from those of Africa and Europe. After over a century of paleoanthropology in Asia this is one of the most basic conclusions which we can draw from the Far Eastern paleolithic record. In retrospect, is not surprising that a large brained hominid responded to new environments with novel solutions.

4

Moving the Moai — Transporting the Megaliths of Easter Island: How Did They Do It?

Jo Anne Van Tilburg

Easter Island's stone statues—sacred objects, emblems of status, and the dominant symbol of a complex ideology—have astounded and perplexed nearly all who have seen or read about them. Pioneering British ethnographer Katherine Scoresby Routledge was the first to investigate the meaning and function of the sculptures, known as *moai*. She and her husband William mounted the 1914-15 Mana Expedition to Easter Island, or Rapa Nui, and mapped Rano Raraku quarry, the volcanic crater where 95 percent of the statues were carved. They discovered and traced the unpaved roads that led from Rano Raraku to ceremonial platforms called *ahu*. Scattered along these roads were 45 statues, presumably abandoned "in transport."

In 1982 I joined the Instituto de Estudios, Universidad de Chile, in its archaeological survey of the island. During the past 12 years my Chilean colleagues and I have located, measured, photographed, drawn, and mapped 883 moai. This number includes visible quarry statues, those on ahu sites, many hidden in caves or partially buried, statues taken from the island to foreign museums, and 47 recorded as "in transport." In mapping Rano Raraku, the Chilean team located 397 of the total number of statues. With 80 percent of the island surveyed, it is possible that another 35-50 moai will be found.

Our goal was to produce a comprehensive description of moai form, style, context, and distribution. In the process we collected a massive amount of data about the political and ideological contexts of the statues. This information holds answers to many questions, not the least of which is how the moai were moved.

To answer this question, I first researched contemporary observations of large stone transport in many parts of the world. In Indonesia, huge gravestones weighing many tons are still hauled on sledges by as many as 150 men, women, and children pulling on attached ropes. In northeastern India, stones of two tons or more were moved over narrow trails as late as the 1940s. Other sources of information are the ethnographically documented cases of stone transport in Madagascar, Tonga, Micronesia, and the Marquesas Islands, and experimental archaeology projects at La Venta in Mexico, at the Giza Plateau in Egypt, and at

Figure 1. Photo of statue at Ahu Akivi, one of seven nearly exactly the same on the same site. This statue defines the metric parameters for the statistically average statue for the entire corpus of Easter Island monolithic figures. (Photo by J. Van Tilburg)

Stonehenge and elsewhere in Great Britain. In virtually all cases, the stones were moved in a horizontal or, occasionally, lateral position on a sledge over rollers.

Next, I studied how eight Rapa Nui statues were collected by foreign museums. In 1886 U.S. Navy Paymaster William J. Thomson and the crew of the USS *Mohican* removed one that is now in the Smithsonian Institution. Islanders and draft animals hauled it two and one-half miles from an inland ahu to Anakena Bay, from which the *Mohican* sailed. The British Museum's statue, called Hoa Hakananai'a ("stolen or hidden friend"), was removed in 1868 from a stone house, then dragged by Rapa Nui people and crew members of HMS *Topaze*, without benefit of a sled. A missionary on the island noted the "precautions" taken to avoid damaging the statue as it was dragged face down, "tracing with its nose, a long furrow on the ground." In 1935 a statue was taken to the Musée d'Art et d'Histoire in Brussels from a site near the village of Hanga Roa. It was wrapped in a cargo net, then placed in a prone position on a wooden sledge, hauled to a nearby bay and loaded on the Belgian training ship *Mercator*. Alfred Métraux, an ethnographer who witnessed the event, took the opportunity to ask questions about prehistoric transport methods. He found that the Rapa Nui were "unable to explain the methods used by their ancestors for transporting the stone images." In 1955 scientists of Thor Heyerdahl's Norwegian Archaeological Expedition attached a 13-foot-tall statue in a horizontal position to a Y-shaped sledge made from a forked tree trunk with cross pieces over the runners. Ropes were attached to the sledge, and between 75 and 180 people hauled it a few yards over flat ground.

Three additional methods of transportation have been suggested. American archaeologist William Mulloy, who directed the re-erection of statues on several restored sites, speculated that a 32-foot-tall, 89-ton statue called Paro could have been moved using a bipod of tree trunks about 30 feet tall. He believed the statue, suspended by ropes from the bipod, could have been inched forward by rocking it on its protruding belly. One or two of the larger statues lying along a transport road may have inspired Mulloy's fulcrum idea, but neither Paro nor the majority of the other larger-than-average statues have sufficient depth through the midsection to make the method feasible.

More recently, a crew directed by Thor Heyerdahl demonstrated that a 13-foot-tall moai could be inched forward in an upright position on completely flat terrain by tilting and rocking the statue back and forth while manipulating ropes attached to the statue's head and base, much as one would move a heavy piece of furniture. The statue they used, which now stands near Ahu Tongariki, was broken at the base during this operation.

Concrete replicas of moai, not particularly well designed or accurately proportioned, have been used in experiments similar to Heyerdahl's. American geologist Charles Love devised a variation on the upright, tilting method by attaching a pod—a small platform of short logs—to the base of his replica. Once upright on the pod, rollers were placed underneath and the replica was pulled forward over flat ground by attached ropes. This was an improvement over the tilting method, but spacing the rollers unevenly caused the replica to come crashing down.

These experiments were largely shots in the dark. I wanted to find a way to experiment with transport methods that didn't endanger a real statue and didn't depend on awkward and inexact replicas. It was also important to conduct experiments that were controlled and replicable, and which could be generalized from

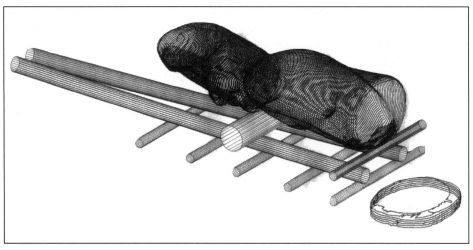

Figure 2. Computer simulation of transport rig capable of supporting and moving the average statue in prone position. It is probable that this was the preferred position for all statues larger and heavier than the statistical average. (Graphic by Mike Ohara)

one statue to many. The moai measurements we so painstakingly gathered over the years would be used to build a computer-simulated moai.

Of the statues inventoried thus far, 134 have ten crucial measurements that define body and head shapes and allow us to determine volume, weight, and center of gravity. All 134 are found on ahu or lying transport" between Rano Raraku and various ahu. Analyses of size, shape, weight, and proportionate relationships of head to body have allowed us to clarify statue forms.

The statistically average statue for the whole island is 14 feet, six inches tall and weighs 14 tons. Of the dozen or more that we could have used as our reference moai, we chose Statue 01 at Ahu Akivi, a restored and dated ahu lying about 460 feet above sea level on the southwestern slope of Maunga Terevaka. Statue 01 is 13

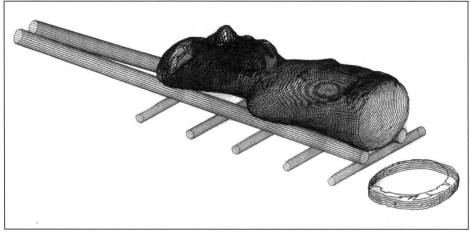

Figure 3. Computer simulation of transport rig capable of supporting and moving the average statue in an alternative, supine position. (Graphic by Mike Ohara)

feet tall and weighs 14 tons. It is five feet wide at its base, almost five feet wide at its head, and has a total depth of three feet through the mid-point of the body. It has a total volume of 210 cubic feet, and its center of gravity is at four and one-half feet. Metric and photogrammetric data collected in 1991 allowed artist Gary Lloyd to sculpt a 1:10 scale model of Statue 01. A computer image of the model produced by laser scan was used to experiment with a variety of hypothetical transport methods.

When Europeans entered the Pacific, the great double-hulled canoes for which Polynesia is now famous were few in number, seen mostly in Samoa, Tonga, and Fiji. Estimates of length vary, but 65 to 70 feet was typical. Canoe hulls from Fiji, Hawaii, and the Society Islands were hewn from massive hardwood tree trunks, weighed from 6 to 12 tons, and were between 108 and 118 feet long. Construction of such vessels was in the hands of master craftsmen with hereditary status and specialized knowledge. The work progressed in accordance with the availability of food. According to Fijian craftsmen, *"a tata tu i kete"* ("the chopping is in the belly"). Sometimes the canoes were built inland, where the best timber was available, and then hauled overland to a beach. In Fiji, the great war canoes are said to have been launched over the bodies of men, sacrificed to serve as rollers allowing the vessel to slide into the water. It is not unreasonable to speculate that moai were commissioned and paid for by Rapa Nui chiefs in much the same way that canoes were built and paid for elsewhere.

We can presume that the Rapa Nui called upon generations of experience in marine exploration and canoe construction and that principles of the fulcrum, lever, forked lever, balance beam, pivot, and moving pivot would have been easily adapted to statue transportation. Ancient skills in the production of stone adzes and chisels, strong cordage, and boring and lashing techniques would have been utilized, as would methods for raising and securing masts using side, back, and fore stays. Fibers from the bark of the hau tree would have been twisted into long, strong ropes. Skilled master carvers would have employed a highly stylized design template, probably using knotted cords and charcoal to mark dimensions on the stone before a statue was roughed out.

We decided—based on Polynesian ethnographies, previous experimental archaeology projects in other megalithic societies, Rapa Nui terrain, and statue attributes—that a horizontal transport method was the most logical. The flat backs of the statues and lines of the shoulders were ideally shaped for such transport. Experiments with our scale model helped us to design a light and economical sledge. When transferred to our computer model, it consisted simply of two simulated, nonparallel wood beams 18 feet long and almost ten inches in diameter. These were placed under our computer reference statue so that they extended and met about three feet beyond the statue's head. The V-shaped alignment of the transport beams would help in pulling the sledge. The weight of the statue alone would hold the beams snugly in place. Fifteen to 20 "rollers" about ten inches in diameter were placed under the simulated beams. The statue was then "pulled" forward with ropes.

Of the 383 statues we have measured to date outside of Rano Raraku, 163 are lying face down, 122 are on their backs, and 31 are on their sides. Does the face down position of "in transport" statues mean they were being moved that way? Perhaps, although the experience of Hoa Hakananai'a being dragged with its nose "tracing a furrow in the ground" suggested to us that adjustments to our model would have to be made. To accommodate the face-down position, two crossbeams six and one-half feet long were required. One was placed at the neck to keep the nose and face clear of the ground, and the other, smaller one was placed at the base. Face-down or face-up, the stone experiences stress at the neck. In the face-up mode, a simple padding of vegetable material under the back of the neck solves the problem, but in the face-down position, the stress is not completely relieved by padding. Some of the statues found "in transport" are broken at the neck, possibly from being transported face-down.

The most difficult aspect of moai transport was positioning and then erecting the statue on an ahu. The statues, whether they were in a face-up or face-down position on the sledge, were probably transported head-first. In the case of Ahu Akivi, statues could have approached the platform in either a face-up or face-down position and from either the front or the rear. Remaining on its transport sledge, the statue was aligned on the site with its base perpendicular to the platform. It was then pulled up a gently sloping earth ramp about three or four times the length of the statue. The base was raised about four feet and positioned on a flat pedestal on top of the platform. Using rocks, earth, rope stays, wedges, and levers, the statue would have been raised to an angle, where it was then guided slowly into place. At this point, the upright, tilting method would have been helpful in adjusting the statue's position on the flat pedestal. Any scars on the smoothly polished surface would have been abraded out with lumps of coral or pumice.

Some coastal ahu were built with high rear walls facing steep seaside cliffs. Moai were moved onto these platforms from the front. Houses and other structures were kept at a distance from the ahu, and the cleared, flat ground in front of the platforms provided ease of access. Earth ramps used in erecting statues were modified and beach cobble paving added to create platform extensions.

Katherine Scoresby Routledge, noting the patterns of breakage on some "in transport" statues, first considered and then rejected the idea that they were being transported upright. Instead, she believed that most had stood erect in place to form a ceremonial road to Rano Raraku. Testing this hypothesis, archaeologist Arne Skjøtolsvold of the Kon-Tiki Museum conducted excavations of two "in transport" statues in 1986. One had a patterned arrangement of stone at the base, suggesting that it had supported the weight of the upright statue, and lending some credibility to Routledge's hypothesis. Her excavation in Rano Raraku quarry, and Skjøtolsvold's own in 1955, revealed human bone, stone bowls, and tools associated with some moai standing on the volcano's slopes. In 1774 Captain Cook's party sought the lunchtime shade of a standing statue that may be one lying "in transport" near Ahu Oroi. This huge moai is almost 30 feet tall, more than double the height of the statistical average. It has a notched base, which suggests that levers were used to help move it while in a horizontal position, but it is shattered in such a way that it appears to have fallen from an upright position. All of this evidence suggests that at least some upright statues in the quarry, and others that *appear* to be "in transport," may actually have been deliberately placed upright at their current non-ahu locations for use in ceremonial activity.

To test Routledge's idea of a ceremonial road further, we plotted the positions and orientations of moai lying along the main road from Rano Raraku to Rano Kau and the populous southeastern coast. The majority of statues either on their sides or face-down are lying with their heads oriented away from the quarry, while the heads of the face-up statues are toward the quarry. This means that nearly all of the statues, if standing upright, were looking southwest toward the massive bulk of the crater Rano Kau. There, from about A.D. 1450-1500 until well after the contact with Europeans in 1722, the pan-island ceremonial center of Orongo flourished as the site of "birdman" rites. Predicated on the seasonal arrival of flocks of sooty terns and other birds following migratory schools of fish such as tuna, the birdman cult was a vital focus of Rapa Nui spiritual life. This cult emerged and evolved, in part, as a response to food resource scarcity and a changing sociopolitical environment. If Routledge's ceremonial road was, in fact, adorned with standing moai, the two spiritual centers of Rano Raraku and Rano Kau would have been visually linked in an extremely dramatic way.

The ahu to which the "in transport" statues were theoretically being moved were not prepared to receive them. None had been cleared of broken sculpture, and their walls had not been strengthened to support the new statues, all of which are larger than average. The cumulative evidence suggests that, at about the time Orongo became important, the ahu were adapted to uses that did not require moai. Instead, the statues remained in Rano Raraku, where many were used in new ways. Taking everything as a whole, it appears to me that Routledge's ceremonial road is a very real possibility.

In our computer modeling we sought the optimal path the Rapa Nui would have taken to haul Statue 01 from Rano Raraku to Ahu Akivi. We invited Zvi Shiller and his engineering graduate students at the University of California at Los Angeles Robotics Lab to participate in this stage of our research. First, they digitized a topographic map of Rapa Nui to produce a three-dimensional map of the terrain. Using their computer programs and our statue data, they proposed three alternate routes.

Path 1 was the shortest, most direct route, requiring the least expenditure of energy. It ran westward and directly inland. Between 55 and 70 people would have been able to haul Statue 01 from Rano Raraku to Ahu Akivi along this route. A concerted pull on the hauling ropes would have moved the statue 14 feet. Taking into account pauses to adjust the statue, move the rollers, and tighten any lashings, the work could have been accomplished in five to seven days, calculated on the basis of a five-hour workday. Paths 2 and 3 were also viable, and neither required substantially more people to move the statue. However, Path 2 was longer and Path 3 the longest. Each demanded that laborers expend substantially more energy, thus requiring more food and water to get the job done.

The maximum force required to pull the statue in a horizontal position is two and one-half tons. In an upright position a 14-ton statue with a flat rectangular base requires two and one-third tons of force to tilt. Thus little energy is saved by tilting, although this transport method does not require wood. Pulling an upright statue on a "pod" over rollers requires nearly the same amount of wood as the horizontal method we designed. Manpower needs, however, are about half. The most obvious argument against upright transport is the Rapa Nui terrain. Our calculations show that an upright statue will fall often on a ten-degree slope and nearly all of the time on a 20-degree slope and nearly all of the time on a 20-degree slope. Tilting an upright statue or pulling one on a "pod" of logs up or down even the gentlest slopes can be tricky and dangerous. Why would the Rapa Nui have resorted to such methods if, in fact, they even did? The only logical explanation would be a lack of wood and/or lack of sufficient manpower. The statues at Ahu Akivi were erected sometime after A.D. 1400 and before the mid-1600s, when the simple, rectangular stone platform was renovated to hold seven statues. Was wood available on Rapa Nui then?

Swamps and lakes in the craters of Rano Raraku and Rano Kau, and on Maunga Terevaka, hold thousands of years of pollen, evidence of the island's history of vegetation and ecological change. Pollen was collected by several investigators, including the Norwegian Archaeological Expedition in 1955. In the early 1980s John Flenley of Massey University in New Zealand and his colleagues analyzed core samples collected on Rapa Nui. They found that the island was once lushly if not lavishly forested, and that a species of palm similar to the gigantic *Jubaea chilensis* was once present, along with other trees.

More recently, Chilean agronomist Gerardo Velasco discovered dozens of large, round holes in ancient, hardened lava flows along the island's coast. The holes are the "prints" left by the trunks of trees once entombed in lava. Close examination reveals patterned ridges in the stone, clearly made by the distinctive trunks of palms. Velasco has measured dozens of these holes, which average 18 inches in diameter. This size is a great deal smaller than that of *Jubaea chilensis*, suggesting that more than one type of palm may have existed on the island. Eighteen inches, however, is a perfect size for transport frames and rollers.

Deforestation took place on the island in various locales at different times, with Rano Raraku probably stripped of its trees by A.D. 1000. American archaeologist Chris Stevenson has found evidence of palms and other as yet unidentified trees at inland sites dating to the 1400s and 1500s. It is safe to assume, therefore, that trees of appropriate dimensions were available for horizontal statue transport at about the time the Ahu Akivi statues were moved.

What about manpower? We used osteological data to calculate the stature of the prehistoric Rapa Nui man who would have transported and erected statues. Our Rapa Nui "reference man" was between the age of 18 and 30, in generally good health. He was five and one-half feet tall and weighed approximately 150 pounds. His daily nutritional requirement would have been 2,880 calories, of which he would have expended roughly 50 percent in energy. According to the ethnographer Alfred Métraux, the typical Rapa Nui family consisted of nine members. Data from western Polynesia clearly show an extended family could be expected to have 45 to 50 members. Virtually every member contributed some form of labor to the economic life of the whole. Conservatively, each extended family would have had eight males of appropriate age and vigor available to haul statues, meaning that between eight and nine extended families would have had to cooperate to move the average moai.

We calculated an optimal daily diet for our Rapa Nui reference man. About 25–35 percent of the 2,880 calories would have been provided by fat. In order to replace the energy and body tissue he was expending in the work task, he would have needed 65–75 grams of protein and 15 grams of iron, in addition to calcium, phosphorous, carbohydrates, and various vitamins. To accomplish this each man would have had to consume either 200 grams of chicken or an equal amount of non-oily fish (preferably tuna or something similar) to gain 500–600 calories of protein. The remaining calories would have been supplied by sweet potatoes, sugar cane, and bananas, all important Rapa Nui crops with a high water content—a key factor in avoiding work fatigue. Water was also available in the crater lake of Rano Raraku and in the vicinity of Ahu Akivi.

To meet the food requirements of the laborers, a Rapa Nui chief *(ariki)* who commissioned an average statue and had it moved along Path 1 would have needed three to six acres per crop above and beyond the normal one-half acre required to feed each person. He would also have required a surplus of crops at least equal to what he was dispensing to pay for the fish or other protein. It is a conservative estimate that agricultural resources provided by 50 acres, or about double the extended family norm, were required to complete the Ahu Akivi transport task.

In the same way that Polynesian chiefs throughout the Pacific commissioned and paid for canoes, Rapa Nui chiefs called upon their communities to make and move statues. Work parties were formed of combined, co-resident family groups or cooperating extended family units at the behest of chiefs who exploited ties of kinship, shared religious beliefs, and personal status to marshall the resources of lineage lands and fishing grounds. Master craftspeople with extensive, formal, and institutionalized knowledge, training, talent, and skill directed work crews. Food, water, and timber were produced on lineage lands or traded for by chiefs, and appropriate ceremonies were conducted at all stages of the work. Polynesians distinguish between food needed for sustenance and feast food, and prodigious amounts of both were required for statue transport.

Transporting and raising seven statues at Ahu Akivi is typical of what a Rapa Nui chief could do, and is no small accomplishment. Transport methods used by Rapa Nui experts would logically have been those that were most efficient and of proven utility, and the horizontal method seems most appropriate. Adaptation to time, manpower, or resource shortages would have required flexibility and could have produced individual innovations.

The evidence throughout the Pacific is that limited island ecosystems with short food chains were dramatically transformed by humans. On Rapa Nui from about A.D. 1000, deforestation and agricultural land-use policies apparently caused serious soil erosion. Birds and eggs, once easily attainable foods, were significantly depleted and consequently more valuable. Natural disasters may have occurred that have not, as yet, been investigated. Rapa Nui cultural practices interacted with the island's marginal and isolated environment to precipitate a series of environmental problems, resource shortages, and probable social crises as yet not fully understood.

Not all Rapa Nui people experienced the same kind of problems at the same time, however. Polynesian people held their island homes in high regard, and chiefs were responsible for maintaining individual lineage land-use rights and managing resources. Some were more successful than others. There is direct archaeological evidence that many people tried to mitigate some of their environmental crises as they recognized and understood them. Practical innovations such as *manavai* (stone garden enclosures), which protected fragile plants from the wind, worked fairly well. The Rapa Nui also conceived the birdman cult and other dramatically new religious practices out of old ideas.

The moai were not abandoned, however. Instead of being transported to ahu, they were used in new ways. It appears that increasingly larger moai were erected on the slopes of Rano Raraku. This may reflect a general movement away from narrowly defined, ahu-based lineage concerns and toward more integrated, supra-lineage ideological practices concentrated on the two main sites of pan-island significance, Rano Raraku and Rano Kau. In the same time frame, however, and possibly less than 200 years before the 1722 arrival of Europeans, our simulated transport studies suggest that a typical Rapa Nui chief was still able to make and move an average-size statue.

The Rapa Nui courageously faced the open and empty sea when they founded and settled their tiny island. As they cleared and used the land and fished the surrounding ocean, they called upon their gods, their leaders, their families, and their own strengths. They interacted with their island environment in traditional ways. Their repertoire of coping skills was shaped by their heritage as Polynesians. Europeans "discoverers" of Rapa Nui perceived the culture, with its fallen statues, as in a state of collapse. This is an ethnocentric Western interpretation rather than an archaeological one. As cultural outsiders, we can now see where the Rapa Nui went wrong. But because the course of Rapa Nui history was interrupted and redirected by the impact of Europeans, we will never know for certain just how successful they might have been in dealing with the environmental crises they faced.

Commentary

Archaeology presents a genuine paradox: we are fascinated with the past, and yet have no direct access to the people whose products we study. European expansion during the 16th and 17th centuries brought Europeans into contact with non-western peoples whose traditional culture provided clues to the functions of artifacts found throughout the Old World. From the 16th century onward, archaeologists have studied technology through replication, through experiment, and through studies of contemporary peoples who still employed similar methods and tools to those found in archaeological sites. Such work has often been described as "experimental archaeology" and "ethnoarchaeology." Not only do these approaches shed light on how people manufactured different kinds of goods, but such studies also help explain changes in technology that we observe through time.

Learning the manufacturing process (and experimenting with different raw materials) tells us something about decisions that prehistoric artisans made during the production process. Replication studies have a long tradition in archaeological research, and most commonly involve tools that we associate with Paleolithic life, like flaked tools and spear points. As the articles in this section demonstrate, however, archaeologists have made a variety of traditional objects, from earthenware pottery and earth lodges to concrete copies of megalithic monuments. Some archaeologists have become so skilled in replicating ancient technologies that they are able to produce near duplicates of artifacts recovered from archaeological sites. Occasionally, we see the development of "living museums" in which people use these traditional technologies to show the public how different life must have seemed in a sometimes distant past. As our sophistication with computer imaging technology continues to grow, it is likely that computer simulations like those described by Van Tilburg with the moai will become just as common as modern-day flint knappers. Archaeologists often combine replication studies with experimental archaeology to study aspects of ancient technology.

A great deal of archaeological research focuses on subsistence and technology, and experimental archaeology provides myriad techniques to study these topics. Archaeologists devote most of their efforts to explain their past, and our field is not strictly an experimental science. The use of experimental archaeology allows us to test the validity of certain assumptions we make regarding how a site is formed, why prehistoric artisans used particular materials, and how much effort they might have expended in making the objects that we study. Some experimental archaeology requires field experiments: in monument construction and moving, in building and destroying traditional architecture, in growing traditional crops (see article by Erickson in PART EIGHT). Still other experimental archaeology takes place in the laboratory, with the assistance of experts in fields as diverse as organic chemistry, structural engineering, and physics. We cannot know, with any certainty, that the experiments we conduct directly mirror the behavior of ancient peoples. By undertaking these experiments, however, we narrow down the range of possible explanations for how ancient technologies were developed and practiced.

Some archaeologists also study technology and technological systems by working with traditional peoples in different areas of the world. Because this approach takes archaeologists into the field to study material culture systems, we call this strategy "ethnoarchaeology." Ethnoarchaeologists have widely divergent interests that they pursue in their fieldwork with indigenous peoples, and generally share an interest in the relationship between human behavior and material culture. Some ethnoarchaeologists pursue research on traditional pottery-making (see also article by William Longacre et al. PART ELEVEN) or groundstone technologies. Others study hunting techniques among foragers, and the range of tools that foragers make and use. Still other ethnoarchaeologists are interested in how garbage heaps form, and in how households organize space. Most of the world is now undergoing rapid modernization, and most indigenous groups are gripped in the midst of profound culture change. In this milieu of culture change, and a time of diminishing cultural anthropological interest in material culture studies, ethnoarchaeologists' observations provide valuable insights on traditional technologies that help us interpret archaeological patterning.

Part Eight

Making a Living

Introduction

Making a living in ancient times was highly varied from one region of the world to the next since individual societies faced different ecological circumstances. Ancient peoples practiced a variety of subsistence strategies that include foraging for wild food and resources (whether fishing or hunting) and food production (horticulture, agriculture, and aquaculture). In many regions and time periods, people exchanged food and other goods with each other to make ends meet, since individual families, communities, or regions could not acquire or produce all of the food and goods that they needed for survival. Articles in this section examine some archaeological studies of subsistence, or how people made their living, in different parts of the world and at different points in time.

When we think of the Pacific region, we often conjure up images of white sand beaches, swaying palm trees, and mossy-looking mountains. It is only through systematic archaeological research that we have begun to learn about the cultural and ecological dynamics of these islands. In their article entitled, "Polynesian Ancestors and their Animal World," Tom Dye and David Steadman examine faunal remains from the colonization of several Polynesian islands to the time immediately before European contact. In Oceania, where ancient peoples practiced a mixed economy comprised of foraging, fishing, and horticulture, (and sometimes "aquaculture"), people significantly impacted the natural environment. Human colonization of the islands contributed to (and likely caused) the extirpation of many bird species. Their faunal analysis suggests a gradual shift from reliance on endemic species to a reliance on domesticated animals like pigs as native species (from birds to turtles) died out. Dye and Steadman argue that Polynesian chiefs encouraged increased levels of food production and fishing to counter the potential shortage of food that was aggravated by extinctions. Not only does this article demonstrate the fragility of island environments in response to external contact. It also shows that some foods we closely associate with Polynesian culture (and particularly pork) only gained prominence toward the end of the period that preceded European contact.

We next turn our attention to a very different part of the world: the Near East. Of the hundreds of sites that archaeologists excavate each year, only a handful produce sufficiently significant dates or finds to become widely recognized. Still less common are those sites whose excavation forces us to rethink the cultural development of a region. The Syrian site of Tell Abu Hureyra, excavated by Andrew Moore, is one of these extraordinary sites. Bruce Fellman describes the field investigations at this site in his article entitled, "The First Farmers." Its occupational sequence spans 4,500 years, and includes the transition to settled farming life in this part of the world. Moore's project produced a detailed reconstruction of changes in local plant use and animal exploitation from 11,500 to 7,000 years ago. Interestingly, clear evidence of plant cultivation, signaled by the dominance of a reduced suite of legumes and pulses, took two thousands years to develop after the settlement's initial occupation. Using ethnobotanical, faunal, and geological information from Tell Abu Hureyra, Moore's team identified the dwindling of wild gazelle populations through time as the human use of the region intensified. Like any great archaeological site, Tell Abu Hureyra is a time capsule, and one that contains important information on how ancient Near Easterners made their living.

We see a roughly similar trajectory—of intensified food production in relation to demographic pressure—elsewhere in the world in places like the Andean highlands. Much like in Syria, the intensification of agriculture at Lake Titicaca was linked to the need to feed an increased population. Clark Erickson's article, entitled, "Raised Field Agriculture in the Lake Titicaca Basin," describes his research on extensive farming systems that once functioned in the highlands of Peru and Bolivia. Erickson's project used aerial photography, survey, and excavations to identify remains of raised fields that were first used nearly 3000 years ago. Contemporary Andean farmers knew little about these fields, whose technological properties provided prehistoric Andean farmers with a highly productive high-altitude farming system. Farmers planted potatoes and quinua (a grain) in the plots, and plants and fish lived in the canals that surrounded raised fields. Erickson and his colleagues believe that the area was first settled ca. 1000 B.C., and that farmers developed raised field agriculture as an adaptation to a harsh, high-altitude environment. As population grew in the region, populations intensified their production systems to feed populations in complex ceremonial and political centers like Pucara and, subsequently, Tiahuanaco. As these centers declined in importance, the area under cultivation contracted as well. One of the intriguing outcomes of Erickson's project was the re-introduction of this farming system to Quechua and Aymara farmers in the region. These revitalized raised-field systems have proven more frost-resistant and productive than contemporary methods, and we see how archaeological findings have the potential to help today's people improve their lives.

We often think of farming when we think of subsistence strategies in traditional societies, but there are other ways of making a living. One of them involves craft specialization: in pottery-making, in manufacturing household utensils, in making textiles, and in making jewelry. In the ancient past, we believe that social groups varied in the degree to which they farmed in a particular territory or region. In some circumstances, for example, some families or communities could have specialized in the manufacture and trade of non-subsistence goods such as shell ornaments, stone tools, and other crafts. Gary Feinman and Linda Nicholas' article, entitled, "Household Craft Specialization and Shell Ornament Manufacture in Ejutla, Mexico," is a well-documented example of this type of activity. Through their research in the Ejutla Valley, they have found clear evidence for shell ornament production from the Classic period (between A.D. 300 and A.D. 800). Analysis of thousands of shell fragments has enabled the archaeologists to reconstruct the ornament manufacturing process and to suggest sources for different species of shell that were used in the process. Although Feinman and Nicholas (1995) do not directly comment on the issue, it is reasonable to wonder if the Ejutla community traded marine shell ornaments to acquire food from their neighbors that were more heavily engaged in agriculture. Documenting such instances of specialized craft production is important for interpreting the archaeological record. It cannot be assumed automatically that all families or communities in an ancient society were directly engaged in subsistence activities to make their living.

1

Polynesian Ancestors and Their Animal World

Tom Dye and David W. Steadman

About four thousand years ago, in an as yet undiscovered homeland in western Melanesia or southeast Asia, a group of seafarers known as the Lapita people set out on a course of migration. The Lapita people produced single outrigger or double canoes capable of crossing hundreds of kilometers of water, and their navigational techniques were sophisticated enough to allow round trips between parent and daughter colonies. Equally important, they had the horticultural, hunting, and fishing technologies needed to sustain fledgling populations on previously uninhabited islands. In the next 2,000 years the Lapita people and their descendants would colonize the rest of Oceania, a vast region spanning 120 degrees of longitude and 70 degrees of latitude—a feat now widely recognized as one of the most far-reaching and rapid of prehistoric migrations (Bellwood 1979; Jennings 1979; Kirch 1984; Rouse 1986).

The movement of the Lapita people and their descendants out of Melanesia and into Polynesia began with settlement of the large, close-set island groups of Melanesia. With no water gap more than 500 km wide between major groups west of Vanuatu and New Caledonia, colonists were able to supplement the diverse resources of their new island homes with materials imported from parent colonies, thus buffering perturbations that might otherwise extinguish a small human population.

This was followed by successful colonization of the remote islands of tropical Polynesia (Fig. 1), beginning with the settlement of Fiji, Tonga, and Samoa by Lapita people some 3,000 years ago and ending with the colonization of Hawai'i by Lapita descendants about a millennium later. The distances traveled by these ancestors of the modern Polynesians were greater than had been navigated ever before— 1,200 km of open ocean from Samoa to the nearest of the southern Cook Islands, 1,000 km from there to the main Society Islands, 1,400 km through the drought-prone atolls of the Tuamotu Islands to the Marquesas, and some 3,500 km from the Marquesas to Hawai'i. Atolls encountered along the way may have served as convenient stopping points but may have been poor in resources. Clearly, the survival of founding populations depended on the ability to gather food in their new island homes rather than on periodic assistance from a distant parent community.

The natural resources on which the initial colonists of tropical Polynesia relied for food were much less diverse than those of Melanesia. Native terrestrial mammals (other than bats) were not to be found east of the main Solomon Islands, native snakes were last encountered in Fiji and Samoa, and large-bodied native lizards were not present east of Fiji and Tonga. On these small islands, with their

Figure 1. The island groups of Melanesia and Polynesia extend across some 12,000 km of the Pacific Ocean. The Lapita people and their descendants migrated out of western Melanesia or southeast Asia in outrigger or double canoes, reaching as far as Hawai·i by about A.D. 400. The stretches of open ocean between islands in Polynesia, some over 1,000 km wide, called for prodigious feats of navigation and meant that colonists must be able to sustain themselves entirely on the resources offered by their new island home. (Graphic courtesy of Tom Dye)

restricted inventories of indigenous plant and animal foods, descendants of the Lapita people developed resources to support densely populated, politically complex societies in which powerful hereditary chiefs ruled polities numbering in the tens of thousands.

The rapid settlement of Polynesia, and the unusual degree to which its natural resources were used to support initial development of politically complex societies, raise intriguing questions for an analyst of the faunal record. To begin with, what kinds of animals were available to the initial colonists of Polynesian islands? Were patterns of human predation consistent from one island to the next? Once viable communities were established and garden lands provided reliable yields, the people would have faced choices on whether and how to manage island faunas. Which species developed into dependable food sources while others became scarce or extinct? As human populations expanded, it became possible to produce sufficient surplus to support a classical Polynesian chiefdom. Which faunal resources were harnessed to sustain this political structure? What role did chiefs play in the production of animals for food? Tentative answers to these broad questions emerge from faunal analyses of several archaeological sites in tropical Polynesia.

The Colonists' Fare

Eight sites, considered by archaeologists to be among the earliest in their respective archipelagoes, have been selected for faunal analysis by means of two criteria. First, their locations, either in calcareous sand dunes or in dry caves, contribute to the preservation of bone. Open sites in volcanic soils, many of which have been disturbed by gardening activities, usually preserve bone too poorly to yield large faunal assemblages. Second, the bones from each site have been analyzed in sufficient detail to be of use in comparisons between sites and taxa. Of first importance here was a report of the weight of remains, from which the relative proportion of meat contributed by each taxon can be estimated. Though meat-weight estimates are rightly viewed with suspicion by faunal analysts (e.g., Grayson 1984), we believe they are important for generalized comparisons between taxa.

Two sites in the sample of eight are found on Tonga: the Tongoleleka site, located in an open dune on Lifuka Island, and the Fakatafenga site, in a sand dune on Tungua Island. It appears from ceramic styles that both date back to the first settlement of Tonga, about 900 B.C. (Dye 1988). Many of the islands of Tonga, such as 'Eua, are being uplifted by tectonic activity. By contrast, no sites from the initial settlement period have been excavated in Samoa, which is located near the subducting margin of the Pacific plate and has been sinking rapidly. The earliest sites there appear to be under water (Jennings 1974).

On present evidence, the next landfall east of Tonga and Samoa was in the Marquesas Islands, an event dated to the late first millennium B.C. (Kirch 1986) or to about A.D. 300 (Sinoto 1979). The single Marquesan site in our sample— the Hane site, located in a sand dune on Ua Huka Island (Sinoto 1966)—contains deposits from this period. Because the late prehistoric deposits at Hane are not particularly rich, we have augmented the Hane sample with remains from the nearby Manihina dune site, also on Ua Huka Island, which yielded a rich, late-prehistoric faunal assemblage.

The earliest dated site in the Society Islands is found below the water table in a sand dune at Fa'ahia on Huahine Island and is confidently dated to the late first millennium A.D. (Emory 1979; Sinoto 1983; Sinoto and McCoy 1975). This finding prompted Sinoto (1979) to hypothesize that the Marquesas served as the homeland for the initial colonists of the Society Islands and other eastern Polynesian island groups. It is possible that there are older sites in the Society Islands, which, like those in Samoa, are now under water (Kirch 1986), although the average rate of subduction is less in the Society Islands than in Samoa. The faunal remains from Fa'ahia support the interpretation that this was an early settlement site in the Society Islands.

Although the Hawaiian Islands have seen more archaeological work than all the other archipelagoes in tropical Polynesia together, the picture of early settlement is not yet clear. The sheer size of the islands, the lack of a highly visible type of early artifact such as pottery, and the extent of modern land development in coastal regions all hamper the discovery and interpretation of early sites. Of the four Hawaiian sites analyzed here, two lie on the southern end of Hawai'i Island: Ka Lae, a sand dune, and Wai'Ahukini, a cave (Emory et al. 1969). Both appear, on the basis of their artifact types, to date back to the early settlement period, in a

Figure 2. Five broad taxa provided the early Polynesian colonists with food: birds, turtles, shellfish, fish, and mammals. The relative proportion contributed by each taxon can vary considerably, as at the eight archaeological sites plotted here, though a general pattern of reliance on birds and/or turtles and a minor role for mammals can be discerned. The proportions are calculated from estimated meat weights, which are derived from allometric formulas by assuming a reasonable mean weight for individuals (Prange et al. 1979; Wing and Brown 1979:128): 1 kg for fish, 50 kg for turtles, 0.4 kg for birds, and 10kg for domesticated mammals. The weight of shellfish is assumed to be 25% of shell weight. (cf. Salvat 1972; graphic courtesy of Tom Dye)

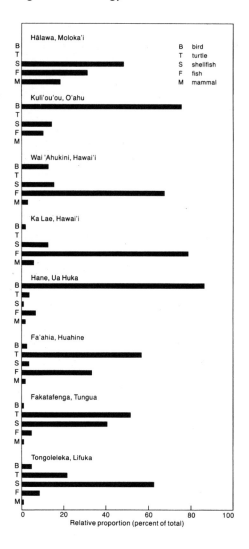

range between A.D. 300 and 750 (Emory and Sinoto 1969; Kirch 1985). The other two Hawaiian sites are Hāmalawa, a sand dune on Molokaʻi Island (Kirch and Kelly 1975), and Kuli'ou'ou, a cave on the dry southeastern coast of O'ahu Island (Emory and Sinoto 1961). Both are thought by their excavators to represent early settlements in their respective regions: A.D. 433-859, for Hāmalawa, and A.D. 680-1392, for Kuliʻouʻou.

Five broad taxa were recovered from the sites: birds, turtles, shellfish, fish, and domesticated mammals. Figure 2 shows the proportion of consumable meat (estimated weight) contributed by each taxon. It is of course possible that problems of differential deposition, preservation, and recovery might call for some revision of the interpretations offered here, although the consistency of the faunal patterns at the eight sites suggests that such changes would be minor.

The estimates presented in Figure 2 show that early colonists relied heavily on the natural resources of their new island homes for food, although the exact mix of taxa varies from archipelago to archipelago and from site to site. At Hane and

Kuliʻouʻou the relative contribution of birds overwhelms that of all other taxa combined. At Tongoleleka, Faʻahia, and WaiʻAhukini, birds made up a substantial portion of the diet, whereas at Fakatafenga, Ka Lae, and Hāmalawa birds were insignificant. Shellfish and fish were regularly exploited by the initial colonists throughout Polynesia. The remains of domesticated pig and dog are rare at all sites except Hāmalawa, where they make up over 10% of the total meat weight in the oldest portion of the cultural stratum and increase steadily in younger deposits.

The "typical" Polynesian island, several or more square kilometers in area, must have supported sizable populations of seabirds and landbirds at the time of human arrival. These birds evolved in an environment free of mammalian predators, and thus had little defense against man and rats. Early birding may have resembled gathering more than hunting, a circumstance that the initial settlers undoubtedly found to their liking.

Given the extensive exploitation of birds of Hane and Kuliʻouʻou, and the significant presence of bird bones at several other early sites, the relative paucity of bird remains from Fakatafenga, Ka Lae, and Hāmalawa demands an explanation. At Fakatafenga, the small size of Tungua Island (1.5 km²) may have limited the size of bird population, so that it constituted a relatively minor resource in comparison with the fish, shellfish, and turtles found on the extensive reefs surrounding the island. Also, because the avifaunas of small islands could be depleted more rapidly than those of large islands, it is possible that archaeological bone samples from small islands must include the first decades of occupation in order to represent the full range of species taken by the earliest colonists.

At Ka Lae, one of the first major excavations in Hawaiʻi, excavation techniques were not as rigorous as those of today; thus it is difficult, for example, to correlate excavated midden material, which was not collected with fine-mesh screens, with stratigraphic layers. Furthermore, the amount of midden analyzed from Ka Lae is comparatively slight, raising the possibility of sampling error. As for Hāmalawa, if this site is accepted as a sample of early settlement in the region, it is difficult to explain the paucity of bird remains. Neither a shortage of territory on the island, nor imprecise methods of excavation, nor sediment type can be invoked to account for the situation at Hāmalawa, which is located at the mouth of a large valley and was carefully excavated.

A second rich animal resource encountered by the initial colonists of several islands was sea turtles, including the green turtle (*Chelonia mydas*), the hawksbill (*Eretmochelys imbricata*), and, to a lesser extent, the loggerhead (*Caretta caretta*). Sea turtles were an important resource at Tongoleleka, Fakatfenga, Faʻahia, and Hane—all sites located in sand dunes. The beaches adjacent to these dunes probably were nesting sites where it would have been easy to capture egg-laying females simply by overturning them.

The lack of turtles from the early Hawaiian sites is puzzling, as green turtles occur today in large numbers in the leeward Hawaiian Islands and in much smaller numbers in the main group (Balazs 1980). Several factors may be involved. The WaiʻAhukini and Kuliʻouʻou cave sites contain volcanic soil, and turtle bone, which is fairly porous, may not have survived the relative acidity of the soil. In this case, however, turtle bone would still be expected at the Ka Lae and Hāmalawa dune sites. One possible explanation for their absence here is that these are not the first settlements in their respective regions, but were established after human predation had altered the patterns of nesting. Alternatively, it may be that the present pattern of minor nesting sites on Lana'i and Moloka'i islands, with major sites restricted to the uninhabited French Frigate Shoals, is not the result of over-predation in the main Hawaiian Islands as is often assumed, but already existed at the time of initial settlement.

Shellfish and fish were regularly exploited by colonists throughout tropical Polynesia. Although the range of taxa taken by the Lapita people in Melanesia and western Polynesia suggests they were already skilled at many forms of marine exploitation (Kirch and Dye 1979; Green 1986), the poor quality of the evidence from many Lapita sites precludes precise estimates of the contribution of fishing to the earliest Polynesian economy (Butler 1988). The ability of eastern Polynesian colonists to adapt to unusual marine environments further testifies to this skill. Adaptation is evident most clearly in the Marquesas Islands, which, with their rocky shores and steeply shelving nearshore waters, contrast strongly with the reef-rich homeland islands in the west.

Early Marquesan archaeological sites such as Hane yield a wide range of fish-hook in different forms and sizes, unmatched by earlier or contemporary assemblages farther west. This variability may reflect a period of experimentation with angling techniques (Kirch 1980). The early Marquesan assemblages include both jabbing and rotating hooks. The fishbone associated with these hooks represents a diverse catch of bottom-dwelling and inshore fish, along with several free-ranging species suggesting that experimentation was successful.

The different contributions of fish and shellfish to the faunal assemblages of the early sites may be associated with differences in the environments. The high relative proportion of fish at Fa'ahia, Ka Lae, and Wai'Ahukini shows that sherma exploited the rich fishing grounds near these sites. The high relative proportion of shellfish at the Tongan sites and at Kuli'ou'ou is probably a function of the proximity of these sites to extensive shoal water reefs, where shellfish were plentiful and easily collected.

The early sites generally show a paucity of domesticated mammals, perhaps reflecting the limited cargo capacity of even the largest voyaging canoes and the length of time needed to establish large breeding stocks. The scarcity is most pronounced at early sites in Tonga, where the only report of pig and dog comes from one site, on Niuatoputapu Island (Kirch 1988). At Hane, pig bone is common in the early layers, but dog bone is extremely rare (Kirch 1980). At Fa'ahia and the four Hawaiian sites, the remains of pig and dog are present in roughly equal quantities. In contrast to the general pattern, two sites in our sample, Ka Lae and Hāmalawa, contain significant quantities of domesticated mammal bone.

These exceptions may be explained by the rather crude excavation techniques at Ka Lae, where material from later layers may have intruded into the base of the site and recovery methods were heavily biased toward relatively large bones; another explanation can be found in the relative lateness of the early layers at the Hāmalawa dune site. In the latter case, the faunal evidence seems to indicate that the Hāmalawa site was deposited when breeding stocks of domesticated mammals were sufficiently developed to provide a reliable source of food, sometime after the initial exploitation of birds.

Three other animals contributed to the diet of the early settlers. Significant quantities of whale and porpoise bone recovered at Fa'ahia attest to the fishing prowess of the early residents of Huahine (Leach et al. 1984), and a large-bodied, iguanid lizard *(Brachylophus* sp.) appears to have contributed to the diet of the early colonists at Tongoleleka (Pregill and Dye 1989).

The Human Impact on Native Faunas

The use of indigenous animals for food, combined with predation by intro-duced rats, had inevitable effects on animal populations that had evolved in rela-tively predation-free contexts. The effects are most clearly reflected in the decline of animals that are in some way dependent on terrestrial habitats—birds, turtles, and large-bodied lizards. In the future, estimates of depletion rates will benefit from improved collection techniques, including the use of fine mesh screens and flotation, and improved chronological control through dating of the faunal re-mains themselves by accelerator mass spectrometry (James et al. 1987).

Predictably, the swiftest declines appear in the large-bodied lizards and birds, the two taxa most directly tied to terrestrial habitats. Of the two extant iguanid lizards in the region, *B. fasciatus* (Brongniart) occurs locally in Fiji and Tonga, and *B. vitiensis* Gibbons is confined to Fiji. The extinct, large-bodied iguana from Lifuka may be added to the list of Oceanic vertebrate taxa whose large-bodied members have become extinct while smaller-bodied forms survived (Cassels 1984; Steadman 1986).

Marked declines are also found in the birds from Hane and Kuli'ou'ou, the two sites with the greatest proportion of birds in early layers. At Hane, the rela-tive contribution of birds to the diet is more than halved within the first 550 years and declines to insignificance in just over a thousand years. The decline at Kuli'ou'ou is even more rapid. The decline of birds is less marked at Wai'Ahukini, where fish always made up the bulk of the diet, and at Tongoleleka, where the rel-atively small size of Lifuka Island (11.4 km²) may have contributed to a decline of birds too rapid to be detailed in available collections.

The decline of bird populations overall was accompanied by the extirpation and extinction of many species. Of the resident species whose bones are recovered at Hane, eight of the 20 seabirds, including shearwaters, petrels, and boobies, are extirpated on Ua Huka, as are 14 of the 16 landbirds, primarily flightless rails, pi-geons, doves, parrots, and songbirds (Steadman 1989). A similar pattern of extir-pation and extinction of birds is found at Fa'ahia.

The contribution of turtles at Tongoleleka falls quickly at first, but is followed by continued exploitation at a stable low level. Sea turtles, like seabirds, are de-pendent on a specific terrestrial microhabitat for nesting sites, and the females are easily taken as they lay their eggs. The seasonal nesting of turtles at selected sand beaches would have been quickly noted and exploited by human colonists. Ini-tially, sea turtles would have seemed an inexhaustible resource. Because of the sea turtle's long maturation period, it would have been possible to take every nesting turtle and egg for 20 to 30 years without affecting the number of recruits arriving at the nesting beach (Bjorndal 1985). After this, however, population declines would be evident, and the hunt for turtles would turn to the open waters, where hunting success by netting, spearing, and hooking would be much lower.

In contrast to the patterns in terrestrial animals of extirpation, extinction, and reduced populations, marine animals appear to have been a relatively stable re-

Figure 3. The relative proportions of the main taxa used for food by the settlers of Polynesia — bird, turtle, shellfish, fish, and mammal — change over time. In the late prehistoric period, domesticated mammals account for a much larger proportion of the total meat weight at each of the five sites, whereas birds and turtles account for a smaller proportion than formerly. (Data from the early period, which were plotted in Fig. 2, are shown here in a lighter shade for comparison.) (Graphic courtesy of Tom Dye)

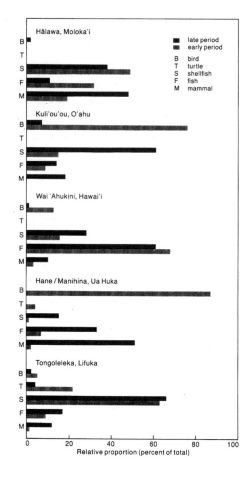

source. Shellfish, especially those restricted to shallow nearshore habitats, occasionally show a diminution in the mean size of individuals deposited in archaeological sites over time, although it may be difficult to distinguish the effects of human predation from environmental change (Spennemann 1987). To date, no changes in fish catches attributable to overexploitation or habitat alteration have been discovered.

The susceptibility of indigenous terrestrial faunas to predation and the alteration of their habitat, and their consequent demise after human colonization, meant that meat needed to support growing human populations now had to come mainly from domesticated mammals, fish, and shellfish. This general pattern is documented in the late prehistoric layers of five sites from Hawai'i, the Marquesas, and Tonga, as shown in Figure 3. In contrast to the early layers of these sites, the late layers contain few bones of native birds or of sea turtles.

The late assemblages from Hane/Manihina and Tongoleleka both lack dog bones, reinforcing historical reports that dogs were not found in the Marquesas or Tonga at the time of European contact (Urban 1961). In the Marquesas, dogs are present in the early prehistoric periods, and although sample sizes are small it appears likely that dogs were extirpated sometime early in the second millennium A.D. (Kirch 1980). Tongan dog populations, if present in prehistory, must have been small and would have played an insignificant role in the economy. In contrast to the patchy distribution of dog bones in tropical Polynesian archaeological sites, pig bones are found in all the late sites.

Fish and shellfish continue to figure importantly in the late assemblages, with relative proportions of the two taxa still a function of environmental conditions. The results of fishing appear to have been fairly constant over time at most sites, with the exception of Hane, where bottom-dwelling and inshore species come to predominate over free-ranging species, a change associated with a striking reduction in the diversity and sizes of fish hooks.

A Basis for Social Stratification

The ability of the Lapita seafarers to exploit the pristine marine environments of newly colonized islands has never been in doubt, and the presumed richness of the sea's resources has traditionally provided a ready explanation for their ability to colonize so successfully. Recent analyses of the faunal remains from archaeological deposits reveal, however, that the earliest colonists of tropical Polynesian islands also found rich and diverse terrestrial faunas, and that species captured on land often played a larger role in subsistence than did fish or shellfish, which became more important later in prehistory. A similar pattern of subsistence change characterized temperate New Zealand as well (Anderson 1983).

For many early colonists, the primary prey was seabirds that nested on or near the ground and landbirds that thrived in virgin forests once devoid of significant predators. Although much has been learned about species richness and diversity (Steadman 1989), reliable data with which to estimate the size of pristine bird populations in tropical Polynesia may never be recovered. Common sense argues that smaller islands would have supported smaller bird populations and that these would decline relatively quickly after human colonization, thus decreasing the probability of yielding a representative archaeological sample. We may infer, too, from the great number of seabird bones recovered from several archaeological deposits, that the present pattern of fewer nesting seabirds on large islands than on small offshore islands reflects pressures brought about by long-term human habitation of the large islands rather than a natural preference of the seabirds.

The pattern of extirpation and extinction of birds described above for Hane and Fa'ahia is repeated at archaeological and paleontological sites through much of tropical Polynesia (Olson and James 1982, 1984; Steadman 1989). Species-level identifications of bones from archaeological sites indicate that a remarkable variety of birds was available to the first human colonists of these islands. The historically surviving avifauna of tropical Polynesia is so badly fragmented by the effects of human colonization that it alone does not reflect natural distributional patterns. Most species of landbirds that occurred in tropical Polynesia before the advent of humans are now extinct, and most of the extant species of seabirds and landbirds are found over greatly reduced ranges. Perhaps the most dramatic example is Abbott's booby (*Papasula abbotti*), known historically only from the Indian Ocean. Bones of this large seabird from Hane and two other Marquesan sites have extended its range about 11,200 km to the east.

The decline of indigenous land-based animals is one result of the widespread transformation of natural environments into culturally managed landscapes. On most islands this transformation meant that tropical Polynesian societies worked harder to produce animal foods, trading raids on bird and turtle nesting grounds for the full-time responsibilities of tending pigs and organizing the production, maintenance, and use of sophisticated boats and other fishing gear.

The spatial organization of animal food production also changed. In the natural environment birds would have been a dispersed resource, with the nesting grounds and favored habitats of many species spread over most of an island's surface. In contrast, pig herds probably were concentrated near settlements, and most of the shellfishing and fishing took place in the relatively narrow band of shoal water immediately offshore. These changed circumstances meant that resources could be monitored with relative ease and thus provided Polynesian leaders an opportunity to expand their control over the production of animal foods.

The authority of tropical Polynesian chiefs derived partly from their ability to oversee the production of food to support a coterie of faithful, who in turn helped the chief administer the realm. The testimony of traditional historians, sea captions, beachcombers, and missionaries all points to the important role played by chiefs in controlling the production of animal foods. The primary tools used for this were taboos against consumption of various flesh foods, and the coordination of labor to produce specialized tools and facilities.

In eastern Polynesia, taboos against the consumption of domesticated mammals were especially stringent, often dividing the community on the basis of gender and social class. In Hawaiʻi, for example, it was taboo for women to eat pork, and they were allowed to eat dog only in certain ritual contexts (Valeri 1985: 115 ff.). Similar restrictions applied in the Society Islands, where pork and dog were further reserved for high-status men (Oliver 1974). Such taboos would have moderated demand for domesticated mammal meat and may have played a major role in preserving herds.

Much fishing in tropical Polynesia seems to have been done by individuals and small groups who possessed the requisite gear and had access to fishing grounds. Nevertheless, various measures carried out under the auspices of chiefly authority served to expand marine production on many islands. Perhaps the most dramatic example comes from Hawaiʻi, where chiefs organized the construction and maintenance of some 449 fishponds (Kikuchi 1976). These ponds, constructed on reef flats or in shallow bays by work gangs numbering in the hundreds and organized by prominent chiefs, produced an estimated yield of almost a million kilograms of fish annually, most of which was consumed or distributed by chiefs. On a smaller scale, chiefs of the Society Islands financed the production of large seine nets and regulated their use in the extensive net-fishing grounds by asserting exclusive rights (Handy 1932). In Samoa the *vaʻa alo*, a fishing canoe specialized for taking skipjack tuna (*Katsuwonus pelamis*), was believed to be ineffective without a decorative row of white *pule* shells (*Ovulum* sp.), which were difficult to obtain and "came in the way of presents to high chiefs" (Hiroa 1930:401).

The widespread use of authority by Polynesian chiefs to increase fishing production lends the Marquesan situation a particular interest. At the time of first extended contact with Europeans, Marquesan chiefs exercised a virtual monopoly over a fleet of fishing canoes that were inferior to canoes elsewhere in Polynesia, and they strictly controlled access to nearshore marine environments, thus strongly curbing the role of individual initiative. In contrast to most other island groups in tropical Polynesia, where fishing skill afforded an individual some measure of prestige, Marquesan fishermen appear to have had low social status. Antagonistic social relations between tribes in neighboring valleys made fishing outside the deeply indented bays a risky adventure, exposing a fisherman to enemies out "fishing for men" (e ika) to sacrifice. These social constraints seem to have rendered the Marquesan fishing industry incapable of intensifying production when prolonged droughts ravaged agricultural production, and many people died of starvation (Dye, 1990).

It is significant that the archaeological evidence for stratified societies appears in tropical Polynesia after indigenous land animals have been depleted and the natural environment has been transformed into a cultural landscape. This transformation was incomplete in most large islands of Melanesia, where societies were usually composed of small, politically autonomous groups. However, in Polynesia, because the authority of the chiefs was rooted in controlled access to important resources, increased opportunities for the control of animal foods may have influenced the development of political institutions. Melanesians generally had the option of striking off on their own if the exactions of a political leader grew onerous; new settlements could be established in the large remaining patches of unaltered environment. In Polynesia, the often complete transformation of natural environments precluded this course.

Future analyses of carefully collected faunal assemblages may add a wealth of interesting detail to the patterns of exploitation outlined here, refining our understanding of the relationships between faunal exploitation and the development of complex societies. The demise of indigenous insular faunas in tropical Polynesia is a fascinating chapter in natural history. By providing an index for the biotic conditions that favor the development of social stratification, it has proved important to cultural history as well.

References

Anderson, A. 1983. Faunal depletion and subsistence change in the early prehistory of southern New Zealand. *Archaeol. in Oceania* 18:1-10.

Balazs, G. H. 1980. Synopsis of biological data on the green turtle in the Hawaiian Islands. NOAA Technical Memorandum NMFS, Honolulu.

Bellwood, P. 1979. *Man's Conquest of the Pacific*. Oxford Univ. Press.

Bjorndal, K. A. 1985. Nutritional ecology of sea turtles. *Copeia* 736-51.

Butler, V. L. 1988. Lapita fishing strategies: The faunal evidence. In *Archaeology of the Lapita Cultural Complex: A Critical Review*, ed. P. V. Kirch and T. L. Hunt, pp. 99-115. Seattle: Thomas Burke Mem. Washington State Mus. Res. Rep. 5.

Cassels, R. 1984. Faunal extinction and prehistoric man in New Zealand and the Pacific Islands. In *Quaternary Extinctions: A Prehistoric Revolution*, ed. P. S. Martin and R. G. Klein, pp. 741-67. Univ. of Arizona Press.

Dye, T. S. 1988. Social and cultural change in the ancestral Polynesian homeland. Ph.D. diss., Yale Univ.

———. 1990. The causes and consequences of a decline in the prehistoric Marquesan fishing industry. In *Pacific Production Systems: Approaches to Economic Prehistory*, ed. D. E. Yen and J. M. J. Mummery. Australian Natl. Univ. Press.

Emory, K. P. 1979. The Societies. In *The Prehistory of Polynesia*, ed. J. D. Jennings, pp. 200-21. Harvard Univ. Press.

Emory, K. P., W. H. Bonk, and Y. H. Sinoto. 1969. *Waiahukini Shelter, Site H8, Ka'u, Hawaii*. Pacific Anthropol. Rec. 7.

Emory, K. P., and Y. H. Sinoto. 1961. *Hawaiian Archaeology: Oahu Excavations*. B. P. Bishop Mus. spec. publ. 49.

———. 1969. *Age of Sites in the South Point Area, Ka'u, Hawaii*. Pacific Anthropol. Rec. 8.

Grayson, D. K. 1984. *Quantitative Zooarchaeology*. Academic Press.

Green, R. C. 1979. Lapita. In *The Prehistory of Polynesia*, ed. J. D. Jennings, pp. 27-60. Harvard Univ. Press.

———. 1986. Lapita fishing: The evidence of site SE-RF-2 from the main Reef Islands, Santa Cruz group, Solomons. In *Traditional Fishing in the Pacific*, ed. A. Anderson, pp. 19-35. Pacific Anthropol. Rec. 37.

Handy, E. S. C. 1932. *Houses, Boats, and Fishing in the Society Islands*. B. P. Bishop Mus. Bull. 90.

Hiroa, T. R. (P. H. Buck). 1930. *Samoan Material Culture*. B. P. Bishop Mus. Bull. 75.

James, H. F., et al. 1987. Radiocarbon dates on bones of extinct birds from Hawaii. PNAS 84:2350-54.

Jennings, J. D. 1974. The Ferry Berth site, Mulifanua District, Upolu. In *Archaeology in Western Samoa*, vol. 2, ed. R. C. Green and J. M. Davidson, pp. 176-78. Aukland Inst. Mus. Bull. 7.

———, ed. 1979. *The Prehistory of Polynesia*. Harvard Univ. Press.

Kikuchi, W. 1976. Prehistoric Hawaiian fishponds. *Science* 193:295-99.

Kirch, P. V. 1980. Polynesian prehistory: Cultural adaptation in island ecosystems. *Am. Sci.* 68:39-48.

———. 1984. *The Evolution of the Polynesian Chiefdoms*. Cambridge Univ. Press.

———. 1985. *Feathered Gods and Fishhooks*. Univ. of Hawaii Press.

———. 1986. Rethinking East Polynesian prehistory. *J. Polynesian Soc.* 95:9-40.

———. 1988. *Niuatoputapu: The Prehistory of a Polynesian Chiefdom*. Seattle: Thomas Burke Mem. Washington State Mus. Monogr. 5.

Kirch, P. V., and T. S. Dye. 1979. Ethno-archaeology and the development of Polynesian fishing strategies. *J. Polynesian Soc.* 88:53-76.

Kirch, P. V., and M. Kelly, eds. 1975. *Prehistory and Ecology in a Windward Hawaiian Valley: Halawa Valley, Molokai*. Pacific Anthropol. Rec. 24.

Leach, B. F., M. Intoh, and I. W. G. Smith. 1984. Fishing, turtle hunting, and mammal exploitation at Fa'ahia, Huahine, French Polynesia. *Oceanistes* 79:183-97.

Oliver, D. L. 1974. *Ancient Tahitian Society*. Univ. of Hawaii Press.

Olson, S. L., and H. F. James. 1982. Fossil birds from the Hawaiian Islands: Evidence for wholesale extinction by man before Western contact. *Science* 217:633-35.

———. 1984. The role of Polynesians in the extinction of the avifauna of the Hawaiian Islands. In *Quaternary Extinctions: A Prehistoric Revolution*, ed. P. S. Martin and R. G. Kline, pp. 768-80. Univ. of Arizona Press.

Prange, H. D., J. F. Anderson, and H. Rahn. 1979. Scaling of skeletal mass to body mass in birds and mammals. *Am. Nat.* 113:103-22.

Pregill, G. K., and T. Dye. 1989. Prehistoric extinction of giant iguanas in Tonga. *Copeia* 505-08.

Rouse, I. 1986. *Migrations in Prehistory: Inferring Population Movement from Cultural Remains.* Yale Univ. Press.

Salvat, B. 1972. La faune benthique du lagon de l'atoll de Reao (Tuamotu, Polynesia). *Cahiers du Pacifique* 16:31-110.

Sinoto, Y. H. 1966. A tentative prehistoric cultural sequence in the northern Marquesas Islands, French Polynesia. *J. Polynesian Soc.* 75:286-303.

———. 1979. The Marquesas. In *The Prehistory of Polynesia*, ed. J. D. Jennings, pp. 110-34. Harvard Univ. Press.

———. 1983. Archaeological excavations of the Vaito'otia and Fa'ahia sites on Huahine Island, French Polynesia. *Nat. Geog. Res. Rep.* 15:583-99.

Sinoto, Y. H., and P. C. McCoy. 1975. Report on the preliminary excavation of an early habitation site on Huahine, Society Islands. *Oceanistes* 31:143-86.

Spennemann, D. H. R. 1987. Availability of shellfish resources on prehistoric Tongatapu, Tonga: Effects of human predation and changing environment. *Archaeol. in Oceania* 22:81-96.

Steadman, D. W. 1986. Holocene vertebrate fossils from Isla Floreana, Galapagos. *Smithson. Contrib. Zool.* 413:1-103.

———. 1989. Extinction of birds in eastern Polynesia: A review of the record, and comparisons with other Pacific island groups. *J. Archaeol. Sci.* 16:177-205.

Urban, M. 1961. *Die Haustiere der Polynesier.* Völkerkundliche Beiträge zur Ozeanistik, Karte 1.

Valeri, V. 1985. *Kingship and Sacrifice: Ritual and Society in Ancient Hawaii.* Univ. of Chicago Press.

Wing, E. S., and A. B. Brown. 1979. *Paleonutrition: Method and Theory in Prehistoric Foodways.* Academic Press.

2

Finding the First Farmers

Bruce Fellman

Flint found in the absence of pottery, the crafting of which began in the region some 8,000 years ago, is a telltale sign of early Neolithic, or "new stone age," settlements. The site's obvious antiquity was especially intriguing to Moore, who was studying the origin and evolution of farming. And the age of the site—radiocarbon dating eventually established that it had been occupied from 11,500 to 7,000 years ago—meant that people had lived there during the period when humans in the Tigris-Euphrates area, the so-called "fertile crescent," learned to cultivate plants and domesticate wild animals. Perhaps, thought Moore, Abu Hureyra might have something important to say about the development of agriculture.

Indeed, it did. The Abu Hureyra material, half of which is now deposited in Aleppo, Syria, with the remainder divided among nine museums in Europe and North America, continues to keep investigators busy, and their research to date has provided unprecedented insights into how humanity made the shift from hunting and gathering to farming. In addition, the ongoing research has enabled scientists to paint an unusually detailed picture of the Neolithic lifestyle, from burial practices and nutrition to family relationships and on-the-job injuries. The work also points to a solution for a puzzle that has long perplexed archaeologists: Why was farming invented in so many places throughout the Middle East—in fact, throughout the world—at about the same time?

Spurred by the impending flood, Moore, his colleagues from English, American, and Australian universities, and scores of Syrian workers in 1972 and 1973 meticulously analyzed the contents of seven trenches, the largest of which was 30 feet long, 40 feet wide, and 25 feet deep, that the researchers had dug into the tell, which was roughly one quarter mile long and 300 yards wide. Their efforts exposed the remains of a village, which consisted of a series of mud-brick houses built on the foundations of those that had been occupied by earlier inhabitants. Sorting the debris with sieves, the archaeologists discovered bones belonging to the villagers and the animals the Abu Hureyrans used for meat. There were ancient tools, such as arrow and axe heads, milling stones, and bone needles, along with the beads and granite carvings that adorned living and dead members of the settlement. Using a special device called a flotation machine, which can separate plant parts from dirt, the researchers were even able to determine, largely by looking at ancient seeds, the kinds of plants that were important to the villagers.

The material the team began to unearth quickly demonstrated that Abu Hureyra was an important site, but it was a chance discovery made at the end of the first digging season that was to establish the village's reputation in archaeology. Moore was running one of the flotation machines as a skeleton crew continued to dig. Suddenly, the soil changed from sticky, brown clay—the remains of mud-brick homes—to a black, organically rich material filled with plant parts. Intrigued, the researcher started to look through the flint debris that had collected in the bottom of the machine. "The flint chips changed in character," says Moore. "They got smaller—they were what we call microliths, which are characteristic of the older, Mesolithic period, the final stage of the time when people were hunters and gatherers."

Clearly, a farming village had been built on top of a much earlier settlement, but what was the relationship between the two? Figuring this out might hold the key to understanding another old puzzle: how our ancestors made the transition from a free-ranging to a more sedentary—and civilized—lifestyle.

Accompanied by a bigger team, Moore returned to the site for a back-breaking second year. "It was a killer," he explains. "We started in the blazing heat, and we finished in weather so cold that our shaving water froze. We were also digging when Israel and Syria went to war. In the end, we excavated only a tiny portion of the site, but we got the essentials we needed."

Putting the story together has required an understanding of both the weather and human ingenuity. Geologists have determined that between 12,000 and 14,000 years ago, the last of the ice ages ended, and cold and dry conditions in the Middle East gave way to a warmer and moister climate. Researchers believe that the improved weather triggered a population increase. Moore's discovery of an early permanent settlement at Abu Hureyra shows that in at least one area,

Figure 1. The mound of Abu Hureyra from the southwest. Note the figures on the summit of the mound around each excavation trench. The trenches were spaced very wide apart to test the deposits across this enormous site. (Photo courtesy of A.M.T. Moore, G.C. Hillman, and A.J. Legge)

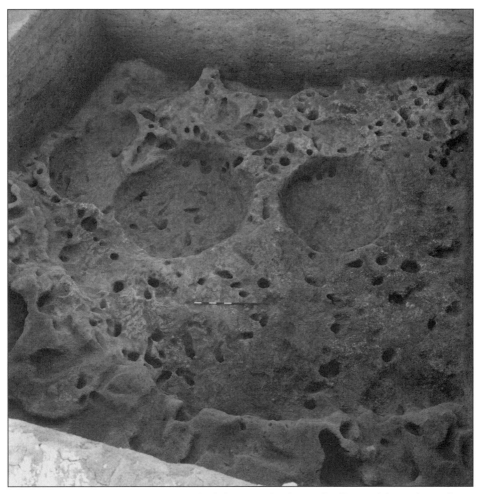

Figure 2. Trench E at the northern end of the mound. The pit dwellings of the earliest village, Abu Hureyra 1 (ca. 11,500–10,000 BP in uncalibrated radiocarbon years). (Photo courtesy of A.M.T. Moore, G.C. Hillman, and A.J. Legge)

people also responded to better conditions by adopting a more settled lifestyle. Even though they remained in one place, however, they had not yet learned to farm. The seeds and bones found at the site, none of them belonging to domesticated plants and animals, show that the Abu Hureyrans depended for sustenance both on gathering the wide variety of plants that grew in the area and on hunting the local wildlife, particularly the Persian gazelle.

But around 11,000 years ago, the geological record shows, the cold returned with a vengeance. "This had a severe impact on people in the Middle East," says Moore.

Finding enough food to feed a growing population must have become difficult since the change in climate caused dependable plants like the wild grains and the pistachio to diminish in abundance. Faced with hard times, the 150 or so people who lived in Abu Hureyra abandoned the little village. For the next several centuries, the place was a ghost town. From time to time, hunters may have camped

Figure 3. Trench E. Abu Hureyra 1. Two basalt querns, used to grind grain, in one of the pit dwellings. (Photo courtesy of A.M.T. Moore, G.C. Hillman, and A.J. Legge)

at the site to take advantage of its proximity to the gazelle migration route, but there were too few plants available to support a permanent settlement. About 9,500 years ago, however, rain and relative warmth returned to Abu Hureyra. And with them returned year-round residents.

It is impossible to determine whether or not the returning villagers were relatives of the former inhabitants, but whatever brought the newcomers to the site—family ties, tales of abundant game, or the availability of fertile soil and ample water—they arrived armed with a revolutionary skill: the ability to grow food plants and raise animals.

Precisely who deserves the credit for these innovations will never be known. Most scientists believe that farming was "invented" almost simultaneously in several places in the fertile crescent region, but contrary to long-prevalent theories that agriculture arose and spread gradually, the evidence from Abu Hureyra paints a picture of an exceptionally rapid event. "The domestication of plants could have easily occurred in a single lifetime," says Moore, pointing out that the

Figure 4. A rectangular, multi-roomed, mudbrick house in the second village, Abu Hureyra 2 (ca. 10,000–7,000 BP). (Photo courtesy of A.M.T. Moore, G.C. Hillman, and A.J. Legge)

considerable variety of seeds—scientists have identified more than 150 floral species—that have turned up in the earlier parts of the site means that people in the area had a superb knowledge of plant lore. They may have already practiced plant cultivation to some degree, and because there are only relatively minor genetic differences between the wild wheat and barley varieties the gatherers exploited and their domestic counterparts, "taming" those plants probably posed little difficulty to the first farmers.

But if the horticultural discoveries that enabled grains and vegetables to be grown rather than gathered took place in just a few spots, the explosive spread of the farming way of life came about because of an equally important innovation.

"There was a communications revolution, with contact between villages and settlements, and trade in ideas and artifacts," says Moore, noting that one indication of the existence of an early information superhighway is the sudden appearance throughout the region during the Mesolithic period both of a volcanic glass called obsidian, which is found naturally only in central Turkey, and of marine

Figure 5. Trench B in the center of the mound. A low doorway in the wall of a mudbrick house in the Abu Hureyra village (ca. 8,000 BP). The doorway connects two rooms in the house. (Photo courtesy of A.M.T. Moore, G.C. Hillman, and A.J. Legge)

shells. "Farming offered a universal solution to a common set of problems in the region, and it had become easy for such knowledge to spread."

And spread it did. Seeds, and the techniques to grow them, arrived from a wide variety of places. Emmer wheat originated in Palestine; einkorn wheat came from northern Syria. Chickpeas were first cultivated in southeastern Turkey, and barley domestication began in many places throughout the region. Within several hundred years, the world's first agricultural revolution was complete.

Moore's seed analysis shows that at Abu Hureyra, as elsewhere, the villagers quickly turned to planting crops and away from foraging for wild plants. While 150 or so species had been used in pre-farming days, the area's farmers depended on a mere eight species, among them emmer, einkorn, oats, barley, chickpeas, and lentils.

Along with domesticating a tiny fraction of the native flora, the inhabitants of the area also tamed some of the animals, first sheep and goats and later, cattle and pigs. But intriguingly, unlike their rapid shift away from plant gathering, the Abu Hureyrans did not abandon their hunting lifestyle for more than a thousand

years. The reason, says Moore, is simple. "The village was clearly sited to inter-
cept the gazelle migration, and as long as the human population stayed relatively
low, there were more than enough of the animals to go around," the archaeologist
explains. "The people there were not living hand to mouth."

In fact, they lived quite well. An analysis of the human skeletons found at the
site, most of which were buried under the floors of the mud-brick houses in which
the villagers lived, showed that the average lifespan approached 60, "not much
different," says Moore, "from that of 19th century rural populations in Europe."

This is surprising, because conditions in Abu Hureyra, particularly as its population swelled past several thousand, seemed tailor-made for epidemics of disease.
Studies showed that their dwellings were exceedingly close together, and chemical
analyses of the soil around each house indicate that trash and human waste were
simply thrown out the nearest window or door. "Forget any sanitized view you
might have of prehistory, this was awful," notes Moore. "And yet, paradoxically,
in this dunghill, the people were healthy."

Figure 6. Filling the flotation machine with water. (Photo courtesy of A.M.T. Moore, G.C.
Hillman, and A.J. Legge)

Figure 7. Pouring sieved soil into the flotation machine. (Photo courtesy of A.M.T. Moore, G.C. Hillman, and A.J. Legge)

Perhaps it was because in sharp contrast to the public squalor of Abu Hureyra, the villagers kept the insides of their homes scrupulously clean. Or maybe the inhabitants owed their relative freedom from disease to a vigorous lifestyle. "We know that everyone worked extremely hard," says Moore. "They had well-developed leg and arm muscles. It shows in the skeletons." Muscles, of course, are attached to bones, and when the muscles grow larger as a result of physical activity, the bones show corresponding and characteristic changes, like increases in thickness and the appearance of buttresses for added support.

But if toil kept infections at bay, it also took its toll on the villagers' bodies. The diggers unearthed more than 150 skeletons, and when Theya Molleson, a member of Moore's research team and a paleontologist at the Natural History Museum in London, examined them, she discovered how a demanding lifestyle had been imprinted on the bones. For instance, the Abu Hureyrans ground grain on a stone mill called a saddle quern; this repetitive and energetic activity eventually caused malformations and arthritis of the spine, the legs, and the big toe, the latter a result of too much time spent working in a kneeling position. These par-

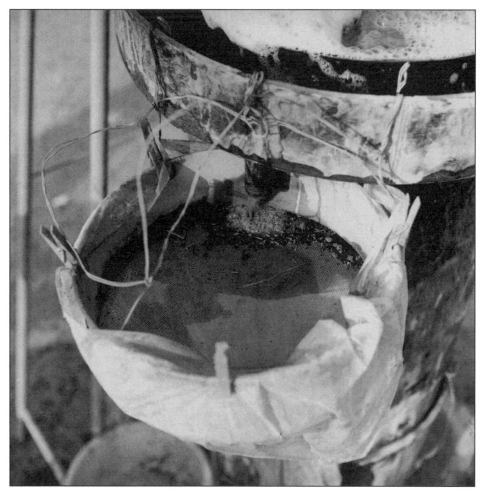

Figure 8. Charred plant remains and charcoal are collected in a fine-mesh sieve at the top of the flotation machine. (Photo courtesy of A.M.T. Moore, G.C. Hillman, and A.J. Legge)

ticular injuries, incidentally, were found in both men and women, indicating that tasks were not yet divided up along strict gender lines.

There is, however, evidence of a different kind of specialization, which was something new in human history. Some of the teeth are grooved, and these marks are similar to those found in other parts of the world among native weavers who would thread canes through their teeth while making baskets. Researchers suspect that, at Abu Hureyra, some of the villagers were using this "technology" to make woven sieves that could separate small stones from grain kernels.

"With farming, we see a redistribution of activities and an entirely new way of life begin to take shape," says Moore. "In a hunting and gathering society, you're always pursuing food, but farming is marked by periods of intense labor coupled with times of relative leisure."

Divorced from the need to constantly find enough to eat, the Abu Hureyrans evidently began to develop a more modern lifestyle, complete with the acquisition of material possessions and the time to enjoy them.

But the village's good fortune didn't last. First, the gazelles began to dwindle. "We see an extraordinary change that took place within the span of a human lifetime," notes the archaeologist. From about the time the village was reoccupied to a point about 8,300 years ago, the researchers found that 80 percent of the animal bones they unearthed were those of gazelles, while 20 percent belonged to domestic species. Suddenly, the percentages reversed. Moore believes that the villagers were victims of their own success. "The human population increased, and the hunting pressure probably became too much for the gazelles," he says.

At night, the elders, no doubt, regaled youngsters with tales of the vast herds that once covered the steppes surrounding the town—and fed the villagers. The children, no doubt, looked out at sheep and goats and found the old-timers' stories hard to believe.

The availability of domesticated animals made up for any losses in protein caused by the collapse of the gazelle population. But the weather was also changing, and the entire region was becoming drier and warmer. In addition, Moore's studies show, the soil was deteriorating in quality, a result of overuse and overgrazing. Life went from easy to tough.

Seven thousand years ago, the villagers departed en masse. The desert buried Abu Hureyra, and there its story slept, until Andrew Moore and his colleagues teased a fascinating tale from old houses, parched seeds, and articulate bones.

3

Raised Field Agriculture in the Lake Titicaca Basin: Putting Ancient Agriculture Back to Work

Clark L. Erickson

The remains of an extensive ancient agricultural system built and used by Andean peoples centuries ago are found throughout the vast high plain surrounding Lake Titicaca in the Andean countries of Peru and Bolivia (Figs. 1, 2). Raised fields are large elevated planting platforms which provided drainage, improved soil conditions, and improved temperatures for crops. The remains of prehistoric raised fields, elaborate sunken gardens, and agricultural terraces cover tens of thousands of hectares in the region, and provide evidence of the impressive engineering abilities of the peoples who lived there in pre-Columbian times.

Our recent investigations of raised field agriculture demonstrate not only the technological expertise of the past cultures, but also that these systems could be reused today to make high altitude lands more productive. In a region such as the Andes, where conditions of soil and climate greatly limit agricultural potential, technological methods to augment productivity have been increasingly necessary to support the growing populations of Quechua and Aymara farmers who live there today. The reuse of raised fields may be an economical and ecologically sound alternative to agricultural development based on expensive imported technology.

Until recently, very little was known about the origins and evolution of raised field technology in the Lake Titicaca Basin. Observant Spanish chroniclers in the 16th century described many aspects of the indigenous agriculture, such as terraces and irrigation canals, but they did not mention raised fields. This omission suggests that raised fields had probably been abandoned before the arrival of the Spanish. Questions such as who constructed the fields, when were they built, what crops were cultivated, why the fields varied so much in size and shape, and how raised field agriculture functioned needed to be answered.

Between 1981 and 1986, I directed a small team of researchers investigating prehistoric raised field agriculture in the community of Huatta in the northern Lake Titicaca Basin of Peru. Huatta is located in the center of the largest block of raised field remains, estimated to cover 53,000 hectares. The project, combining archaeology and agronomy, addressed the important questions raised above, as well as those more relevant to modern agriculture, such as estimating the poten-

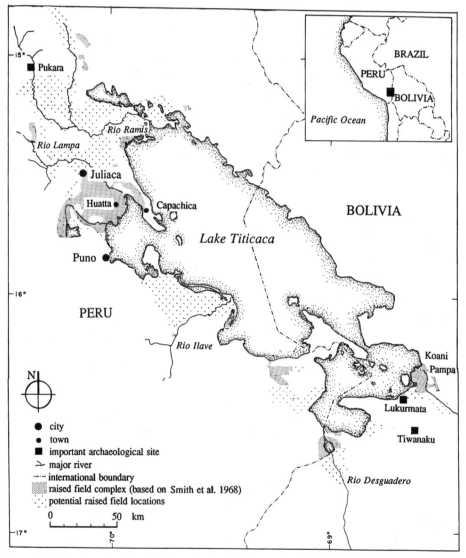

tial productivity of the raised fields and investigating their effects on the local agricultural environment. The investigation was based on archaeological survey and excavation of prehistoric raised fields and selected habitation sites, together with the construction and study of experimental raised field plots. To apply the results of this research, a small-scale development project involving local Quechua farmers was begun in 1982 to put raised fields back into use.

Figure 1. Map showing distribution of raised field remains (based on Smith et al. 1968 fig. 1) and potential raised field sites within the Lake Titicaca basin of southern Peru and northern Bolivia. (Graphic courtesy of Clark L. Erickson)

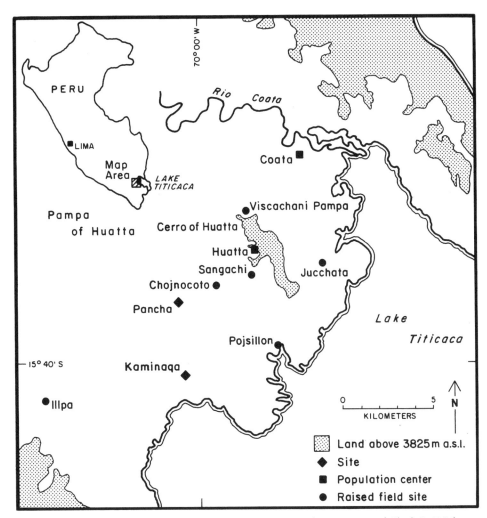

Figure 2. Map showing locations mentioned in text. (Graphic courtesy of Clark L. Erickson; adapted by Ronald Beckwith)

Raised Field Agriculture and the Lake Titicaca Environment

Raised fields are constructed by excavating parallel canals and piling the earth between them to form long, low mounds with flat or convex surfaces. These raised platforms increase soil fertility, improve drainage in low-lying areas, and improve local micro-environments, primarily by decreasing frost risk. The canals between raised fields provide vital moisture during periods of short-and long-term drought. Water in the deep canals might have been used to cultivate aquatic plants and fish, as well as attract lake birds that were an integral part of the pre-historic diet. The raised fields of the Lake Titicaca region are diverse in form and in size, but generally range from 4-10 m wide, 10 to 100 m long, and are 1 m tall.

The prehistoric raised fields, covering some 82,000 hectares of low-lying land around Lake Titicaca in both Bolivia and Peru (Fig. 1), have been badly eroded by a combination of wind, rain, flooding, and modern urbanization, but their remains can be seen clearly on the ground and in aerial photographs. They were specifically adapted to the particular environment, crops, and technology available to the indigenous farmers. Most of the land lies above 3800 m (12,500 feet), and nights can be bitterly cold, despite warm sunny days. The year is divided into distinct wet and dry seasons of roughly six months each, but even this situation may vary greatly from year to year, producing an unpredictable, high-risk agricultural environment. Frosts are most common during the dry season, and at the beginning and end of the growing (wet) season, but may occur locally at any time without warning, especially in low-lying depressions at the bases of hills.

The land immediately adjacent to Lake Titicaca has a somewhat more favorable environment for cultivation, mild enough for special races of corn to be grown in sheltered valleys and on the islands and peninsulas of the lake. The stored heat of the massive body of lake water warms the areas around it, an especially important effect at night when frosts are common. Farther from the lake, this warming effect diminishes, but the entire region around the lake benefits from a slightly higher than average annual rainfall. The major obstacle to lake-side agriculture is that most of the surrounding land is either rocky steep slope or flat, waterlogged lake plain which may be seasonally inundated. Both areas have relatively poor soils and are classified as areas of limited agricultural potential in government studies. Today, large rural populations are located in areas that have better drainage, favorable temperatures, and good soils, combined with access to the lacustrine resources of Lake Titicaca.

The rich and varied biotic resources of the region would have made it an excellent location for prehistoric experimentation with domestication of plants and different cultivation techniques. Once local peoples learned to protect fields from inundation, the *pampa* (the grass-covered low-lying lake plain) would have been a relatively good area for crop production. In fact, botanical and archaeological research indicate that the potato, quinua and cañihua (two seed crops rich in vegetable protein), and many other important Andean crops were probably first domesticated in the Lake Titicaca region. Selection of special traits has produced crop varieties that can withstand harsh environmental conditions, such as high altitude, intense solar radiation, low nocturnal temperatures, and crop pests. The nocturnal cold was put to use by the prehistoric inhabitants in an elaborate freeze-drying technique which enabled vast amounts of agricultural surplus to be preserved and stored indefinitely. This Andean crop complex and its accompanying preservation technology, combined with the herding of llamas and alpacas and exploitation of lacustrine resources, provided a sound subsistence base for the civilizations that developed in the Lake Titicaca Basin.

The indigenous Andean agricultural tool inventory appears limited in technological complexity, but is more than adequate for the needs of the Andean farmer. Traditional tools include the Andean footplow, hoe, and clod breaker which are still the basic tools today, although the stone and wooden blades have been replaced by metal blades. The footplow, a remarkable implement which is excellent for turning over blocks of tough pampa sod for construction of lazy beds for tu-

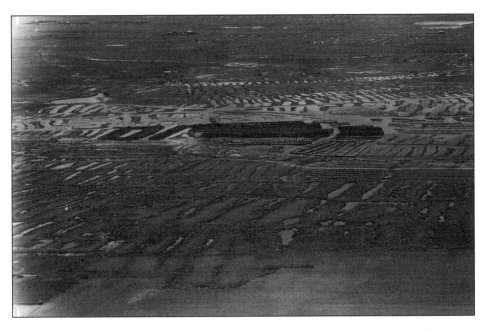

Figure 3. A panorama of ancient raised field remains of the Viscachani Pampa belonging to the residents of Collana Segunda, Huatta, Peru, shows only a small portion of the 82,000 hectares of ancient raised fields in the Lake Titicaca Basin. The lighter surfaces are water-filled canals and the darker surfaces are raised fields or drier pampa. The project's recontructed raised fields are located in the left center of the photograph (May 1986). (Photo courtesy of Clark L. Erickson)

bers and for plowing stony ground on steep hillslopes, played a major role in the development of raised field agriculture.

The Archaeology of Raised Field Agriculture

Our trenches excavated through the prehistoric raised fields showed that those seen today in the pampa (Fig. 3) are only the badly eroded remains of fully functioning prehistoric field systems. The field surfaces were originally much higher, with deep canals between them, which have now become filled with sediment. In some trenches, several distinct phases of construction, use, reconstruction, and re-use of the fields can be delineated (Fig. 4). Some early fields were narrow ridges of 5 m wavelength (distance from canal center to canal center) which at a later time were expanded to larger fields of 10 m wavelength. From each stratum of the trench profile, samples were obtained for pollen and soil laboratory analyses. The data obtained from these analyses provide interesting insights into prehistoric agriculture.

Soil analysis indicates that the canal sediment, composed primarily of organic matter, is rich in nutrients, much more so than the average pampa soil. In addition, soil alkalinity, a major constraint on agriculture in the lake edge soil, is

Figure 4. Archaeological excavations in raised fields provided the archaeologists and agrono-
mists with specific data on original field form, building stages, use period and abandonment,
and samples of soil, pollen, and artifacts. Here, soil stratigraphy is being mapped by archaeological crewmembers. These stratigraphic profiles of prehistoric fields provided the models for
proper reconstruction in the experiments. (Photo courtesy of Clark L. Erickson)

markedly lower in the canal sediments. These rich sediments were periodically removed from the canals and added to the raised fields to improve the crop soils.
Pollen samples from these excavations have been analyzed by Dr. Fred Wiseman
of the Massachusetts Institute of Technology. He finds that pollen grains of
quinua and potato are present in many soil samples from the raised fields, indicating that these may have been the crops grown on the fields. Unfortunately, there is
no way to distinguish between the pollen of the domesticated and wild strains of
these plants.

The precise dating of raised fields presented a problem. Radio-carbon dating of
material recovered from the excavation of two prehistoric habitation mounds associated with raised field agriculture indicated that most of the garbage midden
and construction fill of these sites dates to the period from 1000 B.C. to A.D. 400
(corresponding to the Qaluyu and later Pucara cultures), with a smaller occupation after A.D. 1000 (related to the Aymara kingdoms and subsequent Inca occupation). However, direct dating of the raised fields themselves has proven to be
much more difficult.

Changes in field use were determined through relative dating of the field
stratigraphy, but the duration of each phase could not be ascertained through
stratigraphic analysis alone. Carbonized remains for radiocarbon dating were not
present in raised fields, but six pottery samples recovered from stratigraphic con-

texts in both the construction fill and the canals could be dated by the thermoluminescence technique. This technique determines the time elapsed since the original firing or last exposure to fire of the ceramic vessel. These dates gives us a secure chronology for the raised fields and correlate nicely with the dates from the
occupation mounds. The surprisingly early dates between 1000 B.C. and the beginning of our era, and the successive building stages and abandonment periods,
demonstrate that the raised field system was not a brief late phenomenon as previously suspected. It appears to have been a relatively early agricultural development which was expanded gradually and was used by many generations of Andean farmers.

Our archaeological survey focused on locating the sites occupied by farmers
who constructed and maintained the raised fields around Huatta. Most sites on
the pampa in direct association with raised fields were earthen mounds that had
once been small farmsteads or hamlets. Several larger sites both on the pampa
and in the hills overlooking the plain were once towns with rustic public architecture. All that remains now are the stones that served as the foundations for the
adobe structures. The number and distribution of habitation mounds indicate a
rather dense population in the raised field area throughout the prehistoric period
of raised field use, much larger than that of today, surprisingly.

Two of the larger sites (those mentioned above for which dates were obtained)
were partially excavated, and showed evidence of long-term occupation. These
mounds were the cumulative result of continual rebuilding atop the remains of
older, eroded structures. Many of these mounds are still considered to be ideal
habitation locations due to their elevation, especially during the seasonal flooding
of the pampa. Their garbage middens yielded information about prehistoric subsistence strategies, agriculture, and ceramic and weaving technology.

Plant fragments, direct evidence of agricultural crops preserved by accidental
carbonization, have been recovered by the screening and flotation processing of
soils from the garbage midden and mound fill of habitation sites. These samples

---

Glossary

Aymara: the indigenous peoples of present-day Peru and Bolivia who speak the Aymara
language

cañihua: an Andean grain crop related to our weed lambsquarters; high in protein

chakitaqlla: the Andean foot-plow, composed of a handle, shaft, and footpeg of wood
with a heavy metal cutting blade bound by leather tongs

flotation: a water separation process used by archaeologists for the recovery of small
plant and animal remains from the soils of archaeological sites

pampa: a grass-covered, treeless plain which may be seasonally inundated or waterlogged

pollen analysis: the study of microscopic pollen grains which may give information on
past climatic conditions, local environments, or crops cultivated.

Quechua: the indigenous peoples of present-day Peru and Bolivia who speak the
Quechua language

quinua: an Andean grain crop related to our weed lambs-quarters; high in protein

raised fields: large elevated planting platforms with intervening water-filled canals designed to improve drainage, maximize soil fertility, prevent frosts, and/or provide irrigation

include fragments of potato and possibly other tubers, and quinua. Also identified were aquatic lake plants and other wild plants that could have been used for making mats, nets, and bags, as thatching material, or as forage for domestic animals. Fish, camelids (probably the domesticated alpaca and llama), guinea pig, and various aquatic birds are represented in abundant bone material recovered in the excavations. The floral and faunal remains are found throughout the sequence of occupation and indicate a remarkable economic stability. All of this evidence indicates a prehistoric subsistence pattern similar to that still practiced today by lake-edge dwelling Aymara and Quechua farmers, a pattern based on a combination of potato and quinua cultivation, herding, fishing, and intensive gathering of wild lake resources. The recovery of thousands of basalt hoe fragments, polished through years of use, attests to their importance in the tool inventory of the ancient agricultural technology. These stone hoes were among the implements used to construct the raised fields. Pottery remains included utilitarian serving and cooking vessels, in addition to ceremonial or fine wares decorated with burnishing, incision, and painting. One nearly complete house structure belonging to the Pucara culture (300 B.C.–A.D. 400) was excavated and it has many features similar to those of adobe houses with thatched roofs constructed today in the area.

Interpretations of the Excavations

Our research results show that large farming villages were settled throughout the lake area by 1000 B.C. By 300 B.C., Lake Titicaca society had evolved sufficiently to support large ceremonial and population centers. The site of Pucara in the northern lake basin has approximately 4^2 km of urban sprawl, complete with pyramidal platforms and temples with semi-subtlerranean courtyards. Tiahuanaco (A.D. 300-1000), one of the most impressive Andean sites, probably had its humble beginnings at this time and rapidly grew to influence most of southern Peru and the Bolivian highlands by A.D. 500 through its control of long-distance trade, its colonies, and religious missionization (Browman 1978). Tiahuanaco subsequently collapsed and was replaced by several competing Aymara kingdoms around A.D. 1000. These in turn were conquered by the Inca empire around A.D. 1450. Earlier hypotheses suggested that construction of raised fields and terracing was related to the later cultures, when population stress resulted in the development of labor-intensive agricultural technology, and a centralized bureaucracy was available to plan, direct, and manage the agricultural systems (Smith et al. 1968; Kolata 1986).

Our investigation suggests some alternatives. The growth of the Andean polity of Pucara at the north end of the lake basin was certainly related to the expansion of raised field agriculture; however, this agriculture was well established several centuries earlier. As Pucara's power as a ceremonial center was usurped by Tiahuanaco in the southern lake basin, raised field use appears to have declined in the north, but it was probably never completely abandoned. New research indicates that, as might be expected, raised field construction at the southern end of the lake was related to the growth of Tiahuanaco (Kolata 1986). A later resurgence of raised field construction occurred when a number of independent Aymara kingdoms were established around the lake after the collapse of Tiahuanaco sometime after A.D. 1000. Limited raised field use may have continued during the brief period of Inca domination of the lake basin, sometime after A.D. 1450.

Figure 5. Members of the community of Segunda Collana using footplows to cut sod blocks from old canals for the retaining walls for rebuilding the raised field platforms in Viscachani Pampa, Huatta (October 1985). (Photo courtesy of Clark L. Erickson)

Why was the use of raised fields discontinued in the northern basin after the decline of Pucara and before the arrival of the Spanish? Many ideas have been put forward to account for the abandonment of the system, such as climate change, devastating droughts and floods, and tectonic uplift. I find none convincing. In my opinion, the raised field construction, expansion, and abandonment relate less to environmental factors than to the changes in the relative importance of various ceremonial centers in the Lake Titicaca area. As ceremonial and population centers grew, agriculture expanded to keep pace with them. When power and influence shifted to other areas, production needs dropped and fields were removed from production. Some of the prehistoric communities in the raised field zones may have been depopulated and the inhabitants perhaps even forcibly removed to other locations. Although the area and intensity of cultivation were reduced at various times in the past, raised fields were probably never completely abandoned until the severe depopulation of the region that followed the arrival of the Spanish.

Raised field technology enabled the prehistoric inhabitants of the Lake Titicaca Basin to effectively maximize crop production. The earliest raised fields documented in our project do not appear to have developed as the result of population stress, nor do the earliest phases of field construction and use appear to have been planned and directed by a centralized authority. This technology may have been one of the earliest forms of intensive agriculture, a logical outgrowth of early fishing, gathering, and hunting settled life based on the exploitation of rich lake resources. This subsistence strategy permitted a dense population of wetland-oriented peoples to maintain sedentary lives.

Experiments in Raised Field Agriculture

More detailed information about raised fields as an agricultural technology was gained from the construction and cultivation of several experimental fields. An excavated archaeological trench provides original canal depth and ridge spacing, and the experimental fields were constructed to these specifications by local Quechua farmers using traditional agricultural implements available in all households (foot-plow, hoe, clodbreaker, shovel, and pick). The traditional Andean tools proved to be excellent implements ideally suited for the preparation of raised fields. It was found that the easiest, most efficient method of construction involved teams of three people; two used foot-plows to cut blocks of sod from the old canals between the ridges, while the third tossed the sod blocks onto the old field surface. In this way, a thick layer of rich organic topsoil, a perfect medium for cultivation, was rapidly built up on the eroded field surface. It was calculated that for each hour of work, the team could move three cubic meters of earth, a construction rate much faster than had been expected.

Major crops native to the Andean highlands were cultivated on the experimental raised fields. Of the crops planted, potatoes, quinua, and cañihua (Fig. 6) produced the greatest yields. Potato production during five years of experimentation was between 8 and 16 metric tons per hectare, with an average of 10 metric tons. This figure is much larger than today's average potato production figures of between 1 and 4 metric tons per hectare for the Department of Puno. These larger

Figure 6. Mature potatoes on raised fields in the community of Segunda Collana in Viscachani Pampa, Huatta. Platforms and canals are approximately 10 m wide each (February 1985). The canals, originally between 1.0–1.5 m deep, accumulate rich organic silts and aquatic vegetation that can be periodically used on raised fields for sustained production. The canals collect and store solar energy to prevent frosts, conserve water for use during periodic droughts, and may have been used for raising fish. (Photo courtesy of Clark L. Erickson)

yields are especially significant because we used local and improved potato varieties without fertilizers in the experiments, while most of the potato fields upon which the current regional estimates for Puno are based were fertilized. We have also demonstrated that high yields can be sustained for several years of continuous cropping. Green manure produced in the canals, including nitrogen fixing algae, can be used to replenish depleted soil nutrients on the fields after several years of continuous cropping. The canals were also productive in another way. Various useful aquatic plants, valuable resources in prehistoric times, rapidly colonized the water. Fish might have been raised in the deeper canals, providing a useful source of protein to supplement a diet based on starchy tubers while at the same time increasing the nitrogen content of the canal muck.

The value of raised fields in the cold Lake Titicaca Basin was dramatically demonstrated during a severe local frost in 1982. Crops in nearby fields were severely damaged, while potatoes cultivated on our experimental raised fields suffered only minimal damage and quickly recovered. Several investigators have hypothesized that raised field micro-topography tends to drain heavy dense cold air from the elevated field surfaces into the canals. Frost drainage may have played a role in this effect, but the data indicate that the presence of water in the canals was most important. In order to test this hypothesis, we conducted an investigation of the local climate of the experimental raised fields. Continuous records of incoming and outgoing energy were collected using sensitive meteorological instruments both for an experimental raised field and for nearby non-raised field areas. The study indicated that during a night of light frost in the growing season, soil and air temperatures on the raised fields were a couple of degrees Celsius higher, and the frost was of several hours shorter duration than on nearby regular fields. The water temperatures in the canals between the raised fields were even warmer than that of the soil and air, indicating that the water acts as a heat sink for storage of solar energy. We suggest that this energy is released slowly at night, when frosts are most common, blanketing the surrounding fields in warmer air. Although the increase in temperatures is only slight, our experience indicates that it was enough and that it may have been very important in minimizing the risks due to frosts for the prehistoric farmers of the zone, both lessening crop damage during the growing season and actually extending the season.

Simple cultivation on the floating islands as practiced today by the Uru of the Bay of Puno would have been a preadaptation to raised field agriculture, which was later expanded to include lake and river edge cultivation. Population appears to have grown along with agricultural expansion. Labor figures calculated from the experimental raised fields indicate that construction was not necessarily labor intensive, especially if fields were built and used over many generations. Field maintenance was found to be minimal in the experiments, but may increase after several years of cultivation. If fields can be continually used, with fertility maintained through the periodic application of decomposed organic matter from the canals, the initial labor investment for field construction is offset by the long-term benefits of continuous fertility combined with a high yield.

Raised Field Technology and Rural Development

Countries such as Peru and Bolivia often use models from more technologically advanced nations to develop their agriculture and industry. A succession of apparently sophisticated development projects in the Lake Titicaca region have failed and in some cases we can determine why. For instance, certain projects have attempted to introduce capital-intensive agriculture that depends primarily on petro-chemical fertilizers, heavy farm machinery, imported seed, irrigation pumps, or special animals forage, none of which the small-scale farmer can afford. Other projects have been oriented towards producing cash crops, but small farmers who produce a cash crop on their land often cannot make enough profit to buy food for their family, food they would otherwise produce themselves. In most cases, the majority of the farmers have not benefited from such development projects.

A more effective approach to development is through what is referred to as "appropriate technology." This approach stresses the use of traditional forms of technology and ecologically sound modern forms that are not capital intensive. In the Andes, there is a large work force available, but little capital. Since communal work forces are the traditional form of labor organization, an appropriate technology that is more easily adopted by peasant communities would involve cooperative labor (Fig. 7). Besides increasing productivity of land now under cultiva-

Figure 7. Community lands are cultivated today by representatives from each family household, an old Andean pattern of communal labor. Here, the final construction of a large raised field platform of the Community of Yasin in Chojnocot, Huatta. Loose soil is tossed on the field using carrying cloths to create a convex surface over the sod blacks which make up the fill (September 1985). (Photo courtesy of Clark L. Erickson)

tion, time-tested agricultural systems such as raised fields could be used in areas that are not currently farmed, such as on the vast pampa of the Lake Titicaca Basin.

In order to make the information collected through our archaeological and agronomic studies available as appropriate technology to the present-day Quechua and Aymara farmers of the area, a small-scale development project, the Raised Field Agricultural Project, began in 1982. We formed a multidisciplinary team, combining archaeology, cultural anthropology, agronomy, and agricultural communications that worked directly with indigenous farmers for over five years to rehabilitate the raised field system. Working with the small farmers of communities in Huatta and Coata, 10 hectares of raised fields that had been abandoned or underutilized for centuries were put back into use on communal lands. The Project, in cooperation with the Swiss government and the Peruvian Ministry of Agriculture, designed and prepared a intensive video training program in Quechua, in addition to written textbook materials, to rapidly disseminate the ancient technology.

Our applied archaeological program has finally begun to have an impact. In 1986–87, Ignacio Garaycochea, an agronomist who conducted many of the experiments, directed a government-sponsored project in collaboration with 10 Quechua communities. In our recent 1989 evaluation, we calculate that 100 hectares are now in production. A measure of the success of this project is that many individual farmers have begun to build raised fields on their own private land.

Not only can the Quechua- and Aymara-speaking peoples take great pride in the sophisticated agricultural technology of their ancestors, but they can actually apply it to solve some of the contemporary economic and agricultural problems of Peru and Bolivia. The farmers of the communities participating in rehabilitating raised fields are taking that step. The high productivity of raised field technology not only helps to support the growing populations of the towns and cities of the region where many small farmers have had to migrate in search of a livelihood, but also helps us to understand and preserve this technology for the future. It is ironic that such an immensely important and productive technology is being destroyed in many areas around Lake Titicaca by modern plow farming, urbanization, and road-building.

Bibliography

Browman, David L. 1978. "Toward the Development of the Tiahuanaco (Tiwanaku) State." In *Advances in Andean Archaeology*, ed. David L. Browman, pp. 327-349. The Hague: Mouton.

Erickson, Clark L. 1985. "Applications of Prehistoric Andean Technology: Experiments in Raised Field Agriculture, Huatta, Lake Titicaca; 1981-2." In *Prehistoric Intensive Agriculture in the Tropics*, ed. Ian Farrington, pp. 209-232. British Archaeological Reports, International Series no. 232. Oxford.

———. 1986. "Agricultural en Camellones en la Cuenca del Lago Titicaca: Aspectos Técnicos y su Futuro." In *Andenes y Camellones en el Perú Andina: Historia Presente y Futuro*, ed. Manual Burga and Carlos de la Torre, pp. 331-350. Lima: CONCYTEC.

———. 1987. "The Dating of Raised-Field Agriculture in the Lake Titicaca Basin, Peru." In *Pre-Hispanic Agricultural Fields in the Andean Region*, ed. William Denevan, Kent Mathewson, and Gregory Knapp, pp. 373-384. British Archaeological Reports, International Series, no. 359. Oxford.

Garaycochea, Ignacio. 1986. "Agricultural Experiments in Raised Fields in the Lake Titicaca Basin, Peru: Preliminary Considerations." In *Pre-Hispanic Agricultural Fields in the Andean Region*, ed. William Denevan. Kent Mathewson, and Gregory Knapp, pp. 385-398. British Archaeological Reports, International Series, no. 359. Oxford.

Lennon, Thomas J. 1983. "Pattern Analysis in Prehistoric Raised Fields of Lake Titicaca, Peru." In *Drained Field Agriculture in Central and South America*, ed. J. Darch, pp. 183-200. British Archaeological Reports, International Series no. 189. Oxford.

Kolata, Alan. 1986. "The Foundations of the Tiwanaku State: A View from the Heartland." *American Antiquity* 51(1): 748-762.

Smith, Clifford, William Denevan, and Patrick Hamilton. 1968. "Ancient Ridged Fields in the Region of Lake Titicaca." In *The Geographical Journal* 134:353-367.

4

Household Craft Specialization and Shell Ornament Manufacture in Ejutla, Mexico

Gary M. Feinman and Linda M. Nicholas

Introduction

It has been more than 60 years since Alfonso Caso (1932) discovered the spectacular Tomb 7 at the hilltop center of Monte Albán in the Valley of Oaxaca (Fig. 1). The excavators of this Postclassic-period tomb (see Table 1) were especially impressed by the quantity of gold and jade objects that accompanied the burials. Far less interest was shown in the shell objects. Yet, included with the more than 500 exotic ornaments in the tomb were necklaces made of hundreds of shell beads, especially red ones crafted from the spiny oyster (*Spondylus*). Other necklaces made of small whole shells were used to ornament breastpieces of jaguar skin. There were ornamental shell armbands, earpieces, plaques (little pieces of cut shell; *Pinctada mazatlanica* was the primary species) that were used in mosaics, and perforated shells that served as eyes in mosaics of turquoise. Placed on top of the tomb was an offering of jade ornaments, shell fragments, and a conch-shell trumpet (Marcus 1983a:283).

Earlier, during the Classic period dedication of the great South Platform on Monte Albán's Main Plaza, stone boxes with nearly identical offerings were placed underneath at least three of the corners (Acosta 1958-59:27; Marcus 1983b:175-79). While each box contained a necklace of 7 jade beads, the principal contents were shells—5 large and 5 small spiny oyster shells and 10 tent olive shells (*Oliva*).

The Tomb 7 and South Platform finds attest to the high value that the prehispanic inhabitants of highland Oaxaca, and Mesoamerica more generally, placed on shell. Certain kinds of shell, particularly the red spiny oyster, were especially esteemed. Marine shell ornaments were traded widely, had great symbolic importance, and often were deposited in high-status contexts. Yet, because marine shell has generally been recovered as whole pieces or finished ornaments from dedicatory offerings and funerary contexts, there has been little discussion of the pro-

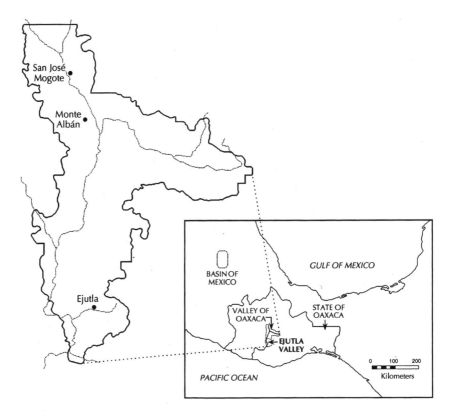

Figure 1. Southern Mexico. Shown are the Oaxaca and Ejutla valleys and site mentioned in the text. (Graphic courtesy of Gary M. Feinman and Linda M. Nicholas)

duction of shell ornaments until recently. Relatively little is known about the technologies utilized (see Suárez 1981 for a notable exception), the range of goods produced, the species used to make specific ornaments, or the scale and context of the production activities—who the artisans were, where they worked, and what they did with their products. Recent evidence from an area of prehispanic shell working at the edge of the modern town of Ejutla de Crespo in Oaxaca is helping to change this picture.

Shell Production in Oaxaca

In the land-locked Valley of Oaxaca, marine shell from both the Pacific and Atlantic coasts was imported as early as the Early Formative period. In the 1970s Kent V. Flannery and Joyce Marcus documented shell working at the Formative period village site of San José Mogote, north of Monte Albán. Several extensively excavated houses at San José Mogote contained areas of 1-2 square meters littered with flint chips, chert knives and drills, fragments of cut shell, and shell ornament fragments that were broken in the process of manufacture (Flannery and Winter 1976:39; see also Parry 1987).

Table 1. Prehispanic chronology of the Valley of Oaxaca	
1500	
1300	Late Postclassic
1100	Early Postclassic
900	
700	Late Classic
500	Early Classic
300	
AD 100	Terminal Formative
100 BC	
300	Late Formative
500	
700	Middle Formative
900	
1100	Early Formative
1300	
1500	

San José Mogote represents an early site for shell ornament production. Most of the shell was from the Pacific Coast, but a significant minority was imported from the Atlantic. Pearl oyster (*Pinctada mazatlanica*) and spiny oyster (*Spondylus*) were the most frequently worked species. The most common ornaments were shell pendants, both perforated whole shells and thin pieces carved in a variety of forms, and flat disk beads.

The formative-period shell assemblage at San José Mogote differs somewhat from the shell recovered from later Classic and Postclassic contexts at Monte Albán. Although *Pinctada* and *Spondylus* were important species used for ornamentation at both San José Mogote and Monte Albán, Atlantic shell species are rare at Monte Albán. In addition, the shell-ornament assemblages vary between the two sites, with Monte Albán having a greater relative abundance of various bead forms and multiple-piece mosaics. These differences raised questions concerning the nature of shell exchange and ornament manufacture in the Valley of Oaxaca during the later prehispanic periods. Given the lack of known shell ornament production sites in Oaxaca for the Classic and Postclassic periods, we also wondered how shell working in these later periods may have differed from shell working in the earlier period represented by San José Mogote.

Ejutla Research

The Ejutla Valley research program was designed to examine the long-term relationship between the Valley of Oaxaca and this smaller, adjacent region to the south. The first step was a regional settlement pattern survey implemented in

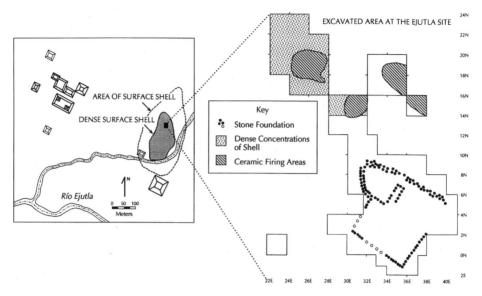

Figure 2. The Ejutla site. The mound complex, which includes several 10-meter-high structures, is located at the center of the modern town. The area with surface shell, where the excavations were carried out, is located at the eastern edge of both the modern town and the ancient site. The excavations recovered a dense midden of shell-working debris, several ceramic firing areas, and the stone foundation of a prehistoric residential structure. (Graphic courtesy of Gary M. Feinman and Linda M. Nicholas)

1984 and 1985. Prior to this research, little was known about the Ejutla Valley in prehispanic times. A cruciform tomb had been excavated in the district head town, Ejutla de Crespo, at the turn of the last century (Diguet 1905), and several sites in the region were recorded decades ago during an extensive reconnaissance of the central valleys of Oaxaca (Bernal 1965).

The hundreds of archaeological sites located and mapped during this recent Ejutla Valley survey (Feinman and Nicholas 1990) have added greatly to our knowledge of the region. One of the largest and most impressive sites is the prehispanic settlement situated beneath the modern town of Ejutla de Crespo, where Diguet had noted the tomb. Although the site has been disturbed by modern occupation, several 10-meter-high prehispanic mounds are still visible in the center of town (Fig. 2). The site was occupied from the Late Formative through the Postclassic; however, the major phase of occupation was the Classic period.

During the survey we discovered a dense concentration of shell debris in several plowed fields at the eastern edge of Ejutla de Crespo. Such finds are rare in land-locked highland areas. Artifact collections from this several-hectare area included shell fragments with obvious signs of work (such as cut marks and perforations), several broken and unfinished shell ornaments, and an unusual abundance of heavily worn stone tools, including obsidian blades. The most well-represented shell taxa on the surface were varieties that generally were used for ornamentation rather than food in prehispanic Mesoamerica.

In 1990, we initiated the first of four seasons of intensive field study at Ejutla. We focused our attention on the area where dense surface concentrations of shell had been encountered previously and on the shell itself, hoping to find answers to a number of questions. What range of items were made and what species of shell were used? What was the nature of the technology? At what scale and in what social context was the craft carried out? Were the items made for local use or were they traded to the neighboring Valley of Oaxaca?

In 1990 and 1991 we concentrated primarily on the excavation of midden deposits composed largely of shell debris, broken pottery, and obsidian and chert tools (Fig. 2). In 1992 and 1993 we focused on the exposure and definition of a nearby prehispanic structure, which included a small sub-floor tomb where four individuals and a dog were interred. During the course of the investigation, at least four ceramic firing areas (pit kilns) were also excavated. In total, a significant proportion of a prehispanic household unit has been excavated, which includes residential and work areas, the pit kilns, and associated midden areas.

Based on surface observations, it is not surprising that we found remains of shell ornament manufacture. However, archaeological indicators for several other craft activities, including ceramic vessel and figurine manufacture, lapidary arts, and possibly spinning, also were recovered (Feinman et al. 1993). Even though we do not detail these other craft activities here, they help place shell-working at the site in a broader context.

Shell Working at Ejutla

In total, more than 24,000 pieces of marine shell have been collected at the Ejutla site. Roughly 5 percent are finished or partially finished ornaments or small unmodified whole shells that could have been perforated to be strung as ornaments. An additional 35 percent show very clear indications of modification, such as drilling, string-cut surfaces and edges, and abraded surfaces. The rest of the shell material consists of broken pieces of varying sizes and minute pieces of chipping debris. No complete shells from large marine species were recovered. Yet the wide range of shell parts represented in the debris indicates that most of the shell was brought into Ejutla as whole (or nearly whole) specimens, and that primary breakage and working of the shells occurred on site.

More than 90 taxa of marine shell have been identified at the Ejutla site; however, only 7 genera account for 95 percent of the identifiable shell. Four of these genera are bivalves (pelecypods): nacreous pearl oysters (*Pinctada*), jewel boxes (*Chama*), spiny oysters (*Spondylus*), and ark shells (*Anadara*); three are snails (gastropods): giant limpets (*Patella*), limpets (*Acmaea*), and conch shells (*Strombus*). Across prehispanic Mesoamerica, each of these taxa was used ornamentally (and not generally for food). In the Ejutla excavations, the genus *Pinctada* alone accounts for approximately 60 percent of the recovered shell by weight.

Most of the Ejutla marine material is from larger species (*Strombus, Pinctada, Patella, Spondylus*), the shells of which were cut and shaped to make various ornaments. Many of the taxa present in low quantities were small gastropods, including olive shells (*Agaronia, Oliva*, and *Olivella*), nutmegs (*Cancellaria*), horn shells (*Cerithidea*), cowries (*Cypraea*), keyhole limpets (*Fissurella*), sea buttons (*Fenneria*), periwinkles (*Littorina*), marginellas (*Marginella*), nerites (*Nerita*, dye shells (*Thais*), and turret shells (*Turritella*). These shells were generally perforated

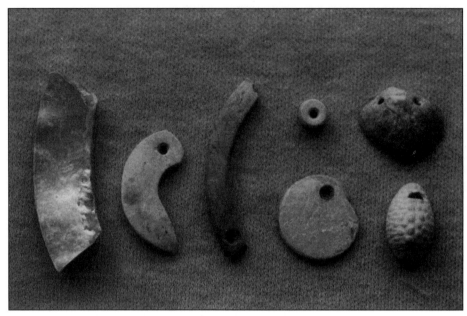

Figure 3. Examples of shell ornaments crafted at the Ejutla site. The whole shell pendant at bottom right is 15.6 mm high. (Photo by Linda M. Nicholas)

and strung whole. Almost the entire corpus of Ejutla shell represents Pacific varieties. Only two Atlantic species were present, including one *Cypraea cinerea* and several *Marginella apicina*.

Shell Ornaments

The prehispanic artisans of Ejutla crafted a range of ornaments from the Pacific Coast shell (Fig. 3). These forms included small plaques that were used in mosaic inlay, disks, beads, pendants, bracelets, and some miscellaneous forms of unknown use. In many cases, certain ornaments were made from only one or a few kinds of shell.

Nacreous pearl oyster (*Pinctada mazatlanica*), the most abundant shell species at the Ejutla site, was used to make the most commonly encountered ornaments, small plaques for mosaics (Table 2, Fig. 4). Many shell disks were cut from *Pinctada*, but depending on the technique used (see below), they were also made from conch and other non-nacreous shell. While bracelets usually were cut from giant limpets (*Patella mexicana*), a small percentage were crafted from *Pinctada*. Beads and pendants were made from a variety of shell species, but rarely from *Pinctada*.

Pearl oyster plaques were cut into a variety of shapes and sizes. Rectangular, trapezoidal, and triangular shapes were especially common. The more finished of these pieces had very straight, smooth cut edges. These pieces could have been used for mosaic inlays, such as those recovered from Tomb 7 at Monte Albán, or sewn onto cloth. Some cut nacreous shell may have been used as incrustations to decorate the teeth of ceramic figurines and urns.

Table 2
Principal ornaments crafted from prevalent shell taxa at the Ejutla site.

Shell Taxa	Common Name	Ornaments
Pinctada mazatlanica	Pearl oyster	Mosaic plaques, disks, bracelets
Spondylus sp.	Spiny oyster	Formed pendants and beads
Chama sp.	Jewel box	Formed beads
Patella mexicana	Giant limpet	Bracelets
Strombus sp.	Conch	Formed beads, blanks
Oliva sp.	Olive	Natural pendants
Various small gastropods		Natural pendants and beads

A much less common type of plaque was cut from the outer wall of certain large gastropods. These non-nacreous pieces were always in the form of small triangles, and may also have been intended for mosaic inlay.

After small plaques, the second most common ornaments were shell disks (Fig. 5). Few entirely finished disks were found. Some circular disks were perforated, evidently to be used as beads, but most were not. Disks may also have been employed in the construction of elaborate mosaics, such as those of shell and turquoise found in Tomb 7.

Beads, both finished and unfinished, were the third most frequently recovered ornaments. In the shell from Tikal, a distinction has been drawn between "natural" and "formed" beads (Moholy-Nagy 1989:141). If the shape of the original

Figure 4. Unfinished shell plaques cut from *Pinctada* shells. Many of the plaques have one or more string-cut edges. The squarish piece at top left is 19.2 by 13.2 mm. (Photo courtesy of Linda M. Nicholas)

Figure 5. Shell disks. The two small nacreous disks on the top row (left) and all the shell disks in the middle row were cut with a hollow tubular drill. The other two small disks on the top row (right) were formed by working the edges of small gastropod pieces. The disks in the bottom row were formed by abrading the edges of small pieces of nacreous shell. Diameter of disk on top left is 9.2 mm. (Photo courtesy of Linda M. Nicholas)

shell is still identifiable, then the bead is considered natural. In contrast, if the shape of the shell has been obliterated in the shell-working process, then the bead is considered formed. The Ejutla beads generally fit Moholy-Nagy's second category, with types including tiny spherical beads, larger cylindrical ones, and tubular beads (Fig. 6) (see Moholy-Nagy 1989 for similar types). At Ejutla, the major-

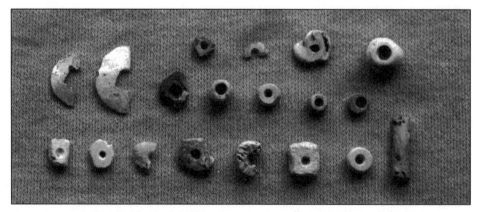

Figure 6. Finished and unfinished shell beads. Diameter of finished bead at top right is 8.5 mm. (Photo courtesy of Linda M. Nicholas)

ity of small beads were made from *Spondylus* or *Chama*, while large beads were crafted from *Strombus* and other large gastropods.

Pendants, bracelet fragments, and blanks were found with less frequency in the Ejutla collections. The majority of the pendants were formed by cutting small tabular pieces from the walls of large shells (*Spondylus* shells were the most frequently identifiable taxa; see Moholy-Nagy 1989:141). Other pendants were made by perforating whole gastropod shells (especially *Oliva*). While many bracelet fragments and debris from bracelet manufacture were recovered, no complete bracelets were found during the excavations.

Shell-Working Techniques

Obsidian and other chipped stone tools were found in close subsurface association with the shell debris, particularly in midden deposits. These tools most likely were used to craft shell ornaments. Thousands of tiny stone flakes, which appear to have been produced during use and retouching of the tools, were recovered from excavated midden strata where we found the densest shell debris. The obsidian at the site included many heavily worn blades. These spent blades would have been effectively dulled by repeatedly cutting and working the hard, abrasive shell. Chert artifacts were also abundant, commonly in the form of small, solid microdrills that have been linked to the perforation of beads and pendants elsewhere in Oaxaca (Parry 1987) and in other parts of the Western Hemisphere (e.g., Mester 1985:107; Yerkes 1989:115).

Careful analysis of the shell artifacts and debris indicates that perishable materials—string and, probably, cane—were also used to modify shell in spite of its hardness. Many of the small plaques and disks were made using these materials. The small tabular shapes frequently were cut from the walls of large nacreous shells using string in conjunction with water and an abrasive such as sand. This method often leaves a small lip on the bottom surface where the shell snaps before being cut completely through. This lip was smoothed away on more finished plaques, but remained in evidence on less finished examples. Many pieces of shell debris at Ejutla also had very smooth string-cut edges or incomplete string cuts across one or more surfaces. In some instances, the nature of these cuts allows us to determine the sequence or steps of manufacture.

Hollow tubular drills, most likely made of cane, were utilized to extract small circular disks from larger pieces of shell (see Fig. 5). The average diameter for the drilled disks was 11 millimeters; more than the three-quarters were between 8.5 and 12.5 millimeters. The nacreous disks were cut from large *Pinctada* shells using these hollow drills. As with string-cut shell, a small lip often remains on the side away from the initial cut.

Another prevalent technique used to make ornaments was to abrade the edges of small pieces of shell against a hard surface to create a smooth rounded edge (Suárez 1981: lámina 14). While many shell disks were made using the hollow drill, a greater number of disks, from both nacreous and hard matte-white shell, were formed by this abrading process. Not surprisingly, the variation in diameter was much greater for the abraded disks than the drilled disks. Abrasion was also used to make most of the shell beads. Many river cobbles were found in the midden and in association with the structure, and these often bore linear marks from abrasion wear.

The production process was not the same for all beads. The crafting of large, thick, formed beads involved more steps and a more labor-intensive process than the production of whole-shell or flat disk beads. To manufacture the more cylindrical beads, an artisan would have to cut a thick piece of matte shell (using string) from either the lip or columella of a large gastropod or the thick upper wall of certain large pelecypods and then abrade the shell into the desired shape (Suárez 1981: láminae 8, 9, 12). The risk of failure during perforation also was greater for the thicker, formed beads. Perhaps due to this risk of breakage, the large cylindrical beads generally were perforated before effort was devoted to final shaping and polishing. In contrast, holes were drilled into smaller, miniature, and flat beads after they were finely shaped and smoothed.

Concluding Thoughts

The shell workers at Ejutla used a variety of techniques to make a diverse range of ornaments, including small plaques, disks, beads, pendants, and bracelets. The majority of shell ornaments recovered were either unfinished or broken, as one might expect in a production context. Likewise, most of the other shell recovered was chipping debris and discarded pieces, the by-products of the manufacturing process.

The Ejutla artisans were involved in a range of craft activities. In some cases similar techniques appear to have been used on different classes of materials. For example, in the midden adjacent to the structure we found onyx drill plugs that would have been the by-products of using a hollow tubular drill to perforate stone. The diameter of most of the plugs was comparable to that of the majority of shell disks that were cut with a tubular drill. Although no finished complete stone ornaments were recovered in the Ejutla excavations, the same hollow-drill technique that was used to fashion the shell disks could have been employed to produce lapidary craft items, possibly small bowls (see Diehl 1983:101-2) or earspools. Involvement in multiple crafts may have enabled this household of Ejutla artisans to concentrate more heavily on non-agricultural production than would have been possible if they focused exclusively on shell or any other single craft.

The excavated structure may not have been the only one involved in multiple craft activities. The intensive study of the Ejutla site located a 5-hectare area with surface shell of which only a small portion was excavated. Included in this larger area was at least one dense concentration of shell artifacts, onyx drill plugs, and building stone that appears to be the location of a second residential structure devoted to a range of craft activities.

Shell ornament manufacture in Classic-period Ejutla was practiced in a household context, as it was in San José Mogote during the Formative period. Yet in contrast to San José Mogote, shell working in Ejutla appears to have been practiced at a higher intensity and in conjunction with a range of other crafts, and seems to have focused almost exclusively on Pacific marine species.

The volume of shell debris at Ejutla eclipses that found at other known sites in highland Oaxaca. Yet the low volume of finished shell artifacts at the site in general, and particularly on the house floor and in the tomb (where only a single shell bead was recovered), indicates that the majority of the finished ornaments were not consumed by their produces. Given the general rarity of evidence for shell working elsewhere in the valleys of Ejutla and Oaxaca (the sole exceptions are San José Mogote [Flannery and Winter 1976; Marcus 1989] and Monte Albán [Blanton 1978]), it seems likely that shell ornaments crafted in Ejutla were transported to other surrounding highland settlements.

Many of the ornament forms and shell species found in Ejutla are strikingly similar to those found at Monte Albán. Although we cannot definitely demonstrate that specific shell artifacts recovered at Monte Albán were made in Ejutla, these artifactual similarities and the rarity of other known shell production sites in the vicinity makes this hypothesis tenable. Firmer assessment, however, awaits a fuller inventory and analytical study of the Monte Albán shell assemblage.

Bibliography

Acosta, Jorge R. 1958-1959. "Exploraciones Arqueológicas en Monte Albán, XVIII Temporada." *Revista Mexicana de Estudios Antropológicos* 15:7-50.

Bernal, Ignacio 1965. "Archaeological Synthesis of Oaxaca." In *Handbook of Middle American Indians*, Vol. 3, *Archaeology of Southern Mesoamerica*, Part 2, ed. Robert Wauchope and Gordon R. Willey, pp. 788-813. Austin: University of Texas Press.

Blanton, Richard E. 1978. *Monte Albán: Settlement Patterns at the Ancient Zapotec Capital*. New York: Academic Press.

Caso, Alfonso 1932. "Monte Albán, Richest Archeological Find in America." *National Geographic Magazine* 62:487-512.

Diehl, Richard A. 1983. *Tula: The Toltec Capital of Ancient Mexico*. London: Thames and Hudson.

Diguet, M. Leon 1905. "Notes d'Archólogie Mixteco-Zapoteque." *Journal de la Société des Américanistes de Paris, Nouvelle Série*, Tome 2:109-16.

Feinman, Gary M., and Linda M. Nicholas 1990. "At the Margins of the Monte Albán State: Settlement Patterns in the Ejutla Valley, Oaxaca, Mexico." *Latin American Antiquity* 1:216-46.

Feinman, Gary M., Linda M. Nicholas, and William D. Middleton 1993. "Craft Activities at the Prehispanic Ejutla Site, Oaxaca, Mexico." *Mexicon* 15:33-41.

Flannery, Kent V., and Marcus Winter 1976. "Analyzing Household Activities." In *The Early Mesoamerican Village*, ed. Kent V. Flannery, pp. 34-45. New York: Academic Press.

Marcus, Joyce 1983a. "Monte Albán's Tomb 7." In *The Cloud People: Divergent Evolution of the Zapotec and Mixtec Civilizations*, ed. Kent V. Flannery and Joyce Marcus, pp. 282-85. New York: Academic Press.

———— 1983b. "Teotihuacan Visitors on Monte Albán's Monuments and Murals." In *The Cloud People: Divergent Evolution of the Zapotec and Mixtec Civilizations*, ed. Kent V. Flannery and Joyce Marcus, pp. 175-81. New York: Academic Press.

———— 1989. "Zapotec Chiefdoms and the Nature of Formative Religions." In *Regional Perspectives on the Olmec*, ed. Robert Sharer and David Grove, pp. 148-97. Cambridge: Cambridge University Press.

Mester, Ann M. 1985. "Un Taller Manteno de la Concha Madre Perla del Sitio Los Frailes, Manabi." In *Miscelánea Antropológica Ecuatoriana* 5:101-11.

Moholy-Nagy, Hattula 1989. "Formed Shell Beads from Tikal, Guatemala." In *Proceedings of the 1986 Shell Bead Conference: Selected Papers*, ed. Charles F. Hayes, III, and Lynn Ceci, pp. 139-56. Rochester Museum and Science Center, Research Records 20. Rochester.

Parry, William J. 1987. *Chipped Stone Tools in Formative Oaxaca, Mexico: Their Procurement, Production, and Use*. University of Michigan, Museum of Anthropology, Memoir 20. Ann Arbor.

Suárez D., Lourdes 1981. *Técnicas Prehispánicas en los Objetos de Concha*. Mexico: Instituto Nacional de Antropología e Historia.

Yerkes, Richard W. 1989. "Shell Bead Production and Exchange in Prehistoric Mississippian Populations." In *Proceedings of the 1986 Shell Bead Conference: Selected Papers*, ed. Charles F. Hayes, III, and Lynn Ceci, pp. 113-23. Rochester Museum and Science Center, Research Records 20. Rochester.

Commentary

Archaeologists study a wide variety of topics today, but we are perhaps most successful in reconstructing how people made a living in the past. One reason for our success is that ancient garbage contains abundant information on what people ate and, in some cases, how they prepared their food. Another reason lies in the range of ancillary disciplines that we use to identify plant and animal remains, and to search for evidence of agriculture on the landscape. Some ethnobotanists concentrate on macrobotanical remains and identify the plant species of charcoal fragments we find in our excavations. Others concentrate instead on pollen contained in the soils of our sites, and distinguish between wild plants and those that were probably domesticated. Still other ethnobotanists study the silica remains of plants, or phytoliths, that are preserved in a wider variety of plants than are pollen. Zoologists identify animal species, and look for signs of domestication in the anatomy of certain animals as they became increasingly dependent on humans for their reproduction and survival. Geologists scour the landscape, using remote sensing techniques, to find scars from ancient plows and alignments from ancient field systems.

Finding information on subsistence, of course, is only the first step in the process of interpreting the occupational histories of our sites and regions. What makes subsistence studies so useful to archaeologists is that, at many key transitions in human history, we see corresponding changes in how people made their living. As the environment changed during the Pleistocene, Paleolithic peoples adjusted their hunting strategies and learned to exploit different animal resources. With the gradual global warming that accompanied the end of the Pleistocene, human populations learned the ways of wild plants and eventually began to cultivate many plant species. As human populations moved into new territories, they assessed available resources and began, through the process of living, to alter the natural landscape that surrounded them. We see this clearly through patterns of localized animal extinction (as in Polynesia) and in technological advances that enabled farmers to resculpt their land (as in the Andes). Studying subsistence provides an essential part of the picture of how people made their living in the past.

Archaeologists often wonder whether our work holds any lessons for today, and it is in some of these subsistence studies that we see potential contributions. In the case of Polynesia, we see that human exploitation of new islands led to widespread devastation of the local flora and fauna. The story of Polynesia might serve as a cautionary tale to human populations today, and as a warning of what awaits us if we do not think about conserving our natural resources. In the case of the Andes, we see that some ancient strategies are more effective than those we use today, despite our abundance of high-technology equipment and knowledge.

In recent decades, anthropologists have worked diligently to persuade economic development specialists to think in terms of appropriate technologies as they make plans to change traditional subsistence systems in developing areas of the world. In the Andes, the revival of raised field systems provides an efficient and economical alternative to new crops, fertilizers, and insecticides for Andean farmers who continue to live in a harsh, highland environment. Archaeology makes different kinds of contributions to the public, and much of the time our contribution lies in illuminating aspects of a cultural heritage. In some cases like those described in this section, however, we can make even broader contributions to our understanding of humans and their world.

Part Nine

Social and Political Life in the Ancient World

Introduction

Studying ancient social and political systems is an enduring interest of anthropological archaeologists throughout the world, whether they work with small-scale or large-scale societies. Interpreting ancient sociopolitical systems is one of the most difficult tasks facing archaeologists, but it is also among the most fascinating. Today we use a variety of methods to study social and political systems of the past, including the study of burials and their associated goods, the study of monumental buildings and architecture, the study of trade and exchange networks, and the study of so-called settlement patterns. Since archaeologists often rely on ethnographic analogy to interpret sociopolitical systems, scholars often use typological frameworks for classifying societies that sociocultural anthropologists originally formulated in the 1960s and 1970s. Archaeologists commonly use classificatory schemes that distinguish between bands, tribes, chiefdoms, or states, or that contrast egalitarian, ranked, and stratified societies with each other when we to interpret ancient sociopolitical systems.

Cross-cultural anthropological research suggests that bands and tribes (which are considered egalitarian societies) are typically small-scale societies or communities, with relatively low populations and most people know each other. On the other hand, chiefdoms and states (which are considered ranked and stratified societies) are much larger and involve hundreds or thousands of people. Anthropologists have found that band and egalitarian societies contain anywhere from a few families to a few hundred people, are often mobile (such as the !Kung Bushmen), and recognize little or no distinctions in status or political power among its members, except according to age and gender. On the other hand, ranked and stratified societies often have high populations, engage in intensive food production, and exhibit marked differences in social status and economic wealth.

Recent discoveries have challenged these generalizations, however, in Australia and France. The article entitled "Cemetery Reveals Complex Aboriginal Society" (Graeme O'Neill) discusses the implications of a newly discovered ancient Australian burial ground with up to 10,000 aboriginal skeletons. Historically and ethnographically documented aboriginal peoples were organized into small groups that were highly mobile. The presence of up to 10,000 skeletons at this site and evidence of a substantial occupation, suggests that aboriginal Australians may have organized themselves quite differently before European contact and had a relatively complex society. Similarly surprising findings from a cave near Boussac, France are described in "Masters and Slaves in an Iron Age Cave?" (by Michael Balter). Archaeologists often assume that Iron Age populations were small-scale societies with little hierarchical organization. The discovery of Iron Age burials in the French cave, which were accompanied by different amounts of grave goods, suggests that social stratification might have begun much earlier than we once thought, perhaps even before state level societies developed.

Studying the development of higher levels of social complexity has proven equally difficult for archaeologists. We often have difficulty in distinguishing so-called "chiefdoms" from so-called "early states," because differences between these types of society may be quantitative, rather than qualitative. The article "Platform Mounds of the Arizona Desert" by Glen Rice and Charles Redman, describes a long-term research program in southern Arizona on developments in the 12th through 15th centuries A.D. Archaeological investigations in the Tonto Basin of east-central Arizona have revealed many sites containing earthen platform mounds, and a network of residential areas surrounding these platform mounds. Work described by Rice and Redman concentrates on learning how these platform mounds were constructed, and on the role of these platform mound villages during the Classic period. They make the point that platform mounds of the southern Southwest pale in comparison to the temple-pyramids of Mesoamerica, and argue convincingly that we can study some processes in the development of sociopolitical complexity more effectively in places (like Arizona), where societies never attained true statehood. Their problem-oriented research, which combines careful architectural analysis and comparison with other sites in the general area, illustrates how much information we can learn from a fine-grained analysis of archaeological sites.

Other societies in the Americas developed still higher levels of complexity that we commonly associate with chiefdoms, rather than states. One of the most remarkable of these was the southeastern United States, whose Mississippian culture contained huge platform mounds, large populations, and a high degree of social stratification prior to European contact. The article "Mighty Cahokia" by William Iseminger, illustrates some of the characteristics of highly developed communities in North America by focusing on the 11th–13th century site of Cahokia. As we have seen in other parts of the world, populations in this region took advantage of fertile farmland, which probably yielded sufficient surpluses to support communities of elites and artisans. What sorts of evidence do archaeologists use to argue that ancient societies were complex? At Cahokia, they use the high number of large earthen platform mounds (and other monumental architecture), the wide array of exotic materials, and mortuary remains that suggest social stratification and status. The association of an opulent male burial with mass burials of females suggests human sacrifice. However we classify Cahokia and the Mississippian society in which it grew, these systems clearly represented a form of complex society.

The mound-building cultures of North America warrant more attention than they have received, since it is in such contexts that archaeologists can study the origins of sociopolitical complexity. When we turn our attention southward to Mesoamerica, however, we find several examples of cultures that evolved into true states or civilizations. One of the most celebrated among these was the Maya, whose culture flourished from the 4th through 9th centuries A.D. during the Classic period. The ancient Maya, once considered a chiefdom, are now believed to have been a highly complex state society. Jeremy Sabloff's article, entitled, "Settlement Patterns and Community Organization in the Maya Lowlands," discusses archaeologists' growing interest in the nature of Maya urbanism in the northern Yucatan through the Sayil Archaeological Project. Through a combination of survey, surface collection, and test excavations, they concluded that much of the space in and around Sayil was used for residences and for farming. These "in-gardens" may have provided a large part of Maya subsistence. They also suggest that Classic Maya sociopolitical organization varied from one part of the lowlands to the next. Manufactured goods circulated widely through the region, and may have been made and exchanged at the household level. Sabloff concludes that certain conditions in the Maya lowlands (such as dispersed populations and the operation of independent farming systems) helped block the growth of the kind of centralized authority that we commonly associate with states.

The splendid temples and city-states seen in the Maya lowlands were latecomers to the civilization scene: Old World civilizations developed 2500 years before the rise of the ancient Maya. One of the heartlands of early civilization lay in the Near East, in a region that archaeologists call Mesopotamia. Anchored along the Tigris and Euphrates rivers, civilization developed—and collapsed—in Mesopotamia by the 3rd millennium B.C. Why did early societies and civilizations like the ancient Maya, the Egyptians, and the Bronze Age Mesopotamians collapse? For the last several decades, many archaeologists believed that these complex societies found their demise through political strife and social unrest. The article entitled "Empires in the Dust" (Karen Wright) considers a theory by archaeologist Harvey Weiss that it was climate, rather than sociopolitics, that was the culprit. According to Weiss, climatic change in the form of a 300-year drought led to the end of Bronze Age communities in Mesopotamia. Not all Near Eastern archaeologists agree with Weiss, in part because it is conventionally thought that peoples in complex societies had the sophistication and technology to overcome poor ecological conditions. Perhaps Weiss' theory that climatological change heavily influenced the course of ancient history might be applicable to interpretations of ancient societies elsewhere in the world. We clearly need to study the relationship between climate, political structure, and economic organization more to resolve such debates over the collapse of ancient states.

1

Cemetery Reveals Complex Aboriginal Society

Graeme O'Neill

In April the dead came out of the ground around the feet of Colin Pardoe and Harvey Johnston. Pardoe, an archaeologist from the South Australian Museum, and Johnston, a researcher for the New South Wales National Parks Service, were walking along a beach dune at Lake Victoria in New South Wales, searching for signs of aboriginal cemeteries, when the skeletons started sliding out of the sand beneath them. "A dozen here, a half dozen there," says Pardoe. "And for every one exposed, we were finding up to five others above or below it."

The two researchers soon realized they were standing atop a huge necropolis, stretching 3 kilometers along the dune and containing as many as 10,000 human skeletons. And archaeologists say this discovery—probably the world's largest assemblage of skeletons from a hunter-gatherer society—is prompting a radical revision of theories about life in pre-European Australia.

Until now, most prehistorians pictured Australia's aborigines as small scattered bands eking a living out of the harsh, arid landscape. But "it's clear we have very seriously underestimated the pre-European population of this continent," says Alan Thorne of the Australian National University in Canberra, an expert on Australian prehistory. The Lake Victoria site, says Thorne, along with several smaller cemeteries found on the banks of the nearby Murray and Darling rivers, indicates that "these were not just isolated tribes existing in desperate circumstances, but substantial communities living in a very rich landscape."

The bones that provoked this reevaluation began eroding out of the dune when Lake Victoria was drained to allow maintenance work on an outlet channel early this year. The Barkindji aboriginal community at Dareton, on the Murray 60 kilometers to the east, asked Pardoe to help them excavate and reclaim the skeletons, which they view as those of their ancestors. That prompted Pardoe and Johnston's April dune walk, accompanied by archaeologist Dan Witter of the parks service and Barkindji elders Roland and Dawn Smith, who supervised the search.

The bones excavated during this search show skull and skeletal similarities that persist from the bottom of the dune to the top. Those similarities are enough to convince Pardoe and his colleagues that the locality was occupied by a single population; geologic dating of the sediments beneath the bones shows that the occupation lasted at least 7000 years.

It wasn't simply a long occupation, however; it was a large one. Pardoe says the main evidence for the enduring presence of a large, organized, sedentary aboriginal community comes partly from the manner of the burials. A human body is heavy, and nomadic aborigines elsewhere in Australia's arid interior left their dead exposed to the elements. Relatives returned later to decorate the bones with ochre before disjointing them and bundling them for burial, often taking the bundles to sacred sites some distance away. Yet at Lake Victoria, most skeletons are intact and the bones are unadorned—signs that people died near the cemetery and were buried while flesh still covered their bones. The vast number of the Lake Victoria dead is also consistent with the notion of a large settled community.

The surrounding flood plain offers further support for the idea of a settled group. The nearby soils are almost devoid of useful stone, but caches of chert—a siliceous rock that flakes easily to a sharp edge—have been found near the dunes, apparently imported from several miles away, near the banks of the Murray. Johnston and Witter believe these imports reflect an organized tool-making industry. In addition, discarded chert blades and scrapers can easily be found within a day's walk of the lake side, but no further—implying the hunters and gatherers weren't traveling far afield and that local food resources were being intensively exploited.

These resources were not, however, exploited to the point of destruction. The simple fact that a large population lived there over thousands of years suggests natural resources were sustained and used—not used up. Elsewhere in the world, this type of adaptation usually involved agriculture, says Witter. And in Australia, he continues, popular history has disparaged aborigines for failing to make this agricultural transition and cited this failure as the reason for their present nomadic lifestyles and small population.

But the evidence from Lake Victoria indicates the aboriginal populations did adapt and expand, and they were able to do so because people found a different but equally valid way to utilize their surroundings. The Lake Victoria community had access to permanent water sources, and they could draw on a diverse larder of plant and animal foods, including reptiles, fish, crustaceans, mollusks, water birds, and a plenitude of game—32 mammal species inhabited the grasslands before Europeans arrived. Amid such plenty, asks Pardoe, why grow crops? Adds Witter: "They achieved a highly flexible, sustainable existence without locking themselves into the technological restraints [such as specialized tools] that accompanied agriculture." (Nor are they the only hunter-gatherer society to do so. Over the past several years, anthropologists have discovered signs that populations in several parts of the world had also developed complex, nonagricultural societies.)

This emerging view of aboriginal life doesn't rest on Lake Victoria alone. Other, smaller, aboriginal cemeteries have been found along the Murray during the past 25 years, and Pardoe says the discoveries had stirred doubts in the minds of researchers about the stereotype of small bands ranging across the landscape. With the Lake Victoria find, he says, the stereotype collapses. "For communities of more than 100 individuals, the logistical problems of moving increase exponentially," he notes. "There are divisions of labor, groups with defined goals, and problems with defense. Even if you do move, you don't scatter. At Lake Victoria, they probably didn't move more than 500 meters to a few kilometers at a time, within a territory only about 20 kilometers square."

2

Masters and Slaves in an Iron Age Cave?

Michael Balter

Death is often described as the great equalizer—but the same can't be said of burial. The rich spend eternity in cushy mausoleums, while the poor elbow each other for space in common graves. And that social distinction isn't new. Nearly 2800 years ago in southern France, 22 people apparently received radically unequal treatment in death, which could help archaeologists understand the origins of social stratification and urban development in this region.

Early this year, explorers and scientists discovered two groups of almost perfectly preserved human skeletons in a cave near the village of Boussac, in the department of Lot. Nineteen of them had gone unadorned to their burials. But three others, apparently interred at the same time in a nearby chamber, were outfitted with jewelry, tools, and weapons.

Such "sharp status differences...could be really interesting," says University of Minnesota archaeologist Peter Wells, possibly indicating that the 19 unadorned bodies were servants or slaves of the other three more "aristocratic" individuals. Almost nothing is known about the structure of the societies that existed during this period—the early Iron Age—in the Western Mediterranean area. And that makes the cave extremely important, says Michel Vidal, the French archaeology services' conservator for the Midi-Pyrenées region and leader of the research team. So important that, although it was discovered in February, the French government kept the cave's existence secret until late April, when the site could be properly secured.

Vidal says that the details of the implements found with the smaller group of skeletons—an iron lance and knife, iron bracelets, and a bronze torque (neck ring)—are typical of the 7th or early 8th century B.C. This would correspond to the early Iron Age societies in temperate Europe known collectively as the Halstatt culture (named for an archaeological site in central Austria), which flourished from the 8th century to the 5th century B.C. The Halstatt connection makes the Boussac discovery "very particular," says Vidal, because cave burials are extremely rare during the Halstatt period. Wells agrees that "cave burials are very unusual....In this period there are hundreds of known cemeteries, but they are all out there in the landscape."

Moreover, most Iron Age graves consisted of burial mounds sheltering only one individual. But not at Boussac—the two groups appear to have been chosen for a single subterranean burial. So not only were there apparent status differences between the two groups, but also between all the buried people and the rest of society. The big question, says Wells, "is why did these individuals get this unusual burial? Is there a social status difference or ritual religious difference between [different] groups in society?" Richard Osgood of the Institute of Archaeology at Oxford University draws an analogy to burials of "the Zulu chiefs of the 19th century....Once the chiefs died, their entire entourage was killed and buried with them." Although it's sheer speculation, he says, a similar relationship could be behind the Boussac interments.

If scientists could determine the family relationships between the individuals in the cave, they might be able to bolster some of these theories or rule them out. To get a handle on genetic relations, Vidal's group of regional archaeologists is teaming up with anthropologists at the University of Bordeaux to extract DNA from the skeletons. They also plan to examine arm, shoulder, and other bones for marks made where muscles were attached. The severity of such marks can reveal whether or not the people were habitually engaged in hard labor. Activity differences might, for instance, provide support for the servant hypothesis. And artifacts on the cave floor near the burials might yield clues about lifestyle.

Archaeologists have been hunting for evidence of social complexity in this region for some time, says Wells. Although the first urban centers, complete with divisions of labor and status among the population, emerged in the Near East during the Bronze Age, about 3500 B.C. the rise of towns in temperate Europe is thought to be an independent development, which begins to show up in the archaeological record at about 600 B.C. "These finds [at Boussac] from a century or two before," Wells says, "might tell us something about the process of social and economic change leading to the formation of these more complex communities."

The first step will be radiocarbon dating of the two groups of skeletons, as well as other organic material—such as bits of wood—that may eventually be found, to confirm that they were buried simultaneously. Vidal expects these tests, the DNA work, and the other studies to be completed later this year. If they do support the notion of social distance between the adorned and unadorned bodies, it would be a discovery to ornament any archaeologist's career.

3

Platform Mounds of the Arizona Desert: An Experiment in Organizational Complexity

Glen Rice and Charles Redman

In the fall of 1989 we began an eight-year project to investigate platform mound communities in the Tonto Basin of central Arizona. The project is being funded by the Bureau of Reclamation as part of an overall plan to study sites that may be affected by proposed modifications to Theodore Roosevelt Dam (see box). We are particularly interested in how the societies that built the platform mounds were organized, and how this organization might have been related to developments either within or beyond the local area. We began the project believing that the platform mounds of the Arizona desert were pretty much part of a single historic movement that swept the region, but as our work has progressed, we have had to rethink our models for the development and organization of the mound-building societies of Arizona.

Platform mounds were built by the prehistoric Salado and Hohokam people of southern Arizona from the 13th through the 15th century A.D., the Classic period. They are basically artificial, flat-topped hills on which the ruling families of the day built their homes. Additional residences and storage rooms were built around the base of a mound, and the whole was enclosed within a compound wall (Fig. 3).

Each mound was the administrative, ceremonial, and economic center for a small-scale political system, or polity, whose settlements were scattered over 5 to 25 square miles (Fish 1989; Rice et al. 1990). At their maximum extent there were probably about 100 of these little political systems scattered across the Sonoran Desert of Arizona.

Platform mound polities were not evenly distributed across the desert floor nor did they completely "fill" the region. They occurred in groups of as few as four to as many as two dozen, and the groups were limited to the floors of the major valleys and low basins (Fig. 4) where agriculture, combined with the gathering of abundant wild foods, allowed for the growth of large populations. Distances of up to 25 miles might separate one cluster from the next, and much of the Sonoran Desert of central and southern Arizona remained uninvolved in the platform mound polities. There is little doubt that some people continued to live in rela-

Figure 1. One or two families live in the four rooms and three courtyards of this 13th century Salado compound. Two rooms are located at the corners of the compound (including the nearest corner) and two rooms are located side by side in the middle of the compound. The backhoe is assisting the archaeologist by removing the dirt that has been blown and washed over the area. (Photo courtesy of the Bureau of Reclamation, U.S. Dept. of the Interior)

tively independent and self-sufficient villages in the areas between the polities, but probably in far fewer numbers than were associated with the platform mounds.

These platform mound polities scarcely compare to the Mesoamerican empires controlled by the Toltecs, Aztecs, or Maya, yet it is their lilliputian scale that we find most interesting. Although the Salado had not formed states, their societies were organized on a scale larger and more complex than the individual village unit. The elites living on top of the platform mounds, who organized the large labor forces needed to construct and maintain the mounds, were much more than tribal elders with temporary authority over a ceremony or a task group. These were full-time leaders who had the authority and power to make demands on the local population for services and for products. In exchange, they provided the organizational structure needed to protect the community, maintain public facilities, and ensure that people were fed.

The large sites in the Chaco Canyon area might indicate another example of a complex society in the prehistoric Southwest. However, some of the researchers working in the area feel that the environment of the Colorado plateau simply could not have generated the levels of surplus food needed to support a complex society (Vivian 1990; Johnson 1989).

On the other hand, the production of a food surplus would not have been a problem for the platform mound people living in the well-watered valleys of the Sonoran Desert (Rice et al. 1990:31-34). The desert climate provides a long growing season, with opportunities for two or more planting cycles per year. To agricultural produce could be added the rich harvests of natural foods such as cacti fruits, agave, and tree legumes. The abundance of the desert is attested by Catholic priests writing in the 18th century who found that the Pima (desert descendants of the Hohokam) frequently left surplus harvests rotting in the fields, having planted far more than they could possibly use. In bad years the extra acreage planted in fields would have come in handy. During the era of the platform mounds, such surpluses could have been harvested and accumulated in central locations for use by the leaders living on the mounds.

The peoples of the platform mounds had taken the first step towards the kind of organizational complexity that functions today throughout much of our industrialized world. Over and over again human societies have taken this road to complexity, and within the last century, human societies have almost completely abandoned the tribal forms of life that had served us so well since the end of the last ice age. As archaeologists we would like to know why and how human soci-

Figure 2. Ceremonies were held in mid summer to celebrate the ripening of the fruit of the saguaro cactus. The pulp can be made into a wine, while the highly nutritious seeds are stored for use later in the season. (Photo courtesy of Brenda Shears)

eties make these changes, but many of the first (or pristine) transitions to complexity took place thousands of years ago, and evidence of them has been obscured, if not eradicated, by the subsequent development of even more complex societies. This is the case for many of the original "cradles" of complex societies, like Mesoamerica, the Middle East, and Asia.

But in southern Arizona, prehistoric peoples of the platform mounds took a small step towards complexity, experimented with it for the relatively brief span of two centuries, then nearly completely disappeared. Small pockets of population remained, but they lacked the size to maintain, much less require, a complex organization. The evidence of this early experiment with complexity has not been clouded by a long archaeological record of subsequent states and empires (Rice 1990:157-58). With the arrival of European American settlers in the last part of the 19th century, however, complex society once again began to spread across the Arizona desert, and true to historical precedence, our own growth is rapidly destroying the evidence of that first experiment in complexity. Even working at a distance of 100 miles from the nearest city, we find our investigations into the Tonto Basin platform mounds constantly beset by problems caused by vandalism and modern construction.

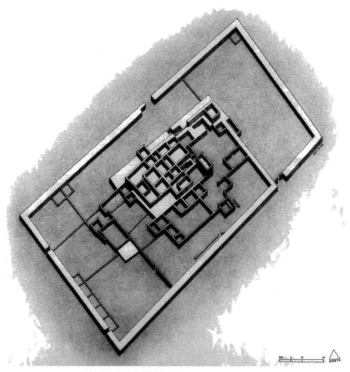

Figure 3. The Cline Terrace mound in Tonto Basin is actually a combination of a big and small mound within a single walled compound. The rooms on top of the mounds are thought to have been used both as residences for the ruling elite and as ceremonial rooms. (Graphic by Glena Cain)

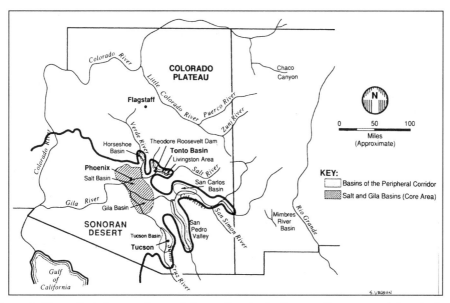

Figure 4. Tonto Basin is one of several river valleys in the Sonoran Desert containing platform mounds. In the Salt and Gila Basins, such mounds developed from an earlier form of dance mound, while in the peripheral basins platform mounds appear to have been preceded by special ceremonial buildings called big houses. (Graphic courtesy of Sharon Vaughn)

Life During the Early Classic Period (A.D. 1200–1325)

For the first two years of the Roosevelt Archaeological Project, our research focused on the excavation of several platform mound communities and a larger number of residential compounds in a portion of the Tonto Basin called Livingston (Fig. 6). Most of the sites in the Livingston area date to the Roosevelt phase (A.D. 1200-1325) and only a few settlements were occupied in the later Gila phase (A.D. 1325-1450). We found a number of surprises in the Livingston area that have forced us to continue to rethink our models of Classic period society (A.D. 1200-1450).

During the Roosevelt phase the people of the Livingston area lived in about 40 small compounds and 5 platform mounds dispersed along a 3-mile stretch of the Salt River valley. We had pored over maps showing similar kinds of dispersed community patterns in the nearby Phoenix basin, but the only extensive excavation of multiple sites (that is, both mounds and compounds) in such a grouping of settlements had taken place more than a century earlier (see Haury's 1945 report on the Hemenway Expedition of 1887 and 1888). Excavation coverage from more recent projects usually focused on only a few compounds or mounds within much larger groupings.

Here in the Livingston area of Tonto Basin was an opportunity to gather fresh data using modern methods and current research orientations. Along with our colleagues from Desert Archaeology (see box), we are paying particular attention to architecture and associated features. Artifacts are being systematically collected

Dams, Problem-Oriented Research, and Salado Platform Mounds

In the first decade of this century Theodore Roosevelt laid out a vision for the development of the abundant natural resources of the western United States, a vision that had as much to do with the creation of the Yellowstone National Park as it did with the construction of the Theodore Roosevelt Dam, the nation's first major hydroelectric and water conservation dam at the confluence of the Salt River and Tonto Creek in Arizona. By storing water, generating electricity, and controlling the unpredictable floods of the Salt River, the dam made possible the phenomenal growth of modern Phoenix.

The building of the dam took nearly a decade, and brought together Italian stone masons, Irish construction workers, and Apache laborers in what was at that time the largest project ever to have been undertaken by the United States government. The project gave birth to a new agency, the United States Reclamation Service, known today as the Bureau of Reclamation.

In the last decade of this century the Bureau of Reclamation has returned to the Roosevelt Dam. The height of the dam will be increased and larger spillways will be constructed. Ironic as it may seem to people not accustomed to life in the Sonoran Desert, the dam is being modified not to store more water but to provide an improved capability for controlling floods that might threaten the Phoenix metropolitan area. These planned modifications will result in a larger reservoir, and could potentially involve the inundation of more than 600 archaeological sites in the Salt and Tonto River valleys.

To deal with the impact to these sites, the archaeological staff of the Bureau of Reclamation sought to develop a program that fulfilled the spirit of the laws on historic preservation. Kathy Pedrick, one of the archaeologists with the Bureau of Reclamation, remembers that "the challenge was to develop a mitigation program that would embrace critical research issues for the area." After nearly a year of study and preparation, a study team of government archaeologists (including Kathryn Pedrick and Thomas Lincoln from Reclamation, Scott Wood from the Tonto National Forest, and representatives from the Arizona State Historic Preservation Office) identified a set of distinct research efforts, each of which was to be undertaken by a different research group.

Those of us on the research team from Arizona State University have the task of documenting the nature of Salado social organization through the excavation of five platform mound communities (i.e., mounds and their associated sites in the surrounding hinterland) located in three areas within the Tonto Basin (Fig. 5). Desert Archaeology, Inc., a private firm directed by William Doelle, is examining two platform mound communities with a slightly different emphasis, to detail the changes in social organization that took place as the platform mound communities developed from the earlier period of pithouse villages. A research team from Statistical Research, headed by Jeff Alschul, has studied a series of small compounds, field houses, and terrace systems in order to document the relationships between "rural" sites and the populations living at the platform mounds. Richard Ahlstrom of SWCA, Inc., has conducted a sample survey in the upper reaches of the *bajadas* (alluvial fans) that surround the valley, and has provided valuable information about the contemporaneous populations living in the upland areas. In the spring of 1993 Arizona State University will excavate some of the bajada sites in order to establish the relationship of the upland populations to those living at the platform mounds. Finally, far to the south, Paul and Suzanne Fish of the Arizona State Museum are mapping and excavating a platform mound community in the northern Tucson Basin. Some of their research was supported by the Bureau of Reclamation (a large aqueduct was constructed by Reclamation through a portion of the 15 square mile community complex).

By the close of this decade the archaeologists working on these various teams will have developed the first comprehensive views of the community systems that envelop platform mounds.

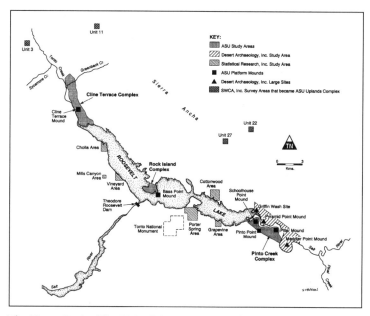

Figure. 5. The Tonto Basin. The United States Bureau of Reclamation has provided funding for three different excavation projects focused on sites around the valley bottom, and a survey by a fourth team which has found numerous Salado sites in the surrounding foothills. (Graphic by Sharon Vaughn)

from screened samples or from carefully recorded locations on the house floors and compound plazas. We are collecting flotation samples (soil from which burned weeds and plant pieces are extracted), pollen samples, charcoal fragments, and archaeomagnetic samples (clay samples taken from hearths for dating) needed to resolve archaeological questions concerning subsistence, chronology, trade, and craft production.

The level of detail in this new information has been gratifying. Inside the walled compounds (Fig. 1) we found the circular bases of granaries, open-air hearths, and small pits for mixing the adobe needed for the regular replastering of the adobe walls. Pollen studies indicate that the granaries were used for the storage of corn and squash. Pine pollen, usually found at higher elevations, was recovered from the plaza areas, suggesting that pine boughs were used in ceremonial processions through the compounds. Fragments of a local form of barley were found clinging to the walls of storage vessels on the house floors. Outside some of the compounds were large roasting pits that our flotation studies showed were used for the baking of agave. We found that many of the compounds were divided in half by a wall, suggesting that perhaps two closely related families, or two generations of the same family, resided within each site.

In a typical residential compound about a third of the rooms contained hearths and were used as residences; other rooms were used as workshops or for storage. One room might contain small flakes and pieces of shattered stone indicating it had been used as a lithic workshop. Other rooms contained polishing stones and chunks of pigments used for pottery manufacture, along with hardened pieces of raw clay that had never been worked.

Just as the rooms within a compound had different functions, so did the compounds within the local area. For example, team member David Jacobs found that compounds that had large pits for roasting agave tended not to have granaries for the storage of corn. Large knives made from polished slabs of schist and used for harvesting agave occurred with great frequency at some compounds, while projectile points and obsidian were found in unusual concentrations at others. Yet the metates and manos that were needed to prepare corn and other grains for cooking were found in all of the sites, as were fragments of agave fibers and the bones of deer and rabbit. The individual sites may have been economically specialized, but the fruit of each family's labor was made available to other families within the polity.

This evidence for the economic diversity and specialization of households was one of the things we had expected to find if our ideas about the complexity of

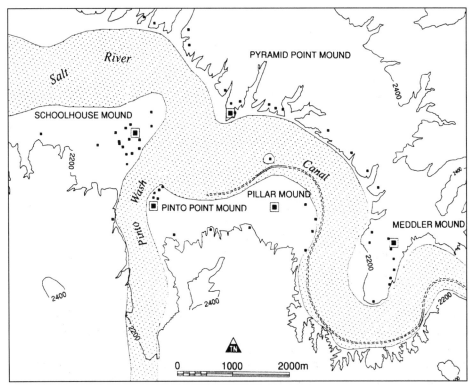

Figure 6. Livingston area. During the Roosevelt phase (ca. A.D. 1250-1325) this part of the Salt River valley contained more than 40 small residential compounds (indicated by small squares). Five platform mounds were built around A.D. 1280. By the Gila phase (A.D. 1325 to about 1450), most of the Salado population in the Tonto Basin had moved into a few very large sites, such as the Schoolhouse Mound. The size of the Schoolhouse Site grew considerably during this later period as people of the Livingston area flocked to it. Some people continued to live at a few small sites near Schoolhouse. (Graphic by Lynn Simon)

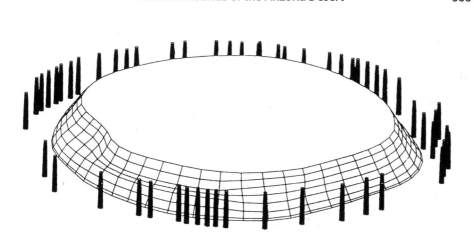

Figure 7. This pre-Classic dance mound at Snaketown was constructed of compacted dirt and was approximately 1 meter in height. Emil Haury suggests that such mounds were used for ceremonial dances. In the Salt and Gila Basins, these dance mounds are frequently the stratigraphic precursors to Classic period platform mounds. (Graphic by Greg Phillips)

Classic period society were correct. One of the benefits for individuals living in a complex society is that the elite rulers provide an administrative framework and the facilities to ensure regular trade and exchange. This made it possible for the families who concentrated on planting and harvesting agave, for instance, to rely on exchange with those families who concentrated on growing corn or specialized in making the projectile points needed to bring down game.

An Unusual Building

While our research was beginning to provide answers to some of our questions, it was producing highly unexpected results in other areas. Based on what was known about platform mounds in the Salt and Gila Basins, we had expected to find buried beneath many of our platform mounds evidence of an earlier and much simpler kind of structure called a dance mound. Dance mounds were frequently circular, although some tended towards the rectangular. They contained no rooms on top and were little more than a slightly raised stage on which ceremonies could have been held. Emil Haury drew on comparisons with the 19th century Pima culture to suggest that these early mounds might have been used for dances celebrating military victories (1976). He excavated a particularly elaborate dance mound at the site of Snaketown that included steps, but was no more than a meter in height (Fig. 7). A circular arrangement of post holes probably represents an adobe wall, reinforced by internal upright posts, that formed the facing of a later mound. It eroded but left a covering of dirt to preserve the earlier dance mound.

As we excavated into the interior of our first platform mound in the Livingston area, however, we found not a dance mound but the remains of a very special kind of ceremonial building that we called a "little Casa Grande." The structure began as a series of two very large rooms (about 38 sq m each) that were entered from a long, narrow courtyard. The doorways of the rooms and the courtyard opened to the east.

Within each room were a pair of adobe columns measuring nearly a meter in diameter and rising to a height of a little over a meter. A socket at the top of each mound held a post used to support the main beam in the ceiling. Neither room had a hearth, and the site had practically no trash.

During the excavation the director, David Jacobs, realized that the columns and doorways in the two rooms of the Pillar Site were aligned in such a manner that for a period of about 10 days during the winter and summer solstices they block all but a thin sliver of light from reaching the back wall of the room (Fig. 9). Modern Native Americans such as the Hopi and Zuni celebration the winter solstice in a 16-day ceremony, and the builders of the Pillar Site may have been similarly concerned with identifying a span of days around the general event rather than the precise day of the solstice.

This was, and still is, an impressive building. It was not, however, an elite residence, nor was it necessarily an indicator of a complex society. It was a ceremonial facility, but it was constructed by a large group of people for the benefit of the entire group. The rooms within the building were very likely used for ceremonial meetings. No other building like this has been found in the Tonto Basin, but a very similar set of rooms with columns was found beneath a small mound in the Tucson Basin.

The First Platform Mounds

Platform mounds appeared throughout Tonto Basin during a very short time span around A.D. 1280; five different platform mounds were constructed within the Livingston area alone. Many of the mounds were built by removing the roofs from the rooms of pre-existing buildings, and filling the rooms with cobbles and dirt to create the platform. Some of the buildings that were modified into platform mounds were large ceremonial structures, such as the one at the Pillar Mound, but others were residential rooms within small compounds. Where some pre-existing building was not conveniently available, a grid-like structure of walled cells was first constructed and then filled to create the platform mound. The use of rooms or cells served a useful purpose in the construction of large mounds by helping to stabilize lateral movements of fill within the mound.

At the Pillar Mound, the large rooms of the building were filled with dirt and cobbles to a height of about 1.2 meters, and new rooms were constructed on top of the resulting platform. The construction of the platform was halted at intervals during which layers of brushy plants were laid over the soil. The purpose of these layers is not known, but radiocarbon analyses of samples of these materials have helped date the construction of the mound. Similar layers have been found in other Roosevelt phase platform mounds. Adobe columns and (for the first time) hearths were built in the elevated rooms, but doorways were omitted in favor of entrance through openings in the roof. If the columns continued to be used as solstitial markers, it was with the aid of windows that have long since disappeared as the walls of the elevated rooms collapsed. In its final form, the entire building had been transformed into an elevated platform mound with four rooms and a small plaza on top.

Although five platform mounds existed within the Livingston area at the same time, the relationships between mounds may have been more cooperative than competitive. Cooperation was needed, for instance, to build and maintain the canal system that traversed the Livingston area. The mounds imply that society had begun to develop important leaders, but as yet there was no single commonly recognized leader for the whole polity. Instead, the Livingston polity was composed of five loosely linked groups, each probably representing closely related kinfolk, and each group constructed a platform mound for its own leader. The Livingston area as a whole, however, was still led by a committee of at least five representatives, one from each of the family groups.

This stage in the development of the society was extremely short-lived. It is exciting to actually have captured it in the archaeological record, for in little more than a generation four of the five Livingston platform mounds were abandoned and apparently rebuilt around the mound at the Schoolhouse Site.

A Late Platform Mound at the Schoolhouse Site

The Schoolhouse Mound, one of the largest in the Tonto Basin, was excavated under the direction of Owen Lindauer in 1990 and 1991. The architecture of the Schoolhouse Mound contains a striking record of the changes that took place during the Gila phase. The site was first occupied in the Roosevelt phase, and our current thinking is that it had a small mound at that time. Three additional mounds may have been added at the start of the Gila phase (Fig. 8a). Through time the mounds expanded and additional rooms were built at ground level. More than a century later, at the end of the Gila phase (A.D. 1450), the mounds had been linked into a nearly continuous unit of rooms and raised patio-like areas. The additional mounds and rooms at the Schoolhouse Mound were built by people who moved in from the other sites and mounds of the Livingston area.

Thus, the small dispersed compounds of the Roosevelt phase disappeared. Only a few continued to be occupied during the growth and expansion of the Schoolhouse Mound. As the people of the Livingston area collected at Schoolhouse, they effectively abandoned nearly all of the area that lay upstream (to the east; see Fig. 6).

As it grew, the Schoolhouse Mound became segregated into very distinct areas (see Fig. 8b). There were three concentric zones within the site, with accessibility decreasing toward the center. Much of the population resided in the rooms at the outside base of the mound. These rooms contained cooking as well as storage vessels, decorated bowls, tools, and frequently one or more granaries. Within this was a second zone consisting of the platform itself. The rooms on the platform were also residences, and while they contained many highly decorated vessels in addition to the various utilitarian artifacts needed for households, very little space was devoted to storage.

At the absolute center of the platform mound, but at ground level, were rooms with massive quantities of stored food and supplies. The central storage rooms were entered through openings in the ceilings, and contained granaries, large storage jars (Fig. 10), and a variety of more portable artifacts including axes, agave knives, serving bowls, and decorated vessels. One of the great mysteries of the Schoolhouse Site is why these rooms were not emptied as the site was vacated.

Figure 8a. The four high areas on the Schoolhouse Mound mark the locations of four clusters of rooms built on a raised platform. The northern mound is the earliest, and is probably the only one of the four that was constructed during the Roosevelt phase. Preliminary analyses suggest that the other three mounds were added during the succeeding Gila phase. (Graphic by Lynn Simon)

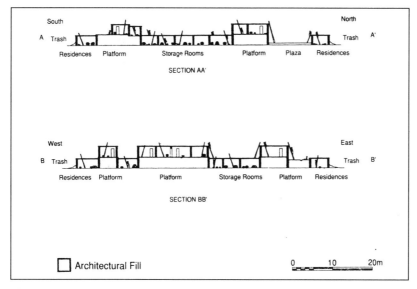

Figure 8b. Cross-sections (AA' and BB' on Fig. 9a) through the Schoolhouse Mound. The elevated portion of the mound was built as a "hollow" square. At the center of the ruin 25 or more rooms were built at ground level and used for storage. Encircling these rooms was an irregularly shaped, elevated mound supporting about 40 rooms and several small courtyards. Around the edges of the ruin were 25 to 30 rooms built at ground level and used as residences. (Graphic by Lynn Simon)

Figure 9. Pillar site. During a ten-day period around the summer solstice, the doorways and columns of the original two rooms block the rising sun so that only a sliver of light extends to the back wall. Although adobe columns also occur in a third room added to the building later, the alignments necessary for this phenomenon exist only in the original rooms. (Graphic by Glena Cain)

The completeness of the assemblages suggests that Schoolhouse may well have been one of the very last sites in the basin to be abandoned.

An intact granary (Fig. 11) was found buried beneath part of the Schoolhouse Mound. This find provided us with badly needed data on the size and construction of these structures. The base of the granary was a circular pedestal of adobe and cobbles, designed to prevent rodents from burrowing into it. The upper part was made of branches coarsely woven into a shape roughly like a bee hive. Both the outside and inside walls were then plastered with mud. Slabs of rock were laid across the opening at the top to seal the granary. It was about 70 centimeters high, with a diameter of 1.14 meters at the base, and had a capacity of 560 liters (about 15.5 bushels).

Assuming that the people living on top of the mound controlled the food amassed in the central storage rooms, Lindauer estimates that the granaries in those rooms alone contained as much as five years' worth of surplus food. This surplus would be increased by approximately another 80 percent if the storage volume of the large vessels were also included. The granaries in the rooms of the peripheral residential zone might have contained three years' worth of surplus food. Both of these figures are considerably higher than the maximum estimate of one year's surplus for the small domestic compounds of the preceding Roosevelt phase. The central storage rooms thus contained the surplus "capital" that would be needed by the leaders in order to feed people while they were involved in construction activities or services on behalf of the entire polity.

Arleyn Simon, the laboratory director for the project, has determined that the Schoolhouse Mound was one of a few pottery-producing communities in the valley. The residents of this site also had a disproportionate amount of turquoise, obsidian tools, pigments, projectile points, and even deer meat. A total of four shell trumpets, five stone "batons," horn cores of mountain sheep, and unusual burial

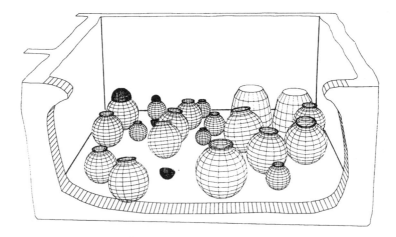

Figure 10. The floor assemblage of this storage room at the center of the Schoolhouse Mound was covered with large vessels, most of the jars, several baskets, and two wattle and daub granaries. The storage rooms at the center of the mound contained from three to five times more food than was needed for the members of the elite families living on top of the mound. After the site was abandoned, the rooms were partially filled in with layers of water-deposited silt and mud washed down from the surrounding walls and roofs. (Graphic by Greg Phillips)

Figure 11. One of the wattle and daub granaries was preserved when the occupants of the site decided to transform this ground level room into part of the raised platform. They filled the interior of the room with dirt and cobbles and constructed a new room on top of the resulting platform. This modification helped to fill in a gap in the elevated area encircling the storage rooms. (Photo courtesy of Brenda Shears)

accompaniments suggests the presence of particularly prestigious individuals living at the mound (Figs. 12, 13). Shell trumpets and elaborate headdresses are still used for important ceremonial occasions by present-day Native American groups in the Southwest.

All of this suggests to us that the platform mound leaders had intensified the extent of their control over the economy of the polity. The architecture of the Schoolhouse Mound reflects this concern with economic matters; ritual was undoubtedly still an important function of the platform mounds, but it was no longer as dominant. The emphasis on amassing considerable surpluses, the control exercised over the production of craft items such as ceramic vessels, and the concentration of prestige items (including prestige foods such as deer meat) reflect a far greater level of centralization than we saw at platform mounds during the Roosevelt phase.

Some Closing Thoughts

The archaeology of the Livingston area has provided new insights into the phenomena of platform mounds. It has shown in surprising detail how a centralized, powerful leadership emerged through a process of gradual amalgamation. The importance of family leaders in the early Roosevelt phase was replaced in the late Roosevelt by a smaller number of important lineage leaders, and in the Gila phase

Figure 12. These shell trumpets and stone batons were found in a ceremonial cache in an abandoned room at the Schoolhouse Mound. During the Classic period, shell trumpets occur only at platform mounds. Ethnographers report that similar kinds of trumpets are still used by the Hopi and Zuni peoples as part of their ceremonies. (Graphic by Glena Cain)

Figure 13. While this scene does not represent any specific ceremony, it does illustrate how some of the artifacts (shell trumpets, stone batons, horn cores from mountain sheep, pollen from pine boughs) and architectural features of the Salado Mounds may have been used. The location is a plaza in front of a tower-like feature at the Cline Terrace site. (Graphic by Glena Cain)

by the authority of a single clan chief. The lower-level leaders did not disappear from the society; every family still had a family head, and every lineage still had their respected elders. But a new level of hierarchy developed, with leaders who assumed greater power and authority.

The amalgamation process in Livingston also exhibited an interesting progression from ceremonial authority toward economic authority. Public buildings at the beginning of the Roosevelt phase were devoted completely to large communal meeting rooms. By the end of the Gila phase, the platform mounds functioned primarily as elite residences and as storehouses for the society's wealth.

Unexpectedly, we found that the mounds in the Livingston group developed from a previous architectural tradition of big houses, rather than from the dance mounds found in the Salt and Gila Basins. We will continue to expand our ideas about platform mounds in the next two years of research, and to think about the powerful forces that were shaping the societies of the Southwest during the 14th and 15th centuries.

Bibliography

Fish, Paul, 1989. "The Hohokam: 1,000 Years of Prehistory in the Sonoran Desert." In *Dynamics of Southwestern Prehistory*, eds. Linda S. Cordell and George J. Gumerman, pp. 19–63. Washington, D.C.: Smithsonian Institution Press.

Haury, Emil, 1945. *The Excavation of Los Muertos and Neighboring Ruins in the Salt River Valley, Southern Arizona.* Papers of the Peabody Museum of American Archaeology and Ethnology, Harvard University, Vol. 24, No. 1. Cambridge, Mass.

1976. *The Hohokam: Desert Farmers and Craftsmen.* Tucson: The University of Arizona Press.

Johnson, Gregory A., 1989. "Dynamics of Southwestern Prehistory: Far Outside—Looking In." In *Dynamics of Southwestern Prehistory*, eds. Linda S. Cordell and George J. Gumerman, pp. 371–89. Washington, D.C.: Smithsonian Institution Press.

Rice, Glen E., ed., 1990. "A Design for Salado Research." *Anthropological Field Studies*, No. 22, Department of Anthropology, Arizona State University. Tempe.

Vivian, R. Gwinn, 1990. *The Chacoan Prehistory of the San Juan Basin.* San Diego: Academic Press.

4

Mighty Cahokia

William Iseminger

It is the time of the annual harvest festival celebrating the fall equinox. Traders from distant territories have brought precious offerings for the lords of Cahokia. Ramadas have been erected everywhere to shelter the merchants and their goods: beads and other ornaments shaped from native copper; drinking vessels and gorgets cut from large whelk and conch shells, many engraved with symbolic designs; baskets of tiny marginella shells; bangles cut from sheets of mica; quivers of arrows tipped with gem-like points; galena, hematite, and ocher from which to make pigments for pottery, clothing, and body paint; and salt from springs and seeps to the south. In exchange the Cahokians offer their own goods: feathered capes; freshwater pearls; finely woven fabrics; fur garments made from otter, mink, and beaver; chert hoes and axes; and corn, dried squash, pumpkin, and seeds from many other plants. These will be taken back to distant places, some in polished black ceramic vessels bearing incised designs of interlocking scrolls, forked eyes, and nested chevrons, symbols of power and prestige because of their place of origin—mighty Cahokia.

This fanciful yet fairly accurate description of Cahokia's harvest celebration is drawn from archaeological studies and early historical accounts of remnant Mississippian cultures in the Southeast. Eight miles east of St. Louis, Cahokia was in its day the largest and most influential settlement north of Mexico. Its merchants traded with cultures from the Gulf Coast to the Great Lakes, from the Atlantic coast to Oklahoma, and they helped spread Mississippian culture across much of that vast area. Some 120 earthen mounds supporting civic buildings and the residences of Cahokia's elite were spread over more than five square miles—perhaps six times as many earthen platforms as the great Mississippian site of Moundville, south of Tuscaloosa, Alabama. At its core, within a log stockade ten to 12 feet tall, was the 200-acre Sacred Precinct where the ruling elite lived and were buried. Atop a massive earthen mound stood a pole-framed temple more than 100 feet long, its grass roof possibly decorated with carved wooden animal figures festooned with glimmering beads, feathers, and cloth. Here Cahokia's rulers performed the political and religious rituals that united the realm. Estimates of the city's population at its zenith, ca. A.D. 1050-1150, range from 8,000 to more than 40,000, though most fall between 10,000 and 20,000. Around A.D. 1200, perhaps having exhausted its natural resources, Cahokia went into a decline that left it virtually empty by 1400.

In 1810 the lawyer and journalist Henry Marie Brackenridge, while surveying the Mississippi and Missouri valleys, visited the site and marveled at the "stupendous pile of earth" at its center. At the time a colony of Trappist monks was growing wheat and fruit trees on the earthen structure, soon to be known as

Figure 1. Central Cahokia area A.D. 1100–1150 looking north between the Twin Mounds, across the Grand Plaza to Monks Mound; painting by L.K. Townsend. (Graphic courtesy of Cahokia Mounds State Historic Site)

Monks Mound. Their plans to build a monastery atop it were abandoned when fever and a shortage of money forced them to leave the site in 1813. The first archaeological excavations at Cahokia took place in the 1920s under the direction of Warren K. Moorehead of the R.S. Peabody Museum in Andover, Massachusetts. Moorehead's work confirmed that the mounds were neither natural hills nor the work of a mysterious race of Mound Builders or Precolumbian colonists from Europe—as imagined by nineteenth-century amateur historians—but had been built by American Indians. In the 1940s and 1950s archaeologists from the University of Michigan, the Illinois State Museum, the Gilcrease Institute of Tulsa, and elsewhere conducted scattered excavations at the site, but the most intensive work began in the early 1960s when Interstate 55-70 was routed through it. Over the years many of Cahokia's mounds have been lost to the bulldozer and the plow, to subdivisions, highways, and discount stores. Today fewer than 80 remain, 68 of which are preserved within the 2,200-acre Cahokia Mounds State Historic Site, managed by the Illinois Historic Preservation Agency.

Cahokia owed its existence to a floodplain 80 miles long at the confluence of the Mississippi and Missouri rivers. Known as the American Bottom, the plain was interlaced with creeks, sloughs, lakes, and marshes. With fertile soil, extensive forests, and plentiful fish and game, the region was an ideal place to settle. During the Palaeoindian (ca. 9500-8000 B.C.) and Archaic (ca. 8000-600 B.C.) periods transient hunter-gatherers set up temporary camps or seasonal villages here. During the Woodland period (ca. 600 B.C.-A.D. 800) the population grew, cultivation of native crops began, and larger and more settled communities, including Cahokia, were established. Settlements spread slowly and grew in size throughout the Emergent Mississippian period (ca. A.D. 800-1000), then expanded rapidly in the Mississippian (ca. A.D. 1000-1400) as more intense farming, especially of corn, made fast population growth possible. Cahokia reached its apex during this period, when it was surrounded by dozens of satellite settlements and scores of smaller villages.

In time, Cahokia's influence spread far beyond the American Bottom. Artifacts made there, including Ramey Incised pottery and hoes of Mill Creek chert from southern Illinois, have been found at sites as far north as Minnesota, as far west as eastern Kansas and Oklahoma, and as far south as the lower Ohio River Valley, Arkansas, and Mississippi. Local imitations of Cahokia's wares, especially pottery, have also been unearthed in these regions. At Cahokia itself we have found copper from the area of Lake Superior; mica from the southern Appalachian Mountains; shells from the Atlantic and Gulf coasts; and galena, ocher, hematite, chert, fluorite, and quartz from throughout the Midwest. Finely made ceramics from the lower Mississippi Valley, perhaps used to carry exotic commodities such as shells from that area, have also been discovered at Cahokia, along with local copies of many of these forms.

The most visible remains of the ancient city are its mounds. Most are rectangular with flat tops (platform mounds) that supported civic buildings and the homes of the elite. Somewhat rarer are conical mounds that may have contained elite burials, as they did in the earlier Woodland period. During the 1920s Moorehead excavated several such burials, but it is often difficult to tell from his records whether they were found in the mounds themselves or in earlier layers. Rarest of all are rectangular ridgetop mounds that may have marked important locations such as community boundaries or mortuary complexes. The destruction of one such mound by farmers in 1931 revealed mass burials laid upon platforms of shell beads and cedar bark.

Monks Mound stands at the center of the site, on the northern edge of the 40-acre Grand Plaza. Covering 14 acres at the base and rising in four terraces to a height of 100 feet, it is the largest prehistoric earthen structure in the New World. Some 19 million man-hours of labor would have been required to excavate, carry, and deposit the estimated 22 million cubic feet of earth needed for this project. Excavations and soil cores indicate that it was built in stages between ca. A.D. 900 and 1200, each possibly related to the accession of a new leader. Probes on the summit have revealed wall trenches for a wooden building 104 feet long and 48 feet wide. Here the leader of Cahokia governed his domain, performed ceremonies, consulted with the spirit world, and may have resided as well. The bones of deceased chiefs may also have been stored here, as was the custom among some historical tribes in the Southeast.

One of the most fascinating discoveries at Cahokia came during the 1967-1971 excavation of Mound 72, a ridgetop one-half mile south of Monks Mound. Measuring 140 feet long, 70 feet wide, and barely six feet high, Mound 72 is oriented along a northwest-southeast axis, one end pointing toward the winter solstice sunrise and the other toward the summer solstice sunset. Excavations revealed that it had originally been three separate, smaller mounds, two platforms and one conical. Around and beneath these three mounds were some 280 burials dating to Cahokia's initial development between ca. A.D. 1000 and 1050. Some of the dead had been borne to their graves on litters or wrapped in mats or blankets, while others had simply been tossed into pits, suggesting that people of different statuses were buried at the same place. Soon after the burials the three mounds were fused into a single ridgetop mound with a final mantle of earth.

In one opulent burial a man about 40 years old, perhaps one of Cahokia's early leaders, was laid upon a bird-shaped platform of nearly 20,000 marine-shell beads. Around him were several other bodies, perhaps of retainers or relatives,

some interred for the first time and others reburied from elsewhere. Heaped atop
six nearby burials were two caches of more than 800 newly made arrowheads,
whose Midwestern cherts and hafting styles suggest possible origins in Wisconsin,
Illinois, Missouri, Tennessee, Arkansas, and Oklahoma. One cache included 15
large concave ground-stone discs, sometimes known as "chunkey" stones, after a
game played with similar stones by historical tribes in the Southeast. Also found
were a large pile of unprocessed mica from the southern Appalachian Mountains,
a three-foot-long roll of copper (possibly a ceremonial staff) hammered from
Lake Superior nuggets, and more marine-shell beads.

Further excavations under Mound 72 revealed several mass burials, most of females between 15 and 25 years old, suggesting human sacrifice. The largest pit
held more than 50 women laid out in two rows and stacked two and three deep;
two others contained 22 and 24 women. A fourth pit, with 19 women, had been
partially redug, and more than 36,000 marine-shell beads, another cache of unused arrowheads (more than 400 of chert and a few hundred more of bone and
antler), and several broken ceramic vessels had been deposited there. Another
burial, of four males whose heads and hands had been removed, may represent
the ritual sacrifice of vassals or retainers, perhaps to accompany their leader in
death. How and why these people were sacrificed remain mysteries, but there may
be parallels with rituals performed by the Natchez Indians of seventeenth- and
eighteenth-century Mississippi, where individuals often volunteered to be sacrificed upon a leader's death to raise their own or their family's status.

In the early 1960s archaeologists working in the remains of a residential area
outside the stockade, to the west of Monks Mound, discovered a number of post-
holes at regular intervals along the circumferences of at least five circles of different diameters. Four of these constructions are thought to have been complete circles, with 24, 36, 48, and 60 posts, respectively. The fifth seems only to have had
12 posts standing along a portion of the circle; if complete it would have had 72.
Why all five circles were formed of multiples of twelve posts is unknown, though
some scholars have speculated that the number may have been related to lunar cycles. Because of their resemblance to the famous English megalithic monument of
Stonehenge, Cahokia's circles of standing wooden posts became known as
"woodhenges." One, with a large center post and 48 evenly spaced perimeter
posts, was 410 feet in diameter and dates to just after A.D. 1100. It is the most
completely excavated of the woodhenges and has been reconstructed in its original location. From a platform atop the central post a priest might have observed
sunrises along the eastern horizon aligning with particular perimeter posts at the
equinoxes and solstices. On the equinoxes the sun would have risen over the front
of Monks Mound, perhaps symbolizing the bond between earthly ruler and solar
deity. Other posts may have marked other important dates, such as harvest festivals or moon and star alignments.

Most of the work at Cahokia has dealt with the everyday life of its people,
many of whom lived outside the stockade in small, rectangular one-family pole-
and-thatch dwellings with walls covered with mats or sometimes daub. Compounds of these dwellings grouped around small courtyards may have housed
kinfolk. Each compound also included buildings used for storage, food processing, and cooking. Excavation of refuse pits around the houses has revealed that
the Cahokians ate mainly cultivated corn, squash, and pumpkin, as well as the
seeds of cultivated sunflower, lambs' quarters, marsh elder, little barley, and may

grass. This diet was supplemented by hundreds of different wild plants and mammals, birds, fish, reptiles, and amphibians.

Household groups were in turn arranged around larger communal plazas that may have defined neighborhoods. Other structures found in each neighborhood included small circular sweat lodges, where water sprinkled upon heated rocks produced steam for ritual cleansing of the body and spirit; community meeting lodges, granaries, and storage buildings; and possibly huts to which women would have been restricted during menstruation.

Ceremonial structures, special-use buildings, and the dwellings of the elite were generally larger versions of the basic house. Many of the elite must have lived within the stockade, but so far none of their residences has been excavated. Elite areas outside the wall include a plaza mound group to the west; another group to the east; Rattlesnake Mound (named for the snakes in the area) to the south; and the North Plaza and Kunnemann (named after a family that once owned the land) groups to the north. We do not know whether the elite living outside the stockade differed from those living inside, although relationship to the leader by lineage or clan affiliation may have been a factor.

Evidence for warfare at Cahokia remains largely circumstantial. A stockade was erected around the Sacred Precinct ca. A.D. 1150 and rebuilt at least three times during the next hundred years. The defensive nature of the wall is suggested by the regular spacing of bastions at 85-foot intervals along its length. From elevated platforms in these projections, warriors could launch arrows at attackers and protect the narrow L-shaped entryways between some bastions. The everyday function of the wall may have been more social, to isolate and protect the Sacred Precinct. Free access may have been limited to the elites who lived there, probably members of the ruling lineage, with the general population admitted only for ceremonial occasions or markets, or in times of war.

The stockade was a monumental construction, built at a great cost of time, labor, and materials. Much of my own fieldwork at Cahokia has involved excavations along the lines of the stockade east of Monks Mound. Based on that work I have estimated that builders would have used nearly 20,000 logs each time the wall was built, and conservatively 130,000 man-hours to fell, trim, debark, transport, and place the posts in excavated trenches. Construction of the stockade, itself designed to protect the city center, may have contributed to Cahokia's decline beginning ca. A.D. 1200. The demands for wood would have been staggering, even for such a renewable resource. Wood was also needed for fires and construction, and people from nearby communities would have been competing for the same resources. The forests around Cahokia, and the animals and plants living there, would have been affected. Soil eroding from deforested slopes may have clogged streams and lakes with silt, increasing localized flooding of valuable farmland.

Beginning in the thirteenth century, a cooling of the climate and concomitant floods, droughts, and early and late frosts may have led to more crop failures and reduced yields. As food and other natural resources became scarce, economic disruption and social unrest could have become problems, perhaps even leading to wars between Cahokia and its neighbors. Eventually its political and economic power base eroded as nearby groups became more autonomous. Although increases in contagious diseases and nutritional deficiencies caused by a heavily corn-based diet may have affected Cahokia's population, more data are needed to determine the role of such health problems in Cahokia's decline.

Figure 2. A four-inch-tall sandstone tablet from Cahokia, dating to ca. A.D. 1300, bears the image of a Bird Man. (Photo by Peter Bostrom/Cahokia Mounds State Historic Site)

Where the people of Cahokia went is one of the site's many mysteries. There is no evidence that the city was destroyed in a single catastrophe. It appears that its people slowly dispersed, breaking up into smaller groups, some establishing new communities and perhaps new ways of life elsewhere. Many small Late Mississippian villages and hamlets have been found in the uplands surrounding the American Bottom and at higher elevations in the bottomlands themselves. Other people may have been absorbed into existing groups elsewhere, possibly where kinship ties already existed. In any event Cahokia was abandoned by 1400, and no positive ties have been established between the great city and any historical tribe.

Because of limited funding and the site's enormous size, only a small percentage of Cahokia has been excavated. Research continues through small field-school programs that include nondestructive remote-sensing projects using electromagnetic conductivity, electrical resistivity, and magnetometry, as well as soil coring. These efforts help locate man-made features underground, providing direction for future small-scale excavations. Detailed mapping projects, combined with soil-core studies, are helping identify the original forms of mounds that have suffered from heavy plowing or erosion. Unpublished data from earlier excavations are being analyzed or reexamined and the results published. In addition, salvage projects at contemporary sites in the American Bottom, such as East St. Louis, are providing insight into Cahokia's interactions with these outlying sites.

Though I have worked at Cahokia for 25 years, I still marvel at what I see. It is an awesome site, massive and mysterious, especially in the predawn hours as I drive past the dark shapes of mounds poking through ground-hugging mist on my way to greet modern-day solstice and equinox observers at the reconstructed woodhenge. Cahokia, the largest prehistoric community north of Mexico, was one of the crowning achievements of the American Indians. Here they established a complex social, political, religious, and economic system and influenced a large portion of the midcontinent. Today, as then, the climb to the top of Monks Mound is breathtaking, literally as well as figuratively, and looking out from the summit one can only imagine what this truly extraordinary place must have been like.

5

Settlement Patterns and Community Organization in the Maya Lowlands

Jeremy A. Sabloff

Since the last century the principal emphasis of Maya studies has been on the ancient Maya elite. This fact is certainly not surprising given the visually spectacular nature of the art and architecture associated with the rulers of the lowland Maya realm. The elaborate tombs, the stelae depicting rulers in full regalia, the polychrome pottery, hieroglyphic inscriptions, temples, and palaces of the ancient Maya became the foci of both scholarly and popular interest.

Because of this emphasis, students of the ancient Maya developed an understanding of Maya civilization that was focused almost entirely on the trappings of elite activities, particularly those of the southern Maya lowlands during the Classic Maya Period (circa A.D. 300–800). For much of this century, for example, it was generally believed that the great Classic centers were non-urban, vacant ceremonial centers in which a few rulers, priests, and their retainers resided. The bulk of the population, it was assumed, lived well outside the centers and only came in to them for great ceremonies or to perform labor for the elite. This was the model popularized in books such as Sylvanus Morley's pathbreaking *The Ancient Maya* (first published in 1946) and Eric Thompson's widely read *The Rise and Fall of Maya Civilization* (which first appeared in 1954).

In retrospect, it can be argued that Maya studies suffered from a sampling bias. With some notable exceptions, significant aspects of the ancient Maya world were generally ignored. It was not until the early 1950s that Maya studies began to undergo a major shift in emphasis. Under the leadership of Gordon Willey of the Peabody Museum at Harvard, Maya studies began to turn, if not away from elite concerns, at least towards the study of overall settlements, including the remains of relatively inconspicuous, perishable peasant houses.

By the late 1950s to early 1960s, new settlement research, in particular that initiated by the University of Pennsylvania Museum and the Guatemalan government at Tikal, began to challenge the accepted wisdom. The picture of vacant, non-urban centers, a complete reliance on extensive shifting agriculture, and a number of other tenets of the traditional or elite-oriented model was changing. For example, as the Tikal archaeologists began to map the central 16-square-kilometer zone of the site and, subsequently, the surrounding suburban and rural zones, they recognized the remains of a large number of apparently non-elite house groups. The urban nature of Tikal soon became undeniable.

This new settlement work, along with path-breaking research in hieroglyphic decipherment, helped overturn a variety of assumptions about the ancient Maya world. Since the 1950s and early 1960s there have been many advances in settlement pattern research. For example, there have been innovations in the technology and instrumentation of this work. EDM total stations, electronic measuring devices which do all the surveying trigonometry, have replaced the archaeologist's laborious and potentially mistake-ridden calculations. These stations allow much more accurate and much faster mapping, as well as the possibility of directly downloading the results into computer plotters. One can now move from field measuring directly to maps and a variety of statistical manipulations of the spatial data. Improved aerial photography has helped archaeologists at the wonderfully named Pulltrouser Swamp in Belize better appreciate how the Maya practiced a variety of agricultural intensification techniques, such as raised-field swamp reclamation. Satellite imagery and side-looking radar have also proved quite helpful.

In addition, there are much better methodologies for recovery of data, including more sophisticated sampling strategies, than there were in the 1950s. Concerns for a wide variety of non-elite activities also have emerged. A good example is the research on chert quarrying and production of chert tools at the site of Colha in northern Belize. Another is the study of the distribution and re-use of chert biface tools that were used to prepare the soil for cultivation at nearby sites such as Pulltrouser Swamp. These and similar studies are illuminating scholarly understanding of the economics and community organization of craft production.

In the realm of analysis we have seen a number of significant and important advances in the interpretation of data and the formulation and testing of hypotheses about the archaeological record. More sophisticated use of analogies drawn from both ethnographic and historic sources (such as the 16th century A.D. writings of Bishop Landa) provides information that can be projected, with care, back into the ancient Maya world.

Despite these many advances, until recently settlement pattern research had not moved beyond the discovery of gross patterns showing the distribution of settlements across varied landscapes. The nature of Maya urbanism was still not well delineated. Ancient house mounds usually showed up on settlement maps as undifferentiated black rectangles, and inferences about household activities, let alone community organization, were at best difficult to make.

In an attempt to rectify these and other problems, I initiated the Sayil Archaeological Project in the Puuc region of northern Yucatan in the early 1980s. Phases I and II of this project were undertaken during five field seasons (1983-88) with the support of the National Science Foundation. Phases III and IV of the project have continued to the present day under the direction of Michael Smyth and Christopher Dore. After the initial season I was joined by Gair Tourtellot (Boston University) as co-director. A number of students and colleagues from both the U.S. and Mexico have contributed to this research. I would like to discuss briefly the nature of our research at Sayil and to indicate what settlement survey can tell us about Sayil community organization in particular, and ancient Maya community organization in general.

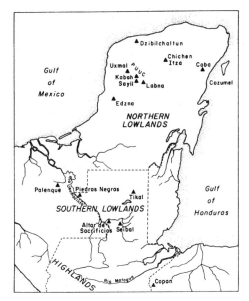

Figure 1. The Maya lowlands, showing the location of Sayil in the Puuc region of Yucatan, Mexico. (Graphic courtesy of Jeremy A. Sabloff)

The Sayil Archaeological Project

Sayil is located in a north-south trending valley of the only hilly area in northern Yucatan (Fig. 1). It is perhaps best known for its three-story building of 90-plus rooms, the so-called Great or North Palace. Scholars have known of Sayil for many years. In fact, the journalist and explorer John Lloyd Stephens and the artist Frederick Catherwood visited Sayil in the mid-19th century. In 1934, the Carnegie Institution of Washington undertook an initial mapping project at Sayil and produced an excellent map for the time. This map, prepared by Edwin Shook under the direction of Harry Pollock, is dominated by standing stone buildings. It is interesting to note that in his write-up Harry Pollock states: "The maps of Sayil and Labna [a neighboring site] are incomplete in that they omit a good number of small constructions, presumably house mounds.... This was done consciously to speed up the mapping, which seemed to be consuming more time than we could afford, and it provides another indication of how we tended to exclude the inconspicuous building remains from our architectural study."

So up until very recently, we had a good map of the standing stone, elite structures at Sayil but no indications of how large the site was, what the nature of its population was, how it was distributed on the landscape, how it was contoured to exploit that environment, or how it was organized. One of the goals of our research was to provide answers to these basic questions as well as to explore a number of hypotheses we had about the nature of urban development at Sayil and surrounding sites.

Turning our attention away from the large, standing structures, we spent the bulk of our time on the remains of small structures or perishable houses. One of the reasons that I chose Sayil for study is that the preservation of the perishable ancient houses was far better than at other sites. Moreover, Sayil was significantly occupied for only a relatively short period of time, and there has been little occupation or disturbance in the thousand years since its abandonment in the 10th century A.D. Typical houses at Sayil were built on small platforms, and their wattle-and-daub walls were set down on one course of foundation stones which would remain after the cane or wood and thatch had decomposed. So even with the wood and thatch gone, we can get some idea of the basal platform, the exact dimensions and nature of the houses, and the activities that took place inside and outside the houses, and on and off the platform.

We studied even more inconspicuous remains. These are small rubble mounds that we think, on the basis of excavations, are all that was left of very small platforms with tamped earth floors and simple perishable structures above them. Some of these lesser structures might have been seasonally occupied houses or perhaps the dwellings of a lower class at Sayil, a group that has been almost totally ignored in Maya studies up until now. Such a group might have included cooks, servants, slaves, or laborers.

Our mapping allowed us to go beyond the simple recognition of house structures and platforms to the details of their composition and growth through time. We cleared wide areas in certain limited survey zones, regardless of whether or not there were visible features on the surface. (This procedure is becoming more common in Maya archaeology, and has been undertaken by Anne Pyburn in Belize, David Webster and his students at Copan, and others elsewhere.) We literally had our crew on their hands and knees in 2-by-2-meter squares, picking up everything in the top 10 centimeters of the soil. We also excavated selected squares to see if there were any hidden features that were not visible on the surface. Fortunately, we were able to conclude that the surface signatures at Sayil accurately reflected what was under the ground. With the relatively short period of settlement at Sayil, the amount of build-up over the limestone bedrock tended to be less than a meter.

We undertook a number of studies of the distribution of pottery and other artifacts—their numbers, their weight, and their size throughout the area, both on top of the platforms as well as in each of the 2-by-2-meter squares that covered this whole area. Geographer Nicholas Dunning (University of Cincinnati) analyzed the soil chemically, particularly for its phosphate content. On the basis of these studies, Thomas Killion (Smithsonian Institution), Tourtellot, Dunning, and I were able to argue that the open areas we had identified were *not* plazas, as had previously been assumed, but were instead filled to a great degree by fertilized vegetable gardens. These were the equivalents of modern truck gardens, which the residents cultivated to provide daily food in addition to the maize, beans, and other crops they grew in more distant fields. In other words, Maya cities were garden cities. What in the past has been taken to be much non-domestic or ceremonial space actually was utilized to provide daily food for the inhabitants. These "infields" might have played as important a subsistence role as the larger but distant "outfields."

We also made a careful study of the location of subterranean cisterns. There are no natural water sources in and around Sayil. In order to live in the Sayil Valley and utilize the very rich soils there, the occupants had to find a way to capture water. Instead of building large community reservoirs, as did the Maya elsewhere,

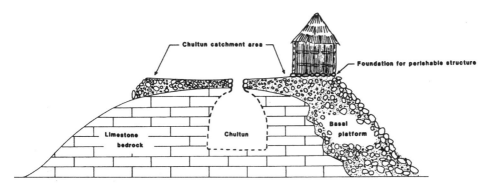

Figure 2. House, house platform, and chultun (water catchment basin). Although the soil is rich, there are no water sources in the Sayil Valley. Ingenious household catchment systems captured rainwater and stored it for use throughout the dry season. (Graphic courtesy of the Sayil Archaeological Project)

they constructed a system of individual household catchment basins to capture water during the rainy season and store it in underground cisterns (*chultun* in Maya). This enabled them to survive during the dry season from February through May, when rainfall either was nonexistent or at a minimum. In studying the nature and distribution of the cisterns, we found that what had initially appeared to be a random settlement pattern did, in fact, have a very recognizable arrangement. These Maya situated their houses on small natural rises where the hard limestone cap was very thin, allowing them to break through to a much softer marl below in which they could excavate their cisterns. They could then use the excavated marl to level the irregular rises and provide a platform to raise their houses off the forest floor. The platform also supported a plastered area to catch the rain and fill the cisterns (Fig. 2). Cisterns had narrow openings to keep the dirt out, as well as to prevent too much evaporation; their stone collars further restricted the openings. As family size grew and new houses were built for the extended family, new cisterns were often dug into the basal platform. So the seemingly random settlement actually had a rationale based, at least in part, on topography and geology, and in part on length of occupation and family size.

In brief, my colleagues and I found at Sayil a fairly well demarcated urban zone of about 5 square kilometers with an inferred population of more than 7,000 at the city's height in the early 9th century. This well-defined, nucleated urban area contrasts with the dispersed pattern found at most Classic Period cities (Fig. 3). As Tourtellot and I have previously suggested, Sayil's pattern may be the result of the city's relatively short occupation. Other Maya sites may have begun with a Sayil-like pattern and through time become more dispersed and amorphous.

Toward a New Model

Although Maya settlement pattern studies are still in their infancy and basic information remains to be uncovered, some preliminary trends are discernible.

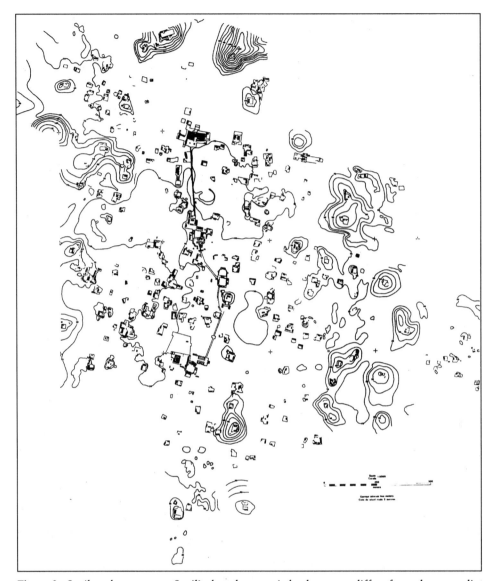

Figure 3. Sayil settlement map. Sayil's densely occupied urban zone differs from the more dispersed patterns of most Classic Period cities. At its peak, the city may have contained more than 7,000 residents in an area of about 5 square kilometers. (Graphic courtesy of the Sayil Archaeological Project)

One, which I wish to emphasize, relates to demographic, political, economic, and religious centralization during the Classic Period. Since the early 1970s, there has been a significant scholarly discussion about whether Classic Maya cities controlled large, extensive territories. Arguments have ranged from those that see the Classic lowlands filled with individual city states to those that envision a few large superpowers. Most of the arguments have centered on differing interpretations of hieroglyphic texts. It now appears that both positions may be correct, with Classic Maya political organization cycling from decentralized to centralized and back again. Whether political and economic centralization co-vary remains to be seen. In relation to the material archaeological evidence, however, the bulk of settlement evidence to date reinforces the picture that I just described for Sayil: particularly that of decentralized political and economic organization.

In the economic realm, we see a widespread distribution of certain elite goods and perhaps some small-scale tribute, but the vast majority of economic exchange was undertaken on the local level. Even where regional distribution can be clearly shown, as in the case of the Colha chert mentioned above, the production/distribution systems do not appear to be under centralized control. And, as the research of Thomas Hester, Harry Shafer, and their colleagues has shown, much production and distribution was undertaken by individual or related households.

The picture that emerges from the hieroglyphic texts indicates that a few states, especially Tikal and Calakmul, were able to hold together large-scale territories for limited periods of time. However, the archaeological picture that has emerged so far indicates that the Maya lowlands were dotted with numerous city-states, with dispersed populations, limited spheres of influence and demographic spread, and relative independence in the realms of politics, economics, and religion. Clearly, more archaeological research is needed to see if the archaeological and hieroglyphic data can be better blended than has been the case to date. Moreover, this picture of dispersed settlements and decentralized power contrasts with that of much of Precolumbian Mesoamerica where dense, compact settlements and centralized political and economic authority appear more frequently.

Can these latter differences be placed in a theoretical context that will provide directions for ongoing and future research? I believe that the answer is yes. In an important 1988 article, Robert Drennan of the University of Pittsburgh provides quantitative evidence to support an argument that agricultural practices could be used to explain these differently organized settlement patterns. In the Maya lowlands during the Late Pre-classic and Classic Periods both slash-and-burn cultivation and forms of intensification such as raised fields and ridged fields encouraged farmers to live near their agricultural plots rather than close to one another. In other parts of Mesoamerica other forms of agricultural intensification, particularly canal irrigation, fomented compact settlements (as well as strong, centralized authority).

What needs to be clarified are the possible links between relatively dispersed populations and decentralized political and economic power (if the latter co-vary). Recent studies that examine rural settlement and others that focus on entire regions (e.g., the vast research at Copan and the greater Copan Valley or the research in the Petexbatun region) certainly will provide some of the data and ideas that are needed to further investigate these links. Nevertheless, many more studies like these are needed. Unfortunately, Drennan's provocative article has not received the attention that I believe it deserves and its suggestions for further investigation have yet to be followed up.

In particular, I would suggest that we may be able to take Drennan's argument a step further. He asserts that certain forms of agricultural production led to compact settlements which in turn were associated with strong centralized leadership in much of Mesoamerica. We could examine a complementary notion that the conditions found in the Maya lowlands helped *block* the growth of a strong central authority. These conditions include the dispersed populations of the Classic Period, the seeming independence of Maya farmers from state control even when they intensified their agricultural production, and the relatively low number of non-food producers (except towards the end of the Classic Period) due to the low level of economic specialization. Why the farmers were able to remain independent would, of course, be one of the prime questions that would need investigation. In addition, as one might expect, there is considerable variability in this picture. In Late Classic times increased nucleation and indications of greater political centralization appear at some of the very largest urban centers such as Calakmul, Tikal, Caracol, and even at a few centers on the peripheries of the lowlands. Clearly, the causes of such variability also need to be explored.

Moreover, archaeologists need to examine the contrasting Late Postclassic (A.D. 1250 to the Spanish Conquest) developments in the northern Maya lowlands. It may be that the denser, more nucleated settlement of cities such as Mayapan, along with the growth of a more centralized political structure for much of the northern lowlands that centered for a couple of centuries at Mayapan, could be directly related to the growth of mercantilism during the Late Postclassic. Restudy of the well-excavated materials from the site, along with new settlement pattern research in its surrounding region, might determine whether the dense population of Mayapan was made up mostly of nonfood producers, as some have suggested.

Our questions are many and our answers are few at the moment. Yet I am optimistic that our understandings of ancient Maya community structure and, ultimately, broad political and economic organization will advance rapidly in the next few years. Our tools, both technical and intellectual, are better than ever before and our questions and research strategies have become more focused. As the nature of ancient Maya organization is elucidated, scholars will have the opportunity to understand why the Maya, especially in the southern lowlands, were able to adapt to their tropical environment so successfully for so long, why they ultimately failed, and how their adaptation compared with that of their neighbors. With such emphases, scholars will be better able to compare, understand, and explain the similarities and differences in cultural development between the Maya and decentralized, pre-industrial agricultural societies in other parts of the Americas and the Old World, as well. They may even be able to make suggestions about the ancient exploitation of the tropical forest environment that will have relevance to problems facing the world today in such areas. As Joyce Marcus of the University of Michigan has cogently stated in a recent article: "Good Maya archaeology will bring to light not merely what is unique and exotic about the Maya, but also what they shared with every other ancient civilization." By moving beyond the temples and palaces and combining the insights of both the new historical understandings of the elite and the settlement-driven understandings of the non-elite, we may confidently hope to achieve "good Maya archaeology."

Bibliography

Coe, W.R., 1965. "Tikal: Ten Years of Study of a Maya Ruin in the Lowlands of Guatemala." *Expedition* 8(1):5–56.

Drennan, R.D., 1988. "Household Location and Compact Settlement in Prehispanic America." In *Household and Community in the Mesoamerican Past*, eds. R.R. Wilk and W. Ashmore, pp. 273–93. Albuquerque: University of New Mexico Press.

Harrison, P.D., and B.L. Turner, eds., 1978. *Pre-Hispanic Maya Agriculture*. Albuquerque: University of New Mexico Press.

Haviland, W.A., 1970. "Tikal, Guatemala and Mesoamerican Urbanism." *World Archaeology* 2:186–98.

Hester, T.R., and H.J. Shafer, 1984. "Exploitation of Chert Resources by the Ancient Maya of Northern Belize." *World Archaeology* 16:157–73.

Killion, T.W., J.A. Sabloff, G. Tourtellot, and N.P. Dunning, 1989. "Intensive Surface Collection of Residential Clusters at Terminal Classic Sayil, Yucatan, Mexico." *Journal of Field Archaeology* 16:273–94.

Marcus, J., 1976. *Emblem and State in the Classic Maya Lowlands*. Washington, D.C.: Dumbarton Oaks.

———, 1993. "Ancient Maya Political Organization." In *Lowland Maya Civilization in the Eighth Century A.D.*, eds. J.A. Sabloff and J.S. Henderson, pp. 111–84. Washington, D.C.: Dumbarton Oaks.

———, 1995. "Where Is Lowland Maya Archaeology Headed." *Journal of Archaeological Research* 3:3–53.

Martin, S., and N. Grube, 1995. "Maya Superstates." *Archaeology* 48(6):41–47.

McAnany, P.A., 1993. "The Economics of Social Power and Wealth Among Eighth Century Maya Households." In *Lowland Maya Civilization in the Eighth Century A.D.*, eds. J.A. Sabloff and J.S. Henderson, pp. 65–90. Washington, D.C.: Dumbarton Oaks.

Morley, S.G., 1946. *The Ancient Maya*. Stanford: Stanford University Press.

Pollock, H.E.D., 1980. *The Puuc, an Archaeological Survey of the Hill Country of Yucatan and Northern Campeche, Mexico*. Memoirs of the Peabody Museum, Harvard University, no. 19. Cambridge, Mass.

Sabloff, J.A., 1983. "Classic Maya Settlement Pattern Studies: Past Problems and Future Prospects." In *Prehistoric Settlement Patterns: Essays in Honor of Gordon R. Willey*, eds. E.Z. Vogt and R.M. Leventhal, pp. 413–22. Cambridge, Mass.: Peabody Museum, Harvard University, and Albuquerque: University of New Mexico Press.

Sabloff, J.A., and G. Tourtellot, 1991. *The Ancient Maya City of Sayil*. Middle American Research Institute, Tulane University, Publication 60. New Orleans.

Sharer, R.J., 1994. *The Ancient Maya*. 5th ed. Stanford: Stanford University Press.

Smyth, M.P., and C.D. Dore, 1994. "Maya Urbanism at Sayil, Yucatan." *Research and Exploration* 10:38–55.

Thompson, J.E.S., 1954. *The Rise and Fall of Maya Civilization*. Norman: University of Oklahoma Press.

Tourtellot, G., and J.A. Sabloff, 1995. "Community Structure at Sayil: A Case Study of Puuc Settlement." In *Hidden Among the Hills*, ed. H. Prem, pp. 71–92. Mockmuhl: Verlag von Flemming.

Webster, D., and N. Gonlin, 1988. "Household Remains of the Humblest Maya." *Journal of Field Archaeology* 15:169–90.

Willey, G.R., W.R. Bullard, Jr., J.B. Glass, and J.C. Gifford, 1965. *Prehistoric Maya Settlements in the Belize Valley*. Papers of the Peabody Museum, Harvard University, no. 54. Cambridge, Mass.

6

Empires in the Dust

Karen Wright

Mesopotamia: cradle of civilization, the fertile breadbasket of western Asia, a little slice of paradise between the Tigris and Euphrates rivers. Today the swath of land north of the Persian Gulf is still prime real estate. But several millennia ago Mesopotamia was absolutely The Place to Be. There the visionary king Hammurabi ruled, and Babylon's hanging gardens hung. There the written word, metalworking, and bureaucracy were born. From the stately, rational organization of Mesopotamia's urban centers, humanity began its inexorable march toward strip malls and shrink-wrap and video poker bars and standing in line at the DMV. What's more, the emergence of the city-state meant that we no longer had to bow to the whims of nature. We rose above our abject dependence on weather, tide, and tilth; we were safe in the arms of empire. Isn't that what being civilized is all about?

Not if you ask Harvey Weiss. Weiss, professor of Near Eastern archeology at Yale, has challenged one of the cherished notions of his profession: that early civilizations — with their monuments and their grain reserves, their texts and their taxes — were somehow immune to natural disaster. He says he's found evidence of such disaster on a scale so grand it spelled calamity for half a dozen Bronze Age cultures from the Mediterranean to the Indus Valley — including the vaunted vale of Mesopotamia. Historians have long favored political and social explanations for these collapses: disruptions in trade routes, incompetent administrators, barbarian invasions. "Prehistoric societies, simple agriculturists — they can be blown out by natural forces," says Weiss. But the early civilizations of the Old World? "It's not supposed to happen."

Yet happen it did, says Weiss, and unlike his predecessors, he's got some data to back him up. The evidence comes from a merger of his own archeological expertise with the field of paleoclimatology, the study of climates past. His first case study concerns a series of events that occurred more than 4,000 years ago in a region of northern Mesopotamia called the Habur Plains. There, in the northeast corner of what is present-day Syria, a network of urban centers arose in the middle of the third millennium B.C. Sustained by highly productive organized agriculture, the cities thrived. Then, around 2200 B.C., the region's new urbanites abruptly left their homes and fled south, abandoning the cities for centuries to come.

Weiss believes that the inhabitants fled an onslaught of wind and dust kicked up by a drought that lasted 300 years. He also believes the drought crippled the empire downriver, which had come to count on the agricultural proceeds of the northern plains. Moreover, he contends, the long dry spell wasn't just a local event; it was caused by a rapid, region-wide climate change whose effects were felt by budding civilizations as far west as the Aegean Sea and the Nile and as far east as the Indus Valley. While the Mesopotamians were struggling with their own drought-induced problems, he points out, neighboring societies were collapsing as well: the Old Kingdom in Egypt, early Bronze Age cities in Palestine, and the early Minoan civilization of Crete. And in the Indus Valley, refugees fleeing drought may have overwhelmed the cities of Mohenjo-Daro and Harappa. The troubles of half a dozen Bronze Age societies, says Weiss, can be blamed on a single event—and a natural disaster at that.

Weiss first presented this scenario in 1993, when soil analyses showed that a period of severe dust storms accompanied the mysterious Habur hiatus. "I was thinking you can't have a microregion drought," he recalls, "because that isn't how climate works. It's got to be much bigger. And I said, 'Wait a minute, didn't I read about this in graduate school? Weren't there those who, 30 years ago, had said that drought conditions were probably the agency that accounts for all these collapses that happened in contiguous regions?' " says Weiss. "Back in the late sixties, we had read this stuff and laughed our heads off about it."

In 1966, British archeologist James Mellaart had indeed blamed drought for the downfalls of a whole spectrum of third-millennium civilizations, from the early Bronze Age communities in Palestine to the pyramid builders of Egypt's Old Kingdom. But when Mellaart first put forth this idea, he didn't have much in the way of data to back him up. Weiss, however, can point to new paleoclimate studies for his proof. These studies suggest that an abrupt, widespread change in the climate of western Asia did in fact occur at 2200 B.C. Samples of old ocean sediments from the Gulf of Oman, for example, show signs of extreme drought just when Weiss's alleged exodus took place. A new model of air-mass movement explains how subtle shifts in atmospheric circulation could have scorched Mesopotamia as well as points east, west, and south. And recent analyses of ice cores from Greenland—which offer the most detailed record of global climate change—reveal unusual climatic conditions at 2200 B.C. that could well have brought drought to the region in question.

"I've got some figures I can show you. Figures always help," says paleoclimatologist Peter deMenocal, swiveling his chair from reporter to computer in his office at Columbia University's Lamont-Doherty Earth Observatory, just north of New York City. On the monitor, deMenocal pulls up a graph derived from the research project known as GISP2 (for Greenland Ice Sheet Project 2). GISP2 scientists, he explains, use chemical signals in ice cores to reconstruct past climates. There are two kinds of naturally occuring oxygen atoms, heavy and light, and they accumulate in ice sheets in predictable ratios that vary with prevailing temperatures. In a cool climate, for example, heavy oxygen isotopes are less easily evaporated out of the ocean and transported as snow or rain to northern landmasses like Greenland. In a warm climate, however, more heavy oxygen isotopes will be evaporated, and more deposited in the Greenland ice sheets.

By tracking oxygen-isotope ratios within the ice cores, the GISP2 graph reflects temperatures over Greenland for the past 15,000 years. Near the bottom of the graph, a black line squiggles wildly until 11,700 years ago, when the last ice age ended and the current warm era, the Holocene, began. The line then climbs steadily for a few thousand years, wavering only modestly, until 7,000 years before the present. From then until now, global temperatures appear relatively stable—"then until now" comprising, of course, the entire span of human civilization.

"The archeological community—and actually segments of the paleoclimate community—have viewed the Holocene as being climatically stable," says de-Menocal. "And so they imagine that the whole drama of civilization's emergence took place on a level playing field in terms of the environment."

Until he met Harvey Weiss, deMenocal wasn't much interested in studying the Holocene; like most of his peers, he was more drawn to the dynamic climate fluctuations that preceded it. In fact, the Holocene had something of a bad rep among climatologists. "It was thought of as kind of a boring time to study," says de-Menocal. "Like, why would you possibly want to? All the action is happening 20,000 years earlier."

Then a few years ago he read an account of Weiss's drought theory and had an epiphany of sorts. It occurred to him that even the smallest variations in climate could be interesting if they had influenced the course of history. What if something was going on in the Holocene after all? He looked up the 1993 paper in which Weiss had laid out the evidence for the Habur hiatus and reported the results of the soil analysis.

"I was pretty skeptical," says deMenocal. "I mean, what would you expect if everyone left a town? It would get dusty. Especially in the world's dustiest place. Big surprise."

Weiss, meanwhile, was getting a similar response from many of his peers. But when he and deMenocal met at a conference in 1994, they hit it off right away—largely because Weiss, too, was dismayed at the paucity of his own evidence. "Peter was immediately sensitive to my moaning about how we needed additional data, different kinds of data," says Weiss. "And he immediately understood where such data could be obtained."

DeMenocal told Weiss that if a large-scale drought had in fact occurred, it would have left a mark in the sediments of nearby ocean floors—the floor of the Gulf of Oman, for example. Lying approximately 700 miles southeast of ancient Mesopotamia, the gulf would have caught any windblown dust that swept down from the Tigris and Euphrates valleys. (The Persian Gulf is closer, but because it's so shallow, its sediments get churned up, thereby confusing their chronology.) And deMenocal just happened to know some German scientists who had a sediment core from the Gulf of Oman.

Analysis of the gulf core is ongoing, but deMenocal has already extracted enough information to confirm Weiss's suspicions. To track dry spells in the sediments, he and his colleague Heidi Cullen looked for dolomite, a mineral found in the mountains of Iraq and Turkey and on the Mesopotamian floodplains that could have been transported to the gulf only by wind. Most of the Holocene section of the core consists of calcium carbonate sediments typical of ocean bottoms.

"And then all of a sudden, at exactly 4,200 calendar years, there's this big spike of dolomite," says deMenocal—a fivefold increase that slowly decays over about three centuries. The chemistry of the dolomite dust matches that of the dolomite in the Mesopotamian mountains and plains, verifying the mineral's source. And not only did deMenocal and his colleagues figure out what happened, they may have figured out how. Studies by Gerard Bond at Lamont-Doherty have shown that the timing of the drought coincided with a cooling period in the North Atlantic. According to a survey by Cullen of current meteorological records, such cooling would have dried out the Middle East and western Asia by creating a pressure gradient that drew moisture to the north and away from the Mediterranean.

"The whole disruption, collapse bit, well, I just have to take Harvey at his word," says deMenocal. "What I tried to do is bring some good hard climate data to the problem." Why hasn't anybody seen this signature of calamity before? Simple, says deMenocal. "No one looked for it."

Weiss's first hints of climate-associated calamity came form a survey of his principal excavation site, a buried city in northeastern Syria called Tell Leilan. Tell Leilan (rhymes with "Ceylon") was one of three major cities on the Habur Plains to be taken over by the Akkadian Empire around 2300 B.C. The city covered more than 200 acres topped by a haughty acropolis, and was sustained by a tightly regulated system of rainfed agriculture that was co-opted and intensified by the imperialist from the south. Weiss had asked Marie-Agnés Courty of the National Center for Scientific Research in France to examine the ancient soils of Tell Leilan to help him understand the agricultural development of the region. She reported that a section dating from 2200 to 1900 B.C. showed evidence of severe drought, including an eight-inch-thick layer of windblown sand and a marked absence of earthworm tunnels.

In his own excavations of the same period, Weiss had already found evidence of desertion: mud-brick walls that had fallen over clay floors and were covered with, essentially, 300 years' worth of compacted dust. And once he made the drought connection at Tell Leilan, he began turning up clues to the catastrophe everywhere he looked. In 1994, for example, Gerry Lemcke, a researcher at the Swiss Technical University in Zurich, presented new analyses of sediment cores taken from the bottom of Lake Van in Turkey, which lies at the headwaters of the Tigris and the Euphrates. The new results indicated that the volume of water in the lake—which corresponds to the amount of rainfall throughout western Asia —declined abruptly 4,200 years ago. At the same time, the amount of windblown dust in the lake increased fivefold.

Weiss came to believe that the effects of the drought reached downriver to the heart of Mesopotamia, causing the collapse of the Akkadian Empire. The collapse itself is undisputed: written records describe how, soon after it had consolidated power, Akkad crumbled, giving way to the Ur III dynasty in—when else?—2200 B.C. The cause of this collapse has been the subject of considerable speculation. But Weiss's studies of early civilizations have convinced him that their economies —complex and progressive though they may have been—were still fundamentally dependent on agricultural production. In fact, he notes, one hallmark of any civilization is that it requires a life-support system of farming communities toiling away in the fields and turning over the fruits of their labor to a central authority. The drought on the Habur Plains could have weakened the Akkadian Empire by drastically reducing agricultural revenues from that region. People fleeing the drought moved south, where irrigation-fed agriculture was still sustainable. For want of a raindrop, the kingdom was lost.

"Well, believe it or not, all my colleagues had not figured that out," says Weiss. "They actually believed that somehow this empire was based on bureaucracy, or holding on to trade routes, or getting access to exotic mineral resources in Turkey." But the drought itself is documented, Weiss says, in passages of cuneiform texts. Images from a lengthy composition called the Curse of Akkad, for example, include "large fields" that "produced no grain" and "heavy clouds" that "did not rain." Scholars had decided that these expressions were mere metaphor.

And many still stand by their interpretations. "I don't agree with his literal reading of the Mesopotamian texts, and I think he has exaggerated the extent of abandonment in this time period," says Richard Zettler, curator of the Near East section at the University of Pennsylvania's Museum of Archaeology and Anthropology in Philadelphia. Zettler doesn't question the evidence for drought, but he thinks Weiss has overplayed its implications. Although Tell Leilan may well have been deserted during the putative hiatus, for example, nearby cities on the Habur Plains show signs of continuing occupation, he says. As for the Curse and other Mesopotamian passages describing that period, says Zettler, "there are a lot of questions on how to read these texts—how much of it is just literary license, whatever. Even if there is a core of historical truth, it's hard to determine what the core of truth is."

Instead of backing down in the face of such commentary, Weiss has continued to document his thesis. Echoing Mellaart, he points out that 2200 B.C. saw the nearly simultaneous collapse of half a dozen other city-based civilizations—in Egypt, in Palestine, on Crete and the Greek mainland, and in the Indus Valley. The collapses were caused by the same drought, says Weiss, for the same reasons. But because historians and archeologists look for internal rather than external forces to explain civilizations in crisis, they don't communicate among themselves, he says, and many aren't even aware of what's going on next door, as it were.

"Very few people understand that there was a synchronous collapse and probably drought conditions in both Egypt and Mesopotamia," let alone the rest of the Old World, says Weiss.

It didn't help Weiss's extravagant claims for third-millennium cataclysm that his alleged drought didn't appear in the GISP2 oxygen-isotope record. The graph in deMenocal's office, for example, has no spikes or dips or swerves at 2200 B.C., just a nice flat plateau. That graph was drawn from an interpretation of the ice-core data. But according to Paul Mayewski of the University of New Hampshire in Durham, who is chief scientist of GISP2, there are plenty of reasons a drought in western Asia might not make it into the oxygen-isotope record in the Greenland glacier. Greenland might be too far away to "feel" the regional event, or the drought may have left a different kind of chemical signature. Only a climatologist like Mayewski could explain these reasons, however. And no one asked him to.

"As a consequence, a lot of people called Harvey Weiss and said, `Well, the GISP2 record is the most highly resolved record of Holocene climate in the world. And if it's not in there, you're wrong, Harvey,' " says Mayewski. "I didn't realize that poor Harvey was being abused for not existing in our record."

Fortunately Mayewski, like deMenocal, is a curious sort with interests a bit broader than his own specialty. When he happened upon Weiss's 1993 paper, he'd already lent a hand on a few archeological projects, including one on the disappearance of Norse colonies from Greenland in the mid-1300s. But he figured other scientists had already looked for the Mesopotamian drought in the climate record. When he finally met Weiss in 1996, he learned otherwise. Mayewski began reanalyzing his core data with Weiss's theory in mind, and he uncovered a whole new Holocene.

"We can definitely show from our records that the 2200 B.C. event is unique," says Mayewski. "And what's much more exciting than that, we can show that most of the major turning points in civilization in western Asia also correlate with what we would say would be dry events. We think that we have found a proxy for aridity in western Asia."

Earlier interpretations of the GISP2 data had measured a variety of ions in ice cores that would reveal general information about climate variability. To look for the 2200 B.C. drought in particular, Mayewski used tests based on 2.5-year intervals in the climate record instead of 50-to 100-year intervals. He also collected a broader set of data that allowed him to reconstruct specific patterns of atmospheric circulation—not only over land but over land *and* oceans. When Mayewski focused on the movement of air masses over oceans, he found that air transport from south to north in the Atlantic—so-called meridional circulation—hit a significant winter low some 4,200 years ago. Mayewski and deMenocal are studying how this event relates to drought in western Asia.

"But it seems on the basis of the paleoclimatic data that there is no doubt about the event at 2200 B.C.," says Weiss. "What the qualities of this event were, and what the magnitude of this event was, that is the current research frontier now."

Trouble is, even though the drought may seem like a sure thing, its effects on Mesopotamia are still unproved, as Zettler points out. They will remain controversial, Weiss admits, until archeologists better understand the contributions of politics, agriculture, and climate in the formation of ancient societies. That mission grows more urgent as more archeologists seem ready to grapple with models of "climatic determinism." In the past few years, drought and flooding have been cited in the demise of several New World civilizations, including the Maya of Central America, the Anasazi of the American Southwest, and the Moche and Tiwanaku of Peru and Bolivia.

"Until climatic conditions are quantified, it's going to be very difficult to understand what the effects of climate changes—particularly controversial, abrupt ones—were upon these societies," says Weiss. The precise constellation of forces that led to the collapse of Bronze Age cultures around 2200 B.C. will probably be debated for a very long time. But paleoclimatology has assured Mother Nature a place in that constellation. And the notion that civilizations are immune to natural disaster may soon be ancient history.

Commentary

Most archaeologists interpret their data through a combination of preconceived notions (influenced by particular theoretical frameworks) and analysis of patterning in their data. What some articles in this section have illustrated is how new findings from archaeological and paleoenvironmental research force us to reassess continually how we view social and political life in the ancient world. The cemetery finds in Australia remind us that what we see in the ethnographic record is a picture influenced by centuries of population loss and reorganization following European contact. In the French Iron Age, clear evidence for status differentiation suggests a more advanced form of sociopolitical organization than archaeologists previously suspected. In adjusting our explanations to fit the data, archaeologists rely on empirical data to help them refine their interpretations.

For archaeologists who profess an interest in the origins of complex society, studying cultures like the mound-builders of the American Southwest and the American Southeast is an invaluable opportunity. In such societies, we can monitor the development of community-level organization. We can calculate how much labor (and organization) was needed to construct the public architecture that leaves archaeological remains. The scale—of human populations, of architectural construction, and even of settlement—is large but manageable in such societies, and the period of time involved lasts only a few hundred years. An enduring question for archaeologists who study these early complex societies is why they did not evolve into full-fledged states. What were the environmental and social constraints on complexity? Piece by piece, we begin to find answers to these questions as we undertake the painstaking research required to study sites from these ancient ranked societies.

Ancient states and empires have always dazzled the public and fascinated archaeologists. We can hardly resist the allure of monumental architecture, vast cityscapes, complex irrigation systems, and the high arts that characterize ancient civilizations. How did they develop, and why did they fall? Archaeologists use cross-cultural comparisons to examine and interpret similarities and differences in the development—and demise—of sociopolitical systems that emerged in the ancient world. Many archaeologists today have begun to suggest that we need to look more closely at environmental factors, which may have played a larger role than we previously imagined. Despite the technological complexity and organizational sophistication of these ancient states, they may have been susceptible to the same kinds of environmental calamities that affect our society today. Although further work on refining our interpretations of past sociopolitical systems is certainly warranted, articles in this section reveal how anthropological archaeology is producing exciting insights on this dimension of ancient life.

Part Ten

Art, Ritual, and Ideology

Introduction

Anthropologists believe that art reflects the cultural values of a society, through oral traditions (myths, legends, tales), performance, and visual arts. Some art and rituals are intended for a public audience; other art and rituals are undertaken in private, sacred places. In most traditional societies, art and ritual are intimately related through a shared belief system, or ideology. Archaeologists acknowledge that art, ritual, and ideology are integral dimensions of human life, yet we are often frustrated in our attempts to study these aspects of ancient cultures. They often leave few archaeological traces, and where such traces exist, we rarely know how to interpret them. We cannot ignore these phenomena: they are a part of human culture and they played an important role in helping societies deal with an uncertain world. Archaeological examples of art, ritual, and ideology, to name only a few, include petroglyphs (etchings) and pictographs (paintings) on panels of rock; pendants and fetishes carved from stone and ivory; pyramids and other monuments; and human burials and their associated grave-goods. The richness and variety of this record suggest that art and ritual played essential roles in ancient societies, and the challenge is to find methods of interpretation.

Ancient petroglyphs are particularly common in some areas of the world, including (but not limited to) western North America and southwest France. We call petroglyphs and pictographs rock art, and rock art is sometimes extremely old. Cave paintings in France are more than 25,000 years old, and we suspect that artistic traditions have been a part of human culture as long as modern humans have existed. Why, exactly, did ancient people make petroglyphs and pictographs? Are they simply mindless "doodles," made by adults and children? Or did they have important symbolic meanings? Who knows? Until recently, a vast majority of archaeologists have overlooked some material evidence of ritual and ideology, such as petroglyphs and pictographs. Recently, however, more archaeologists are devoting serious attention to interpreting petroglyphs and pictographs, and they are proposing some startling ideas and theories. In "Reading the Minds of Rock Artists," archaeologist David Whitley combines insights from ethnography and neuropsychology to examine thought processes of ancient peoples in what is now western North America. His research on artistic traditions of traditional hunter-gatherers in the west (and particularly in California) revealed close links between rock art and the supernatural world. Many native American societies had shamans, or religious specialists, who communicated with supernatural entities to help their communities. Whitley uses examples from the Great Basin of eastern California to test his hypothesis that rock art sites were localities for shamanistic vision quests. He also uses findings from neuropsychology to explain why rock art is linked to trance states, and why rock art shares design similarities over such broad regions of the world.

We move from North America's Great Basin to the French coast to examine the earliest dated rock art in the world. Jean Clottes and Jean Courtin report on recent findings from the Cosquer cave in their article entitled, "Neptune's Ice Age Gallery." What makes this new site extraordinary is not simply its great antiquity (27,000 years old) and its beautiful cave painting, but the fact that a rising sea level in the last 12,000 years sealed this site from the world's view. An intrepid professional diver discovered the site, by exploring a 450-foot-long tunnel under the ocean that led to this magnificent rock art gallery. Most of the images are weathered but decipherable. Clottes and Courtin believe that the earliest art consisted of images of human hands, and that the zoomorphic tradition began approximately 18,500 years ago. Findings from Cosquer help us to develop a chronology for the development of Paleolithic cave art. They also include some of the earliest evidence of sea mammals (specifically seals), and ocean creatures that had only been recorded previously at a few sites. Archaeologists have recorded fish and sea creatures that resemble jellyfish or squid on the walls of Cosquer, besides land mammals (like bison, ibex, and deer) that are also found at famous sites like Lascaux. The site of Cosquer is extraordinary for its preservation, and will provide great insights for archaeologists who study the Paleolithic mind.

When we think of art in anthropological archaeology, we often think of rock art. As old as rock is in some cases, we know that humans in Europe began fashioning portable art at least 13,000 years earlier than rock art. Portable art took many forms in the Paleolithic that survive today, from carved ivory disks and stone beads to pierced fox teeth, pendants of many different materials, and anthropomorphic figurines. "The Dawn of Adornment," by Randall White, describes some of this ornamentation and suggests what this portable art might have meant to early human societies. Why did people manufacture ornaments and figurines from ivory, bone, marine shells, steatite, jet, pyrite, and other materials that people often imported through long-distance trade? White suggests that the motivations of Paleolithic peoples to make these goods were aesthetic rather than purely utilitarian. Archaeologists often find quantities of these ornaments placed in human burials, and the Cro-Magnons used certain materials like ivory almost exclusively for ornaments. Why did these Paleolithic peoples spend thousands of hours creating art, unlike their predecessors? What was the purpose of representational images like the famous Venus figurines? White offers the intriguing hypothesis that these artifacts represent new forms of communication and organization within and among social groups. Such goods might have been used to signal one's sex, age, or status, and clearly prove our direct link to the modern humans of the Ice Age.

Evidence from the European Paleolithic has changed our views about the aesthetic impulses and cognitive potential of our ancestors. The nature of the evidence remains mysterious, however, and we can never hope to reconstruct fully the ideological system in which Paleolithic rock art was made. It is when we turn our attention to early complex societies that we have the potential to study the relationship between art, ritual, and belief systems. Archaeologists have been reluctant to offer interpretations of ancient ideology even in societies that lacked writing, since we cannot question religious practitioners from those cultures nor read their texts about their practices. One of the most spectacular cultures of ancient Mesoamerica developed in the Basin of Mexico, and had its capital at the site of Teotihuacan during the Classic period (A.D. 200–600). John Carlson's article, en-

titled, "Rise and Fall of the City of the Gods," describes a complex social and ideological system that involved powerful rulers, warfare, astronomy, ritual centers,
and human sacrifice. Archaeologists study this complicated ideological system by
analyzing beautifully painted murals and elaborate human burials found at Teotihuacan. Carlson outlines the rise and fall of this great settlement and its society
and discusses how archaeological investigations of the Feathered Serpent Pyramid
reveal aspects of ritual and ideology. Sixteenth-century chronicles, left by early
Spanish visitors, have greatly enriched these archaeological interpretations, since
the Aztec religion seems to have built on an earlier ideological base. Carlson's
analysis of art, iconography, and writing (as glyphs) suggests that these ancient
Mesoamericans structured their lives around astrologically-based almanacs and a
religion whose primary deity is known as the "Great Goddess." Images of this
deity are found in sculptures, murals, and abstract iconography, as are Feathered
Serpent images and serpentine creatures that closely resemble the Quetzalcoatl of
the Aztecs some six centuries later. Carlson believes that warfare and human sacrifice were necessary in the Teotihuacano world to keep the world in balance, and
that those very traditions were also involved in the demise of this ancient metrop-
olis.

1

Reading the Minds
of Rock Artists

David S. Whitley

Pictographs and petroglyphs are very different from potsherds and projectile points, the staples of traditional archaeological research. Painted (in the case of pictographs) or engraved (as petroglyphs), rock art adorns the faces of caves, cliffs, and boulders. Rock art isn't subject to the natural processes of stratigraphic burial that affect most aspects of the archaeological record. It's as visible on the landscape today as it was when first created hundreds and, in some cases, thousands of years ago. Yet its very visibility and accessibility have made rock art the ultimate archaeological tease: So easy to see and find, yet so hard to understand.

The enigma of American rock art is an old one. Decades before Thomas Jefferson's famous excavations of earthen mounds in Virginia, Cotton Mather (of Puritan fame) wrote about Dighton Rock, a Massachusetts petroglyph site, for the Royal Society of London, giving rock art research pride of place in the history of American archaeological reporting. However, Mather's view of petroglyphs—that they were a kind of proto-writing which would eventually succumb to linguistic analysis—was misguided. His efforts, along with those of subsequent researchers, did little to advance the interpretation of the art.

Proving that perseverance pays, a new generation of archaeologists is finally making headway in understanding rock art, nearly 300 years after Mather's initial report. Breakthroughs have come via an analysis of the ethnographic record (the published and unpublished studies of historically known American Indians conducted by anthropologists since the early part of this century), combined with a much less obvious method—the examination of human neuropsychology. This combination is shedding light on who made this art, why they made it, and what it symbolizes.

Reopening the Records

Often the most profound discoveries aren't the hardest to find, but those longest overlooked. Nowhere is this truer than in rock art research. For generations, archaeologists ignored the ethnographic record in favor of striking out into the prehistoric unknown, with no real clue as to why people might have made rock art, or what it may have meant. There are a number of reasons why researchers ignored the ethnographic record, one of which is the fact that most ar-

Figure 1. Pictograph from Pleito Creek Cave, a Chumash pictograph site in the mountains above the Santa Barbara Channel, California. Colors are red and blue; scale is 10 centimeters. This motif is a human figure (note the hands and fingers). It "explodes" at the shoulders creating another human torso that "explodes" again into the starburst at top. The psychedelic quality of paintings like this one caused Alfred Kroeber to suggest, in 1925, that this art originated in shaman's hallucinogenic trances. Subsequent analyses of the ethnographic record have proven him correct. (Photo by David Whitley)

chaeologists lack intensive training in ethnographic interpretation. In my own case, I disregarded ethnography for a simpler reason: When I began my research, all the published authorities claimed the ethnographic sources contained no useful information on rock art. To my detriment, I believed this bold traditional claim for many years.

My perspective changed in the mid-1980s. Inspired by the research of South African archaeologist David Lewis-Williams with San (Bushmen) rock art, some of my colleagues and I began systematically reexamining the ethnography of far-western North America. This region includes the art of California, the Great Basin, and the Columbia Plateau, or essentially the hunter-gatherer West, as opposed to the farming Puebloan Southwest. With Julie Francis, James Keyser, Larry Loendorf, and others, we've found that substantial ethnographic information exists on the making and meaning of rock art—information that confirms, in dramatic fashion, hypotheses that had been suggested but never proven. This information connects much far-western rock art with shamanism, the pervading religious system of hunter-gatherer Native America.

Although there were slightly different expressions of it, all shamanistic religions believed that humans may directly interact with the supernatural world by entering a trance. While in this state, the shaman could obtain supernatural power (often in the form of an animal spirit helper), or conduct supernatural undertakings, such as healing the sick, making rain, finding lost objects, or bewitching an enemy.

Anthropologist Alfred Kroeber was the first to suggest that rock art might be linked to shamanism in his 1925 *Handbook of the Indians of California*. Although archaeologists were aware of Kroeber's hypothesis, no firm evidence confirmed it. Indeed, the few widely recognized ethnographic passages about rock art seemed to indicate a fundamental lack of American Indian knowledge about this art. A good example of this belief involved many informants' claims that rock art was made by a "rock-" or "water-baby." Archaeologists incorrectly equated "water baby" with traditional European tales of wood sprites and faeries, concluding as a result that the Indian informants knew nothing about rock art. Recent, more detailed studies of the ethnography show that rock- and water-babies weren't inconsequential spirits. On the contrary, they were among the strongest spirit helpers of the shaman. As anthropologist Carobeth Laird notes in her book *Mirror and Pattern*, the actions of shamans and their spirit helpers were considered indistinguishable, so claiming that art was made by a water baby was a way of saying it was done by a shaman. This deception was necessary in order to avoid speaking the names of the dead.

The ethnographic record clearly indicates that many rock art motifs portray the visionary images of trance. American Indian informants of anthropologist Harold Driver claimed that rock art symbols are the "spirits" seen in a trance. In much of California and the Great Basin, shamans were the only individuals making rock art, while in southwestern California, the Columbia Plateau, and along the Colorado River, puberty initiates also made art.

Rock art sites, then, were vision-quest locales. In California's Southern Sierra Nevada, sites were called various names (in different languages and dialects) that translate as "shaman's spirit-helper place." Among the Numic of the Great Basin, a rock art site was known as a "house of supernatural power." The sites were portals into the supernatural, with the motifs themselves representing images of this sacred realm.

Conserving Sacred Images

Rock art has long captivated the imagination of the American public. Kokopelli, the hump-backed flute player of the Southwest, is so renowned that a Las Vegas casino lounge now bears his name. Disney's *The Lion King* includes a scene featuring Rafikki (a monkey shaman) painting pictographs. Rock art has insinuated itself into our popular cultural awareness like no other aspect of the archaeological record, yet no other aspect of this record is so inherently fragile or so greatly imperiled.

The difficulties in conserving rock art sites are numerous: wind and rain erode unprotected art; livestock rub against rocks and scratch away the art; natural freeze-thaw cycles break off rock panels. But the bigger problem is irresponsible human visitation. As Jannie Loubser, a specialist in rock art site management with New South Associates, puts it: "People can destroy in an instant what has lasted for thousands of years." While most people are familiar with the negative effects of graffiti, they often don't realize that chalking the outlines of motifs, taking castings or rubbings, touching motifs-even trampling one's feet near a site (which allows dust to accumulate on and obscure the art)—all have immediate and longterm adverse consequences for rock art.

Recognizing rock art's importance, The Archaeological Conservancy has acquired two important California rock art sites (a number of the Conservancy's Southwestern sites also contain rock art components). The Rock Hill site, near the town of Exeter, is an archaeological resource of world-class significance. It is the largest concentration of pictographs in California, containing more than two dozen paintings associated with a Late Prehistoric/Historic-period Wukchumni Yokuts village site.

The second site, Willis Wells, in the Mojave Desert outside of Barstow, is a good example of a "typical" desert petroglyph site. Situated near a spring, Willis Wells contains about 50 petroglyphs and adjacent habitation debris. While the Conservancy's acquisition and management of these sites represent a key step in safeguarding California rock art, only time will tell whether we can preserve our rock art sites for posterity.

The Coso Range Example

The importance of shamanism to the understanding of rock art is well illustrated by the petroglyphs of the Coso Range in eastern California. The Cosos are a western extension of the Great Basin, occupied historically by Numic speakers (the Shoshone and Northern and Southern Paiute). The range contains between 75,000 and 100,000 petroglyphs, but no one really knows how many motifs are in this isolated and rugged region of basalt flows and volcanic domes. Regardless, it is undoubtedly the biggest concentration of rock art in North America. About half the petroglyphs at Coso sites depict bighorn sheep. Other identifiable motifs include humans, weapons, "medicine bags," and a smaller number of other animal species. Geometric forms of myriad shapes represent about one-quarter of the total.

Figure 2. Petroglyphs from the Coso Range near Death Valley, eastern California. Scale is 10 centimeters. These human figures depict shamans wearing the ritual hide shirts that they painted with their "signs of power": entopic images that they had seen during their visions. Like the central figure, they are commonly portrayed with a concentric circle face. According to Native American informants, this symbolizes the whirlwind, which was believed to concentrate supernatural power and to "carry" the shaman into the supernatural world. The central figure wears a quail topknot feather headdress, the special ceremonial headgear of the Numic rain shaman. (Photo by David Whitley)

Figure 3. Bighorn sheep petroglyph from the Coso Range, eastern California. The bighorn was the spirit helper of the rain shaman. Ethnohistorical accounts indicate that Numic shamans traveled to the Cosos from as far away as northeastern Utah to acquire rain-making power from this spirit helper. Note that the head and snout are shown in profile while the horns and ears are twisted, as if seen directly from the front. This signals the fact that this bighorn is not intended as a portrait of a "real" animal, but instead is a supernatural being. (Photo by David Whitley)

Knowing that Great Basin petroglyphs were made by Numic shamans allows archaeologists to use their understanding of Numic shamanistic beliefs and practices as a guide to interpreting their art. The early research of anthropologist Isabel Kelly indicates that the bighorn was a specialized kind of spirit helper, one who imparted power to make rain. Certain locations were associated with specific kinds of supernatural power, and shamans sometimes traveled great distances to these spots to obtain desired types of potency. Given the predominance of bighorn petroglyphs, shamans obviously saw the Cosos as a source for rain-making power. Shamans often traveled from as far as northern Utah to the Cosos for their ritual activities.

Recently, scholars have tried to expand their understanding of rock art beyond historical cases to identify the human "universals" underlying the making of this art. One approach to the problem has involved the study of how the brain functions during trance. Since we know that rock art was made historically to portray the visions of trance, it follows that understanding the biological and mental effects of trance should give us additional insight.

"All human beings are *Homo sapiens sapiens* regardless of where they live," explains New Mexico State University's Larry Loendorf. "Neuropsychology gives us an anatomical opportunity to explore an area of human uniformity in culture."

In other words, our reactions to trance are broadly similar, which means scientists can use the similarities as analytical guides to test our ethnographic interpretations against prehistoric rock art, or to study rock art regions with no ethnographic records.

Still, the question remains: Why did shamans create rock art? Although every culture throughout the world had different reasons for making the art, neuropsychology gives us one important clue. Laboratory studies have shown that, during a trance, chemical changes in the brain result in impaired short-term memory. Ethnographic accounts reflect this neuropsychological universal, with a number of informants recounting the great importance and difficulty attached to remembering the hallucinations the shamans experienced in the supernatural realm. By "fixing" visionary images on the landscape with hammerstone or paintbrush, shamans ensured their permanence as records of easily forgotten sacred experiences.

Neuropsychology also helps explain the frequent occurrence of geometric motifs found in much hunter-gatherer rock art. During a trance, our optical system commonly generates a series of mental images—light patterns known as entoptic ("within the eye") phenomena, including designs such as zigzags, meanders, grids, and spirals. (These entoptic patterns may also occur during a migraine headache, or after a blow to the head, or even if we stare at a bright light and then close our eyes and press on our eyelids.) Different cultures interpret these motifs in different ways, but neuropsychology tells us that geometric forms can be expected in rock art that portrays the mental imagery of trance.

Another insight from neuropsychology concerns the emotions of the prehistoric artists—a subject long assumed to be archaeologically unknowable. Abundant emotions are a common characteristic of trance and, although we usually think of trance as euphoric, clinical studies have shown that unpleasant emotions such as grief and rage are also typical. Ethnographic accounts confirm this by emphasizing the dangerous and frightening (rather than beneficent) nature of the supernatural. It was commonly stated that shamans were required to pass immense grizzly bear and rattlesnake spirits to enter the supernatural, or to fight off attacks by skeletons or ghosts—all events that are tied to unpleasant rather than ecstatic emotions.

As we now realize, far-western North American rock art is more than just quaint imagery, useful only for embellishing the covers of archaeological monographs or decorating T-shirts. Rather, it is a valuable record of the American Indian's view of their sacred realm. It is also a glimpse inside the consciousness of the shaman, taking us beyond the technology of stone and ceramic artifacts, to examine the prehistoric mind responsible for making the archaeological record.

2

Neptune's Ice Age Gallery

Jean Clottes and Jean Courtin

In 1985, Henri Cosquer, a professional deep-sea diver, discovered a narrow, underwater opening, barely nine feet by three, beneath the base of a cliff rising from the Mediterranean Sea. Located in the Calanque area between Marseille and Cassis, the cave was 110 feet below sea level. Cosquer dived down several times and cautiously explored his way along a 450-foot-long sloping gallery. Eventually he emerged in a huge, air-filled chamber with many stalactites and stalagmites. However, it was not until a return dive, in July 1991, that he happened to notice the silhouette of a handprint on the cave wall—a common feature of Paleolithic art, made by blowing or spraying pigment around the artist's hand. After photographing it, he noticed two more handprints. Sometime later he returned to the cave with friends to search for additional artworks. This time the explorers began to discern many paintings and engravings of animals on the rock walls.

News of Cosquer's discovery of apparently prehistoric cave paintings circulated among the diving community, and on September 1, three divers from another region went into the cave on their own, could not find their way out, and died there. Hoping to prevent further accidents, Cosquer belatedly reported his discovery to French government officials and submitted photographs that reached us through the Ministry of Culture.

Judging from the pictures he had taken, the paintings and engravings seemed genuine. Many were partly obscured by bright, white calcite deposits, and most of the engravings seemed to be covered by a patina, formed by a natural process that requires long periods of time. However, we could not authenticate the art unless we could examine it directly.

An expedition would require investigators who were both specialists in prehistoric rock art and experienced divers, an uncommon combination. Our exploration of the painted chamber was organized in late September 1991 by R. Lequément, director of the Department of Submarine Archaeological Research (DRASM) and included Cosquer, archeologists from DRASM, several divers from the French navy, and coauthor Courtin.

Even after only a preliminary inspection, Courtin became convinced that the art was genuine. All the figures were weathered, so that when they were examined under a magnifying glass, numerous minute bare spots were visible where the ancient pigment no longer adhered to the cave walls. Many drawings were coated not only with calcite but also with small stalactites that had grown on top of the coating. A patina, often the same as that of the surrounding walls, partly filled in engraved lines of the petroglyphs. Microcrystals had formed on them as well. On the walls were dozens of animal figures, a number of stenciled hands, and thou-

Figure 1. Cape Morgion, near Marseille; the opening of Cosquer Cave is located at the base of the rocky point (center) at a depth of 37 meters. (Ministère de la Culture, Direction du Patrimoine, photo courtesy of A. Chené, CNRS)

Figure 2. Map showing location of Cosquer Cave along the coast of France. (Graphic by Ronald Beckwith)

sands of tracings made by human fingers in the once-soft surface coating. A hoax was out of the question. This was a major find.

A close examination of its contents showed that the cave had not been lived in. Two fires had been made but they were quite small, about a foot in diameter, and no bones or flint flakes could be seen around them. Unlike hearths found in Paleolithic cave dwellings, usually surrounded by a large amount of refuse from human activities, these fires were used for light, not cooking. Hundreds of pieces of charcoal littered the hard calcite floor, probably the remnants of torches used by the Paleolithic artists.

Stéphanie Thiébault, of the National Center for Scientific Research, examined a number of charcoal samples from the site and determined that they belonged to two varieties of pine (*Pinus silvestris* and *P. nigra*) that no longer grow in the Calanque area; nowadays the Alep pine grows there, but this species was not found among the charcoal we analyzed. A preliminary pollen analysis by Thiébault's colleague Michel Girard also revealed that the ancient cave painters had inhabited a bleak landscape with only a few species of trees, among them *P. silvestris* and birch. Radio-carbon dating methods applied to the charcoal samples indicated that they were 18,440 years old.

These analyses confirmed what Courtin's on-site observations and the photographic studies had already indicated: the art was genuine, and it belonged to a pre-Lascaux period. However, after the discovery was announced in late October 1991, a few specialists publicly expressed doubts about its authenticity. Despite the fact that our evidence had been made public, the controversy went on for months, petering out only after we published a comprehensive technical analysis of the cave in July 1992.

One of the main reasons for this lingering skepticism was that a really important discovery does not always fit into familiar patterns of expectation. Sometimes experts find it painful to have to change long-held assumptions. Therefore, whenever a new painted or engraved cave is discovered, its authenticity can be more convincingly established through physical studies and analyses than by comparing the art with what is known elsewhere. To evaluate newly discovered artworks by the comparative method alone would imply that our knowledge of the 20,000 years of Upper Paleolithic cave art is so complete that it cannot admit of any significant modifications.

The evidence tells us that ancient people went into the Cosquer cave during at least two different periods. During Paleolithic times, the sea level was about 360 feet lower than it is now, and the coast was several miles away from the cliff. When the sea rose dramatically at the end of the Würm Glaciation (about 12,000 years ago) and even later—it is still slowly rising today—more than half the cave was flooded. The whole entrance passageway and the lower part of the main chamber remain underwater, but their huge stalagmites and stalactites could not have formed unless these areas had been free of water for a very long time. Some digital tracings in the soft wall surface are covered with calcite and are still preserved underwater, but only for the first two feet. Below that, the walls have been eroded by water and scoured by tiny mollusks. We can thus safely assume that what remains above water is just part of the art in what must have been one of the greatest decorated caves in Europe.

The first period of activity at the Cosquer cave produced the forty-five stenciled handprints and thousands of finger tracings discovered so far. The two forms

Figure 3. The narrow entrance of the cave (to right of the diver), at 37 meters below the ocean's surface. The cord serves as a guide for making one's way in the tunnel to the cave. (Ministère de la Culture, Direction du Patrimoine, photo courtesy of A. Chené, CNRS)

must be contemporaneous because although handprints are usually on top of finger tracings, occasionally it is the other way around. This period can also be differentiated from the one that followed because animal paintings and engravings are always superimposed on either digital tracings or handprints and were therefore made later. What we have called Phase 1 is now well dated at about 27,000 years ago by four radiocarbon analyses performed in the laboratory at Gifsur-Yvette, France. In addition, one piece of charcoal found on the ground was dated at approximately 27,870 years ago and another at 26,360 years. The late Abbé Breuil, France's premier prehistorian, always attributed hand stencils and finger tracings to the beginnings of cave art; radiocarbon results for the handprints confirm his idea of a very early date. In fact, our date of 27,000 years ago is the oldest-known direct date not just for hand stencils but for any painting anywhere in the world.

The hand stencils in Cosquer cave can be compared with those of Gargas, a well-known cave 250 miles away in the Pyrenees. In both caves, the prints were produced by applying hands to the walls and by blowing red or black paint on top of and around them, so that they left a stenciled outline. As in other prehistoric caves, a majority of the hands seem to have incomplete fingers. Early twentieth-century researchers explained the missing finger joints as examples of ritual mutilation, a gruesome hypothesis that has long since been abandoned. Some later specialists argued that severe frostbite or diseases such as ainhum or Raynaud's syndrome could have caused the loss of fingertips, while others thought they were more likely a sort of sign language such as hunters use. Experiments have demonstrated, however, that the Gargas "mutilations" could be duplicated with normal hands. The Cosquer discovery may put an end to the debate since it seems unlikely that the same disease would have struck different human groups such a long distance apart and, even if it had, that both groups would then have recorded their mutilations on cave walls.

Sixteen of the stenciled hands in the Cosquer cave have been tampered with in one way or another. Some have been criss-crossed with deep engravings and are now hardly visible; sections of the calcite on which other handprints had been painted have been deliberately broken off; red dots or lines have been applied to a few more. Compared with other painted caves, this is most unusual. There is no way to tell exactly when this defacing was done. It may well have happened shortly after the hands were stenciled—perhaps they had served their purpose, whatever it was, and were no longer useful. (However, although ours is an untested hypothesis, we believe much more time passed before the tampering took place. When the people of Phase 2 went into the cave, they could not have missed seeing the handprints that bore testimony to long-forgotten magical practices. They may have wanted to eradicate any power the handprints retained, either by destroying them outright or by putting their own signs on top of them.)

Finger tracings in Cosquer cave have no discernible pattern, and this technique is not used to draw animals as it is in other caves. However, hardly any soft area was left untouched; in some cases digital tracings can be as high up as twelve or even fifteen feet, so getting there may have involved the use of a climbing device. Some wall panels are entirely covered with such tracings, perhaps reflecting a desire to demonstrate possession of the whole cave. The stenciled handprints may also have been a symbol of power and possession, so the conjunction of the two during the same period is probably significant.

Figure 4. The large chamber remains inundated; the ceiling contains engravings (Ministère de la Culture, Direction du Patrimoine, photo courtesy of A. Chené, CNRS)

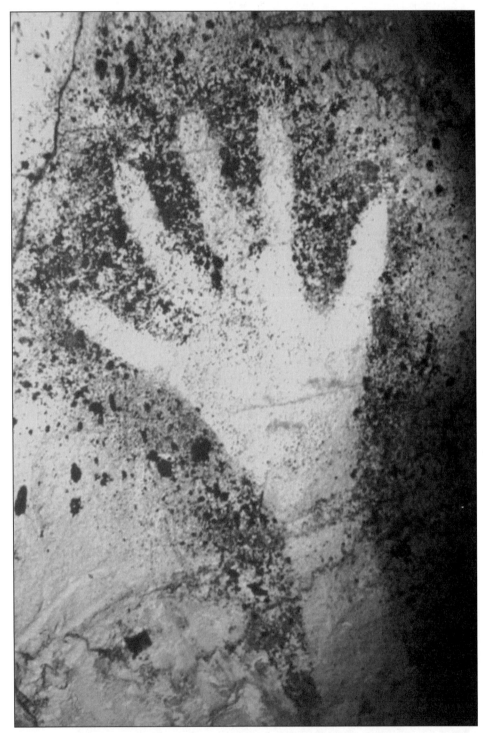

Figure 5. Stenciled hand made in ocher. (Ministère de la Culture, Direction du Patrimoine, photo courtesy of A. Chené, CNRS)

Following Phase 1, the cave was abandoned for about 8,000 years, unless people used it without leaving any evidence of their presence. We will never know whether this abandonment was deliberate, perhaps because the cave had a reputation for being sacred or maleficent—many such cases are known to ethnographers—or whether it was deserted because the entrance was blocked by rock falls or bushes. Whatever the case, it was probably not abandoned because it was flooded, since so far as we know water entered the chamber only after the end of the last glaciation, thousands of years later.

We believe it was during Phase 2 that all the animal paintings and other engravings were made. This period is well dated at about 18,500 to 19,000 years ago by radiocarbon analyses of the charcoal in some of the paintings, as well as by some charcoal lumps found on the floor. Shortly after the cave's discovery, one of these lumps was dated at 18,400 years old. Another was unfortunately mixed with calcite and sediment and thus gave a less reliable date of between 15,570 and 20,370 years ago. However, three paintings of animals made with charcoal were directly dated (two of them twice) by the recently developed accelerator mass spectrometer. This apparatus requires much less material—about half a milligram of charcoal—than the usual radiocarbon dating technique, and it can therefore be applied to minute charcoal samples from Paleolithic paintings or drawings. Using this technique, the Gif-sur-Yvette laboratory dated the image of a feline head at about 19,000 years old and a horse drawing at 18,500 years.

Animal paintings and engravings seem to have been placed where they are because of the smoothness and the availability of particular surfaces. Sometimes they appear on a wall and at other times on a ceiling. In one case, several large animals—one red deer, two horses, and one ibex—were painted in black on a very low roof, barely one and a half feet from the floor, perhaps by a supine artist.

We have now documented about one hundred images of animals. Horses are the most numerous, making up nearly one-third of the total. In some drawings they are represented by a single head; in others, by the whole animal. Such minute details as the difference in coat color between belly and flank are discernible on one painting. On the same panel are three black horses with an ibex engraved over one of them. Horses are the animals most often depicted in other Upper Paleolithic caves, so their dominant presence in the Cosquer cave is not unusual.

The next most commonly depicted animals are ibexes and chamois, animals that favored the rocky environments that existed during Paleolithic times. All but one of the black ibexes are engraved. Their bodies are accurately proportioned, except for the horns, which in some cases are disproportionately large. Male ibex horns grow longer as the animal ages, so representing an ibex with huge horns may have been a way of emphasizing the animal's maleness and possibly its age.

Also represented are several European bison—some engraved, others painted black. Bison are pictured very frequently in Paleolithic art, but some of the Cosquer cave renditions are unusual. In one example, the bison's body is in profile, the horns are seen frontally, and the head is in three-quarter profile. In another engraving the animal's head is lowered as though in readiness to attack. Among the other images found on the cave walls are deer: one buck is painted and two others engraved, as are several hinds. In addition, two strange animals, one

Figure 6. Timeline for Upper Paleolithic rock art. (Graphic by Ronald Beckwith)

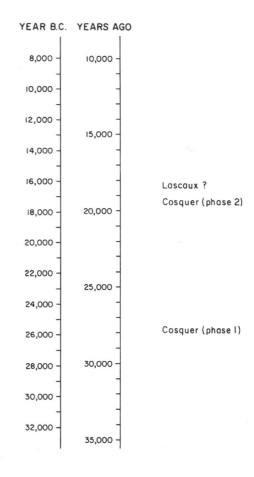

YEAR B.C.   YEARS AGO

8,000 —   10,000 —

10,000 —

12,000 —
              15,000 —

14,000 —

16,000 —   Lascaux ?
                                Cosquer (phase 2)
18,000 —   20,000 —

20,000 —

22,000 —
              25,000 —

24,000 —

26,000 —   Cosquer (phase I)

28,000 —   30,000 —

30,000 —

32,000 —
              35,000 —

Figure 7. Archaeologist Jean Courtin in front of charcoal images of horses (images from Phase 2: 18,500 B.P., Solutrean). (Ministère de la Culture, Direction du Patrimoine, photo courtesy of A. Chené, CNRS)

painted and one engraved, each with the same massive body and huge hump, seem to be giant deer, rather like Irish "elk." A feline's head painted in black is also present.

One of the most delightful surprises of the Cosquer cave was its depiction of sea animals. A few paintings and engravings of saltwater fish are known in Upper Paleolithic cave art, but drawings that look like seals had so far only been recorded in two caves, at La Pileta and at Nerja in Andalusia. In the Cosquer cave we found three painted auks, eight seals, three strange engraved figures that might be fish, and seven painted sea creatures that resemble either jellyfish or squid. All this is highly unusual and can only be explained by the cave's seaside location. The seals may have had a special symbolic significance, because unlike the other sea animals depicted in the caves, all of them are represented with spearlike signs on top of them.

The unvarying conventions used in the drawing of the land animals lend unity to Phase 2 and tell us that the period did not last long. Bodies are well proportioned but stiff and lacking anatomical detail. Horns and antlers—and at times ears and legs—are seen from the front, in twisted perspective. An ibex's horns bracket a skull that is not drawn in. Legs are always sketchy and spindly, without hoofs, drawn quickly in the form of a Y. These distinctive artistic conventions indicate an early phase of Paleolithic art, well before Lascaux; and in fact the great age of the paintings was obvious on first examination. The radiocarbon datings of Phase 2 came more as a confirmation than as a surprise. The best comparisons can be made with Ebbou, a cave in the lower valley of the Ardègeche, about 100 miles west of the Cosquer cave, where similar animal representations have long been known. In Upper Paleolithic times, people traveled, met other groups, and shared their knowledge as well as their goods. Therefore, we find an overall unity in most Paleolithic art, with "styles" confined to definite periods. Recognizable conventions may have been common to contemporary peoples living hundreds of miles apart, while at the same time unique local features arose in various cave paintings. From this point of view, the Cosquer cave does not depart from the norm.

The discovery of the Cosquer cave is an important event in the history of European Paleolithic art—probably the most important discovery since Lascaux in 1940. There are enough animals represented to allow a detailed analysis of the species chosen and their relative importance, of specific artistic conventions, and of the paintings' relationships to one another and to accompanying symbols. Both phases occurred before Lascaux, adding important new data to our knowledge of that period. Even more important, the solidity of the new dating provides a baseline for understanding the chronology of less well defined sites. Not all departures from the expected norm reflect profound changes in symbolism or culture. Use of sea-animal themes shows the importance of local environment in influencing the choice of images—a lesson that can also be applied elsewhere.

The Cosquer cave will never be open to the public. That cave art should have survived under such conditions is a sort of miracle, due only to the gallery's being sloped up and the cave's not being flooded in its entirety. Changing the natural conditions that prevail now could have disastrous consequences for the paintings, an unacceptable risk. In the next few years, the climate of the cave will be thoroughly studied by means of sensors that will transmit information from the main chamber to an outside laboratory. Meanwhile, the cave will remain sealed, although our photographs enable us to share these remarkable paintings with the world.

Figure 8. Engraved image of feminine symbol (length: 20 centimeters). (Ministère de la Culture, Direction du Patrimoine, photo by A. Chené, CNRS)

3

The Dawn of Adornment

Randall White

Some 2.5 million years after our ancestors began hammering out stone tools, early members of our own subspecies, *Homo sapiens sapiens*, started sculpting animal and human figurines from ivory, engraving and painting images on limestone blocks, and carefully crafting personal adornments of ivory, shell, soapstone, and animal teeth. In Europe, these creations, as well as innovative stone tools and weapons, first appeared about 40,000 years ago, well before the famous 17,500-year-old cave paintings at Lascaux. They were the work of the Cro-Magnons, successors to the Neanderthals (*H. sapiens neanderthalensis*). Although they had successfully occupied Europe and western Asia from about 200,000 years ago, the Neanderthals had shown only glimmerings of symbolic representation, doing little more than collecting fossils, minerals, and other objects that held some attraction for them. They vanished from Europe several thousand years after the Cro-Magnons appeared.

The rapid emergence of personal ornamentation in particular may have marked, not a difference in mental capabilities between Cro-Magnons and Neanderthals, but rather the emergence of new forms of social organization that facilitated and demanded the communication and recording of complex ideas. As anthropologist Andrew Strathern has observed,

> What people wear, and what they do to and with their bodies in general, forms an important part of the flow of information—establishing, modifying, and commenting on major social categories, such as age, sex and status, which are also defined in speech and in actions. Whatever the precise origins of clothing, then, they can be sought only within the general context of the development of social communication and of society itself.

A clue that social factors played a key role in this cultural watershed is that significant innovations in technology seem to have been developed not so much to improve hunting or gathering efficiency as to achieve aesthetic goals. For example, during the Aurignacian cultural period (about 40,000 to 28,000 years ago), the Cro-Magnons devised various techniques for working ivory, including the preparation and use of metallic abrasives (notably powdered hematite) for polishing. They used ivory in the creation of beads, pendants, and figurines, but almost never for manufacturing utilitarian weapons and tools.

In addition to ivory, the Cro-Magnons made representational objects from mammal bones and teeth, antlers, fossil and contemporary species of marine and freshwater shells, fossil coral, limestone, schist, talc-schist, steatite, jet, lignite, hematite, and pyrite. They did not choose these raw materials at random. Some came from sources hundreds of miles away, possibly obtained by trade. Only a

Figure 1. The sequence of bead making is illustrated: blanks of ivory (top center) were shaped (lower left) and perforated by gouging and then ground and polished (lower right). (Photo by Randall White)

dozen or so of the thousands of shell species available on the Atlantic and Mediterranean shores were transformed into personal ornaments. Only the teeth of certain animals were chosen. In some cases, the Cro-Magnons crafted ivory and soap-stone facsimiles of these same marine shells and animal teeth.

Techniques for producing Aurignacian ivory and stone beads varied from one European region to the next. In France, the most common beads, represented by more than 1,000 specimens dated to between 33,000 and 32,000 years ago, were created in several steps. The Cro-Magnons first fashioned pencillike rods of ivory or soapstone, inscribed them circumferentially at intervals of one-half to three-quarters of an inch, and then snapped off cylindrical blanks. These they thinned and perforated by gouging from each side, rather than by drilling (the technique of choice elsewhere). The roughed-out beads were then ground and polished into their final form, using hematite as an abrasive.

At the 36,000-year-old site of Kostenki 17 in the Don Valley of Russia, archaeologists have discovered ornaments made from fossil coral and from belemnites, the fossilized, cigar-shaped shells of a kind of extinct squid. Beads made from belemnites are a translucent gold or brown and are easily mistaken for amber. The bead maker began with the naturally cylindrical belemnites, cut them into segments, split each segment to make semicylindrical blanks, perforated them by drilling from each side, and polished them into final form. Similar techniques were used to make ivory beads at contemporaneous sites in central and western Europe.

The inhabitants of the Russian site of Sungir, an open-air camp, wore elaborate personal ornaments of ivory and schist and carved geometric and animal forms out of ivory. At 28,000 years, the site is one of the oldest in which archeologists have discovered ornaments on human skeletons. The remains include the skeleton of a sixty-year-old man, buried in one trench, and the skeletons of two children (one aged seven to nine, the other about thirteen) buried head to head in another. Based primarily on differences in the grave goods, Russian physical anthropologists believe the younger child was a girl and the older one was a boy.

These three burials were decorated with thousands of painstakingly prepared ivory beads arranged in dozens of strands, perhaps originally basted to clothing. Although the three who died apparently were members of the same social group, the burials differed in the details of body decoration and grave offerings. For example, the man's forearms and biceps bore a total of twenty-five polished mammoth-ivory bracelets, some showing traces of black paint. Around his neck, he wore a small, flat schist pendant, painted red with a small black dot on one side.

As was common elsewhere, the beads were mass produced in a methodical, step-by-step fashion. They were scored across each face so that when strung they would fall into an interlocking, criss-cross pattern. Careful analysis shows that the scoring was done on each blank bead before the hole was drilled, indicating that the creator had the desired aesthetic effect in mind at even the earliest stages of production. Experiments reveal that each bead took more than an hour to make.

The adult male burial contained about 3,000 beads, while each child's burial contained 5,000. Thus the man's beadwork required more than 3,000 hours of labor, while that of each child took more than 5,000 hours. The other objects placed on and alongside the children's corpses also represented a greater investment of labor. The extra attention lavished on the children may simply show that those who buried them felt a very deep loss. But it could mean the children had inherited a high social rank. If so, hierarchical societies arose—contrary to what some have assumed—well before economic systems based on agricultural production.

In creating representational images, the Cro-Magnons applied many of the techniques employed in the production of personal ornaments. They shaped

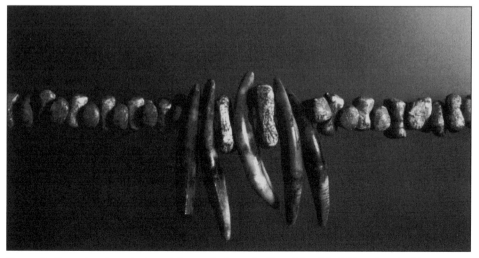

Figure 2. Ivory beads and pierced fox teeth from the Sungil burial yield an interlocking pattern when strung. (Photo by Randall White)

three-dimensional ivory and steatite sculptures by gouging, grinding, and polishing. Such sculptures were often perforated for suspension. An experimental reconstruction of an ivory horse from the south German cave site of Vogelherd took archeologist Joachim Hahn nearly forty hours. The Cro-Magnons also marked limestone slabs. Frequently they first smoothed the surface by abrasion. Then they used diverse techniques—engraving, pecking, chiseling, gouging, and occasionally painting—to make desired lines.

The several dozen Aurignacian engraved blocks that have been discovered are difficult to interpret. Their arrays of punctuations, cup marks, incisions, and notches form few recognizable images. The dominant engraved sign—an oval or triangle partly bisected by a line—has been commonly identified as a representation of the vulva. An alternative interpretation is that such signs, as well as other arrangements of cuplike marks, represent hoof prints. Such symbolism could have arisen from a very natural association between animals and their tracks.

Perhaps the most unexpected object that has survived from Aurignacian times is a flute from the site of Isturitz in southwestern France. Made of bird bone, which is naturally hollow, it had at least three finger holes. This flute indicates that in addition to other forms of expression, the Aurignacians also had music. At least a dozen more such flutes are known from the succeeding cultural period, the Gravettian (roughly 28,000 to 22,000 years ago).

The Gravettian period also witnessed the emergence of the first fired ceramics, which appeared in central and eastern Europe about 26,000 years ago. Many thousands of fragments of animal and human figurines, as well as kilns for their production, have been recovered from sites in Moravia, in what is now the Czech Republic, and Russia. The figurines were shaped from moistened loess, a fine sediment underlying the campsites where they have been found, and fired at high temperatures. This invention preceded by at least 10,000 years the first known ceramic vessels. Because the figurines are often fragmented, some archeologists suggest that the kilns were purposely designed to explode them.

By far the most famous Gravettian representations are the female statuettes and bas-reliefs popularly (but inappropriately) called Venuses. Some are ceramic, but others are sculpted from a variety of materials—ivory, limestone, steatite, and calcite. Varying regionally in form and manufacturing technique, they are found throughout Europe. At the 26,000-year-old site of Avdeevo, in Russia, Maria Gvozdover and her colleague Gennadi Grigoriev have excavated more than a dozen such figurines, nearly as many as have been found at all of the other sites of this age in western Europe combined. Most were sculpted from the tusks of woolly mammoths and depict women in the late stages of pregnancy, frequently in birthing postures. Many were buried in pits, sometimes more than one to a pit. In some cases, different fragments of a broken statuette were buried in pits dug several yards apart. This careful placement must have reflected some ritual concern.

Gravettian sites have also yielded numerous animal engravings, often done in a rather stiff, flat style, with the lower limbs left unfinished. Finally, the Gravettian is famous for its numerous hand stencils, found at habitation sites beneath rock overhangs and in shallow to medium-depth caves. One French cave, Gargas, has more than 150 hands stenciled on its walls. In Grotte Cosquer, the underwater cave recently discovered near Marseille, the charcoal-based paint used to spray the numerous hand stencils has now been radiocarbon dated to about 27,000 years ago (see "Neptune's Ice Age Gallery," Part Ten, this volume).

This great commitment of labor, technological innovation, and creativity implies that ornamentation and representation served practical, adaptive functions for early Cro-Magnon people. Neanderthals and their contemporaries outside of Europe may have had the mental capacity to use lines and materials to represent natural objects—some apparently did so when exposed to Aurignacian cultures—but on their own they do not seem to have appreciated the advantages of such exercises. Cro-Magnons used two- and three-dimensional forms of representation systematically—to render concepts tangible, to communicate, and to explore social relations and technological possibilities. This powerfully enhanced their evolutionary fitness. As University of Miami archeologist Heidi Knecht has argued, the ability to simulate visually things that do not yet exist is essential to any degree of innovation.

Around the world today, images and icons—from tattoos to national flags—are frequently brandished to assert social and political authority. Personal ornaments, constructed of rare, sacred, or exotic materials or requiring great labor, knowledge, or skill, serve universally to distinguish people and groups. Modern culture in any of its diverse forms is unimaginable without the kind of material symbols that humans first devised 40,000 years ago.

4

Rise and Fall
of the City of the Gods

John B. Carlson

Teotihuacan (TAY-OH-TEE-WAH-KAHN)...To millions of visitors each year, it is known simply as "The Pyramids," a vast ruined city whose brooding grandeur fills most of a tributary valley 30 miles northeast of Mexico City. I first visited the site in the summer of 1973, when I was a young graduate student in astronomy. Stepping out of an air-conditioned bus into the dry heat and bright blue sky, I was quite unprepared for the magnitude of the ruins. Its Street of the Dead, broad and straight, sloped northward across the valley for almost three miles, flanked by scores of temples and temple complexes including the Pyramid of the Sun, whose base is comparable to that of the Great Pyramid at Giza. At the northern end of the street stood the Pyramid of the Moon, whose architecture mimics the sacred mountain of Cerro Gordo in the distance. Exploring its southern end, I discovered the monumental Ciudadela Complex, which surrounds a great rectangular courtyard large enough to have held 100,000 people. On the east side of the complex were the remains of palace and administrative buildings flanking the city's third largest monument, the Feathered Serpent Pyramid. Dozens of stone fanged monster heads, arranged in pairs, gazed out from its layered tableros and balustrades. One with a protruding jaw and plumed collar was surely the legendary Feathered Serpent so often depicted in Mesoamerican art. The other, sporting goggle-like rings on its mosaic-beaded forehead above inlaid obsidian eyes, was far more enigmatic.

As I searched for the best camera angles, my head spinning from the heat, altitude, and excitement, I was approached by one of the ubiquitous local guides. Teotihuacan was an ancient city of the Aztecs who, he proudly explained, were his ancestors. It was named Teotihuacan (Place of the Gods) because their gods, whom they worshiped with human and animal sacrifices, had been born here. The Aztecs, he told me, called the feathered serpent Quetzalcoatl, a powerful creator god of the winds, legendary warrior, and hero of the Aztec's spiritual ancestors, the Toltecs. The goggle-eyed monster was Tlaloc, a god of rain and fertility. Children were sometimes sacrificed to Tlaloc, their tears invoking the spirits of the rains.

Local guides at archaeological sites worldwide are notorious for supplying a creative mixture of fact and fiction, and this fellow was no exception. Teotihuacan was neither Aztec nor Toltec. In fact, it lay in ruins for nearly six centuries before the nomadic Mexica tribes, whom we now call the Aztecs, wandered into the Basin of Mexico and were awestruck, according to their own accounts, by its splendor. For them, Teotihuacan was the birthplace of the gods. In truth, they probably knew little more of the site's history than my guide.

Leaving Teotihuacan that day with more questions than answers, I vowed to learn as much as I could about this ancient city and its relationship to the other cultures of Mesoamerica. This decision led to a change in my career from extra-galactic astronomy to archaeology. I began to focus on the astronomical practices, celestial lore, mythologies, and world-views of the ancient peoples of the Americas.

Who were the Teotihuacanos? What language or languages did they speak? Why did the Valley of Teotihuacan become so important in the Classic period rather than the much larger and ecologically richer Valley of Mexico just to the south? What was the nature of their political, religious, and social systems? The tombs of the rulers have never been found and, unlike the Lowland Maya to the east, they left no obvious portraits of their leaders. Did they have a system of writing similar to the Maya? We know that the two cultures were in contact from Early Classic times. But, most important, what led to the rise of this extraordinary people around the beginning of the first millennium A.D., what was the key to their long-term success, and what precipitated the violent destruction of their city in the early eighth century?

We do know that Teotihuacan rose rapidly to become the largest urban center in the Americas. Its power and influence extended across Mesoamerica, east into the Maya and Gulf Coast areas, and southeast into Zapotec Oaxaca. The concurrent florescence of these cultures created what we call the Mesoamerican Classic period. Teotihuacan was a key player, and its fall precipitated a profound collapse of all of the Classic civilizations.

Our current understanding of Teotihuacan stems largely from the last 30 years of scientific excavation of the site. In 1960, Eric Wolf initiated the comprehensive Valley of Mexico Project, which addressed the natural history of this unique environmental zone as well as its complex cultural heritage. This work led to the remarkable Teotihuacan Mapping Project, headed by the University of Rochester's René Millon, which focused on the city itself, and the Teotihuacan Valley Project, directed by William T. Sanders of Pennsylvania State University, which examined the rural environs of the valley. These efforts provided the scientific bedrock for a series of further archaeological excavations beginning in 1980 under the auspices of the Mexican National Institute of Anthropology and History (INAH) and headed by Rubén Cabrera Castro. During 1988-89, Cabrera and George Cowgill of Arizona State University directed further excavations in which Saburo Sugiyama, also of Arizona State, penetrated the heart of the Feathered Serpent Pyramid, which yielded explicit evidence for both militarism and abundant human sacrifice. My own research has focused on the Pan-mesoamerican practice of sacred warfare and ritual sacrifice regulated by the motions of Venus in the heavens. These efforts have yielded insights into Teotihuacan's spectacular rise to power, what sustained it and, moreover, what led to its violent demise.

Ancient Mesoamerican astronomers were well aware of Venus's 584-day celestial journey. Of the 16 or so surviving Precolumbian codices, five contain almanacs documenting Venus's position relative to Earth's 365-day solar year. According to two volumes, the Dresden and Grolier codices, Venus first appears just before sunrise in the east as Morning Star, where it can be seen for 236 days. Venus then disappears, reappearing 90 days later at dusk in the west as the Evening Star. Then, 250 days later, Venus disappears a second time only to appear once again as Morning Star eight days later, thus completing its cycle. New World

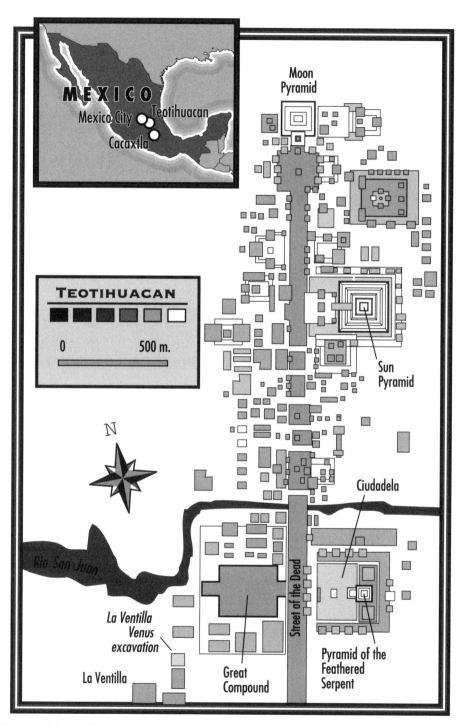

Figure 1. Map of Teotihuacan showing the locations of pyramids at the site. (Graphic by Joe Le Monnier)

astronomers noted that five 584-day Venus cycles equal eight 365-day years and they used this astronomical resonance as the basis of their almanacs, which span 2,920 days. The Dresden and Grolier codices contain 104-year almanacs, which tie the cycles of the Sun and Venus into the 260-day Mesoamerican sacred calendar.

Why did the Mesoamericans create such elaborate Venus almanacs? The reason became clearer in the early 1980s when Floyd Lounsbury of Yale University discovered that certain war events or battles in Classic Maya texts, whose glyphs contained the Maya symbol for Venus, were timed to coincide with certain positions of the planet in the heavens. Dubbed "Star Wars" after the popular movie's title, these astrologically timed battles were soon recognized as practices that extended well beyond the Maya realm. We have identified glyphs associated with at least three Venus-cult traditions practiced in Mesoamerica. One tradition was shared by the Maya and Gulf Coast peoples, one by the Zapotecs of Oaxaca, and another by the Teotihuacanos and cultures of the Mexican Highlands. In addition to military conquest, the Venus cult was concerned with the symbolic transformation of blood into water and fertility through the ritual execution of captives. Teotihuacan's Feathered Serpent was a representation of Venus, a god of warfare and blood sacrifice, as well as of water and fertility. The goggle-eyed Storm God has also been linked with both warfare and water. The key to our understanding of this cult has come only recently with the discovery of spectacular murals at Cacaxtla, a seventh-century site 80 miles east of Teotihuacan.

But let's start at the beginning. Sometime early in the second century B.C., a remarkable transformation began to take place within the small farming communities along the Río San Juan and the spring-fed marshes of the Teotihuacan Valley. At an elevation of more than 7,000 feet and with an annual rainfall of no more than 20 inches, the Teotihuacan Valley would appear to have been a marginal agricultural zone. However, numerous springs watered the valley's rich volcanic soil, making it a particularly fertile region. In addition, its proximity to valuable deposits of obsidian and its location on a major trade route to the Gulf Coast and Maya Lowlands gave the site strategic importance. At the beginning of the first century B.C. the region was dominated by Cuicuilco, a town of about 10,000 inhabitants in the southern Valley of Mexico. Fortunately for Teotihuacan, natural disaster soon shifted the balance of power in its favor when the volcano Xitle erupted around 100 B.C., destroying Cuicuilco and its surrounding agricultural land. Following the eruption 90 percent of the valley's population moved northward to Teotihuacan.

The eruption of the volcano, however, seems not to have been the sole cause for the migration. Millon and a number of other scholars, including myself, believe that religion played a major role in attracting people to the site. In the 1960s Mexican archaeologists discovered that the Pyramid of the Sun, the last phase of which was completed sometime before A.D. 200, had been built atop an important shrine—a dry four-chambered lava-tube cave. Archaeologist Doris Heyden of Mexico's INAH has argued convincingly that this cave had long been an important sacred site, a place from which the Teotihuacan ancestors had emerged—its four chambers were likely interpreted as representations of the four parts of the Mesoamerican cosmos. In time, it became a Mesoamerican mecca attracting an increasing number of pilgrims as Teotihuacan prospered.

A second critical ideological factor in the city's development involved the rise of a primary deity who, in all of her forms, is known to us only as the "Great

Goddess." First recognized as a female entity in the 1970s by Peter Furst, then at the State University of New York at Albany, and Esther Pasztory of Columbia University, the goddess is apparent throughout the site, in monumental stone sculptures and murals and highly abstracted iconography. Exhibiting both creative and destructive aspects, the goddess would seem to have been the physical embodiment of Cerro Gordo, the sacred mountain from which the springs that nourish the valley flow. She is often depicted with a bird of prey in her headdress, a well-known Teotihuacan warrior emblem. Streams of liquid flow from her mouth and cave-like womb. With a characteristic open-hand gesture, she scatters precious liquids, seeds, and flowers. Her priests bear bags of incense and likewise participate in the scattering rites—their chanting illustrated by flower-decorated scrolls emanating from their mouths.

By the middle of the second century A.D., the ground plan of the city had been worked out, apparently taking into consideration the location and layout of the underground cave, the surrounding mountains, including Cerro Gordo, and important elements of the cosmos. Several structures, most notably the Pyramid of the Sun and the Pyramid of the Feathered Serpent, face the northwestern horizon where the star cluster Pleiades sets and approximately where the sun sets twice a year when it passes directly overhead.

During the second half of the second century A.D. a brilliant new phase of municipal architecture south of the Pyramid of the Sun, including the Great Compound and the Ciudadela Complex with its spacious plaza, Feathered Serpent Pyramid, and flanking residential-administrative compounds, was completed. The Great Compound is likely to have served as a central market area for the city while the Ciudadela became its new administrative center. Even the Río San Juan, which cut through the site, was rerouted to conform to the city's design. Throughout its early years Teotihuacan was probably ruled by a succession of charismatic leaders. Millon, Cowgill, and others have argued convincingly that the Great Compound and Ciudadela were the work of the last such ruler, and have suggested that the Feathered Serpent Pyramid may have served, in part, as his mortuary monument.

After this extraordinary period of construction, there were no further monumental building projects, and attention was paid almost exclusively to renovating the city's residential areas. From A.D. 200 to 600, the city continued to flourish with long-distance trade becoming an important factor in its prosperity. Teotihuacanos extended their influence to the far reaches of Mesoamerica, with contacts, and even enclaves or colonies, in such areas as Zapotec Oaxaca (Monte Albán), the Guatemalan Highlands (Kaminaljuyú), the Gulf Coast (Matacapan), and the Maya Lowlands (Becan and Tikal, for example). These incursions were unquestionably associated with Highland-Lowland trade in goods such as obsidian, jade, shells, salt, rubber, cacao, exotic bird feathers, animal skins, incense, medicines, and textiles. More than 2,000 walled apartment compounds were built during this time, of which only a few have been excavated. Nonetheless, the results of these excavations, combined with surveys and surface collections, indicate a diverse society engaged in numerous craft specializations and diverse foreign populations. A Oaxaca barrio and a so-called Merchants' barrio, housing a Veracruz gulf coast group, have been identified by their material culture, architectural style, and mortuary practices.

We also now know that Teotihuacan's prosperity during these years involved the practice of sacred warfare and human sacrifice timed by the position of Venus.

Ample evidence for this practice has been found at the Feathered Serpent Pyramid. The pyramid took its name from its remarkable façade of serpentine "Quetzalcoatl" and goggle-eyed "Tlaloc" masks revealed in the 1918-22 excavations of the Mexican archaeologists Manuel Gamio and Ignacio Marquina. In the intervening decades many speculative theories have been offered concerning the identity of these figures, the meaning of the building's iconography, and the ultimate function of the temple and its surrounding Ciudadela Complex.

From the start, there has been essential agreement that the fanged figures with collars of blue-green feathers jutting out from the tableros and stairway balustrades are representations of the Feathered Serpent of Mesoamerican mythology. Images of this rattle-tailed serpent undulate along the pyramid and swim within bands of marine shells, including white conch and various pink-painted bivalves—all symbols of water and fertility. Debate, however, has arisen over whether these serpentine creatures represent the same deity that the Aztecs knew as Quetzalcoatl more than six centuries after the fall of Teotihuacan. Quetzalcoatl was many things to the Aztecs, including a god of wind and legendary hero of the Toltecs. Quetzalcoatl could also manifest himself as Tlahuizcalpantecuhtli (Lord of the House of Dawn), a death-dealing warrior aspect of Venus whose rays speared victims. I have shown that the Feathered Serpent of Teotihuacan was also a manifestation of Venus, a god of warfare and blood sacrifice.

The other fanged monster head, with inlaid obsidian eyes and goggles on its mosaic forehead, has proved far more difficult to identify. Although the goggles and the fanged upper jaw are indeed characteristic of the Teotihuacan Storm God as well as the Aztec Tlaloc, this figure appears to be a different creature, one scholars have termed a Storm God-related serpent. It is occasionally depicted in full form with a rattle tail, forked tongue, and often covered with scales. Sugiyama and Karl Taube of the University of California have demonstrated that in these representations the goggle-eyed creature, lacking a lower jaw, represents a war helmet worm by members of the militaristic Feathered Serpent cult.

Teotihuacan's Great Goddess appears to have played a major role in this militaristic cult. In Teotihuacan art, her attendant priests are virtually indistinguishable from the goggle-eyed warriors responsible for providing captives for sacrifice. Cult priests are shown marching in processions with blood-dripping hearts impaled on great obsidian skewers. They also scatter the blood and related offerings as does their patroness, the Great Goddess, as she presides over a religion that justified war and conquest as a source of water and fertility.

The sixteenth-century Spanish chronicler, Bernardino de Sahagún, vividly described such Venus-related sacrificial practices among the Aztecs of his day: "Of the morning star, the great star, it was said that when...it newly emerged, much fear came over them; all were frightened. Everywhere the outlets and openings [of houses] were closed up. It was said that perchance [the light] might bring a cause of sickness, something evil, when it came to emerge. But sometimes it was regarded as benevolent. And also [captives] were slain when it emerged, [that] it might be nourished. They sprinkled blood toward it. With the blood of captives they spattered toward it, flipping the middle finger from the thumb; they cast [the blood] as an offering; they raised it in dedication." [Sahagún (1953: Book 7, Ch.3, 11-12), The Florentine Codex].

The Feathered Serpent Pyramid was painted almost entirely in hematite red, a dark blood-red color, with decorative bands of the blue-green circles representing the goggles worn by the Storm God. The structure represented nothing less than the Great Goddess herself, the Mother of Waters, made manifest in an architectural mountain. The Aztec word for city, actually the concept of city and community inextricably bound, was *Altepetl*, meaning "water-mountain." The Feathered Serpent Pyramid was the ultimate statement of Teotihuacan as the Altepetl. The gruesome physical evidence of the Venus-regulated warfare cult, however, lay beneath the pyramid's structure.

In 1925, the Mexican archaeologist Pedro Dosal found burials of single individuals, evidently sacrifices, placed in pits just outside each of the pyramid's four corners. Then, during INAH-sponsored excavations conducted in 1983-84, Sugiyama and Cabrera uncovered three symmetrically placed burial pits along the southern side of the pyramid while excavating exploratory trenches. The largest, Burial 190, was a 25-foot trench placed midway along the side. It was flanked by two smaller interments (Burials 153 and 203). Burial 190 contained 18 young males, 169 obsidian projectile points, and more than 4,000 pieces of worked shell. Many of the skeletons wore collars made of imitation human maxillae (upper jaws) with artificial teeth carved from shell, as well as several real maxillae and mandibles. Behind the pelvic regions of several were small slate disks resembling *tezcacuitlapilli*, pyrite-inlaid mirrors often worn by Aztec warriors and regularly depicted as part of Toltec and other Highland Mexican military costumes. Most of these 18 individuals were found with their hands crossed at the wrists behind their backs, implying that they had been bound when placed in the tomb. The conclusion of the investigators was that these were sacrificed military personnel who, judging from the positions where they fell when buried, had been placed seated, facing away from the center of the pyramid as if to guard it and whatever it contained. The two interments flanking Burial 190 each contained one individual—a female in Burial 153 and a male in Burial 203. These interments have been likewise interpreted as sacrificial. Stratigraphic evidence has verified that all of these burials were associated with the construction of the pyramid.

The symmetry of the graves strongly suggested that similar multiple burials might exist along the north side and perhaps even on the east and west sides of the structure. This hypothesis was verified when another linear trench (Burial 204) with 18 sacrificed people with similar costume elements and offerings was found in 1986 on the north side. This trench was also flanked by two single interments completing the dedicatory pattern. Further excavations conducted by Cabrera, Sugiyama, and Cowgill in 1988-89 revealed still more burials along the east side of the pyramid. Again, multiple and single burials included large numbers of obsidian projectile points, numerous worked shell ornaments, and cut shell imitation maxillae that formed elaborate collars. Slate disks were again found beneath most pelvic bones. In Burial 5, one person with pronounced cranial deformation was found interred with a massive collar composed of nine real human maxillae. Interestingly, in Burial 6, opposite Burial 5, another individual was found with a collar of shell teeth made to resemble those of wolves, coyotes, or dogs.

During the 1988-89 field season, Sugiyama began tunneling directly into the south face of the pyramid in part to search for a central tomb. About a third of the way to the center, he found two additional mass burials. The first was a simple one containing eight young individuals ranging in age from ten to 25 years. They were found in the flexed position; some clearly had had their hands tied behind

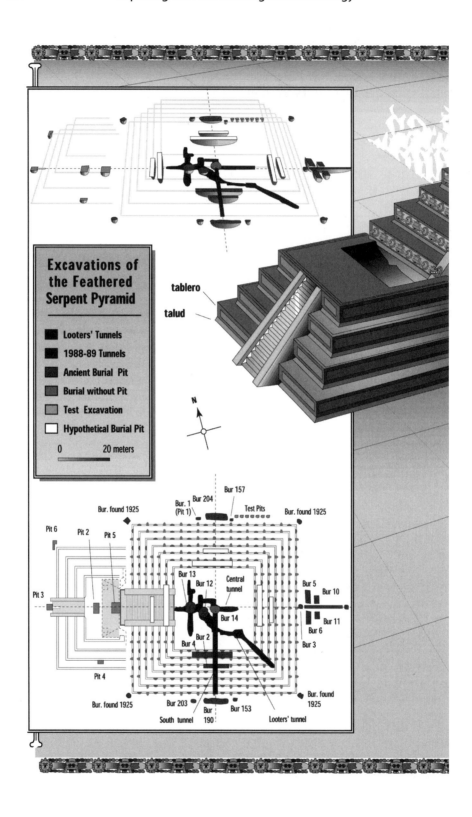

Excavations of the Feathered Serpent Pyramid

- Looters' Tunnels
- 1988-89 Tunnels
- Ancient Burial Pit
- Burial without Pit
- Test Excavation
- Hypothetical Burial Pit

0   20 meters

tablero

talud

N

Figure 2. Three-dimensional perspective of Feathered Serpent Pyramid at Teotihuacan. (Graphic by Joe Le Monnier)

their backs and had been buried facing the center of the pyramid. These people may have represented the number of solar years in the Venus almanac. The second interment held 18 men with substantially richer offerings, 18 slate disks, numerous projectile points, and additional necklaces of either artificial or real human and canine jawbones.

Near the heart of the pyramid, excavators broke into an ancient looters' tunnel. The looters had entered at the southeastern corner, moving diagonally. Modern measurements show that they missed the center by six feet, but that they had located and looted two mass burials to the west side of the center. Both of these (Burials 12 and 13) were badly disturbed, but the quantities of remaining grave goods suggest that these tombs contained the remains of some of the highest-status individuals yet found. Burial 13 still had one partially undisturbed and one complete skeleton found with a fine pair of earspools, 21 large beads, and a rectangular nose ornament, all of greenstone, as well as a large unusually shaped obsidian projectile point. The discovery of a carved wooden baton in the form of a stylized serpent head suggested that at least some of the high-status individuals interred there may have held priestly office.

Working east, from the old looters' tunnel, Sugiyama finally reached the center of the pyramid where he found a mass grave with 20 undisturbed skeletons. These remains, known collectively as Burial 14, were placed directly on the ground in an elliptical pattern along with the richest offerings found to date. All appear to have been adult males laid out in a complex scheme indicating some attention to orientation. Six skeletons were aligned along the pyramid's east-west axis, while the others tended to face the easternmost individual in the burial. However, this skeleton was indistinguishable from the others, and the rich collection of offerings was seemingly distributed randomly over the whole interment. The offerings, not yet analyzed in detail, included more than 400 greenstone items—among them 18 unique conical objects, figurines, earspools, nose ornaments, beads, and headdress-shaped plaques known as *resplandores*. More than 800 fine obsidian objects, 3,400 shell pieces, slate disks, animal and plant remains, and items of wood and fiber were found. In addition, archaeologists recovered nine groups of artifacts surrounded by vegetable material—possibly textile fragments. These were most likely specially prepared bundle offerings. There were only a few ceramic finds, including the remains of two vessels modeled in the shape of the Storm God. These offerings appear to have been deposited as part of the sacrificial rite rather than as the personal property of those buried under the pyramid.

It is clear that both the number of individuals within each burial as well as their placement are directly related to the pyramid's function within the religious life at Teotihuacan. Numbers such as eight, 18, and 20 immediately suggest calendrical significance. The months of the Mesoamerican calendar are 20 days in length. There are 18 full 20-day months in the traditional Mesoamerican 365-day year. Most significant, there are eight years in the Venus almanac. Although the four-directional pattern of the burials is not yet fully understood, it may, like the shape of the underground cave, reflect fundamental concepts of space and time.

Although the remains of more than 100 individuals have been found, the symmetrical placement of the burials suggests that as many as 200 people may have been sacrificed prior to the building's construction. But who were they? Cowgill favors the idea that they were loyal Teotihuacanos, sacrificed to serve as eternal guardians of a great charismatic leader buried in the structure. There is ample precedent for this practice in Mesoamerica and elsewhere in the world. However, I believe that the remains may be those of enemy warriors and other prisoners captured in battle for sacrifice as part of the Venus warfare cult. The presence of the Storm God vessels in the central burial, a well-known ceramic form associated with water and fertility rites, fits my hypothesis.

Cowgill's theory and my own, however, are not mutually exclusive. The pyramid, believed to have derived sustenance from sacred sacrifices, may also have been the tomb of a powerful ruler. Those sacrificed there may include palace guards or royal retainers as well as prisoners of war. Certainly the discovery of an undisturbed royal burial would have helped to support the pyramid-tomb hypothesis. Because of the ancient grave-robbers, we may never know if such an individual was ever interred in the structure. Future archaeometric analysis including DNA scanning may provide a key to the identities of the sacrificial victims. Excavations into the core of the Pyramid of the Moon, thought to be undisturbed, may answer the question of whether *any* of Teotihuacan's great pyramids was constructed as a ruler's tomb.

For half a millennium, Teotihuacan prospered. By the mid-seventh century, however, the city appears to have fallen into decline. Although no one dominant cause stands out, factors deriving from its long-term success seem to have spawned the seeds of its dissolution. The general health of the Teotihuacan people was poor and infant mortality high. There are also indications that environmental degradation was taking its toll. Centuries of harvesting wood had drastically depleted the forests, permanent springs were less bountiful, clean drinking water was difficult to obtain, and disease was endemic. But what caused the city's violent end?

It is an ironic turn of fate that Teotihuacan, which was baptized in a rain of volcanic fire, was consumed in a great man-made conflagration. The archaeological evidence shows unequivocally that sometime before A.D. 750 the ceremonial and administrative heart of the city, all along the Street of the Dead, was systematically and selectively sacked and destroyed by fire. Outlying temple structures were likewise put to the torch, though the majority of residential complexes were left untouched. But who did it and why?

Clues to Teotihuacan's demise may lie on a hilltop, about 80 miles to the east at the ruins of Cacaxtla, a fortified acropolis in the state of Tlaxcala, apparently established around A.D. 650-700 by elite Gulf Coast warrior-merchants known as the Olmeca-Xicalanca. The site had received little attention until the mid-1970s when some of the most spectacular murals ever seen in Mesoamerica were unearthed there. These included life-sized jaguar and bird-costumed warriors standing posed on the backs of jaguar serpents and plumed serpents, respectively, framed in water bands with numerous aquatic creatures. Further excavations revealed a great tableau of what appeared to be a fearsome battle between dark-painted jaguar-skin costumed Cacaxtla warriors and soldiers in elaborate bird costumes. The murals, which are marvelously preserved, were painted in a Lowland Maya style yet with an eclectic mix of iconography from Oaxaca, the Gulf Coast, the Maya region, and Teotihuacan.

Although the scene has been interpreted as a battle, the losers—the bird-costumed soldiers—have no weapons. Furthermore, some of them are dressed as sacrificial victims, painted blue with their hands bound with characteristic sacrificial white paper or cloth ties, a Panmesoamerican symbol of sacrifice. I believe that this is *not* a battle scene but a mass public sacrifice directly linked to the Venus cult practiced at Teotihuacan. On the west wall, the vanquished Bird Warrior Captain stands, hands folded in submission, guarded by a victorious Cacaxtla warlord named Three Deer. The Bird Captain stands in front of a strange white backdrop framed in red Teotihuacan Venus glyphs.

The meaning of this backdrop became clearer after the recent discovery of two new and equally spectacular groups of murals at Cacaxtla. The first was painted on two rectangular columns of a cloistered chamber on the west side of the site. They depict a blue-painted scorpion man and woman. The couple, members of the militaristic Venus cult, stand with upraised arms in a dancing posture above the blue water bands on a red background, framed in Teotihuacan Venus glyphs. Each figure wears a jaguar-skin kilt with a massive Oaxaca-style Venus glyph buckle. The upper torso and head of the female did not survive the centuries; the scorpion-tailed man clearly wears a goggle-eyed mask of the Teotihuacan Venus war cult.

When I saw this painted chamber, I realized in one of those moments that all archaeologists live for, that this was the very sacrificial chamber where the humiliated Bird Warrior Captain had been prepared for sacrifice. The Venus glyph backdrop behind the defeated Bird Captain in the "battle" scene was a representation of this very room. Moreover, a representation of this same chamber is included in a previously undeciphered glyph at Cacaxtla—the glyph shows a rectangular box decorated with Teotihuacan Venus glyphs terminating in the well-known scattering hands of the Great Goddess and her attendants. The Bird Warrior's blood must have been offered in rites evoking the forces of fertility under the auspices of Venus. Nowhere is this concept more graphically represented than in a portrait of one of the Cacaxtla jaguar warriors. He holds a great bundle of darts bound up in blue cloth tied with the same strips of fabric worn by sacrificial victims. From the darts' obsidian tips, large droplets of blood fall down, filling the water bands that frame the scene. These blood drops are bright blue, having been transformed into the nourishing waters of life.

The last group of murals was found in a sunken chamber called the Templo Rojo. Amid myriad symbols of natural bounty such as mature maize plants and cacao trees, a Cacaxtla merchant warrior named Four Dog is dressed in the costume of a well-known Maya trader deity. His merchant pack, laden with Lowland products such as quetzal feathers, rubber for the ball game, jaguar skins, and possibly cacao, is propped up on his lance. Below him, laid out on the floor for all to walk on, is a remarkable tableau of emaciated captives with sacrificial ties bound around their heads. Between the legs of one of these victims is a burning five-stepped temple-pyramid consumed by flames, a ubiquitous symbol for conquest in the Aztec world. The Templo Rojo murals show us for the first time that this symbol was in use at least 600 years earlier when Teotihuacan was destroyed by fire. Furthermore, on the step riser directly below these captives are the name glyphs of at least seven places Cacaxtla conquered. Two of these places are illustrated with Teotihuacan-style temples. I propose that these place names may be temples or enclaves in or around Teotihuacan. The warrior merchants of Cacaxtla had migrated up along one of their well-traveled routes and established themselves in Tlaxcala as the power of the old city waned. Some of them may have also been part of the foreign population represented in enclaves such as the Merchants' barrio at Teotihuacan. In time, they, aided by other like communities, simply overran and destroyed the city.

These are immensely exciting times in Teotihuacan research. Current excavations by Cabrera and others are producing wonderful surprises. Just this past August, I visited Cabrera's new dig in the La Ventilla area, just southwest of the Ciudadela. Surrounded by an army of archaeologists, conservators, and field workers, we walked from one ancient building to the next, passing by city streets that had not been trodden in 1,500 years. I was startled by what I saw in one small room where young workers were carefully removing the dry fill from the face of a red-painted band of murals along the lower walls. To my astonishment, I realized it was a sacrificial chamber just like the one at Cacaxtla. I had been scouring the literature for images of just such a room at Teotihuacan. Here, the red basal band was decorated with Teotihuacan Venus glyphs with red droplets falling in between, and at the corners were goggles of the Storm God Venus warriors. Other rooms in the compound bore murals of the plumed jaguars or pumas of the elite Teotihuacan military orders. Was this the kind of place in which those buried beneath the Feathered Serpent Pyramid had been prepared for sacrifice? I will always remember that special day as the twentieth anniversary of my first visit to the mysterious City of the Gods. I could never have imagined that, in 20 years time, stars on walls would be as fascinating as those in the heavens.

Commentary

As we have seen in these articles, humans everywhere create art to serve various needs, even when these needs are as amorphous as an artistic impulse. Humans are creative by nature, and art is just another reflection of our creativity that also finds a voice in technological innovations and in political change. Cultural anthropologists study art and ritual to understand a culture's world view or ideology. Many anthropologists maintain that these qualities of culture are among the most resilient: environmental catastrophes can force a village to move, long-term droughts can encourage people to shift crops, and growing populations may compel groups to adopt technological innovations. Religious beliefs, expressed in art and in ritual, are more resistant to change. In some parts of the world, like the American Southwest, it is possible for indigenous peoples like the Hopi to interpret ancient iconography precisely because that iconography has changed so little. We know, then, that ritual and ideology, are enduring elements of every culture, even when we have no way of measuring just how old these practices may be in a particular place.

Archaeology gives us one tool for exploring the time-depth of art, ritual, and ideology. In Europe, we know that these qualities of culture have played an important role in human existence for at least 40,000 years. Just how long ago did people first experiment with art and ritual? For how long have humans structured their lives around an ideology that we now equate with religion? Modern humans have lived in the Near East for at least 90,000 years, and we wonder whether artistic and ritual expressions began with the appearance of *Homo sapiens sapiens*. Problems with preservation and limitations of our current dating techniques may explain why we have not found still older evidence. As our investigations continue and our dating techniques improve, perhaps we will find still older artistic expressions around the world.

We know that art, ritual, and ideology are just as essential for cultural survival as are a culture's subsistence practices and its technological systems. For many years, however, archaeologists have been reluctant to interpret aesthetic and ideological systems. What we study best is material culture, and we have used scientific techniques to make great strides in our research on subsistence and technology. Scientific techniques are only marginally useful in studies of art and ideology: we can use conservation science to recover and preserve ancient art, and we can use experimental techniques to test possible construction sequences of this art. When it comes to explaining why ancient peoples crafted stone figures and cave murals, we must look elsewhere for our explanations. This search takes us into the world of ethnography, whether we work directly with indigenous peoples to interpret material culture or whether we read ethnohistoric or early 20th century descriptions of traditional cultures in the Americas. Because interpretations of art and ideology lie largely outside the domain of scientific interpretation, we also find it difficult to evaluate competing interpretations. Archaeology is clearly still a very young field, with room for developing how we evaluate different explanations of the past.

Part Eleven

Experiment and Ethnography in "Living Archaeology"

Introduction

It is often said that archaeology is the study of the remains of past behavior. Interpreting what really happened in the past is an extremely difficult challenge for archaeology, since eyewitnesses whom scientists can consult died long ago. Rather, scientists must rely on the mute, frequently unspectacular remains that we find in the archaeological record, such as bits of pottery, broken bricks and adobe from collapsed buildings, food refuse (fragments of animal bone, carbonized plant remains), and sometimes even human skeletal remains from burials or episodes of violence and warfare. Try as we might, interpreting such archaeological remains leaves many questions unanswered: these artifacts often only reflect patterns of prehistoric trash disposal and other unwanted by-products of everyday life. Archaeologists study the motivations and patterns of trash behavior, but we also want to know how artifacts were made and used, and the significance that different types of material goods had in the cultures that used them. As should be clear from the previous section on art, ritual and ideology, some dimensions of ancient life like religious practices are especially difficult to understand without data or information that can supplement our interpretation of the archaeological record.

Articles in this section illustrate particularly interesting approaches that scientists have developed for answering questions about past societies. When archaeologists undertake ethnographic fieldwork, we do so with an eye toward the archaeological record and often concentrate on topics such as technology and subsistence. We call the study of material culture in living societies ethnoarchaeology (or "living archaeology"), and this research strategy provides important clues for archaeologists in their studies of past societies. In "The Last Stone Ax Makers," by Toth, Clark, and Ligabue, we have the rare opportunity to observe traditional lithic technology among the Langda of highland New Guinea. The Langda, who had little exposure to the outside world before 1984, still make and use stone tools regularly. With contact and access to metal tools, their stone tool tradition may quickly disappear; the imminent threat of change is one compelling reason for ethnoarchaeologists to study this technology. Studying how the Langda make stone axes gives archaeologists some idea of the distance people will travel to raw material sources, and demonstrates the manufacturing steps required to make these polished stone objects. Ethnoarchaeological research also illustrates the effi-

413

ciency of these tools: using stone axes, Langda men can chop down small trees in three minutes, and trees as thick as telephone poles in five to ten minutes. These insights, combined with experimental archaeological research, help archaeologists to reconstruct the technology and use of stone tools in the prehistoric past.

We move next to the Cordillera highlands of the northern Philippines, where ethnoarchaeologists have studied traditional pottery-making for more than two decades through the Kalinga Ethnoarchaeological Project. This project is described in the article entitled, "Ethnoarchaeology at the Top of the World," by William Longacre, James Skibo, and Miriam Stark. William Longacre's research among the Kalinga began in the early 1970s, and his project has now involved many members with diverse research interests regarding archaeological studies of ceramics. In this article, the authors describe the history of the project and point out how research interests in the project have changed in step with changing issues in archaeological ceramic studies. Kalingas in the Pasil River Valley have welcomed project members to study topics as diverse as pottery exchange networks and technological change to pottery use-life studies. This article highlights three recent subjects studied by Kalinga Project members: ceramic production and distribution, pottery use-alteration, and cases of technological change. Archaeologists who study craft specialization may find insights in studies of emergent part-time craft specialization in the Kalinga village of Dalupa. Archaeologists who undertake residue analysis and use-wear studies with prehistoric ceramics might find research on Kalinga use-alteration instructive. Studies of technological change detailed in this article also illustrate the intricate relationship between the world system, technological constraints, market demand, and performance characteristics that produce particular types of innovations in Kalinga pottery.

Ethnoarchaeologists often work in traditional societies in developing countries around the world, from Asia to Latin America. Yet archaeologists also engage in ethnography with contemporary peoples to understand aspects of particular pasts, and this work has been especially useful in North America. The article, "Understanding the Past Through Hopi Oral History" (by Kurt Dongoske, Leigh Jenkins, and T.J. Ferguson), illustrates how archaeologists can learn about ancient religious meanings encoded in the archaeological record by talking with the living descendants of ancient cultures. Here we see a case of successful, long-term collaboration between Hopis and archaeologists in the American Southwest. The authors focus on recent archaeological research in the Tonto Basin (east-central Arizona), and on the coincidence of oral tradition and archaeology in the study of ancient migrations. Working together, Hopis and archaeologists have linked many late prehistoric sites to places described in clan histories as stopping points along the migration routes that brought ancient Hopis to what is now northeastern Arizona. Archaeologists can give indigenous peoples like the Hopis information about specific places, while peoples like the Hopi can teach archaeologists how such knowledge fits into indigenous views of the past.

Traditional technologies are becoming increasingly rare as globalization and economic development has brought Western technology to cultures throughout the world; in some regions today, ethnoarchaeology is no longer feasible because cultures have undergone modernization. Some types of experimental archaeology offer archaeologists a method to study and interpret ancient technologies when its practitioners have disappeared. It may surprise beginning students to learn that some "experiments" that archaeologists conduct take place far outside the labo-

ratory! We often correlate scientific experiments with researchers in white laboratory coats who work in rooms full of test tubes. Previous articles in this reader
(see especially articles in Part Six: New Techniques in Archaeology) have illustrated kinds of experimental research that resemble that model. Another kind of
experimental archaeology relies on replication studies, in which an archaeologist
will try to understand a particular ancient technology by actually practicing it.
The manufacture of stone tools by archaeologists has been an especially active
area of experimental archaeology, although replicative studies have also involved
hunting and butchering wild game, constructing houses and monuments, and
many other activities. In rare and important cases, experimental studies can resolve archaeological debates. Ben Finney's article, entitled, "Putting Voyaging
Back into Polynesian Prehistory," describes such a study, whose impetus lay in understanding how ancient Polynesians could have colonized most Pacific islands
before European contact, and without modern navigational devices. His study
displays an unusually dramatic form of experimentation designed to reconstruct
ancient transportation technologies. He worked with native Pacific Islanders to
build and sail a traditional voyaging canoe from Hawai'i to Tahiti, and the
process yielded many insights regarding the logistics involved in these ambitious
Pacific voyages. This experiment also provided data that changed archaeological
interpretations of ancient Polynesian colonization and the peopling of the Pacific
Ocean.

1

The Last Stone Ax Makers

Nicholas Toth, Desmond Clark, and Giancarlo Ligabue

Only 10,000 years ago all human societies made and used stone implements. In modern times the relentless advance of more complex technologies has left but few remnants of that primeval world, and even these will surely disappear before this century is out. Anthropologists must therefore hurry to study contemporary Stone Age craftsmen for clues they may provide about our early ancestors.

The study of modern humans from an archaeological perspective is called ethnoarchaeology. Unfortunately, it comes on the scene very late in the day. The scholars of the 19th century often paid more heed to such artisans as Britain's gunflint makers than to the contemporary stone knappers of the Americas, southern Africa, Australia, New Guinea and the Pacific Islands.

We sought to help fill this gap in 1990 by visiting a group of horticulturalists of Langda village, in the central mountains of Irian Jaya, western New Guinea. These people had made and traded stone axes in almost complete isolation from the outside world until 1984, when Gunter Konrad, a German urologist, and one of us (Ligabue) met them while on an expedition to the area. Because the later establishment of a Christian mission and the encroachment of a cash economy had begun to transform the traditional culture, the Ligabue Research and Study Center funded the expedition explicitly for the purpose of studying the stone technology. This report is based on that study.

The Langda ax makers live some 2,000 meters (about a mile) up in the southern slopes of the central cordillera of New Guinea, an altitude that makes for a generally cold and damp climate. Clouds often shroud the village, but when they clear, a superb vista of snow-capped peaks appears. We saw the peaks at their most awe-inspiring while flying by helicopter at a level halfway up the V-shaped walls of a river valley that runs from Wamena, 200 kilometers (120 miles) to the northwest.

The villagers call themselves the Kim-Yal; their language, which belongs to one of the many Papuan families, they call Uni. The average Kim-Yal man stands about four feet, six inches tall, far shorter than populations who live at lower altitudes, such as the Dani of the central highlands and the Asmat of the southwest coast. It is not yet clear whether the highlanders' short stature stems from an adaptation to local conditions caused by natural selection or merely from nutritional factors.

The stone ax makers cultivate sweet potato and taro root and raise pigs and chickens, a diet they supplement with wild plants and small game. They grow their crops in fields, usually on steeply terraced slopes of the river valleys. To clear a new field, they must often fell trees and chop out the residual roots. Historically they have done such work with stone axes, although these implements are slowly yielding to imported metal axes.

The Kim-Yal form open village clusters in which about 200 people occupy from 10 to 15 huts. Each hut typically contains a man, his wives and their children. Adult males may also choose to reside part of the time in a communal hut that serves as a kind of men's club. The residence pattern is patrilocal: men generally stay in the village in which they were born, whereas women marry men from different villages. There are 10 village clusters in the Langda area, most of them situated on a plateau or at the top of a mountain ridge.

The craft of ax making confers high status to the male specialists who practice it and to their sons, who traditionally learn the work in lengthy apprenticeships. Today every man at Langda owns at least two stone axes and each woman at least one. Most children older than five years also tote an ax to the fields, where they work alongside their elders.

An archaeologist would normally classify these implements as adzes, because in side view their ground edges assume an asymmetric, plano-convex shape rather than the symmetric shape typical of axes. Moreover, they are hafted with the working edge at right angles to their handles, whereas ax edges generally lie in the same plane as the handle. But we call them axes because they are used to chop wood and fell trees and because the literature has generally classified such implements according to their use rather than their design. In some other groups, adzes are commonly used not to chop down trees but to shape wood.

An ax begins as a large piece of unflawed stone of a kind that will fracture predictably and carry an edge. Best of all are the large boulders of fine-grained, blue-gray andesite lava that are carried from their volcanic source by the Hei River, which flows some 800 meters below the Langda village. The ax makers descend into the river valley along steep trails that wind through forest and field to the stream bed, a walk that normally takes about 60 minutes going down and about 90 minutes coming back up. They seek not only boulders but also smaller lava stones to use as hammers.

The worker typically holds in both hands a large stone hammer, some 25 centimeters (10 inches) in diameter, and then swings it against the edge of a lava boulder core. If he strikes it correctly, he detaches large flakes from the core. We were quite surprised to find that workers usually swing the hammerstone through their legs, much like the motion of an American football center. This technique, to our knowledge, has never before been described ethnographically; we believe it could have been used in antiquity for detaching such large flakes.

Suitable flakes may also be produced by throwing one boulder hammer against another boulder core or by kindling a fire alongside a boulder to initiate fractures. On rare occasions a properly proportioned, water-worn cobble will also serve as a blank. A typical blank measures about 24 centimeters long, 14 centimeters wide and seven centimeters deep (about 10 by six by three inches).

Half an hour of quarrying will produce, on average, from five to 10 blanks for ax manufacture. Hundreds or even thousands of smaller fragments, used-up boulder cores and hammerstones also come out of the quarrying operation. The workers discard such detritus by the riverside, where the next flood will sweep it away.

Paleolithic archaeologists would recognize the three major manufacturing steps that the Langda stone workers themselves regard as integral. Each stage has its characteristic ax morphology and waste products, which tend to be discarded in different places on the landscape. In the first stage the craftsman uses a hammerstone from 10 to 12 centimeters (four to five inches) long to remove large flakes from both faces of the lava blank, leaving bold scars on the flake surface. Normally he does this work at the riverside quarry. The resultant biface is quite crude: a jagged outline and an irregular, sinuous edge run around its entire circumference. The "rough-outs" are then reduced by flaking so as to minimize carrying weight—especially if a hidden defect should cause the stone to break.

The second stage of ax manufacture may take place back at the village, although it is often carried out in a field hut situated on a terrace about 100 meters above the riverbank. There the ax maker can work in the shade of the hut, build a fire if it is cold and perhaps roast sweet potatoes or game as he continues flaking. He normally does so while sitting on his haunches, holding the hammerstone in his right hand and the rough-out in the left. (All of the stone workers we observed were right-handed.)

The ax maker keeps several stone hammers of different sizes, shapes and degrees of hardness, and he switches from one to another as flaking proceeds. As our earlier reconstructions of stone-knapping techniques had predicted, the craftsman tends to use ever smaller hammerstones as his ax approaches its final shape. But we did not foresee that such hard hammerstones would be used for fine work. Most archaeologists would have labeled this retouch flaking as "soft hammer"—that which is done with a piece of wood, bone or other soft material.

Each flake sets up further flaking by preparing what is called the striking platform. The object is to steepen the edge angles by lightly flaking, crushing and abrading them with the hammerstone. If all goes well, flat, thin flakes can then be removed from the ax surface. In this way, the overall shape of the ax becomes progressively thinner, narrower and more symmetric.

A man may work alone or sit with other ax makers, creating an occasion for talking, singing and showing off one's handiwork. Members of such groups invariably sit in a line and face in the same direction so that sharp waste flakes will not fly into anyone's face. These flakes, which become smaller and proportionately thinner as flaking proceeds, are usually found outside the perimeter of the field hut. Sometimes, however, they appear around a hut in the village, evidence that some rough-outs are carried there before being worked to any great extent.

Women from the village, most often relatives of the stone workers, typically transport rough-outs from the valley to the village. The women protect themselves from cuts and scratches by wrapping the axes in vegetation. They put the implements in carrying nets that they sling over their backs, supporting the load on a strap that loops around the forehead.

The final reduction of the ax normally takes place back at Langda, often next to the hut of an ax maker. Here the worker prepares his striking platform with extreme delicacy so as to detach tiny trimming flakes; he also abrades the surface. The final product of flaking is a long, thin ax with nearly parallel sides, a triangular cross section and a bit end having a slightly convex outline and an edge beveled at about 50 degrees. A typical stage-three ax measures about 20 by four by three centimeters, but substantially larger and smaller ones are occasionally made as well. The time spent flaking—from quarry blank to stage three—varies from about 30 to 50 minutes. Between 10 and 20 percent of the blanks tend to be lost to breakage.

The waste flakes produced in Langda village are much smaller than those produced in the earlier stages. The complete sequence of ax manufacture, from the quarry blank to the finished flaked ax, in a typical case produced a total of 225 flakes and fragments larger than two centimeters in length (and many more smaller bits, grading to microscopic size). Of these, approximately 100 could be expected to end up at Langda village, dropped there during the later stages of flaking. They are generally strewn in a circular or oval-shaped pattern, often near an ax maker's hut, with the vast majority of fragments concentrated in an area of one square meter. Such a concentration would probably be dispersed over time by humans or pigs walking over the ground. Ultimately, the flaking debris would be trampled underground, at times when the ground is soft and muddy.

After the final flaking, the craftsman grinds the working end of the ax against a wetted slab of fine-grained sandstone. These grinding stones are highly prized and come from a distant river valley some six hours' walk away. They are stationed close to a water source in the village. The worker squats down with the grind-stone in front of him, adds water to the worn surface on the stone and then grinds the ax against the stone. The fine sandstone and lava particles mix with the water to form a paste that serves as the grinding medium. The axhead is inspected at regular intervals and more water added, with special attention being paid to the working edge. An hour or so of grinding turns out an axhead with a polished bit and an extremely regular edge.

One might wonder why the Kim-Yal would grind flaked edges, which are already as sharp as they can be. The reason is simple: ground tools hold their edges longer and lend themselves more readily to resharpening. Grinding thus makes sense mainly for woodworking tools and other implements that are used intensively over long periods. It is no accident that the so-called age of polished stone began with the development of agriculture, when people began clearing forests in order to plant their crops.

Aesthetic considerations also motivate the Kim-Yal grinders, otherwise they might not bother to polish more than a few millimeters from the leading edge. In fact, they polish nearly to the point where the axhead disappears into the binding of the haft. Prehistoric craftsmen in New Guinea and other parts of the world often went further, polishing the entire surface of the tool. Additional evidence of aesthetic intent appears in the Kim-Yal's use of red ochre and other locally occurring pigments to fill in the unground depression spots on their axes. Such use of pigments for aesthetic or symbolic purposes has been widely documented in modern nonindustrial societies, as well as in prehistoric cultures over the past 35,000 years.

Hafting allows a tool to be used at length and to greater effect. The workers haft the finished axhead onto a T-shaped wooden handle, made from a flattened tree trunk or branch from which a thinner branch projects at an angle of approximately 45 degrees. The stone rests against several strips of wood and frayed bark, which help to absorb shock. The worker then lashes the composite tightly with split vine, creating a design that distributes the force of a chopping blow throughout a flexible binding. Without this flexibility, the stone would tend to snap across its short axis.

A Langda villager equipped with such an ax can fell a tree as thick as a telephone pole in five to 10 minutes. The villagers also use these axes to cut out roots from a field, to build fences to protect crops from pigs and to make wooden digging sticks, containers and other wooden tools. A well-ground edge can often last for several hours of use without requiring resharpening. When it begins to dull, it can easily be resharpened by rubbing it against a grindstone using water as a lubricant; the axhead generally remains mounted in its haft.

The villagers will use an ax until it breaks or until regrinding has reduced the tool to the point where it can no longer function. Broken-off tips may be lost in the field, but interestingly, most worn-out or broken specimens end up in the village. The ax makers say they "feel sorry" for their handiwork and take pains to bring it home for final discard. Although such personal attachment to tools figures in the *Iliad* and the *Odyssey*, few anthropologists probably have suspected that it might explain distribution patterns in prehistoric sites. Henceforth, we and our colleagues must take such factors into account.

The stone axes carry cultural significance that goes beyond their practical function. Feasting villagers often exchange axes to cement their social bonds, and men give them in payment of the bride price—compensation to a father for the privilege of marrying his daughter. Our informants tell us that in the days before the cash economy intruded, a stone ax could be traded for a pig, the most prized food. Today three stone axes can be traded for one metal ax.

The Langda people trade their axes to other villages that lack suitable stone for such implements. Some six days' journey northward, the people of Bima barter their goods for Langda axes. Southward, the main trading post, at Lukan village on the edge of the highlands, attracts Kopkaka tribespeople from the lowlands, who pay for the axes with bowstaves, vine, fibers for mats, bird-of-paradise feathers or animal pelts. In the past the Langda axes were traded as far away as the southern coast, mainly in exchange for shells. Such specialization of labor as the ax industry requires must, in any case, have depended on long-distance trade. Traces of such far-reaching trade networks become obvious in the prehistoric record only after about 35,000 years ago.

Interestingly, the Langda villagers do not commonly use other stone tools in their daily activities. The exception is a small, flat knife ground from slate or some softer stone. Villagers use these knives—which come in oval, kidney or subtriangular form—to cut off the leaves and stem from a taro root, scrape the outer surface clean and then split the root for cooking. They also use the knives to split the long leaves from which women's skirts are made. For other purposes, however, organic materials work better. We saw men butchering pigs, for example, with razor-sharp pieces of split bamboo. One resharpens such a tool by simply tearing off a strip of bamboo with the thumbnail or teeth. The serviceability of bamboo has been invoked to explain the simplicity of stone tools in East Asian sites that were inhabited by protohumans for many hundreds of thousands of years.

The Langda ax makers provide many other interesting insights to the archaeologist. They show how horticulturalists use stone tools in a natural and economically sensible context. The by-products of their labor, at each of the three stages of manufacture, may mirror patterns preserved in the archaeological record. Finally, the ax makers are of intense archaeological interest because various stages of their ax manufacture appear to recapitulate the evolution of stone technology.

The first stage—quarrying flake blanks from boulder cores—strikingly recalls the manufacturer of the Acheulean hand axes and cleavers of the Early Stone Age. Acheulean technology was invented by *Homo erectus* some 1.7 million years ago, and it continued unchanged into the age of archaic *H. sapiens* some 200,000 years ago [see "The First Technology," by Nicholas Toth; SCIENTIST AMERICAN, April 1987]. The second stage is recapitulated in the Langda villagers' roughouts, which resemble the so-called Sangoan and Lupemban core axes of the Middle Stone Age of Equatorial Africa. Unhafted Sangoan tools are believed to have been used to work wood in tropical Africa between 200,000 and 100,000 years ago. The third stage of ground and hafted axes corresponds almost perfectly to the axes associated with early farming communities in both the Old and New World.

The earliest evidence of ground stone axes comes, however, from sites in New Guinea and Australia that date to more than 20,000 years ago. Still, such tools do not appear frequently in the archaeological record until after the rise of farming communities some 10,000 years ago. The Langda axes are clearly one of the last remnants of this Stone Age tradition.

We do not wish to create the impression, however, that any ethnoarchaeological study that might have been undertaken in modern times could have revealed all the secrets of Early Stone Age technological culture. The Kim-Yal, unlike some of those earlier inventors, are anatomically modern humans possessed of language systems and cultures as complex as anyone else's today. Their modes of operation are almost certainly much more complex than those of protohuman toolmakers.

We suspect, for example, that the Kim-Yal's tendency to "pity" the ax that has outlived its usefulness would not have been seen in many archaic hominids that could probably have mastered the ax-making craft. Anthropologists caution that one should not confuse similarity of performance with identity of mind. One could easily teach modern hunter-gatherers how to fly and land a Boeing 747 airliner. But such might not be the case for an *H. erectus* a million years ago, even one that had been adopted at birth into modern society.

One can try to reconstruct the earliest stone technology in other ways. Experimental archaeologists make and use stone tools with materials and methods that were available to prehistoric people. Primatologists study tool use among chimpanzees in the wild. Recently the two lines of inquiry converged in a fascinating experiment at the Language Research Center in Atlanta, operated by Georgia State University and the Yerkes Regional Primate Research Center.

There Susan Savage-Rumbaugh, Duane Rumbaugh and Rose A. Sevcik collaborated with one of us (Toth) and Toth's co-worker, Kathy Schick, in teaching stonecraft to a bonobo, or pygmy chimpanzee. The bonobo, named Kanzi, has demonstrated the ability to grasp the most basic skills required to detach flakes from stones and to use the flakes as cutting tools and has even taught himself new skills—such as breaking up big stones by throwing them on a tiled floor. Ongoing research also seeks to discover whether Kanzi can impart tool making knowledge to other bonobos. Such studies may help workers estimate the limits bounding toolmaking among modern humans, nonhuman primates and protohuman populations.

How much longer will stone ax manufacture and its complex exchange network continue? It is likely that the network will disappear in a few short years as stores providing metal tools are introduced in the highlands and mountains and a cash economy replaces the traditional system of barter. Given that none of the younger members of the tribe is currently apprenticed in this craft, it is likely that most of this skilled ax-making technology will be lost within one or two generations.

We have felt privileged to visit and learn from these friendly peoples, to examine their stone ax exchange system, to observe the relationships between technological processes and their products, and to describe this technology from an archaeological perspective. We hope these observations will provide information that archaeologists will be able to draw on when attempting to decipher the Stone Age past.

Further Reading

EXPLORATION IN ETHNOARHAEOLOGY. Edited by Richard A. Gould. The School of American Research, University of New Mexico Press, 1978.

A PREHISTORY OF AUSTRALIA, NEW GUINEA AND SAHUL. J. Peter White and James F. O'Connell. Academic Press, 1983.

QUARRYING IN A TRIBAL SOCIETY. John Burton in *World Archaeology*, Vol. 16, No. 2, pages 234–247; October 1984.

INDONESIA: LA GRANDE DERIVA ETNICA. Edited by Gilda M. Ronzoni. Erizzo Editrice, 1986.

THE FIRST TECHNOLOGY. Nicholas Toth in *Scientific American*, Vol. 256, No. 4, pages 112–121; April 1987.

2

Ethnoarchaeology at the Top of the World: New Ceramic Studies Among the Kalinga of Luzon

William A. Longacre, James M. Skibo,
and Miriam T. Stark

I. History of the Project

The Kalinga are a tribal society inhabiting the high mountains of Luzon in the northern Philippines. Here, on ridges and in valleys overlooking swift flowing rivers, they make their living by growing rice in irrigated, terraced fields. Why, in 1973, did a Southwestern archaeologist leave his dig in Arizona and travel some 10,000 miles to live with and learn from these people? The answer lies in the theoretical climate of the day.

The Kalinga Ethnoarchaeological Project was forged during the era of the "New Archaeology." Reacting against traditional archaeological approaches, proponents of the New Archaeology emphasized explanation over description. One of their aims was to develop the means to infer aspects of past societies that are difficult or impossible to excavate, such as social organization and certain behaviors of interest to the archaeologist. New Archaeologists frequently used excavated pottery in making their inferences. Could the abundant pottery the Kalinga still make and use in their daily lives hold a key? We thought it could.

Over the 18 years that have passed since the Project began, the face of archaeology has changed dramatically. So, too, have the goals of the Project, now encompassing concerns about the formation of the archaeological record, performance characteristics of pottery, experimental studies, production and distribution of pottery, and much more. Reviewing those changes in historical context provides a look at the changing nature of archaeology itself.

Selecting an Appropriate Society

Why did we choose the Kalinga? In one of the first case studies of the "New Archaeology," the senior author analyzed the distribution of painted pottery decoration at a prehistoric Pueblo ruin in Arizona called the Carter Ranch Site (Longacre 1970). In that study, he argued that certain aspects of social organization could be inferred through such a distributional study. If pots are made by women, as they are in nearly every known case where pottery is made for domestic consumption, then subtle styles of decoration might develop that reflect the learning of pottery making from one's mother. And if that is so, then micro-traditions of pottery decoration might reflect the making of pots by a group of related women—sisters, for example.

Some societies favor the husband leaving his natal home at the time of marriage and moving in with his wife's family. If that were the rule at the Carter Ranch Pueblo during prehistoric times, then clusters of decorated pottery should be found in architecturally defined groups of rooms. Although Longacre's study found a correlation between pottery designs and architectural units, by 1973 serious doubts were raised about that study and others like it. Concern was expressed about whether or not micro-traditions reflected learning frameworks in such a society.

Also, the study of prehistoric pottery did not unravel factors (other than kinship) that affected the distribution of the pottery as it was excavated from the prehistoric village. Some of these factors include where the pottery was produced, how the pottery was used, and how the pottery was affected by environmental processes after the village was abandoned. It had been assumed in the original study that the distribution reflected directly the locus of use and production of the pots themselves.

It was clear that the only place where one could begin to address such concerns was not in the archaeological record, but among a living society. The problem was to find an appropriate society with which to work. Ideally, it should be a group that makes and uses pots on a household basis. That is, each household makes pots for its own use and not for sale in a market. It should also be a culture whose customs and traditions had already been studied by cultural anthropologists (e.g., Barton 1949; Dozier 1966, 1967; Scott 1958, 1960; Takaki 1977, 1984), providing a foundation for ethnoarchaeological research. Finding such a society was difficult in the modern world. At the time, the Kalinga, a tribal society living in the rugged mountains of north central Luzon in the Philippines, seemed the most likely candidate. An initial trip was made to the Kalinga-Apayao province in 1973 to ascertain if the people still made pots on a household basis and to seek their permission to undertake a long-term study if such were the case (Longacre 1974).

The Kalinga Ethnoarchaeological Project focused its efforts on villages within the Pasil municipality (Fig. 1). The village of Dangtalan was the first place visited. Pottery was in use everywhere: the Kalinga used pottery vessels to cook their rice and their vegetables and meat, as well as to carry and store water from the spring and even to brew *bayas*, a sugar cane wine. Women made the pots and learned how to do it from their mothers, and virtually every household made its own pottery. This seemed the perfect place for the envisioned study.

After getting to know the senior author over a week and hearing about the planned research, the Kalinga agreed to let him return for a year-long study, and that was carried out during 1975-1976 (Longacre 1981). The main objective was

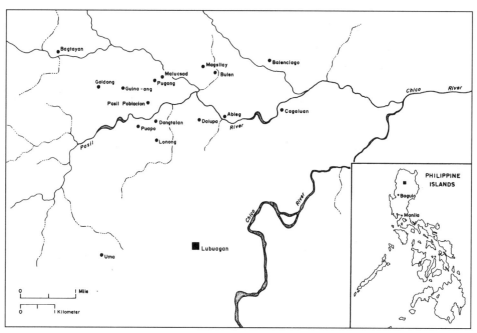

Figure 1. Villages studied during the Kalinga Ethnoarchaeological Project all fall within the political boundaries of the Pasil municipality, whose borders largely coincide with the Pasil River drainage system. Ethnoarchaeological research has been conducted in 7 of the municipality's 13 communities. (Graphic by Brigid Sullivan)

to collect information (and pots) that reflected the learning frameworks in order to test some of the ideas generated in the Carter Ranch study. During the course of the field work it became apparent that the Kalinga potters tended to work in informal groups based upon neighborhoods, so data and pots from particular work groups were also collected to measure the impact of potting together. In addition, information on ceramic decorative style was collected for each Dangtalan potter.

Virtually all Dangtalan pots are decorated with incised designs that are known as *gili* around the vessel neck (Fig. 2a, b). The number of *gili* bands on a particular vessel ranges from one to four or more. Many *gili* designs have names, and bands may be combined in a variety of patterns. After the Kalinga field work was completed and a large collection of pots made, analysis of the *gili* decoration was undertaken by Michael Graves as part of his dissertation research (Graves 1981). Combinations of *gili* designs were analyzed using multivariate techniques to see whether micro-traditions reflected the Kalinga potter's learning frameworks, as had been hypothesized. Graves found only weak support for that hypothesis, but discovered a strong link between the age of the potter and the degree of complexity of decoration: the older potters tended to make far more complex decorations than their younger counterparts.

Figure 2. This vessel is undergoing the final stages of decoration after it has been incised below the rim with a bamboo stylus (*gili*). (Photo by Miriam T. Stark)

New Research Goals

By 1975, new concerns and questions were being raised about the "formation processes" responsible for the archaeological record. What types of processes transform artifacts after they are discarded within a living system and before archaeologists excavate the artifacts centuries or millennia later? The Kalinga setting offered an appropriate research venue for investigating such issues, and they were added to the research plan that guided the field work that year.

One of the new concerns involved the general question of how long items last before they are discarded. Thus, the use-life of different types of pots among the Kalinga became of interest. But how could we measure the use-life of pottery? In 1975 and 1976, all the pots in use in two Kalinga villages, Dangtalan and Dalupa, were inventoried. The type of pot, the name of the potter, and the year the pot was made were recorded for each household; in all, data on over 2,000 pots in use were collected.

By 1980, political turmoil caused by Kalinga resistance to a government-sponsored hydroelectric project made the Kalinga area too dangerous to continue the study. In 1979 and 1980, the senior author's principal Kalinga assistants re-inventoried each household. New and replacement pots were added to the inventory, and information about each pot missing from the original inventory was collected. Many of these vessels had been broken or had simply worn out, and the dates of their departure from the ceramic assemblage were noted.

This information formed the basis for detailed estimates of the use-life of the various types of Kalinga pots (Longacre 1985). A general principle emerged that seems to hold true for other pottery-using societies as well: the large pots last longer than do the smaller-sized vessels in regular use. This principle has important implications for the prehistorian trying to draw chronological inferences from pieces of pottery recovered from an archaeological site. The archaeologist has a better chance of defining chronological differences by focusing upon the pieces from the smaller pots. Smaller pots likely broke more often and required replacement more frequently, promoting faster stylistic change, change that could be observed archaeologically.

Return to the Kalinga

By 1986, problems in the Kalinga subprovince had subsided and conditions were sufficiently peaceful to resume the project. A major ethno-archaeological project was planned, and in the summer of 1987 the senior author, along with six University of Arizona graduate students and several more from the University of the Philippines, began 12 months of field work.

By the late 1980s archaeology had changed a great deal, and the new research plans reflected some of those changes. But the main theme continued to be the investigation of the relationships between variation in material culture and variation in behavior and organization. Some of the questions that guided the earlier research continued to be addressed. Thus, collecting data and pots from younger potters was planned to test the Graves hypothesis, that design complexity was decreasing among the younger Dangtalan potters. We also planned to continue the detailed inventory to pursue the use-life study.

Of course, over the years the Kalinga had been changing as well. The entry of government forces and of commercial mining and logging interests introduced outsiders to Kalingas and brought various forms of progress. In addition, Dangtalan ceased to be a major pottery-producing community for the Pasil municipality. By 1987 few potters were active there. Instead, Dalupa had become the center for pottery making in the Pasil River Valley, and a great deal of experimentation was evident. New decorative styles had appeared, and a variety of nontraditional ceramic forms were being made.

A number of new studies were undertaken by the 1987–1988 Kalinga Ethnoarchaeological Project. The first ethnoarchaeological study of basketry was undertaken. Kalinga baskets are made by men; thus this research formed a parallel study to that of the pottery produced by women. Additional studies focused on vessel breakage, refuse disposal behaviors, ceramic production and distribution, and ceramic use-alteration. Still other projects focused upon the material correlates of wealth and status and the ecology of irrigation rice agriculture.

II. The Kalinga Ceramic Studies

Here, we present the results of only a few of the timely and interesting studies conducted by the Kalinga Ethnoarchaeological Project: ceramic production and distribution, and pottery use-alteration. Two other studies are summarized briefly in boxes accompanying the text: a study of technological change and a study of the development of a new decorative ceramic tradition.

Ceramic Production and Distribution

One hallmark of "Neolithic" communities that archaeologists study worldwide has been pottery making. Pottery is ubiquitous in the archaeological record and constitutes one indicator of prehistoric economy. Many archaeologists believe that economic factors are vital in the emergence of prehistoric states. Examining how the organization of pottery production is related to social and political aspects of prehistoric societies, then, sheds light on broader archaeological issues, such as the nature and development of social complexity.

Pottery-making systems worldwide vary greatly in their organization and scale. At one end of the continuum lie those tribal societies in which pottery is produced at the household level for household use. At the other end of the continuum are large-scale ceramic industries, such as the Wedgwood manufactories of 18th century England. This continuum in the organization of ceramic production is also present in the archaeological record, where pottery making among simple agriculturalists stands in stark contrast to ceramic production in the state-controlled craft industries of early Mesoamerican and Mesopotamian civilizations.

The Kalinga Case Study

Within the Kalinga-Apayao province, the Kalinga section has been divided into eight municipalities that roughly coincide with the valleys that encase major rivers and tributaries. That pottery making—and the pots themselves—continues to be an integral part of Kalinga life is evidenced by the fact that pottery-making centers were to be found in each of these municipalities during the 1980s

The Switch to Metal Pots: A Case Study of Technological Change

A unique feature of the archaeological record is that it can document long-term change. But what are the factors that govern technological change and how do alterations in material items relate to other aspects of society? These questions, though important to archaeologists, cannot be answered by looking at the prehistoric record alone; the process of technological change must be addressed through research such as experimental archaeology and ethnoarchaeology. As part of the pottery use-alteration study, information was collected on one component of change in Kalinga society: the replacement of ceramic with metal cooking pots.

Nearly all households in the village of Guina-ang have enough metal pots for all their cooking needs, but ceramic vessels are still widely used. Metal pots are used most frequently for cooking rice, but ceramic vessels are still used for cooking vegetables and meat. Interviews with Kalinga pottery users, as well as laboratory experiments, demonstrated that the performance of the two types of pots is important in the transition from ceramic to metal vessels. Pots, or any technology, can have performance characteristics that relate to the actual use of the pot as a tool (i.e., techno-functions), but also social or ideological functions.

Metal pots are now used to cook rice because they boil the rice faster and are more durable. Ceramic vessels are still used for cooking vegetables and meat because the food can boil without boiling over, and they are easier to wash than metal vessels. Durability and heating properties of the vessels relate to techno-functions, but ease of washing is a performance characteristic that relates to non-techno-functional factors. Metal pots are more difficult to wash because the Kalinga insist upon making them shine by removing all of the soot that adheres to and has penetrated the metal surface. Wealthier households have more metal vessels, and they appear to be a sign of modernization. Metal pots of all sizes are usually stored in conspicuous locations, whereas ceramic vessels are often stored out of sight.

Thus, it was found that the performance characteristics important in the transition from ceramic to metal vessels relate primarily to techno-functions but that social functions also play a role.

(Fig. 3). Even the provincial capital of Tabuk, where many homes have electricity and running water, contained at least three pottery-making neighborhoods, where emigrant potters from rural areas have continued to make and sell their products.

The Kalinga Ethnoarchaeological Project focused its research on several communities along the Pasil River. These villages were initially selected for study because pottery making there represented a traditional, small-scale industry in which pots were produced and used primarily for the potters' own households. During the Project's most recent field study, two villages were engaged in production of earthenware goods and formed the focus of research on ceramic production and distribution: Dalupa and Dangtalan.

Kalinga pottery making is a combination of coil-and-scrape manufacture, which yields the initial shape of the vessel, and paddle-and-anvil techniques, which produce the final shape of the even globular vessel bodies (Fig. 4). Although the initial vessel-forming sequence lasts just 15–25 minutes, the entire pottery-making process involves clay preparation, vessel forming, drying, and firing. An active Kalinga potter can finish between 10 and 15 vessels in a week; this

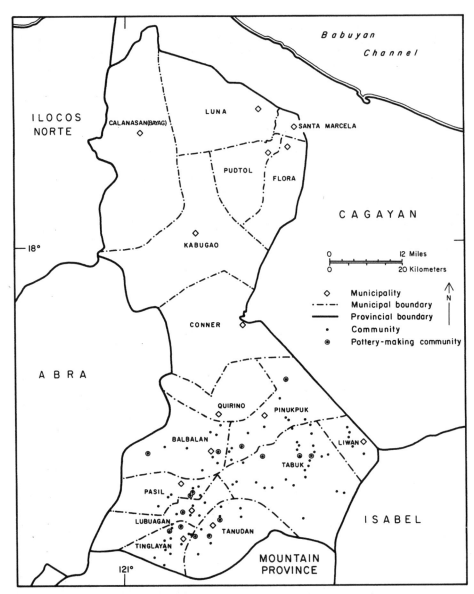

Figure 3. Because archaeologists frequently analyze the distribution of particular ceramic types, understanding the relationship between Kalinga ceramic production and distribution provides a comparison with archaeological cases. In the Kalinga area of Kalinga-Apayao province, each municipality (or river valley) contains one or several pottery production centers that service the needs of the surrounding population. Population density, topographic relief, and the reliance on non-ceramic alternatives all help to determine the placement of Kalinga pottery production centers, as seen in this illustration. (Graphic by Ronald Beckwith)

Figure 4. A woman fabricating a ceramic vessel. (Photo by Miriam T. Stark)

Figure 5. Group of women sitting with ceramic vessels in the village of Dalupa. The vessels will be given as gifts to their neighbors. (Photo by Miriam T. Stark)

number varies according to other household and farming demands that the potter may confront, including childcare and cooking, along with rice farming activities such as transplanting, weeding, or harvesting.

An Historical Perspective on Kalinga Pottery Making

Changes in the location and activity levels of pottery-making villages can be seen at the regional and local levels. Three decades ago, villages to the east (Cagalwan) and west (Balatoc) of Dalupa and Dangtalan also made and traded pots. In the last 20 years, several changes in the local environment and economic structure have discouraged pottery production in areas where alternative modes of subsistence can be pursued. These changes include the reactivation of gold mines, the establishment of major logging operations and subsequent deforestation of neighboring areas, and the developing importance of coffee as a cash crop for villages having access to suitable crop land. Dalupa and Dangtalan, then, have only recently emerged as the only pottery-making centers for the Pasil River Valley.

Changes have also been observed in the communities of Dalupa and Dangtalan during the 16-year history of the Kalinga Ethnoarchaeological Project. What was once a thriving pottery industry in Dangtalan has now become a sporadic practice, while Dalupa potters have accelerated their activity since the early 1980s. One goal of the 1987–1988 research was to document this change in Dalupa from household production to a household industry.

The Development of Part-time Craft Specialization

Upon the Kalinga Ethnoarchaeological Project's return in 1988 it was no small surprise to find that the organization of Kalinga pottery production had undergone major changes. At least half of the Dangtalan potters had virtually ceased to make pottery at all, while their Dalupa neighbors had joined the potter ranks in full force. Dalupa potters had become semi-specialists, and the organization of production had shifted from production for household consumption to pottery making for exchange (Stark 1991).

Changes in pottery production can first be examined from an ethnographic perspective. Through the ethnographic lens, household and village-level economic structures can be compared and contrasted. Labor outputs by family members, as well as the number of household members to support, can be assessed. Regarding the potters themselves, rates of pottery production and of exchange may be recorded and correlated with patterns of household affluence. Analysis is currently underway regarding the scale of pottery production and exchange, using this holistic approach.

Taken as a whole, the ethnographic data reveal that the development of Dalupa pottery specialization may be largely explained through diminishing resources, insufficient rice field landholdings, and a population boom, all of which have collectively strained the ability of Dalupa households to sustain themselves. Pottery production for exchange in nearby communities and farflung villages garners rice to feed family members, as well as clothing, lumber to construct new homes, and, occasionally, cash that pays for children's educational fees while attending high school or college in the provincial capital of Tabuk.

Changes in Kalinga ceramic production can be examined through an archaeological perspective as well by focusing on Kalinga material culture. Previously mentioned influences include the reactivation of gold mines and the establishment of logging companies in the area. Perhaps the most profound impact on the general Pasil area occurred as a result of the Marcos government's efforts regarding the Chico River Dam Project. Governmental employees were unsuccessful in their efforts to woo the Kalinga into accepting the hydroelectric project that would displace 10,000 Kalingas from their land to provide electricity for Cagayan Valley residents living 40 miles to the northeast. Massive resistance to the project by the Kalinga and the neighboring Bontoc groups prevailed, and the project was cancelled.

During this period, however, non-Kalinga customs and values were introduced that had an impact on traditional lifeways. Governmental employees (including the military) sought Dalupa ceramic "souvenirs"; figurines and religious plaques were developed that have now become a standard part of the Dalupa potter's repertoire. One means by which the Marcos government attempted to curry favor with the Kalingas was through the establishment of centralized workshops to promote and revitalize traditional crafts such as backstrap-loom weaving. Interaction between Dalupa potters and weavers in the center of Lubuagan during the Chico River Project encouraged Dalupa potters to modify both the shape and the decoration of their water jars (*immosso*). Dalupa-produced water jars now sport festive ocher decorations of floral motifs, geometric designs, and an occasional anthropomorphic depiction.

Pottery Use-Alteration

Since the work of the Russian archaeologist Semenov (1964) was introduced to the west, lithic use-wear analysis has become common-place. From the polish and microchips on the edges of stone tools archaeologists are now able to infer how a tool was actually used. Though it has been several decades since the first lithic use-wear analyses, comparable studies with pottery have not been done. This is not for lack of need. Ceramic data are often employed to determine things such as prehistoric exchange patterns, diet, population size, and social organization. Many of these inferences rely on a fundamental but often unresolved question: How was pottery used?

Accurate estimates about household size from pottery, for example, require that one can determine which pots were used for daily cooking, water storage, and serving, and which pots were not in use. Similarly, before one can determine that a type of pottery was controlled and distributed by elites in an elaborate exchange network, it is necessary to understand the way pottery functioned in everyday life. Nearly all inferences about past society that employ pottery must rely ultimately on assumptions about how the pottery functioned. The purpose of this component of the Kalinga Ethnoarchaeological Project is to link pottery use with alterations to the vessel. This will help prehistorians determine how pottery was used in the past.

The data for this project were collected from March through May 1988 in the Kalinga village of Guina-ang; Masashi Kobayashi was the co-director of the pottery use-alteration study. Guina-ang is across the river and about an hour's walk from Dangtalan. It is the largest village in the Pasil Valley and is thought to be the oldest. Guina-ang consists of slightly over 100 houses that cluster atop a ridge overlooking the Pasil river.

The data for the pottery use-alteration study were collected in two phases. The first phase involved inventorying all the vessels in the 102 households. This information was collected by Kalinga assistants and it included not only data about each pot, such as the age, the dimensions, and the maker of the pot, but also information about pottery use. For all 2481 vessels in the village of Guina-ang we know things such as what each pot is used for, when it was last used, whether it is ever used to cook other foods, and some basic information about use-alteration traces.

The second phase of data collection involved day-long observations of pottery use. In 40 households the use of pottery was carefully documented from before the first meal until after the final meal of the day. Any activity that involved pottery, such as cooking, cleaning, and storing, was recorded. In these households new vessels were exchanged for the old ones in order to create a use-alteration study collection of about 200 vessels. These vessels were wrapped carefully to avoid further alterations to the surfaces and then shipped to Tucson where they now reside in the Arizona State Museum.

The analysis of pottery use-alteration concentrated on three lines of evidence: absorbed residues, attrition, and carbon deposition. The analysis focused on the two forms of Kalinga cooking pots (Fig. 2a, b): *ittoyom*, used to cook rice, and *oppaya*, used to cook vegetables and meat. The rice and vegetable/meat pots provide a good contrast because they are used to cook different foods, and there are a different set of activities associated with each vessel type.

The analysis of absorbed residues concentrated on fatty acids. All plant and animal species have different combinations of fatty acids, which can, potentially,

New Kalinga Ceramic Traditions

Early ethnoarchaeological research indicated that Kalinga pottery was made for use within the potter's own household, and that pottery making occupied the slack periods in the farming cycle. Potters produced a narrow range of items to be used in daily activities: cooking pots (*oppaya, ittoyom*), water jars (*immosso*), pot lids (*sukong*), and basins used for feeding domestic animals (*kannogan*). When the Kalinga Ethnoarchaeological Project resumed field work in 1987 a metamorphosis had occurred in pottery production. Activity in Dalupa had escalated in the late 1970s as the village emerged as the heartland of ceramic innovation. Once uniformly red water jars (*immosso*) now sported festive incised and painted decorations and pronounced shoulders, while a dazzling array of non-traditional forms appeared in the Dalupa potter's repertoire.

A wide range of decorative items were now in demand, from flower pots and religious plaques to money banks in the shape of water buffalos. To the Kalinga, these non-traditional forms are known as ay-ayam or toys. Ay-ayam are the embodiment of individual creativity and provide a needed source of cash. Ideas for new designs are found in elementary school textbooks, the rare Manila magazine that winds its way into the remote Kalinga highlands, and in orders placed by customers for flower vases and plaques emblazoned with the words "God Bless Our Home."

Explaining why this new ceramic tradition developed requires attention to political, ecological, and economic processes during the late 1970s and early 1980s. The failed Chico River Dam Project brought non-Kalingas into the region with non-Kalinga values and a desire for "souvenirs." Regular motor transport was also begun that made travel between communities easier and encouraged Dalupa potters to expand their regional exchange network and diversify their products. Wage labor trickled into the traditional barter economy through the reactivation of gold mines and dam-related construction efforts. The introduction of new ideas and values, the access to motor transport, and the availability of cash in the Kalinga economy all contributed to the development of the Dalupa ay-ayam tradition.

Fascinating as the birth of the ay-ayam tradition may be, its future is equally intriguing for anthropologists. Increasing contact between the industrial world and tribal societies often stimulates the development of ethnic and tourist art forms. Carved Eskimo ivory, North American Pueblo pottery, and African wood carvings have all found a firm niche in an international ethnic art market. Is the Kalinga ay-ayam tradition a passing fancy or a nascent ethnic art tradition? Kalingas often express a desire for "progress," and such progress means improved transportation, increased wage labor opportunities, better health care, and population increases. With "progress" will come rapid culture change, and this change will in part be reflected in the Kalinga ceramic traditions. How, and in what ways, Kalinga ceramic traditions will change can only be examined with the long-term approach that characterizes the Kalinga Ethnoarchaeological Project. As archaeologists, we concern ourselves with the past; as ethnoarchaeologists, we also look toward the future.

survive long periods in the depositional environment. Fatty acids were extracted from a sample of vessels and a set of Kalinga foods and then identified with gas chromatography/mass spectrometry. The results demonstrated that fatty acids can be used to discriminate pots used to cook different items. The residue absorbed into the vessel wall of the rice cooking pots could be clearly linked to rice. Although the vegetable/meat cooking pots were more problematic because they were used to cook a variety of foods (e.g., chicken, pork, dog, and various forms of garden-grown vegetables and wild plants), the residue analysis did determine that a variety of both plant and animal foods were prepared in the vessels.

To determine how well the fatty acids survive in the depositional environment, a sample of sherds excavated from a Kalinga midden were also analyzed. Fatty acids were still present in the walls of the sherds but there was some evidence of fatty acid decomposition. Research in this area is ongoing.

Attrition to the vessel surfaces as a result of use is also an instructive trace. There are nine areas on the Kalinga cooking pots that have evidence of distinct activities, such as stirring, methods of heating the contents, and washing. The use-attrition traces were identified with the help of low-power optical and scanning electron microscopy. It was found that the exterior surfaces of the rice and vegetable/meat cooking pots have similar use-attrition patterns, but that the interiors have distinct use traces that reflect different cooking activities. For example, the vegetable/meat cooking pots have evidence of stirring and manipulation of the contents during cooking, but the rice cooking vessels do not. Moreover the rice cooking pots have thermal spalls on the interior midsection suggesting that they were placed next to the fire. The attritional data are so patterned that it is even possible to identify the pottery users in the community that are lefthanded.

The final form of use-alteration analyzed in this study is interior and exterior carbon deposits. Interior patches of carbonized food provide information on what the food was and how it was cooked. Exterior carbon, or soot, can demonstrate how the vessel was positioned over the fire. The rice and vegetable/meat cooking pots have different patterns of carbon deposition that represent different ways of cooking. For example, the rice cooking pots often have a carbonized patch on the interior mid-section from being placed next to the fire in the final stage of rice cooking. The Kalinga pots offered firsthand evidence of pottery carbon deposition, and this has led to a more complete description of the factors that control both interior and exterior carbon formation.

This is the first ethnoarchaeological study to concentrate exclusively on pottery use-alteration. It was demonstrated that all three forms of use-alteration—residues, carbon deposits and surface attrition—do reflect pottery use activities. The rice and vegetable/meat pots could be discriminated based on all three forms of use-alteration traces (Skibo 1992). This has led to a more general discussion of the factors that control the ways in which pottery can reflect activities. The ultimate objective of this research was to provide the means for the prehistorian to make more refined inferences about pottery use. This component of the Kalinga Project demonstrates that patterned activities of pottery use alter the vessels in ways that can be interpreted by the archaeologist, leading to better inferences of pottery use and therefore to more accurate reconstructions of the past.

III. Conclusions

Change is a unifying theme in the history of the Kalinga Ethnoarchaeological Project. During the last 18 years, much has changed in both the types of research topics pursued on this project, and in the nature of Kalinga society. The project was initiated in the 1970s as an attempt to explore ceramic styles and residence, but has been sensitive to changing trends in archaeology. Research within the Kalinga project today ranges in focus from pottery use-life, use-alteration, and refuse disposal to regional studies of ceramic production and distribution. One of the major strengths of the Kalinga Project lies in its efforts to integrate experimental, ethnoarchaeological, and archaeological approaches to ceramic analysis. The other strength is its long-term perspective, enabling us to track material culture change, a uniquely archaeological concern. Kalinga research continues, and the next two decades promise to provide even greater contributions for archaeologists.

Bibliography

Barton, Roy F. 1949. *The Kalingas, Their Institutions and Custom Law*. Chicago: University of Chicago Press.

Dozier, Edward P. 1966. *Mountain Arbiters: The Changing Life of a Philippine Hill People*. Tucson: University of Arizona Press.

—— 1967. *The Kalinga of Northern Luzon, Philippines*. New York: Holt, Rinehart and Winston.

Graves, Michael W. 1981. *Ethnoarchaeology of Kalinga Ceramic Design*. Ph.D. dissertation, University of Arizona. Ann Arbor: University Microfilms, Inc.

—— 1985. "Ceramic Design Variation Within a Kalinga Village: Temporal and Spatial Processes." In *Decoding Prehistoric Ceramics*, ed. B. A. Nelson, pp. 9–34. Carbondale: Southern Illinois University Press.

Lawless, Robert 1977. "Societal Ecology in Northern Luzon: Kalinga Agriculture, Organization, Population, and Change." *Papers in Anthropology* 18(1):1–36.

Longacre, William A. 1970. *Archaeology as Anthropology: A Case Study*. University of Arizona Papers 17. Tucson: University of Arizona Press.

—— 1974. "Kalinga Pottery-Making: The Evolution of a Research Design." In *Frontiers of Anthropology*, ed. Murray J. Leaf, pp. 151–159. New York: D. Van Nostrand Company.

—— 1981. "Kalinga Pottery: An Ethnoarchaeological Study." In *Essays in Honor of David Clarke*, ed. I. Hodder, G. Isaac, and N. Hammond, pp. 49–66. Cambridge: Cambridge University Press.

—— 1985. "Pottery Use-Life Among the Kalinga, Northern Luzon, the Philippine:" In *Decoding Prehistoric Ceramics*, ed. B. A. Nelson, pp. 334–346. Carbondale: Southern Illinois University Press.

Longacre, William A., ed. 1991. *Ceramic Ethnoarchaeology*. Tucson: University of Arizona Press.

Longacre, William A., Kenneth Kvamme, and Masashi Kobayashi 1986. "Southwestern Pottery Standardization: An Ethnoarchaeological View from the Philippines." *The Kiva* (53)2:101–112.

Scott, William Henry 1958. "Economic and Material Culture of the Kalingas of Madukayan." *Southwestern Journal of Anthropology* 14(3):318–337.

—— 1960. "Social and Religious Culture of the Kalingas of Madukayan." *Southwestern Journal of Anthropology* 16(2):174–190.

Semenov, Sergei A. 1964. *Prehistoric Technology*. Trans. M. W. Thompson. London: Cory, Adams and Mackey.

Skibo, James M. 1992. *Pottery Use-alteration: An Ethnoarchaeological and Experimental Approach*. New York: Plenum Publishing.

Stark, Miriam T. 1991. "Ceramic Production and Community Specialization: A Kalinga Ethnoarchaeological Study." *World Archaeology* 23(1):64–78.

Takaki, Michiko 1977. *Aspects of Exchange in a Kalinga Society, Northern Luzon.*
Ph.D. dissertation, Yale University.
————— 1984. "Regional Names in Kalinga: Certain Social Dimensions of Place
Names." In *Naming Systems: 1980 Proceedings of the American Ethnological
Society*, ed. Elisabeth Tooker, pp. 55–77. Washington: The American Ethnolog-
ical Society.

3

Understanding The Past Through Hopi Oral History

Kurt Dongoske, Leigh Jenkins, and T.J. Ferguson

Out of respect for their ancestors, and a desire to know about their past, the Hopis want to collaborate with archaeologists in contemporary research conducted at their ancestral sites. It is the position of the Hopi Tribe that in order to perform a thorough archaeological investigation and interpretation, it is essential that research be conducted in conjunction with the living descendants of the people who created the archaeological sites.

The Hopis want to be treated as peers in archaeological research projects, so that their knowledge, values, and beliefs are regarded with the same respect that archaeologists afford one another when there are differences in research methods and interpretation of the archaeological record. The Hopis do not, however, want to indiscriminately superimpose their sacred knowledge on the archaeological record or to unfairly constrain archaeological interpretation. They have no desire to censor the ideas of archaeologists, nor do they wish to impose research designs on archaeologists.

Archaeological research concerns the Hopis particularly when their ancestors are the subject of that research. The findings of archaeologists are important and have real impact on how the Hopis perceive themselves. The destruction of archaeological sites by construction projects and land development, or by scientific excavation, is of great concern to the Hopis, in part because the record established by their ancestors is obliterated. Hopi participation in archaeological research will help ensure that Hopi perspectives and concepts are incorporated in the written record that will remain after archaeological sites are destroyed. Inclusion of the Hopi information and interpretation in the written history of an archaeological site will help offset the losses that occur with the destruction of a site created by Hopi ancestors.

The migrations of the Hopi people throughout the western United States and northern Mexico are marked by numerous archaeological sites.

The Hopis emerged into this, the Fourth World, from the Sipapuni, a limestone cone located in the gorge of the Little Colorado River near the Grand Canyon. Upon emerging, they encountered *Ma'saw*, the guardian of the Fourth World. A spiritual pact was made with Ma'saw, wherein the Hopis would act as stewards of the world. As a part of this pact, the Hopis vowed to place their footprints throughout the lands of the Fourth World as they migrated in a spiritual quest to find their destiny at the center of the universe. Hopi clans embarked on a lengthy series of migrations that led them throughout the Southwest and beyond, settling for a time in various places. Eventually, their priests would receive omens and

Figure 1. Wilcox Kooyahoema, Victor Masayesva, Robert Sakiestewa, and Leigh Kuwan-wisiwma discuss Hopi history at an ancestral archaeological site at Nankoweap during research in the Grand Canyon. (Photo by T. J. Ferguson, October 8, 1994)

spiritual signs, either through some supernatural phenomenon, or a natural event like a pestilence or earthquake, that directed the people to continue their migrations. After many generations, the Hopis finally arrived at their rightful place on the Hopi Mesas.

During the migrations, the Hopi people established themselves throughout the land by cultivating and caring for the earth. As directed by Ma'saw, the setting of Hopi "footprints" included the establishment of ritual springs, sacred trails, trail markers, shrines, and petroglyphs. As the Hopi people moved on to new areas, they left behind ruins, potsherds, and other physical evidence that they had vested the area with their spiritual stewardship and fulfilled their pact with Ma'saw. From the Hopi perspective, these archaeological sites provide physical evidence verifying Hopi clan histories and religious beliefs.

The Hopi believe that these archaeological sites were not abandoned by their prehistoric ancestors, but rather are places with which the Hopi people retain a strong emotional and ancestral affiliation. The Hopi people believe that their ancestors who were laid to rest at these archaeological sites were intended to—and continue to—maintain a spiritual guardianship over those places. Many of the sites continue to be referred to specifically by the Hopi during the recounting of particular clan histories by clan elders within the ceremonial rooms known as kivas.

A very large archaeological excavation project is currently underway in the Tonto Basin of central Arizona. The Hopi Tribe claims cultural and ancestral affiliation to the prehistoric culture in the Tonto Basin, as established in Hopi clan oral migration histories. The Hopi clans of Water, Snake, Tobacco, Reed, Grease-wood, Sun, Sand, Badger, and Corn have oral histories of having once resided within the area of the Tonto Basin as part of their divinely directed spiritual migrations.

Because of this cultural and ancestral affiliation, representatives of the Hopi Tribe and archaeologists from Arizona State University's project in the Tonto Basin have begun to meet to discuss issues of mutual interest. Jointly, they are seeking to bring together information from all sources to better understand the past in the Tonto Basin. The Hopi Tribe and Arizona State University are in the process of developing a research proposal which will address the integration of Hopi clan history and knowledge concerning the prehistoric inhabitants of the Tonto Basin with the findings from archaeological excavation and analysis.

An initial visit by Hopi elders to prehistoric sites being studied by Arizona State University in the Tonto Basin provided a taste of the sorts of information that will be developed through collaboration between scholars and Hopis. During examination of artifacts in the laboratory, for example, Hopi elders were able to identify the esoteric function of ritual artifacts. Some, but not all, of this sensitive information could be shared with the archaeologists. A representative from the Water Clan pointed out the symbols of his clan that appear in both the decoration of pottery and in rock art in the area. The interpretation of Hopi symbols that appear in completely different artifact types is a kind of analysis rarely attempted by archaeologists, and it provides an example of how Hopis can help archaeologists see data in new ways. The Hopis also recognized enigmatic rock pile features in the field as Hopi shrines, thus helping archaeologists ascribe a function to a type of site that they would otherwise know little about. At the large platform mounds, Hopi elders remarked on the similarities and differences that are evident with the villages they now occupy.

Much of the information about Hopi clan history in the Tonto Basin is known through "oral history": information and explanations about life in the past, conveyed through the generations by the spoken word. The Hopi distinguish four basic types of oral narrative. *Navoti* is historical knowledge of events to which the speaker has a direct and personal link, either by virtue of having experienced the events being discussed, or because the information is ritual knowledge the speaker has been entrusted with as a member of a religious society. The theological and prophesying aspects of Hopi narratives are described as *tutavo* and *wuknavoti*. *Tutavo* are teachings, instructions, and guidance. *Wuknavoti*, literally "old people's knowledge," is more properly defined as prophecy. *Tuuwutsi*, in contrast to *navoti*, is a reiteration or remembrance of something today by people who do not have a direct link to the past that is the subject of the story. Tuuwutsi can include both oral history learned from another person and stories that non-Indians commonly label myths, legends, or folk tales. The Hopi distinction between *navoti* and *tuuwutsi* must be kept in mind when conducting and evaluating oral history interviews by noting what people know based on their life experience, as contrasted to what they know based on what other people have told them.

Navoti, *wuknavoti*, and *tutavo* are powerful narratives that inspire and guide the Hopi way of life. These narratives incorporate the unfolding of historical events in real places in past time, and they provide conceptual bridges between those events and the present. The Hopi people hold these narratives as precious aspects of their cultural patrimony and do not share them indiscriminately with

Cooperation and Partnership
by Glen E. Rice and Charles L. Redman

In the Summer 1992 issue of NATIVE PEOPLES Magazine (and this volume; see "Platform Mounds of the Arizona Desert: An Experiment in Organizational Complexity"), we described several highlights of our archaeological excavations at Salado sites in the Tonto Basin of central Arizona. For two centuries, the Salado people prospered in this and many of the other desert valleys of southern Arizona and New Mexico. Then, shortly after AD 1450, they left their well-planned communities and disappeared from the region. As archaeologists, we are fascinated by the 200-year-long success story of the Salado and equally puzzled by their sudden departure.

The Roosevelt Platform Mound Study is gathering information that archaeologists need to understand Salado history and solve these puzzles, but not all of that knowledge will come from excavation and scientific analysis. Archaeology is only one of several ways to understand the past.

Cooperation and partnership between Native Americans and archaeologists, and bringing together our different kinds of historical evidence, can result in a more complete reconstruction of the past, which all of us seek.

The fourteenth and fifteenth centuries in the American Southwest were a fascinating time. The archaeological record suggests a period of great movement and communication. People were training, traveling, and migrating throughout the region and deep into the heart of Mexico. Ideas and societies were in flux. This milieu, which we archaeologists call the "Salado," was an important chapter in the history of many Native Americans of the Southwest, particularly agricultural peoples such as the Pima, the Tohono O'Odham, the Zuni, and the Hopi. In this article, representatives of the Hopi Tribe express their desire to collaborate in archaeological projects. Other tribes are joining, too, in cooperative research efforts.

Our archaeological project in the Tonto Basin can help illuminate the history of modern Native American groups, and modern Native American groups can contribute information that we need to interpret our archaeological findings. We welcome the participation of Native Americans in the archaeological undertaking.

Glen E. Rice and Charles L. Redman are the principal investigators of the Roosevelt Platform Mound Study, a decade-long research project being undertaken by archaeologists at Arizona State University. The study is funded by the Bureau of Reclamation under a permit from the Tonto National Forest. It is one of a set of projects to study prehistoric sites in the Tonto Basin area that may be impacted by modifications now being made to Theodore Roosevelt Dam for improved flood control.

non-Indians. *Navoti, wuknavoti,* and *tutavo* are very sensitive topics, and the ethical documentation and use of these narratives in research can be done only in close collaboration with Hopi tribal members in a study in which Hopis are peers to project scientists.

The history embedded in the archaeological record and the history in Hopi narratives of *navoti* and *wuknavoti* operate in different conceptual frameworks. Relating one set of evidence to the other is not always simple. Occasionally, the places where critical events took place are well-known in terms of contemporary geography but at other times an exact correspondence is not possible, based on current knowledge. The Hopis know, however, that their ancestors were real people who traveled over a real landscape in real time. For this reason, they believe there is an important correspondence between their oral narratives and the archaeological record in the Southwest, even if current archaeological method and theory are not refined enough to elucidate this. They are interested in sharing a portion of their oral traditions to help archaeologists learn more from the archaeological record since they believe that sharing this knowledge will, in turn, help them better understand their tribal history.

The Hopis recognize that the past was different in many respects from the present. Archaeology provides a means to learn about that past and to understand how it is linked with our contemporary world. The collaboration the Hopis are proposing with Arizona State University archaeologists in the Tonto Basin presents exciting intellectual prospects that would not otherwise be possible. Collaboration will lead to new knowledge of value to both Hopis and scholars—an exciting prospect that augurs well for the future of archaeology in the Southwest.

4

Putting Voyaging Back Into Polynesian Prehistory

Ben Finney

Voyaging canoes, those graceful twin-hulled vessels which we thought had disappeared forever from Polynesian waters, are once more sailing between Hawai‘i, Tahiti, Rarotonga, Aotearoa and other widely separated islands. In the 1960s this revival of canoe voyaging was initiated, along with the art of navigating by naked-eye observations of celestial bodies, ocean swells and other natural phenomena, for two purposes: to provide realistic information on canoe sailing and navigation needed to help resolve a controversy over how Polynesia had been explored and settled; and to enable contemporary Polynesians to learn about and experience the technology and skills of their seafaring ancestors.

Questions about Polynesian migration and voyaging have been widely debated ever since European explorers first chanced upon the islands and found to their surprise that stone age voyagers had preceded them into the Pacific. Late in the 19th century and early in the 20th century such scholars as Abraham Fornander (1878–1885), S. Percy Smith (1898, 1913–1915), Elsdon Best (1923), E.S.C. Handy (1930), and Peter Buck (1938) developed scenarios, based primarily upon the analysis of oral traditions and the distribution of languages and culture traits, of the intentional settlement of Polynesia by seafarers sailing east across the tropical Pacific, and of post-colonisation voyages made widely around Polynesia to exchange valued goods, make pilgrimages to sacred places, and for romance, raiding and other "adventurous" purposes.

At mid-century, this orthodoxy was forcefully challenged by Thor Heyerdahl and Andrew Sharp, largely on the basis of their negative assessments of Polynesian voyaging capabilities. Stressing that Polynesians could not have sailed eastward across the tropical Pacific against the prevailing easterly trade winds and ocean currents, Heyerdahl (1947, 1953) hypothesised that the islands must therefore have been first settled by South Americans pushed westwards before the trade winds and currents. Sharp (1956, 1961) accepted that the Polynesians came from the west, but claimed that their canoes did not sail well enough, and that their non-instrument navigation methods were not sufficiently accurate, for them to have intentionally explored and colonised the Pacific, and then to have sailed back and forth between distantly separated outposts. The historian maintained that the islands must therefore have been settled accidentally by chance arrivals of drifting canoes that had been blown off course or had strayed through navigational error, or by fortuitous landfalls of canoes bearing desperate exiles fleeing

Figure 1. The *Hokule‘a* in 1995 as she was returning to Hawai‘i from the Marquesas Islands. (Photo courtesy of the Bishop Museum)

war or famine, and that the resultant colonies remained isolated from all but their nearby neighbours except for the random arrival of drift or exile canoes.

Although Heyerdahl's theory found little acceptance among students of Polynesian prehistory, Sharp's model of accidental, random settlement followed by relative if not absolute isolation appealed to many prehistorians, particularly those who were then introducing new archaeological methods into the Pacific and wanted to make a break with previous ways of interpreting Polynesia's past. Sharp's rhetoric about the impossibility of long, intentionally-navigated canoe voyages reinforced scepticism about the extreme "migration mentality" of previous scholars, and their portrayals of canoes sailing freely back and forth across the Pacific and how successive waves of migrants shaped island societies. Moreover, Sharp's thinking fit comfortably with the shift then occurring within archaeology away from a culture historical concentration on migration and diffusion toward a focus on cultural reconstruction and on processes of change internal to the development of a particular culture (Adams et al. 1978, Kirch 1985:52–53, Dunnell 1986, Trigger 1989:330–36, Anthony 1990), as well as with closed system modelling of the evolution of individual Polynesian societies then being attempted by some social anthropologists (Goldman 1955, Sahlins 1958).

Although Roger Green and some of the other archaeologists starting to work in Polynesia during the late 1950s and the 1960s sought to combine these new approaches with the older culture historical perspective, many of the new archaeologists focused solely or primarily on ahistorical reconstructions and processual analyses of individual island or archipelago cultures. This led to such fascinating studies as how islanders from the tropics adapted to temperate Aotearoa (Golson and Gathercole 1962), and how highly stratified chiefdoms evolved in Hawai'i (Earle 1978, Cordy 1981), but ones in which the rich Polynesian seafaring heritage was conspicuously missing.

By the early 1970s, however, a number of other studies began to appear that challenged thinking about the random, accidental settlement of Polynesia and the subsequent development of local cultures in isolation. Computer simulations indicated that it was highly unlikely that random drift voyaging could account for the Polynesian thrust to the east, and their dispersion to Hawai'i, Rapa Nui, and Aotearoa (Levison, Ward and Webb 1973). Ethnographic studies of traditional navigation on remote islands where it still survived demystified the art and demonstrated how well it was adapted for interisland voyaging (Gladwin 1970, Lewis 1972). Linguist Bruce Biggs (1972) decried the "simplistic view of Polynesian settlement" inherent in unidirectional, least-moves modelling, reminding prehistorians that the spare, family-tree diagrams of Polynesian languages are models of language relationships not diagrams indicating one-way colonisation with no return voyages or communication back and forth between settlements. Above all, the evidence uncovered by Green and other archaeologists in their excavations across the South Pacific indicated that ancestral Polynesians had expanded into the Pacific much faster than a random, accidental model could explain, that they traded Lapita pottery and other goods widely back and forth along this migration route, and that they and their Polynesian descendants took plants and animals with them on planned colonisation voyages (Ambrose and Green 1972, Yen 1973, Green 1974).

These challenges undermined random, least-moves thinking about Polynesian settlement, but they did not explain how Polynesians and their ancestors were able to expand so swiftly across the Pacific, sail to distant islands including many located far upwind in relation to the trades, and, if oral traditions were to be believed, travel back and forth between widely separated outposts. Basic information was needed, ideally gathered over the actual routes and in the wind and sea conditions in question, on how well canoes sailed and how well non-instrument navigation worked. Since voyaging canoes and their navigators were no longer sailing, and reports on them from the contact era were incomplete and subject to various interpretations, it became obvious that in order to obtain the needed information we had to reconstruct the canoes, relearn ways of navigating, and then test these over the long sea roads of Polynesia.

Experimental Voyaging

The first steps toward developing this experimental approach were taken in the mid-1960s when David Lewis (1966) used non-instrument methods to navigate from Tahiti to Rarotonga and then to Aotearoa, and my students and I reconstructed and tested a Hawaiian double canoe. The results of these trials, which demonstrated the long-range capability of non-instrument navigation and that double canoes were well adapted for trade wind sailing, led me to challenge the contention that Polynesian canoes and ways of navigating were inadequate for long, navigated voyages by proposing that we sail a voyaging canoe navigated by traditional means over the legendary sea route between Hawai'i and Tahiti (Finney 1967).

In 1973 artist Herb Kane, racing canoe paddler Tommy Holmes and I formed the Polynesian Voyaging Society, and began designing a voyaging canoe, raising funds for its construction and planning the voyage. Unfortunately, we could not follow the experimental archaeology canon of recreating the artefact to be tested from an archaeologically-recovered example using only traditional materials and tools (McGrail 1975, Coles 1979). No ancient voyaging canoes had been recovered from excavations on land or the seafloor to provide exact models, and we did not have the resources, time or skills necessary to replicate all the traditional materials, tools and construction techniques. The design was therefore developed from drawings made at the time of European contact of voyaging canoes from throughout Polynesia to come up with a vessel that incorporated common, presumably archaic, features, and non-traditional materials and tools were used to fabricate major components of the craft.

In 1975 we launched our double canoe, christening her *Hōkūle'a* after the bright star Arcturus which now passes directly over the island of Hawai'i. Her twin hulls, each 19 m long, are lashed together with cross beams which also support a deck. Two masts are mounted on the deck and rigged a pair of upward-curving Polynesian sprit sails (Finney 1977). Because the hulls were fabricated from layers of cold-moulded plywood, and synthetic line and other modern materials were used for some other components, our experiments cannot directly address issues of strength and durability. Since, however, *Hōkūle'a* follows traditional precedents in terms of her lines, weight (displacing around 11.4 metric tons fully loaded) and sail plan, we believe that her performance provides data useful for estimating how voyaging canoes sailed, and that she serves as a realistic platform for navigational trials.

In 1976 we sailed *Hōkūleʻa* from Hawaiʻi to Tahiti and return and since then have made three more major round-trip voyages: Hawaiʻi–Tahiti in 1980; Hawaiʻi –Aotearoa (via Tahiti, Cooks, Tonga, Samoa, and the Tuamotus) in 1985–1987; Hawaiʻi–Cooks (via Tahiti) in 1992 (Finney 1977, 1994). All but three segments of these round-trips (Tahiti–Hawaiʻi in 1976, Aotearoa–Tonga in 1986, Maʻuke– Aitutaki in 1992) were navigated without instruments. Altogether, *Hōkūleʻa* has logged some 50,000 miles on these long voyages and on shorter trips around the Hawaiian archipelago and other island groups she has visited.[1]

Sailing, Seamanship, and Practical Meteorology

Although the double canoe was one of the finest ocean vessels of the ancient world, those employed in the original expansion probably did not sail as fast, nor point as close to the wind, as do their modern descendants, racing catamarans, or the Micronesian-Polynesian hybrids which were coming into vogue at the time of Cook's voyages: the *kalia* of Tonga, *ʻalia* of Samoa, and *ndrua* of Fiji. Nonetheless, even though archaic double canoes may have lacked the huge sails and deep-V shaped hulls of racing catamarans, or the racy lateen-rigged, double-ended configuration of late prehistoric *kalia* type canoes, judging from *Hōkūleʻa's* performance, they were seaworthy craft well adapted for long range voyaging. In brisk trade winds *Hōkūleʻa* cruises easily in the 6–7 knot range, and can accelerate to 10–12 knots when broad reaching across strong winds. On long voyages, however, the inevitable calms and periods of light winds, as well as squalls and storms when sails have to be lowered, bring her average speed down to a little over 4 knots, or around 100 miles a day. Although she sails best when reaching across the wind, *Hōkūleʻa* can sail to within at least 75° off the wind.

The four voyages *Hōkūleʻa* has made so far from Hawaiʻi to Tahiti demonstrate that a double canoe with such a modest windward ability can make long, shallow slants into the wind. Whereas the windward (with respect to the easterly trades) position of Tahiti over 300 miles to the east of Hawaiʻi allows a canoe to sail freely across and slightly before the wind from Tahiti to Hawaiʻi, a canoe sailing southward from Hawaiʻi must be sailed hard into the wind to make enough easting to reach Tahiti. Figure 2 shows how in 1980 *Hōkūleʻa* followed a curving course against first the northeast trades and then the southeast trades to arrive at Tahiti after 31 days of hard sailing (Finney et al. 1986).

Such a modest windward ability does not, however, explain how the Polynesian and their Lapita ancestors managed to move so far east against the trade wind direction. Judging from late 18th and early 19th century reports of Polynesian sailing practices, as well as two unsuccessful attempts in the 1970s to tack reconstructed outrigger canoes from West to East Polynesia (Siers 1977, 1978), Polynesians did not normally attempt to force their canoes directly against wind and sea to reach distant upwind destinations. Instead, they waited for favourable winds. Heyerdahl's (1978:332) claim that the easterly trade winds barred ancestral Polynesians from sailing east across the tropical Pacific founders on his false assumption of trade wind permanence. Although the trades may be among the

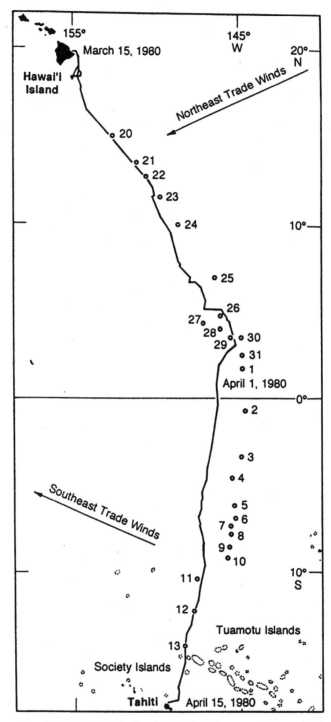

Figure 2. Hawai'i to Tahiti 1980: Track of *Hokule'a* (from satellite positioning) and daily dead reckoning positions (from tape-recorded estimates of the canoe's progress charter after the voyage).

globe's steadiest winds, periodically they are replaced by winds blowing from other directions. In the western South Pacific there is marked monsoon alternation between the winter trade wind season and the summer westerlies season, ideal conditions for the rapid expansion eastward and subsequent movement back and forth along the migration route indicated in the Lapita archaeological record. Summer westerlies extend into the eastern Pacific, although they are generally more episodic and short-lived there except during El Niño events when they spread widely over the region and can prevail for months at a time. Even during the height of the winter trade wind season, westerly winds may periodically disrupt the trades. The Tahitian savant Tupaia told Captain James Cook how his countrymen exploited westerly winds to return to Tahiti after sailing before the trades to islands to the west (Beaglehole 1955:154). As Cook's reaction to this intelligence suggests, it seems likely that the early Polynesians employed spells of westerly winds to mount the original exploration and colonisation voyages into unknown eastern seas, and then subsequently exploited alternating easterly and westerly winds to sail back and forth between at least some of the resultant colonies.

Why did Lapita and Polynesians colonists brave unknown seas to expand eastward across the Pacific against the direction of the prevailing winds to find and settle islands they had never seen? To begin with, their ancestral seafaring experience virtually dictated that they expand eastward: it told them that the sea was filled with islands, and that those to be found to the east would be uninhabited. Furthermore, exploring to the east, to windward with respect to the dominant trade wind flow, made good sailing sense. An exploring party that found a promising new land to the east could return home with news of their discovery by waiting for the trades to return and then running west before them. Or, if they failed to find land, they could exercise the life-saving option of running home before the trades—unless they had the misfortune of sailing when the westerlies were unusually persistent. In addition, the Austronesian stress on primogeniture encouraged migration to the uninhabited islands of the east by a ruling chief's younger sons who had little hope of succeeding to leadership at home. Instead of resorting to rebellion or fratricide, they could create a chiefdom of their own by building a voyaging canoe, recruiting followers and setting sail to find and colonise a new island to the east.

During the winter of 1986 we demonstrated how to move from west to east across Polynesia directly against the trade wind direction by sailing *Hōkūleʻa* from Samoa to Tahiti, utilising westerly wind shifts brought about by troughs extending into the tropics from low pressure systems passing to the south. *Hōkūleʻa* left Samoa, first sailing south across the trades, and then east when a passing trough brought several days of westerlies that enabled the canoe to get within range of the Southern Cooks before the trades returned. After stopovers at Aitutaki and Rarotonga, the canoe headed due east for Tahiti, sailing before northwest winds associated with another trough. Unlike on the previous leg, *Hōkūleʻa* stayed with this slow-moving trough for practically the whole crossing. In fact, she was driven to the east of Tahiti by the northwesterlies before the trades finally returned, and allowed her to be turned back to the west to reach the island (Fig. 3) (Finney et al. 1989).

Once, however, Hawaiʻi, the Marquesas, Tuamotu-Gambiers, and Australs had been colonised, and at least one canoe reached lone Rapa Nui, the Polynesians had run out of colonisable islands in the tropical Pacific. Somehow, however, canoes did fetch up on a huge uninhabited land far to the southwest in temperate

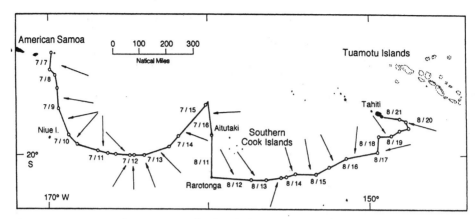

Figure 3. Samoa to Tahiti 1986: Track of *Hokule'a* (from satellite positioning) and daily wind directions.

latitudes. Linguistic and archaeological research indicates that Aotearoa was probably settled from central East Polynesia, and some Māori migratory traditions specify that colonising canoes sailed from Hawaiki, arguably located in the Societies, Cooks, or both. Yet doubt has been cast upon the idea that canoes could have been deliberately sailed there from central East Polynesia particularly because of the difficulty migrants would have had in moving out of the favourable trade winds and warm seas of the tropics, and into colder latitudes with their periodic spells of strong, stormy westerlies that could force back or even overwhelm any canoe headed southwest for Aotearoa. We discovered, however, that Māori traditions of canoes sailing to Aotearoa late in the spring make good meteorological sense, for that is when high pressure systems dominate the seas to the east of Aotearoa, bringing easterly winds along their northern flanks ideal for sailing southwest. During the late spring of 1985 we used easterlies from a succession of slow moving high pressure systems to sail *Hōkūle'a* from Rarotonga to Aotearoa, covering the 1650 mile route in 16 days (Fig. 4) (Babayan et al. 1987).

Access to meteorological data and knowledge unavailable to traditional navigators does not invalidate these experiments. We are more impressed by the deep knowledge of local wind and sea conditions exhibited by Polynesian seafarers whom Cook and other early European explorers met than by our own knowledge. For example, the Spanish navigator Andia y Varela (Corney 1915, Vol. 2:266) wrote how two Tahitians who sailed with him were able to predict

> the weather we should experience the following day, as to winds, calms, rainfall, sunshine, sea and other points, about which they never turned out to be wrong: a foreknowledge worthy to be envied, for, in spite of all that our navigators and cosmographers have observed and written anent [about] the subject, they have not mastered this accomplishment.

Surely, people so well attuned to the sea and the sky were able to anticipate and then detect the coming of favourable winds and employ them to sail where they wanted to go.

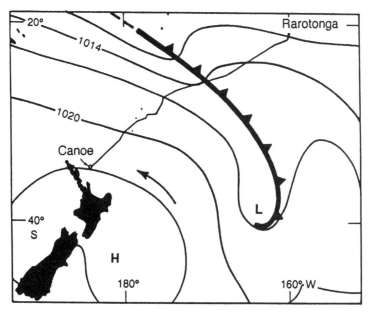

Figure 4. Rarotonga to Aotearoa 7 December 1985: Track of Hokuleʻa (from satellite positioning) showing her sailing toward Aotearoa with favorable easterly winds brought by the third high-pressure system encountered on the crossing.

Navigation

The historian Sharp (1961) declared that Polynesians could not have intentionally navigated between islands more than 300 miles apart; Cook (Beaglehole 1955:154), the consummate Western navigator, accepted that Polynesians sailed "from Island to Island" for great distances, "the Sun serving them for a compass by day and the Moon and Stars by night." Subsequent research by Lewis (1972) and others has expanded our understanding of Polynesian navigation beyond the sketchy remarks of Cook and other European explorers. At night, navigators oriented on the rising and setting points of key stars and constellations; by day, on the sun when low in the sky (its changing position having been calibrated against the fading star field of the dawn sky). When clouds obscured the stars or sun, (or the moon, a secondary guide), and when the sun was too high in the sky to yield a bearing, they oriented on the dominant swells, the direction of which they had previously established in relation to star or sun bearings. They compensated for current set and leeway drift across a course by steering on the appropriate star or sun bearing to one side of the course and made course corrections during the voyage as indicated by dead reckoning estimates of the canoe's progress, and by changing wind and sea conditions. To expand the range at which an island could be detected, they watched for such signs as cloud build-up over high islands, interference in the swell pattern, and the flight of land-nesting birds that daily fly out to sea to fish.

Using methods closely related to Polynesian ones, in 1976 Mau Piailug, a master navigator from Micronesia, successfully guided *Hōkūle'a* to Tahiti. Since 1980, Nainoa Thompson, a Hawaiian who learned how to navigate without instruments through self-study, planetarium simulations and instruction from Mau Piailug, has guided *Hōkūle'a* on her long crossings except in 1992 when his students took over for major portions of the voyage from Hawai'i to Rarotonga and return. Although Nainoa and his students may think in terms of miles and degrees, and use some techniques of Nainoa's own invention, because their system is based on star, sun, and swell orientation and other Polynesian methods, and because at sea they use no instruments, charts, or even paper and pencil, their experiences can tell us much about the capabilities of traditional navigation. Furthermore, by comparing after each crossing the navigator's dead reckoning, based on verbal position estimates recorded daily, with the actual track of the canoe, determined remotely by satellite position, we have been able to analyse closely non-instrument navigational performance.

Our prior geographical knowledge of Polynesia of course meant *Hōkūle'a* could only retrace post-colonisation crossings back and forth between already known islands and archipelagos. Nonetheless, we contend that our voyages have amply demonstrated that basic Polynesian navigational skills would have enabled explorers to follow deliberate search strategies to find new islands, and to mount return voyages back to their homeland to fetch cultigens, more colonists or whatever was needed to make newly founded outposts viable.

If reaching the desired destination is the ultimate arbiter of navigational success, our navigators have repeatedly passed this test, for on every experimental crossing they have been able to bring *Hōkūle'a* to the target island. Almost all of these crossings have been longer than the 300 mile limit Sharp placed on navigated canoe voyages. In fact, the distance covered by *Hōkūle'a* in curving to windward on the crossing from Hawai'i to Tahiti approaches 3,000 miles, ten times Sharp's artificial limit, a performance that demolishes any notion that traditional navigation methods were inadequate for long distances.

Sharp, Akerblom (1968) and other critics posed the navigational debate in terms of a degree of accuracy inappropriate to Polynesian geography. They exaggerated the challenge of navigating long distances by, in effect, demanding that the navigator sail unerringly and exactly from one isolated island to another. They then stressed the impossibility of taking precise bearings off the stars, sun and ocean swells, of steering the correct course by them and of accurately dead reckoning when the effects of current and leeway are unknown, concluding that the inevitable errors in orientation, steering and dead reckoning would accumulate during the voyage to throw the navigator farther and farther off course. In contrast, our experiments indicate that despite its seemingly inherent inaccuracy, non-instrument navigation works on long as well as short voyages.

Although Nainoa Thompson has at times navigated across hundreds of miles of open ocean and hit a small island target exactly, the problems of orientation, steering and dead reckoning are such that he cannot rely on being able to do so. What he can do repeatedly is bring a canoe close enough to the target island so that it can eventually be reached. Nainoa relies, of course, on a central fact of Polynesian geography: virtually all the islands there are part of archipelagos, some stretching for hundreds of miles. With few exceptions, the navigator does not have to sail directly and precisely to a lone island, but rather to an archipelago of islands. Once landfall is made on one island within an archipelago, he can then reorient himself and head directly for the target island.

For example, in sailing from Oʻahu to Tahiti we do not have to hit Tahiti exactly, any more than we have to sail directly and unerringly back to Oʻahu. Tahiti is imbedded in a screen of islands, formed by the Societies extending hundreds of miles to the west and the Tuamotus extending even farther to the east, and Oʻahu is part of the long Hawaiian chain. In sailing from Hawaiʻi to Tahiti we try to gain enough easting to make landfall on one of the atolls of the western Tuamotus just to the north-northeast of Tahiti, and then sail directly from there to Tahiti. When returning home we try to come within range of the comparatively huge island of Hawaiʻi on its windward side, turn downwind to make landfall, and then work our way along the chain to Oʻahu.

Whereas Sharp and other critics had assumed that navigational errors would necessarily accumulate in one direction to throw a canoe far off course, our experience indicates that errors often fall randomly around the desired course line. The direct cancelling out of opposing errors in estimating current can be seen in the 1980 voyage to Tahiti (Fig. 2). On March 31, just after leaving the doldrums, *Hōkūleʻa* apparently crossed through one of those swift, narrow current jets that periodically appear near the equator, but which are difficult to perceive without a land referent, and Nainoa did not detect that the canoe had been quickly set some 90 miles to the west of where he thought it was sailing. With this omission embedded in his reckoning, as the canoe headed south over the next ten days Nainoa's position estimates paralleled the actual track, but were 90 miles to the east of it. Then, on April 11 Nainoa revised his thinking. Because he reasoned that the slow progress of the canoe below the equator was exposing it to more of the westward-flowing South Equatorial Current than allowed for in his calculations, Nainoa factored in more current set to the west, which, as we discovered later, placed his dead reckoning positions some 90 miles to the west, almost directly on *Hōkūleʻa*'s actual track. Contemporaneous tracking of this current by radio buoys showed, however, that it was particularly weak then. Nevertheless, Nainoa's overestimate of current strength below the equator, in effect cancelled out missing the current jet north of the equator, and brought his mental picture of where the canoe was sailing almost directly onto the actual track (Finney et al. 1986).

On a few crossings, however, dead reckoning "errors" have accumulated in one direction, although not with fatal consequences. As planned, on all four voyages from Hawaiʻi to Tahiti *Hōkūleʻa* made landfall on one of the three westernmost atolls of the Tuamotus: Mataiva in 1976 and 1992, Tikehau in 1980 and Rangiroa in 1985. On three of the voyages the navigator's dead reckoning correctly predicted landfall in that section of the Tuamotus. On the 1985 crossing, however, an overestimate of the westward flowing current, or an underestimate of the canoe's windward performance, or both, led Nainoa to reckon that the canoe was going to make land in the leeward Societies, well to the west of the actual landfall on Rangiroa. This experience underlines how the location of a target island within a wider screen of islands helps navigators reach their destinations. Keeping the canoe sailing hard against the trades to gain maximum easting had actually brought her to the desired, western Tuamotu, section of the island screen, but even if *Hōkūleʻa* had made landfall in the western Societies she could have been worked from there to Tahiti (Finney 1994:200–24).

Discussion

These and other findings and insights from *Hōkūle'a*'s voyages have been widely cited by prehistorians who, as Roger Green has long been suggesting, have come to accept that voyaging canoes and highly skilled ways of sailing, exploiting changing wind patterns and navigating formed an adaptive complex that enabled seafarers to expand into the remote reaches of the Pacific.[2] For example, Geoffrey Irwin has recently developed a comprehensive theory of the deliberate exploration and colonisation that depends upon systematic search strategies, return voyaging and other capabilities that were so categorically dismissed before our experiments (Irwin 1989, 1992, Irwin et al. 1990). Other prehistorians now have no qualms about searching for evidence of widespread intra- and inter-archipelago exchange in the distribution of basalt adze blades, obsidian tools and other materials that can be precisely sourced, as well as hypothesising about how two-way, multi-archipelago voyaging may have shaped regional cultural developments (Kirch 1986, F. Leach et al. 1986, Anderson and McFadgen 1990, Walter 1990, Best et al. 1991, H. Leach 1993, Rolett 1993). Some even dare to suggest that such once-anathematised migration scenarios drawn from tradition as the arrival in Aotearoa of a number of migratory canoes during the same period, the settlement of islands from multiple sources and the impact of new migrants on an already established Hawaiian population, may be reflected in the archaeological record (Spriggs 1988, Dye 1989, Anderson 1991:790, Cachola-Abad 1993, Law 1994).

In addition to helping to make voyaging once more central to the study of Polynesian prehistory, our experimental initiative has also led to a voyaging renaissance whereby empowered Polynesians are now seeking to learn about their maritime past by sailing *Hōkūle'a* and other reconstructed canoes over the sea roads pioneered by their ancestors. Not only did the Hawaiians re-introduced to canoe voyaging quickly learn to sail and navigate *Hōkūle'a*, but they soon assumed control of the project and then proceeded to extend the canoe's voyaging programme far beyond the initial expedition to Tahiti and back. In addition, they have reached out to their fellow Polynesians by recruiting Marquesans, Tahitians, Cook Islanders, Māori, Tongans and Samoans as crew members and by working closely with leaders from the various islands along the canoe's routes to make *Hōkūle'a*'s visits cultural celebrations of the technology, skills and courage that made possible the settlement of their islands—indeed the very existence of the Polynesian people. Furthermore, their efforts have stimulated other experimental voyaging projects such as the joint Māori-Tahitian effort led by Matahi Whakataka and Francis Cowan to construct *Hawaiki-Nui*, a double canoe which sailed from Tahiti to Aotearoa in 1985 just a few weeks after we did, and the Cook Island effort to build *Takitumu*, a project led by the former premier Sir Tom Davis who recently sailed the canoe from Rarotonga to Tahiti and return.

The *Hōkūle'a* veterans have also helped Māori and Cook Island groups to build canoes and learn navigation for participation in the 1992 Pacific Festival of Arts held at Rarotonga where the declared theme was canoe voyaging. The *Te Aurere of Aotearoa*, a double canoe built by the Māori leader Hector Busby and his apprentices from the Tai Tokerau region of the North Island and five smaller double canoes built, respectively, by the communities of Ma'uke, Mangaia, Mitiaro, Atiu and Aitutaki in the Southern Cooks, all sailed to Rarotonga for the festival where they were met by the *Takitumu*, *Hōkūleʻa* and canoes from elsewhere in the Pacific. Most recently, the Hawaiians have launched the *Hawaiʻi-Loa*, a double canoe built primarily with native materials, which in 1995 sailed, in company with canoes from elsewhere in Polynesia, from the Marquesas to Hawaiʻi to retrace the route arguably taken by the first discoverers of Hawaiʻi, or at least by some of its early settlers.

A few cautionary words are in order about what we have learned from sailing *Hōkūleʻa* around Polynesia and about the renaissance in Polynesian voyaging. For example, the route-specific nature of our experience in two-way voyaging should not be overlooked. Repeatedly sailing *Hōkūleʻa* between Hawaiʻi and Tahiti does not mean that earlier voyagers could have so successfully sailed back and forth between all other pairs of distantly spaced islands. Whereas the wide targets formed by the Hawaiian archipelago and the Societies-Northern Tuamotus spread of islands and the favourable alignment of Hawaiʻi and Tahiti across the trades are conducive for voyaging back and forth, conditions for sailing between some other sets of islands are much less favourable. For example, Rapa Nui's location far upwind with respect to the trades and its lack of surrounding islands are far from ideal for two-way communication with the archipelagos 2000 miles to the west. Although voyagers leaving Rapa Nui could have easily sailed west before the trades to these large archipelagic targets, the exact navigation and timing of westerly wind shifts required to sail back to Rapa Nui, and the lack of surrounding islands to facilitate landfinding, would have greatly challenged any voyagers wanting to return to this tiny, isolated outpost.[3]

However, although isolationist assumptions may therefore make some sense for Rapa Nui it is equally obvious that they do not for the archipelagos to the west—the Australs, Tuamotus, Marquesas, Societies and Cooks. Both our voyaging experiments and recent reinterpretations of archaeological evidence support the hypothesis that these central East Polynesia archipelagos formed a cultural region within which, particularly in the centuries soon after settlement, people, ideas and artefacts may have flowed freely (Kirch 1986, Finney et al. 1989:291-97). This suggests an integrated answer to such long-standing questions as on which island or group did ancestral East Polynesian culture develop and spread therefrom and why archaeological dates for settlement appear earlier than estimated dates of separation between languages. If island populations in this multi-archipelago region were in frequent contact with one another for some centuries after settlement, linguistic and cultural differentiation would have been delayed, and the whole region or a major portion thereof would have become, in effect, a greater East Polynesian homeland. The uniqueness of Rapa Nui, as marked by the great elaboration of the huge stone statues and other features of their culture, may therefore be a function of isolation from regional cultural developments shared among these central archipelagos—not, as has been suggested, because Rapa Nui was settled significantly earlier than other East Polynesian islands, or directly from West Polynesia or an even more exotic source (Biggs 1927:134–52, Langdon and Tryon 1983, Pawley and Green 1984:123).

Although *Hōkūleʻa*'s record of sailing repeatedly to various islands in the South Pacific and then back to Hawaiʻi without major incident might seem to indicate that long-distance canoe travel was a fairly safe, even routine, enterprise, our experiences and those of other experimental voyagers, as well as historical reports of canoe disasters, actually suggest otherwise. When *Hōkūleʻa* sails on long voyages she is followed by an escort boat and carries safety gear dictated by Coast Guard regulations as well as by the bitter experience of two swampings (one of which resulted in a capsize) that occurred while sailing unescorted in the rough seas between the islands of the Hawaiian chain. Both times the canoe was towed to shore, though in the case of the capsize not before a crewman disappeared while attempting to summon help by paddling a surfboard through stormy seas to land. Had these accidents happened while sailing alone in heavy weather and without safety gear, the craft and everyone on board would probably have been lost.

Two reconstructed canoes built just after *Hōkūle'a* was launched were lost at sea in attempts to make long crossings. The *Spirit of Nukuhiva*, a double canoe modelled on the late-prehistoric *kalia* of Tonga, broke up in 1975 when the cross beams connecting the hulls failed during squally weather while sailing from the Marquesas to Hawai'i. The *Taratai II*, an outrigger canoe modeled along Micronesian lines, broke up in 1977 when her outrigger support beams gave way during an attempt to sail from Tonga to Tahiti (Siers 1978). (Fortunately, the yacht escorting the *Spirit of Nukuhiva* picked up her crew, and a rare passing ship just happened to spot the *Taratai II's* rubber raft and took all the survivors aboard). To be sure, the dangers of the sea did not deter Polynesians from seeking new lands, or sailing to already known ones for a variety of purposes, but their expansion into the Pacific and subsequent voyaging activities were not undertaken without cost.

Finally, some words must be said about canoe design and performance. *Hōkūle'a* was designed to sail no better than ancient canoes of her kind so that her performance would enlighten us about voyaging possibilities in the past. This conservative strategy has been repeatedly challenged by those who have wanted to add jibs to the sail rig, keels to the hulls, or other non-traditional features to make *Hōkūle'a* sail faster or closer to the wind and by those who insist that we had handicapped our endeavour from the very beginning by emulating a slow, clumsy type of canoe when we should have copied the true race horse in the Polynesian stable of canoes, the Tongan *kalia*. Attempts to argue that adopting modern innovations or following the late-prehistoric *kalia* design which combined the Micronesian lateen rig and double-ended hull with the Polynesian double canoe configuration (Haddon and Hornell 1938:41–44), would have obviated our experimental research strategy have not always won the day against those who insist that *Hōkūle'a*, and subsequently built canoes like *Te Aurere* and *Hawai'i-Loa* that were designed according to the same philosophy, are too conservative in design and performance. The dispute between Herb Kane, *Hōkūle'a's* designer and Tom Davis over whether *Hōkūle'a* or the *kalia*-inspired *Takitumu* best represents archaic voyaging canoes of 800 or so years ago provides a case in point. It seems likely that as this canoe renaissance proceeds such disputes will multiply as competing authorities champion this or that design, and as sailors bored with sailing the same old way experiment with new sail rigs and other innovations. However much such developments may muddy our ideas about ancient voyaging capabilities, they should also be regarded as a sign that canoe voyaging has truly been reborn and is alive and growing.

Notes

1. Nautical miles and knots (nautical miles per hour) are used throughout. One nautical mile equals 1.15 statute (land) miles, and 1.85 kilometres.

2. Coles (1979:66–69), Green (1981), Davidson (1984:27–28), Kirch (1984:83), Rouse (1986:41), Terrell (1986:73), Bellwood (1987:43–44, 1989:19), Keegan and Diamond (1987), Kirch and Green (1987:440), Sutton (1987:144), Irwin (1989:168), Thorne and Raymond (1989:259), Irwin et al. (1990:39), Irwin (1992:51–52, 60, 97, 105–106, 219).

3. The decrease following colonisation in the number of migratory birds flying to and from Rapa Nui, as well as of land-nesting birds daily flying out to sea to fish, would have made it even more difficult for subsequent voyagers to find the island.

References

Adams, W.Y., D.P. Van Gerven and R.S. Levy, 1978. The retreat from migrationism. *Annual Review of Anthropology*, 7:483–532.

Akerblom, K., 1968. *Astronomy and Navigation in Polynesia and Micronesia*. Ethnographic Museum Monograph 14. Stockholm.

Ambrose, W.R. and R.C. Green, 1972. First millennium B.C. transport of obsidian from New Britain to the Solomon Islands. *Nature*, 237:31.

Anderson, A.J., 1991. The chronology of colonization in New Zealand. *Antiquity*, 65:767–95.

Anderson, A. and B. McFadgen, 1990. Prehistoric two-way voyaging between New Zealand and East Polynesia: Mayor Island obsidian on Raoul Island, and possible Raoul Island obsidian in New Zealand. *Archaeology in Oceania*, 25:37–42.

Anthony, D.W., 1990. Migration in archeology: The baby and the bathwater. *American Anthropologist*, 92:895–914.

Babayan, C., B. Finney, B. Kilonsky and N. Thompson, 1987. Voyage to Aotearoa. *Journal of the Polynesian Society*, 96:161–200.

Beaglehole, J.C. (ed.), 1955. *The Journals of Captain James Cook on his Voyages of Discovery. I. The Voyage of the Endeavour, 1768–1771*. Cambridge, Hakluyt Society.

Bellwood, P., 1987. *The Polynesians: Prehistory of an Island People*. Revised ed. London, Thames and Hudson.

——— 1989. *The colonization of the Pacific: Some current hypotheses*. In A.V.S. Hill and S.W. Serjeantson (eds.), The Colonization of the Pacific: A Genetic Trail, pp. 1–59. Oxford, Clarendon Press.

Best, E., 1923. *Polynesian Voyagers: The Maori as a Deep-sea Navigator, Explorer, and Colonizer*. Dominion Museum Monograph 5. Wellington.

Best, S., P. Sheppard, R.C. Green and R. Parker, 1992. Necromancing the stone: Archaeologists and adzes in Samoa. *Journal of the Polynesian Society*, 101:45–85.

Biggs, B.G., 1972. Implications of linguistic subgrouping with special reference to Polynesia. In R.C. Green and M. Kelly (eds.), Studies in Oceanic Culture History Volume 3. *Pacific Anthropological Records* 13:143–52. Honolulu, Department of Anthropology, Bernice P. Bishop Museum.

Buck, P.H. [Te Rangi Hiroa], 1938. Vikings of the Sunrise. Philadelphia, Lippincott.

Cachola-Abad, C.K., 1993. Evaluating the orthodox dual settlement model for the Hawaiian Islands: An analysis of artefact distribution and Hawaiian oral traditions. In M.W. Graves and R.C. Green (eds.), *The Evolution and Organisation of Prehistoric Society in Polynesia*. New Zealand Archaeological Association Monograph 19, pp. 13–32. Auckland.

Coles, J.M., 1979. *Experimental Archaeology*. New York, Academic Press.

Cordy, R., 1981. *A Study of Prehistoric Social Change: The Development of Complex Societies in the Hawaiian Islands*. New York, Academic Press.

Corney, B.G., 1913, 1915, 1919. *The Quest and Occupation of Tahiti by the Emissaries of Spain During the Years 1772–1776*. 3 vols. London, Hakluyt Society.

Davidson, J., 1984. The Prehistory of New Zealand. Auckland, Longman Paul.

Dunnell, R.C., 1986. Five decades of American archaeology. In D.J. Meltzer, D.D. Fowler and J.A. Sabloff (eds.), *American Archaeology Past and Future 1935–1985*, pp. 23–49. Washington, Smithsonian Institution Press.

Dye, T., 1989. *Tales of two cultures: Traditional historical and archaeological interpretations of Hawaiian prehistory*. Bishop Museum Occasional Papers, 29:3–22. Honolulu.

Earle, T., 1978. *Economic and Social Organization of a Complex Chiefdom: The Halele'a District, Kaua'i, Hawai'i*. Anthropological Papers of the Museum of Anthropology, University of Michigan 63. Ann Arbor.

Finney, B., 1967. New perspectives on Polynesian voyaging. In G.A. Highland, R.W. Force, A. Howard, M. Kelly and Y. Sinoto (eds.), *Polynesian Culture History: Essays in Honor of Kenneth P. Emory*, pp. 141–66. Bernice P. Bishop Museum Special Publication 56. Honolulu, Bishop Museum Press.

———— 1977. Voyaging canoes and the settlement of Polynesia. *Science*, 196:1277–85.

———— 1994. *Voyage of Rediscovery*. Berkeley, University of California Press.

Finney, B., P. Frost, R. Rhodes and N. Thompson, 1989. Wait for the west wind. *Journal of the Polynesian Society*, 98:261–302.

Finney, B., B.J. Kilonsky, S. Somsen and E.D. Stroup, 1986. Re-learning a vanishing art. *Journal of the Polynesian Society*, 95:41–90.

Fornander, A., 1878, 1880, 1885. *An Account of the Polynesian Race. Its Origin and Migrations and the Ancient History of the Hawaiian People to the Times of Kamehameha I*. 3 vols. London, Trübner.

Gladwin, T., 1970. *East is a Big Bird*. Cambridge, Harvard University Press.

Goldman, I., 1955. Status rivalry and cultural evolution in Polynesia. *American Anthropologist*, 57:680–97.

Golson, J. and P.W. Gathercole, 1962. The last decade in New Zealand archaeology [Parts I and II]. *Antiquity*, 36:168–74, 271–78.

Green, R.C., 1974. Sites with Lapita pottery: Importing and voyaging. *Mankind*, 9:253–59.

———— 1981. Location of the Polynesian homeland: A continuing problem. In J. Hollyman and A. Pawley (eds.), *Studies in Pacific Languages & Cultures in Honour of Bruce Biggs*, pp. 133–58. Auckland, Linguistic Society of New Zealand.

Haddon, A.C. and J. Hornell, 1938. *Canoes of Oceania*. Volume 3. Honolulu, Bishop Museum Press.

Handy, E.S.C., 1930. *The problem of Polynesian origins.* Bishop Museum Occasional Papers, 9(8):1–27. Honolulu.

Heyerdahl, T., 1947. Le "Kon-Tiki" à Papeete. *Bulletin de la Société d'Etudes Océaniennes,* 7:345–355.

——— 1953. *American Indians in the Pacific.* Chicago, Rand McNally.

——— 1978. *Early Man and the Ocean.* London, Allen and Unwin.

Irwin, G.J., 1989. Against, across and down the wind: A case for the systematic exploration of the remote Pacific Islands. *Journal of the Polynesian Society,* 98:167–206.

——— 1992. *The Prehistoric Exploration and Colonisation of the Pacific.* Cambridge, Cambridge University Press.

Irwin, G.J., S.H. Bickler and P. Quirke, 1990. Voyaging by canoe and computer: Experiments in the settlement of the Pacific Ocean. *Antiquity,* 64:34–50.

Keegan, W.F. and J.M. Diamond, 1987. Colonization of islands by humans: A biogeographical perspective. *Advances in Archaeological Method and Theory,* 10:49–92.

Kirch, P.V., 1984. *The Evolution of the Polynesian Chiefdoms.* Cambridge, Cambridge University Press.

——— 1985. *Feathered Gods and Fishhooks: An Introduction to Hawaiian Archaeology and Prehistory.* Honolulu, University of Hawaii Press.

——— 1986. Rethinking East Polynesian prehistory. *Journal of the Polynesian Society,* 95:9–40.

Kirch, P.V. and R.C. Green, 1987. History, phylogeny, and evolution in Polynesia. *Current Anthropology,* 28:431–56.

Langdon, R. and D. Tryon, 1983. *The Language of Easter Island: Its Development and Eastern Polynesian Relationships.* Laie, Institute for Polynesian Studies.

Law, R.G., 1994. The likelihood of multiple settlement in Eastern Polynesia—A stochastic model. In D. G. Sutton (ed.), *The Origins of the First New Zealanders,* pp. 77–95. Auckland, University of Auckland Press.

Leach, B.F., A. Anderson, D. Sutton, R. Bird, P. Duerden and E. Clayton, 1986. The origin of prehistoric obsidian artefacts from the Chatham and Kermadec Islands. *New Zealand Journal of Archaeology,* 8:143–70.

Leach, H.M., 1993. The role of major quarries in Polynesian prehistory. In M. W. Graves and R. C. Green (eds.), *The Evolution and Organisation of Prehistoric Society in Polynesia.* New Zealand Archaeological Association Monograph 19, pp. 33–42. Auckland.

Levison, M., R.G. Ward and J.W. Webb, 1973. *The Settlement of Polynesia: A Computer Simulation.* Minneapolis, University of Minnesota Press.

Lewis, D., 1966. Stars of the sea road. Journal of the Polynesian Society, 75:84–94.

——— 1972. *We, the Navigators.* Honolulu, University of Hawaii Press.

McGrail, S., 1975. Models, replicas and experiments in nautical archaeology. *Mariners' Mirror,* 61:3–8.

Pawley, A.K. and R.C. Green, 1984. The Proto-Oceanic language community. *Journal of Pacific History,* 19:123–46.

Rouse, I., 1986. *Migrations in Prehistory.* New Haven, Yale University Press.

Rolett, B.V., 1993. Marquesan prehistory and the origins of East Polynesian culture. *Journal de la Société des Océanistes,* 96:29–47.

Sahlins, M.D., 1958. *Social Stratification in Polynesia.* Seattle, University of Washington Press.

Sharp, A., 1956. *Ancient Voyagers in the Pacific*. Wellington, The Polynesian Society.

———1961. Polynesian navigation to distant islands. *Journal of the Polynesian Society*, 70:219–26.

Siers, J., 1977. *Taratai, A Pacific Adventure*. Wellington, Millwood Press.

———1978. *Taratai II, A Continuing Pacific Adventure*. Wellington, Millwood Press.

Smith, S.P., 1898. *Hawaiki: The Whence of the Maori*. Wellington, Whitcombe and Tombs.

———1913–1915. *The Lore of the Whare Wananga*. 2 vols. New Plymouth, T. Avery.

Spriggs, M.J.T., 1988. The Hawaiian transformation of Ancestral Polynesian society: Conceptualizing chiefly states. In J. Gledhill, B. Bender and M.T. Larsen (eds.), *State and Society*, pp. 57–73. London, Unwin Hyman.

Sutton, D.G., 1987. A paradigmatic shift in Polynesian prehistory: Implications for New Zealand. *New Zealand Journal of Archaeology*, 9:135–55.

Terrell, J.E., 1986. *Prehistory in the Pacific Islands*. Cambridge, Cambridge University Press.

Thorne, A. and R. Raymond, 1989. *Man on the Rim: The Peopling of the Pacific*. North Ryde, N.S.W., Angus and Robertson.

Trigger, B.G., 1989. *A History of Archaeological Thought*. Cambridge, Cambridge University Press.

Walter, R.K., 1990. *The Southern Cook Islands in Eastern Polynesian Prehistory*. Unpublished Ph.D. thesis, University of Auckland, Auckland.

Yen, D.E., 1973. The origins of Oceanic agriculture. *Archaeology and Physical Anthropology in Oceania*, 8:68–85.

Commentary

In a world of rapid modernization, anthropologists have increasingly fewer opportunities to learn about traditional cultures through ethnographic research. Ethnoarchaeology is a kind of last-chance or "salvage" ethnography, and represents one of the last opportunities to study traditional systems before processes of global change absorb them. Although ethnographers in the early twentieth century often studied traditional technological systems in great detail, changing research orientations in cultural anthropology has left an open niche for ethnoarchaeological research. We are finding, through such research, that archaeologists can gain insights on the archaeological record of the ancient past by watching and studying living peoples and cultures that still practice a traditional life way. Contemporary people such as the Kalinga who still make and use traditional pottery, and the Kim-Yal of Highland New Guinea, who were still making stone axes in 1984, offer archaeologists rare opportunities to enrich their understanding of ancient pottery-making and stone ax-making. Still other ethnoarchaeological research has clarified our understandings of how foragers move in seasonal rounds, how farmers practice different types of cultivation systems, and even how sedentary peoples use their domestic and public space.

At its best, ethnoarchaeological and experimental research help us to strengthen our inferences regarding the archaeological record. Some of the most useful ethnoarchaeological research comes from projects with the greatest time-depth. A handful of projects in Africa, Asia, and Central America are now entering their third and fourth decades and provide longitudinal data on many topics that archaeologists study. One benefit of this longitudinal approach, detailed in the Kalinga article, lies in its ability to adapt to changing research interests in the archaeological world at large. An equally important benefit of a longitudinal study is that ethnoarchaeologists can document processes of change: in production, in use, and in organization. We know that archaeologists work in much longer time-frames than do ethnoarchaeologists, and that many archaeologists observe change over a period of centuries rather than the decades that any ethnoarchaeological project can study. Yet the ability to document the causes and directionality of change in traditional systems provides much food for thought, and occasionally gives archaeologists new ideas for their interpretations of ancient societies.

As we have tried to show in this section, the study of "living archaeology" involves more than simply ethnoarchaeological research; it also involves experimental approaches and ethnographic work. For pragmatic and research-oriented reasons, increasing numbers of archaeologists have begun to integrate ethnographic consultation with descendants of the cultures under study. This collaboration between archaeologists and indigenous peoples adds new perspectives to our interpretations, while giving respect and importance to the oral traditions of cultures. Such collaboration also holds the potential for archaeologists to give something back to indigenous peoples, whether that contribution involves information about sacred places that are now archaeological sites (as in the Hopi case) or the re-intro-duction of long-extinct agricultural practices (as in the Aymara Indians in the Titi-caca Basin of Bolivia; see Part Eight). Articles in this section illustrate only a few of the many possibilities for archaeologists who use experiment and ethnography in "living archaeology." The only limits to this intriguing and insightful scientific pur-suit are the willingness of our consultants, and our archaeological imaginations.

Part Twelve

Archaeology and the Contemporary World

Introduction

In the popular imagination, archaeology is far removed from the worries and concerns of everyday life in its study of ancient times and life ways. Even when we abandon our stereotypes of intrepid, Indiana Jones-like archaeologists who slash their way through tropical jungles to find long-concealed ruins, we still conjure up images of bespectacled academics who spend their lives hunched over piles of sherds and writing up obscure reports on their work in remote parts of the world. In this second stereotype, the archaeologist lives in an academic world in which only other academics read his or her work. Today, nothing could be further from the truth. In the United States, for example, most funding for archaeology comes from the public sector, and many archaeologists are employed outside universities and colleges. For practical and ethical reasons, archaeologists can no longer afford to live in an "ivory tower" that buffers them from the problems of the contemporary world. As we begin to study the history of archaeology, we are learning that archaeology has always been affected by the social milieu in which it was practiced and that contemporary political views affect how we interpret the past.

Many archaeologists now believe that our interpretations can never be as neutral and dispassionate as we desire, and that we can no longer afford to practice our profession as a detached scientific discipline. In most of the world's countries, archaeologists work for their governments, and their archaeological findings are directly relevant to the history of that nation. In recent years, many archaeologists have concluded that archaeology is neither neutral nor objective, and that forces beyond our profession shape how we practice our trade. Advocating this stance does not preclude more conventional research, but it certainly changes the priorities we accord to different kinds of archaeological work. Articles in this section illustrate several examples of the important relevance of archaeology to the contemporary world, whether political or environmental.

Unfortunately, archaeology can (and has) been used for terribly destructive purposes, including the oppression and genocidal treatment of specific ethnic and religious populations. We begin with the example of Nazi Germany, where archaeologists played a vital role in developing the notion of a shared German heritage. Bettina Arnold's article, entitled, "The Past as Propaganda," describes the close linkage between the development of prehistoric archaeology in Germany and the rise of the Nazi state in the first half of our century. Before the 1930s, the most prestigious German archaeologists concentrated on either the Near East or Roman archaeology. Few archaeologists studied German prehistory, which seemed culturally backward in contrast to the contemporary Roman civilization. Germany, after all, only became a recognized nation during the latter half of the nineteenth century. By the 1930s, the National Socialist regime in Germany recognized the propaganda value of prehistoric archaeology and followed efforts by Gustav Kosinna to glorify the German past. Nazi Germany used archaeology to unite the nation and to legitimize their territorial expansionism into other countries like Poland and Czechoslovakia that, archaeologists maintained, were once populated by ancient Germans. As is well known, Nazis promoted the idea of "Aryan superiority" to eliminate complete ethnic and religious groups from their area of control, such as Jews and Gypsies. During this period of intense nationalism, Germany's leaders were intensely aware of how they could make the past serve the present. German archaeologists who were trained during the 1930s and 1940s had to completely revise their explanatory frameworks during the postwar era.

The example of Nazi archaeology is just one example of how archaeological practice has been subordinated to the needs of a particular state. We need look no further than the United States, however, to see social and political relevance of archaeology to the lives of the descendants of the people whom we study. Not only are Native Americans increasingly vocal about their concerns with archaeology, but so are African Americans. Spencer Harrington's article, entitled, "Bones and Bureaucrats: New York's Great Cemetery Imbroglio," describes the recent discovery of a colonial period African American cemetery that now sits in the middle of New York city. Despite a widespread belief that colonial New York lacked slaves, the unexpected exposure of this 17th-18th century cemetery through construction activity sparked widespread controversy. New York's African-American community was outraged by the government's lack of regard for this cemetery and by its pressure on archaeologists to finish mitigation quickly so that construction could begin on the property. Through a long and complex process, the African-American community successfully demanded that descendant communities must have a role in decisions regarding the preservation of the site and the analysis of its remains. Harrington's article describes the process of negotiation required to find a workable collaboration between the African-American community and the federal government. Through such long and problem-filled negotiations, the Federal government has established a precedent for future collaboration in such field investigations.

Until quite recently, archaeologists and federal agencies frequently overlooked the concerns of Native Americans, and this attitude set the stage for inevitable conflict over the treatment of archaeological remains. Nowhere has this problem been more pronounced than in the treatment of Native American graves and collections of mortuary goods that are now housed in museums. Fortunately, this situation has begun to change as archaeologists increasingly work with Native Americans to present different interpretations of the past. Janet Spector's article, entitled, "Collaboration at Inyan Ceyaka Atonwan (Village of the Rapids)," discusses historical obstacles to building collaborative relationships between Native Americans and archaeologists, and notes that many deal with how we have traditionally practiced anthropology in the United States. She also urges archaeologists to learn more about the history of relations between Native Americans and archaeologists in different regions of the New World. The article describes Spector's long-term archaeological interest in contact-period archaeology of the upper Midwest (south-central Minnesota), and chronicles the development of an interdisciplinary, multicultural team to study the site of Little Rapids. Her ambitious project shows how building cooperative relationships helps both Native Americans and archaeologists by enriching their understanding of the Native American heritage.

As archaeology comes of age, its practitioners have begun to acknowledge that we undertake our work through the approval and sponsorship of a multicultural public. The two previous examples illustrate how archaeologists have begun to work more closely with stakeholders, who in these cases may be the direct descendants of the ancient communities that we study. This increasing relevance of archaeology to Native Americans and African- Americans mirrors a growing interest in archaeology by the public. Archaeology is an increasingly popular subject, and most people first learn about archaeology through television and movies. Not only do people like to learn about archaeology, but increasing numbers of people want an opportunity to *do* archaeology. In "Archaeology Returns to the Public," Charles Redman describes several ways in which the public can now participate in archaeological research. Civic organizations and amateur archaeology organizations throughout the United States now provide opportunities for public involvement through fieldwork and labwork opportunities. Among the most prominent public programs are those in Cortez, Colorado (Crow Canyon Archaeological Center) and in southern Illinois (Center for American Archeology [Kampsville]). Organizations like Earthwatch and University Research Expeditions give paid volunteers opportunities to work with research archaeologists around the world. Governments, from city to federal levels, have developed archaeological sites into monuments and built museums. Many Native American groups have now established tribal museums and cultural centers designed to educate the public about their respective tribal heritages. What archaeologists are increasingly realizing is that our work has greater significance beyond our narrow scientific goals; our greatest challenge is to learn how to make our work understandable to a variety of publics.

As some previous articles in this reader have shown (see Erickson, Part Eight), archaeology can provide clues regarding how people can practice sustainable resource management in different kinds of environments. Anabel Ford's article, entitled "Signatures Across the Landscape: the El Pilar Archaeological Reserve for Maya Flora and Fauna — Belize/Guatemala" is an excellent case study in the role that archaeologists can play in resource conservation. Her settlement survey studied prehistoric Maya land-use strategies, and used findings from this work to develop a community resource management plan based on ancient Maya practices. Local residents have established a cooperative association to encourage community enterprises in tourism and agriculture. The El Pilar program has worked with local groups to run training programs to educate local residents about their cultural resources, and to train potential guides and hotels in preparation for tourism in the region. Governments around the world have begun to demand that archaeologists contribute to the development of the heritage industry. The El Pilar program shows one model of how archaeologists can work with local communities to conserve the world's natural resources and develop sustainable life ways.

1

The Past as Propaganda

Bettina Arnold

The manipulation of the past for political purposes has been a common theme in history. Consider Darius I (521–486 B.C.), one of the most powerful rulers of the Achaemenid, or Persian, empire. The details of his accession to power, which resulted in the elimination of the senior branch of his family, are obscured by the fact that we have only his side of the story, carved on the cliff face of Behistun in Iran. The list of his victories, and by association his right to rule, are the only remaining version of the truth. Lesson number one: If you are going to twist the past for political ends, eliminate rival interpretations.

The use of the past for propaganda is also well documented in more recent contexts. The first-century Roman historian Tacitus produced an essay titled "On the Origin and Geography of Germany." It is less a history or ethnography of the German tribes than a moral tract or political treatise. The essay was intended to contrast the debauched and degenerate Roman Empire with the virtuous German people, who embodied the uncorrupted morals of old Rome. Objective reporting was not the goal of Tacitus's *Germania*; the manipulation of the facts was considered justified if it had the desired effect of contrasting past Roman glory with present Roman decline. Ironically, this particular piece of historical propaganda was eventually appropriated by a regime notorious for its use and abuse of the past for political, imperialist, and racist purposes: the Third Reich.

The National Socialist regime in Germany fully appreciated the propaganda value of the past, particularly of prehistoric archaeology, and exploited it with characteristic efficiency. The fact that German prehistoric archaeology had been largely ignored before Hitler's rise to power in 1933 made the appropriation of the past for propaganda that much easier. The concept of the *Kulturkreis*, pioneered by the linguist-turned-prehistorian Gustav Kossinna in the 1920s and defined as the identification of ethnic regions on the basis of excavated material culture, lent theoretical support to Nazi expansionist aims in central and eastern Europe. Wherever an artifact of a type designated as "Germanic" was found, the land was declared to be ancient Germanic territory. Applied to prehistoric archaeology, this perspective resulted in the neglect or distortion of data that did not directly apply to Germanic peoples. During the 1930s scholars whose specialty was provincial Roman archaeology were labeled *Römlinge* by the extremists and considered anti-German. The Römisch Germanische Kommission in Mainz, founded in 1907, was the object of numerous defamatory attacks, first by Kossinna and later by Alfred Rosenberg and his organization. Rosenberg, a Nazi ideologue, directed the Amt Rosenberg, which conducted ethnic, cultural, and racial research.

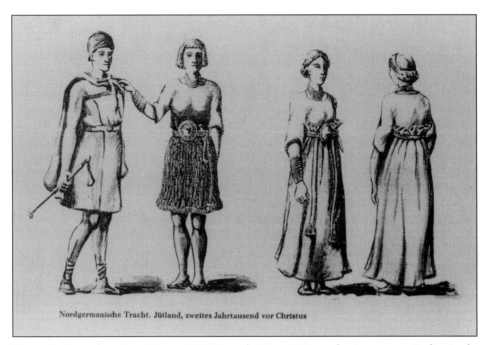

Nordgermanische Tracht. Jütland, zweites Jahrtausend vor Christus

Figure 1. Image from Curt Biging 1933 Deutsche Vorzeit, Deutsche Gegenwart. Berlin: Buchmeister Verlag. This was a popular text published the year Hitler came to power attempting to directly link the German prehistoric past to the present (this is the literal meaning of the title). The image shows a reconstruction of "northern Germanic" (actually Scandinavian) costumes from Bronze Age burials. (Graphic courtesy of Bettina Arnold)

Altered prehistory also played an important role in rehabilitating German self-respect after the humiliating defeat of 1918. The dedication of the 1921 edition of Kossinna's seminal work *German Prehistory: A Preeminently National Discipline* reads: "To the German people, as a building block in the reconstruction of the externally as well as internally disintegrated fatherland."

According to Nazi doctrine, the Germanic culture of northern Europe was responsible for virtually all major intellectual and technological achievements of Western civilization. Maps that appeared in archaeological publications between 1933 and 1945 invariably showed the Germanic homeland as the center of diffusionary waves, bringing civilization to less developed cultures to the south, west, and east. Hitler presented his own views on this subject in a dinner-table monologue in which he referred to the Greeks as Germans who had survived a northern natural catastrophe and evolved a highly developed culture in southern contexts. Such wishful thinking was supported by otherwise reputable archaeologists. The *Research Report of the Reichsbund for German Prehistory*, July to December 1941, for example, reported the nine-week expedition of the archaeologist Hans Reinerth and a few colleagues to Greece, where they claimed to have discovered major new evidence of Indogermanic migration to Greece during Neolithic times.

This perspective was ethnocentric, racist, and genocidal. Slavic peoples occupying what had once been, on the basis of the distribution of archaeological remains, Germanic territory, were to be relocated or exterminated to supply true

Germans with *Lebensraum* (living space). When the new Polish state was created in 1919, Kossinna published an article, "The German Ostmark, Home Territory of the Germans," which used archaeological evidence to support Germany's claim to the area. Viewed as only temporarily occupied by racially inferior "squatters," Poland and Czechoslovakia could be reclaimed for "racially pure" Germans.

Prehistoric archaeologists in Germany, who felt they had been ignored, poorly funded, and treated as second-class citizens by colleagues specializing in the more honored disciplines of classical and Near Eastern archaeology, now seemed to have everything to gain by an association with the rising Nazi party. Between 1933, the year of Hitler's accession to power, and 1935, eight new chairs were created in German prehistory, and funding became available for prehistoric excavations across Germany and eastern Europe on an unprecedented scale. Numerous institutes came into being during this time, such as the Institute for Prehistory in Bonn in 1938. Museums for protohistory were established, and prehistoric collections were brought out of storage and exhibited, in many cases for the first time. Institutes for rune research were created to study the *futhark*, or runic alphabet in use in northern Europe from about the third to the thirteenth centuries A.D. Meanwhile, the Römisch Germanisches Zentral Museum in Mainz became the Zentral Museum für Deutsche Vor-und Frühgeschichte in 1939. (Today it has its pre-war title once again.)

Germanische Tracht zur älteren Bronzezeit um 1600 v. Chr.

Figure 2. Image from Richard Ströbel 1935 Unseres Volkes Ursprung: 5000 Jahre nordish-germanische Kulturentwicklung (The Origins of Our People: 5000 years of nordic-germanic cultural development). Berlin: Propaganda-Verlag Paul Hochmuth. This volume was part of a series of "educational" text intended to be used in schools. Again there is an explicit linking of past and present. The caption translates as "Germanic costume of the late Bronze Age around 1600 BC." (Graphic courtesy of Bettina Arnold)

Open-air museums like the reconstructed Neolithic and Bronze Age lake settlements at Unteruhldingen on Lake Constanz were intended to popularize prehistory. An archaeological film series, produced and directed by the prehistorian Lothar Zotz, included titles like *Threatened by the Steam Plow, Germany's Bronze Age, The Flames of Prehistory*, and *On the Trail of the Eastern Germans*. The popular journals such as *Die Kunde* (The Message), and *Germanen-Erbe (Germanic Heritage)* proliferated. The latter publication was produced by the Ahnenerbe ("Ancestor History") organization, run as a personal project of Reichsführer-SS and chief of police Heinrich Himmler and funded by interested Germans to research, excavate, and restore real and imagined Germanic cultural relics. Himmler's interests in mysticism and the occult extended to archaeology; SS archaeologists were sent out in the wake of invading German forces to track down important archaeological finds and antiquities to be transported back to the Reich. It was this activity that inspired Steven Spielberg's *Raiders of the Lost Ark*.

The popular journals contained abundant visual material. One advertisement shows the reconstruction of a Neolithic drum from a pile of meaningless sherds. The text exhorts readers to "keep your eyes open, for every *Volksgenosse* [fellow German] can contribute to this important national project! Do not assume that a ceramic vessel is useless because it falls apart during excavation. Carefully preserve even the smallest fragment!" An underlined sentence emphasizes the principal message: "Every single find is important because it represents a document of our ancestors!"

Amateur organizations were actively recruited by appeals to patriotism. The membership flyer for the official National Confederation for German Prehistory (*Reichsbund für Deutsche Vorgeschichte*), under the direction of Hans Reinerth of the Amt Rosenberg, proclaimed: "Responsibility with respect to our indigenous prehistory must again fill every German with pride!" The organization stated its goals as "the interpretation and dissemination of unfalsified knowledge regarding the history and cultural achievements of our northern Germanic ancestors on German and foreign soil."

For Himmler objective science was not the aim of German prehistoric archaeology. Hermann Rauschning, an early party member who became disillusioned with the Nazis and left Germany before the war, quotes Himmler as saying: "The one and only thing that matters to us, and the thing these people are paid for by the State, is to have ideas of history that strengthen our people in their necessary national pride. In all this troublesome business we are only interested in one thing—to project into the dim and distant past the picture of our nation as we envisage it for the future. Every bit of Tacitus in his *Germania* is tendentious stuff. Our teaching of German origins has depended for centuries on a falsification. We are entitled to impose one of our own at any time."

Meanwhile archaeological evidence that did not conform to Nazi dogma was ignored or suppressed. A good example is the controversy surrounding the Externsteine, a natural sandstone formation near Horn in northern Germany. In the twelfth century Benedictine monks from the monastery in nearby Paderborn carved a system of chambers into the rock faces of the Externsteine. In the mid-1930s a contingent of SS Ahnenerbe researchers excavated at the site in an attempt to prove its significance as the center of the Germanic universe, a kind of Teutonic mecca. The excavators, led by Julius Andree, an archaeologist with questionable credentials, and supported by Hermann Wirth, one of the founders

Figure 3. Image from Paul Vogel 1939 *Deutsche Vorgeschichte: Eine erste Einführung* (German Prehistory: An Introduction). Frankfurt am Main: Verlag Moritz Diesterweg. This is another school text, and the image attempt to combine actual archaeological evidence (in this case of the so-called "sun cult" represented by the bronze disc being pulled on a four-wheeled wagon) in a reconstruction of "early Germanic life." The link between past and present was here supposed to prepare the way for state-controlled neo-pagan religion replacing Christianity. (Graphic courtesy Bettina Arnold)

of the SS Ahnenerbe, were looking for the remains of an early Germanic temple at the Externsteine, where they claimed a cult of solar worshipers had once flourished. The site was described in numerous publications as a monument to German unity and the glorious Germanic past, despite the fact that no convincing evidence of a temple or Germanic occupation of the site was ever found.

So preposterous were the claims made by Andree, Wirth, and their associates that numerous mainstream archaeologists openly questioned the findings of the investigators who became popularly known as *Germanomanen* or "Germanomaniacs." Eventually Himmler and the Ahnenerbe organization disowned the project, but not before several hundred books and pamphlets on the alleged cult site had been published.

By 1933 the Nazis had gone a step further, initiating a movement whose goal was to replace all existing religious denominations with a new pseudo-pagan state religion based loosely on Germanic mythology, solar worship, nature cults, and a Scandinavian people's assembly or *thing*, from which the new movement derived its name. Central to the movement were openair theaters or *Thingstätten*, where festivals, military ceremonies, and morality plays, known as *Thingspiele*, were to be staged. To qualify as a Thingstätten, evidence of significant Germanic occupation of the site had to be documented. There was considerable competition among

Figure 4. Image from the cover of one of several National Socialist journals dedicated to "racial hygiene": the title Volk und Rasse translates as "The People and Race". The volume shown dates to August 26, and shows an "ideal" Aryan facial type. The journal regularly sponsored photo competitions for the "purest" example of both male and female "Germanic" facial types. (Graphic courtesy of Bettina Arnold)

municipalities throughout Germany for this honor. Twelve Thingstätten had been dedicated by September 1935, including one on the summit of the Heiligenberg in Heidelberg.

The Heiligenberg was visited sporadically during the Neolithic, possibly for ritual purposes; there is no evidence of permanent occupation. It was densely settled during the Late Bronze Age (1200–750 B.C.), and a double wall-and-ditch system was built there in the Late Iron Age (200 B.C. to the Roman occupation), when it was a hillfort settlement. Two provincial Roman watchtowers, as well as several Roman dedicatory inscriptions, statue bases, and votive stones, have been found at the site.

When excavations in the 1930s failed to produce evidence of Germanic occupation the Heiligenberg was granted Thingstätte status on the basis of fabricated evidence in the published excavation reports. Ironically, most of the summit's prehistoric deposits were destroyed in the course of building the open-air arena. The Heiligenberg Thingstätte actually held only one Thingspiel before the Thingmovement was terminated. Sensing the potential for resistance from German Christians, the Ministry of Propaganda abandoned the whole concept in 1935. Today the amphitheater is used for rock concerts.

Beyond its convenience for propaganda and as justification for expansion into countries like Czechoslovakia and Poland, the archaeological activities of the Amt Rosenberg and Himmler's Ahnenerbe were just so much window dressing for the upper echelons of the party. There was no real respect for the past or its remains. While party prehistorians like Reinerth and Andree distorted the facts, the SS destroyed archaeological sites like Biskupin in Poland. Until Germany's fortunes on the eastern front suffered a reversal in 1944, the SS Ahnenerbe conducted excavations at Biskupin, one of the best-preserved Early Iron Age (600–400 B.C.) sites in all of central Europe. As the troops retreated, they were ordered to demolish as much of the site's preserved wooden fortifications and structures as possible.

Not even Hitler was totally enthusiastic about Himmler's activities. He is quoted by Albert Speer, his chief architect, as complaining: "Why do we call the whole world's attention to the fact that we have no past? It's bad enough that the Romans were erecting great buildings when our forefathers were still living in mud huts; now Himmler is starting to dig up these villages of mud huts and enthusing over every potsherd and stone axe he finds. All we prove by that is that we were still throwing stone hatchets and crouching around open fires when Greece and Rome had already reached the highest stage of culture. We should really do our best to keep quiet about this past. Instead Himmler makes a great fuss about it all. The present-day Romans must be having a laugh at these revelations."

"Official" involvement in archaeology consisted of visits by Himmler and various SS officers to SS-funded and staffed excavations, like the one on the Erdenburg in the Rhineland, or press shots of Hitler and Goebbels viewing a reconstructed "Germanic" Late Bronze Age burial in its tree-trunk coffin, part of the 1934 "Deutsches Volk—Deutsche Arbeit" exhibition in Berlin. Party appropriation of prehistoric data was evident in the use of Indo-European and Germanic design symbols in Nazi uniforms and regalia. The double lightning bolt, symbol of Himmler's SS organization, was adapted from a Germanic rune. The swastika is an Indo-European sun symbol which appears in ceramic designs as early as the Neolithic in western Europe and continues well into early medieval times.

German archaeologists during this period fall into three general categories: those who were either true believers or self-serving opportunists; those (the vast majority) who accepted without criticism the appropriation and distortion of prehistoric archaeology; and those who openly opposed these practices.

Victims of the regime were persecuted on the basis of race or political views, and occasionally both. Gerhard Bersu, who had trained a generation of post-World War I archaeologists in the field techniques of settlement archaeology, was prematurely retired from the directorship of the Rauomisch Germanische Kommission in 1935. His refusal to condone or conduct research tailored to Nazi ideological requirements, in addition to his rejection of the racist Kossinna school, ended his career as a prehistorian until after World War II. The official reason given for the witch-hunt, led by Hans Reinerth under the auspices of the Amt Rosenberg, was Bersu's Jewish heritage. By 1950 Bersu was back in Germany, again directing the Rauomisch Germanische Kommission.

It should be noted that some sound work was accomplished during this period despite political interference. The vocabulary of field reports carefully conformed to the dictates of funding sources, but the methodology was usually unaffected. Given time this would have changed as politically motivated terms and concepts altered the intellectual vocabulary of the discipline. In 1935, for example, the entire prehistoric and early historic chronologies were officially renamed: the Bronze and pre-Roman Iron Ages became the "Early Germanic period," the Roman Iron Age the "Climax Germanic period," the Migration period the "Late Germanic period," and everything from the Carolingians to the thirteenth century the "German Middle Ages."

It is easy to condemn the men and women who were part of the events that transformed the German archaeological community between 1933 and 1945. It is much more difficult to understand the choices they made or avoided in the social and political contexts of the time. Many researchers who began as advocates of Reinerth's policies in the Amt Rosenberg and Himmler's Ahnenerbe organization later became disenchanted. Others, who saw the system as a way to develop and support prehistory as a discipline, were willing to accept the costs of the Faustian bargain it offered. The benefits were real, and continue to be felt to this day in the institutions and programs founded between 1933 and 1945.

The paralysis felt by many scholars from 1933 to 1945 continued to affect research in the decades after the war. Most scholars who were graduate students during the 12-year period had to grapple with a double burden: a humiliating defeat and the disorienting experience of being methodologically "deprogrammed." Initially there was neither time nor desire to examine the reasons for the Nazi prostitution of archaeology. Unfortunately prehistoric archaeology is the only German social-science discipline that has still to publish a self-critical study of its role in the events of the 1930s and 1940s.

The reluctance of German archaeologists to come to terms with the past is a complex issue. German prehistoric archaeology is still a young discipline, and first came into its own as a result of Nazi patronage. There is therefore a certain feeling that any critical analysis of the motives and actions of the generation and the regime that engendered the discipline would be ungrateful at best and at worst a betrayal of trust. The vast majority of senior German archaeologists, graduate students immediately after the war, went straight from the front lines to the uni-

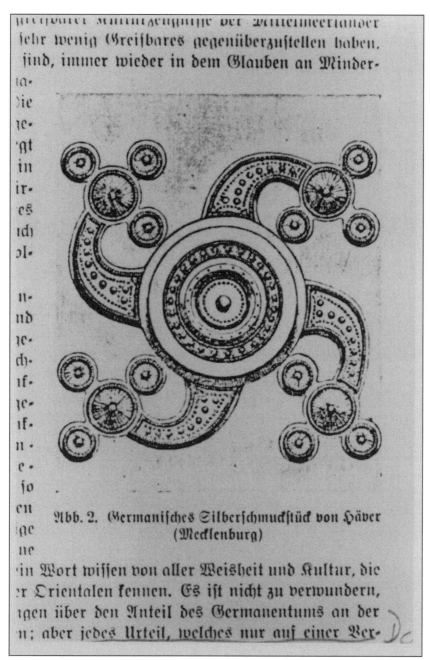

Figure 5. Image from Wilhelm Teudt 1934 Germanische Heiligtümer. Lippe. This Migration-Period silver brooch from the Prussian state of Mecklenburg in the form of a swastika was reproduced frequently in various Nazi party publications, appearing at least once on the cover of Germanenerbe, the popular publication on archaeology and history funded by Heinrich Himmler's SS-Ahnenerbe (Ancestor Heritage Society). (Graphic courtesy of Bettina Arnold)

versities, and their dissertation advisers were men whose careers had been determined by their connections within the Nazi party.

The German system of higher education is built upon close bonds of dependence and an almost medieval fealty between a graduate student and his or her dissertation advisor. These bonds are maintained even after the graduate student has embarked on an academic career. Whistle-blowers are rare, since such action would amount to professional suicide. But in the past decade or so, most of the generation actively involved in archaeological research and teaching between 1933 and 1945 have died. Their knowledge of the personal intrigues and alliances that allowed the Nazi party machine to function has died with them. Nonetheless, there are indications that the current generation of graduate students is beginning to penetrate the wall of silence that has surrounded this subject since 1945. The remaining official documents and publications may allow at least a partial reconstruction of the role of archaeology in the rise and fall of the Nazi regime.

The future of prehistoric archaeology in the recently unified Germany will depend on an open confrontation with the past. Archaeologists in the former East Germany must struggle with the legacy of both Nazi and Communist manipulation of their discipline. Meanwhile, the legacy of the Faustian bargain struck by German archaeologists with the Nazi regime should serve as a cautionary tale beyond the borders of a unified Germany: Archaeological research funded wholly or in part by the state is vulnerable to state manipulation. The potential for political exploitation of the past seems to be greatest in countries experiencing internal instability. Germany in the years following World War I was a country searching for its own twentieth-century identity. Prehistoric archaeology was one means to that end.

2

Bones and Bureaucrats: New York's Great Cemetary Imbroglio

Spencer P.M. Harrington

The bones of 420 enslaved Africans found last year under a parking lot two blocks north of New York's City Hall comprise the largest and earliest collection of African-American remains, and possibly the largest and earliest collection of American colonial remains of any ethnic group. The excavation of the old Negros Burial Ground has challenged the popular belief that there was no slavery in colonial New York, and has provided unparalleled data for the Howard University scholars who will study the remains of New York's first African Americans. But as archaeologists removed the remains one by one, they dug up age-old resentment and suspicion with every trowel-full of earth. Scholarly excitement was tempered by the protest of the city's black community, which felt its concerns were not being addressed in decisions about the excavation and disposition of the remains. In the flurry of protests, negotiations, and political maneuverings, the controversy took on an undeniably racial cast. The African Burial Ground, as it is known today, became a "microcosm of the issues of racism and economic exploitation confronting New York City," says Michael L. Blakey, a Howard University anthropologist and the burial ground's scientific director.

In a national context, the controversy over the burial ground excavation became an important episode in a larger struggle of descendant communities to reclaim their heritage. But more specifically, the story was about African-American empowerment: about how a black congressman, acting on the advice of New York City's first black mayor, stopped the excavation of the burial ground; about how the African-American community chose Washington D.C.'s Howard University, the country's most prestigious black research university, as a venue for the study of the remains, thereby ensuring that black researchers and students would study and interpret the remains of their ancestors; and about how the city's black community lobbied for and received a $3 million appropriation from Congress for a memorial and commemorative museum. Equally important were the hard lessons learned by the General Services Administration, the federal agency that supervised the excavation—lessons about the importance of descendant-community involvement in salvage archaeology.

The story of the African Burial Ground begins in 1626, when the Dutch West Indies Company imported its first shipment of slaves, 11 young men from today's Congo-Angola region of Africa. Two years later, the company brought over three

African women "for the comfort of the company's Negro men," according to Dutch West Indies records. Like the British who governed Manhattan after them, the Dutch encountered difficulties attracting European settlers to the new colony. Grave manpower shortages threatened the profitability of the Dutch West Indies trading enterprise, and the company was quick to import slave labor to farm its fields. In 1664, just before the Dutch ceded Manhattan to the British, enslaved Africans made up about 40 percent of the colony's total population. The British continued the slave trade, importing as many as 6,800 Africans between 1700 and 1774, many of whom had worked previously on Caribbean plantations. By the mid-eighteenth century, New York had become a thriving port town, and enslaved Africans loaded and unloaded cargo at the docks, wharves, slips, and warehouses along the East River. They also piloted boats ferrying produce from the farming villages of Long Island, repaired and expanded city streets, and worked in shipbuilding and construction. On the eve of the American Revolution, New York City had the largest number of enslaved Africans of any English colonial settlement except Charleston, South Carolina, and it had the highest proportion of slaves to Europeans of any northern settlement. Though seldom acknowledged, Africans were essential to the functioning, as well as the building of colonial New York.

In November 1697, New York City adopted a policy of mortuary apartheid, declaring lower Manhattan churchyards off-limits to blacks. Forced to look for a place to bury its dead, New York's African population, which then numbered about 700, chose unappropriated property outside city limits two blocks north of today's City Hall. There, from 1712 until 1790, in an area characterized by David Valentine, an early city historian, as "unattractive and desolate," Africans conducted last rites for their people. "So little seems to have been thought of the race that not even a dedication of their burial place was made by church authorities," wrote Valentine of what was known then as the Negros Burial Ground. Under the British, Africans were subject to a sunset curfew and city ordinances that prohibited unsupervised gatherings of more than three slaves. They were, however, allowed to gather in large numbers and with regularity at the burial ground. Some 10,000 to 20,000 people, both black and lower-class white, are believed to have been buried in the five-to-six-acre plot of land.

The growth of the city's population in the late eighteenth and early nineteenth centuries led to a northward expansion along main thoroughfares such as Broadway. Street plans were drafted, and blocks over the burial ground were divided into lots for residential and commercial development. By the end of the century, ten- and 15-story buildings with deep foundations and with vaults that were used for storage and coal delivery were going up. The Negros Burial Ground, now paved or built over, was all but forgotten, noted only in a few historical maps and documents. Meanwhile, African Americans were now burying their dead on the Lower East Side, near what are now Chrystie and Delancey streets.

Nearly 200 years later a section of the burial ground lay beneath a parking lot between Duane and Reade streets. In December 1990, New York sold this property and another plot on nearby Foley Square to the General Services Administration (GSA), the federal agency charged with constructing and managing government buildings. The GSA paid $104 million for both properties, which it hoped to develop simultaneously. It planned to build a $276 million, 34-story office tower and adjoining four-story pavilion on the parking lot area. A federal court-

Figure 1. One of the many rallies protesting the excavation of the African Burial Ground. Congress allocated 3 million dollars to finance the planning for the memorialization at the site. Some believed that "3 million dollars nor any amount" would compensate for the desecrated burials. (Photo courtesy of the U.S. General Services Administration)

house was envisioned for the Foley Square property. The tower, designated 290 Broadway, would contain the offices of the United States Attorney, a regional office of the Environmental Protection Agency, and the downtown district office of the Internal Revenue Service. The pavilion would house a day-care center, an auditorium, and a pedestrian galleria.

Five months before the GSA bought the sites from the city, the agency hired Historic Conservation and Interpretation (HCI), an archaeological salvage and consulting firm, to write the archaeological portion of an environmental impact statement for the 290 Broadway site. Such statements are a legal requirement before any new construction using federal funds can begin. HCI's report identified the area as a section of the old Negros Burial Ground and included historical maps indicating its approximate location. But the impact statement predicted that nineteenth- and twentieth-century construction at the site would have destroyed any significant archaeological deposits. It read in part: "The construction of deep sub-basements would have obliterated any remains within the lots that fall within the historic bounds of the cemetery."

Still, the statement left open the possibility of some human remains being preserved under an old alley that once bisected Duane and Reade streets. That the GSA purchased the land despite this possibility suggests that the agency was betting on HCI's overall assessment that few, if any, human remains would be found there. In retrospect, GSA regional director William Diamond admits that the agency would never have bought the land if it had known it would have to remove hundreds of skeletons before sinking the office tower foundation.

In May 1991, six months after purchasing the land, the GSA hired HCI to investigate the possibility that there were undisturbed burials in the alley area. By the end of the summer the firm started to find human bones. In September a full-scale excavation was underway, and on October 8 Diamond held a press conference to announce the discovery of the remains. One year later, the last of some 420 skeletons had been removed from the site to Lehman College in the Bronx, where they were undergoing conservation before being transferred to Howard University for more detailed study.

African-American outrage over the handling of the excavation stemmed from a perception that the black community had no control over the fate of its heritage—that decisions about the burial ground were being made by white bureaucrats with little insight into African-American history and spiritual sensitivities. "Religious, Afrocentric people believe that to disturb burials in any way is the highest form of disrespect," says Gina Stahlnecker, an aide to State Senator David Patterson, who represents Harlem and the Upper West Side. "There were some people who believed the archaeologists were releasing evil." According to Peggy King Jorde, of the Mayor's Office of Construction, an early monitor of the project, the GSA initially was calling the site a "potters' field," which she felt divorced it from its African origin and diminished its importance. There were even rumors, she says, that the bones were to be removed without any archaeological study. Jorde says that the GSA had only vague ideas about what to do with the remains that were coming to light.

The black community was also upset because it was not alerted at the outset to what might lie beneath the parking lot between Duane and Reade streets. While the GSA did distribute both draft and final environmental impact statements to more than 200 federal, state, and city agencies and local community groups, the agency did not alert civic groups in predominantly black neighborhoods that the buildings would be constructed on top of the old burial ground. "I spoke to hundreds and hundreds of people in the black community, and no one had ever heard about it," says Stahlnecker. While distributing environmental impact statements to descendant communities may seem like a good idea, it is not customary for private or government developers to do so. Peter Sneed, the GSA's planning staff director, argues that the distribution list was formulated in accordance with federal regulations. "We didn't include the Harlem community board because the project isn't in Harlem, it's in lower Manhattan," he says. "We felt it was incumbent upon the Mayor's office to spread the word. It's unreasonable to expect a federal agency to know every interest group in the community."

African-American fury over the excavation increased dramatically after a backhoe operator digging the tower's foundation accidentally destroyed several of the burials. The incident was reported by Dan Pagano, an archaeologist for the city's Landmarks Preservation Commission, who was photographing the site through a telephoto lens when he spotted HCI archaeologists sifting through human remains outside the excavation area, where the backhoe had scooped up earth so that a concrete footing could be poured for the tower. Pagano says jawbones and leg and arm bones were among the remains scooped up by the backhoe. The GSA blamed the accident on an out-of-date drawing that the construction crews were using to determine which part of the site was "culturally sterile." Diamond halted tower construction pending further investigation by archaeologists. The incident led State Senator David Patterson to form an oversight committee to monitor the burial ground excavation.

Stories the Bones Will Tell

The skeletal remains and associated artifacts from the African Burial Ground are the only concrete evidence recovered to date of the life of Africans who lived in colonial New York City. The burials were found 16 to 28 feet below street level, many coffins stacked one on top of another—an urban mortuary practice of the period. Although the majority of burials are people of African descent, about seven percent appear to be Europeans. Physical anthropologists determine racial differences by studying characteristic features of the skull, pelvis, and limb bones. The 420 skeletons found at the New York City site represent a fraction of the entire graveyard population. The condition of the remains varies considerably, from good to extremely poor. There were no grave markers or burial maps, and other than wood, coffin nails, and shroud pins, few artifacts associated with the burials were found. "These were not wealthy graves," says Howard University's Michael L. Blakey, the African Burial Ground's scientific director. "The most striking artifacts were the glass beadwork on one woman, and cowrie shells," he says. "Cowrie shells had a symbolic function in West African funeral practice. They were symbols of the passage in death across the sea and have been variously interpreted as a return to Africa or the afterlife."

In the vast majority of the burials the deceased's head faces west, which prompted journalists to report that the bodies were arranged according to Christian burial practice so that they could sit up and see the rising sun on Judgment Day. But Blakey warns that there was considerable overlap between African and Western burial practices during this period, and it is unclear just how Christianized the Africans were. Blakey points out that a few graves facing east may indicate Moslem burials.

Spencer Turkel, an anthropologist with the Metropolitan Forensic Anthropology Team, estimates two-thirds of the remains found at the site were male, and that 40 percent of the sample were children. He says that sex ratios may change after lab study because the hard physical labor demanded by slavery affected the musculoskeletal structure in such a way that some female skeletons look male. The soil in which the bodies were buried was highly acidic and corrosive to human bone, causing further complications for researchers. "One problem we've been having is trying to determine the difference between damage to the bone caused by life experience and that caused by post-mortem soil exposure," says Turkel.

He notes that field examination revealed some obvious causes of death—a musket ball lodged in a rib cage, and a case of rickets, a nutritional deficiency. Diagnosis of other causes of death will have to await further study. "The major epidemics of that period were cholera and yellow fever, but here we're dealing with vague written descriptions," he says. "Many of the children would have died from diarrhea, which is a form of malnutrition. Poorly nourished children would also have been susceptible to pneumonia."

Meanwhile, Howard University scientists are contemplating the skeletal sample's research potential. Because seventeenth- and eighteenth-century historical sources tend to dismiss or ignore New York's enslaved Africans, anthropological research becomes all the more important for scholars interpreting what their life was like. "This is a unique opportunity to gain a better understanding of the biology, health, and culture of the first generation of people who would become the African-American people," says Blakey.

The primary focus of the research conducted at Howard will be the social and economic conditions affecting the health of the enslaved Africans. The interdisciplinary team studying the skeletal population will consider questions dealing with demography, epidemiology, nutrition, social history, and cultural transformation. Demographic research will attempt to provide information on the African ethnicity of the sample. "We hope to bring attention to the great variety of cultural groups that were brought over from Africa," says Blakey. "Some of these individuals may have spent time in the West Indies or

South America, and we may be able to pick that up," he says. Meanwhile, epidemiologists will study the Africans' adjustment to New York's disease environment. Turkel notes that such bone-scarring diseases as tuberculosis and syphilis were relatively rare in Africa, and finding them in this population would yield interesting data on the community's acculturation to Western diseases. Research on the skeletons may also reveal information about nutrition in the colonial period, while study of mortuary practices at the site will show the extent to which African burial traditions were retained or modified.

Because the sample is large enough to account for human variation, accurate statistical analysis will be possible. And because of the age of the burial population, the sample provides baseline data against which hypotheses about the development of specific pathologies in the African-American population can be tested, such as the relatively high incidence of hypertension in today's black community. The data will also yield information on toxic-element levels in pre-industrial America.

The draft research design submitted by Blakey this past fall notes that earlier studies of African-American skeletal populations tended to be descriptive of physical characteristics such as sex, age, and height rather than focused on biohistorical information such as diet, African nationality, and adaptation to disease. According to Blakey, carefully conceived, large-scale academic research plans for African-American archaeological sites are rare. "The growth of African-American archaeology reflects the randomness of the discoveries resulting from development projects," he says, adding that specialists in African-American archaeology often find themselves responding to "emergency situations," in which burial grounds or other sites are threatened by development projects. Theresa Singleton, an archaeologist at the Smithsonian Institution, says that "quick and dirty" salvage archaeology has compromised historical sites in general, and African-American sites in particular, because "you need time to study sites thoroughly, and most contractors don't have time." She adds that "many contract archaeologists don't know much about African-American archaeology." Blakey notes that contract archaeologists "have not often taken advantage of the rich literature and perspectives of Afro-American scholarship on Afro-Americans. That needs to change. And that's one of the things all the protest in New York brought about."—S.P.M.H.

Miriam Francis, a member of Patterson's committee, says that the involvement of African-American anthropologists in the excavation was among the group's most pressing concerns. "If it was an African find, we wanted to make sure that it was interpreted from an African point of view," she says. But the committee soon learned that the GSA had picked physical anthropologists from the city's Metropolitan Forensic Anthropology Team (MFAT) to conduct field analyses of the remains and that the bones would be stored at the group's Lehman College facility. "We didn't know anything about MFAT, whether they were butchers, bakers, or candlestick makers," says Francis. She notes that when the committee introduced the GSA to African-American specialists like Howard University's Michael Blakey, it was either stonewalled or ignored.

Meanwhile, the GSA was having difficulty getting HCI, its archaeological salvage contractor, to produce a research design stating conservation measures and scientific study goals for the burial project. The GSA had managed to obtain extensions on the report's due date from the Advisory Council on Historic Preservation, the government agency that reviews all federal projects that might have an impact on historic sites. Still, the missing research plan sent further signals to the black community that something was wrong with the way work was progressing. "Any archaeological excavation is useless without a research design," noted Landmarks Preservation Commission Chair Laurie Beckelman at a congressional hearing on the burial ground. "It's like driving a car in a foreign country without a road map or destination."

HCI's Edward Rutsch, the project's archaeologist, says that although he was responsible for the research design, he felt too overworked to get it done properly. "They [GSA] had us working seven days a week and overtime every day," says Rutsch. "Many times it was expressed to me that millions of dollars of public money were being lost. There was terrific pressure to get the excavation done—to finish it."

Last April, black activists staged a one-day blockade of the site in an effort to prevent the GSA from pouring concrete for the tower's foundation. Among other things, they were concerned that there was little African-American involvement in the scientific aspects of the excavation; they were visibly unhappy at the choice of Lehman College as the site for the conservation of the remains. Bones from the site had been wrapped in newspaper and placed in cardboard boxes before being shipped to Lehman. One problem, according to Dan Baer of Edwards and Kelcey, an engineering firm hired to manage the site, was that "We were digging them out faster than [storage] cases could be made." But in the African-American community there was concern that the bones were being damaged at Lehman. "They had some remains up there in boxes ten or 11 months," says Abd-Allah Adesanya, director of the Mayor's Office of African American and Caribbean Affairs. "They were wrapped in newspaper longer than they should have been. They had to be rewrapped in acid-free paper." Baer says, "The bones were stored in newspaper, which may be scientific protocol, but it didn't appear respectful to those who visited the site. It was a mistake that was made. But the bones were in good shape and Dr. Blakey said so after touring the facility."

Blakey's tour of Lehman resulted from pressure by Senator Patterson's committee. "We kept asking them [MFAT], 'Can we go up there?' And that involved more waiting, more delays," says Miriam Francis. "It wasn't that we were against Lehman, we just wanted to see how our ancestors were being stored." Blakey's visit to the facility confirmed the community's suspicion of inadequate conservation. In a letter to ARCHAEOLOGY, Blakey wrote "We intervened in time to prevent the potential for further deterioration, such as the spread of mold in the skeletal remains due to inadequate environmental controls, and improper storage of skeletal materials on top of fragile bone."

As the excavation progressed, the GSA began briefing the public on the burial project's progress. But there was a widespread perception among African Americans that the GSA was merely paying lip-service to the public, that they were digging the bones as fast as they could so the tower foundation could be poured. "People would tell them [the GSA] their gripes, then they went off and did what they wanted," says Adesanya. "The community wanted to be let in on the decision-making process, to influence the direction of the project." While descendant-community input into decisions about the course of contract excavations seems desirable when human remains are involved, consultation is not part of standard archaeological practice. Nonetheless "the [African-American] community was very unhappy," says Diamond, "and I understood that and kept saying to them, I wish I could help you with this but my obligations by law are contrary to your wishes, and the only way we can get this changed is by an act of Congress or an agreement from the administrator of the GSA.' And I was in consultation with them [GSA administrator Richard G. Austin and members of Congress] and they were telling me to continue the construction."

Figure 2. Burial 37—intact male skeleton considered to be in a good state of preservation. (Photo courtesy of the U.S. General Services Administration)

At the GSA's public meetings, African Americans also questioned the propriety of continuing with the removal of remains from the area where the pavilion would be built. They also hoped that the GSA would consider not building the pavilion, or at least modify the plans so there would be no further removals. "There were several conflicting demands," recalls Diamond. "Some wanted the exhumation to stop, others wanted nothing built on the site, and still others wanted a museum built on the site.... But I had no authority but to continue under the law with the construction."

The GSA eventually replaced Historic Conservation and Interpretation with John Milner Associates (JMA), a West Chester, Pennsylvania, archaeological contractor. JMA had recently completed a successful excavation of an early nineteenth-century cemetery associated with the First African Baptist Church in Philadelphia that brought to light information on that city's early black history. "JMA had done this sort of job before," says Baer. "We didn't feel we had involved the community enough and we thought that JMA would improve that situation."

But reports by agencies monitoring the excavation were becoming increasingly critical. One report filed by the Advisory Council on Historic Preservation stated, in part, that: "...the GSA was proceeding without any clear focus on why the remains were being removed; how they were to be analyzed; how many more bodies were involved; or, what the African-American community's desire was for the treatment of the burials." Mayor David Dinkins sent a letter to Diamond complaining about the lack of a research design and requesting "that the GSA suspend all excavation and construction activities in the pavilion area and bring the project into compliance with the terms outlined in the Memorandum of Agreement [a document specifying the terms of archaeological work to be undertaken in advance of construction]...." There is "no basis for discontinuance of ongoing excavations" was Diamond's response a week later. "I would not be put in a position of abrogating important government contracts because of political pressure," he later recalled.

The final act in the drama was played out before the congressional committee that appropriates funds for the GSA, the House Subcommittee on Public Buildings and Grounds. Meeting in New York, the subcommittee was chaired by former Representative Gus Savage, an Illinois Democrat, who heard testimony from the GSA, the Advisory Council, the city's Landmarks Preservation Commission, and concerned citizens. At the meeting, the GSA argued that stopping the excavation would jeopardize the exposed human remains, and it estimated that relinquishing the pavilion site would cost taxpayers as much as $40 million: $5 million in interest payments, $10 million in land acquisition costs, and $25 million in initial construction costs.

Savage then subjected GSA representatives to intense questioning, during which it became apparent that at the outset the GSA was aware that a historic burial ground had once occupied the land it intended to purchase and develop, and that the agency had made no contingency plans for construction in the event that human remains were found. The meeting also revealed that the building prospectus for 290 Broadway the GSA had submitted for Congressional approval did not mention the burial ground, nor was Savage's subcommittee alerted by the agency when HCI's impact statement mentioned the possibility of intact graves. Savage ended the hearing early, noting that he would not approve any further GSA projects until he received "a more honest and respectful response" from the agency regarding its excavation of the burial ground. "And don't waste your time asking this subcommittee for anything else as long as I'm chairman, unless you can figure out a way to go around me! I am not going to be part of your disrespect," Savage said.

Three days later, Savage halted excavation on the pavilion site, and last October former President Bush signed Public Law 102-393, ordering the GSA to cease construction of the pavilion portion of the project and approving $3 million for the construction of a museum honoring the contribution of African Americans to colonial New York City. Meanwhile, JMA removed the last of the exposed burials.

In a statement to the House Subcommittee on Public Buildings and Grounds, GSA head Richard G. Austin acknowledged that "in hindsight we could have handled some things better." Austin's statement made it clear to all parties that the GSA recognized the need for descendant-community cooperation in salvage excavations. Its office tower would be built, but African Americans would determine the course of research on the remains. The agency hired Blakey to develop a research design, which he produced in consultation with JMA and numerous black scholars. Blakey was also appointed scientific director of a five-year research program on the remains that will take place at Howard University. Sherill D. Wilson, an urban anthropologist and ethnohistorian, calls the sudden involvement of black scholars "very revolutionary." Such scholarship, she says, "is going to set a precedent for what happens to African burial grounds in the future, and how African heritage will be viewed by the public."

Meanwhile, a chastened GSA has also set up a federal advisory committee chaired by Howard Dodson of New York's Schomburg Center for Research in Black Culture that will address plans for reburial of the remains, an African Burial Ground memorial, a burial ground exhibition in the office tower, and a museum of African and African-American History in New York City. State Senator David Patterson's burial ground oversight committee seeks to create a museum that will honor African-American heritage, "a place similar to Ellis Island, something that can attest to Afro-American history." The city Landmarks Preservation Commission has also proposed that the burial ground be designated a city landmark and has requested that it be considered for National Historic Landmark status. These efforts stemmed in part from a massive petition drive spearheaded by Senator Patterson's oversight committee and jazz musician Noel Pointer that yielded more than 100,000 signatures. Among other things, the petition called for the creation of a museum and landmark status for the burial ground.

The burial ground controversy and its attendant publicity have had important repercussions nationwide. "The media exposure has created a larger, national audience for this type of research," says Theresa Singleton, an archaeologist at the Smithsonian Institution who has done pioneering research on African-American sites. "I've been called by dozens of scholars and laypeople, all of them interested in African-American archaeology, all of them curious about why they don't know more about the field. Until recently, even some black scholars considered African-American archaeology a waste of time. That's changed now."

Things have indeed changed. Public curiosity about this country's African-American past has been aroused by the New York experience. And it is probably safe to assume that in the future government and private developers will take a hard look at how to include descendant communities in their salvage excavations, especially when human remains are concerned. "Everyone could have talked more to everyone else," concludes the GSA's planning staff director Peter Sneed. "There would have been a lot less heartache...the GSA has certainly been sensitized to archaeology."

3

Collaboration at *Inyan Ceyaka Atonwan* (Village at the Rapids)

Janet D. Spector

In my 30-year career as an archaeologist, the first occasion I ever had to work with Indian people was in fieldwork at Little Rapids, a 19th-century Wahpeton Dakota summer planting village located in south-central Minnesota. Our collaborations began somewhat late in the project, in 1986, the fourth and final year of fieldwork. The effects were nonetheless dramatic, transforming the character of our field program and my perception of the 19th-century Wahpeton community.

Why did it take so long to become involved in a collaborative project? Nothing in my disciplinary training at the University of Wisconsin (1960s–1970s) predisposed or prepared me to work collaboratively. On reflection, I see that there were many disincentives for doing so—few of them deliberate but powerful nonetheless. My training was fairly conventional for a specialty in the history and culture of Indian people in the Upper Midwestern U.S.—in my case, during the period of colonial expansion. This apprenticeship discouraged me from even imagining productive collaborations between Indian and non-Indian people in archaeology. These are some of the messages I absorbed:

Message 1—I learned that Indian people did not participate in archaeology as teachers, authors, or excavators. I had no models—positive or negative—of non-Indian archaeologists working with Indian educators, spiritual or community leaders.

Message 2—There is very little connection between contemporary Indian people in our region and the people we study archaeologically even in fairly recent time periods. "Contact" with Europeans quickly led to acculturation, dislocation, cultural disintegration, and a breakdown of cultural distinctiveness and vitality. Our training implied that modern Indian people had little knowledge about the past. Too much time had elapsed; too much had been lost.

These presumed ruptures between past and present are reinforced in the ways our discipline is sub-divided, our majors are organized and courses taught, and our research designed. Anthropology fragments our knowledge about Indian histories and cultures by breaking the field into cultural anthropology and archaeology. The former conventionally studied "traditional Indian cultures" in the timeless, "ethnographic present"; while the latter studied groups known primarily through the archaeological record, and neither showed much interest in contemporary people, or, until recently, the period of colonization. Archaeological "cul-

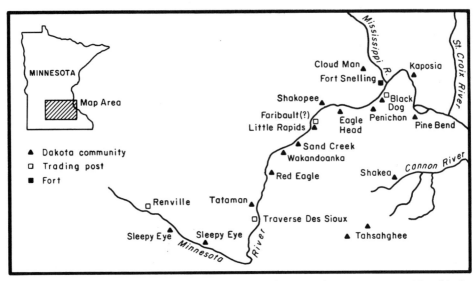

Figure 1. Map showing the location of Little Rapids in southern Minnesota. (Graphic by Ronald Beckwith)

tures" are very distinct from those known ethnographically. We define cultures taxonomically, on the basis of characteristic material objects and we name groups after geographic or time periods (Mississippian, Woodland, Archaic, and Oneota) rather than ancient Winnebago, Dakota, or Anishinabe, in our area, as if these groups had no relationship to one another.

Message 3—Indian people today are interested in archaeological sites artifacts for "political" reasons, not because of cultural or historical interests. This cynical view is reinforced by the general absence of courses about local colonial history and the lingering legacies of those distressing times, particularly from the Indian perspective. In our region, transcripts of 19th-century treaty negotiations document a 150-year history of Indian concerns about the desecration of burial and other sacred sites. These protests predate by just a few decades the extensive archaeological surveys and later excavations of mounds and other earthworks which laid the foundation for regional archaeology—projects done without Indian participation or consent. Archaeology students would be well served by knowing about this history of relations between Indians and archaeologists.

These are just some of the messages I received during my enculturation into archaeology and they created real barriers against imagining active, mutually respectful relationships with Indian people. These barriers began to diminish for me only after becoming involved in feminist anthropology and archaeology. Over the last two decades feminist, third world, African-American, Chicano, and American Indian scholars, activists, and their allies have seriously challenged many academic disciplines including anthropology and archaeology. What are the ramifications of the fact that until fairly recently academic knowledge has been produced almost exclusively by white, middle-class men of European descent, socialized in cultures that discriminate on the basis of race, sex, and class? How has this domination by a rather narrow segment of the population determined the curriculum and the content of courses we teach? our research priorities? the projects that get funded? the manuscripts that get published?

Across the disciplines we have exposed pervasive androcentric and eurocentric (less delicately put sexist, racist, heterosexist, and classist) portrayals of human life, past and present. We have shown that who we are—our gender, cultural background, social and economic position, and personal histories—shapes the character of our work in significant ways. And we have called for more responsible academic work, acknowledging that those of us who produce public knowledge about other people hold a powerful and privileged position.

As my own criticisms of archaeology became increasingly pointed with respect to the treatment of women as subjects of study, I also became acutely aware of the exclusion of Indian people from the creation of archaeological knowledge about their histories and cultures. For some time, the dissonance between my critique of archaeology and its exclusions, and my lack of contact with Dakota people on the Little Rapids project became almost unbearable. At that point I became more active in pursuing a collaboration.

Collaborations at Little Rapids

Initiated in 1979, the goal of the Little Rapids project was to learn about the Wahpeton community life during a turbulent and poorly known period—a time of rapidly accelerating Euroamerican settlement and escalating tensions between cultures as U.S. government officials and Protestant missionaries pressured Dakota people to give up their lands and ways of life. I was particularly interested in understanding more about how these pressures affected men and women and how gender roles, relations, and beliefs shaped the character of encounters between Dakota people and Euroamerican colonists.

Though I was unsure of how to begin, I was committed to making contact with Indian people. In the process of securing permission to excavate at Little Rapids from the landowners and the State Archaeologist, I sent my project proposal to the (now) Minnesota Indian Affairs Council. Within a few weeks, the Council's Executive Director Donald Gurnoe sent me a copy of his letter to Norman Crooks, then chairman of the Prior Lake Sioux Community, the Dakota community geographically closest to Little Rapids. "Many times in the past," Gurnoe wrote,

> the scientific community has run afoul of Indian people through failure to communicate and their insensitive approach to the concerns of the community. This, apparently, is not the case in respect to this project, as Professor Spector has made every effort to enlist the support of Indian people through our offices (Gurnoe to Crooks, April 7, 1980)

This response encouraged me to pursue direct contacts with Dakota people. Dr. Chris Cavender, now Professor of American Indian Studies at SW State University in Marshall, Minnesota, was referred to me as a well known Dakota educator. He was not available at that time and I began the project without further Indian participation.

We excavated at Little Rapids from 1980 to 1982 through the University of Minnesota's archaeological field school program, then suspended excavations to

Figure 2. Chris Cavender, Carolynn Schommer and some crew members at the 1986 archaeological excavation at Little Rapids. (Photo courtesy of Janet Spector)

complete the analysis of those materials. In 1984–1985, while on sabbatical, I felt I could no longer, in good conscience, continue doing Dakota archaeology without their involvement.

I tried again, this time successfully, to reach Dr. Cavender. Our initial conversation was awkward. It seemed late to be consulting him about a project designed several years earlier without any Dakota input. Chris had never heard of Little Rapids, and although he was cordial, he was distant, and I suspected, suspicious. Candid about his views of "anthros" as he calls us, Chris was quite open in his cynicism about the motives of academics, including me.

In our initial conversation I mentioned that 19th century written records consistently named Mazomani as a prominent leader at Little Rapids. Chris said nothing about this at the time, but later he asked if we could visit the site together. Mazomani, it turned out, was related to him through his mother, Elsie Cavender, who was raised by her grandmother, daughter of Mazomani and Blueberry Woman. Over the next few months Chris and I made a number of trips to Little Rapids, often bringing other family members along. We had long conversations about the tensions between archaeologists and Indian people. I learned a good deal about Chris's family history. His mother was a well known oral historian, particularly knowledgeable about the 1862 conflict between some Dakota people and some of the newly arrived American settlers and U.S. soldiers that ultimately led to the forced exile of Dakota people from Minnesota.

Being at the site with people having a direct kinship link to it was a profoundly moving experience. We shared a deep respect for the place that, unlike many Indian sites in our area, had been shielded from plowing, construction and other modern destructions. The only major disturbances there had been done by decades of amateur archaeologists drawn to Little Rapids by the burial mounds at the southern end of the site, their activities permanently etched into the landscape. Though Indian visitors knew we were not digging in or near the cemetery, it was excruciating to walk near the scarred, sacred mounds with them.

As the 1985–86 school year began, Chris and I planned to teach together at Little Rapids. We secured university funding and recruited other instructors for the field program: Carolynn Schommer, a Dakota language instructor at the University of Minnesota and also a descendant of Mazomani, introduced crew members to the Dakota language, tailoring her lessons to our specific work. Ed Cushing, a university ecologist, led students on environmental field trips teaching them about the natural history of the area. He, Chris, and Carolynn compared Dakota and non-Dakota names for and ideas about the local plants that were—and still are—important to Dakota people. Sara Evans, a history professor, helped us critically evaluate 19th-century written records, and Chris shared what he knew from Dakota sources about the people and events described in those documents.

Finally, a project felt right to me. We worked as an interdisciplinary, multicultural team. Every day Chris and Carrie talked about Dakota family, community, and spiritual life; about Dakota philosophy, place names, and the Dakota council fires; and we talked about the Conflict of 1862 and its tragic aftermath. We also talked about racism—19th century and contemporary—including incidents that erupted during the field season.

Before we began to dig, Chris spoke briefly in Dakota, expressing our collective respect for the spirit of the place and our hopes to be guided by wisdom and sensitivity in our treatment of the people who once lived there. A pipe ceremony was conducted by Amos Owen, a Dakota elder and spiritual leader who communicated in words that had been spoken at Little Rapids for centuries before the voices were silenced there in the 1850s.

Those of us with previous field experience appreciated the 1986 season even more than the novice crew members who had no basis for program comparisons. We found it extraordinary to work with people who had direct family ties to the place and history we were studying; extraordinary to hear Dakota spoken there after the silences of more than a century and a half; extraordinary to share the pipe with a Dakota spiritual leader. The student apprentices could not imagine archaeology being done any other way.

It was hard to resist romanticizing our Dakota colleagues. Just as we sometimes fantasized about finding an ideal archive or a key artifact that would reveal elusive aspects of the past, most of us also hoped that Chris and Carrie would have special insights about the site or the recovered artifacts. Though they connected us to the past in very tangible ways each day, neither was particularly interested in the archaeology or the materials we unearthed. This was true of most of the Indian visitors to the site. Given the long history of tensions between Indians and archaeologists, I was grateful that Chris and Carrie had agreed to participate in the project at all. I know it was not without considerable ambivalence.

Writing About Little Rapids

In 1987 I began to write my book *What this Awl Means: Feminist Archaeology at a Wahpeton Dakota Village* (Minnesota Historical Society Press, 1993). I wanted to produce an accessible, human scale portrayal of the community; a rendering that would give readers an empathetic sense of the times as a feeling of the connections between that past and the present. I wanted to claim my own voice and authorship while simultaneously introducing other voices, visions, and perspectives. But each time I began to write I found myself tethered by the conventions of archaeological writing—the dull, lifeless, distanced, detached, and taxonomic rhetoric of our field—a rhetoric that subordinates the people we study.

I turned my attention to an artifact we had discovered in 1980 in a garbage dump, a 3" antler awl handle, delicately inscribed with a series of dots and lines. The handle would have held a short, pointed, iron tip for perforating leather hides to be made into tipi covers, clothing, bags and other accessories.

In response to this evocative find, after discovering the meaning of the inscriptions—they were tallies women kept marking their hide-working accomplishments—I wrote a short interpretive narrative encapsulating a good deal about what we had learned about the Little Rapids community. This story sets the scene and the tone environmentally, culturally, and historically; it introduces some of the people associated with the site; it reveals what the awl might have meant to the woman who used it and to her community; and it suggests how the awl handle might have been discarded. The rest of the book unravels the narrative, layer by layer exposing what we learned through excavations, documents, and Dakota sources. I discuss how awls are traditionally treated by archaeologists (typologically if at all) and describe the history of relationships between Dakota and non-Dakota people including fur traders, military men, missionaries, and archaeologists. Mazomani's 19th-century family and their contemporary descendants are prominently featured throughout the book. The book is partly a critique of archaeology, partly a professional memoir and story of the dig, and partly a community study, all presented with as little archaeological jargon as possible.

The collaborative relations continued throughout the writing and publication process. I presented early versions of the interpretive narrative to Chris and his family members and to Indian studies classes on numerous occasions. These were important facets of revising the manuscript. Editors at the Minnesota Historical Society Press continued consultations with Indian people. The manuscript was sent to both archaeologists and Indian educators for review. The Indian readers urged me to write more about the damages done by amateur archaeologists at Little Rapids, more about Indian criticisms of archaeology and about repatriation issues and laws, and to say more about the ethics of digging one part of the site that might have been a Medicine Dance area.

Conclusion

The collaborative work on the Little Rapids project was an entirely rewarding experience. My relationships with members of Mazomani's family have broadened and deepened since I first worked with Chris and Carrie, enriching my work and life. Regretfully, there are still major barriers against collaborative work in archaeology in our area and in a university setting: it is very costly to support team-taught field programs; few Indian faculty resources or students are at the University and potential colleagues are more likely found outside of the academy and often without the credentials required for staff appointments; and many archaeologists are still resistant to sharing the power and privilege of setting archaeological priorities and standards involved in serious collaborative work. Nonetheless, I can't imagine doing the archaeology of Indian people without their active and vital participation. An inclusive archaeology will entail more than simply adding the voices of so-called "others." It will transform the ways we practice archaeology and the way we view and portray the past, enriching our discipline. Our future depends on it.

4

Archaeology Returns to the Public

Charles Redman

Archaeology is returning to the public, where it was born. Intrigued by the new science that excavates buried evidence from the past, many early professional archaeologists were individuals whose first careers had been in other areas. Whether it was Thomas Jefferson excavating an Indian burial mound in Virginia in 1784, Heinrich Schliemann revealing the walls of Troy in 1871, or Austin Layard unearthing the great sculptures of ancient Assyria, early archaeologists were lured from diverse occupations by a curiosity about the past. Their primary audience and source of support was the general public; early archaeology was not the exclusive domain of scholars or academics. And in the United States today, public participation in archaeology is back.

Because much of early North American archaeology was funded by wealthy members of the public, the findings of early expeditions had to be understandable to the layman. Even an expedition's objectives were defined in cooperation with interested private individuals. The overarching goal of anthropology, and archaeology as part of it, was to discover and explain the full diversity of human existence, past and present. The excitement inherent in this quest was shared alike by scientists and the public and often was most clearly articulated by the layperson. The public set North American archaeology on its course 100 years ago, and today the public is playing an active role in charting its future.

There are three major avenues through which the public is participating in archaeology: civic organizations, corporate activities, and amateur archaeology societies.

Local and state officialdom and the federal government are increasingly active in archaeological affairs. Governmental involvement has been most conspicuous in the enactment of laws to protect archaeological resources from vandalism and pothunting—the practice of pillaging a site for treasure. Laws now provide stiff penalties for almost any disturbance of archaeological sites on public lands in order to protect these resources for future generations. Local governments have begun to demonstrate sensitivity to the presence of archaeological sites when decisions are made about zoning or building permits. Thousands of sites are known to have been lost to the bulldozer of development, but there is hope now that we will be able to protect a portion of what is left with the help of supportive new laws and attitudes at all levels of government.

As important as the new laws are, it is in the area of outreach and public education that the greatest strides are being made toward reinvolving the public. For

Figure 1. Sifting through excavated earth and stone, members of the Arizona Archaeological Society and visitors strain their eyes as they search for artifacts. (Photo by Brenda Shears/Arizona State University)

example, in 1985 the Arizona Legislature created an advisory commission to oversee public involvement in archaeology. This panel has worked closely with the State Historic Preservation Officer, and one of the major activities of this cooperative venture has been the creation of an annual Archaeology Week. During that week, public talks, tours and open houses at archaeological sites, new museum exhibits and special events promote a wider appreciation and enjoyment of archaeology. Posters, flyers and media broadcasts are used to make the public aware of these activities. In 1988 it was estimated that fifty organizations took part in the Sixth Annual Archaeology Week in Arizona, and more than 15,000 people attended.

The "open-house" concept has been a particularly effective way of sharing with the public the excitement of archaeology and the insights it offers into local prehistory. The reality of archaeological open houses grew from the thought that visitors to sites should have an active, participatory experience. This approach is being experimented with at the Pinnacle Peak Village dig in Arizona, as well as in other parts of the country, most notably in Annapolis, Maryland, where the public is invited to watch historic buildings undergoing excavation.

Open houses are a unique educational activity for the non-professional because they bring learning about archaeology into a real excavation setting. They are a powerful tool for teaching because visitors are able to witness archaeologists in action, ask them penetrating questions, and even help them work. Demonstrations of various aspects of prehistoric technology are presented at an open house, some of which, like pottery-making or stone-tool fashioning, can be attempted by the visitor as well. A uniquely effective aspect of the open house is that visitors come to the actual location where ancient people lived. There is something very special about treading the same paths, climbing the same landforms and viewing the same local vegetation as the Native American did a thousand years ago.

Although laws and governmental agencies control archaeological sites on public lands, they can do little to protect historic resources on private land. This fact is especially troubling in areas destined for development. Recently, however, some outstanding examples of enlightened behavior by land developers appear to signal a new attitude on the part of business people toward archaeological sites. A few development corporations have retained archaeologists to investigate sites located on their land, and in some cases they have planned their developments carefully with the protection of sites in mind.

Certainly the Salt River Project pioneered consciousness to the point of employing a full-time anthropologist. Archaeologists from the Institute for American Research in Tucson have worked with Fairfield Properties and Del Webb Corporation to record, excavate and save whatever was of value at every site before residential development began. Norton Development Company in Phoenix worked with Arizona State University archaeologists years before construction began on their Spur Cross Ranch property north of Cave Creek, Arizona. From the outset, these developers wanted what they were doing to have minimal impact on the ar-

Figure 2. Volunteers at Pinnacle Peak Open House sift a tripod screen. Under supervision, all "finds" are given to ASU archaeologists to be logged and photographed. (Photo by Brenda Shears/Arizona State University)

Figure 3. Onlookers surrounding a platform mound room listen to an explanation of the life-ways of ancient peoples by archaeologist Dr. Owen Lindauer at Roosevelt Platform Mound Study site tour. (Photo by Brenda Shears/Arizona State University)

chaeological resources, and they have gone so far as to designate one of the major Hohokam sites on their land as open space protected from construction. In fact, all across America, public concern for protecting archaeological resources is beginning to affect approaches to land development.

A particularly exciting example of environmental awareness and corporate responsibility has been the Pinnacle Peak Land Company's efforts to investigate and preserve the Pinnacle Peak Village site in Scottsdale, Arizona. Having learned of this potentially important site on his land, company president Jerry Nelson approached Arizona State University archaeologists and asked them to devise a plan for preserving the site. What followed has been an exemplary case of corporate, university and community cooperation. Construction was delayed and rerouted to protect the site. Cadres of local citizens volunteered their labor through the amateur archaeology society. Two full seasons of excavation under professional supervision were provided by Arizona State University and financially underwritten by the land owners. School groups were encouraged to visit the dig, and open houses were held to give the public a chance to learn about archaeology and about the native peoples who had once inhabited this location. The heartening final chapter to this story of corporate involvement is that several acres of land formerly designated for residential construction will now be an open space in perpetuity.

A special combination of factors made each of these situations work. Corporate executives in charge of the development projects were sufficiently aware of

cultural and environmental issues to recognize the value of the archaeological remains. Community interest supported the projects, volunteers helped in the work
and archaeology professionals were available to guide it. The rewards have been
manifold to all participants. Sites have been preserved, archaeologists have gained
a better understanding of the native peoples who lived in the areas, participation
in archaeology has broadened and the people now living in the affected areas
have been enriched by awareness of the prehistoric past.

There are many ways for members of the public to become actively involved in
archaeological projects without specialized university training or the commitment
to becoming a full-time professional. Societies for amateur archaeologists exist in
all parts of the country. Groups typically have monthly meetings with guest
speakers, and they often organize field trips to sites of special interest. They also
provide more intensive experiences such as academic courses, opportunities for
excavation training and cooperation with professional groups. Any well-planned
effort by government and university professionals to make archaeology available
to a broader public will use trained and energetic amateurs. Notwithstanding supervision by university professionals and financing from corporations, there could
have been only a fraction of the achievements to date without the dozens of volunteer amateur archaeologists who carried out the excavations and staffed open
houses. Through this participation, many amateurs have become proficient at archaeological fieldwork and have moved into supervisory roles in subsequent excavations.

Along with the increasing number of chances for amateurs to become involved
in excavations near home, there are a few national organizations that provide
such activity in many locales. Near Cortez, Colorado, a group has built a major
research station called Crow Canyon. Groups and individuals of all ages and levels of experience are provided carefully supervised field and laboratory experiences by the Crow Canyon staff. Their excavations center on a series of important
Anasazi sites in a majestic setting. Another group that facilitates amateur participation is Earthwatch, which is based in Watertown, Massachusetts, but under-
writes archaeology and naturalist expeditions in all parts of the world. Earthwatch usually works with ongoing research projects that seek additional funds
and labor. In return, volunteers are able to take part in an advanced research project, often in an exotic environment.

Amateur archaeologists do more than gain experience for themselves; they can
be very active in public education, and many are leaders in the movement to protect archaeological sites from vandalism. In such roles, amateurs become part of
some important and exciting activities in Arizona. Under the administrative um-
brella of the state's Archaeological Advisory Commission, volunteers and government land-management agencies together have formed the Arizona Site Stewards
program. In an effort to protect the remaining archaeological treasures on public
lands, the stewards visit sites on a regular basis and monitor whether they are
being disturbed. Law enforcement personnel are notified if site stewards discover
vandalism or other disruption. A statewide director and twenty regional offices
have been created and staffed entirely by volunteers. More than one hundred
local volunteers have been trained and are already taking part in the program. As
the site steward program grows, it is expected that local groups of amateurs will
take on even more responsibility for protecting archaeological resources by discovering and recording new sites and formulating public education programs.

Figure 4. Treasures and techniques of Hohokam pottery-making are discussed by visitors at excavation site displays. (Photo by Brenda Shears/Arizona State University)

Where do contemporary Native Americans fit in the new public archaeology? What for the past century has been a case of outsiders researching and exploring Native American archaeological resources is increasingly becoming a joint venture. In some instances, Native American groups are acting on their own. This change is part of the growing control by Indian communities over the exploration and interpretation of their local histories and tribal heritages.

Several Indian-based archaeological programs are in place. The Zuni tribe in New Mexico has been especially active in protecting sites on its reservation and in having Zuni people participate in excavations. The Zuni Archaeological Program, involving both Indian and non-Indian staff, has been in operation for fifteen years. The Zunis are seeking national monument status and federal financial support for some of their more important sites, and they envision creating visitor attractions from the most visible of these.

Many Indian groups have now established tribal museums to showcase their heritage from their own perspective. An impressive example of this is the recent work at the Salt River Pima-Maricopa Indian Community in Scottsdale. This group has great pride in the Hohokam people who preceded them in the area and has taken a special interest in excavations on and near their reservation. A small museum was established in 1987 to present local prehistory to all tribal members, and to children in particular. Along with the museum, the Salt River Community is conveying to the next generation some of its traditional lifeways through such means as demonstrating the construction of pit houses and ramadas.

The Hopi people in Arizona have long been actively involved in the archaeology on their lands and the surrounding countryside. They were instrumental in the creation of a new state park at the ancestral site of Homolovi near their present villages. They have currently secured funding to study the establishment of a national monument at Awatovi, an important protohistoric site on reservation land. The Hopis are also the first tribal group to officially become part of the Site Steward Program. In their concern with preserving and communicating the past, the Hopis are typical of many Indian groups nationwide.

For long-range public involvement in archaeology there are three major forecasts. First, greater public awareness and participation in archaeology lies ahead; there is an almost universally shared interest in our past. Archaeology not only provides the key to the past, but it combines science and humanities into a holistic study of ourselves that, unlike many other scholarly disciplines, can be directly experienced by members of the public.

Second, efforts to preserve what we have left of our precious archaeological resources will accelerate in the coming years, and this responsibility will be shared by private citizens and corporate directors, as well as the professional archaeological community.

Third, a cooperative spirit between Native Americans and archaeologists will grow. Native Americans will take a larger part in archaeological planning, fieldwork, interpretation and site preservation and management.

Perhaps a harbinger of future cooperative relations among Native Americans, professional and amateur archaeologists and the business community occurred in the cool evening hours after the open house at the Pinnacle Peak Village site. Emmet White, a traditional holy man from the Gila River Indian Reservation had come to the site to see what was taking place and to provide a blessing on the land to be preserved. He performed a ceremony saying a blessing toward each of

Figure 5. Visitor observes firsthand the time-consuming labors of the ASU Archaeological Research Team at the Shoofly Village Ruins north of Payson, Arizona. (Photo by Brenda Shears/ Arizona State University)

the four directions. He asked the ancient Hohokam spirits who lived there to forgive the archaeologists for disturbing their rest. He asked for their blessing on all who gathered there. Finally, he made a special request that the spirits reveal to the archaeologists many important things about the ancient ways of life.

In the quest to have the past revealed, it appears that there is a place for every interested person to participate.

5

Signatures Across the Landscape: The El Pilar Archaeological Reserve for Maya Flora and Fauna —Belize/Guatemala

Anabel Ford

Introduction

Conservation of cultural and natural resources is one of the most important global long-term goals for the coming century. Yet, efforts to accomplish this have led to the compromise of important short-term economic needs at regional and local levels. This is clearly evident in the Maya forest region of Mesoamerica (Fig. 1). Programs aimed at resource conservation must balance short-term needs with long-term objectives to attain a viable management framework. This requires a collaborative program of scientific research, field exploration, and development designs to effectively stage implementation.

The El Pilar Program, under my direction, has attracted an international and multi-disciplinary research and development team with the momentum to evolve an unique conservation plan incorporating local community needs, government development agenda, and international environmental concerns. The core of the El Pilar vision comes from research on the evolution of the ancient Maya landscape. The essence of this program acknowledges that clues to sustaining the complex habitats of today's Maya forest environment are embedded in ancient Maya prehistory. The blueprint for the new El Pilar Archaeological Reserve for Maya Flora and Fauna in Belize/Guatemala is based on ancient Maya settlement patterns and is designed to develop a resource management model that conserves environmental diversity and preserves the irreplaceable cultural heritage of the ancient and contemporary populations in the region. This vision has been adopted by an international group of professionals, supported by the diplomatic community, and endorsed by the governments of Belize and Guatemala.

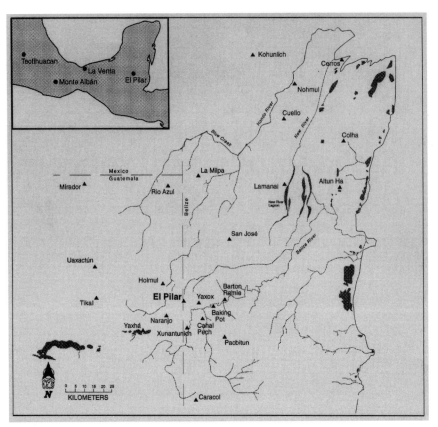

Figure 1. Central Maya Lowlands with El Pilar and other major sites indicated. (Graphic courtesy of Anabel Ford)

The Scientific Research Base: Archaeological Research

Research on the Maya civilization demonstrates that it was built on the wealth of their economic base: agriculture. Regional settlement distribution, local community subsistence patterns, and individual household organization of the ancient Maya provide material evidence for the evolution of sustainable economies in one of the planets last frontiers: the tropics. Archaeological research on the Maya underscores the complexity of interrelationships between cultural systems and environment over time. These patterns and their interpretations provide alternatives with implications for the future of the Maya forest and the people who live there today.

The staged project of the Belize River Archaeological Settlement Survey (BRASS) was designed to compile regional settlement data, identify local community patterns and investigate household organization evident in the archaeological record of the central Maya lowlands (Fig. 2). The research results present a picture of the ancient Maya economic landscape as a continuum of land use strategies from densely settled, intensively-used uplands with public centers, dispersed and extensively-used transitional zones loosely organized around resident elite, to unsettled swamps (Fig. 3). This is evidence of the ancient land use mosaic that is mirrored in the contemporary botanical and zoological distributions of the region which is the result of 30 centuries of cultural selection. This research provides a basis for a new appreciation of the relevance of the past in conceiving alternatives for the future.

The regional center of El Pilar stretches over an area of more than 45 hectares and was constructed over the course of 16 to 20 centuries, beginning in the Middle Preclassic before 600BC. This important ancient Maya center is composed of several sectors unified by causeways, one of which connects across a contemporary political boundary, linking Belize and Guatemala (Fig. 4). Today, this Maya causeway is symbolic of the diverse ways that El Pilar can benefit the communities of two nations at the local, national and international levels, at the same time enhancing our knowledge of the ancient Maya.

Exploration of the construction histories of El Pilar's temples, plazas, and palaces reveal clues to the development of Maya civilization, and survey of surrounding residential sectors detail the tapestry of the ancient urban economic landscape. Stabilizing the ruins, consolidating representative buildings and tem-

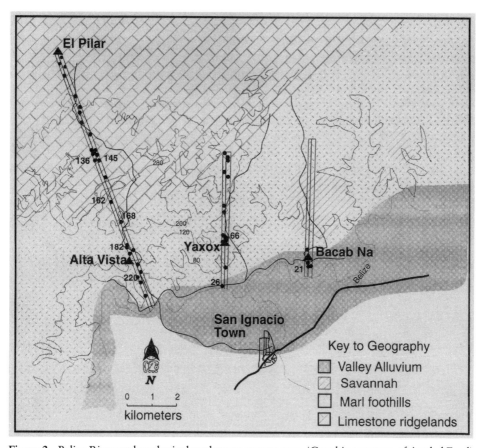

Figure 2. Belize River archaeological settlement survey area. (Graphic courtesy of Anabel Ford)

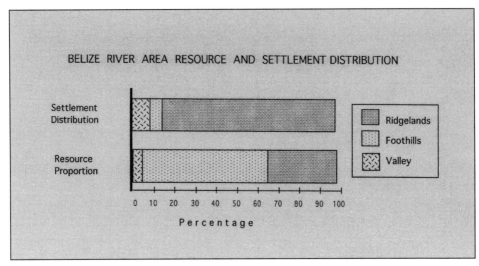

Figure 3. Belize River area resource and settlement distribution. (Graphic courtesy of Anabel Ford)

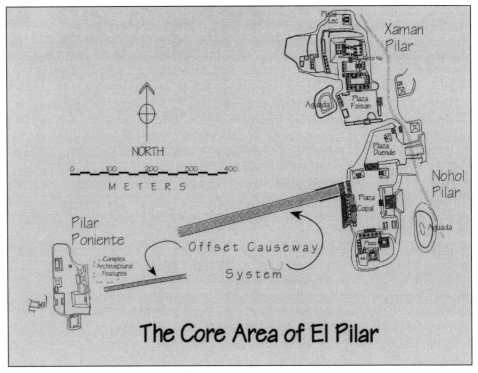

Figure 4. The core area of El Pilar. (Graphic courtesy of Anabel Ford)

ples, conserving preserved architecture, along with reconstructing examples Maya houses within their forest gardens help to educate local, regional, and international visitors in the values of archaeological inquiry. The revival of ancient traditions at El Pilar provide a context for a new perception of Maya prehistory, one that takes into account the complexity of the Maya forest along with its peoples past and present.

The BRASS/El Pilar Program is rooted in the study of the human/environment relationship. It draws on the foundation of cultural ecology, interpreting evolutionary changes in strategies for survival. The composition of the Maya forest today bears the imprint of ancient human habitation and resource management. The goal of the El Pilar Program is to evaluate continuities and shifts in the evolution of the human/environment relationship through time and across space and found a model conservation design that envisions the viable development of the region.

Agricultural Design and Technology: Implications for the Structure of the Maya Forest

Agricultural technologies evolve to fulfill the subsistence needs of society. Traditional agriculture is focused on the household. Relying on strategies that emulate the native environmental structure, traditional polycultivation strategies involve an "industrious evolution" of skilled labor rather than an industrial revolution based on scarce capital. This was the foundation of the Maya civilization.

The ecological structure of the Maya forest is a relic of the dynamic relationship in which humans have played an integral part. This relationship extends back more than four millennia to the initial agricultural pioneers of the Maya forest region, the ancestors of the ancient Maya civilization, and the heritage of contemporary farmers. The large contiguous stands of forest are a testimony to the efficacy of ancient Maya practices. While the Classic Maya collapse affected the human populations, plants and animals survived only to be threatened with extinction today. Therein lies the ecological lesson that must be perceived to build a sound basis for conservation in the future.

Traditional production systems in the tropics world-wide are as complex as the environment within which they developed. Mimicking the forest structure, a polycultivation system evolved to minimize instability, prevent degradation and integrate both intensive and extensive labor techniques that maximize production. Heterogeneous and biodiverse, the forest gardens constituted the strength of the Maya community in the past, as well as today, by relying on the traditional knowledge of local farming households. Essential linguistic terms speak to these traditions and describe a continuum of economic qualities of the forest, denoting a long-term human coexistence with the environment. *Kanan K'ax* describes a "well cared for" forest, evoking a concept of stewardship; *K'ax il kab* refers to a forest with beehives; and *Ka'kab K'ax* indicates a forest with good agricultural soil quality. Yet today, villagers are rapidly abandoning time-proven methods in exchange for introduced technologies.

At El Pilar, the development of a polycultivation design is a process that is based on a household plan and includes annuals and perennials interspersed with tree crops. This will provide an ongoing source of innovation for the community and foster resource conservation and community development that aligns with, rather than opposes, the natural regenerative processes of the tropical forest. Through farmer participation and networking, shared experience and knowledge will extend beyond the boundaries of the reserve to help restore the local landscape to a state of greater biological diversity.

Community Involvement, Investment, and Stewardship

To accomplish the goal of improving living standards and self sufficiency of the regional community of the Maya forest, the immediate and short-term needs of families must be incorporated into the long-term agenda of stainability. No reserve exists within a vacuum and, in order to survive and thrive, the local population must assume a stewardship role or the ultimate conservation aims may not be achieved.

A cooperative association has already been established with Amigos de El Pilar, a community-based organization promoting local participation in the reserve. Their goal is to develop community enterprises in tourism and agriculture that increase villagers' economic stakehold in the reserve. Through education and participation, the links between the community and the reserve will strengthen local investments in conservation and develop the stewardship responsibility. The leadership role they are assuming and the self determination they are gaining in the process is the foundation upon which the future success of the El Pilar model depends.

Promoting Ecotourism at El Pilar

The tourism industry has become increasingly focused on traditional communities and cultures as well as the natural environmental wonders. Mesoamerica has become a flourishing travel destination, and the Maya world has evolved as a vital niche for adventurers and eco-tourists. Links between specialty travel firms in the international arena and regional travel services in the Maya area are essential to the development of this market, and new destinations contribute significantly to its appeal.

The El Pilar Program has set the stage for ecotourism with local guides and hotels, regional publications, and international promotion in media and tour books. The program has worked through the village council and Amigos de El Pilar in education and training workshops, given lectures and tours with the schools, and encouraged participation in the archaeological search. Further, the program has hosted events, such as the annual Fiesta Pilar, that draw national and regional attention. Lectures and articles in Belize, Guatemala, and Mexico have increased knowledge and appreciation of the site. Public relations information has been circulated to international guide books, reported in journals such as American Archaeology, posted on the World Wide Web, and featured in Archaeology Magazine in 1997. Funding from international agencies, such as Central American Commission for Environment and Development (CCAD), Ford Foundation, MacArthur Foundation and U.S. Agency for International Development (USAID) has also elevated the visibility of El Pilar on the global front, providing a springboard for development.

The Foundation for the El Pilar Model

Park management and planning is fundamental to the reserve's future. Informed designs are based on assessments of the ecological and cultural resources within the protected area. Further, identification of stakeholders, incorporation of public interests, articulation of the mission, and a clear set of objectives for sustainable maintenance of the reserve is essential. Finally, the extent of conservation goals, issues of access and education, and the long-term funding needs must be developed. To address these requisites, the program organized the Mesa Redonda

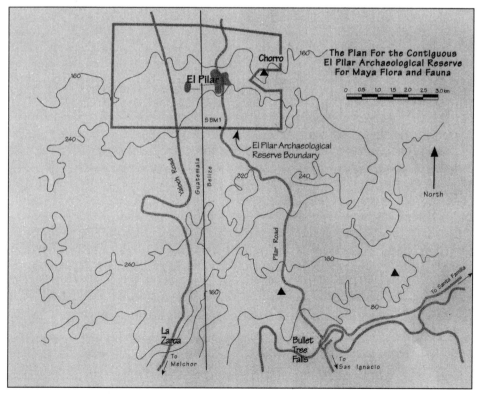

Figure 5. The plan for the contiguous El Pilar Archaeological Reserve. (Graphic courtesy of Anabel Ford)

El Pilar in January 1997 (sponsored by Ford Foundation) that brought together 28 professionals in research and development to initiate the master planning process. This plan is scheduled for publication this year by World Monument Fund and U.S. Man and the Biosphere Program.

The objectives of the El Pilar Management Plan incorporate the diverse dimensions of the program. It must include the concerns and desires for both resource conservation and economic development. Short-term strategies for community involvement are essential. Long-term concerns for conservation of the ancient architecture and the environment are to be integrated into the plan. Educational and interpretive designs for the park and surrounding landscape are also considered. These aspects are crucial to establishing the reserve on a lasting base.

The management plan also takes into account the location of El Pilar between Cayo, Belize and El Petn, Guatemala. This unusual setting impacts every aspect of research and development activities at El Pilar. The overall size of the civic center is presently unknown as the most comprehensive studies have thus far been concentrated in Belize. Despite this, preliminary surveys into the western section of El Pilar, in Guatemala, demonstrate its importance. Interviews in the Guatemalan community of La Zarca and Melchor de Mencos suggest that there is considerably more monumental architecture to be discovered, identified, mapped, and inventoried as part of the greater site core. There is also the greater environmental context of the escarpment and ridges between Belize and Guatemala that needs to be explored.

The physical situation of El Pilar raises the requisite for protection both in Belize and Guatemala. The establishment of the contiguous park around one resource in two countries is a landmark (Fig. 5). Research projects and resource management designs for El Pilar have been drafted with the contiguous sections of Belize and Guatemala considered as a whole. The natural environment, cultural resources, access for tourism, and adjacent contemporary peoples all figure prominently in this master research and development plan. The challenge now is to see that this plan takes the shape of the ultimate product: The El Pilar Archaeological Reserve for Maya Flora and Fauna.

Commentary

Archaeologists who worked a century ago might be surprised and pleased at the technological advances we have made in how we study the past. In many respects, however, archaeological field investigations today are only improvements on models established during the 19th century. Many analytical techniques that we now use would seem familiar to a 19th century archaeologist, if somewhat more sophisticated. If there is an area of archaeological practice that seems alien to 19th century archaeologist, then it would probably lie in the realm of social responsibility. In the closing decades of the 20th century, archaeologists around the world are becoming ever more aware of how contemporary national policies affect our practice, and how our findings reach a diversity of audiences. Articles in this section have illustrated some aspects of archaeology's role in the contemporary world. Archaeology is often used for political ends: it can be melded to fit nationalist agendas (whether benign or malignant), and it has become increasingly important in indigenous claims on land and on artifacts. Archaeology is no longer an ivory-tower field, and the public nature of our sponsorship and our constituencies obliges us to consider how our practice is influenced by, and affects, the contemporary world.

The recognition that archaeology is affected by (and influences) the modern world is difficult to reconcile with our notion of archaeology as a field of research. What is the identity of our field? Are we primarily scientists? To what extent should our commitment to the public and to our constituencies shape the nature and practice of archaeology? Charles Redman points out that 19th century archaeology was more accessible to the public, in part because wealthy patrons sponsored field investigations and archaeologists were obliged to convey their findings to a general audience. In the 20th century, as archaeology has developed into a professional discipline, it has moved further and further from the public and into the realm of science. This maturation of our field has a deeply positive side: work is more systematic, archaeologists must publish their work, and laws and regulations have been passed to prevent nonprofessionals from destroying archaeological sites. Yet this development of the field has a potentially negative side as well if archaeologists refuse to participate in a public archaeology. Archaeological sites and regions are now preserved as monuments and parks at the municipal, tribal, state, and federal levels. Who will convey the past to descendants of various cultures and to the public if trained archaeologists will not? One lesson from articles in this section is that archaeologists must actively participate in interpretations of the past and to fulfill our obligations to those who support our work.

Fortunately, archaeologists have great incentives for doing so. The public interest in archaeology has surged in recent decades, and provides essential support for

515

funding the work that archaeologists undertake throughout the United States. Public concern for protecting archaeological resources has also benefitted archaeologists in their efforts at cultural resource management. Archaeologists have valuable insights to share with this public, and with stakeholders in different regions of the world. One lies in our study of successful (and not so successful) adaptations of past peoples to their natural environments. Ford's article illustrates that archaeology is in a unique position to inform contemporary societies on strategies for living that will conserve scarce natural resources and help ensure the long-term survival of humanity.

Part Thirteen

Archaeology's Future

Introduction

The archaeological record is a finite and nonrenewable resource, much like primary forests and fossil petroleum reserves throughout the world. Like other resources, the archaeological record is now being destroyed through modern development. Cultural resources include sites, monuments, historic buildings, and other remains of our common past. Cultural resources are symbols of the past that create a shared sense of identity, that forge links between the past and the present, and that can be used for economic ends. As a major cultural resource, the archaeological record is threatened by collectors and "looters" in search of valuable antiquities, and even by professional archaeologists engaged in scientific field research. As looters and development further diminish the archaeological record of ancient life, the very survival of our cultural heritage — and of the field of archaeology — depends on whether we can devise effective solutions for historic preservation and heritage management.

In Part Twelve, we have tried to show that many interest groups (private citizens, indigenous peoples, and professional archaeologists) are concerned with, and committed to, conserving the archaeological record. In many areas of the world like the Middle East, Asia, and Europe, archaeological sites are an important economic resource that attracts tourists and visitors, not simply material for study by scientists and researchers. Consequently, conservation of the archaeological record has important economic implications besides social, political, and scientific implications. Concern with guarding the human past is worldwide, and is certain to increase as the destruction of the archaeological record accelerates. This task of saving our natural and cultural resources is overwhelming and the need is immediate.

We begin this section with a thoughtful essay by Sharman Russell entitled, "In our Grandmother's House." Today in much of the western world, archaeology is at once a scientific enterprise, a bureaucracy, and a business. Protecting the past is a complex process that involves archaeologists, legislators, private landowners, and a supportive public who work together to promote historic preservation. The passage of key historic preservation laws in the last thirty years has led to a boom in applied archaeology in North America. In fact, the majority of archaeologists today are employed in the world of cultural resource management (or CRM), and spend most of their professional careers involved in what has been called "salvage archaeology" (applied research). Despite the large budgets of CRM projects, work in this field is also demanding, difficult, and complicated in any number of political ways. Contract archaeologists must constantly develop strategies to negotiate between different (and sometimes competing) values of Native Americans, developers, and archaeologists in the management of the archaeological record.

Still another challenge confronts archaeologists and law enforcement specialists who are charged with protecting the archaeological record from looters on public and private land. Russell's interviews with archaeologists reveals a variety of responses to demands in the CRM world, and demonstrates how the archaeological record, as one part of our shared cultural heritage, is under persistent threat.

How can we protect our cultural resources? The answers to this question lie, in part, in identifying what cultural resources are, and by determining why they are important to different interest groups. Articles such as "The Destruction of the Past: Nonrenewable Cultural Resources," by Catherine Cameron, emphasize the fragility of the archaeological record and the value of preserving the past. Her article explains the nature of cultural resource management around the world, and discusses the reasons why the archaeological record is currently under threat. Archaeological sites are a source of profit for commercial looters and artifact dealers in many parts of the world, and a troubling relationship has existed for centuries between these looters and museums in the western world. Some of the finest museum collections today consist of looted artifacts, that lack locational information and were recovered through illegal methods. Countries around the world are now developing legislation to protect cultural resources from looting, and some regions are also using education as a long-term solution to the looting problem. Simple solutions do not exist in the world of cultural resources management, and Cameron's article identifies some of the factors that make this world so complex.

One of the greatest threats to cultural resources in the United States is the growing market for antiquities. Although we have laws that prohibit unauthorized excavations on public land, these laws are difficult to enforce in rural areas like the American Southwest. Moreover, we still lack comprehensive legislation to protect archaeological sites on private lands. Does land ownership imply proprietary control over its archaeological sites? In his article, "Fingerprints in the Sand," Richard Monastersky describes important steps that law enforcement officials have taken to stop the theft of antiquities on public land in the United States. Working as detectives, archaeologists and other scientists now use forensic techniques to link evidence from archaeological sites and artifact collections. Sometimes, the best evidence lies in the dirt: specialists have used soil analyses to link suspects to the sites that they looted. By 1998, public land made up about a third of the United States; National Park Service archaeologists estimate that this land contains six or seven million archaeological sites. Protecting and managing this vast tract of public land is a Herculean task, and we must increase our efforts to curb looting through legislation, education, and the kind of archaeological criminal investigation that Monastersky reports in his article.

The international illegal antiquities trade is another looming problem that we must confront more aggressively in today's world. As Cameron pointed out in her article, a global antiquities market creates a demand of illicit trafficking in archaeological artifacts. Unfortunately, museums and private, wealthy collectors that comprise most of this market frequently do not acknowledge the impact that their collecting exacts on the archaeological record. As some antiquities have become increasingly scarce, their value has mushroomed and site looting has intensified. Circumstances that may compound the international destruction of antiquities sometimes include warfare or neglect, such as happened in Central America and in Southeast Asia. Site conservation and heritage management programs are often expensive and difficult to sustain in developing countries, where limited economic resources are often channeled in other directions.

In the article entitled, "City Lost in the Jungle," by Fergus M. Bordewich, examines efforts by the World Monuments Fund to protect some of Cambodia's spectacular monuments in the Angkor Wat region from further deterioration. Angkor Wat is one of the largest ancient religious buildings in the world, and it is surrounded by a twenty-five square mile area filled with sandstone and brick temples built between the 9th and 14th centuries A.D. The Angkor area is Cambodia's heritage and legacy, and the main tourist attraction that draws visitors to the country. Its enchanting temples are decorated with delicate bas-reliefs, and the temples were once filled with sculptures. For the Angkorian sites, destruction takes two forms. The first is looting, which has emptied the temples of their sculptures and removed architectural elements from structures. The second is natural decay, in which luxuriant tropical vegetation constantly threatens to reclaim the ruins as happened in the centuries following the collapse of Angkor. Restoration and preservation efforts at Angkor began in earnest more than seventy years ago, when Cambodia was still under French colonial rule. Today, after decades of regional conflict and civil war, the ruins of Angkor demand attention. Work at the ruin of Preah Khan by the World Monuments Fund provides an excellent model for historic preservation and architectural conservation in Southeast Asia.

1

In Our Grandmother's House

Sharman Russell

In most religious traditions the world is whole, and humans are not in charge. For many of us today the world has been broken into confusing parts for which we are directly responsible. We must save the rainforest, clean up the rivers, prevent soil erosion, close the hole in the sky, limit our population growth—and watch for hot viruses. Undereducated and undertrained, we are the middle managers of a very complicated planet. We feel plagued by doubt and office burnout. Our sense of urgency increases. Maybe we were promoted too fast? Maybe we're not management material?

American archaeologists have a similar headache. Roads, houses, factories, farms, restaurants, shopping malls, office buildings, parking lots, tennis courts, and swimming pools are stripping away our archaeological record. An exploding interest in "primitive and prehistoric art" means that many sites are also being looted. By necessity archaeology has become dominated by the phrase CRM, or Cultural Resource Management, a changing system of laws that regulate how we deal with ancient artifacts and remains. The linchpin remains the National Historic Preservation Act of 1966, which mandated federal agencies to seek out and conserve important archaeological sites. In 1979 the Archaeological Resources Protection Act further defined cultural resources on public land and set penalties for vandalism and looting. NAGPRA helped clarify the legal relationship of some artifacts and remains to modern tribes. Other rules and regulations try to fill in the holes and alleviate our basic bewilderment—how do we "manage the past?"

Perhaps more than any academic field, archaeology has been absorbed into a government bureaucracy. Archaeologists like Joanne Dickenson, Todd Bostwick, Brad Lepper, Larry Benallie, and Roger Anyon work for a variety of tribal, federal, state, or city agencies. Their jobs range from educating the public to tracking down pothunters. Paperwork is no longer a research project. The telephone has invaded the ivory tower.

Because of CRM, archaeology is also a business. When federal laws require a survey of potential sites, it is often contracted out to a private company. If a site must be excavated, that is also often done through bids and contracts. State laws may require a "licensed archaeologist" to deal with human remains on private land. The yellow pages of any phone book in any major city have a new listing: archaeological services.

But CRM is not just a new part of archaeology; it is the largest part. Perhaps one out of a hundred students graduating with a degree in archaeology will find a job as a university professor, an academic like Pat Watson or Kathleen Deagan in-

volved in teaching or pure research. The other ninety-nine will go into some form
of CRM.

Catherine Cameron (whose husband is Steve Lekson) is on the President's Advisory Council on Historic Preservation, established to help federal agencies conform to national laws. "We have the best program for historic preservation in the world," Cathy says—as a prelude to saying something quite different.

Our preservation program worked, for example, when the Central Arizona Project spent 4 billion dollars to bring Colorado River water to farms, cities, and Indian communities in central Arizona. The construction included a 330-mile-long canal and a huge distribution network, as well as new dams and reservoirs. By 1995, 35 million dollars had been diverted into archaeology.

Lynn Teague was head of the CRM Division at the Arizona State Museum at the University of Arizona. She directed the work on a major aqueduct in a river valley filled with Hohokam sites. "It was very stressful," she remembers. "At one point we had more than a hundred people on the project, in the field. We had deadlines, deadlines, like you always do in CRM. I was out working all the time. Finally I had to go to the doctor. When the nurse called back, she said the results were positive. 'Which ones?' I asked. 'Oh, all of them,' she said, `You have strep throat, Valley Fever, pneumonia...' " Lynn laughs.

"But we learned a tremendous amount. No one had ever dug these kinds of sites before, these small outlying settlements. In the 1960s you could have held a meeting of Hohokam archaeologists in your bathroom. Now we have big conferences. We've totally revised our understanding of Hohokam history and chronology. It's going on right now. All this contract and CRM work is producing a tremendous amount of information."

"When I started, CRM was just taking off, driven by laws that were so new no one had a handle on them. The University of Arizona was doing the contract work then, with maybe a half-dozen people. By the early 1980s we were employing as many as 180. We eventually stopped because private companies grew to the point where we couldn't compete—and we didn't have to. The companies around here are excellent."

Lynn Teague jokes that she was "one of those good little girls" who went into archaeology because it allowed her to get dirty. After fifteen years the thrill wore off. Today she is out of the field and in charge of repatriation for the state of Arizona. She echoes Todd Bostwick: things are going smoothly. "Developers often find it really interesting when tribal elders come to do a ceremony or a prayer on their construction site. They are getting to meet new types of people." She repeats Larry Zimmerman. "Archaeologists benefit more from getting closer to these cultures in their living form than whatever they lost in any kind of analysis." She agrees with Larry Benallie. "The native peoples of Arizona have a right to manage their own heritage. There are some things a tribe might wish that aren't my personal preference. But that's not the issue. I don't doubt their right to make these decisions."

Like Lynn, most CRM archaeologists have no territory to protect, no research questions they must control. Reburial is simple. It's the law. CRM often aligns with the Native American view because it is essentially preservationist. Sites are dug when they are imperiled, because they are imperiled.

Although cultural resource management usually takes place outside the university, it can still further research. Salvage archaeology produces information that would otherwise be lost. Sometimes government agencies and private companies have more money to use state-of-the-art technology. Also, they are geared toward publication. They must produce a timely written report. CRM archaeologists don't procrastinate or hoard data. They are on a deadline. They go on to the next project.

Cathy Cameron drops the other shoe. For a successful program, "the best in the world," CRM has a lot of critics.

"Oh, in Arizona," Cathy says, "they've done some wonderful work. Fantastic stuff. But in other states the situation can be horrible. We have this continuum from wonderful to horrible. We have to bring everyone up to the same level."

Cathy thinks CRM is "a program that's broken." She rattles off the ways. "Students at the university aren't being trained in CRM. They graduate without the slightest idea how to do this kind of work. All these reports, the gray literature that CRM produces, isn't widely available. Academic archaeologists aren't using the material appropriately. When we're talking contract archaeology, by private businesses, there's no interactive monitoring. No one is peer-reviewing the data. Most of all, CRM isn't tied to anything larger, to any larger picture. There's no effort or money to synthesize the information. It can get very costly, all this feature-by-feature excavation. A road goes in here, and so we excavate these sites. But it's work that's not always done well or that gives us particularly good information. We have to be more accountable. These preservation laws have to benefit the public or they could go away. They could be repealed. *That* would be a disaster."

Most of these problems have solutions. They require creativity—and cooperation. Archaeology has any number of schisms; the one between CRM and academia may be the most self-destructive. One side is accused of being unprofessional and commercial. The other is labeled elitist and impractical. They have, at times, very different interests. A tribal archaeologist believes that a nonthreatened site should never be excavated. A private contract company tries to maximize its profits by doing as much archaeology as possible. A professor wants particular research done as a way of furthering his or her career. As the bulldozer approaches, CRM archaeologists, academics, and Native Americans can hardly afford to be in the middle of an argument.

"Archaeology is an expensive activity that requires public support," Catherine Cameron says. "Americans have a right to good archaeology for their money, with some sort of cost-benefit analysis."

Recently, funding for the Advisory Council and for the entire National Historic Preservation Act was threatened by budget cuts in Congress. In the "management of the past," both nouns are cultural constructions, open to interpretation. "We don't manage the past," Roger Anyon says, "we manage the present."

Who expected it to be easy?

Allen Funkhouser wears his gun even in the halls of the Gila National Forest Supervisor's Office, decorated with happy pictures of Smoky the Bear. Allen is a criminal investigator for the Forest Service in southern New Mexico. Crime in the Gila includes drug traffic, theft, range trespass, and the looting of archeological resources. For thousands of years Mogollon and Mimbres tribes lived in this area, and their sites still scatter these 3 million acres of public land. The people who work in this office have a reputation for vigorously pursuing pothunters. James Adovasio, from the Meadowcroft Rock Shelter, calls them "rabid." That's a compliment.

No one knows how much of our archaeological heritage is being stolen, because no one knows how much we have left. A 1987 government report estimated that only 7 percent of sites had been surveyed on America's 104 million acres of Forest Service, Bureau of Land Management, and National Park Service land. In 1989 a group of federal land managers concluded that vandals and thieves had damaged at least 90 percent of known sites in the Southwest, including almost all of the Classic Mimbres sites. Another estimate is that 50 percent of sites on American public and private land have been destroyed.

For the archaeologist the loss is profound. "Analyzing a site," Catherine Cameron says, "is like the reconstruction of a crime scene. The context in which artifacts and structures are found is vitally important to understanding the culture of which they were once a part. Artifacts out of context may appear beautiful, exotic, or mundane, but they have lost their power to tell the story of past peoples and cultures."

Much of the damage is done by professional looters. Allen Funkhouser describes a scene both similar and tied to drug dealing. Often the same people are involved, an organized network of criminals whose buyers are commonly overseas. Working at night on isolated public land, pothunters can make a tremendous amount of money. Locally, an especially fine Classic Mimbres bowl might fetch $1,000; sold in Albuquerque, it could net $45,000; auctioned in New York, it gets $95,000; taken to Europe, it reaps $400,000.

People like Allen fight back with undercover cops, informants, bullet-proof vests, and back-country Broncos bristling with antennas. They set up sting operations and find themselves leaping into dingy hotel rooms, flashing badges, barking clichés, "Federal officers! Up against the wall!" One National Park Service archaeologist posed as the mistress of a wealthy collector; her fashionable sweater, tank top, and Lycra tights concealed a harness with two mikes and a tape recorder. Deliberately "bitchy," she convinced a pothunter to take her on a helicopter to a looted site. Later she was heard to murmur as she packed away a tiny woven cotton sandal from Utah, stored in an evidence vault in Santa Fe, "Archaeologists *never* find these. We find little bits of cloth. Now I know why. Someone has already been there."

Commercial looters are also homegrown. In my valley families have pot hunted Mimbres sites for generations. On private land that's legal. On public land it's not. For some Westerners the difference between private and public land is still confusing. The idea that a dirty pot equals money is still miraculous—a sweet deal for a short day's work.

"At some point they have to sell it or show it," Allen says. "That's where we get them. We go to the dealers, we go to the museums, we go to the sales. If you're going to dig, the chances are good you're going to be caught."

The penalties for getting caught vary. Under the Archaeological Resource Protection Act of 1979, any vehicle or tool used in looting can be seized, with fines up to $100,000 and a year in jail for a misdemeanor, which is defined as damages to a site of $500 or less. For a first felony conviction the fine can be as high as $250,000, with two years in jail. In reality convictions are few, and judges are lenient. Typically, in 1993, a building supply dealer who looted a rock shelter in the Gila National Forest was fined $5,000, given three years of probation, and ordered to perform 300 hours of community service. Slowly, stiffer sentences are becoming more common.

"But not in the Southwest," Allen admits. "Not yet. We have a culture here that pretty much condones pothunting."

A disincentive that Allen willingly exploits is "hex mythology," the belief in angry spirits who guard Native American graves. "When you are dealing with illegal dealers, they talk about it. There are certain things hardcore diggers won't touch. They might be out there in the forest, and they'll get an eerie feeling. There have been plenty of cases where pothunters have had problems, at the site, or afterwards. When I'm with these guys, I'll say, kind of meaningfully, you take *care* now. Don't get *unlucky*."

At Chaco Canyon the National Park Service warns tourists of misfortunes that befall people who take potsherds. Recently two looters voluntarily confessed to stealing ancient Hopi ceremonial figures—fifteen years ago. They have believed themselves cursed ever since. One man tried burning the kachinas in an effort to lift the spell. Archaeologists who work closely with Native Americans don't scoff. Both Larry Zimmerman and Roger Anyon have had experiences outside their "scope of cultural perception."

Louis Redmond suggests, "When you are on a site, I ask you to act as if you were in your grandmother's house. That's how we view the people who lived there. Be gentle. From some of the things I've seen on desecrated sites, I'd strongly advise it."

Thieves steal because they have customers. Behind the pothunter is the dealer, and behind the dealer is the collector. In the public's eye the first is sinister, the second is sleazy, and the third is cultivated. Amassing large piles of old objects is still something educated upper-class people do to gain status and prestige. Moreover, most of our great public collections have been looted from sites around the world. Often we see these artifacts exhibited as art—beautiful, exotic, out of context.

"The problem with looting is not here in the Four Corners area," one archaeologist told a congressional subcommittee. "It is in the drawing rooms of Washington, D.C., on the mantles of Boston fireplaces, and on the walls of Los Angeles condominiums.... Until the reaction to the private display of such artifacts is one of scorn rather than approval, those artifacts will continue to find a market."

Another archaeologist complains of the hypocrisy. "We are saying that it is okay, in fact admirable, for rich people to collect pothunted artifacts and donate them to museums, but it is not okay for destitute Costa Ricans or St. Lawrence islanders to pothunt them or for middle-class artifact dealers in Ohio to trade in them."

If wealthy people are drawn to the cachet of antiquity, so are the poor, the working class, the Boy Scout troop, the senior citizen, the hiker, the biker, the grade school teacher. An important category in pothunting is the casual or hobby collector. One-to-one, commercial looters do more harm. But hobby collectors have a cumulative effect. Huge numbers of people visit our national forests and parks. When a woman on a picnic takes an arrowhead, her act is magnified by a million picnickers. Their interest is often personal, intelligent, and sincere. In that case it can be redirected.

"The real answer is not enforcement," Allen Funkhouser says. "It's public education. We have to get the public on our side or nothing is going to work."

Cautiously Allen sees an improvement. "I think casual pothunting is on the decline or, at least, it has stabilized. We have lots more public archaeology now, site steward programs, Passports in Time, things like that. We go to schools and talk to kids, and I know we're reaching them. We have people come in and confess, 'Hey, I found this basket in a cave, and it was so *neat*, and I took it, but I want to give it back now' or 'My family has had these pots for years and I think some of them came from federal land.' We don't prosecute, of course. We're just happy to have the artifacts returned."

As we chat comfortably I don't admit this to Allen Funkhouser, but I am one of the people he has helped educate. There was a time I didn't know that taking a potsherd from the national forest was wrong or illegal. So I did. It was so neat. I had found the Easter egg, the treasure, the thing that sent me spinning back a thousand years. Greedily I desired that little bit of clay. Casually I put it in my pocket. Now I tell my children they may not do this, and I watch their struggle. Like ravens, we are naturally acquisitive. We want to take the magic home.

Instead, my husband and I insist on the archaeological etiquette and say, righteously, "Yes, it's wonderful. It's pretty. Now you've touched it. Now put it back, right where you found it." My children are too young to argue the point. But I understand their resentment. This is, after all, just a broken sherd, a jagged memento, an inch big. This site isn't important, and it isn't pristine. Moreover, the next person who finds this sherd will take it, or the next, or the next. Why not me?

We can hardly imagine a bit of the world not being owned, and so we insist on owning everything, snapping our beaks at the flash of silver. It is a hard lesson— to let things be. It is important, I think, to tell my children, "Put it back where you found it. Leave it alone. Carry it in your mind." It is important to have faith, a belief in each other and in the future, that the next person, and the next, and the millionth will have the same respect and control.

Truthfully, I am not sure that I don't want this bit of earth to dissolve in the ground and become earth again. That's a new kind of archaeology, of cultural resource management, which I find attractive. Perhaps only some sites should be studied, and others left to live differently in the mind. This might shock friends like Steve Lekson. I know his arguments, and I agree with many of them. We have a lively discussion in which I play both parts. In these ways I am learning about myself.

Our country is one of the few which does not protect cultural resources on private land. Nations as diverse as Mexico and England assume that archaeology is part of the common good. Important sites—rock art, ruins, mounds, earthworks—belong to no one in particular, to everyone in general. Americans, of course, have fierce views on the sanctity of private property rights. Like grizzled wolverines, we hold on to that legbone. Laws now protect human and cultural remains on federal and Indian land. Many states also ensure that a landowner no longer owns the bones or burial goods that came with his or her deed. Beyond that, if it's on your property, you can blow it up, level it, or paint it blue. We are free to rampage through the house of our grandmother.

"Americans are newcomers," Roger Anyon explains. "They don't have a long involved relationship with the land. The linkage just isn't there. Instead there's all this fragmentation, subdividing the land into little pieces. It's a parochial view of the world. There's an attitude in Anglo society of take, take, take. Eventually you have to give back.... There's a lot of greed, a lot of greed, and a lot of racism against Indians. In pothunting the motive is usually money. But somewhere behind this, I think, is the notion that if we wipe out all these traces of people who have been here before, then we won't have to acknowledge any of their claims. Manifest Destiny. It's an underlying theme."

I see Roger's point. But it's not the whole story. Ultimately pothunting is fueled by the desire to connect with the past by buying it. There are larger issues of materialism and alienation. Do we feel so separate now that we can put everything— time, history, the whole world—in our pocket?

Certainly the way we respond to a potsherd on the ground reflects our sense of cultural heritage. For non-Indians there must be the recognition of difference, of those who were here then and who are here now. At the same time we are also touching our own tribal self, a shared past of evolution and migration. We are holding something made of the land we have made our home.

When Larry Zimmerman and Roger Anyon point to the racism in their profession, they are right to do so. But if I thought archaeology were inherently racist, I would not be writing a book about it. American archaeology is grounded in the belief that our national heritage extends back thousands of years, that we are deeply, truly multicultural and multiracial.

How we manage cultural resources can be compared to how we manage other resources. Scientists are just beginning to trace the interweavings of the natural world. They have returned, roundabout, to a kind of pantheism: the universe conceived as a whole is God. All the parts make up this whole, and all the parts work together. We cannot destroy our rivers and forests, our midges and minnows, without destroying ourselves.

The same may be true of archaeological resources. Our past, present, and future may form a whole, much as they do in a single human life. As a culture, when we sever the connections to our own past, we may be giving up our emotional connection to the future, to the seventh generation to come. We lose our place on the continuum. We are out of context. At this point our mistakes can be profound.

In archaeology, and within archaeology, the acceptance of cultural diversity is an exercise in survival. Diversity appears to be the will of the universe. No war, no form of oppression, can obliterate it. Our instincts tell us to cherish the familiar, that small group bound by trust and blood. Evolution tells us to bloom into difference, a thousand ways of speaking and behaving and seeing the world. Somehow we have to do both. With a network of technology that includes the nuclear bomb, we've invented the oxymoron "global village." Now we have to live in it.

As we hold that potsherd, warm from the sun and gritty with dirt, we have the choice to fill this moment with all the power of our imagination. We can fit into a physical and cultural landscape, finding our place there, enfolded in time. This, of course, is not management at all. It is an embrace.

2

The Destruction of the Past: Nonrenewable Cultural Resources

Catherine M. Cameron

Introduction

Cultural resources—ruins, monuments, historic buildings, and other concrete remains of our common past—are some of humanity's most important yet most threatened nonrenewable resources.[1] Cultural resources are threatened by modern development, looters, vandals, and not-so-benign neglect. Destruction of cultural resources has increased dramatically in the last quarter of the 20th century as a result of two forces: first, development and construction, and second, the astonishing explosion of demand for "primitive" and prehistoric art.

The magnitude of the yearly loss of cultural resources can be only grossly estimated because just a fraction of these places and structures have been formally recognized. By some estimates, given current trends, 98 percent of all archeological sites will be destroyed by the middle of the 21st century (Knudson, 1989). Modern development is probably taking the largest toll on cultural resources because construction is pervasive and destructive. Although looting has proportionately less of an effect, looters often target those properties that have the most significant structures and artifacts.

---

1. The term cultural resources as used here follows the definition in: The United States Department of Defense, Office of the Deputy Assistant Secretary of Defense for the Environment, *Legacy Resource Management Program*, Report to Congress September 1991 (no author), p. 156:

> For the purposes of Legacy, the term "cultural resource" refers to both archeological and architectural resources. For archaeology, it includes, but is not limited to, traditions, lifeways, cultural and religious practices, and other institutions to which a community, neighborhood, Native American tribe, or other group ascribes cultural significance, together with any artifacts and real property associated with such elements. For architecture, it includes, but is not limited to, buildings, sites, districts, structures, or objects, landscapes, and vistas. In addition, the term encompasses historic documents and relics.

Development and looting are coming under increasing scrutiny in many countries as the pace of destruction accelerates. The scale of the issue is immense, and difficulties in attacking the problem are intricate and constantly changing. Attempts to counter the impact of development on cultural resources generally center on "cultural resource management" (CRM) programs that tend to be more highly evolved in developed countries than elsewhere. Looting is being addressed through (1) international, national, and local laws, (2) educational programs that focus on the cultural values of these resources, and (3) studies of looters and their varied motivation (for example, King, n.d.).

Efforts to protect cultural resources have been complicated in the past few decades by an emerging ethical debate. Who owns the past? Are cultural resources the property of the political entities on whose land they are found or do they belong to the lineal descendants of the individuals who produced them? Should looted artifacts that have been transported, exported, or appropriated into foreign lands be returned to their country of origin? Are poverty-stricken looters from underdeveloped countries justified in destroying archeological sites to acquire antiquities for sale to feed their hungry families (Howell, 1992)? Are wealthy art collectors innocent in purchasing these looted artifacts (Elia, 1993; Renfrew, 1993)? What role should ethnic or indigenous minority groups play in the ownership, management, and treatment of their sacred places on public lands?

None of these questions will be resolved before century's end, but the destruction of cultural resources proceeds at a dizzying pace. The following discussion touches on major issues related to cultural resources and outlines measures being developed to halt their destruction.

Why Are Cultural Resources Valuable?

Ancient sites and antiquities have probably been recognized and valued by every culture, past or present. Each culture imbues its cultural resources with a different set of values, but scholars group these values into the following broad categories (Lipe, 1984; Cleere, 1989b):

1. Cultural resources are symbols of the past that create a sense of continuity and cultural identity; in some cases, the identity is religious in nature.
2. Cultural resources are sources of data from which we can learn about the past through archeological and other studies.
3. Cultural resources are economically important in the tourist and antiquities markets.
4. Cultural resources can be perceived as objects of beauty without any link to their cultural origins (Lipe, 1984, p. 7).

Most cultures have used the past, to some extent, to glorify themselves and to create a shared sense of ethnic identity. In modern developed societies, cultural heritage becomes especially important as symbols of those things that make that society great. These symbols can include buildings, statuary, objects, textiles, texts, or virtually any object that has been endowed with cultural values; in other words, those things that we call cultural resources. In Greece, the Parthenon is a potent symbol of Greek national pride. The French are proud of cave paintings produced by their Paleolithic ancestors more than 20,000 years ago. The immense city of Teotihuacan in Mexico, with its remarkable Temples of the Sun and the Moon, is a treasured part of pre-Columbian Mexican heritage. Upon gaining independence, the former British colony of Southern Rhodesia became Zimbabwe, after the great ruined prehistoric city of the same name (Cleere, 1989b, p. 8). Even the Nazi Government used twisted versions of German prehistory as propaganda to legitimize its existence (Arnold, 1992).

In less technologically developed societies, the past is no less—and perhaps even more—important, as myth, history, and ancestor worship interact to produce an enhanced group awareness and essential social cohesion (Cleere, 1989a, p. 5–10). The legends of the Greeks and Romans, the Dreamtime of the Australian Aborigines, and the migration stories of the Pueblo Indians of the southwestern United States function to create a group identity and a shared past to which an individual member of the culture can relate. Archeological sites, structures, or even landscapes may be incorporated as components of the religious systems of such groups, with the past as a living part of ongoing oral tradition. A rock art panel may be simply an interesting glimpse into another culture to a Euro-American tourist, but to an Australian Aborigine, it was once, and may still be, a potent method for interacting with the forces of his world (Gray, 1993).

Cultural resources are a critical source of knowledge about the past; in fact, archeological sites are our only scientific source of knowledge about the prehistoric past. The development of the field of archeology is arguably one of the major scientific achievements of the modern era (Fagan, 1989, p. xv), because it allows the study of human cultures that have existed around the world and through time for which no written records exist. Through archeology, we can study human development over a vast span and gain knowledge about human nature and society that may be critical in understanding our current complex society. Archeologists have discovered that our earliest ancestors lived in the savannahs of Africa more than 2.5 million years ago; they have studied the shift from hunting and gathering to food production that began to occur worldwide 7,000 or 8,000 years ago; they have explored the development of cities, states, and empires in the past. With the recent fragmentation of the Soviet Union, an event with worldwide repercussions, studies of the rise and fall of ancient states and civilizations may be essential for charting our own future.

Archeologists learn about the past by studying material remains—artifacts, architecture, and other structures—unearthed in archeological sites. The interpretation of these archeological materials is, in some ways, like the reconstruction of a crime scene. The context in which artifacts and structures are found is vitally important to understanding the culture of which they were once a part. For example, if a single house in a prehistoric village contains the majority of all valuable items and, in comparison to other houses, has the greatest amount of storage space, it may be assumed to have been the home of a village chief or headman. From this observation, much can be learned about the social organization of the culture of which the village is a part: that it had a social hierarchy, the characteristics of individuals who held high positions in the hierarchy, the relationship of high-ranking individuals to others in the society, the nature of trading or political relationships with nearby societies, and much more. If these valuable items are removed from their archeological context, then they are useless for such interpretations; their value in understanding the past is largely gone.

Archeological sites are a nonrenewable resource, finite in number and irreplaceable; when sites are looted or destroyed, we lose vital knowledge about our past. Artifacts out of context may appear beautiful, exotic, or mundane, but they have lost their power to tell the story of past peoples and cultures—how they lived, how they interacted with their environment and other cultures, and the secrets of their survival that may be essential to our own. Archeologists work slowly and painstakingly to retrieve every scrap of information from the archeological sites they excavate. The result is not simply objects of beauty or interest, but knowledge and understanding of the broad sweep of human history on Earth.

Aesthetic and economic values of cultural resources go hand in hand. Beauty perceived in an object, structure, or building enhances the desire of people to view, visit, inhabit, own, or otherwise interact with it. In the last decades of the 20th century, increased wealth and greater ease of travel have made the farthest reaches of the world accessible; the treasures of thousands of past and present cultures can be visited and viewed—for a price. Many communities and even national economies depend heavily on tourism. Cultural resources, from the Greek Parthenon to Machu Picchu in Peru, are a major draw for tourism. Unfortunately, development for tourism may be as damaging to cultural resources as looting. The controversial attempts at conservation and the accompanying rush of tourists at the Cambodian royal complex of Angkor (Garfield, 1992) are only one example.

Countering the Effects of Development— Cultural Resource Management

The number of cultural resources being destroyed throughout the world can be presumed to be vast, simply because of the almost unlimited extent of modern development. In Jordan, for example, the cutoff of Iraqi oil after the Gulf War has led to the strip-mining of oil shale in a 100-square-mile area east of the Dead Sea where archeologists have identified over 550 sites that range from 250,000-year-old rock shelters to Roman forts (Di Giorgio, 1993). The Jordanian Government is now weighing the economic needs for oil against the importance of preserving a vital part of its history. In the remote Pacific island of Palau, construction of a new road system threatens dozens of prehistoric and historic sites, many of which have traditional cultural importance to the people of Palau. In the southwestern United States, the U.S. Bureau of Reclamation has constructed a canal more than 300 miles long across central Arizona, diverting water from the Colorado River to supply the cities of Tucson and Phoenix and adjacent farmland. Numerous archaeological sites in the path of the canal were disturbed during the project. In every part of the world, development is ongoing, but the magnitude of the cultural loss is unknown.

Cultural Resource Management Legislation

Although efforts to combat the loss of cultural resources began as early as the 17th century in a few European countries, it was not until the mid-20th century that measures to protect cultural resources were in place in most countries of the world (Cleere, 1989a, p. 1). Widespread growth and development in the years after World War II, and especially after 1960, resulted in an international focus on environmental protection (Cleere, 1989a). Demand for the protection of cultural resources accompanied the environmental movement, and governments throughout the world hurried to develop or revise antiquities legislation.

Implementing new cultural resource management legislation has proved to be difficult because, initially, no policies concerning what should be preserved, how management was to take place, and what costs were justifiable for the process had been established. Archeologists, trained in academic research, were accustomed to excavating archeological sites purely for research purposes. They were ill-prepared to deal with the complex problems of cultural resource management. For example, should excavation for the purposes of research take precedence over preservation of sites for the future? Should sites be stabilized or reconstructed (both are processes with high immediate and long-term costs) for purposes of local education or for tourism? When should funds be expended on salvage archeology in advance of construction projects, and how much public money should be spent on such efforts?

In the early 1970's, the United States took the lead in developing cultural resource programs and policies to combat the rapid destruction of cultural resources (McGimsey, 1972; Lipe, 1974), but, by the end of the decade, the effort had become international. Most frequently called cultural resource management but also archeological heritage management or simply historic preservation, these programs are now found in virtually every nation, although they function with varying degrees of effectiveness (Cleere, 1989b).

What CRM Programs Do

In general, CRM programs establish which properties are to be protected by the state, define the ownership and treatment of historic properties discovered on public or private land, and set punishment for looting and destruction of sites. Unfortunately, most countries have little idea of the extent and nature of their cultural resources. Even in the United States, where public lands have been extensively surveyed for cultural resources, only a small fraction of the total number have been located and catalogued.

In the United States, all Federal projects are subject to review under Section 106 of the National Historic Preservation Act (NHPA), which requires that Federal agencies " ...consider the effects of their undertakings on historic properties." (*Historic property* is the U.S. Government's term for significant cultural resources.) Although the NHPA, enacted in 1966, is an effective program that requires Federal agencies to consider the effects of their projects on all types of significant cultural resources (including buildings, bridges, outhouses), perhaps its greatest impact has been in the field of archeology. Regulations that implement Section 106 of the NHPA state that professional excavation of an archeological site can result in the recovery of what the legislation calls the "values" that make the site a significant historic property; these values, in most cases, are the information the site may contain about the past. If Federal agencies cannot avoid archeological sites during construction projects, they may arrange to have them excavated, and information about the past that was contained in the sites retrieved, thereby fulfilling their obligations under NHPA. These Federal requirements have resulted in an explosion of CRM archeology; today a very large percentage of the archeological excavations in the United States are performed to fulfill Federal requirements under NHPA (McManamon, 1992, p. 32).

Although the protection of cultural resources in the United States seems to be comprehensive (and is, compared with many other countries in the world), the provisions of the NHPA extend only to Federal "undertakings." Federal undertakings include projects that occur on Federal lands, use Federal funds, or require a Federal permit or license, regardless of land ownership. In addition, most State and some local governments require consideration of cultural resources when development projects occur on lands that they own. Cultural resources on private lands, however, are completely unprotected (except in the case of a Federal undertaking) and may be disturbed or destroyed at the discretion of the landowner. In the past decade, some states have passed laws that protect unmarked graves on private lands from disturbance (Price, 1991); this is a measure aimed primarily at protecting Native American graves, but the effectiveness of these laws has yet to be determined.

CRM in Underdeveloped Countries

In underdeveloped countries, the desire to protect cultural resources must compete with other economic and cultural requirements. In many of these countries, cultural resources are often handled through poorly funded departments of antiquity whose programs are limited to emergency salvage projects or restoration for tourism (Simmons, 1992, p. 80–81). In the Philippines, for example, cultural resource legislation is curative rather than preventative; that is, measures are often taken only after road projects or looters have already damaged important archeological sites (Henson, 1989). Lack of professionally trained staff and inadequate funding severely hamper the development of more responsive CRM programs in many underdeveloped countries.

Underdeveloped countries are just as concerned with preserving their cultural heritage as are developed countries. The effectiveness of CRM programs in underdeveloped countries can be expected to improve if funding increases. International agencies such as the World Bank, the U.S. Agency for International Development (USAID), and the United Nations Educational, Scientific, and Cultural Organization (UNESCO) are important potential sources of funding for CRM activities in the Third World (Simmons, 1992, p. 87). Support from these development organizations should open important avenues for protecting and preserving cultural resources in the future, in countries without adequate domestic funding sources.

Looting and the Destruction of Cultural Resources

Looting and destruction of archeological sites has become epidemic in the second half of the 20th century. Archeologists in the United States have begun to study the varied motivations of those who disturb archeological sites for pleasure or profit in order to deal more intelligently with them (King, n.d.). The term *looters*, although a handy catch-all for nonarcheological use of archeological sites, actually includes individuals with a variety of motivations. Some people who disturb archeological sites, especially in the United States, are simply the interested public, for example, families who enjoy spending Sundays hunting for arrowheads or digging for pots. Others are vandals who destroy the works of others for no rational reason. Rock art panels are the frequent target of wanton destruction—defaced by scratched-in or painted-on graffiti, bullet holes, and sometimes spray paint (King, n.d.). In one tragic case, a significant rock art panel in southern Utah was covered with a chemical solvent that obliterated the figures (Nickens, 1991, p. 79).

Destroying Archeological Sites for Financial Gain

Most destructive, however, are individuals who destroy archeological sites for commercial purposes and artifact dealers who traffic in pieces of the past for personal gain. Commercial looting has long been recognized as a serious problem; more than two decades ago, Meyer's (1973) popular study vividly documented the international scope of the looting problem. Commercial looters see dealing in antiquities as a quick way to wealth. These individuals are often well equipped and well funded and use high-technology equipment, including helicopters and high-elevation aerial photography, to locate and loot sites. Their illegal ventures are not unlike, and are sometimes allied with, the drug trade (Harris, 1989, p. 155).

Not all those who destroy sites for financial gain are well-heeled outlaws. Especially in the Third World, sites are often looted by people desperate for some means of making a living (e.g., Peruvian huaqueros, Howell, 1992). For example, *The New York Times* reported, on July 11, 1993, that destruction of archeological sites has increased dramatically in the Israeli-occupied West Bank and Gaza Strip since March 1993 when these areas were sealed off by the Israeli Government, leaving thousands of Arabs without access to jobs in Israel. Many Arabs have found that furtive excavations in prehistoric mounds and underground caves yield artifacts that can bring enough money to feed hungry families.

Regardless of whether they are commercial looters or hungry laborers, these individuals supply a market at the demand of wealthy Western art collectors who pay fantastic sums for pieces of the past. The result of looting is the destruction of archeological sites that could speak volumes about past cultures if they had been carefully excavated using scientific methods. Artifacts that could serve (and, in some cases, have served) as symbols of cultural heritage and national pride are sold to private collectors in other countries as art pieces.

Cultural Looting *Is* an International Problem

Cultural looting is not a new phenomenon. The spoils of war have often been the antiquities of a defeated culture. The Roman Empire looted Greece of its classical statuary. Napoleon filled the Louvre with pillaged antiquities. These were cases of military conquest; the development of an extensive market in antiquities began only in the late 19th century. Then, in the late 1960's, a new emphasis on "primitive" and prehistoric "art" dramatically increased traffic in antiquities. The United States provides one of the largest markets for antiquities, although other countries, such as Germany and Canada, are also heavily involved. More recently, Japan and Australia have become major players (Pendergast and Graham, 1989, p. 52).

The Maya area of Mesoamerica is one of the most tragic examples of the results of looting. In the Peten region of Guatemala, looting began in the late 19th century when explorers discovered enormous Maya sites, such as Tikal and Uaxactun (Archaeology, 1991). Pieces of these sites, which include altars, carved stelae, and other irreplaceable objects, were removed for sale to museums and dealers. With the increased demand for Precolumbian art in the late 20th century, looters began in earnest to pillage the remains of the Maya civilization. Consequently, almost 85 percent of known Maya archeological sites have been looted to greater or lesser degrees (Archaeology, 1991). The resulting loss of archeological information on Maya prehistory is catastrophic.

Attempts to halt looting in the Maya area have not been successful. Pendergast and Graham (1989) noted that in Belize, the discovery of looters and their successful prosecution is rare because government agents are hampered by dense jungle and there are legislative limitations that allow looters who are brought to trial to go free. Indeed, looters are more numerous and better funded than the country's military force. Pendergast and Graham (1989, p. 58) suggested that collectors in the United States, Canada, and other developed countries be subject to raids and seizure of illegally obtained artifacts. Focusing a spotlight on the illegal activities of wealthy collectors who flout the laws of their own country and those of other countries might do more to end the antiquities trade than legislation has been able to do (Pendergast and Graham, 1989, p. 58).

The looting of Native American cultural heritage in the southwestern United States also began more than a century ago. The wonders of southwestern Indian cultures, both past and present, were reported by a series of exploratory expeditions sponsored by the U.S. Government during the mid-19th century—reports that stimulated the Eastern intelligentsia. As Euro-Americans settled the Southwest, many became aware of the money to be made by selling antiquities to museums and private collectors. Rancher Richard Wetherill and his brothers were the first Euro-Americans to view the cliff dwellings of Mesa Verde in the 1880's, and the publicity about these spectacular sites and their well-preserved remains increased the market for artifacts. In fact, the Denver Historical Society paid Wetherill several thousand dollars for his collections (Hutt and others, 1992, p. 19).

In the 20th century, looting became a cottage industry in some southwestern communities. Almost 1,000 years ago, the Mimbres culture of southwest New Mexico produced some of the most beautiful and elaborate pottery ever made in North America; but Mimbres architecture was far less interesting to the profes-

Figure 1. The Pruitt site in the Mimbres Valley of southwestern New Mexico. Archaeologists examine the jumbled remains of the site where a looter's bulldozer has cut through it. (Photo by Stephen H. Lekson)

sional archeologist than the magnificent ruins of Mesa Verde (Brody, 1977; LeBlanc, 1983; Lekson, 1990). As a result, Mimbres sites were largely ignored by early southwestern archeologists while local residents mined them and sold the pottery to collectors and museums. In the late 1960's, the new emphasis by collectors on "primitive" art created an enormous demand for Mimbres pots and led to the use of bulldozers on archeological sites (Fig. 1) (Lekson, 1990). Useful scientific information can sometimes be salvaged by archeologists from sites that have been looted using hand tools, but when bulldozers push entire sites into a jumbled heap in an effort to retrieve pots buried with human remains below ancient floors, virtually no useful information remains.

Looting in the southwestern United States continues today. For example, looting and vandalism rose 1,000 percent on Navajo Nation tribal land between 1980 and 1987 (Frazier, 1993). Of 137,000 archeological sites recorded on Federal lands in the Four Corners area alone, almost a third have been damaged by looting (Hutt and others, 1992, p. 13).

The Role of Museums and Collectors in the Destruction of Archeological Sites

The historical role of museums and private collectors in the traffic in antiquities and the resulting destruction of archeological sites is complex. In Europe and the Americas, museums and collectors evolved together over the past several centuries as the study of antiquity became an admired occupation for the aesthete. Museums were (and still are) supported by wealthy patrons who had a personal interest in the past, but sometimes little understanding of or concern for how knowledge of the past is gained. For these individuals, and the museums they supported, the collection of ancient objects became a goal in itself. Many museums sponsored excavations aimed primarily at acquiring objects for display, and some showed little interest in the context or culture from which the objects came.

The troubling relationship among museums, collectors, and looting continues today. The crux of the problem is the treatment of prehistoric artifacts and the cultural remains of "primitive" (that is, non-Western) cultures as art objects rather than as keys to understanding the past or as important elements of cultural patrimony. Neither museums of arts nor museums of anthropology are immune to making such transformations of cultural objects into "art." In a critique of exhibits at the Museum of Modern Art (MOMA) and the American Museum of Natural History (AMNH), Clifford (1988, p. 200) notes "At MOMA, treating tribal objects as art means excluding the original cultural context ... [the assumption is that] cultural background is not essential to correct aesthetic appreciation and analysis; good art, the masterpiece, is universally recognizable." The artistic value of such pieces, bestowed upon them by the Western art world, divorces them from whatever value or importance they may have had to their maker. "[And at AMNH,] ... ethnographic exhibits have come increasingly to resemble art shows....While these artistically displayed artifacts are scientifically explained, an older, functionalist attempt to present an integrated picture of specific societies or culture areas is no longer seriously pursued" (Clifford, 1988, p. 203). Such attitudes allow museums to focus on objects rather than on the values of these objects to the culture of which they were once a part.

The debate over separating primitive or prehistoric objects from their culture can be illustrated with a case from Greece. Elia (1993) recently reviewed a volume on Cycladic figurines, small statues made in the third millennium B.C. in the Aegean Islands (Renfrew, 1991). The book discusses the collection of Dolly and Nicholas Goulandris, which is now housed in a museum in Greece. Elia (1993) points out that virtually every piece in the Goulandris Collection had been purchased on the international art market or in Greece; ultimately all the pieces had been obtained through looting. In purchasing these figurines, the Goulandris were supporting and encouraging the work of looters. He estimated that approximately 460 tombs were plundered to supply the Goulandris Collection. Reacting to Elia's (1993) criticism that he downplayed the origin of the figures as looters' spoils, Renfrew (1993, p. 16) agrees with his critic that " ... collectors are the real looters."

As Clifford's (1988) critique and the Greek example illustrate, ethics relating to cultural resources are conflicting. Currently, a paradox exists—collectors and museums are respected elements of modern society, yet some of their activities lead to the destruction of archeological sites and the knowledge these sites contain. The conundrum was illustrated by King (1991, p. 88–89) in an anecdote about the Arthur M. Sackler Gallery of Asian art at the Smithsonian Institution. King notes that the objects on display, donated from Sackler's personal collection, were clearly obtained through looting, yet no mention is made of this fact in the display. He describes the incongruity (1991, p. 89): " ... if we are not ready to inscribe such warnings on the walls of the world's art galleries, then our educational message is discordant. We are saying that it is OK, in fact admirable, for rich people to collect pothunted artifacts and donate them to museums, but it is not OK for destitute Costa Ricans or St. Lawrence Islanders to pothunt them or for middle-class artifact dealers in Ohio to trade in them." Whereas King (1991), in fact, advocates a rapprochement with individuals who disturb archeological sites for personal pleasure or financial gain, others, like Elia (1993) and Renfrew (1993), are far less conciliatory.

Protecting Cultural Resources from Looting

Efforts to protect cultural resources from those who would destroy them for pleasure or profit have taken two primary directions: legislation and education. Laws for the protection of cultural resources have been enacted in most countries, although the scope of the legislation is highly variable (Cleere, 1989b). As previously discussed, legislation in many countries is often ineffective in preventing the looting of archeological sites. Legislation is often aimed at controlling the antiquities market by restricting the export of cultural objects. Some countries prevent export of only the most important cultural objects; others have a total export restriction; and some countries, such as China and Mexico, declare that all types of cultural resources are the property of the state (Herscher, 1989, p. 118; Min, 1989, p. 102).

International Laws

As with the illegal drug trade, international attempts have been made to control antiquities. In 1970, UNESCO adopted the "Convention on the Means of Prohibiting and Preventing the Illicit Import, Export and Transfer of Ownership of Cultural Property." Unfortunately, many countries that are major consumers of illicit antiquities (Germany, Switzerland, the United Kingdom, Japan) have not ratified this convention. Perhaps as a consequence, it has not been particularly effective internationally in halting the looting of archeological sites or the sale of looted artifacts, and the pace of destruction has increased dramatically in some areas in spite of the convention (Pendergast and Graham, 1989, p. 51). In the United States, legislation to implement the convention was passed in 1983, after a decade of debate in Congress. As a result of the legislation, bans on the import of certain types of antiquities from several countries (El Salvador, Bolivia, Guatemala) (U.S. Information Agency, 1993) are in place. Remarkably, this legislation deals only with the import of cultural property, not with the export of United States cultural property.

Although the United States does not have export restrictions on its cultural property, it does have legislation such as the Archeological Resource Protection Act of 1979 (ARPA) that prohibits excavation of archeological sites on Federal lands without a permit (Hutt and others, 1992). ARPA provides penalties for persons who are caught disturbing archeological sites on Federal lands and for transporting or selling artifacts illegally obtained from federal land. Unfortunately, monitoring vast tracts of sparsely populated Federal land and catching offenders has proven difficult. Successful prosecutions under ARPA have been infrequent (but see Munson and others, 1993), and the strength of the legislation has yet to be fully tested (Hutt and others, 1992, p. 51).

Education as an Approach to the Looting Problem

Education is another approach, especially in the United States, to solving the looting problem. Programs have been developed by Federal, State, and local governments and even by private organizations (Smith and Ehrenhard, 1991). Targeted groups range from school children to the elderly. In Arizona, the Arizona Archaeological Council developed a weekend workshop for precollege teachers that presents the basic concepts of archeology and offers lesson plans that can be used in the classroom (Rogge, 1991). The program aims at educating a large segment of the local population about the values and relevance of archeology.

In a Canadian experiment, archeologists and educators in Toronto developed the Archaeological Resource Center (ARC) as part of the public school system (Smardz, 1991). Through ARC, school children are allowed to participate in urban archeology projects; this instills in them a sense of pride in their city's cultural heritage and, presumably, a desire to protect that heritage. In southwestern Colorado, Crow Canyon Archaeological Center enables lay people to participate with professional archeologists in scientific research on sites in the Mesa Verde area; participants achieve an appreciation of the importance of careful archeological excavation. In 1992, the Center was the recipient of the President's Award for Historic Preservation, the nation's highest honor to a private organization dedicated to the preservation of America's heritage.

Programs have also been designed to actively protect sites (Smith and Ehrenhard, 1991). In the United States, Arizona has a program, "Site Stewards," in which carefully trained volunteers patrol and monitor archeological sites on public lands (Hoffman, 1991). These volunteers record site conditions and report any evidence of damage to land-managing agencies. Because of their active interest in preserving archeological sites, Site Stewards convince the public of the importance of these resources and they have created a heightened public sensitivity to the problem of looting in Arizona.

Who Owns the Past?

Efforts to preserve cultural resources have opened a new arena of debate concerning rights to and ownership of these resources. The debate is part of a worldwide change in attitude toward the ownership and treatment of cultural resources that has developed in the past few decades, especially during the last 10 years. Social upheavals in the 1960's and 1970's and philosophical developments in Europe and the United States, manifested in Post-modernism, have had a dramatic effect on both public and professional attitudes toward cultural resources. Archeology "...has become part of a struggle to recapture a cultural identity that was lost during colonization and industrialization...it has also become part of claims for rights over land and resources (Kristiansen, 1989, p. 24)." Changed attitudes have resulted in changes in public policy and the enactment of legislation whose most far-reaching effects seek redress for the leftover attitudes of the colonial era.

Repatriation and Reburial in the United States

In the United States, the repatriation and reburial issue is a significant example of the attempt to grapple with changed attitudes toward ownership of cultural resources. During the 1970's, Native Americans began to express publicly their long-held dismay at the anthropological treatment of Native American human remains. They asked that the remains be given to them for the appropriate, traditional reburial and that associated grave goods also be returned (repatriated).

The repatriation and reburial debate amounted to a clash of culturally based ethics between scientific archeology and Native American religion (Goldstein and Kintigh, 1990). For archeologists, human remains provide an extremely valuable store of information on prehistoric society; they were, literally, the human context behind the artifacts so long admired in museums and by collectors. Bones can tell us what people ate, how healthy they were, the demographic parameters of the prehistoric population, what sorts of trauma they experienced, and much more. Artifacts associated with graves contain a wealth of information on individual social status, the social structure of the prehistoric group, the kinds of exotic or highly valued items people had access to, and what kinds of possessions they used in their daily lives.

For some Native American groups, human remains and other things of the past should return to the earth. For example, the prehistoric Pueblo people of the southwestern United States often buried their dead in what Euro-Americans might call refuse mounds. Silko (1987, p. 83), a Pueblo writer, explained the practice: "Corn cobs and husks, the rinds and stalks and animal bones were not regarded by the ancient people as filth or garbage. The remains were merely resting at a mid-point in their journey back to dust. Human remains are not so different. They should rest with the bones and rinds where they all may benefit living creatures—small rodents and insects—until their return is completed."

Native Americans have implied that there is a culturally based double standard in the treatment of the dead in the United States (Frazier, 1993, p. 8A). Would a scientist be allowed unrestricted permission to excavate and study bodies in a Civil War cemetery? Why, the Native Americans asked, was it proper to excavate, disturb, destroy, and display Native American dead? Anthropologists had not been aware of a double standard; they were as comfortable studying prehistoric individuals from the Old World (such as the Bog People, Egyptian mummies, or the Ice Man recently found in Austria's Tyrol Mountains) (Muller, 1992) as from the New World. To anthropologists, prehistoric human remains represent anonymous individuals from the past—fair game for investigation. The oral traditions of most Native American groups, however, do not recognize a "prehistoric" period—oral traditions are, for them, history; and ancestors, whether recent or ancient, are to be treated in a respectful and traditional manner.

The Native American Graves Protection and Repatriation Act (NAGPRA), which was passed in 1990, finally legislated how human remains found on Federal lands will be treated, and required all Federal agencies and museums that receive Federal support to inventory Native American human remains and associated grave goods in their possession and to report these items to the appropriate affiliated Native American group (Price, 1991, p. 32–33). The way repatriation and reburial will play out on a national level is unknown because the inventories of museums mandated under NAGPRA are just now nearing completion (completion required November 1993). Some museums have already repatriated a few human remains and objects. Partly as a result of NAGPRA, Native American concerns regarding human remains and other issues are being given new attention in the treatment of cultural resources, especially in CRM archeology.

Sacred Places and Traditional Cultural Properties

Controversy over the ownership, use, and conservation of cultural resources, of course, extends far beyond artifacts and human remains. The ownership of and access to historic and prehistoric *places* (archeological sites, rock art, sacred sites, and so forth) has been debated worldwide. In Australia, legislation was enacted in 1972 to protect places of special significance to Aborigines. This was defined as "any place, including any sacred, ritual or ceremonial site, which is of importance or of special significance to persons of Aboriginal descent" (Flood, 1989, p. 81). Aboriginal cultural resources are, however, divided into two types, sacred (as defined above) and nonsacred, even though Aboriginal people consider all sites to have strong symbolic value and, significantly, to constitute tangible proof of their prior ownership of and rights to Australia (Flood, 1989, p. 82). The definition of a significant place was broadened by legislation passed in 1986 to include newly discovered archeological sites. The Australian Government has attempted to separate the protection of sacred sites from questions of land rights (Flood, 1989, p. 83), but the issue still sparks much contention.

In the United States, the Federal Government recognizes the "traditional cultural property" as a special type of historic property. Traditional cultural properties are places that have been used by a community for more than 50 years and "... [have] significance derived from the role the property plays in a community's historically rooted beliefs, customs, and practices" (Parker and King, 1990, p. 1). Traditional cultural properties are varied in nature, and adequate management and treatment of these places is often quite difficult. Traditional cultural properties identified in the southwestern United States, for example, include locations as diverse as the San Francisco Peaks, which cover an area of 1,500 km^2 in northern Arizona and are sacred to several Native American groups, and a small set of sandbars in the Rio Grande River in New Mexico, where the people of Sandia Pueblo have traditionally conducted ceremonies (Parker and King, 1990). For the people who hold traditional cultural properties sacred, however, publicly communicating the exact location and significance of the property may detract dramatically from its value or violate the informant's cultural rules; the users of these places, therefore, often resist attempts to identify and define them. These problems sometimes make traditional cultural properties difficult for Federal land managers to adequately identify and protect, although the 1992 amendments to the National Historic Preservation Act have strengthened the protection afforded these properties.

Especially difficult are those cases in which the meaning and values placed on traditional cultural properties differ dramatically among the groups who wish to use them. In Wyoming, a prehistoric circular stone structure, called the Medicine Wheel, is a sacred religious spot to a number of Plains Tribes. Part of the power of the Medicine Wheel is in the pristine nature of its location. The Medicine Wheel is located in a National Forest, and it was named a National Historic Landmark in 1969. In addition to the Native American users, the Medicine Wheel had come to be valued by practitioners of the "New Age" movement, almost entirely non-Native Americans whose beliefs are an eclectic blend of Native American and other religions. New Age practitioners feel that they have a valid right to religious expression through the use of such structures as the Medicine Wheel. Their excursions to the Medicine Wheel pushed visitation in 1992 from an average of about 12,000 persons per year to almost 70,000, causing damage to the structure from excessive foot traffic and deposition of trash to increase dramatically. Native Americans were outraged by what they perceived as desecration and damage to their traditional cultural property. Clearly, decisions had to be made about who was to have access to the Medicine Wheel and what the nature of that access was to be.

After several years of delicate negotiations among the U.S. Forest Service, the Native American groups, and the Advisory Council on Historic Preservation (a Federal regulatory group), the resulting Memorandum of Agreement stipulated when and how the Medicine Wheel could be used. Native Americans were allowed exclusive access during certain times of the year to conduct private ceremonies. During the remainder of the year, visitors were to be kept at a specified distance from the structure and instructed on appropriate behavior near this sacred place. A monitoring team, which included representatives of the concerned Native American groups and the U.S. Forest Service, were charged with ensuring adequate protection of the Medicine Wheel. Although the agreement does not satisfy any of the users of the Medicine Wheel completely, it represents the sort of compromise that is becoming standard in deciding who will own and manage the past.

The Medicine Wheel illustrates one of the most critical problems in cultural resource management in the field of archeology. Should archeology sites and structures be preserved and managed only by and for the descendants of the people who created them? Should they be allowed to disintegrate if these descendants so desire [a desire expressed by some Pueblo people in regard to their unique architecture (Swentzell, 1990; see also Silko, 1987, quoted previously)? Or should cultural resources be managed and preserved for the larger public for educational, aesthetic, scientific, and even economic purposes? These are questions under current heated debate, and answers are not yet apparent.

Conclusions

Cultural resources are pieces of the past that retain value in the present and are irreplaceable. Reassembling a disturbed or destroyed archeological site is not possible, nor is it possible to rebuild a Maya temple or replace a defaced rock art panel. The value of these cultural resources is in their age and history and in the meaning placed on them by people today. Value and meaning are, of course, the key to the problem; because not everyone places the same value and meaning on cultural properties, a consensus on how they should be treated is difficult to reach. How do we weigh the costs and benefits of a development project against the costs and benefits of preserving or excavating an archeological site? How much can we afford to spend on cultural resource management? Some people gain enormous pleasure in collecting artifacts; for these people, the value of artifacts is in their beauty or the joy of recovering them from the ground (King, n.d.). Should these simple pleasures be denied to protect the fragile knowledge that archeological sites can provide? What claims do native peoples have over the sites that their ancestors created or over sites on public land that they hold sacred?

The world's cultural heritage is vanishing at an appalling rate. Despite recent legal efforts to halt this trend, the rate of destruction is increasing. Cultural resources are nonrenewable. They must be conserved and managed. Management of nonrenewable resources looks to the future; in the case of cultural resources, managers and planners must address the future of humanity's past.

References

Archaeology, 1991, Protecting the Peten. *Archaeology*, v. 44, no. 4, p. 20.

Arnold, Bettina, 1992, The past as propaganda. *Archaeology*, v. 45, no. 4, p. 30–37.

Brody, J.J., 1977, *Mimbres painted pottery*. Albuquerque, University of New Mexico Press, 253 p.

Cleere, Henry, 1989a, *Archaeological heritage management in the modern world*. London, Unwin-Hyman, 318 p.

——— 1989b, Introduction: The rationale of archaeological heritage management, in Cleere, Henry, ed., *Archaeological heritage management in the modern world*. London, Unwin-Hyman, p. 1–19.

Clifford, James, 1988, *The predicament of culture*. Cambridge, Harvard University Press, 318 p.

Di Giorgio, Roberta, 1993, Salvaging ruins in Jordan. *Archaeology*, v. 46, no. 3, p. 23–24.

Elia, R.J., 1993, A seductive and troubling work. *Archaeology*, v. 46, no. 1, p. 64–69.

Fagan, Brian, 1989, Foreword, in Messenger, P. M., ed., *The ethics of collecting cultural property: Whose culture? Whose property?* Albuquerque, University of New Mexico Press, p. xv–xvii.

Flood, Josephine, 1989, "Tread softly for you tread on my bones": The development of cultural resource management in Australia, in Cleere, H. F., ed., *Archaeological heritage management in the modern world*. London, Unwin-Hyman, p. 79–102.

Frazier, Deborah, 1993, *Looters of the artifacts*. Denver, Rocky Mountain News, May 9, p. 8A, 28–30A.

Garfield, Donald, 1992, Saving grace. *Museum News*, v. 71, no. 3, p. 42–47.

Goldstein, Lynne, and Kintigh, Keith, 1990, Ethics and the reburial controversy. *American Antiquity*, v. 55, no. 3, p. 585–591.

Gray, D.D., 1993, Champion of aboriginal art. *Archaeology*, v. 46, no. 4, p. 44–47.

Harris, Leo J., 1989, From the collector's perspective: The legality of importing pre-Columbian art and artifacts, in Messenger, P. M., ed., *The ethics of collecting cultural property: Whose culture? Whose property?* Albuquerque, University of New Mexico Press, p. 155–175.

Henson, F.G., 1989, Historical development and attendant problems of cultural re-
source management in the Philippines, in Cleere, Henry, ed., *Archaeological heritage management in the modern world*. London, Unwin-Hyman, p. 109–117.

Herscher, Ellen, 1989, International control efforts: Are there any good solution? in Messenger, P.M., ed., *The ethics of collecting cultural property—Whose culture? Whose property?* Albuquerque, University of New Mexico Press, p. 117–128.

Hoffman, T.L., 1991, Stewards of the past: Preserving Arizona's archaeological resources through positive public involvement, in Smith, G.S., and Ehrenhard, J.E., ed., *Preserving the past*. Boca Raton, CRC Press, p. 253–260.

Howell, C.L., 1992, Daring to deal with Huaqueros. *Archaeology*, v. 45, no. 3, p. 56–58.

Hoving, Thomas, 1993, *Making the mummies dance*. New York, Simon and Schuster, 348 p.

Hutt, Sherry, Elwood, W., and McAllister, M.E., 1992, *Archaeological resource protection*. Washington, D.C., The Preservation Press, National Trust for Historic Preservation, 179 p.

King, T.F., 1991, Some dimensions of the pothunting problem, in Smith, G.S., and Ehrenhard, J.E., ed., *Protecting the past*. Boca Raton, CRC Press, p. 83–92.

———— [n.d.], *Looters or lovers—Studying the non-archaeological use of archaeological resources*. Prepared for the Society for American Archaeology, 65 p.

Knudson, Ruthann, 1989, North America's threatened heritage. *Archaeology*, v. 42, no. 1, p. 71–73.

Kristiansen, Kristian, 1989, Perspectives on the archaeological heritage: History and future, in Cleere, Henry, ed., *Archaeological heritage management in the modern world*. London, Unwin-Hyman, p. 23–26.

LeBlanc, S.A., 1983, *The Mimbres people*. London, Thames and Hudson, p. 183.

Lekson, S.H., 1990, The Southwest's remarkable Mimbres people. *Archaeology*, v. 43, no. 6, p. 44–48.

Lipe, William, 1974, A conservation model for American archaeology. *The Kiva*, v. 39, no. 1-2, p. 213–43.

———— 1984, Value and meaning in cultural resources, in Cleere, Henry, ed., *Approaches to the archaeological heritage*. Cambridge, Cambridge University Press, p. 1–11.

McGimsey, C.R., 1972, *Public archaeology*. New York and London, Seminar Press, 265 p.

McManamon, F.P., 1992, Managing America's archaeological resources, in Wandsnider, LuAnn, ed., *Quandaries and quests, visions of archaeology's future*. Carbondale, Occasional Paper No. 20, Center for Archaeological Investigations, Southern Illinois University at Carbondale, p. 25–40.

Meyer, Karl, 1973, *The plundered past*. New York, Atheneum, 353 p.

Min, Zhuang, 1989, The administration of China's archaeological heritage, in Cleere, Henry, ed., *Archaeological heritage management in the modern world*. London, Unwin-Hyman, p. 102–108.

Muller, Scott, 1992, Iced mummy. *Archaeology*, v. 45, no. 3, p. 24.

Munson, Cheryl Ann, Jones, M.M., and Fry, R.E., 1993, General electric mound and ARPA—Current status. *Society for American Archaeology Bulletin*, v. 11, no. 3, p. 3–4.

Nickens, P.R., 1991, The destruction of archaeological sites and data, in Smith, G.S., and Ehrenhard, J.E., ed., *Protecting the past*. Boca Raton, CRC Press, p. 73–82.

Parker, P.L., and King, T.F., 1990, *Guidelines for evaluating and documenting traditional cultural properties*. Washington, D.C., National Register Bulletin 38, National Park Service, Interagency Resources Division, 22 p.

Pendergast, David, and Graham, Elizabeth, 1989, The battle for the Maya past: The effects of international looting and collecting in Belize, in Messenger, P.M. ed., *The ethics of collecting cultural property: Whose culture? Whose property?* Albuquerque, University of New Mexico Press, p. 51–60.

Price, M.H., 1991, *Disputing the dead, U.S. law on aboriginal remains and grave goods*. Columbia, University of Missouri Press, 136 p.

Renfrew, Colin, 1991, *The Cycladic spirit—Masterpieces from the Nicholas P. Goulandris Collection*. New York, Harry N. Abrams, 208 p.

———— 1993, Collectors are the real looters. *Archaeology*, v. 46, no. 3, p. 16–17.

Rogge, A.E., 1991, Teaching with archaeology—An Arizona program, in Smith, G.S., and Ehrenhard, J.E., ed., *Protecting the past*. Boca Raton, CRC Press, p. 129–134.

Shestack, Alan, 1989, The museum and cultural property: The transformation of institutional ethics, in Messenger, P.M., ed., *The ethics of collecting cultural property: Whose culture? Whose property?* Albuquerque, University of New Mexico Press, p. 93–102.

Silko, L.M., 1987, Landscape, history, and the Pueblo imagination, in Halpern, Daniel, ed., *On nature—Nature, landscape, and natural history*. San Francisco, North Point Press, p. 83–94.

Simmons, A.H., 1992, Global cultural resource archaeology in the early twenty-first century, in Wandsnider, LuAnn, ed., *Quandaries and quests, visions of archaeology's future*. Carbondale, Occasional Paper No. 20, Center for Archaeological Investigations, Southern Illinois University at Carbondale, p. 79–97.

Smardz, Karolyn, 1991, Teaching people to touch the past: Archaeology in the Toronto school system, in Smith, G.S., and Ehrenhard, J.E., ed., *Protecting the past*. Boca Raton, CRC Press, p. 135–142.

Smith, G.S., and Ehrenhard, J.E., 1991, *Protecting the past*. CRC Press, Boca Raton, 314 p.

Swentzell, Rina, 1990, Remembering Tewa Pueblo houses and spaces. *Native peoples*, v. 3, no. 2, p. 6–15.

U.S. Information Agency, 1993, *Looting, theft, and smuggling, a report to the President and the Congress, 1983–1993*. Cultural Property Advisory Committee, United States Information Agency, 28 p.

3

Fingerprints in the Sand

Richard Monastersky

The moon rises heavy over New Mexico's high desert, casting its rays on scattered juniper trees, pinyon pines and a crime in progress. Two men have just plundered the remnants of an ancient dwelling in the Gila National Forest and are loading up sacks with prehistoric pots and bead jewelry. As their truck swings homeward, they think about the handsome price these relics will fetch from dealers who sell fine antiquities.

That theft in New Mexico last year is but one case in a little-heralded crime wave sweeping the United States. Although the federal government and many states prohibit the unauthorized removal of artifacts from public lands, "pot hunters" illegally raid thousands of archaeological sites each year, ranging from prehistoric burial grounds in Washington state to the graves of Civil War soldiers in Virginia.

"While we tend to think of [archaeological] looting as a phenomenon that occurs outside the United States, the scale of looting inside this country is massive," says James Adovasio, an archaeologist at Mercyhurst College in Erie, Pa., who has investigated several such crimes.

Over the past two decades, the pace of pot hunting has grown steadily, reflecting a burgeoning antiquities market hungry for pretty legacies of the past. Archaeologists and law enforcement agents have responded by stepping up their own efforts. But it's often difficult to put the guilty behind bars, because savvy thieves can claim they collected artifacts legally on private property.

In the last three years, scientists have developed their own "dirty" tactics to circumvent that defense. Using X-rays and electron microscopes, they analyze soil particles recovered from stolen antiquities in an effort to prove the items were illegally removed from protected sites. So far, the high-tech soil tests have contributed to convictions in only a handful of cases. But those who investigate archaeological crimes believe the technique holds great potential in the battle against artifact thieves.

"Soils are probably *the* most important weapon in our arsenal against these people right now, because it's pretty hard to dig in an archaeological site without taking soil away too," says Martin McAllister, an archaeologist and consultant who trains investigators to handle artifact crimes.

The New Mexico case illustrates how a criminal investigation can benefit from some snooping in the soil. The pillaged site once housed members of the Mimbres culture, who lived in the region around 1100 A.D. The looters not only carted off artifacts but also disturbed a Mimbres grave and left human bones strewn about the ancient dwelling, says Linda Kelley, a U.S. Forest Service archaeologist involved in the investigation.

Figure 1. A looted rockshelter site along the Snake River in southern Idaho. (Photo courtesy of Martin McAllister/Archaeological Resource Investigations)

As often happens, authorities did not learn of the crime until long after the thieves had fled. But with the help of informants, federal agents tracked down a pair of suspects and searched the house where they lived. The agents found several bits of evidence there, including a bag of pottery fragments and some reconstructed pots as well as dirt-covered coveralls and excavation tools. The suspects claimed they had collected the artifacts from private property with permission from the landowner.

Because police had not caught the suspects in the act of robbing the Mimbres site, archaeologists had to find circumstantial evidence that would convince a jury the seized material came from national forestland. Focusing on the dirt encrusting the tools, clothing and pottery found in the suspects' home, Kelley called in a team of soil sleuths who had pioneered a technique for analyzing sediments in cases of archaeological theft.

Adovasio, working with geologist Gary A. Cooke of the R.J. Lee Group, Inc., in Monroeville, Penn., and sedimentologist Jack Donahue from the University of Pittsburgh examined the recovered dirt and two other soil samples: one collected at the Gila site and another from the private property where the suspects claimed to have found the artifacts. Using a computer-controlled scanning electron microscope, the researchers drew up a list of the minerals and elements in each sample.

Donahue says such analyses provide a distinctive profile of the soil samples. "This is essentially a fingerprint, but you're fingerprinting sediment rather than a person," he explains.

The forensic tests struck pay dirt, revealing that the soil on the seized pottery and tools matched the sediment from the national forest rather than the sediment from the privately owned site.

Kelley found other clues implicating the purported thieves. During excavations at the Gila site she collected more than 8,000 pottery shards left behind by the looters. In scrutinizing the fragments, she found one that matched a pot shard recovered from the suspects' home. The clay bits fit together like adjoining pieces of a jigsaw puzzle.

Such a match might seem irrefutable, but this type of evidence hasn't always ensured convictions in the past. For that reason, Kelley says the additional evidence from the soil analysis will prove important when the case goes to trial. "We need this scientific analysis to get rid of the kinds of doubt that an attorney could raise," she says.

When Donahue, Adovasio and Cooke joined the New Mexico investigation, they already had a forensic success record of 2-0, having used soil analyses to provide hard evidence against suspected looters twice before.

The first of those cases involved a man named Earl Shumway, who discovered a spectacular cache of thirteenth-century Anasazi baskets in southeastern Utah, "the likes of which hadn't been collected in over 50 years," says Adovasio. Archaeologist suspected Shumway had looted the baskets from Manti-La Sal National Forest, but he claimed they came from private land.

Although Shumway had cleaned the baskets, Donahue and colleagues managed to collect a small sample of dirt from under the stitching, which enabled them to demonstrate that the baskets had come from the national forest. Prosecutors used this analysis in their case against Shumway, who eventually confessed to the crime.

In the second incident, a man was convicted of stealing a 1,500-year-old mummified infant from a site known as Tin Cave in Arizona's Tonto National Forest.

Figure 2. Ancient Mimbres ceramic pots recovered during a criminal investigation in New Mexico. (Photo courtesy of Martin McAllister/Archaeological Resource Investigations)

Authorities arrested him in 1988 after he tried to sell the infant's remains for $20,000 to an undercover agent. Through soil analysis, the researchers linked sediment from inside the cave with dirt found with the mummy. Because the man never denied having taken the mummy from the cave, the soil analysis wasn't crucial to his conviction, but the trial provided an important test of the technique's reliability.

In the Utah and Arizona investigations, the scientists analyzed soils using X-ray fluorescence and X-ray diffraction rather than the electron microscopy technique applied to the New Mexico soils. While the X-ray tests can provide an equally accurate portrait of the minerals and elements within soil, the computer-controlled scanning electron microscope technique is faster and easier, says Donahue, who described the three cases in Dallas this October at the annual meeting of the Geological Society of America.

Soil analysis has long played a role in investigations of artifact poaching, notes McAllister, a veteran in the field of archaeological criminology. But until the last five years, he says, authorities have used relatively simple techniques that lack the fingerprint-like accuracy of X-ray and electron microscope analyses.

Investigators have used the high-tech tests in only a few cases so far, primarily because news of the advances has yet to spread and the tests can cost up to $5,000 per case. But Donahue says many universities and research organizations have the necessary equipment to perform this type of analysis.

"I think the soil tests will be used more commonly in the future," McAllister says, noting that it's very difficult to prove that purloined artifacts came from a protected area without such evidence. "Even if you find someone driving down a road through a national forest with a truckful of pots or other artifacts in their possession, you're not necessarily going to be able to prosecute them," he says.

Paradoxically, the new tests may lose some of their power against criminals as they gain popularity with investigators. That's because looters pay close attention to new legal tactics and adjust their methods to stay ahead of the law.

Several years ago, authorities started using an approach that capitalized on looters' disregard for the environment. Pot hunters often left cigarettes, beer cans and other garbage at the scene of the crime, and investigators collected the trash as evidence. But the looters soon caught on to that technique. "They're running a much cleaner operation now," says J. Scott Wood, an archaeologist at the Tonto forest who worked on the Tin Cave case.

Investigators have also drawn evidence from distinctive footprints and tire tracks found near excavation sites. Looters have responded by buying boots with common soles and tires with unremarkable treads.

Most archaeological thieves are tightly "networked," readily passing on information about new forensic techniques. Already, many have begun fastidiously cleaning off their artifacts and tools, Wood says. As this trend continues, he says, "the success of soil techniques will depend on when we catch them. If we can get them before they clean their stuff off, then we have a chance."

Part of the problem, says Adovasio, is that the techniques work best when soil samples are large enough to allow several tests. "But if worse comes to worse, as was the case with the Shumway business, we can use extremely minuscule portions to do the job—thimble-size or smaller," he says.

Donahue recounts one instance in which the team scraped tiny bits of sediment from within the grooves in an arrowhead and found the sample sufficient for analysis. Thus, he says, "even if [the looters] clean it off very carefully, we still have a chance of finding material that can be analyzed."

Although experts lack detailed statistics showing the extent of archaeological looting in the United States, they say the problem has worsened in recent decades as antiquity prices have reached staggering levels. Most of the plundered material ends up gracing coffee tables of wealthy U.S. collectors, although an increasing proportion reaches Japan, Europe and Saudi Arabia, says McAllister.

"It's going on everywhere in the United States, anyplace you find an historic or prehistoric artifact that has collector interest. You'll find people stealing from public lands, tribal lands and even off private property without the permission of the owner," he says.

People outside the archaeological community may wonder whether this looting truly represents a serious problem. After all, the United States has thousands of archaeological sites, and museums have countless artifacts stored away in dusty basements.

Yet that reasoning belies the real impact of pot hunting. There are only a finite number of archaeological sites holding information about prehistoric life; no more will ever exist. The raiding of these sites wipes out our record of past peoples. When looters ransack a site, they not only remove artifacts but also rearrange critical archaeological clues, destroying the contextual information researchers need to understand a particular site, Kelley says.

That information cannot be recovered even if police locate the stolen goods. "A looted artifact has lost 95 percent of its value to tell us what was going on in the prehistoric or historic period," McAllister says.

4

City Lost in the Jungle

Fergus M. Bordewich

I watched the saffron-robed Buddhist monks move by, oblivious to the stifling tropical heat. I had been to Cambodia before, but never to this place. Up I climbed through a stone gateway, up dark, ancient stairwells. Courtyard upon courtyard rose toward a central tower, more than 200 feet above the jungle floor. I was in the temple of Angkor Wat.

This was a site that had fired my imagination since childhood, when my father gave me the *Complete Book of Marvels* by globe-trotting author Richard Halliburton. The book swept me away to exotic places. But nothing gripped me like the photos of a vine-shrouded city in the jungle, its origins hidden in the haze of time.

The days of Angkor's glory were between the ninth and 14th centuries. The Khmers, as the Cambodians were known, ruled over much of Southeast Asia, including parts of Thailand, Laos and Vietnam. Their prosperous capital, Angkor, covered an area the size of modern Paris, and its population dwarfed that of any city in Europe at the time.

Today the ruins, including massive stone temples and a sophisticated water system, testify to a splendid, advanced civilization. Spread over 100 square miles, the city's one million inhabitants lived at the crossroads of China and the Indian subcontinent. It was a teeming city of fabulous wealth, its markets overflowing with exotic silks, rhinoceros horn, ivory, spices and rare woods.

Angkor's glory began to fade and finally disappeared after the city was abandoned when the Thais attacked in 1431. Eventually, it was forgotten by most of the world. By the time French colonizers began exploring Angkor in the middle of the 19th century, the temples were covered with a carpet of jungle.

As archeologists began to peel back Angkor's green veil, it became clear that one of the true wonders of human achievement was being revealed.

"Angkor is the ultimate jungle ruin," John Stubbs, vice president of the World Monuments Fund, had told me before I left to visit the fabled site. His New York-based organization is sponsoring major restoration work at Angkor. "It easily ranks as one of the all-time great human achievements. It's in the same league as the Parthenon, Chartres Cathedral and the Forbidden City in Beijing."

Hopes for its rebirth were brought to an abrupt halt in the mid-1970s by the murderous onslaught of the Khmer Rouge. In the span of a few short years, the Communist zealots took control of Cambodia and killed more than one million of their own people.

The Khmer Rouge also showed raw contempt for Angkor. Giant statues of Buddha were blown up and smashed by sledgehammers. Painstakingly prepared

Figure 1. View of Angkor Wat in Cambodia. (Photo courtesy of Wilhelm Solheim)

blueprints and notebooks were destroyed. Experts on Angkor's history were executed.

After Vietnamese forces ousted the Khmer Rouge regime in 1979, Angkor succumbed to looting. For the next ten years the presence of Khmer Rouge guerrillas made travel to the site a dangerous proposition. Isolated by war and under relentless attack by the encroaching jungle, Angkor seemed destined to be lost again to the world.

It was only in 1989 that Cambodia's conflicts shifted enough to enable foreigners to visit Angkor. One of the first on the scene was a ruddy-faced British architect named John Sanday. He led a team sponsored by the World Monuments

Fund as part of a worldwide effort to help save Angkor's treasures from further deterioration.

Sanday was overwhelmed when he saw the ruins. Entire buildings were crushed in the embrace of gigantic roots, while labyrinths of ancient courtyards unfolded in dizzying patterns.

First Sanday had to create a work force from scratch. He sent messengers to scour the surrounding villages for men who had experience working with stone.

Sanday and a team of restoration experts from half a dozen nations soon began work as war raged nearby in northwest Cambodia. There were nights when Sanday and a crew that had grown to 100 fell asleep to the sound of gunfire and the distant boom of artillery.

Grabbing a machete, Sanday often took the lead at work. He and the crew lugged fallen stones and propped up unsteady walls. They stapled some of the stones together with steel clamps and reinforced others with fiberglass and stainless-steel rods.

Sanday also began to train a new generation of Cambodian architects and archeologists to love Angkor and Cambodia's ancient past. One of them was Chhan Chamroeun.

As a child under the Khmer Rouge, Chhan Chamroeun had once caught a brief glimpse of Angkor Wat rising over the jungle as he trekked across the war-torn country with his family. "I saw it for only a few minutes," the serious young archeologist told me one day, as we walked to the ruins of a recently uncovered shrine. "But I never forgot it. It was always in my dreams."

Raised at a time when knowledge was treated as a crime, Chhan had grown up completely ignorant of his country's past. "I knew nothing about Cambodian history," he said, as we made our way through the under-brush.

After the overthrow of the Khmer Rouge regime, he enrolled in the national university. He was so poor that he slept in a classroom and cut up cement bags to use as notebooks. Still, he remembered the crumbling city that he had glimpsed in the jungle. The very image of it gave him hope to go on.

"We cannot go back to the past, but we can show that we once were great," Chhan told me with quiet passion. "I want to help my culture, to raise it up and keep it alive."

In the ensuing days of my visit, I wandered from temple to temple. In one area laborers cleared brush from some 300,000 blocks of stone that will in the coming years be used to rebuild a nearby temple. Round and square columns, lintels, cornices, roof tiles, moldings and sculptured panels stretched away as far as I could see.

With a sense of awe I walked through one temple. First, I climbed stairs so steep and narrow that I had to go up sideways. Dark towers rose all around me. Everywhere I turned, giant faces gazed down at me: scores, perhaps hundreds of them, ineffably mysterious and smiling enigmatically. From every tower they stared off toward the points of the compass.

As my journey neared its end, dancers from a recently re-established academy of classical dance came to perform. Parakeets swirled overhead as drums and cymbals rang out through the ruined halls. The dancers appeared one by one, dressed in dazzling costumes of gold, scarlet and cobalt blue.

I sat on a toppled column and watched the dancers as they acted out age-old myths and tales of nymphs and demons. Cambodians believe that the air of

Figure 2. Jungle growth is accelerating destruction of buildings in Angkor Thom complex. (Photo courtesy of Wilhelm Solheim)

Angkor is thick with the living spirits of the dead. I could almost feel the mysterious Khmers of long past hovering near, drawn by the exquisite music and the forms of a dance that had changed little since the days when Angkor was young.

And I thought of those evenings long ago when, with Richard Halliburton's book opened on my knees, I had stared at Angkor's temples and towers crumbling in the grip of the jungle. I remembered how I had dreamed of entering that mysterious realm. Now, at last, I had stepped into the picture.

Commentary

The last two sections of this reader illustrate that archaeology has many publics, and that to be an archaeologist now requires more than simply academic training in excavation, survey, and stratigraphic interpretation. Pressing issues are at stake in the world of archaeology today that concern historic preservation, cultural resource protection, and heritage management. Although these three topics fall outside the traditional academic domain, institutions of archaeological training can no longer afford to ignore them. Many different interest groups today find value in some aspect of the archaeological record: some are descendants of people who inhabited these residential and cemetery sites, others are conservation-oriented citizens who understand that cultural resources are nonrenewable, and still others are amateur and professional archaeologists. We must not only listen to voices of various interest groups, but we must actively find ways to protect a fragile archaeological record. The question is how best to go about doing this.

Protecting the archaeological record is not easy, even with proper legislation in place, because the preservation task forces society to face compelling ethical and legal issues. Who owns the past? Should subsurface archaeological remains be legally treated like subsurface minerals or water? Since we cannot save everything, what part of the past shall we preserve? We can find no easy answers to these questions. Articles in this section show how archaeologists must constantly try new strategies in the quest to protect and manage cultural resources. Additional legislation protects archaeological remains on federal and state land, but provides almost no protection for materials found on private land. As Cameron notes in her article, federal enactment of the Native American Graves Protection and Repatriation Act (or NAGPRA) has changed the way in which archaeologists deal with human graves in the United States. Passage of this (and other recent) legislation prohibits looting of sites on private land that contain mortuary remains. Since most ancient village sites have some evidence of human burials, this new legislation may finally provide the necessary tools to stem unauthorized excavations on some private land.

The world of cultural resource management is more dynamic today in developing countries than ever before, since CRM is now an established aspect of archaeology in North America. Most archaeologists working in such countries are involved in applied research, and we see a growing interest in developing protective legislation to slow (or halt) the trafficking in antiquities. Students in many countries now seek college-level training in archaeology to become professional archaeologists. One reason for this trend surely lies in the expansion of cultural tourism in recent decades, and the fact that tourists now visit nearly every corner of the earth. Trained professional archaeologists are needed who can manage cultural resources in national forests, archaeological parks, and departments of antiquity. Another reason for this surge in archaeological interest lies in the accelerated rate of economic development, which inevitably threatens cultural resources. Yet even as the world's number of archaeologists grows, so, too, does the destruction of sites through looting and economic development. International organizations have developed to protect the world's cultural heritage, like the World Monuments Fund, ICOMOS (International Committee on Monuments and Sites), and UNESCO (United Nations Educational, Scientific and Cultural Organization). We know that change is irreversible, but more work is needed in finding better methods of cultural resource management to protect the world's archaeological record.

Our cultural heritage is important to indigenous, ethnic, and religious groups, to nations, and to the international community. Archaeologists fear that eventual destruction of the archaeological record may one day make the study of the ancient past all but impossible. Today, members of many indigenous communities whose ancestors used these sites are just as anxious. Some are archaeologists themselves, while others develop and administrate tribal and cultural museums. As archaeological resources become potential tourism locations, governments around the world are paying increasing attention to planning for sustainable development. Emerging nation-states around the world have also become increasingly concerned with the destruction of their heritage, since the archaeological record offers tangible evidence of their community histories and self-identity. Whatever the outcome of debates concerning the management of the archaeological record, people worldwide clearly share a deep interest in our human past. Our responsibility as archaeologists is to study, manage, and protect that heritage for future generations.

Index

absolute dating, 82–83, 161–162, 167, 171, 187

Adovasio, James, 525, 549–552

Advisory Council on Historic Preservation (ACHP), 486, 489, 524, 545

aerial photography, 190, 209, 262, 352, 537

aerial survey, 209, 262

Africa, 25, 28, 40–41, 93, 96–97, 104, 109–110, 112–113, 115–116, 162–163, 165–166, 173–174, 183–184, 187, 222, 242–243, 245, 247, 417, 422, 465, 481, 485–486, 533

African-Americans, 437, 468, 487

Agriculture, 93, 127, 152, 187, 261–263, 279, 282, 289, 291–302, 315, 322, 325, 351, 359, 361, 364, 366, 420, 430, 439, 464, 469, 510, 513–514

Altamira (Spain), 80–81, 109

America, 4–5, 7, 15, 24, 30, 33–34, 36, 55, 65, 67, 94, 119–123, 159, 161, 171, 181, 192, 203, 209–210, 279, 302, 313, 318, 359, 366, 369–370, 375–376, 414, 465, 486, 504, 519–520, 526, 538, 542, 547, 552, 559

analogy, 28, 317, 324

Andes, 289, 300, 315–316

Angkor, 147, 157, 521, 534, 555–558

Angkor Wat, 521, 555–557

Anthropology, 3, 9, 18, 55–56, 63, 77, 81, 119, 121, 125, 140, 144, 192, 230, 301, 314, 341, 365, 398, 439, 461–465, 468, 485–486, 493–494, 501, 540
  archaeology, 3, 63, 77, 81, 125, 301, 365, 439, 461, 464, 493–494, 501

antiquities market, 520, 538, 541, 549

Anyon, Roger, 523, 525, 527–529

archaeological data. See data, 357

archaeological method, 42, 140, 161, 444, 463

archaeological record, 25, 28, 45, 63, 93, 114, 159, 219, 225, 247, 263, 324, 328, 335, 352, 373, 376, 379, 413–414, 421–422, 425–426, 429–431, 441, 444–445, 453, 458, 465, 493, 510, 519–520, 523, 553, 559–560

archaeological research, 4, 28, 68, 90, 125, 127–128, 161, 187, 219, 221–222, 247, 259, 261, 292, 318, 329, 357, 359, 367, 373, 381, 414, 429, 439, 441–442, 444, 454, 465, 467, 469, 480, 486, 508, 510, 519, 542
  and CRM, 519–520, 523–525, 532, 535–536, 544, 559

Archaeological Resource Protection Act, 526

archaeology, 3–5, 8, 10–12, 14, 16, 18, 20, 22, 24–43, 45–46, 48, 50–56, 58, 60, 63, 65–66, 68, 70, 72, 74, 76–83, 85–86, 88–91, 93–94, 96, 98, 100, 102, 104, 106, 110, 112, 114, 116, 120, 122–123, 125, 127–128, 131–132, 134, 136, 138–142, 144, 148, 150, 152, 154, 156, 159, 161–162, 166, 168, 170, 172, 174, 178, 180, 184, 186, 189–190, 192, 194, 196, 198, 200, 202–204, 206, 208, 210–212, 214, 216, 219–220, 222, 224, 226, 228, 230, 232, 234, 236, 238, 240, 242, 244, 246, 249–250, 252–254, 256, 258–260, 262, 266, 268, 270, 272, 274–276, 279–280, 282, 284, 286,

288–290, 292–294, 296, 298,
300–302, 304, 306, 308, 310,
312–314, 316, 318, 322–324, 326,
328–330, 332, 334, 336, 338–341,
344, 346, 348, 352, 354, 356,
358–359, 362, 364–367, 370, 374,
376, 378, 382, 384, 386, 388, 390,
392, 394, 398, 400, 402, 404, 406,
408, 411–415, 418, 420, 422–423,
425–426, 428–432, 434, 436,
438–440, 442, 444–445,
448–450, 452, 454, 456, 458,
460–469, 471–474, 476–482,
484, 486–488, 490–491,
493–499, 501–508, 510, 512,
514–520, 523–529, 531–532, 534,
536, 538, 540, 542, 544, 546–548,
550, 552, 556, 558–560
academic, 4, 93, 423, 462, 486,
    494, 523, 525, 559
and anthropology, 3, 63, 77, 81,
    125, 301, 365, 439, 461, 464,
    493–494, 501
and racism, 529
and the future, 29–30, 220, 445,
    462, 480, 499, 501, 519, 529,
    546–548
contract, 486, 525
experimental, 413, 466
goals of, 219, 501
historical, 65, 91, 139, 358, 425,
    449, 462, 486, 498
history and, 3, 63, 65, 78–79, 89,
    91, 128, 205, 397, 442,
    444–445, 463, 467, 479, 494,
    547–548
popularization of, 3, 467, 469,
    472, 479
world archaeology, 3–4, 7, 33, 51,
    65, 72–73, 96, 120, 127–128,
    161–162, 189, 196, 217, 220,
    261, 316, 359, 369, 389, 414,
    423, 439, 445, 464, 467–468,
    480, 494, 505, 515, 517, 519,
    547, 559
architecture, 3, 31, 69, 90, 259, 295,
    317–318, 329, 335, 339, 351,
    367, 397, 401, 513, 516, 531,
    533, 538, 545

Arizona, 4, 8–9, 14, 17–19, 95, 275,
    277, 318, 325, 327–331, 333,
    335, 337, 339, 341, 398, 414,
    425–426, 429, 436, 439,
    442–445, 502–508, 524–525,
    534, 542, 544, 547–548, 551–552
    Garbage Project, 4, 8, 14, 18–19
Arnold, Barto, 128, 141
Arnold, Bettina, 467, 471–473,
    475–476, 479, 546
art. see also cave art
    Paleolithic, 81, 165, 175, 221,
        228, 370, 381, 383, 387–389
    rock, 162, 185–186, 369–370, 373,
        375–376, 378–379, 381, 388,
        443, 528, 533, 537, 544–545
    symbols, 183, 375, 443, 537
artifacts, 3–5, 7, 11–12, 14, 18, 26–29,
    31–34, 36–37, 39, 45, 47, 50,
    55–56, 63, 65, 67, 69, 73, 78–79,
    82–83, 88, 93–96, 102, 104–107,
    110, 115, 120–121, 128, 131–134,
    138, 142–145, 156–157, 161–162,
    184, 193–194, 196, 211, 214–216,
    222–223, 227, 231, 233, 235, 241,
    243, 245–247, 259, 283, 294,
    311–313, 324, 329, 335–336, 340,
    345, 354, 370, 379, 406, 413, 429,
    443, 485, 494, 497, 502, 517, 520,
    523, 526–528, 531–534, 537–538,
    540–541, 543–544, 546, 549–550,
    552–553
Askra (Greece), 131, 133–134,
    136–138
Atapuerca (Spain), 111, 114–115, 117
Australia, 162, 166, 171, 183–185,
    187, 191, 317, 321–322, 367,
    417, 422–423, 538, 544, 546
bamboo, 96, 222, 239–241, 243–247,
    421, 428
Bang Pakong valley, 128, 147
Beck, Colleen, 5, 45
belief. see also cognitive archaeology;
    cult; ideology; religion; ritual, 65,
    119, 222, 369–370, 375, 468,
    481, 527–529
Bintliff, John L., 128, 131, 140
birds, 269, 271
Blakey, Michael, 481, 485–487, 490

blood, 89, 189, 191–194, 212, 219,
  400, 402, 408, 529
  residues, 192
  residue technique, 189, 219
bone, 34, 41–43, 58, 68, 80, 85, 87, 93,
  97–98, 109–110, 113–114, 116,
  152–153, 165, 167–168, 172, 174,
  193, 195, 197, 216, 222, 231–238,
  254, 267, 269–270, 279, 296, 346,
  370, 394, 413, 419, 485, 487
  animal, 231, 235, 237, 413
Boucher de Perthes, Jacques, 76, 79
Brain, C. K., 93, 95, 97
bronze. see also metals; metallurgy, 4,
  26–27, 39, 68, 70, 78–79, 82–83,
  131, 145, 156–157, 319, 323–324,
  361–362, 366, 472–475, 477–478
Brooks, Alison, 17, 162, 165–167,
  169, 171–174
Cahokia, 318, 343–349
Cambodia, 147, 521, 555–557
Cameron, Catherine, 520, 524–526,
  531, 559
careers in archaeology, 480, 519
Carlson, John B., 370–371, 397
Carter, Howard, 8, 211
CAT also see computed axial tomography, 190, 213
cave art, 81, 183, 186, 223, 228, 230,
  369–370, 381, 383–384, 387,
  389, 411
  painting, 186, 221, 370, 384
ceramics, 145, 345, 394, 414, 439
Chhan, Chamroeun, 557
chipped stone, 56, 79, 311, 314
chronology, 22, 68, 70–71, 75–78,
  82–83, 110–111, 113, 161, 295,
  305, 331, 363, 370, 389, 461, 524
civilizations, 12, 147, 187, 292, 313,
  318–319, 361–362, 364–367,
  398, 430, 533
  New World, 3, 31, 33, 36, 50, 65,
    67, 72, 91, 94, 119–121, 123,
    187, 189, 220, 242, 316, 345,
    352, 359, 366, 398, 413, 417,
    420, 422, 425, 429, 437, 439,
    468, 535, 543, 546, 555, 559
  Old World, 65, 68, 94, 161, 242,
    259, 319, 358, 361, 365, 422

Clark, Desmond, 41, 417
classification, 219
Clottes, Jean, 370, 381
Clovis (New Mexico), 56, 58, 120
computer applications, 195
Connor, Melissa, 5, 51, 63, 141
conservation. see also preservation, 58,
  145, 192, 330, 411, 469,
  483–484, 486–487, 489, 509,
  513–516, 519–521, 534, 544, 547
Cook, Captain, 254, 453, 461
Courtin, Jean, 370, 381, 383, 388
crops, 33, 256–257, 260, 284, 289,
  292, 294–295, 298–300, 316,
  322, 344, 354, 411, 417, 420, 514
  bread wheat, 27, 213
  einkorn, 284
  emmer, 42, 284
  rice, 19, 147, 149–150, 152, 156,
    318, 325, 327–328, 341,
    425–426, 430–431, 434–438,
    444
cross-dating, see also sequence comparison, 33
cultural change, 174, 260, 275–276,
  411, 449, 542, 560
cultural ecology, 513
cultural evolution, 241–242, 276, 462
cultural resource management (crm),
  519, 523, 532, 559
Darwin, Charles, 65, 76–77, 95, 109
data, 9, 15, 19–20, 22–24, 27, 29, 33,
  49, 52, 54–55, 75, 91, 115, 123,
  128, 133, 154, 159, 179–181, 183,
  195, 199–200, 209, 213, 220, 229,
  241, 249, 253, 255–256, 272–273,
  275, 293–294, 299, 329, 338, 347,
  349, 352, 357, 361–367, 389, 413,
  415, 427, 429, 435–436, 438, 443,
  450, 454, 465, 471, 477, 481, 486,
  510, 525, 532, 548
  gathering, 181, 329
  interpretation, 54, 220, 367
dating methods, 82–83, 161–162, 167
deBeaune, Sophie A., 221, 223,
  226–227, 230
dendrochronology, 161
destruction of archaeological sites,
  441, 534, 548, 560

disease, 21, 39, 285–286, 385, 407, 486
DNA testing, 191
Dongoske, Kurt, 414, 441
Dye, Tom, 261, 265–266, 268, 272
Easter Island, 222, 249–250, 463
ecology, 275–276, 430, 439, 513
economy, 138, 156, 261, 270, 273,
    339, 417, 421–422, 430, 437
Egypt, 4, 41, 83, 159, 162, 178–181,
    197, 211, 249, 362, 365
    ancient, 181, 197
Egyptology, 177
Eisele, Judith A., 192–194
Ejutla (Mexico), 262, 303–313
El Pilar (Belize), 469, 509–516
Erickson, Clark L., 260, 262, 289–291,
    293–294, 297, 299, 301–302, 469
ethnoarchaeology, 25, 259–260,
    413–414, 417, 425, 427, 429,
    431, 433, 435, 437, 439, 465
ethnography, 369, 375, 411, 413–414,
    465–466, 471
    and archaeology, 413, 466
Europe, 3, 27, 65, 67–69, 72, 76,
    78–79, 82–83, 94–96, 105,
    109–117, 121, 162–163, 165, 168,
    171, 173–175, 183–184, 186–187,
    190, 211, 213, 217, 221–223,
    230–232, 242, 247, 279, 285,
    323–324, 344, 370, 383, 391–392,
    394–395, 411, 471–473, 477, 519,
    526, 539, 542, 553, 555
evolution, 3, 74, 77, 79–80, 93–94,
    96, 99–100, 109, 114, 116–117,
    125, 222, 239–243, 245, 247,
    276, 279, 289, 313, 421, 439,
    449, 462–463, 509–510, 513, 529
excavation, 8–10, 13, 18, 24, 29, 35,
    42, 48, 51, 53, 55–56, 59, 67,
    78–79, 81–82, 85–90, 111, 114,
    120–121, 127–129, 131–132,
    139–140, 147, 150–152, 154,
    156–157, 159, 165, 187, 190, 194,
    254, 261, 269–270, 277, 280, 290,
    294, 307, 329–331, 334, 341,
    345–346, 364, 398, 441–444, 474,
    477, 481, 483–484, 486–487,
    489–490, 496, 502, 504–506,
    525, 535, 541–542, 550, 552, 559

experimental archaeology, 227, 249,
    253, 259–260, 300, 394,
    414–415, 431, 439, 450, 462, 465
farming, 26, 42, 65, 156, 190–191,
    213, 261–262, 279–280,
    282–284, 287, 296, 302, 319,
    344, 364, 375, 400, 422, 434,
    437, 482, 513
fatty acids, 438
Feinman, Gary M., 262, 303–304,
    306–307, 313
Ferguson, T. J., 414, 441–442
field projects, 9, 127, 289–290, 298,
    301, 352, 431, 437, 484, 493, 524
    project design, 486–487, 489
Finney, Ben, 415, 447, 450–451, 453,
    457, 459, 461–462
flakes. see also stone tools, 94,
    102–107, 114, 185, 243, 246,
    311, 322, 331, 383, 418–420, 422
flotation, 4, 41–43, 88, 271, 279,
    285–287, 295, 331
Ford, Anabel, 469, 509–512, 515
formation processes, 324
fossils, 69, 111
Fresh Kills, 7–10
Funkhouser, Allen, 525–528
Garbage Project, 4, 8–10, 14–15, 17–24
geochronology, 168, 187
Giza. See also pyramids, 7, 159, 162,
    177–181, 249, 397
Giza Plateau, 177–181, 249
    Egypt, 178–179, 249
Great Hopewell Road, 190, 203–210
Great Pyramid, 7, 162, 177, 371, 397,
    401, 407
ground survey, 47, 209
Guatemala, 314, 359, 469, 509, 511,
    514, 516, 538, 541
Gwisho Hot Springs (Zambia), 40
Haliartos (Greece), 128, 131, 134,
    136–138
Hantman, Jeffrey, 65
Hawaii, 253, 276–277, 463
Herodotus, 28, 197
Heyerdahl, Thor, 251, 447, 449, 451,
    463
Higham, Charles, 128, 147–152, 154,
    156–157

historical archaeology, 65, 91, 139, 358, 425, 449, 462, 486, 498
hominids, 125
    early, 96, 110
Hohokam, 325, 327, 341, 504, 506–508, 524
Hokule'a, 448, 452, 454–455
Howard University, 193, 211, 481, 484–486, 490
Hublin, Jean-Jacques, 94, 109
human remains, 3, 51, 65, 69, 71–72, 75–76, 85, 95–96, 110–111, 113, 115, 125, 147, 153, 170, 221, 318, 367, 393, 413, 483–484, 487, 489, 491, 523, 528, 539, 543–544, 559
    Information from, 221, 539, 543
ice age, 5, 33–34, 50, 76–77, 80, 83, 98, 109–110, 119, 165, 186, 221, 223–235, 237–238, 327, 362, 370, 381, 383, 385, 387, 389, 394
ideological systems, 411
    reconstruction of, 370
Incas, 153, 294, 296–297
interpretation, 13, 16, 28, 42, 65, 91, 113–114, 117, 155, 200, 215, 246–247, 258, 267, 352, 365, 369, 373, 375, 394, 412–413, 441, 443, 474, 483, 489, 507, 525, 533, 559
    From analogy, 28
    In cultural history, 258, 474
Iron Age, 68, 78–79, 82–83, 317–318, 323, 367, 477–478
Iseminger, William, 318, 343
isotope analysis, 226
Jefferson, Thomas, 65, 85, 159, 373, 501
Jenkins, Leigh, 414, 441
Jodry, Margaret, 5, 56–58, 60–61
Johnson, William Gray, 45
Jones-Miller Site (Colorado), 55, 59–60
Ka Lae (Hawai'i), 267, 269–270
Kalinga (Philippines), 240–241, 414, 425–427, 429–432, 434–440, 465
Kanzi, 93–94, 100–107, 422
Katanda (Zaire), 165–166, 169, 172–174
Kao Pah Nam (Thailand), 239, 242, 245–246
Khmer (Cambodia), 156, 555–557

Khok Phanom Di, 128–129, 147–152, 154–157
    bone, 152
    social organization, 129
Knecht, Heidi, 221, 230–231, 233–235, 238, 395
Kuli'ou'ou (Hawai'i), 268–271
La Salle (Texas), 128, 141–145
Lake Titicaca (Bolivia and Peru), 262, 289–293, 295–302
Lake Turkana (Kenya), 25
Lake Victoria (Australia), 321–322
Lamps, 221, 223–230
Landscapes, 5, 274, 352, 531, 533
Langda (Irian Jaya), 413–414, 417–422
Lepper, Bradley T., 190, 203, 523
Lewin, Roger, 93, 99
Ligabue, Giancarlo, 413, 417
Little Rapids (Minnesota), 468, 493–498
Little Salt Spring (Florida), 4, 33–34
Longacre, William A., 260, 414, 425–426, 429, 439
looting, 520–521, 523, 525–527, 531–532, 534–535, 537–542, 548–549, 553, 556, 559–560
Loy, Thomas, 191, 193
Lyell, Charles, 65, 75–77, 161
macrobotanical remains, 129, 315
manufacture, 39, 73, 94, 104, 227, 233, 235–236, 241, 243, 262, 303–305, 307, 311–312, 331, 370, 415, 418–419, 421–422, 431
mapping, 4–5, 29, 35, 51–53, 133, 204, 249, 330, 349, 352–354, 398
Mary Rose (England), 4, 36–40
material culture, 51, 63, 260, 276, 395, 401, 411, 413, 429, 435, 439, 471
Maya, 4, 187, 203, 206, 209, 318–319, 326, 351–359, 366, 398, 400–401, 407–408, 469, 509–511, 513–514, 516, 538, 545, 548
    agriculture, 359, 469, 510, 513
    classic, 318–319, 351, 356–359, 398, 400, 513
        Classic Maya collapse, 513
McAllister, Martin, 547, 549–553
Melanesia, 265–266, 270, 275

Mesoamerica, 31, 33, 303, 306–307, 313, 318, 328, 357, 370, 398, 400–401, 407, 509, 514, 538
Mesolithic, 40, 238, 280, 283
Mesopotamia, 319, 361–366
metallurgy, 187, 215
Mississippian culture, 314, 318, 343–344, 349, 494
models, 82, 125, 159, 187, 189–190, 294, 300, 325, 329, 366, 449–450, 463, 493, 517
Mogollon, 525
Montelius, Gustav Oscar, 82–83
Moore, Andrew, 261, 288
multivariate strategy, 427
museums, 78, 520
nationalism, 468
Native Americans, 444, 468, 543, 545
Anasazi, 203, 206, 366, 505, 551
Hopi, 334, 340, 411, 414, 441–445, 466, 507, 527
Hohokam, 325, 327, 341, 504, 506–508, 524
Mimbres, 525–526, 538–539, 546–547, 549–551
Salado, 325–326, 330–332, 340–341, 444
Neandertal see also Neanderthal, 26, 109–110, 113–114, 117
Neanderthal, 77, 80, 112, 170–171, 174, 184
Near East, 42, 96, 109–110, 127, 161, 222, 261, 319, 324, 365, 411, 467, 482
Neolithic, 27, 29, 79, 81, 83, 211, 213, 279, 430, 472, 474, 477
Nevada Test Site (Nevada), 45–46
New Archaeology, 14–15, 26–27, 33, 35, 55, 65, 72, 77, 80, 120, 123, 144, 189, 199, 220, 316, 339, 352, 359, 415, 417, 425–426, 429, 439, 445, 461–465, 468, 501–502, 505, 507, 523–524, 528, 538, 546–548
New Guinea, 28, 413, 417, 420, 422–423, 465
Nicholas, Linda M., 303–304, 306, 308–310, 313
Oaxaca, Valley of, 303–307, 313

ornamentation. see also jewelry, 165, 305–306, 370, 391, 395
Paleolithic, 79, 81, 99, 107, 162, 165–166, 172, 174–175, 183, 186, 221–222, 224–230, 238, 240, 247, 259, 315, 370, 381, 383, 387–389, 418, 533
Perthes, Jacques Boucher de Cr(ve-coeur, 76, 79
Peru, 121–122, 262, 289–290, 292–293, 295–296, 300, 302, 366, 534
Lake Titicaca, 262, 289–290, 292–293, 295, 302
physical anthropology. see also biological anthropology, 3, 125, 464, 486
Pillar Mound (Arizona), 334
platform mound, 318, 325–327, 329–330, 333–337, 339–340, 444, 504
Pleistocene, 94, 110–111, 116–117, 227, 242, 246, 315
pollen, 56, 83, 115, 129, 147, 149–150, 216, 256, 293–295, 315, 331, 340, 383
Polynesia, 222, 253, 256, 265–267, 269–270, 272–277, 315, 447, 449–451, 453–454, 456, 459, 461–463
Pope, Geoffrey G., 96, 239, 247
pottery, 13, 45, 75, 82, 131, 133–134, 137, 140, 147, 149–150, 153–154, 189, 246, 259, 267, 279, 294, 296, 307, 331, 343, 345, 351, 354, 413–414, 425–426, 429–432, 434–439, 443, 449, 462, 465, 538–539, 546, 550–551
public archaeology, 316, 376, 467, 469, 490, 495, 501–505, 507, 515, 517–518, 525, 527, 547
radiocarbon dating, 161, 167–168, 172, 174, 183–185, 220, 294, 324, 387
raised fields, 262, 289–291, 293–294, 298–302
Rapidan River mound (Virginia), 85–88
Rathje, William L., 4, 7
reconnaissance. see also surface survey, 127–128, 190, 206, 306

Redman, Charles, 318, 325, 444, 469, 501, 517

refuse. see also garbage project, 10–11, 15, 21, 34, 42, 153, 346, 383, 413, 430, 438, 517, 543

relative dating, 161–162, 167, 187, 294

religion, 4, 20, 72, 357, 371, 400, 402, 411, 475, 543

remote sensing, 190, 219, 315

repatriation, 498, 524, 543–544, 559

residue analysis, 189, 191, 193, 219, 414, 437

rice agriculture, 430

Rice, Glen, 318, 325, 341, 444

ritual, 13, 32, 88, 153, 155–156, 190, 203, 212, 274, 277, 324, 339, 346–347, 369–371, 377–378, 384, 394, 398, 400, 411, 413, 442–443, 477, 544
  iconography, 411

Robbins, Lawrence, 4, 25, 128

rock art, 162, 185–186, 369–370, 373, 375–376, 378–379, 381, 388, 443, 528, 533, 537, 544–545

Sabloff, Jeremy, 318–319, 351, 353, 359, 462

Salado, 325–326, 330–332, 340–341, 444

salvage archaeology, 142, 481, 486, 519, 524

Savage-Rumbaugh, Sue, 93, 99, 422

Sayil Archaeological Project, 319, 352–353, 355–356

scanning electron microscope, 88, 550, 552

Schliemann, Heinrich, 501

Schoch, Robert M., 162, 177

Schoolhouse Mound (Arizona), 332, 335–340

Schurr, Theodore G., 122–123

science, 3, 18, 29, 58, 63, 65, 68, 91, 119, 125, 144, 165, 177, 184, 193, 219, 247, 259, 276–277, 314, 352, 411, 462, 474, 501, 507, 517
  and archaeology, 29, 58, 65, 144, 259, 474, 501, 507

scientific method, 3, 5

settlement archaeology, 267, 305, 352, 356, 358, 449, 478, 512

shell, 34, 39, 145, 152–155, 262, 268, 303–314, 338–340, 345, 391–392, 403, 406

Sillen, Andrew, 93, 95

sites, 3–5, 9, 23, 25–31, 33, 35, 40–43, 45, 50, 53, 56, 58, 60, 63, 79, 81–82, 85–86, 94–96, 109–115, 117, 119–121, 123, 127–128, 133–134, 141–142, 153, 156, 161–162, 165, 167, 170–171, 173–175, 183–184, 186, 189–190, 206, 208, 219, 222, 224–225, 228–229, 231, 233, 236, 238, 241–242, 246, 249, 251, 256–257, 259, 261, 266–274, 276–277, 290, 294–296, 305–306, 312–313, 315, 318, 322, 325–326, 329–332, 335, 338, 345, 349, 352–355, 367, 369–370, 375–376, 389, 392, 394, 397, 414, 421–422, 441–444, 462, 466, 469, 477, 483, 486, 490, 494, 496, 501–505, 507, 510, 517, 519–521, 523–528, 531–542, 544–546, 548–549, 552–553, 559–560
  as data, 52, 133
  dating of, 58, 111, 161–162, 172–174, 187, 191, 279
  discovery of, 505
  interpretation of, 128
  surveying of, 127, 133, 135, 305, 364, 523

Skibo, James M., 414, 425, 438–439

Skudelev (Denmark), 34–36, 40

slavery, 136, 481, 485

Smithsonian Institution, 55–56, 58, 85, 119, 121, 167, 194, 208, 251, 341, 354, 462, 486, 490, 540

Snodgrass, Anthony M., 128, 131, 140

social systems, 317, 393, 398, 430, 440

Sonoran Desert, 325, 327, 329–330, 341

Southeast Asia, 96, 147, 155–157, 222, 240–247, 265–266, 520–521, 555

Spector, Janet, 468, 493, 495–496

Stanford, Dennis, 5, 55, 57, 60–61, 119

Stark, Miriam T., 240–241, 244, 246, 425, 428, 433–434, 439

Steadman, David W., 261, 265, 271, 273, 277

stratigraphy, 79, 87–88, 96, 161–162, 170, 172, 179, 187, 219, 294

state society, 203–204, 318, 464, 502, 504

Sungir (Russia), 392

surface survey, 127–128, 131, 133, 135–136, 139, 319, 354

Teague, Lynn, 524

technological systems, 260, 289, 411, 422, 465
    change in, 414

Tell Abu Hureyra (Syria), 261–262

Tell Leilan (Syria), 364–365

Teotihuacan, 7–8, 313, 370–371, 397–403, 405–409, 533
    mapping, 398
    Pyramid of the Moon, 397, 407
    Street of the Dead, 397, 407

Teotihuacan, Mexico, 8, 370, 397–398, 400, 533

Thailand, 128, 147–149, 151, 153, 155–157, 239, 244–247, 555

thermoluminescence (TL), 162, 168, 172, 184, 187

Thespiai (Greece), 128, 131, 134–139

Three Age System, 68, 78–79, 161

Thomsen, Christian Jurgensen, 53, 78–79, 82, 161

Thosarat, Rachanie, 128, 147

Tikal (Guatemala), 7, 309, 314, 351, 357–359, 401, 538

Tonto Basin (Arizona), 318, 325, 328–332, 334–335, 414, 442–445

Tools, 3–4, 12, 19, 26–27, 34, 40–41, 53, 55–56, 58, 65, 67–69, 73, 75–77, 79–80, 88, 91, 93–96, 98–100, 102, 104–107, 109–111, 116, 121, 143, 157, 165, 167–168, 170–172, 175, 184, 189, 191–194, 211, 215, 219, 221–222, 230–233, 238, 240–243, 247, 254, 259–260, 262, 274, 279, 292, 298, 306–307, 311, 314, 322–323, 335, 338, 352, 358, 391, 413–415, 420–422, 436, 450, 458, 539, 550, 552, 559

Toth, Nicholas, 99, 101, 104, 413, 417, 421–423

tree-ring dating. see also dendrochronology, 161

Ubeidiya (Israel), 110

underwater archaeology, 25–27, 29, 31, 33, 35, 37–39, 41–43, 128, 141–142, 144

UNESCO, 536, 541, 560

uniformitarianism, 77

urban archaeology, 351, 356, 511

Valley of Mexico, 33, 262, 313, 353, 397–398, 400, 539

Valley of Oaxaca (Mexico), 303–307, 313

watercraft, 123

Weiss, Harvey, 319, 361–366

White, Randall, 186, 221, 223–224, 226, 230, 238, 370, 391–393

Whitley, David S., 369, 373–374, 377–378

Wisseman, Sarah, 195–201

Woodland period, 89, 344–345

X-ray, 190, 197–198, 213, 552

Yellen, John, 162, 165, 172–173

Zhoukoudian (China), 95–96

zooarchaeology, 276